Rare Social & Political Pamphlets

A SELECTION OF THE SOCIAL AND POLITICAL PAMPHLETS OF ANNIE BESANT

Also in

Rare Social & Political Pamphlets

A SELECTION OF THE POLITICAL PAMPHLETS OF CHARLES BRADLAUGH

A SELECTION OF THE SOCIAL AND POLITICAL PAMPHLETS OF ANNIE BESANT

WITH A PREFACE & BIBLIOGRAPHICAL NOTES

BY

JOHN SAVILLE

AUGUSTUS M. KELLEY · PUBLISHERS

NEW YORK 1970

First Published in This Edition 1970

Reprinted 1970 by
AUGUSTUS M. KELLEY · PUBLISHERS
REPRINTS OF ECONOMIC CLASSICS
New York New York 10001

. . . .

S B N 678 00638 5
L C N 78 114024

. . . .

PRINTED IN THE UNITED STATES OF AMERICA
by SENTRY PRESS, NEW YORK, N. Y. 10019

A SELECTION OF THE POLITICAL AND SOCIAL PAMPHLETS OF ANNIE BESANT (1847-1933)

Mrs. Besant was born on the 1st October 1847. Her father died when she was five years old and much of her younger life was spent with Miss Ellen Marryat, the sister of the novelist, to whom she was indebted for an excellent education. She went back to her mother at the age of sixteen and remained in the family home until she married the Rev. Frank Besant in December 1867. Among the close friends of her family was W. P. Roberts the 'pitman's attorney' and it was Roberts, as she wrote later in her *Autobiographical Sketches,* who was her 'first tutor in Radicalism'.

Her marriage was unsatisfactory and unhappy from its beginning, and in the course of the next few years her personal difficulties were compounded by an increasing scepticism concerning the christian religion. She separated from her husband in the autumn of 1873 and within a year had fully accepted atheism. In August 1874 she joined the National Secular Society and within a few months had become a staff writer on Charles Bradlaugh's journal, the *National Reformer.*

This was the beginning of the extraordinary partnership between Bradlaugh and Annie Besant. She wrote voluminously, became an outstanding platform speaker and stood by Bradlaugh during the turbulent years of the next decade. The most sensational of the many campaigns they engaged in was the famous trial of 1877, in which they were prosecuted for re-publishing Charles Knowlton's *Fruits of Philosophy.* The trial, and the publicity which attended it, was the beginning of the modern movement for birth control in Britain, and one personal consequence for Mrs. Besant was that she was deprived of the custody of her daughter by the action in court of her husband.

The revival of socialist ideas and of a socialist movement in the early 1880's saw a further shift in Mrs. Besant's career. On the 21st January 1885 she made her first public declaration of faith as a socialist, at a meeting of the Dialectical Society at which Bernard Shaw was the main speaker. She joined the Fabian Society and for the next five years she was a major figure in the young socialist movement. She continued to work within the Secular Society and her relations with Bradlaugh, although always affectionate, were somewhat strained at times. By the spring of 1889 the next chapter in her life was beginning. She joined the Theosophical Society on the 10th May 1889 and quickly attained a leading position in the international movement. She visited India first in 1893 and from then until her death on the 20th September 1933, she spent most of her life there. She became the outstanding representative in the world of the Theosophy movement, and at the same time played an important part in the development of the national movement for Indian independence.

Annie Besant was one of the great women of the past century. The pamphlets in this collection illustrate the ideas of her radical and socialist years, between 1874 and 1889. Most of those reprinted here are exceedingly rare and many are not to be found in the major libraries of the world. Section I contains typical statements of the radical position of the 1870's on domestic issues, and are similar in argument to the writings of Bradlaugh in the same years. No. 7, *The Trades Union Movement,* written at the end of her socialist period, is an excellent example of the careful statement of fact and argument characteristic of her journalism. Section II collects together some of her best known work on the social position of women and on neo-malthusianism, and it includes the famous *Law of Population,* which is probably the best known, and possibly the most widely circulated, of all her writings. Section III contains a selection of her radical pamphlets on foreign policy questions and includes three on Ireland. Together they afford a representative statement of the accepted radical attitudes towards the handling of foreign affairs by both Conservative and Liberal governments. Section IV illustrates the Fabian position she accepted after 1885, with the argument between herself and Bradlaugh (No. 25) providing a good introduction to the radical-socialist debate in the 1880's. The final pamphlet is Mrs. Besant's acceptance of Theosophy.

The literature written about her is considerable, and the items which follow are only a selection of the more important. The story of her early years is given in her *Autobiographical Sketches* (1885) and *Annie Besant An Autobiography,* the first edition of which was 1893 and the second 1908. There have been a number of biographies, among them Geoffrey West, *Annie Besant* (London and New York, 1928) ; Theodore Besterman, *Mrs. Annie Besant: A Modern Prophet* (1934) ; Arthur H. Nethercot, *The First Five Lives of Annie Besant* (1961) and *The Last Four Lives of Annie Besant* (1963). Her relations with Bradlaugh are discussed in

Nethercot (1961) *op. cit.*, in H. P. Bonner, *Charles Bradlaugh: A Record of His Life and Work,* 2 vols. (1894) and J. M. Robertson, *The Life of Charles Bradlaugh* (1921). On neo-malthusianism and the trial of 1877 see Norman E. Himes, *Medical History of Contraception* (New York, 1936; reprinted 1963) with an excellent bibliography; and a more recent volume, Peter Fryer, *The Birth Controllers* (1965) with bibliography to supplement that of Himes. For her years in the socialist movement, in addition to Nethercot and the other biographies already noted, see Margaret Cole, *The Story of Fabian Socialism* (1961) ; H. Pelling, *The Origins of the Labour Party* (2nd ed. Oxford, 1965) ; C. Tsuzuki; *The Life of Eleanor Marx, 1855-1898* (Oxford, 1967).

J. S.

BIBLIOGRAPHICAL NOTES

Section I

1. *Landlords, Tenant Farmers, and Laborers.* Fourth edition, 1880, 8 p.

   First serialised in the *National Reformer,* 20 and 27 September and 4 October 1877, under the pseudonym of Ajax, which Annie Besant used in the first year or so of her contributions to the *National Reformer.* The text of this fourth edition is identical with that of the first.

2. *The English Land System.* First edition, 1880, 8 p. Originally published in two parts in the *National Reformer,* 11 and 18 January 1880. This, as far as can be discovered, was the only edition.

3. *Liberty, Equality, Fraternity.* Third edition, n.d. 8 p.

   Originally appeared as one of the essays in *Essays by Mrs. Besant* (1875). This third edition of the pamphlet must have been published between 1877 and 1882, the years when the Freethought Publishing Company was at 28 Stonecutter St.

4. *Civil and Religious Liberty. With Some Hints Taken From the French Revolution.* Second edition, n.d., 24 p.

   First published in *Essays by Mrs. Besant* (1875) and at the same time as a pamphlet. This second edition must have been issued sometime between 1877 and 1882; it was in its sixth thousand in 1885.

5. *English Republicanism.* First edition, 1877, 8 p. As far as can be discovered this was the only edition.

6. *The Redistribution of Political Power.* First edition, 1885, 30 p.
   First published in *Our Corner,* March 1885; and no further editions, as far as can be discovered.
7. *The Trades Union Movement.* First edition, 1890, 29 p.
   First serialised in the *National Reformer,* 22 and 29 December 1889, 5 and 12 January 1890. No later editions.

Section II

8. *The Political Status of Women.* Third edition, n.d., 14 p.
   The text of Annie Besant' first formal lecture after she had joined the National Secular Society, given at the Co-operative Institute, Castle St., London on 25 August 1874. Issued as a pamphlet in September 1874 and therefore her first pamphlet for the secularist movement. This third edition published between 1877 and 1882.
9. *The Legalisation of Female Slavery in England.* First edition, 1885, 8 p.
   Originally published in the *National Reformer,* 4 June 1876. No further editions have been traced. The pamphlet was issued in January 1885 as a contribution towards the last stage in the campaign to repeal the Contagious Diseases Acts. The Repeal Act was passed on 16 April 1885.
10. *The Law Of Population: Its Consequences, And Its Bearing Upon Human Conduct And Morals.* 1891, 46 p.
    First edition 1877. A version of the first edition was earlier published in the *National Reformer,* 7, 14, 21 and 28 October, 4 November 1877, but this did not include the details of the contraceptive techniques which were given in the first edition of the pamphlet, as summarised by Peter Fryer, *The Birth Controllers,* pp. 164-165. Himes, *Medical History of Contraception,* p. 245 ff, was wrong

in dating the first edition as late 1878 or January 1879, but his discussion of the various editions of the pamphlet was careful and thorough. The bibliographical problem is that there do not appear to have been different editions as such, specifically listed, but the text was several times altered as new issues were made. This present reprint of 1891 was almost certainly the final text to be published, for when Mrs. Besant became a Theosophist in the summer of 1889, she was gradually persuaded that the neo-malthusian ideas in the pamphlet were wrong and she refused to allow further reprints or to sell the copyright (*Autobiography*, p. 237 ff.). This 1891 edition, as with most of the earlier editions, has interesting advertisements for contraceptive appliances, etc.

11. *Marriage, As It Was, As It Is, And As It Should Be: A Plea For Reform.* Second edition, 1882, 60 p. First serialised in the *National Reformer,* 17 February, 10, 17, 24 and 31 March, 7 and 14 April 1878. The first edition was 1878, and there is no evidence of any edition after the second, which was still being advertised in 1886.
12. *The Social Aspects of Malthusianism.* First edition, n.d., 8 p.

    Published either December 1880 or January 1881. No evidence of later editions.

Section III

13. *The Story of Afghanistan; Or, Why The Tory Government Gags the Indian Press. A Plea For the Weak Against the Strong.* First edition, 1879, 16 p.

    Published first in the *National Reformer,* 14 and 21 December 1879 and issued immediately as a pamphlet. The only edition.
14. *The Transvaal.* First edition, 1881, 8 p.

    Probably the only edition. It was advertised in the *National Reformer* in April 1887 as being in its

4th thousand, but it was not specified whether this was still the first or a revised edition.

15. *Egypt*. First edition, 1882, 16 p.
Published first in the *National Reformer,* 27 August 1882 and 3 September 1882. Second edition 1885.
16. *The Atheistic Platform. V. The Story of the Soudan*. Second edition, 1885, 16 p.
First edition, 1884. The text of this second edition was unchanged from that of the first.
17. *Gordon Judged Out Of His Own Mouth.* First edition, 1885, 16 p.
First published in the *National Reformer,* 26 April and 3 May 1885, and issued immediately as a pamphlet. It is unlikely to have had further editions.
18. *Force No Remedy.* First edition, 1882, 8 p.
Since the pamphlet arose out of a specific incident, namely, the Phoenix Park murders, it is unlikely to have been revised later, but the pamphlet was still being advertised in the *National Reformer* in February 1885, although there was no indication whether this was the original or a revised edition.
19. *Coercion In Ireland And Its Results. A Plea For Justice.* First edition, 1882, 8 p.
First published in the *National Reformer,* 30 April 1882 and issued immediately as a pamphlet. Since it was mainly directed against a specific piece of legislation, the pamphlet is unlikely to have had further editions.
20. *England's Jubilee Gift to Ireland.* First edition, 1887, 8 p.
First published in the *National Reformer,* 8 May 1887 and issued within a fortnight as a pamphlet. It is unlikely to have had further editions.

Section IV

21. *Why I Am A Socialist.* First or second edition, 1886, 8 p.

First published in *Our Corner,* September 1886 and issued as a pamphlet in late October or early November 1886. It is not certain whether there were revised editions at a later date, but it is unlikely. The Bradlaugh-Besant pamphlets were often published in editions of 5,000 and this is clearly the second 5,000 to be issued before the end of 1886, an indication of the drawing power of its author. The text of this edition was unchanged from that of the first.

22. *The Evolution of Society.* First edition, 1886, 24 p. First published in *Our Corner,* July, August, September and October 1885. This is almost certainly a first edition, with no changes in the text from its original publication. It continued to be advertised in the *National Reformer* until 1893 with no indication of any revision in its text.
23. *The Socialist Movement.* First edition, 1887, 24 p. First published in the *Westminster Review,* July 1886, and issued as a pamphlet in June 1887. No evidence of later editions.
24. *Radicalism and Socialism.* First edition, 1887, 20 p. First published in *Our Corner,* November and December 1886. It is unlikely that there were any further editions.
25. *Socialism: For And Against.* By Charles Bradlaugh and Annie Besant. First edition, 1887, 31 p. First published in *Our Corner,* March, April, June 1887; and unlikely to have had later editions.
26. *Modern Socialism.* Second edition, 1890, 51 p. First published in *Our Corner,* February, March, April and May, 1886 and the first edition of the pamphlet was issued in June 1886. There is no evidence of later editions after the second of 1890.
27. *Why I Became A Theosophist.* First Edition, 1889, 31 p. One of the first statements of Mrs. Besant's intellectual position after joining the Theosophist Society in May 1889. A second edition was published in 1891.

SECTION I

LANDLORDS, TENANT FARMERS, AND LABORERS.

BY ANNIE BESANT.

— *Fourth Edition.* —

AMID the din and the whirl of a great contest, when men range themselves on the one side or on the other, according as their temporary interests, their passions, or their prejudices bid them, those who ought to stand side by side, and shoulder to shoulder, sometimes get thrown face to face, and are found striking at each other. Some petty squabble, some superficial disagreement, turns into enemies those who ought to be friends; and thus, those whose interests are at bottom the same, are transformed into opponents, because their temporary interests appear to clash. The truth of these remarks has been sadly proved by the contests between laborers and farmers; and the position I am anxious to establish is, that the interests of the farmers and the laborers are identical, and they would, if they were wise, combine to form one strong union of the agricultural interest, in antagonism to the interests of the land-owners. To see this, it is necessary to lay down clearly the two positions of farmer and laborer, and to see with what amount of justice each claims to be the injured party.

To give the farmer the precedence. It is perfectly true that there are some wealthy farmers, who keep carriages for their wives and daughters, ride to hounds, train greyhounds, breed hunters, send their sons to college, their daughters to Paris and to Bonn. The laborer eyes his master's wife as she rolls in her easy carriage, and looking round, as he leans on his cottage gate, at the wretched hovel he calls his "home," he feels bitterly that the land which he labors on, and which his labor enriches, gives to him starvation diet during life, and at last a workhouse to die in; while it gives to his master, who just rides about over-looking everything, luxury and ease, which appear to him insulting and unendurable. The laborer, on the whole, is wrong, because he forgets that the wealthy farmer is wealthy, not because he has earned his wealth by farming, but because he had large capital to start with. If a man has capital, and invests it well, it will inevitably yield him a rich harvest; but the man who desires to use his capital to the best advantage will not, if he be wise, use it in farming. Capitalists are often attracted towards farming because of its accessories. The life of a rich farmer is a pleasant and easy one; it gives employment, but it is employment of an unlaborious kind; it gives excitement, but excitement which is gentle, and only bracingly stimulating. The farmer is free from the hurry, the unrest, the fever, the strain of town life, and of the whirlpool of business toil. His is a wholesome, sturdy, free, and manly existence. Therefore, instead of trying to double or treble it in trade he is content to gain only small profits from his invested capital. The laborer, if he reasoned justly, would take all this into account; he would remember that his employer draws his income, *not from the land only, but from the capital he previously held, and which he has invested in the land.* If a man be poor, and takes to farming for a livelihood, he must expect to have a sharp struggle even to keep his head above water. The small farmer's life is as laborious, and is more anxious and responsible, than that of the laborer he employs. The profits drawn from farming are, on the whole, small; they are precarious, and are dependent on circumstances beyond the farmer's control. "A bad year"—*i.e.*, unfavorable weather, disease among the stock, failure of crops—is a thing that presses on the farmer more than on the laborer; for the laborer's wages are certain, the farmer's returns are doubtful. From all this it results that the sore and indignant feeling manifested by the farmers during agrarian struggles has its source in a true and natural idea. The farmers feel that their own lot is hard and precarious, that their profits are small, that their position is unassured, and they resist with a blind and bitter determination the action of the laborers to force them into giving a rate of wages which they are conscious, *and justly conscious*, that the profits drawn from the land do not authorise.

To turn to the laborer. One is almost ashamed to have said a word of blame, when one remembers what is the laborer's lot in England. *We* rail against slavery! So far as physical comfort goes, a slave is in an enviable position when his lot is compared with that of our free (?) English laborers. The slave is, at least, housed and fed sufficiently well to keep him in fair working health, for his owner's interests require it; when he is old and worn out, a contemptuous kindness leaves him free air and sunshine, food and home. But the laborer? a hovel, where his master's dogs and horses would not house, is hired to him for shelter; if he is ill, there are plenty of others to take his place; he has no claim on any; when he is old, there is parish pay for him; if he is too helpless to live in his hovel, there is the workhouse open to him; if he dies, there is the parish coffin for him, the pauper's grave. I know that even nominal freedom is better than slavery, and that it is a higher thing to be an English peasant than a slave; but, as regards physical comfort, the lot of the slave is infinitely more desirable. I know, too, that kindly charity brightens the laborer's path, that gentle womanly hands will bring comforts to the suffering, and soft voices cheer his sick room, and gladden his weary heart; but it is not just nor right that the man who labors honestly should be dependent on charitable neighbors, nor that he should be degraded by being forced into accepting with gratitude, as a favor, that which his right hand should have won for him as a right. Besides, as a matter of fact, only some laborers receive even charity. Personally I have known cases of want and suffering, at the very remembrance of which the heart aches, and the eyes fill. I have seen a laborer's home, one small room, with a bed, a table, a few chairs; on that bed slept father, mother, a child sick with scarlet fever, and a dead child; in that room the daily life went on, dressing, eating, living; and farmers round said reprovingly that the man drank, and was a "demagogue," an "ill-conditioned agitator." The man was not a habitual drunkard, though he did drink now and then, driven to the "public" to escape from his miserable, fever-stricken, death-haunted home. He did "agitate;" but who has a word of condemnation for a man who felt that his lot was an unjust one, and strove, however blindly, to remedy a state of things which was driving him to desperation? Ay, and I have known grandfather, grandmother, daughter, and grandchild, and three unmarried men lodgers, sleeping in one room, in two beds. True, the mother was unmarried, the daughter unmarried, though both were mothers. But, O Englishwomen, nurtured in innocence and purity, sedulously guarded from stranger's look, and shielded from prying eyes, have you the heart to blame these women for immodesty and indelicacy, when, if they would, they could not be anything but brazen-faced and coarse? Stern censors talk of the sad immorality of our country villages; but if you herd men and women together like beasts, you have no right to expect from them anything higher than the natural gratification of natural tendencies. My own marvel is, *not* why the laborers are rough, and coarse, and sensual, but how there grow up from these terrible hot-beds of vice, so many sweet, pure blossoms of tender womanhood and noble manhood, worthy to take their place beside the offshoots of pure and happy homes. My own marvel is, *not* why the laborers are agitating now, but how it comes to pass that they have not agitated long ago; *not* why they claim justice now, but why they have endured injustice silently so long. I render my heart's homage to the noble patience, the strong self-control, the pathetic dignity, the steadfast endurance, which have waited, and borne, and suffered so long, and which, even now, do not break out into wild excesses, but quietly and firmly set to work to alter a state of things which would excuse an armed revolt, and to redress injustices which would condone a revolution.

We are then forced to acknowledge that the farmer has justice on his side when he refuses to give higher wages to his laborers, pleading that his profits do not justify larger out-goings; we are forced to acknowledge also that the laborer has justice on his side when he demands higher wages, pleading that he and his family cannot live in decency, much less in comfort, on the miserable pittance he earns week by week.

Various remedies are suggested whereby to help the laborer to better his position; but they none of them go to the root of the matter, and they all have the grave defect that they are aimed against the farmer, and will, if successful, render farming impossible. I contend that the farmer and laborer are natural allies; that their interests are inextricably intertwined; that they must stand or fall together. I pass by all the sentimental arguments about patriarchal feeling, and so on; doubtless kindly feeling between employers and employed is valuable, if it be *mutually* respectful, generous, and true; but at present, while condescension meets servility, and arrogance scowls at independence, the loyal, frank co-operation of man with man in honest friendliness is scarcely attainable, and we must perforce be content, for the present, with a simple contract, fairly carried out on both sides. But my position is grounded on an undeniable fact, and that radical fact is, that the farmer and the laborer *together* form the agricultural interest; without the farmer's capital the land must remain unfertilised, and without the laborer's thews and sinews the land must remain uncultivated. But all the proposed remedies only try to alter the state of the labor market; if laborers abound in one place, and the rate of wages is low, the superabundant labor is to be drafted off elsewhere. This is all very well to a certain extent, but the stern fact remains that wages must be limited by the paying-power of the farmer; and if there are so few laborers left that he is obliged to give to one the sum he formerly gave to three, he will be compelled, as he cannot afford to treble his expenditure, to decrease his staff of laborers, and therefore his power of putting work into the land. To put pressure of this kind on the employer in cases where the profits arising from the business are very large, is a fair and just way of forcing him to allow the men who make his wealth to share in its advantages; but in farming, where the profits are small, the pressure can only result in one of two ways: either the farmer will resign his work and invest his capital in some more profitable business, or he will decrease the quality and quantity of the labor he employs, and will thereby deteriorate the land he farms. Emigration is another, and still more fatal, remedy. Besides being open to the objections stated above, it has the far worse fault of taking out of the country the men who are invaluable to the State. Emigration takes from us the cream of the agricultural working classes: the thrifty, the steady, in a word, the superior peasantry leave our shores, embittered by failure and privation, and are gladly welcomed in other lands, where the labor, despised here, enriches and beautifies the new Fatherland. To England are left the inferior workmen, the careless, improvident, unsteady. The ultimate effect of undue encouragement of emigration is to deprive the State of the energetic men and women who form its life-blood and backbone, and to burden the State with weaker and more helpless citizens. English land will be less well and less intelligently cultivated, and the poor-rates will, it may be added, be indefinitely increased, if the now popular scheme of emigration be carried out with sufficient success to relieve the labor market to an extent which will increase appreciably the scale of wages. There are other suggestions, such as those about co-operative farming by laborers who cannot possibly get sufficient capital to start with, of small allotments at low rental, etc., all of which are based on the good old Conservative idea, that when a wall is thoroughly rotten, the best plan is to conserve it by sticking in a sounder brick here and there. and so trying to tinker it up, instead of knocking the crumbling thing down and building a new and stronger wall in its place. It would take too much time to discuss one by one these dilettante, kid-glove schemes; the reformation needed is a radical one. It will justly be asked: If farmer and laborer both have justice on their side, and if the laborer's wages cannot be largely increased without entailing the ruin of the farmer, what possible remedy is there for the present state of things? Deliberately and firmly I answer: The extinction of the present land-owning class, and the radical revolution of the present idea as to the right of appropriating land.

We will take the latter half of the sentence first, and point out, though necessarily very briefly, why the present idea that one citizen has a right to appropriate land, and to will it to his heirs, is an injustice to the whole body of citizens. "The essential principle of property," says J. S. Mill, "being to assure to all persons what they have produced by their labor, and accumulated by their abstinence, this principle cannot apply to what is not the produce of labor, the raw material of the earth." The "rights of property" are not in any way touched by a discussion on the appropriation of land by individuals; land is not property in the strict sense of the term, and ought not to be allowed to be held as such. The soil of the globe is the life-estate of the inhabitants of the globe, and cannot rightly or justly be monopolised by a few for their own benefit, to the exclusion of the rest. The proprietorship of the land should be vested in the Government, as the trustee of the nation, to be used for the good of the nation, and not for the good of a few favored individuals. The soil of England is, in justice, the possession of the whole people of England, inherited by the people by natural right as Englishmen—their birthright, in fact. Natural gifts can never be rightfully monopolised by a section of mankind. If, then, no right can be manufactured by law which gives individuals a just claim to hold land as their own property, and to will it as such to their heirs, it is manifest that the existence of the present landowning class is an injustice, and as such ought to be put an end to. A man who owns land, draws money from it, and does nothing to improve it, is an anomaly that must simply be extinguished. For it must be remembered that, although land is a natural gift, yet the improvement of land is the result of human labor, and comes therefore under the head of property. If unfertile and barren land is rented by a man who invests his capital in the land, and thus renders it fertile and rich, that man has a just claim to reap the return of his capital and his labor. The land is not his property; the improvement in the land is. It is manifestly for the benefit of the nation that the nation's land should be highly cultivated, and should be made to return as rich harvests as possible. Therefore, the Government, as trustee, might rightly and wisely rent large portions of the land to capitalists; and it must also, from the nature of the business, give to the capitalists security of tenure, so that the farmer may feel certain that, in putting his capital into the ground, he will be able in due time to reap his fair and just reward. In this sense, property in land is justifiable; land may be held by individuals, on condition that they cultivate it, improve it, enrich it. But this does not justify the landowner's existence; it justifies only that of the farmer and the laborer. What do the great landlords do for the land they own? *Simply Nothing.* They own it; *voilà tout.* These fortunate individuals let out their so-called "property" to the farmers; they do nothing to improve the land, and therefore they have no right to hold the land; they draw vast incomes from the soil, and put nothing into it. Their existence is an injustice to the community, and, as landowners, they must disappear. The present holders have, it should be said in passing, a right to compensation from the State when the State deprives them of the land they hold by long prescription; the landlords must not be unjustly treated because they have been born the heirs of an injustice.

It is an error to imagine that the State, in thus "confiscating the land" as it is called—*i.e.*, in resuming rights that it should never have allowed to be taken from it, will be doing anything new, or unprecedented. Not at all; it will only be doing on a large scale what it is continually doing on a small. When a railway is needed for the public good, Parliament has no scruples about passing a Bill to compel the occupiers of the land through which the line must go, to sell their "property." If this land were really property, it would be unjust to force the owners to part with it, but it is seen, in these cases, that the land may rightfully be claimed when it is required for the good of the State. Carry out this same principle, and the landowners will cease to exist.

The farmer has too often joined hands with the landowner against the laborer; that is to say, half the agricultural interest has allied itself with its natural enemy, in order to crush the other half. What do the farmers owe the landlords that they should make common cause with them against the class on whose labor the value of the land depends? The landlord lets land—to which he has no right—to the farmer; that is, to the man whose improvement of the land gives him a real property in it; he exacts a high rent; he gives no lease, or a short lease. When the farmer's care, and energy, and money have doubled the value of the land, the owner, who has done nothing to it, steps in to raise the rent; that is, he claims the interest of the farmer's capital. The owner expects the farmer to feed from his crops some thousands of wild creatures, which the owner shoots, but which the farmer may not touch. In fact, the farmer very generously invests capital, works the year round, rises early, lives hardly, preserves game, and improves farm-buildings, in order that the landowner may draw a larger income, live idly and in luxury, shoot in the autumn, and in time let his enriched farm to a new man at a still higher rental. And this is the farmer's friend! In order to be at peace with a class to whom he owes nothing, but which fattens on his toil, the farmer quarrels with his laborers, on whom he himself depends.

The low wages of the laborer are the ruin of the farmer. They oblige the peasant to live from hand to mouth, to put by nothing against "the rainy day" of sickness and old age; and thus they throw the laborer on "the parish" for every week during which he is out of work, and make him a burden on the rates in his old age. These rates fall on the farmer, and therefore every man who earns sufficient to keep himself and his family "off the parish" is so much less weight thrown ultimately on the farmer's purse. Higher wages to the laborer mean the lessened taxation of the farmer. Therefore, as the farmer cannot give higher wages while he is being ground down by heavy rent and heavy taxes, the first step to free the farmer and the laborer is for them to combine into an union which shall make it its one object to strike against landlordism. The tremendous power such an Union might wield, in case of need, by sternly refusing to rent or cultivate land at all, would simply bring the landlords to their knees, and enable the agriculturalists to demand whatever terms they chose. But, before proceeding to this extremity, the Union would bend all its efforts to alter the incidence of taxation, to abolish the Game Laws, and to reform the Land Laws. The first step forwards would be to extend the county franchise, so that the farmers and laborers might combine to send into Parliament men who would represent the agricultural interest, instead of that of the landlords. This is a necessary preliminary. The next step is to throw the weight of taxation on the land. In 1692 there was a land tax consisting of "one-fifth of the whole annual value," and land thus contributed about a third of the annual revenue raised by taxation. If this proportion were restored, the relief to the mass of the nation would be enormous, and all the taxes which at present throw so unfair a proportion of the taxation on the middle and lower classes might be swept away. But towards the end of the 18th century Parliament passed an Act that the taxes contributed by land should remain at the figure fixed in 1692: that is, that land should contribute to the State, not a fifth of its annual value, but a fifth of the value at which it was estimated in the year 1692. Thus the whole contribution of land for State purposes is now a little over one-eighty-sixth part of the total taxation, instead of being about one-third. The tax paid by the present Duke of Westminster for his land in London, being one-fifth of its value in 1692, must really represent its present value very justly! And the fact that that eminent nobleman has done so much to earn his vast wealth is one which is very interesting to the contemplative and admiring bystander. When the agricultural interest shall have altered these little anomalies, and forced those who, owning land, do nothing for it, to pay their fair share of taxation, the farmers will find themselves in a position to pay their laborers better, and to have their own pockets fuller. The abolition of entail, the easier buying and selling of land, and other reforms in this direction, would facilitate the ultimate transfer of the ownership of the land to the people themselves, as represented by their elected government. It is very important that small—even the smallest—capitalists should have it in their power to acquire land in small holdings on the same terms as to security of tenure on which the large farmers would hold theirs from the State. A large number of peasant proprietors are the safeguard of a State. There is a steadiness, a dignity, an independence, about the men who cultivate their own little farms that no other employment seems to give. The old English "yeomanry" were men of this description; such are now some agriculturalists in Cumberland and Westmoreland; such are the Swiss peasants, the Norwegian, the Flemish, the Rhenish. All observers unite in reporting that, to quote M. de Sismondi, "wherever we find peasant proprietors we find also the comfort, security, confidence in the future, and independence, which assure at once happiness and virtue." This sturdy, independent peasantry would form a strong backbone to the country in times of trouble; it might easily be drilled and trained sufficiently to replace a standing army in England, and would offer a reliable guarantee of steady progression without hasty revolution. Certainly, it would not yield to the "higher classes" a supple obedience or a servile courtesy, for it would be a class which would secure England for ever against domestic tyranny or class despotism.

To end with the proposition with which I started: it is to the union of farmers and laborers that we must look for the solution of the present difficulty: the farmer and the laborer, the two classes whose capital and labor give them a property in the soil, must stand shoulder to shoulder to push off from the land he burdens the landlord who takes all, and gives nothing back. One in interest, as they are one in work, the two must combine against the class whose flourishing depends on their ill-requited labor. The interests of the landlord and the farmer are opposed, the interests of the farmer and the laborer are identical.

ONE PENNY.

London: Printed by Annie Besant and Charles Bradlaugh, 28, Stonecutter Street E.C. 1880.

THE ENGLISH LAND SYSTEM.

BY ANNIE BESANT.

"In no sound theory of private property was it ever contemplated that the proprietor of land should be merely a sinecurist quartered on it.'—JOHN STUART MILL.

NINETEEN centuries ago Tiberius Gracchus said of the Roman people: "They are called the masters of the world, but there is no clod of earth they can call their own." What was true of Romans in the olden days is true of Britons to-day. Their armies conquer many a country. Their navies ride over many a sea. Their "empire," their wide dominion, their mighty power, is a constant boast. Yet the masses of the people are "landless men." The adjective which was the shame of their free Saxon forefathers is the one which describes the condition of the vast majority of the modern British nation.

Yet no country can be sure of its freedom, no nation can maintain its prosperity, when—as Cobden said of England—the majority of the cultivators are "divorced from the soil they till." In France, over five millions of Frenchmen own the soil of France. In Prussia, a wise legislation has created peasant proprietors by the thousand. In Switzerland, the greater part of the land is owned by the cultivators. In Denmark, Sweden, and Norway the same system prevails. In Italy a share of the produce forms the rental of the farm. In Great Britain and Ireland an artificial class is found—the survival of feudal times—which is "quartered on the soil," a class that does not work, but exists on an inherited right to live on the produce of the land which it does not till, on the results of labors which it does not share. This class draws yearly from the country a rental of £200,000,000 sterling, and gives in return—the fact that it exists. "The greatest burden on the land," it has been bitterly said, "is the landlord." Is it necessary that this burden should always bow down the shoulders of labor?

Five persons own estates exceeding 2,000,000 of acres in extent, seven persons own estates of 3,455,864, and twenty persons own estates considerably exceeding 5,000,000 of acres. Less than 2,200 individuals own considerably more than one-third, but less than one-half of the United Kingdom. The owners of these huge estates claim some rights as landlords that can only be designated as monstrous. They claim (*a*) the right to evict; (*b*) the right to raise rents when land is improved by tenants; (*c*) the right to appropriate the results of the labor and capital of others. (*a*) This right to evict has been largely exercised, more especially in Scotland. It includes the right to retain barren and useless land that might be utilised for the common good. Her Majesty the Queen and the Prince of Wales have "cleared out the people" to a considerable extent round their respective homes. The grandfather of the present Marquis of Huntly evicted forty families, who owned 9,000 head of sheep and goats and 200 head of cattle. The result of the exercise of this "right of property" has been the creation in Scotland during 61 years of 65 deer forests, in which are to be seen "the ruins of numerous hamlets, with the grass growing over them." Even between 1870 and 1873, 680,000 acres of land were added to the 1,320,000 acres of desert already created in Scotland. I deny the right of the idle to "clear out" the industrious. I deny the right of the wealth-consumers to evict the wealth-producers. If this right be admitted, then the wealthy few might legally buy up England, and turn out the English nation from their own land. It is right and good that some land should be kept for amusement; but such land—being taken out of the national wealth of the nation —should be used for the good of the nation. It is well that the Welsh hills, the Westmoreland valleys, the Scotch mountains, the Irish lakes, should not be handed over to the mill or to the plough. They are needful for the playgrounds of the nation, lest the sense of beauty, of admiration, of awe, should die out of the lives of the people. But they should be open to all alike. No individual should own the pass of Killiecrankie, the lakes of Killarney, the paths of Snowdon, the mighty crest of Helvellyn. They should be national, not private, property; the birthright of all, not the appanage of the few.

(*b*) A landlord lets a farm at a low rental. The land is overgrown with weeds, covered with stones. Hedges are neglected, buildings decayed. An energetic farmer takes it. He grubs up the old hedges and plants new ones; he pays laborers to clear off the weeds, to gather the stones. He builds strong sheds for his cattle, warm shelter for his stock. Manure repairs the losses of the soil, careful husbandry tends it. The crops become heavier, the flocks and herds more fruitful; capital, science, and labor have trebled the value of the land. The landlord rides by with his bailiff. "Smith, that farm's worth more than it was ten years ago. You must have it re-valued." Why? The landlord has not wrought and toiled and spent thought and money on it. Why should he share a profit he has not helped to make? The added value of the land is the tenant's interest on his capital and his labor; to raise the rent—*i.e.*, to take a share of the profit—is to rob the farmer of the interest of that which he has invested.

(*c.*) Of the same character is the right of the landlord to buildings erected on his land when he has let it on building leases. The Duke of Bedford leases land on building leases. He lets the land at the value which it is worth to him. The builder works, and invests capital. Streets, crescents, squares, arise on every side. Years pass away. The lease expires. The Duke of Bedford becomes the landlord of all the house property created. Why? He has not planned, and toiled, and builded. Not his the energy and the skill that have transformed the empty plot into the crowded market. Why should he become the owner of the wealth made by the toil of many? No injustice would be done to him if the State secured to him his original rental—the rent which was the value of the land to him—and poured the surplus wealth into the national exchequer, so that what was made by the general industry should be utilised for the general good.

It is sometimes pretended that the owners of these vast estates act as a kind of special providence for their less wealthy neighbors, and are the fathers of their "happy tenantry." The Royal Commission on the employment of children and women in agriculture gave a somewhat sarcastic commentary on the "beneficial results" of the English land system. It told us of ill-built hovels, badly roofed huts, starvation wage; it revealed to us a mass of hideous suffering, of long drawn-out patient endurance of ill-requited labor; it drew aside the veil over English agricultural life, and showed us little children driven to toil from babyhood, growing up neglected, untaught, untrained; women knee-deep in manure filling the carts; a population living and dying in dense brutal ignorance, continually falling back on charitable or parish relief, regarding "the parish" as the natural maintenance for old age.

To-day the discontent has risen higher in the social scale. Land is falling out of cultivation by thousands of acres, because the landlords' drain on it makes farming unprofitable. In Ireland "between 1877 and 1878, 92,000 acres of land lapsed into 'bog and waste unoccupied.'" Farmers are emigrating by the score, carrying their energy and their capital to a land where the profits made by their investment will belong to themselves and not to the landlord. Meanwhile food is being imported in ever increasing quantities, and the men who ought to be raising it from our own fields are driven into the cities, to increase the glut in the labor-market.

The principle on which the land should be dealt with is that laid down by all political economists—*i.e.*, the land of a country is the possession of the people of the country, and should be dealt with for the general good. Property in land differs wholly from property in manufactured goods. What man can make, man can own. What no man made, no man can claim as exclusively his. To quote the words of John Stuart Mill:—

"When the 'sacredness of property' is talked of, it should always be remembered that any such sacredness does not belong in the same degree to landed property. No man made the land. It is the original inheritance of the whole species. Its appropriation is wholly a question of general expediency. When private property in land is not expedient, it is unjust. It is no hardship to any one to be excluded from what others have produced; they were not bound to produce it for his use, and he loses nothing by not sharing in what otherwise would not have existed at all. But it is some hardship to be born into the world, and to find all nature's gifts previously engrossed, and no place left for the new-comer."

The limited nature of property in land is, as a matter of fact, acknowledged by English law. If a railway is wanted in a neighborhood an Act of Parliament compels the landowners to part with such part of their land as is required. If a new street is to be made, the owners of the property through which it is to pass are forced to sell. No such interference would be tolerated if it dealt with really private property; but, to quote once more J. S. Mill: "The claim of the landowners to the land is altogether subordinate to the general policy of the State."

Not only is it admitted that property in land is subordinate to the general good, but it is also to some extent recognised by law that property in land must not conflict with individual safety. If I buy a piece of land near a public thoroughfare and dig a large hole in it, the law will step in and say: "Fence that hole." I answer: "I will not fence it. The land is mine. I will dig as I please. Have I not a right to do as I will with mine own?" "No," the law answers, "you have so such right. The property in land is limited. It does not include a right to endanger your neighbor." Thus we find that in England there exists by law no right so to hold land as either to exclude the control of the State or to use it to the common injury. It is true that the last principle—legal though it be—is only partially recognised. By storing dynamite on your land you run the chance of blowing up your neighbors; by preserving game you run the chance of starving them. In each case the act is injurious. But in the one the law forbids, in the other it sanctions, the abuse of the landholder's power. Morally, the twain are on a level; legally, they are utterly distinct.

The central principle of Land Reform is also the central principle of the English Land Law: namely, the supreme right of the State, as represented by Parliament, to control the conditions on which the land may be held. The object of modern Reformers is not to introduce a new principle, but to apply and enforce the old. We complain that the supreme right of the Nation, while theoretically admitted, is practically subordinated to the pleasure of the few.

We demand a change in certain conditions of Land Tenure which are antagonistic to the common good, and are therefore opposed to the central principle of English Law. The chief of these which need to be destroyed are: (1) The Game Laws. (2) Primogeniture and Entail. The main changes which need to be introduced are: (1) The compulsory cultivation or sale of cultivable land. (2) The simplification of Land Transfer. (3) The re-adjustment of the Land Tax. (4) The graduated taxation of large estates. (5) The establishment of a Peasant Proprietary.

First, the abuses which need to be destroyed. (1) The Game Laws. Any defence of these relics of a barbarous feudalism seems absurd in these modern times. That poor men should have their crops—on which they often depend for their rents—destroyed by wild animals kept for their landlord's amusement would be ridiculous, if it were not monstrous. I carefully cultivate some cabbages and turnips, hoping to sell them in the market at a fair profit. Some hares and rabbits stray in and nibble away at my cherished crops. I set traps round my vegetables, among my cabbages. I catch one or two hares, half a dozen rabbits. I am haled before the magistrates, and sent to gaol as a poacher. I ought quietly to have watched the destruction of the results of my labor, of my care; I should have let my children pine in order that my landlord's hares might fatten. And I—appealing to that right to life which is higher than the right to play; I—challenging that right to amusement which gives to others the right to starve; I—industrious and thrifty face to face with the idle and the extravagant; I proclaim that England's children are more precious than England's brutes, and that the peasantry have a right to the soil they till, more sacred than the right of the game. Every man should have the right to kill on his own land wild animals that stray on to it. Tame animals should be pounded, and restored to their owners on the payment of any damage that may have been done by them. Each man's right to his own property should be protected. No man should be allowed to injure his neighbor with his game, any more than with his oxen or his sheep.

(2) Primogeniture and entail should be abolished. No dead

hand should be permitted to strangle the living. Primogeniture is unjust, both to the family and the State. Why should one son profit by the loss of his brothers and sisters? All children, whether they be first or last born, have an equal claim on their parents. By no right of nature, by no reasonable award, can the eldest claim that the wealth of the common parents shall pass to him alone. The consequences of this monstrous law are patent. First, the accumulation of vast wealth in the hands of a small minority. The eldest son is the representative of "the House." Each newly acquired farm, each gap in the estate filled in, each increase of rent-roll is an addition to the power of the heir. Each means territorial influence, social position, political power. Meanwhile, the younger children must be provided for: hence family livings, and sinecures in Civil List, ornamental positions for the cadets of great houses. For a tramp to live on the rates is despicable. For a Lord Cecil to live on the taxes is honorable. Destroy primogeniture, and one of the great incentives to increasing estates is gone: if the owner knows that the estate, at his death, will be divided among all his children alike, he will be less anxious to add to it. Destroy primogeniture, and the taxes will be relieved from the constant drain now made upon them for the benefit of the younger sons of our landed aristocracy.

The constructive work is even more important than the destructive. And first in the list of reforms stands the compulsory cultivation or sale of cultivable land. At the present time at least eleven million acres of cultivable land are left barren. At the present time millions of tons of food are being imported into the country. At the present time thousands of strong arms are wasting in idleness. Barren lands; scanty food supply; idle arms. Add the barren lands and the strong arms together and the sum will be a wealth of food. Separated, they are alike useless; united, they would mean national prosperity. If landlords refuse to cultivate, they should be forced to sell. Just as a man is compelled to sell land wanted for a railway, so he should be compelled to sell land wanted for food-supply. The landlord should be paid a fair price for his land. But the fair price is not the value of the land cultivated, corn-bearing, cattle-fattening, but the value of the land untilled, barren, deer-trodden. The landlord suffers no wrong if he receives the value of the land *as he held it*. The nation is not bound in justice to pay him its potential, but only its actual, value.

(2) The simplification of Land Transfer. Why should it be more difficult to sell a piece of freehold land than to sell a piece of cloth? Yet to buy a small plot of such land will entail almost as much in fees to lawyers as the land itself will cost. If all titles were registered no difficulty would arise, and an intending purchaser might as readily deal with the seller of land as the seller

of coats. (3) The re-adjustment of the Land Tax. Land is supposed to pay—nominally as tax, really as rental to the State —4s. in the £, or one-fifth of its value. This amount was levied on the land as a fair rental by the landowners themselves in 1692. At that time the land was valued, and the tax was duly levied on the assessment. Even in 1798, on a rental of £22,500,000, the landowners paid to the State £2,037,627 net. To-day, on a rental of over £200,000,000 they pay a little over £1,000,000 gross. They still pay at the rate of 4s. in the £, *bien entendu*, but they pay on the valuation of 1692, while they receive the value of the land in 1880. A real tax of 4s. in the £ would yield to the national exchequer some £40,000,000 a year. The landowners pay some £1,090,000. Under such circumstances the claim of Land Reformers to re-adjust the Land Tax can scarcely be regarded as an unfair one. (4) More objection may be made to the principle of the next reform—*i.e.*, the graduated taxation of large estates. Yet it is our English habit to tax luxuries, and where land is held as a luxury why should it alone be exempt from the general rule? The carriage is taxed while the business cart goes free: so also should land which is not wanted for cultivation be taxed more heavily than that which supports life. Taxation should fall more and more heavily, as the amount of land held by one man grows larger and larger. An estate of 5,000 acres should pay more than five times as much as an estate of 1,000 acres. In an old and thickly-populated country, huge estates are huge wrongs.

(5) The establishment of a Peasant Proprietary. Lord Burleigh "does not know" how a peasant proprietary can be formed, and the *Standard* sapiently opines that if a peasant has no money the permission to buy land is not a very useful gift to him. Fortunately, the ungauged depth of Lord Burleigh's ignorance affords no measure of other people's knowledge, and all thinkers do not confine their attention to England alone. In Prussia a peasant proprietary has been created by law, not by revolution, and to Prussia we therefore turn for information. Lord Burleigh has probably never heard of Baron Stein. Stein was a Prussian Minister in the early years of the present century, and, seeing his country's weakness, he resolved to "create a free peasant class" which, their interests being one with those of their Fatherland, would be steady and reliable in its defence. The first step was taken by the law of October, 1807, which enabled peasants to own land, but did nothing more; in 1811 another act passed, giving the peasantry the right to "become proprietors of their holdings, after paying to the landlord the indemnity fixed by this edict." Thus a second step was taken: not only was the peasant permitted to buy, but the landowner was compelled to sell. There remained still the difficulty raised by the *Standard*. To the moneyless man permission to buy is not

very valuable. The difficulty was removed by the legislation of 1850. In this year an act was passed establishing "Rent Banks" in every district. These banks issued rent debentures to the landlords, paying four per cent. on a capital sum equal to twenty years' purchase of the land the peasant desired to buy. Thus the claims of the landlords were satisfied. On the other hand, the peasant paid each month to the tax-gatherer, with his usual rates and taxes, 1-12th part of a rent amounting to four-and-a-half or five per cent. on the same capital sum; if he paid at four-and-a-half his land was free in fifty-six 1-12th years; if at five his land was free in forty-one 1-12th years; in either case the one or the one-and-a-half per cent. over the payment to the landlord by the State, at compound interest during the term of years, extinguished the debt due to the State, and enabled the peasant by easy instalments to pay the twenty years' purchase of his land. The result of this reform has been the creation of some 80,000 peasant proprietors in Prussia. They are free, prosperous, self-reliant; they ask no charity; they require no support; their industry maintains them while their freedom elevates them. We ask for such a class in exchange for our laborers.

Richard Cobden, ere his too-early death, proclaimed that Free Trade in Land was as necessary as Free Trade in Manufactures. In his last speech he cried: "The English peasantry has no parallel on the face of the earth, you have no other country in which it is entirely divorced from the land. There is no other country in the world where you will not find men turning up the furrow on their own freehold." Cobden's words are as true to-day as they were when he spoke them. England has still the bad pre-eminence of possessing the worst land system in the world. Will Cobden's countrymen allow the reproach to lie unremoved? Or will they be wise ere it be yet too late, and by timely Land Reform prevent Land Revolution?

PRICE ONE PENNY.

London: Printed by ANNIE BESANT and CHARLES BRADLAUGH, 28, Stonecutter Street E.C.

LIBERTY, EQUALITY, FRATERNITY.

BY

ANNIE BESANT.

THIRD EDITION.

LONDON:
FREETHOUGHT PUBLISHING COMPANY,
28, STONECUTTER STREET, F C.

PRICE ONE PENNY.

LONDON:
PRINTED BY ANNIE BESANT AND CHARLES BRADLAUGH,
28, STONECUTTER STREET, E.C.

LIBERTY, EQUALITY, FRATERNITY.

FREEDOM, JUSTICE, BROTHERHOOD: such, in other words, is the legend which is inscribed on the Republican banner, which is the motto on the Republican shield. With these words gleaming on her brow, Republican France fought and conquered; with this war-cry ringing from her lips, Republican France unsheathed the sword which struck at the tyrants of the people, and at "the priests of an evil faith." Alas! that France, maddened by oppression, and by most cruel outrage, blinded with furious hate and passionate indignation, conscious that she was strong enough to defy her gaolers, allowed herself to be betrayed by the emissaries of monarchs, and permitted some of her citizens to be bribed by English coin, until the golden letters were tarnished with blood, and their brightness shone lurid through a mist of terror. And yet France—glorious in spite of her madness and of the despair of her anguished fear—France clung fast to the grandest thought ever struck out of the human soul: men are free; men are equal; men are brothers. The shame of the Revolution we fling back on her tyrants; on the kings who had made France their playground, and had rioted while the people were starving; on the nobles who, evil courtiers, fluttered round an evil monarch, and wrung from the peasants' food the money for their feasting, and took from the poor man's home its brightest ornaments, the honour of his wife, and the purity of his daughter; on the Church, whose priests were corrupt, and whose Bishops were the worst of a bad court, foul with the double foulness of a hypocrisy which knelt to God in order the better to rob Man. On these be the disgrace of the Reign of Terror, of the massacres of September. These men had taught the people that Liberty meant the power to grasp at everything which gratified the whim of the moment; that Equality meant that, when possible, those above should be dragged down to a lower level; that Fraternity meant that brother should slay the brother and betray the sister. Little wonder that the evil seed bore evil fruit, and that Republican France did not shake off at once the ingrained habits of France Monarchical. Yet at the worst she did not torture her victims, as the Monarchy had tortured Damiens; or commit them to long-drawn agony, as the Monarchy did with its *lettres de cachet;* the massacres of September were scarce so bloody as the massacre of St. Bartholomew, or the guillotine so devouring as the *dragonnades* of Louis. True, the Republic shed the blood of nobles, while the Monarchy shed only the blood of the people; *there* is the secret of the execrations that arise against the Revolution, and of the hatred which blackens it and defames. In spite of her faults and her errors, the Republic held fast to the thought embodied in her motto; she was based on principles that were pure and strong; her creed was noble, even though muttered by lips that were red with blood. And to-day we repeat it, we Republicans, enthusiasts, dreamers, as men call us, we proclaim that the words are true, that the thought is perfect; we own as the ideal we worship, "Liberty, Equality, Fraternity."

It is well, however, that we should attach to each word of our motto a clear and distinct meaning, so that we may never be led away into making an indefensible statement, or be betrayed into a foolish and untenable position. What is Liberty? Not, as some seem to fancy, the power to impose upon others a political constitution of which they do not approve, or a form of Government which they do not desire. Not the fact that our own opinion is uppermost, and our own ideas triumphant. Not the discovery that we have grown strong enough to bend the wills of others to our will, and to make the world as we would wish to see it. Liberty means that every individual is left perfectly free to follow his own will, to pursue his own objects in his own fashion, with no limit whatsoever imposed upon him by others; this complete freedom being bounded only by the equally complete freedom of every one of his neighbours. Nothing less than this is liberty; nothing more than this is possible. This liberty is the birthright of every man and of every woman. The right to life comes with the fact of birth; and life implies something more than mere existence; it implies the right to exercise every physical and every mental faculty, to grow, to develop, to become perfect. No one has a right to maim another's body; all admit this; and yet men claim a right to maim the faculties of another, to break his mental arms, and to stunt his mental growth. No man can exercise his faculties to the fullest extent unless he has complete freedom to do so; but no man has a greater right to complete freedom than his fellow; and, therefore, we are driven to the conclusion that every individual has a right to complete freedom of action, but that he has no right to infringe on the complete freedom of any one else. Liberty, then, implies the right to live the fullest and happiest life of which the individual is capable by the constitution with which he is born into the world; it implies the right to property, to all which the individual has acquired for himself by his own skill and his own power, provided that, in acquiring it, he has not trespassed on his neighbours either by force or by fraud; it implies the right to make what contracts or arrangements he pleases with other individuals, provided, again, that the contract contains nothing which trenches on the rights of other parties. The free man is king of himself, but he is ruler of none other; self-respecting, he must respect the rights of others; jealous of his own liberty, he must be equally jealous of the liberty of every one else; stern defender of his own dignity, he must equally sternly repress any personal inclination, or any inclination of the many, to injure the same dignity which is in each individual alike. There is no picture of a nation possible to imagine which is sublimer than this: a nation of men and women, each free to develop into that beautiful variety which is one of the marvels and the glories of Nature, each a law to himself, each the defender of the liberty of each, strong and dignified as only free citizens can be, with the strength which grows from self-confidence and from confidence in others, with the dignity which is born of the knowledge that he who lives on the highest level he can reach, deserves the respect of his own heart, and wins the respect of all who surround him.

Equality is a word which is used as carelessly and as lightly as Liberty, and with as little thought of its only possible meaning. Equal in natural endowments, equal in possibilities of achievement, equal in physical and in mental strength, equal in moral virility, men are *not;* in this sense they are not born equal, in this sense they never can be equal; this equality is nowhere found in Nature, for throughout her mighty realms there is an endless variety, a marvellous interweaving of higher and lower elements, but never a dead level of equality, wherein none is afore or after other, none is greater or less than another. As a simple matter of fact, does any one pretend that men can be born equal in power and in possibilities? Take the children of drunken and unhealthy parents, born with enfeebled nerves, with stunted limbs, with dwarfed brain and diseased blood; take the child of hardy, sound, and temperate parents, with strong round limbs, and well-strung muscles, and all the bright vitality of young new life thrilling and bounding within him; are the two babes born equal? Could they be equal under any possible system of government? Let them be born, if you will, where waves the flag of a true Republic, and let no factitious superiority raise the one over the other; let each have a fair chance, and let neither be unjustly weighted; but Nature, before birth, has handicapped the one, and there is no equality between them. It may be pleaded that where equality was recognised and taught, *there* drunkenness and criminality would have fewer victims, and that then our poor little ones, foredoomed to misery and vice, would be one of the horrors of the past, no longer to be found in England. Take it that so it would be, as to a great extent it would be, although no glory of governmental purity and nobility can raise men without the will of men to raise themselves; take it so, because the ideal Republic is not possible until the men and women who *are* the Republic have grown into true manhood and true womanhood, and have left behind the weaknesses of childhood; yet, even then, no absolute equality will be found; some brains will be larger than others, and some bodies stronger than others; never will man be as the work of a craftsman, turned out by the dozen from the same mould. What, then, does Equality mean, when we place it in our Trinity of Hope and of Love? Is it only an empty word without meaning, with the false jingle of which we seek to deceive, babbling a falsehood which can never be a truth? Not so; Equality has a meaning which makes it worthy of its high place, mid-way between the Freedom and the Brotherhood of Man. Equality is Justice; absolute Justice to all alike; Justice which denies to none the right which is his; Justice which gives to none a right which is not his. Equality means that in rights, all men are equal; that before the law, all men are equal; that in law-given opportunities, all men are equal; that in advantages bestowed, all men are equal. It means that in life's race none shall start in artificial advance of another; that, although strength, and agility, and endurance must tell in the race itself, yet the racers shall be placed equal at the starting-post; that the superiority must be *in the runner*, and not gained by an advantage in the position from which he begins the race. Equality implies also that men shall really be born more equal than they are at present, because from our present inequalities, from our swollen wealth on the one side and from our ghastly poverty on the other, we actually labour to increase the slighter inequalities which Nature would produce, and we literally breed an inferior race with which to fill our workhouses and our gaols. Where equality of right is recognised, we shall gradually decrease inequalities of Nature, and we shall raise the race itself to a higher level, until, in the march upwards, until, in the developments of a more glorious Humanity, the poorest and the lowest in those happier times will be the superiors of the noblest and the proudest of our heroes of to-day.

There remains Fraternity: Fraternity, without which no Liberty is possible, except the fierce liberty of the beast of prey, living alone and in enmity with all; Fraternity, without which no Equality can exist, unless it be an equality of barbarism, where each lives by himself and through himself, and owes nought to his fellow. For Fraternity none need plead in theory, although we trample it under our feet in our daily practice; all acknowledge the beauty of brotherly love, and all would gladly extend its sway; many are careless of Liberty, and few seek for Equality, but all would raise an altar to Fraternity, where the smiling goddess might sit, garlanded in flowers, with the child Love in her arms, with the moon Peace at her feet, and clothed with the sun of Joy. And brotherhood may be cultured among us, yet more easily than Freedom and Justice; it is the hand which shall pluck the others, it is the magic wand which shall create them. Fraternity binds us together, each to each; fraternity is the strong cord which shall give to one the power of the whole. Liberty and Equality can only be won by *combined* effort, and combination is only possible as brotherhood is recognised and felt. This principle can be acted upon and spread by each of us: in our homes, in our lives, we can show its beauty; by the genial word and the helpful act; by the mere cordial clasp of the hand, which recognises the brotherhood of the labourer as reverently as that of the noble; by the steady refusal to deny the right of e lowest and most degraded, and the constant readiness to own the brotherhood and sisterhood of those whom the world makes outcasts; by crushing down jealousy and by following true greatness loyally; by working hand-in-hand with others to further every noble cause; by joyful self-sacrifice for the common good, and glad free labour for the benefit of all, we may so spread the principle of Fraternity in our ranks that, by the force of unity among us, we may stand all-powerful for attack, and may wrest Liberty from the grasp of oppressors, and erect the statue of Equality on the ruins of privilege and favouritism. Liberty, Equality, Fraternity: it is our motto, our cry, our badge. As the Christian wears the cross, and the Mahommedan is known by the crescent, so might Republicans be known by this symbol of their creed; engraven on the ring, on the locket, on the ornament, it might speak with silent eloquence of the hope which we struggle to realise, of the faith in which we work, of the aspirations by which we live; and, dead, it might hallow our tombs, as the sacred ideal to which we strove to conform our lives, and as the promise of the dawn of a gladder to-morrow, which shall be won for those who come after us by our labour or by our deaths.

CIVIL & RELIGIOUS LIBERTY.

WITH SOME HINTS TAKEN FROM

THE FRENCH REVOLUTION.

A Lecture

BY ANNIE BESANT,

(SECOND EDITION).

LONDON:
FREETHOUGHT PUBLISHING COMPANY,
28, STONECUTTER STREET, E.C.

PRICE THREEPENCE.

LONDON
PRINTED BY ANNIE BESANT AND CHARLES BRADLAUGH,
28, STONECUTTER STREET, E.C.

CIVIL AND RELIGIOUS LIBERTY.

"O Liberty! how many crimes are committed in thy name!" So exclaimed Madame Roland, one of the most heroic and most beautiful spirits of the great French Revolution, when above her glittered the keen knife of the guillotine, and below her glared the fierce faces of the maddened crowd, who were howling for her death. But Madame Roland, even as she spoke, bowed her fair head to the statue of Liberty which—pure, serene, majestic—rose beside the scaffold, and stood white and undefiled in the sunlight, while the mob seethed and tossed round its base. Madame Roland bent her brow before Liberty, even as the sad complaint passed her lips; for well that noble-hearted woman knew that the guillotine, by which she was to die, had not been raised in a night with the broken chains of Liberty, but had been slowly building up, during long centuries of tyranny, out of the mouldering skeletons of the thousands of victims of despotism and misrule. The taunt has been re-echoed ever since, and lovers of repression have changed its words and its meaning, and they have said what noble Madame Roland would never have said: "O Liberty, how many crimes are committed by thee, and because of thee!" They have never said, they have never cared to ask, how many crimes have been committed *against* Liberty in the past; how many crimes are daily committed against her in the England which we boast as free. They have never said, they have never cared to ask, whether the excesses which have, alas! disgraced revolutions, whether the bloodshed which has ofttimes stained crimson-red the fair, white, banner of Liberty, are not the natural and the necessary fruits, not of the freedom which is won, but of the tyranny which is crushed. Society keeps a number of its members uneducated and degraded; it houses them worse than brutes; it pays them so little that, if a man would not starve, he must toil all day, without time for relaxation or for self-culture; it withdraws from them all softening influences; it shuts them out from all intellectual amusements; it leaves them no pleasures except the purely animal ones; it bars against them the gates of the museums and the art galleries, and opens to them only the doors of the beer-shop and the gin-palace; it sneers at their folly, but never seeks to teach them wisdom; it disdains their "lowness," but never tries to help them to be higher; and then, when suddenly the masses of the people rise, maddened by long oppression, intoxicated with a freedom for which they are not prepared, arrogant with the newly-won consciousness of their resistless strength, then Society, which has kept them brutal, is appalled at their brutality; Society, which has kept them degraded, shrieks out at the inevitable results of that degradation. I have often heard wealthy men and women talk about the discontent and the restlessness of the poor; I have heard them prattle about the necessity of "keeping the people down;" I have heard polite and refined sneers at the folly and the tiresome enthusiasm of the political agitator, and half-jesting wishes that "the whole tribe of agitators" would become extinct. And as I have listened, and have seen the luxury around the speakers; as I have noted the smooth current of their lives, and marked the irritation displayed at some petty mischance which for a moment ruffled its even flow; as I have seen all this, and then remembered the miserable homes that I have known, the squalor and the hideous poverty, the hunger and the pain, I have thought to myself that if I could take the speakers, and could plunge them down into the life which the despised "masses" live, that the braver-hearted of them would turn into turbulent demagogues, while the weaker-spirited would sink down into hopeless drunkenness and pauperism. These rich ones do not mean to be cruel when they sneer at the complaints of the poor, and they are unconscious of the misery which underlies and gives force to the agitation which disturbs their serenity; they do not understand how the subjects which seem to them so dry are thrilling with living interest to the poor who listen to the "demagogue," or how his keenest thrusts are pointed in the smithy of human pain. They are only thoughtless, only careless, only indifferent; and meanwhile the smothered murmuring is going on around them, and grim Want and Pain and Despair are the phantom forms which are undermining their palaces; and "they eat, they drink, they marry, and are given in marriage," heedless of the gathering river which is beginning to overflow its banks, and which, if it be not drained off in time, will "sweep them all away." If they knew their best friends, they would bless the popular leaders, who are striving to win social and political reforms, and so to avert a revolution.

The French Revolution is so often flung, by ignorant people, in the teeth of those who are endeavouring to extend and to consolidate the reign of Freedom, that it can scarcely be deemed out of place to linger for a moment on the threshold of the subject, in order to draw from past experience the lesson, that bloodshed and civil war do not spring from wise and large measures of reform, but from the hopelessness of winning relief except by force, from over-taxation, from unjust social inequality, from the grinding of poverty, from the despair and from the misery of the people. It shows extremest folly to decline to study the causes of great catastrophes, to reject the experience won by the misfortunes and by the mistakes of others, and to refuse to profit by the lessons of the past.

Of course I do not mean to say, and I should be very sorry to persuade any one to think, that our state to-day in England is as bad as that from which France was only delivered through the frightful agony of the Revolution. But we have in England, as we shall see as we go on, many of the abuses left of that feudal system which the Revolution destroyed for ever in France. The feudal system was spread all over Europe in the Middle Ages, those Dark Ages when all sense of equal justice and of liberty was dead. It concentrated all power in the hands of the few; it took no account of the masses of the people; it handed over the poor, bound hand and foot, to the power of the feudal superior, and it cultivated that haughty spirit of disdainful contempt for labour, which is still, unfortunately, only too widely spread throughout our middle and upper classes in England. This system gradually lost its harsher features among ourselves; but in France it endured up to the time of the Revolution; and in this system, added to the fearful weight of taxation under which the people were absolutely crushed and starved to death, lies the secret of the bloodshed of the Revolution.

Therefore, before passing on to the parallel between our state and that of ante-revolutionary France, I would fain put into the mouths of our friends an answer to those who say that the excesses of the French Revolution are the necessary outcome of free thought in religion and of free action in politics. It is perfectly true that the determination to shake off a cruel and unjust yoke was implanted in the bosoms of the French people by the writings of those who are commonly called the Encyclopædists. These men *were* Freethinkers; some of them—as Holbach and Diderot—might fairly be called Atheists; some were nothing of the kind. These men taught the French people to think; they nurtured in their breasts a spirit of self-reliance; they roused a spirit of defiance. These men rang the tocsin which awoke France, and *so far* it is true that Freethought produced the Revolution, and *so far* Freethought may well be proud of her work. But not to Freethought, not to Liberty, must be ascribed the excesses which stained a revolution that was in its beginning, that might have been throughout, so purely glorious. For do you know what French Feudalism was? Do you know what those terrible rights were, which have branded so deeply into the French peasant's heart the hatred of the old nobility, that even to the present day he will hiss out between clenched teeth the word "aristocrat," with a passionate hatred which one hundred years of freedom have not quenched?

In the reign of Louis XIV. there was a Count, the Comte de Charolois, who used to shoot down, for his amusement, the peasants who had climbed into trees, and the tilers who were mending roofs. The *chasse aux paysans*, as it was pleasantly termed, the "hunt of peasants," was remembered by an old man who was in Paris during the Revolution as one of the amusements of the nobility in his youth. True, these acts were but the acts of a few; but they were done, and the people dared not strike back Then there was another right, a right which outraged all humanity, and which gave to the lord the first claim to the serf's bride. The terrible story in Charles Dickens's "Tale of Two Cities" is no fiction, except in details, if we may judge from some of the chronicles of the time. (Dufaure gives many interesting details on French feudalism.) Then they might harness the serfs, like cattle, to their carts; they might keep them awake all night beating the trenches round their castles, lest noble slumbers should be disturbed by the croaking of the frogs. When any one throws in the Radical's teeth the excesses of the French Revolution, let the Radical answer him back with these rights, and ask if it is to be wondered at that men struck hard, when the outrages and the oppressions of centuries were revenged in a few wild months? Marvel not at the short madness that broke out at last; marvel rather at the cowardice which bore in silence for so long.

I pass from these hideous rights of feudalism to its milder features, as they existed in France before the Revolution, and as they exist among us to-day in England. The laws by which land is held and transmitted, the rights of the first-born son, the laying-on of taxation by those who do not represent the tax-payer, a standing army in which birth helps promotion, the Game Laws—all these are relics of feudalism, relics which need to be swept away. It is on the existence of these that I ground my plea for wider freedom; it is on these that I rely to prove that Civil and Religious Liberty are still very imperfect among ourselves.

In France, before the revolution, people in general, king, queen, lords, clergy, thought that things were going on very nicely, and very comfortably. True, keener-sighted men saw in the misery of the masses the threatened ruin of the throne. True, even Royalty itself, in the haggard faces and gaunt forms that pressed cheering round its carriages, read traces of grinding poverty, of insufficient food. True, some faint rumour even reached the court, amid its luxury, that the houses of the people were not all they should be, nay, that many of them were wretched huts, not fit for cattle. But what of that? There was no open rebellion; there was no open disloyalty. What disloyalty there was, was confined to the lower orders, and showed itself by a fancy of the people to gather into Republican clubs, and other such societies, where loyalty to the Crown was *not* the lesson which they learned from the speakers' lips. But such disloyalty could of course be crushed out at any moment, and the court went gaily on its way, careless of the low, dull growling in the distance which told of the coming storm. We, in England, to-day, are quite at ease. True, some of our labourers are paid starvation-wages of 10s., 11s., 12s., a week, but again I ask, what of that? Has not Mr. Fraser Grove, late M.P., told the South Wiltshire farmers that they had a right to reduce the labourer's wage to 11s. a week, if he could live upon it, and, if he did not like it, he could take his labour to other markets? Why should the labourer complain, so long as he is allowed to live? Then the houses of our people are scarcely all that they should be. I have been into some so-called homes, composed of two small rooms, in one of which father and mother, boys and girls growing up into manhood and womanhood, were obliged to sleep in the one room, even in the one bed. I have seen a room in which slept four generations, the great-grandfather and his wife, the grandmother (unmarried), the mother (unmarried), and the little child of the latter, and in addition to these relatives, the room also afforded sleeping accommodation to three men lodgers. Yet people talk about the "immorality of the agricultural poor," as though people could be anything except immoral, when the lads and lasses have to grow up without any possibility of being even decent, much less with any possibility of retaining the smallest shred of natural modesty. The only marvel is how, among our poor, there do grow up now and then fair and pure blossoms, worthy of the most carefully-guarded homes. But a very short time since there were worse hovels even than those I have mentioned. Down at Woolwich there were "homes" composed of one small room, 12 feet by 12, and 8½ feet high in the middle of the sloping roof, and the huts were built of bad brick, the damp of which sweated slowly through the whitewash, and the floor was made of beaten earth, lower in level than the ground outside, and in front of the fire they kept a plank all day baking warm and dry, in order that at night they might put it into the bed, to keep the sleeper next the wall from being wet through by the drippings as he slept. And in other such huts as these four families lived together, with no partition put up between them, save such poor rags as some lingering feeling of decency might lead them to hang up for themselves—and these huts, these miserable huts, were the property of Government, and in them were housed her Majesty's married soldiers, housed in such abodes as her Majesty would not allow her cattle to occupy near Windsor or near Balmoral. Yet among us there is no open rebellion; there is no open disloyalty. Among us, too, what disloyalty there is, is chiefly confined to the lower orders, and that, as everyone knows, can be snuffed out at a moment's notice. Among us, it also shows itself in that fancy of the people to gather into Republican clubs and other such societies, where loyalty to the Crown is not the lesson most enforced by the speakers. The quiet, slow alienation of the people from the Throne is going on unobserved; a people who are loyal to a monarchy will not form themselves into Republican Clubs; yet our rulers never dream that the people are discontented, and that these clubs are signs of the times. They fancy that the agitation is only the work of the few, and that there is no widely-spread disaffection behind the Republican teachers; only the leaders of popular movements know the vast force which they can wield in case of need, but the Government will never listen to these men, any more than in France they would listen to Mirabeau, until it was too late. Yet do sensible people think that a sound and a healthy society can rest upon the misery of the masses? and do our rulers think that palaces stand firm when they are built up upon such hovels as those which I have described? It appears they do; for our Queen and our Princes seem to believe in the lip-loyalty of the crowds which cheer them when they make us happy by driving through our streets, loyalty that springs from the thoughtlessness of custom, and not from true and manly reverence for real worth. For I would not be thought to disparage the sentiment of loyalty; I hold it to be one of the fairest blossoms which flower on the emotional side of the nature of man. Loyalty to principle, loyalty to a great cause, loyalty to some true leader, crowned king of men by reason of his virtue, of his genius, of his strength—such loyalty as this it is no shame for a freeman to yield, such loyalty as this has, in all ages of the world, inspired men to the noblest self-devotion, nerved men to the most heroic self-sacrifice. But just as only those things which are valuable in themselves are thought worthy of imitation in baser metal, so is this true golden loyalty imitated by the pinchbeck loyalty, which shouts in our streets. For what true loyalty is possible from us towards the House of Brunswick? Loyalty to virtue? as enshrined in a Prince of Wales? loyalty to liberality, and to delicacy of sentiment? as exemplified by a Duke of Edinburgh? loyalty to any great cause, whose success in this generation is bound up with the life of any member of our Royal House? The very questions send a ripple of laughter through any assemblage of Englishmen, and they are beginning to feel, at last, that true loyalty can only be paid to some man who stands head and shoulders above his fellows, and not to some poor dwarf, whom we can only see over the heads of the crowd, because he stands on the artificial elevation of a throne.

The court in France was very extravagant; it spent

£34,000,000 in eight years, while the people were starving, our princes do not spend so much ; *they dare not;* but that the spirit is the same is clearly seen when a wealthy queen sends to Parliament to dower her sons and her daughters : when the scions of a family so rich as are the Brunswicks, become beggars to the nation, and pensioners on the pockets of the poor. However, courts are expensive things, and if we want them we must be content to pay for them. Now, in France, the nobles, the clergy, the great landed proprietors, paid next to nothing : the heavy burden of taxation fell upon the poor. But the poor had not much money which they could pay out to the State, and it is not easy to empty already empty pockets with any satisfactory results ; so, in France, they hit upon the ingenious system called indirect taxation ; they imposed taxes upon the necessaries of life ; they squeezed money out of the food which the people were obliged to buy. Also, those who imposed the taxes were not those who paid them : they laid on heavy burdens, which they themselves did not touch with one of their fingers. We, in England, also think that it conduces to the cheerful paying of taxes that they should be laid chiefly upon those who have no voice wherewith to complain of their incidence in Parliament. If you want to knock a man down, it is very wise to choose a dumb man, who cannot raise a cry for help. A large portion of the working classes, and all women, have no votes in the election of members of Parliament, and have therefore no voice in the imposition of the taxes which they are, nevertheless, obliged to pay. It is a long time since Pitt told us that "taxation without representation is robbery ;" it is a yet longer time since John Hampden taught us how to resist the payment of an unjust tax, and yet we are still such cravens, or else so indifferent, that we pay millions a year in taxation, without determining that we *will* have a voice in the control of our own income. We are crushed under a heavy and a yearly increasing national expenditure, partly because of our extravagant administration, partly because the burden falls unequally, weighing on the poor more than upon the rich, and wholly because we have not brotherhood enough to combine together, nor manhood enough to say that these things shall not be. Our system of taxation is radically vicious in principle, because it must of necessity fall unequally. Those who impose the burdens know perfectly well that it is impossible for the poor to refuse to pay indirect taxes, however onerous those taxes may be: they *must* buy the necessary articles of food, whether those articles be taxed or no; a refusal to pay is impracticable, and no combination to abstain from buying is possible, because the things taxed are the necessaries of life. Yet as long as indirect taxation is permitted—and the major part of our annual revenue is drawn from Customs and from Excise—so long must taxation crush the poor, while it falls lightly on the rich.

On this point I direct your attention to the following extract, taken from the *Liverpool Financial Reformer*, and quoted by Mr. Charles Watts in his "Government and the People":—

"A recent writer in the *Liverpool Financial Reformer*, divided the community into three divisions—first, the aristocratic, represented by those who have an annual income of £1,000 and upwards; the middle classes were represented by those who had incomes from £100 to £1,000; and the artisan or working classes were those who were supposed to have incomes under £100 per year. He then assessed their incomes respectively at £208,385,000; £174,579,000; and £149,745,000. Towards the taxation, each division paid as follows. The aristocratic portion contributed £8,500,000, the middle classes £19,513,453, and the working classes £32,861,474. The writer remarks: 'The burden of the revenue, as it is here shown to fall on the different classes, may not be fractionally accurate, either on the one side or the other, for that is an impossibility in the case, but it is sufficiently so to afford a fair representation in reference to those classes on whom the burden chiefly falls. Passing over the middle classes, who thus probably contribute about their share, the result in regard to the upper and lower classes stands thus:—Amount which should be paid to the revenue by the higher classes (that is, the classes above £1,000 a year), £23,437,688; amount which they do pay, £8,500,000; leaving a difference of £14.937,688, so that the higher classes are paying nearly £15,000,000 less than their fair share of taxation. Amount which should be paid by the working classes (or those having incomes below £100), £16,846,312; amount which they do pay, £32,861,474; making a difference of £16,015,162; so that the working classes are paying about £16,000,000 more than their fair share. In other words, the respective average rates paid upon the assessable income of the two classes are—by the higher classes, 10d. per pound; the working classes, 4s. 4d. That is to say, the working classes are paying at a rate five times more heavily than the wealthy classes.'"

The whole system of laying taxes on the necessaries of life

is radically vicious in principle; to tax the necessaries of life is to sap the strength and to shorten the life of those men and those women on whose strength and whose life the prosperity of the country depends; it is to enfeeble the growing generation; it is to make the children pale and stunted; it is, in fact, to undermine the constitution of the wealth-producers. To tax food is to tax life itself, instead of taxing incomes; it is a financial system which is, at once, cruel and suicidal. As a matter of fact, taxes taken off food have not decreased the revenue, and when this policy of taxing food shall have become a thing of the past, then a healthier and more strongly-framed nation will bear with ease all the necessary burdens of the State. Indirect taxation is also bad, because it implies a number of small taxes (some of which are scarcely worth the cost of collecting), and thus necessitates the employment of a numerous staff of officials, whereas one large direct tax would be more easily gathered in.

It is also bad, because, with indirect taxation, it is almost impossible for a man to know what he really *does* pay towards the support of the State. It is right and just that every citizen in a free country should consciously contribute to the maintenance of the Government which he has himself placed over him; but when he knows exactly what he is paying, he will probably think it worth while to examine into the national expenditure, and to insist on a wise economy in the public service. I do not mean the kind of economy which is so relished by Governments, the economy which dismisses skilled workmen, whose work is needed, while it retains sinecures for personages in high places; but I mean that just and wise economy which gives good pay for honest work, but which refuses to pay dukes, earls, even princes, for doing nothing. This great problem of fair and equal taxation ought to be thoroughly studied and thought over by every citizen; few infringements on equal liberty are so fraught with harm and misery as are those which pass almost unnoticed under the head of "collection of the revenue"; few reforms are so urgently needed as a reform of our financial system, and a fair adjustment of the burdens of taxation.

In France they had Game Laws. If the season were cold the farmers might not mow their hay at the proper time, lest the birds should lack cover; they might not hoe the corn, lest they should break the partridge eggs; the birds fed off the crops, and they might not shoot or trap them; if they transgressed the Game Laws they were sent to the galleys; herds of wild boar and red deer roamed over the country, and the farmers and the peasants were forbidden to interfere with them. Englishmen! who call yourselves free, do you imagine that these relics of barbarism, swept away by the French Revolution in one memorable night, are nothing but archæological curiosities, archaic remains, fossilised memorials of a long-past tyranny? On the contrary, our Game Laws in England are as harsh as those I have cited to you, and the worst facts I am going to relate you have no parallel in the history of France. These cases are so shameful that they ought to have raised a shout of execration through the land; they have been covered up, and hushed up, as far as possible, and I have taken them from a Parliamentary Blue-book; and I have taken them thence myself, because I would not quote at second-hand deeds so disgraceful, that had I not read them in the dry pages of a Parliamentary Commission I should have fancied that they had been either carelessly or purposely exaggerated in order to point a tirade against the rich. I allude to the deer-forests of Scotland.

But before dealing with these it is interesting to note the curious points of similarity between our Game Laws and those of the French. In France, they were sometimes forbidden to mow the hay because of the cover it yielded to the birds: in England, you will sometimes find a clause inserted in the lease of a farm, binding the farmer to reap with the sickle instead of with the scythe, that is, to reap with an instrument that does not cut the corn-stalks off close to the ground, so that cover may be left for the birds; thus the farmers' profits are decreased by the amount of straw which is left to rot in the ground for the landlord's amusement. In France, the game might not be touched even if the crops were damaged; in England, the hares may ruin a young plantation, and the farmer may not snare or shoot them. In France, those who transgressed the Game Laws were sent to the galleys; in England, we send them to prison with hard labour, and we actually pay for the manufacture of 10,000 criminals every year, in order that our Princes of Wales and our landed proprietors may make it the business of their lives "to shoot poultry." In France, the herds of wild boar and red deer might not be molested; in England we manage these things better; we have, unfortunately, no wild boar, but we clear our farmers and our peasants out of the way in order that we may be sure that our deer are not interfered with. As the son of a Highland proprietor said, when planning a new deer-forest: "the first thing to do, you know, is to clear out the people." *The first thing to do is to clear out the people?* Yes! clear out the people: the people, who have lived on the land for years, and who have learned to love it as though they had been born landowners; the people who have tilled and cultivated it, making it laugh out into cornfields which have fed hundreds of the poor; the people, who have wrought on it, and toiled with plough and spade; turn out the people and make way for the animals; level the homes of the people and make a hunting ground for the rich. "It is no deer-forest if the farmers are all there," said a witness before the Commission; and so you see the farmers *must* go, for of course it is necessary that we should have deer-forests. No less than forty families, owning seven thousand sheep, seven thousand goats, and two hundred head of cattle, were turned out from their homes in the time of the present Marquis of Huntly's grandfather, their houses were pulled down, and their land was planted with fir-trees; some of the leases were bought up; in cases where they had expired the people were bidden go. And thus it comes to pass, according to the evidence of one witness—a witness whom members of the Commission tried hard to browbeat, but whose evidence they utterly failed to shake—thus it comes to pass that "you see in the deer-forests the ruins of numerous hamlets, with the grass growing over them." A pathetic picture of homes laid desolate, of the fair course of peaceful lives roughly broken into; of helpless and oppressed people, of selfish and greedy wealth. "From Glentanar, thirty miles from Aberdeen, you can walk in forests until you come to the Atlantic." And this evil is growing rapidly; in 1812 there were only five deer-forests in Scotland: in 1873 there were seventy. In 1870, 1,320,000 acres of land were forest; in 1873, there were 2,000,000 acres thus rendered useless. Under these circumstances, it is scarcely to be wondered at that the population is decreasing; the population of Argyleshire in 1831 was 103,330; in 1871, forty years later, when it ought to have largely increased, it had, on the contrary, decreased to 75,635; in Inverness it was 94,983; during the same time it has gone down to 87,480.

But this is not all. While some farmers and peasants are "cleared out" altogether, those who are allowed to remain suffer much from the depredations of the deer and other game. In Aberdeenshire alone no less than 291 farmers complained of the enormous damage that was done to their crops by the deer. The deer-forest is not generally fenced in; and as deer are very partial to turnips, it naturally follows that the herds come out of the forest and feed off the farmers' crops. One proprietor graciously states that he does his best to keep the deer away from the farms, but—judging by the complaints of the farmers—these laudable efforts scarcely appear to be crowned with the success that they deserve. Not only, however, do the deer stray *out* of the forests, but the farmers' sheep stray *in*, and as sheep are not game he is not permitted to follow them to fetch them out. When such evidence as this comes out, and we know the pressure that is put upon tenants by their landlords, and the danger they run by giving offence to their powerful masters, we can judge how much more remains behind of which we know nothing. And, in the name of common justice, what is all this for? Why should a farmer be compelled to keep his landlord's game for him? Why should the farmer's crops suffer to amuse a man who does nothing except inherit land? This wide-spread loss, these desolated homes, these ruined lives, what mighty national benefit have these miseries bought for England? They all occur in order that a few rich men may occasionally—when other pleasures pall on the jaded taste, and *ennui* becomes insupportable—have the novel excitement of shooting at a stag. Verily we have a right to boast of our freedom when thousands of citizens suffer for the sake of the amusement of the few.

But these deer-forests do not only injure the unfortunate people who are turned out to make room for the deer, and the farmers who lose the full profit of their labour; *to turn cultivable land into deer-forests is to decrease the food-supply of the country*. Some people say that only worthless land is used for this purpose; but this is not true, for pasture-ground has been turned into forests. In one place, 800 head of cattle and 500 sheep were fed upon one quarter of the land which now supports 750 red deer. That is to say, that 1,300 animals good for food were nourished by the land which is now devoted to the maintenance of 187½ useless deer. Judge then of the decrease of the food-supply of the country which is implied in the fact that one-tenth part of Scotland is now moor and forest. A baillie of Aberdeen calculates the loss to the country at no less than 20 millions of pounds of meat annually. In England things are not so bad; but in England, also, the cultivation of the land wasted in game-preserving would increase to an almost incalculable extent the food supply of the country. There is the vast estate of Chillingworth, kept for a few wild cattle, in order that a Prince of Wales may now and then drive about it, and from the safe eminence of a cart may have the pleasure of shooting at a bull. But at this point the question of the Game Laws melts insensibly into that of the Land Laws, for under a just system of Land Tenure such deeds as these would be impossible; then, men could not, for their own selfish amusement, turn sheep-walks into forests, and farms into moors.

With our great and increasing population it is absolutely necessary that all cultivable land should be under cultivation. To hold uncultivated, land which is capable of producing bread and meat is a crime against the State. It is well known to be one of the points of the "extreme" Radical programme that it should be rendered penal to hold large quantities of cultivable land uncultivated. Then, instead of sending the cream of our peasantry abroad, to seek in foreign countries the land which is fenced in from them at home; instead of driving them to seek from the stranger the work which is denied to them in the country of their birth; we should keep Englishmen in England to make England strong and rich, and give land to the labour which is starving for work, and labour to the land which is barren for the lack of it. "Land to labour, and labour to land" ought to be our battle-cry, and should be the motto engraven on our shield.

But it is impossible to throw land open to labour so long as the laws render its transmission from seller to buyer so expensive and so cumbersome a proceeding. It is impossible also to effect any radical improvement so long as the land is tied up in the hands of the few fortunate individuals who are now permitted to monopolise it. Half the land of England, and four-fifths of the land of Scotland, is owned by 160 families. These few own the land which ought to be devoted to the good of the nation. Land, like air, and like all other natural gifts, cannot rightly be held as private property. The only property which can justly be claimed in land is the improvement wrought in the soil. When a man has put labour or money into the land he farms, then he *has* a right to the advantages which accrue from his toil and from his invested capital. But this principle is the very contrary of that which is embodied in our Land Laws. The great landowners do nothing for the land they own; they spend nothing on the soil which maintains them in such luxury. It is the farmers and the labourers who have a right to life-tenancy in the soil, or, more exactly, to a tenancy, lasting as long as they continue to improve it. The farmer, whose money is put into the land—the labourer, whose strength enriches the soil—these are the men who ought to be the landowners of England. As it is, the farmer takes a farm; he invests capital in it; he rises early to superintend his labourers; the land rewards him with her riches, she gives him fuller crops and fatter cattle, and then the landlord steps in, and raises the rent, and thus absolutely punishes the farmer for his energy and his thrift. The idle man stands by with his hands in his pockets, and then claims a share of the profits which accrue from the busy man's labour. Meanwhile the labourer—he whose strong arms have guided the plough, and wielded the spade, he who has made the harvest and tended the cattle—what do our just Land Laws give to him? They give him a wretched home, a pittance sufficient—generally at least—to "keep body and soul together," parish pay when he is ill, the workhouse in his old age, and he sleeps at last in a pauper's grave. O! just and beneficent English Law! To the idle man, the lion's share of the profits; to the man who does much, a small share; to the man who does most of all, just enough to enable him to work for his masters. But if this gross injustice be pointed out, if we protest against this crying evil, and declare that these crimes shall cease in England, then these landowners arise and complain that we are tampering with the "sacred rights of property." Sacred rights of property! But what of the more sacred rights of human life? The life of the poor is more holy than the property of the rich, and famished men and women more worthy of care than the acres of the nobleman. If these vast estates are fenced in from us by parchment fences, so that we cannot throw them open to labour, so that we cannot make the desert places golden with corn, and rich with sheep and oxen; if these vast estates are fenced in from us by parchment fences, then I say that the plough must go through the parchment, in order that the people may have bread.

The maintenance of a standing army, in which birth helps promotion, is another blot upon our shield. A Duke of Cambridge, General Commanding-in-Chief, and Colonel of four regiments, who holds these offices by virtue of his "high" birth, and in spite of the most palpable incapacity, is an absurdity which ought not to be tolerated in a country which pretends to be free. A Prince of Wales, who has never seen war, made a Field-Marshal; a Duke of Edinburgh, created a Post-Captain; such appointments as these are a disgrace to the country, and a bitter satire on our army and our navy. Carpet-soldiers are useless in time of war, and they are a burden in time of peace; and to squander England's money on such officers as these, simply because they chance to be born Princes, is a distinct breach of equal Civil Liberty.

The need of Electoral Reform is well-known to all students of politics. No country is free in which all adult citizens have not a voice in the government. A representation which is based upon a property qualification is radically vicious in principle. But not only is our civil liberty cramped by the fact that the majority of citizens are not represented at all, but even the poor representation we have is unequally and unjustly distributed. In one place 136 men return a member to Parliament; in another, 18,000 fail to return their candidate. In Parliament 110 members represent 83,000 voters. The next 110 represent 1,080,000. A group of 70,000 voters return 4 members; another group of 70,000 return 80. In one instance, 30,000 voters outweigh 546,000 in Parliament by a majority of 9. Hence it follows that a minority of electors rule England, and, however desirable it may be that minorities should be represented, it is surely not desirable that they should rule. Our present system throws overwhelming power into the hands of the titled and landowning classes, who, by means of small and manageable boroughs, are able to outvote the masses of the people congregated in the large towns. As long as this is the case, as long as every citizen does not possess a vote, as long as the few can, by means of unequal distribution of electoral power, control the actions of the many, so long England is not free, and civil liberty is not won.

To strike at the House of Lords is to strike at a dying

institution; but dying men sometimes live long, and dying institutions may last for centuries if only they are nursed and tended with sufficient care. A House in the election of whose members the people have no voice; a House whose members are born into it, instead of winning their way into it by service to the State; a House which is built upon cradles and not upon merit; a House whose deliberations may be shared in by fools or by knaves, provided *only* that the brow be coronetted—such a House is a disgrace to a free country, and an outrage on popular liberty. As might be expected from its constitution, this House of Lords has ever stood in the path of every needed reform, until it has been struck out of the way by hidden menace or by stern command. Is there any abuse whose days are numbered? be sure it will be defended in the House of Lords. Is there a monopoly which needs to be abolished? be sure it will be championed in the House of Lords. Is there any popular liberty asked for? be sure it will be refused in the House of Lords. Is there any fetter struck from off the limbs of progress? be sure that some cunning smith will be found to weld the fragments together again, under the name of an amendment, in the House of Lords. The only use of the thing is, that it may act as a political barometer by which to prognosticate the coming weather; that which the House of Lords blesses is most certainly doomed, while whatever it frowns upon is crowned for a speedy triumph. It has not even the merit of courage, this craven assemblage of toy-players at legislation; however boldly it roars out its "No," a frown from the House of Commons makes it tremble and yield; like a reed, it stands upright enough in the calm weather; like a reed, it bows before the storm-wind of a popular cry. As a question of practical politics, the House of Lords should be struck at almost rather than the Crown, because the whole principle of aristocracy is embodied in that House, the whole fatal notion that the accident of birth gives the right to rule. Our puppet kings and queens are less directly injurious to the commonwealth than is this titled House. The gilded figure-head injures the State-vessel less than the presence of hands on her tiller-ropes which know naught of navigation. And with the fall of the House of Lords must crash down the throne, which is but the ornament upon its roof, the completion of its elevation; so that when the toy-house has fallen at the breath of the people's lips, and we can see over the near prospect which it now hides from our gaze, we shall surely see, with the light of the morning on her face, with her golden head shining in the sun-rays, with the day-star on her brow, and the white garments of peace upon her limbs, with her sceptre wreathed in olive-branches, and her feet shod with plenty, that fair and glorious Republic for which we have yearned and toiled so long.

Having seen the chief blots upon our Civil Liberty, let us turn our attention to the defects in our religious freedom. And here I plead, neither as Freethinker nor as Secularist, but simply as a citizen of a mighty State, and member of a community which pretends to be free. For every shade of Nonconformity I plead, from the Roman Catholic to the Atheist, for all whose consciences do not fit into the mould provided by the Establishment, and whose thought refuses to be fettered by the bands of a State religion. I crave for every man, whatever be his creed, that his freedom of conscience be held sacred. I ask for every man, whatever be his belief, that he shall not suffer, in civil matters, for his faith or for his want of faith. I demand for every man, whatever be his opinions, that he shall be able to speak out with honest frankness the results of honest thought, without forfeiting his rights as citizen, without destroying his social position, and without troubling his domestic peace. We have not to-day, in England, the scourge and the rack, the gibbet and the stake, by which men's bodies are tortured to improve their souls, but we have the scourge of calumny and the rack of severed friendship, we have the gibbet of public scorn, and the stake of a ruined home, by which we compel conformity to dogma, and teach men to be hypocrites that they may eat a piece of bread. The spirit is the same, though the form of the torture be changed; and many a saddened life, and many a wrecked hope, bear testimony to the fact that religious liberty is still but a name, and freedom of thought is still a crime. Public opinion, and social feeling, we can but strive to influence and to improve; what I would lay stress upon here, is the existence of a certain institution, and of certain laws, which foster this one-sided feeling, and which are a direct infringement of the rights of the individual conscience.

First and foremost, overshadowing the land by her gigantic monopoly, is the Church as by law established. This body —one sect among many sects—is given by law many privileges which are not accorded to any other religious denomination. Her ministers are the State-officers of religion;

her highest dignitaries legislate for the whole Empire; national graveyards are the property of her clergy; and the best parts of national buildings are owned by her rectors. So long as the State was Christian and orthodox, so long might the Establishment of the State-religion be defensible, but the moment that the Church ceased to be co-extensive with the nation, that same moment did her Establishment become an injustice to that portion of the nation which did not conform to her creed. Every liberty won by the Nonconformist has been a blow struck at the reasonableness of the Establishment. She is nothing now but a palpable anachronism. Jews, Roman Catholics, even "Infidels" (provided only that they veil their Infidelity), may sit in the House of Parliament. They may alter the Church's articles, they may define her doctrines, they may change her creed; she is only the mere creature of the State, bought by lands and privileges to serve in a gilded slavery. The truth or the untruth of her doctrines is nothing to the point. I protest in principle against the establishment by the State of any form of religious, or of anti-religious, belief. The State is no judge in such matters; let every man follow his own conscience, and worship at what shrine his reason bids him, and let no man be injured because he differs from his neighbour's creed. The Church Establishment is an insult to every Roman Catholic, to every Protestant dissenter, to every Freethinker, in the Empire. The national property usurped by the Establishment might lighten the national burdens, were it otherwise applied, so that, indirectly, every non-Churchman is taxed for the support of a creed in which he does not believe, and for the maintenance of ministrations by which he does not profit. The Church must be destroyed, as an Establishment, before religious equality can be anything more than an empty name.

There are laws upon the Statute Book which grievously outrage the rights of conscience, and which subject an "apostate"—that is, a person who has been educated in, or who has professed Christianity, and has subsequently renounced it—to loss of all civil rights, provided that the law be put in force against him. The right of excommunication, lodged in the Church, is, I think, a perfectly fair right, *provided that it carry with it no civil penalties whatsoever.* The Church, like any other club, ought to be able to exclude an objectionable member, but she ought not to be able to call in the arm of the law to impose non-spiritual penalties. But the "apostate" loses all civil rights. The law, as laid down, is as follows: "Enacted by statute 9 and 10, William III., cap 32, that if any person educated in, or having made profession of, the Christian religion, shall by writing, printing, teaching, or advised speaking, assert or maintain there are more Gods than one, or shall deny the Christian religion to be true [this Act adds to these offences, that of "denying any one of the persons in the Trinity to be God," but it was repealed *quoad hoc*, by 53 George III., c. 60] or the Holy Scriptures of the Old and New Testaments to be of divine authority, he shall upon the first offence be rendered incapable to hold any ecclesiastical, civil, or military office, or employment, and for the second, be rendered incapable of bringing any action, or to be guardian, executor, legatee, or grantee, and shall suffer three years' imprisonment without bail. To give room, however, for repentance, if within four months after the first conviction, the delinquent will, in open court, publicly renounce his error, he is discharged for that once from all disabilities." Some will say that this law is never put in force; true, public opinion would not allow of its general enforcement, but it is turned against those who are poor and weak, while it lets the strong go free. Besides, it hangs over every sceptic's head like the sword of Damocles, and it serves as a threat and menace in the hand of every cruel and bigoted Churchman, who wants to extract any concession from an unbeliever. *No law that can be enforced is obsolete;* it may lie dormant for a time, but it is a sabre, which can at any moment be drawn from the sheath; the "obsolete" law about the Sabbath closed the Brighton Aquarium, and Rosherville Gardens, and is found to be quite easy of enforcement; though people would have laughed, a short time since, at the idea of anyone grumbling at its presence on the Statute Book. Poor, harmless, half-witted, Thomas Pooley, in 1857, found the Blasphemy Laws by no means "a dead letter" in the mouth of Lord Justice Coleridge. And there are plenty of other cases of injustice which have taken, and do take place under these laws, which might be quoted were it worth while to fill up space with them, and but little is needed to fan the smouldering fire of bigotry into a flame, and to put the laws generally in force once more. Already threats are heard, murmurs of the old wicked spirit of persecution, and it behoves us to see to it that these swords be broken, so that bigots may be unable to wield them again among us.

I do not, as I have said, protest now against these laws as a Secularist; I challenge them only as unjust disabilities imposed on men's consciences, and I appeal to all lovers of liberty to agitate against them, because they impose civil disabilities on some forms of religious opinion. And to you, O Christians! I would say: fight Freethought, if you will; oppose Atheism, if you deem it false and injurious to humanity: strike at us with all your strength on the *religious* platform; it is your right, nay, it is even your duty; but do not seek to answer our questions by blows from the statute book, nor to check our search after truth by the arm of the law. I impeach these laws against "infidels," at the bar of public opinion, as an infraction of the just liberty of the individual, as an insult to the dignity of the citizen, as an outrage on the sacred rights of conscience.

I do not pretend, in the short pages of such a paper as this, to have done more than to sketch, very briefly and very imperfectly, the chief defects of our civil and religious liberty. I have only laid before you a rough draft of a programme of Reform. Each blot on English liberty which I have pointed to might well form the sole subject of an essay; but I have hoped that, by thus gathering up into one some few of the many injustices under which we suffer, I might, perchance, lend definiteness to the aspirations after Liberty which swell in the breasts of many, and might point out to the attacking army some of the most assailable points of the fortress of bigotry and caste-prejudice, which the soldiers of Freedom are vowed to assail. I have taken, as it were, a bird's-eye view of the battle-ground of the near future, of that battle-ground on which soon will clash together the army which fights under the banner of privileges, and the army which marches under the standard of Liberty. The issue of that conflict is not doubtful, for Liberty is immortal and eternal, and her triumph is sure, however it may be delayed. The beautiful goddess before whom we bow is ever young with a youth which cannot fade, and radiant with a glory which nought can dim. Hers is the promise of the future; hers the fair days that shall dawn hereafter on a liberated earth; and hers is also the triumph of to-morrow, if only we, who adore her, if only we can be true to ourselves and to each other. But they who love her must work for her, as well as worship her, for labour is the only prayer to Liberty, and devotion the only praise. To her we must consecrate our brain-power and our influence among our fellows; to her we must sacrifice our time, and, if need be, our comfort and our happiness; to her we must devote our efforts, and to her the fruits of our toil. And at last, in the fair, bright future—at last, in the glad to-morrow—amid the shouts of a liberated nation, and the joy of men and women who see their children free, we shall see the shining goddess descending from afar, where we have worshipped her so long, to be the sunshine and the glory of every British home. And then, O men and women of England, then, when you have once clasped the knees of Liberty, and rested your tired brows on her gentle breast, then cherish and guard her evermore, as you cherish the bride you have won to your arms, as you guard the wife whose love is the glory of your manhood, and whose smile is the sunshine of your home.

Printed by ANNIE BESANT and CHARLES BRADLAUGH, 28, Stonecutter Street, London, E.C.

ENGLISH REPUBLICANISM.

BY

ANNIE BESANT.

LONDON:
FREETHOUGHT PUBLISHING COMPANY
28, Stonecutter Street, E.C.

PRICE ONE PENNY.

ENGLISH REPUBLICANISM.

BY

ANNIE BESANT.

Republicanism in England is a feeling that is ever growing beneath the surface, but that only rarely shows itself above ground; its strength is real though little apparent, sturdy though not fiery. Very seldom does absolute Republicanism break out in Parliament, as in Mr. Cowen's eloquent protest against the assumption by the Queen of the imperial title, but the Republican spirit is the very core of English progressive thought, and influences political action even among those who are most opposed to it. Self-reliance, self-government, decentralisation, these are at once the essence of Republicanism and of the English political genius, and no Republic that the world has yet seen will be so strong, so stable, so free, as that British Republic which will be the completion of the work of the Long Parliament and of the Revolution of 1688. Milton, Vane, Marten, Algernon Sidney, are types of English Republicanism; the effacement of one-man government was their chief object; the gradual recession of the royal personality has been the gradual realizing of their ideal, and its complete disappearance will be the blossoming of the tree they planted two hundred years ago. Great Britain has been slowly broadening into a Republic during these centuries, and it may well be hoped that the ultimate form of our Republic will be shaped on the lines they drew, and will thus avoid those perils which have been exhibited in the working of other Republican constitutions. It is worthy of notice, that the consciously Republican feeling is strongest in those parts of the country in which politics are most studied by the people, and education is most general. The mining population of Northumberland and of a great part of Durham stands, taken as a whole, head and shoulders above any other labouring class for independence, self-respect, thoughtfulness, and political earnestness; in the pit cottages of that district politics are discussed with an amount of shrewdness and sound knowledge which would astonish some of our dilettante clubsmen; Republicanism is there the political creed of the large majority: as one said, amid the approving cheers and laughter of a crowded mass meeting: "We pitmen don't care to keep more cats than there's mice to catch," and the royal cats are, in their eyes, wholly unprofitable domestic animals. The growing pressure of want will much quicken the Republican feeling, and the Tory increase of taxation tells in the same direction. Unfortunately, pressure of suffering, though a convincing, is the most unwholesome teacher of Republicanism which can be sent through any nation. Republics should be born of thought, not of suffering; of reason, not of despair; they should be slowly evolved through Reform, not burst, Minerva-like, full-formed and clad in mail, from the Jove of Revolution.

What is a Republic, and what its most perfect form? The essence of Republicanism is that the Government shall be made and controlled by the nation, and that every legislative and executive office shall be elective, not hereditary. Hereditary right to rule can find no place in a Republic, since a Republic is built by reason, and inherited authority is of all things the most irrational. "One of the strongest natural proofs of the folly of hereditary right in kings," says Thomas Paine, "is that Nature disapproves it, otherwise she would not so frequently turn it into ridicule by giving mankind an ass for a lion." The winner of a title is ennobled because he is a lion; his descendants too often inherit only the lion's skin.

It matters little what name is borne by the chief magistrate of a Republic; it is not what he is called, but what he is, which is important. The chief magistrate may be elected for life, and decorated with some imperial title: this is the unwisest form of all, and ever grows into a tyranny. He may be elected for a term and styled a President, as in America for four years, and as now in France for seven;

this also is unwise, and shares in the vice of royalty, making a master instead of a minister. A nation should never give itself away into the hands of one man for a fixed term of years. Most wisely, it may elect its chief only through its elected Parliament, and styling him either President or Prime Minister, make him only the responsible head of the Executive Council, holding power while he keeps a Parliamentary majority; this is the safest, the freest plan of all; this at once utilizes the best brains of the nation, and yet forbids a despotism; it is orderly and free, preventing alike tyranny and confusion. For Great Britain, this form of Republic is the natural outcome of its Parliamentary history; the power of the monarch has grown less and less, while that of the Cabinet has increased more and more; the new name would give no shock, would not even be a new departure; it would be the orderly and peaceful completion of our national growth. The throne has long been empty in fact, save for that injurious secret influence which it has substituted for its old open authority—and the empty throne would be carted away to the national museum of antiquities: *voilà tout.*

A Republic can only exist by virtue of the free action of the nation; a Republican form of Government in a country where a portion of the community is unenfranchised is a nominal, but not a real, Republic; only by possession of the vote can a man assent to or dissent from political action, and therefore universal suffrage is a *sine quâ non* of a true Republic. But universal suffrage is the bugbear of timid politicians, as Mr. Lowe has lately demonstrated to a marvelling, but not admiring world. It is strange, in reading his pathetic cries of fear, to reflect that England is behind most continental countries in this respect. Universal manhood suffrage is the rule on the Continent, the nominal restrictions being of the lightest character; no country, as yet, has real universal suffrage, *i.e.*, manhood and womanhood suffrage; all maintain at the urn a despotism of sex, while rejecting a despotism of birth. In France, Switzerland, Denmark, Greece, and Germany, there is no suffrage restriction save that of age; when a male attains his majority, he enters, as a matter of course, on his rights as citizen. Now, whatever Tories may say about France, or however dangerous Germany or Greece may be as a home, surely the most timid would feel safe either in Switzerland or in Denmark; no countries are more free from disorder or violence than those inhabited by the sober, thrifty and industrious Danes and Swiss. Universal suffrage, subject to very slight restrictions, prevails as follows: Belgium, all males paying direct taxes of 43 francs annually; the Netherlands, all paying £1 13s.; Italy, all paying £1 12s.; Servia, all paying direct taxes; Portugal, all with an annual income of £22; Roumania, all who can read and write. Why should the English be counted less worthy of the suffrage than all these nations? Is the country which boasts of its self-governing genius less fit to be trusted with the control of its own destinies, and less capable of self-rule than Germany or Portugal, or even than Roumania and Servia?

Great Britain has another peculiarity of government in which, once more, she is behind all her neighbours, viz.: an hereditary legislative body. Whether an Upper House is wanted at all is a matter to me extremely doubtful, but there can be no doubt whatever that if there is to be a Senate it should be wholly composed of those who are peers by right of merit, and not by right of birth. The large majority of continental nations have a second chamber; Greece has only one, elected for four years, and seems none the worse for the absence of an Upper House. Spain, in her Senate, has some grandees who sit by right of birth, but these are counterbalanced by the non-hereditary senators, 100 of whom are nominated by the king, and 130 who are elected by the corporations. Italy has, perhaps, the next worst second chamber to our own, the members being nominated for life by the king; and Portugal labours under the same disadvantage. In Belgium, the people elect the Upper House, the only difference between it and the Lower, so far as election is concerned, being that the Upper is elected for eight years, half the members retiring every four years, while the Lower is elected for four years, half the members retiring every two. In Denmark, twelve senators are appointed for life by the crown, and fifty-four are elected for eight years. In France, seventy-five are nominated by the National Assembly, and elected by the senate for life, while the remainder are elected for nine years, one-third retiring every third year. In the Netherlands, the Upper House is elected by provinces. In Sweden, it is elected by landstings and corporations. In Norway, the whole assembly is elected annually, and it then divides itself into two chambers. In Roumania and Servia, the senate is elected. Thus Great Britain preserves the barbarous feudal traditions which other nations have swept away, and still, with simple faith, trusts to Providence to supply legislative brains to all eldest sons of "our old nobility."

To make the Republic possible, far more is needed than arguments as to its theoretical desirability; some practical gain must be shown before people will take the trouble to make a change. The real, though not material, gains of more conscious independence, of a higher sense of personal responsibility, of feeling self-ruled, instead of being ruled by others, all these, which make the difference between men and machines, between citizens and serfs, are not measureable nor ponderable; their value is recognised when some great crisis comes upon the nation, and the country's freedom depends upon the patriotism of her children. Let us reckon gains more readily acknowledged. One great objection to our monarchical and aristocratic form of government is its enormous expense and its relatively small results. It is not only the million a year which we spend on our royalties, but it is the vast number of pensions, of sinecures, of ornamental offices, of useless posts, kept up for the benefit of younger sons of the nobility, of noble idlers, of aristocratic connections; the hereditary title draws with it the hereditary lands, and they being assigned to the wearer of the title, it is necessary to have places in Church and State which may be filled by interest rather than by merit, so that the cadets may, by living on the nation's money, "keep up their positions:" to add to the splendour of "the house" neighbouring estates are greedily bought up when they come into the market; land is made a luxury for the wealthy, and primogeniture masses it in a few hands to the impoverishment of the nation.

Pensions (except for services actually performed by those who hold them), sinecures, and useless offices, will be gradually abolished by the Republic. Our army shows as in a microcosm the abuses of our system of government; a Royal Duke, Commander-in-Chief, useless in the field of battle, but highly paid for his uselessness, and holding, among his many offices, the colonelcies of regiments to which he performs no duty save that of drawing his pay; a Royal Prince, Field-Marshal and manifold Colonel, as ignorant of military duties as is the rawest of subalterns; but the catalogue is too long to go through, the result being an army over-officered and under-manned, costing, last year, £15,421,356, in addition to compensation for the abolition of purchase in the English budget, as well as a further sum reckoned in the Indian; all this with the monarchical form of Government. The heavy taxation increases the cost of living and embitters the feeling of the poor. Government extravagance and home difficulties contrast over forcibly, and the swollen expenditure seems to invite a reform which shall lighten the burden on the country.

But how can a Republic be made? when will an opportunity occur when the Monarchy can be abolished without a civil convulsion? The opportunity is clear enough; there is no need to empty the throne; it will become empty after awhile without interference of ours; once empty, it is for us to see that no new monarch ascends to the vacant seat. The throne in England is elective, and not hereditary as of right. Mr. Justice Foster well says: "The Crown is not merely a descendable property, like a laystall or a pigstye, but is put in trust for millions, and for the happiness of ages yet unborn, which Parliament has it always in its power to mould, to shape, to alter, to fashion, just as it shall think proper." Lord Abingdon, during the reign of George III., argued that "the right to new model or alter the succession rests in the Parliament of England without the king, in the Lords and Commons of Great Britain solely and exclusively." The right of the people, through the Parliament, over the chief magistracy of this realm is not a matter of theory alone; not to allude to earlier cases, James II. was dispossessed of the throne, his son the Prince of Wales was excluded from the succession, and the next nearest heirs after Anne, being Catholics, were passed over in favour of the descendant of the Electress Sophia; and all this as a matter of right. Since the Brunswick family only succeeded to the throne by virtue of an Act of Parliament, an Act of Parliament would be sufficient to bar the succession, and the nearest heir would then be only a Pretender, as in the time of William and Mary, Anne, and George I. A strong Republican feeling in the people would suffice to return members to Parliament who would repeal the Act of Settlement, and thus deprive the Brunswick princes of any claim to the English throne. A burdensome foreign war, a large increase of taxation, a few defeats abroad, would very rapidly awaken this feeling; for the Crown in England is no longer really loved by the masses of the people, but is simply regarded with an indifference nearly akin to contempt. The publication of the third volume of the "Life of the Prince Consort" is a valuable assistance to the Republican cause, since it unveils the secret influence of the Crown on the conduct of foreign affairs; it shows us our royal family in close and amiable friendship with the perjured ruler of France, Napoleon III., and tells how the Prince Consort "threw his whole heart into the war" with Russia, while the Queen fanned the flame. The moment that it is understood that the Crown claims and exercises power, that moment it will be deprived of a position so full of peril to the interests of the nation. That Great Britain will become a Republic none can doubt; the only question is—When? Our cousins on the other side the Atlantic set us a good example one hundred years ago, and have just celebrated the centenary of their independence; when another century has rolled away, may two uncrowned Republics stretch greeting hands across the ocean, two Republics which to the old memories they both inherit of the English Commonwealth, may add the newer bond, that one in the eighteenth century and the other in the nineteenth shook from off their necks the weight of a German yoke.

Printed by ANNIE BESANT and CHARLES BRADLAUGH, 28 Stonecutter Street, London, E.C.

THE

REDISTRIBUTION

OF

POLITICAL POWER.

BY

ANNIE BESANT.

LONDON:
FREETHOUGHT PUBLISHING COMPANY,
63, FLEET STREET, E.C.
1885.

PRICE FOURPENCE

LONDON:
PRINTED BY ANNIE BESANT AND CHARLES BRADLAUGH,
63, FLEET STREET, E.C.

[Reprinted from *Our Corner*.]

THE REDISTRIBUTION OF POLITICAL POWER.

Results of the Reform Bill of 1832.

Standing as we do face to face with the enfranchisement of two million men and the redistribution of electoral power in the community, it seems well to look back on earlier Reform Bills and to endeavor to judge of the probable results of the present measures from the results that have followed their predecessors. My object in the following pages is to trace out the most important tendencies which have shown themselves after each Reform Bill; to mark the chief activities manifested after each "infusion of new blood"; to present a picture of certain steadily developing modifications of the national organism, modifications which are likely to become very pronounced in the near future. I am not aware that any attempt has been made to distinguish the transitory from the permanent tendencies, the reforms done once for all amid great excitement from the apparently less important measures which none the less initiate new eras and serve as the starting-point for new developments. Yet in sociology as in geology, the most far-reaching changes are not made by the volcanoes and the earthquakes, but by the slow action of countless silent ever-working forces.

Each Reform Bill has been followed by a great outburst of reforming energy, and amid the many measures carried in the reformed Parliaments those are, I think, of the most permanently important character which have dealt with the conditions of Labor, with the extension of Religious Liberty and Equality, with the Tenure of Land, with the Education of the People.

One marked change has come over the nation apart from any legislative enactment—the decrease of the power of the hereditary peers after each Reform Bill. That of '32 swept away from them their control of the House of Commons; after '67, their legislative chamber became less and less able to hold its own against the increased power of the popular representatives; on the Bill of '84 they nearly shipwrecked their House, and when the new constituencies have had their say we may hope that the abolition of their hereditary right of obstruction will be within measurable distance.

We shall not be able to estimate the changes brought about after 1832 without glancing at the England of the pre-reforming period. The power of the great houses then controlled the elections of so many boroughs that the peers practically made the government; in the list given by Lord John Russell in 1831, we find boroughs returning members in which the constituencies consisted of 13, 18, 5, 10, 12, persons, and in one case of no persons at all. In these dukes, marquises, earls, and great untitled commoners, appointed whom they would as the members to serve in Parliament. Molesworth says: "In most of these boroughs the seats were sold by the proprietors. Sometimes they themselves or some of their relatives or dependents were nominated to represent them. Bribery was also practised with little or no reserve or concealment where it was necessary, but in many instances the constituency was so dependent on the proprietor that no expenditure of this kind was requisite" (History of the Reform Bill, page 116). Lord John Russell urged that a stranger visiting the country "would be very much astonished if he were taken to a ruined mound, and told that the mound sent two representatives to Parliament—if he were taken to a stone wall, and told that three niches in it sent two representatives to Parliament—if he were taken to a park, where no houses were to be seen, and told that that park sent two representatives to Parliament" (Ibid., p. 104).

Complaints of a similar nature were put even more forcibly in a petition presented to the House of Commons as early as 1793, in which the petitioners stated that "seventy of your honorable members are returned by thirty-five places, where the right of voting is vested in burgage and other tenures of a similar description, and in which it would be to trifle with the patience of your honorable house to mention any number of voters whatever, the elections at the places alluded to being notoriously a mere matter of form"; further that two hundred and twenty more were elected by places in which the electors varied from less than fifty to less than two hundred; that one hundred and fifty-seven members were sent to Parliament by the direct authority of eighty-four individuals, and one hundred and fifty more "not by the collective voice of those they appear to represent, but by the recommendation of seventy powerful individuals", one hundred and fifty persons thus returning a majority of the House (Ibid., pp. 342, 343, 347).

The agitation outside against this intolerable political condition was sharpened by poverty and distress among the people. Then, as now, social suffering was widespread and alarming. The Non-intercourse Act, passed by the United States, shut the American market against England, while the introduction of machinery into various manufactures threw numbers of persons out of employment, and the year 1811 was marked by the "Luddite riots", in which the new and hated machines were destroyed by the infuriated workers. But these, isolated by ignorance, could enter into no effective and organised action for their own good; they could make riots, they could burn a castle; they could not formulate their demands and enforce them. In 1819, at Peterloo, the savage yeomanry rode at the helpless crowd, cutting with their swords in every direction, till six hundred and eighteen people were wounded and fourteen were killed. (See Hunt's speech, reported in "Molesworth", p. 126.) But the answer to this was not Reform, but the infamous "Six Acts" of Lord Sidmouth, generally called "Castlereagh's Six Acts", which gave more speedy execution of justice in certain cases, prevented unauthorised military training, punished so-called "libels", gave authority to seize arms, forbad "seditious" meetings, and imposed a stamp duty.

Even when at last a Reform Bill was introduced, it met with bitter opposition. Sir Charles Wetherell railed against it in the true Tory style, prophesying all sorts of mischiefs as the consequences of Reform. "I say that the principle of the Bill is Republican at the basis; I say that it is destructive of all property, of all right, of all privilege; and that the same arbitrary violence which expelled a majority of members from that House at the time of the Commonwealth, is now, after the lapse of a century from the Revolution, during which the population has enjoyed greater happiness than has been enjoyed by any population under heaven, proceeding to expose the House of Commons again to the nauseous experiment of a repetition of Pride's purge" (Ibid., p. 132). Spite of all these terrible forebodings the Bill passed into law, receiving the Royal Assent on June 7th, 1832.

The general result of the Act was to throw political power into the hands of manufacturers and capitalists, in a phrase to "enfranchise the middle classes". The direct influence of the working classes was, if anything, slightly diminished by the Act, since it disfranchised a few places in which they had previously possessed the suffrage. It struck a fatal blow at the privileges of the possessors of hereditary authority, and gave representation to the commercial interests of the nation. One striking proof was given that the class which then won political power was not unworthy of the freedom it had gained. One of its first reforms was the introduction of a Factory Act to protect the more helpless of the operative class, and it ought never to be forgotten that effective legislative interference with employers was due to a Parliament elected principally by that very same *bourgeois* class which it is now the fashion to so unsparingly denounce.

In 1801 the first Act limiting the hours of labor was passed, and by this it was forbidden that apprentices should work for more than twelve hours a day; in 1819 Sir Robert Peel was defeated in a Bill which proposed to limit the working day for young persons under sixteen years of age to eleven hours and a half, and the Act of 1801 appears to have been systematically evaded. When the Reformed Parliament met in 1833, a Bill was introduced in the preamble of which it was stated that "it has become a practice to employ a great number of children and young persons of both sexes an unreasonable length of time, and late at night, and in many cases all night";

this Bill enacted that no child should be employed in any factory or mill (except a silk manufactory) under ten years of age, and limited the working day to nine hours for children under fourteen. In silk mills children under the age of thirteen were still allowed to work for ten hours a day. The hours of labor for young persons over fourteen and under eighteen were fixed at sixty-nine a week or eleven-and-a-half a day. Inspectors were also appointed to see to the proper carrying out of the law, but it was nevertheless evaded, and in 1838 Lord Ashley proposed another measure for the protection of children, but his Bill was thrown out by 121 votes against 106. In 1842, the same gentleman successfully carried through a Bill prohibiting the employment of women and children in coal mines, and thus put a stop to the torture of young children, and to the wholesale demoralisation which accompanied the working together of men and women stripped to the waist in the mines. Lord Londonderry, as a large coal-owner, bitterly opposed the Bill, affording one more example of the fact that "humanity" vanishes before the greed for wealth, and that the life and happiness of the employed weigh little when put in the balances against increased profit for the employer. In 1844 an unsuccessful attempt to limit the working of women and children in factories to a Ten Hours' Day, brought in by Lord Ashley, was opposed by the Government and was defeated, and a similar fate befell the same measure when re-introduced in 1846 by Mr. Fielden. In 1847, however, Mr. Fielden carried a bill reducing the working day to ten hours for young persons up to the age of eighteen.

This group of measures, passed by the Reformed Parliaments, may be taken as laying down the principle of legislative interference between employers and employed, of protecting the latter by law against the former. That this principle will, in time to come, be carried considerably further is, to my mind, not a matter of doubt, and those who object to further legislation in the interests of labor ought in consistency to advocate the repeal of all the laws on that matter already passed. They should send back women to work half naked in the coal-mines. They should bid the young children leave the schoolroom and the playground, and go back to the factory to toil all day "and late at night and in many cases all night", till they fall asleep over their work, and till, lying at home on their pallets, their little hands in sleep still toss the shuttle to and fro.[1] They should call on the law to stand aside and to let the wild struggle for life go on unchecked. They should allow the workers to trample each other down in the fearful competition for bread, and the employers to wring from their necessities the greatest amount of labor at the lowest wage. So shall the sacred "freedom of contract" remain untouched, and the beautiful spectacle of anarchical competition unrestrained by law shall be offered as the outcome of civilization. Wild beasts rend each other in their strife over the carcase of their prey; why not men in their strife for bread and wealth?

With regard to Religious Liberty the Reformed Parliaments made vast changes between 1833 and 1867. In 1833 a Bill for abolishing the civil disabilities of the Jews was passed by the House of Commons but rejected by the Lords, and thus began the long struggle which ended only in 1860 by the Act which abolished the Christian oath for members of Parliament. In 1834 the Commons passed Bills for the abolition of University Tests, for the abolition

---

[1] *From Evidence from the Report of the Committee of the House of Lords,* 1819.—*T. Wilkinson.*—"What are the hours of working in the factories you are acquainted with?—From six to seven in the summer, and from seven to eight in the winter. What time is allowed for dinner?—An hour. Is any other time allowed for meals?—No. Are the children ever obliged to be at the factory before or after the common hours of work?—Yes. Are they ever beaten to make them work?—I have seen hundreds beat, to keep them awake and drive them on." *John Farebrother.*—"How old were you when you first went in?—Between five and six. When the children have to eat their meals in the factory, do they generally finish it?—No. Do they leave much of it?—Yes; I have seen it all left many times. Is that owing to its being covered with dust?—Yes. How do they get their breakfast and afternoon meal?—As they can catch it; when the machinery is moving they eat it as they are piecing. How soon do you begin to see a difference in a child's health?—I have seen a difference in one week." *Evidence before the House of Commons Committee in* 1816.—*J. Moss.* "He had on one occasion known children to work in the mill from eight o'clock on Saturday night to six on Sunday morning. The same children resumed work on Sunday night at twelve o'clock, and worked until five in the morning. . . . He had known children to work for three weeks together from five in the morning till nine or ten at night, with the exception of one hour for meals; he had frequently found the children asleep on the mill floors, after the time they should have been in bed."

of Church Rates, for allowing marriages in Dissenters' chapels, but all these were rejected by the Lords, the struggle over University Tests lasting until 1871, after a second Reform Act. In 1836, the right of registering births, marriages, and deaths was taken from the clergy of the Established Church, and in the same year a Bill was passed permitting Dissenters to be married in their own chapels. In 1837 an attempt was made to relieve Dissenters from the payment of Church Rates, but the Bill was withdrawn in consequence of the opposition raised to it, and the measure was not carried until 1868, after the impulse of a new Reform. In 1840 a small instalment of justice to Ireland in religious matters was made by the Irish Tithe Bill, which had been originally introduced in 1834, and rejected in 1835, 1836, and 1837; in 1857 another small instalment was paid by the abolition of a tax called "Ministers' Money" which had been levied for the support of the Establishment. The great agitation for the disestablishment of the Irish Church was commenced in Parliament by Mr. Dillwyn in 1865; it was endorsed by the Liberal Party in Mr. Gladstone's famous resolutions for disestablishing and disendowing it, carried in the unreformed Parliament in March 1868, and the way was thus opened for a Bill on the subject after the general election. The claim of Dissenters to be allowed to bury their dead without the intrusion of the State-paid priests went too far on the path of religious equality for the Parliaments between 1833 and 1867; the establishment of cemeteries whereof a part remained unconsecrated for their use was permitted, but complete freedom of burial was only obtained by them in 1880, and this is not even yet extended to thorough-going heretics.

With respect to the Tenure of Land, nothing of any importance to the nation was done between 1832 and 1867. A number of bills affecting land were passed, but they were all on points touching only the landowners, and nothing was even suggested which could imply that the nation had the smallest interest in its own soil. The great Corn Law struggle, which ended with the passing of the Anti-Corn Law Bill in 1846, was, however, really a struggle between the masses of the people wanting cheap bread and the landlords wanting to keep out foreign corn; only by protection could farmers, they thought, continue to pay high rents for the land they cultivated, and the "protection of agriculture" then, as now, was nothing more than an attempt on the part of the landlords to tax the community for their own benefit. Here, as everywhere else, the interests of the small land-monopolising class were in direct conflict with the interests of the masses of the people. The people need cheap food; the landlords want food to be dear, so that the farmers who supply it may be able to pay high rent; every attempt to keep out foreign corn, foreign cattle, foreign food of any kind, is an attempt to maintain unfair rents by forcing up the prices of farmers' produce, and to levy a tax on the consumers for the maintenance of an evil system.

The roots of our present system of National Education are struck in the first Parliament after the Reform Act of 1832. In 1833 a grant of £20,000 a year was made for the purposes of National Education, but it was placed for administration in the hands of the National Society and of the British and Foreign School Society; so that although the grant implied a recognition of the duty of the community towards its children, the recognition took the unhealthy form of placing State funds in the hands of unofficial societies. Practically most of the money was disposed of by the clergy, and was used for denominational purposes. In 1839 the grant was raised to £30,000 a-year, and an Educational Committee of the Privy Council was appointed to receive and administer the money: this was the foundation of State Education, for not only was the money kept under State control, but inspectors were appointed over the schools assisted by the State, and so began the system which received such vast development after the Reform Rill of 1867, and which is likely to develop yet further in the near future. Those who oppose its development are bound in reason to object to the recognition of the whole principle of State Education, and to agitate for the abolition of the huge system which has grown out of the seeds planted in 1833 and 1839. Those who would leave education to "voluntary effort" should see what was its condition before the State stepped in on behalf of its helpless children, and should gravely ask themselves whether they really desire that the ignorance of the early part of the nineteenth century should return to shroud its close, and that the children of the twentieth century should be robbed of the knowledge which is raising the children of to-day.

While Parliament was thus laying the basis of a system of National Education for children, the yearning of the workers outside for wider knowledge forced on it other legislation, which was also essentially educational. This yearning took the form of a resolute agitation for an unstamped press, for the fourpenny stamp imposed on all newspapers placed them entirely out of the reach of the poorer workers. Never was a struggle for a noble object carried on with more resolute heroism, with more strenuous patience. It was waged almost entirely by the poor, men and women selling unstamped papers, going to gaol, and continuing the sale on their release. Glancing over the list of those prosecuted in the year ending September, 1834, I see a few well-known names, and many to me unknown. There are Henry Hetherington, John Cleave, James Watson, all prominent men; but few know Edmund Wastneys of Newcastle, Isabella Rose of Southampton, Richard Lee and Edmund Stallwood of Holborn, John Smith of the Strand, George Baker of Worcester, Edmund Somerside of Winlaton, W. Nicholls of Tottenham Court Road, Patrick Bready and Edward Gleave of Sheffield, John Chappell of Clifton, James Guest, Richard Jenkinson, Julius Faulkner, William Plastans, William Guest, Thomas Watts, all of Birmingham, Alexander Yates of Coventry; yet all these suffered imprisonment for the crime of selling unstamped newspapers. And so I might go on with list after list of these, the privates in Liberty's army, who were struck down in the battle, who by their sufferings won for us our freedom, and on whose unknown graves we cannot even lay a leaf of memory and of thanks.

In 1836 the stamp was reduced from 4d. to 1d., despite the argument that the reduction would "introduce a cheap and profligate press, one of the greatest curses that can be inflicted on humanity". This penny duty was levied on papers containing "news", or remarks on news, published periodically at intervals of less than twenty-six days, and "published for sale for a less price than sixpence, exclusive of the duty" (6th and 7th William IV., cap. 76, quoted in the Report of the Select Committee on Newspaper Stamps, 1851, p. iv.). The agitation continued against the 1d. stamp, and the Committee of 1851 reported against it because of "the impediments which it throws in the way of the diffusion of useful knowledge regarding current and recent events among the poorer classes" (Report, p. xii.). The stamp was abolished in 1855.

In 1860, Mr. Gladstone proposed and carried in the House of Commons a clause in his Budget Bill repealing the paper duties, so as to still further cheapen literature, but the Lords struck out the clause by a majority of 89. In 1861, however, Mr. Gladstone made the repeal a part of his financial measure in such fashion that the Lords would have been obliged to reject the Budget if they rejected the repeal clause, and as they did not venture on so dangerous an aggression the "taxes on knowledge" were taken off.

Of all the work done by the Reformed Parliaments that connected with education was perhaps the most vitally important and the most far-reaching. Without a cheap press, political education is impossible for the masses, and without political education reforms are either unattainable or inoperative. Education is the lever whereby political and social inequality shall be overturned, and with this lever in one hand and the trowel of political power in the other, Democracy will be armed to overturn the Wrong and to build up the Right.

II.—Results of the Reform Bill of 1867.

The question of Parliamentary Reform again took definite shape in 1858, after the convulsions caused by the Crimean War and the Indian Mutiny. In that year, the Tories being in power, Mr. John Bright formulated a new scheme of Reform, which proposed to give the franchise to all who paid the poor-rate in boroughs, to all who paid a £10 rental in counties, and to lodgers paying a similar rental. Voting by ballot was also adopted by the Reformers, for the protection of the poorer voters who were subjected to intimidation by their employers. In 1859 Mr. Disraeli introduced a Reform Bill containing a most extraordinary collection of fancy property franchises, and on this the Government was defeated, and Lord Derby went to the country. After the general election Lord Palmerston came into power, and in the following year, 1860, Lord John Russell introduced a measure which gave a £6 franchise in boroughs, and a £10 in counties; in this Bill appeared for the first time the proposal to make "three-cornered constituencies", in which a minority might secure representation by electing one member out of three. The Bill made but slow progress in the House, and excited no enthusiasm out-of-doors, and it was finally withdrawn by the Government on June 11th. The question of Reform then slept until 1865, when Mr. Baines brought up some resolutions in its favor, and the Government declined to take any action in the matter; the feeling outside had, however, been growing steadily, and after the general election of 1865—in which Mr. Gladstone was defeated at Oxford and returned for South Lancashire—the Liberal party found itself stronger than ever. On the assembling of Parliament, Earl Russell being Premier, Parliamentary Reform found a place in the Queen's speech, and Mr. Gladstone introduced the Government Bill on March 13th; the proposed was by no means a Radical one, the county franchise being fixed at £14, and the borough at £10, but the famous "Cave of Adullam" was formed against it, and the Whigs and Tories together defeated the Government. Lord Derby took office at the end of June, and the agitation in favor of Reform now rose to fever heat; the Government tried at first to coerce the people, but succeeded only in irritating them, as when it closed the gates of Hyde Park against a meeting of the Reform League, and a new way was made into the Park over the pulled-down railings. On this the Government decided to yield to the popular demand, and in March, 1867, Mr. Disraeli, after bringing forward some abortive resolutions, startled Whigs, Tories, Liberals, and Radicals by introducing his famous Reform Bill which gave household suffrage to ratepayers in the boroughs, and reduced the county franchise to a £15 qualification. The latter was further reduced to £10, and householders who paid their rates in their rents received also the franchise. The Bill, characterised by Lord Derby as "a leap in the dark", passed the House of Lords in August, and thus the second great Reform Bill of the century became law, the working classes in the towns winning their enfranchisement and becoming, so far as the boroughs were concerned, the real depositories of political power.

It was manifestly impossible for the Tories long to delay the appeal to the new electorate, working, as they were, with a minority in the House of Commons. Lord Derby resigned office, and was succeeded by Mr. Disraeli, at the beginning of the Session of 1868, and the opening of a new period of reforming energy was announced in the famous resolutions of Mr. Gladstone, carried by a majority of 66, proposing to disestablish and disendow the Irish Church. Parliament was dissolved and a general election took place in November, resulting in the return of a large Liberal majority to the House of Commons. Mr. Gladstone, who in 1865 had proved too Liberal for Oxford, was in 1868 proved to be too Liberal for the county constituency of South Lancashire, but was returned by the working men of Greenwich, and became Premier of the new Liberal Ministry.

The Labor legislation of the period between the Reform Bills of 1867 and 1884 continued steadily on the lines laid down in the preceding period, and though fewer in number the Bills introduced were of the most valuable kind. In 1871 the Trade Union Act was passed, by which were repealed the iniquitous laws against combinations of workers. The law of 39 and 40 George III., cap. 106, to take an example of past legislation, punished combination by imprisonment, and rendered illegal all agreements between workmen for obtaining any advance of wages. Various Acts had been passed from time to time, partly repealing, partially re-enacting, this and similar oppressive measures, and the common law of conspiracy was constantly used against the Trades' Unions, the most outrageous sentences of penal servitude being passed on men under this law for combination and picketing. The natural result of oppression, secret outrages, appeared in many large towns; a strong agitation was carried on, and various Select Committees were appointed to consider the laws affecting the relations between employers and employed. The result was the passing of the Trade Union Act, which rendered the associations legal. This emancipating legislation was completed by the Employers and Workmen Bill, passed by Mr. Disraeli's Government in 1875, an Act which repealed all the oppressive penal laws under which labor had been so long suffering.

This same year 1875 was noticeable for the passing of the Artisans' Dwellings Bill, a well-meant measure, but which has proved inoperative, in consequence of its being permissive. A Shipping Bill, due to Mr. Plimsoll, was also passed during this year, and did something, though but little, to protect sailors' lives.

In 1874 a Bill introduced by Mr. Mundella, for extending the operation of the Factory Acts, had been taken up by the Government and passed; and in 1878 Mr. Cross succeeded in carrying another Bill, which had also been previously proposed by Mr. Mundella, for the consolidation and amendment of the Factory and Workshops Acts. This Act insisted on a sanitary condition for factories and workshops, and on the safeguarding of machinery; it limited the hours of labor for children, young persons, and women, prohibited the employment of children under ten years of age, provided for the education of child employees, set apart certain holidays and half-holidays, and required certificates of fitness for employment for children under sixteen years of age. On the whole the measure was a good one, though permitting too long hours of labor.

The Employers' Liability Bill of 1880, earnestly pleaded for by the representatives of labor in the House, made another important step forwards, by declaring that the employer might be made responsible for injuries received by his employees where such injury resulted from neglect by himself or by his agents.

Looking at the whole of this legislation, we find recognised as a definite principle the right of the community to interfere, by means of law, for the protection of the workers from the greed of those who employ them, whether it be to save sailors from "coffin-ships", or miners and other operatives from preventible injury, or factory and shop-workers from excessive hours of labor. We also find that the community recognises its interest in the wholesome housing of its laboring class, in the health of those producers on whom the wealth of the nation depends.

Some of the greatest blows struck for Religious Liberty and Equality during the century were dealt between 1867 and 1884. It is mentioned above that in 1868 Mr. Gladstone's resolutions against the Irish Establishment were carried in the unreformed Parliament by a majority of 66, and when Mr. Gladstone came into power as a result of the general election, the Liberal party was thereby pledged to attack the Irish Church without delay. On March 1st, 1869, Mr. Gladstone introduced a Bill for the

Disestablishment and Disendowment of the Irish Church. As the Church of the landlords and of a very small minority of the population, and as a badge of conquest, the Irish Church was quite peculiarly indefensible, yet it is needless to say that the Tory party loudly denounced the Bill as sacrilegious and confiscatory. It passed the Commons in May, but was returned to them so altered that they declined to accept it; after much wrangling the usual compromise was effected, and the Bill received the Royal Assent on July 26th. The great blunder of the Act lay in its clauses for compensating the officials of the defunct Establishment. Every official—including schoolmasters, clerks, and sextons—who was in office on January 1st, 1871, was declared to be entitled to payment of the net income which he was previously receiving so long as he discharged his office, such income to be further commutable for a capital sum, calculable on the value of the income as a life-annuity. The consequence of giving a seventeen months' period during which fresh interests could be created was, of course, to add largely to the class which had to be compensated, and so to diminish the funds applicable to national purposes. But the Act is of utmost value, in that it declared that the "ultimate surplus" was available for "the relief of unavoidable calamity and suffering", and that "the said proceeds shall be so applied accordingly, in the manner Parliament shall hereafter direct". That is, it laid down the precedent of treating the Church merely as a department of the State, the funds administered by which were national funds, to be used as the nation may direct.

The same year 1869 saw the passing of the Evidence Amendment Act, allowing witnesses without religious opinions to affirm in courts of law. As first introduced by the Hon. George Denman, it only permitted affirmation to those who should "object to take an oath". Charles Bradlaugh, now junior member for Northampton, pointed out that this would not enable Atheists to affirm, since they had been held "incompetent" to swear, whether they objected or not, and after some insistance a modification was made which authorised the taking of an affirmation by anyone who should "object to take an oath", or who should be objected to as "incompetent to take the oath". Unhappily the insulting words were added that the presiding judge must be "satisfied that the taking of an oath would have no binding effect on his conscience". This phrase has been constantly used as though Atheists stated that the oath was not binding on them, whereas the words were merely words of insult used by a Parliament in which Christians were in a large majority. The Evidence Further Amendment Act, passed in the following year, only extended the meaning of the word "judge" to "include any person or persons having by law authority to administer an oath for the taking of evidence". This Act was passed in consequence of the rejection of Mr. Bradlaugh's evidence by an arbitrator, the Court of Common Pleas holding that the evidence was rightly rejected, the Act of 1869 only admitting evidence given in a court of justice before a judge.

Since 1880, in consequence of Mr. Charles Bradlaugh's claim to affirm as a member of the House of Commons, various attempts have been made to legalise affirmation in Parliament. In June 1882 Lord Sundridge introduced a Bill permitting any member of either House to affirm if he intimated in writing that he had "a conscientious objection to the form of the oath required by the law, or that the taking of an oath would have no binding effect on his conscience". Objection was raised that the Government ought to deal with the matter rather than a private member, and the Bill failed to pass. In February, 1883, the Government introduced a similar Bill, but instead of making the conditions above stated, proposed that every member "may, if he thinks fit," affirm instead of swearing. The Government foolishly did not make their Bill a cabinet question, and it was lost by a majority of only three votes, proving that the least energy on their part would have ensured its success. In February, 1885, Mr. Hopwood, Q.C., introduced a far better measure, legalising affirmation "in all places and for all purposes where an oath is or shall be required by law". The fate of this new attempt to widen religious liberty is still doubtful when I write.

In 1871, the University Tests Bill, abolishing religious tests in the Universities, was at last passed, bitterly opposed as it was by the Tories, who denounced it in unmeasured terms; and by this funds usurped by the Church were rendered available for the education of Churchmen and of Dissenters alike. An attempt to do a similar service for Ireland, by the creation of a University from which theology should be excluded, was made by Mr. Gladstone in 1873, but this Bill was rejected by a majority of three. A Bill was, however, passed in this year abolishing tests in Trinity College, Dublin, and so a small step towards equality was made. In 1877, a Burial Acts Consolidation Bill was introduced in the House of Lords, which permitted "silent burial" in churchyards by Dissenters; but it was ultimately withdrawn, and quarrels over the coffins of dead Dissenters continued until 1880, in which year a Burials Bill was passed which permitted dissenting ministers to bury members of their sects in parish churchyards with any "religious and orderly service" they preferred. A strong effort was made to include all orderly forms of burial, Mr. Ashton Dilke pointing out that as he had no "religious" opinions the permission would not include himself, but the Christian majority was too intolerant to extend to extreme heretics the liberty it claimed for its own members, and an amending Burials Act is still required. It may be noted in passing that in 1879 Mr. Martin succeeded in passing through Parliament a Bill which made it incumbent on local authorities to provide cemeteries for the burial of Dissenters.

The prosecutions in 1883 of Messrs. Bradlaugh, Foote, Ramsey, and Kemp, for blasphemy, the conviction of the three latter, and the brutal sentences passed on them by Mr. Justice North, roused public feeling strongly against the Blasphemy Laws, and a Bill for their repeal was drafted by Mr. Justice Stephens. No member of the House of Commons, however, could be found bold enough to introduce it, and the abolition of these cruel laws is left to a more enlightened Parliament, chosen by a wider electorate.

Enormous progress was made in questions affecting the Tenure of Land between 1867 and 1884. First in order and in far-reaching importance comes Mr. Gladstone's great measure, the Irish Land Act. It was introduced in the Commons on February 15th, 1870, and became law on August 1st. By this Act the right of a tenant to his own improvements was recognised, and an attempt was made to prevent the confiscation by the landlord of the tenant's property by imposing on the landlord the obligation to compensate an outgoing tenant for his improvements. The right of the tenant to security of tenure was admitted by compelling the landlord to "compensate for disturbance" if he ejected his tenant, and by authorising the tenant to keep possession of his holding until the money was paid. In cases of dispute, the amount of compensation was to be decided by the Civil Bill Court (County Court); a scale, however, limiting to far too low a sum the maximum amount that could be fixed as compensation for disturbance, was inserted in the Act. Unfortunately the object of the Legislature in passing the Bill was foiled, for it made no provision for preventing the landlord raising the rent when improvements were made by the tenant, and so confiscation went on unchecked; if the tenant tried to avoid the penalty by giving notice to quit on the raising of the rent he received no compensation for disturbance, the compensation being only paid when he was "disturbed in his holding by the act of his landlord". The attempt to create a peasant proprietary also proved a failure, for though the Government was authorised to advance two-thirds of the purchase-money to a cultivator desiring to buy land, the legal expenses were so heavy as to prove practically prohibitory. A fairly extensive sale of Church lands, however, took place, the legal cost being far less, and between five and six thousand peasant proprietors were thus made.

The failure of this effort to settle the Irish land question, and the sufferings inflicted on the people by famine, led to continued agitation, and one of the first measures introduced by Mr. Gladstone's Government in the short session of 1880 was the Compensation for Disturbance Bill (Ireland). It was rejected by the House of Lords by a majority of 232, and the agitation in Ireland passed, as Mr. Gladstone had predicted, into a state which was practically one of civil war. In 1881 the second great Irish Land Act was passed, which laid down the important principle of a "judicial rent". It also established Land Courts, which were empowered to fix these judicial rents, and these Courts have largely reduced the rack-rents before exacted.

While these two great Irish measures are of vital importance as laying down the principle of State interference between landlord and tenant, other measures affecting the Tenure of Land were passed during this same fruitful period. The Agricultural Holdings Act of 1875 was, like the Artisans' Dwellings Act, permissive, and those whom it is most necessary to coerce thus escape from its provisions. In 1879 an attempt to abolish distraint for rent of agricultural holdings was made by Mr. Blennerhassett, but he was defeated by a majority of 110, and nothing was done for tenants until a Liberal Government was again in power. In 1880 the Ground Game Bill was passed, authorising farmers to kill ground game on their own farms, so relieving them from the obligation of feeding their landlords' animals, so far as quadrupeds were concerned. The landlords are still allowed to keep winged game at their tenants' expense, and avail themselves largely of this legalised form of theft.

The system of National Education, commenced in 1839, assumed definite shape and wide extent in 1870. In that year Mr. Forster brought in his famous Bill of Elementary Education and carried it to a successful issue. By this Act it was declared that "there shall be provided for every school district a sufficient amount of accommodation in public elementary schools (as hereinafter defined) available for all the children resident in such district for whose elementary education efficient and suitable provision is not otherwise made". Religious liberty was guarded by enacting that "it shall not be required, as a condition of any child being admitted into or continuing in the school, that he shall attend or abstain from attending any Sunday school, or any place of religious worship, or that he shall attend any religious observance or any instruction in religious subjects in the school or elsewhere": any religious instruction given at the school was to be given at the beginning or end of the schoolhours, and any parent might withdraw his child; the inspector was not to have the duty of examining in religious knowledge. Each child was to pay a weekly fee, unless excused on the ground of the parent's poverty, and if "a school board satisfy the Education Department that, on the ground of the poverty of the inhabitants of any place in this district, it is expedient for the interests of education to provide a school at which no fees shall be required from the scholars, the board may, subject to such rules and conditions as the Education Department may prescribe, provide such school, and may admit scholars to such school without requiring any fee". Expenses were to be met out of the "school fund", which consisted of moneys received as fees, provided by Parliament, raised by loan or by rate: further, one district might be directed to "contribute towards the provision or maintenance of public elementary schools in another school district or districts". School Boards, to carry out the duties imposed by the Act, were to be elected by the ratepayers by the cumulative vote, and these Boards might pass a bye-law rendering education compulsory for children between the ages of five and thirteen, any child over ten years of age being exempted from the bye-law if he was certified as having reached the standard of education fixed by the Board. Such is an outline of the famous Education Act, the first effective attempt to educate the children of the poor. The amending Act of 1873 contains nothing but matters of detail, with the exception of the proviso that if any parent was receiving out-door relief, it was to "be a condition for the continuance of such relief that elementary education in reading, writing, and arithmetic" should be given to any child between the ages of five and thirteen. In 1876 another Education Act was passed. By this it was declared that "it shall be the duty of the parent of every child to cause such child to receive efficient elementary instruction in reading, writing, and arithmetic, and if such parent fail to perform such duty, he shall be liable to such orders and penalties as are provided by this Act". The Act forbade the employment of children under ten years of age, and of children above that age if they had not reached a certain standard of education, unless such children were attending school during part of the day. Local authorities were empowered to authorise the employment of children over eight years of age, for not more than six weeks in the year, in husbandry or ingathering of crops. Provision was made for compelling the parent to send his child to school, and in case of non-compliance with the order a court of summary jurisdiction was authorised to send the child to a certified day industrial school. In such schools meals were to be provided, and were to be paid for "out of moneys provided by Parliament" and by fees paid by the parents, the latter to be excused if the parent were too poor to pay them, and to be charged on the rates. It is noteworthy that in all cases of payment of fees for parents, provided for in this and in the Act of 1870, the payment is not to be taken as making the parent a pauper; thus, in this Act of 1876 it is laid down: "The parent shall not by reason of any payment made under this section be deprived of any franchise, right, or privilege, or be subject to any disability or disqualification".

As in the former period, from 1832 to 1867, the struggle for a free press accompanied Parliamentary action in favor of education, so in the period we are now considering, another great step was taken towards freeing the press from its shackles. The combatant in this struggle was Charles Bradlaugh, and the battle was over the Act imposing sureties against blasphemy and sedition, 60 George III., cap. 9. This Act was intended to stop "pamphlets and printed papers, containing observations upon public events and occurrences, tending to excite hatred and contempt of the Government and constitution of these realms, as to law established, and also vilifying our holy religion". It applied only to publications sold at less than sixpence per copy. Mr. Bradlaugh, as editor of the *National Reformer*, a Republican and Freethought twopenny journal, declined to give sureties, on the ground that so doing would make the conduct of the paper too costly for his means. For some years the paper went on its way, all applications for the security being met with a bland refusal. At last, in 1868, the Tory Government resolved to prosecute, and the paper appeared with a line under its heading: "Published in defiance of Her Majesty's Government, and of the 60th George III., cap. 9" (*National Reformer*, May 3rd, 1868, p. 281). Mr. Bradlaugh's answer to the notice of prosecution was characteristic:

"TO HER MAJESTY'S COMMISSIONERS FOR THE DEPARTMENT OF INLAND REVENUE.

"GENTLEMEN,—You have taken the pains to officially remind me of an Act of Parliament, passed in 1819, avowedly for the suppression of cheap Democratic and Freethought literature, and you require me to comply with its provisions, such provisions being absolutely prohibitory to the further appearance of this journal. With all humility, I am obliged to bid you defiance; you may kill the *National Reformer*, but it will not commit suicide. Before you destroy my paper we shall have to fight the question, so far as my means will permit me.

"I know the battle is not on equal terms. You have the national purse, I an empty pocket; you have the trained talent of the law officers of the Crown, I my own poor wits. But it would be cowardly indeed in me to shrink in 1868 from a contest in which my gallant predecessor, Richard Carlile, fought so persistently more than a quarter of a century since."

This is not the place to record the varying events of the long struggle; it must suffice to say that Sir John Karslake failed, in consequence of the adroit legal fencing of his lay opponent, and that the Gladstone Government, coming into office, disgraced itself by taking up the prosecution in 1869. The Crown gained a verdict, which Mr. Bradlaugh upset; a *stet processus* was then entered, the Government introducing a Bill to repeal the Acts. Mr. Ayrton had previously endeavored to get rid of these oppressive laws, having described them as "laws which could never have been placed upon the statute-book except in the most evil times, when the old Tory party was engaged in desperate struggles to repress the expression of public opinion, and to maintain its hold of political power". Now his bill passed rapidly through its stages, and the freedom of the press was won as far as political discussion was concerned. From that time forward cheap newspapers could circulate, criticising all flaws, advocating all reforms, without fear of having to pay for their boldness by the forfeiture of their recognisances, and that freedom they owe to that small but gallant party which since the time of Thomas Paine has fought and suffered for the liberty of all.

III.—Results of the Reform Bill of 1884.

In the previous pages I have tried to trace the results of Reform as seen exemplified in our past. In the following ones I propose to outline results which are yet in the future, but which lie in the direct line of evolution, and are but an expansion and a development of principles already accepted by the Legislature. What legislative action is likely to be taken by the Reformed Parliament with respect to the conditions of Labor, Religious Liberty and Equality, the Tenure of Land, the Education of the People? As in the past, so in the future, the new Parliament will be full of reforming energy; again we stand on the threshold of great changes, changes to which some look with fear and some with hope.

We have already seen that the principle of legislative interference between employers and employed has been largely acted on by Parliament since 1832. There is no reason to suppose that the new Parliament will be more careless of the interests of the workers than its predecessors have been; indeed, elected as it will be, by a larger number of handworkers than have ever before taken part in the choice of representatives of the Commons, it will probably be more inclined to legislate in the interests of Labor than any Parliament we have yet seen.

The hours of labor have been shortened at successive intervals since 1801, and it is not unreasonable to suppose that a further shortening of these hours will soon be made. The ordinary London operative now works for a ten hours' day, from 6 a.m. to 5 p.m. with an hour's interval for dinner. Mr. Howell says on this: "If we take the metropolis we shall find that a building operative has to be at his work at six o'clock in the morning, and he now leaves at five o'clock at night. But he has often to walk four or five miles to his work, so that he has to leave home at five and cannot reach home again until six, making a total of thirteen hours. . . . An hour's walk is often very exhilarating to a business man, shut up in an office all day, but to a mason, carpenter, bricklayer, or plasterer, who has frequently to plod through the rain or drifting snow, it is painfully exhausting, especially when it has to be done before six o'clock in the morning."[1]

There can be no doubt in the minds of reasonable people that a ten hours' day is too long. But if that be so, what shall we say to the hours of labor of shopmen and shop-women, who in most large shops in London begin at 8 a.m. or 9 a.m. and continue at work until 7 p.m. or 8 p.m.? In the smaller shops things are still worse, and, going through a poor neighborhood, we see provision shops open until 10 p.m. or even 11 p.m. served by exhausted men and women, whose pale cheeks and languid movements tell of the strain which is destroying their vitality. The new Parliament should pass an Eight Hours Bill, making the legal day a day of eight hours only, and giving one half-holiday in the week, so that the weekly hours of labor shall not exceed forty-four. In time to come I trust that the hours of labor will be yet further shortened, but the

---

[1] "The Conflicts of Capital and Labor." By G. Howell. Pp. 295, 296.

passage of an Eight Hours Bill would mark a good step forward. Looking at the question from a rational point of view, it is surely clear that a human being should not be required to give more than eight hours out of the twenty-four—one third of his time—for absolute bread-winning. Another seven or eight hours must be given to sleep, leaving eight for meals, exercise, recreation, and study. The last eight are short enough for their varied uses, and I look forward to a time when the first section shall be shortened and the third lengthened; but if every worker had even eight hours of freedom in the day, his life would be a far more human and far more beautiful thing than it is at the present time.

The establishment of an eight hours' day would also help to distribute toil a little more evenly than it is distributed now; the same amount of work will have to be performed, and if each pair of hands only does $\frac{4}{5}$ of the work it now does, additional pairs of hands must execute the remainder. At present some are being worn out with excessive labor, while others are clamoring for employment; shorter hours for the present workers mean work for the now idle hands.

Legislation on the sanitary—or rather insanitary—conditions of various trades is urgently required. I need only mention the whitelead makers, the Sheffield grinders, the miners in dangerous workings, to remind my readers of well-known scandals. Some would leave all remedial measures to voluntary effort and to the influence of "humanity". But humanity looks on them indifferently to-day: it shops at all hours, careless of the suffering inflicted: it says "How sad!" when it reads of special distress, and goes on with its dinner: it contemplates the conditions under which they live who feed and clothe and serve it, and murmurs platitudes about "differences of ranks", and happiness being "pretty evenly distributed, after all": and so it will remain until the strong arm of the law shall compel it to do justice, and shall force it to yield as obedience what it will never yield to prayer.

We may reasonably hope that Religious Liberty and Equality will be rendered complete by the new Parliament. The liberty to make an affirmation in all cases in which an oath is now required will, I trust, be granted by the present Legislature; if not, the passage of an Affirmation

Bill will be one of the first duties of the Reformed Parliament. An amending Burials Bill, giving to unbelievers the right to an "orderly service" at the graveside (see p. 18), will probably pass without much difficulty. Nor is there much likelihood of serious opposition to a Bill for repealing "all the statutes inflicting penalties for opinion, or placing hindrances in the way of lectures and discussions", and for annulling "the present penal and disabling effect of the common law".[1] The general confession by hostile Christians that the latest prosecutions for blasphemy have only injured their religion and strengthened Freethought, shows that the rusty sword of persecution is not likely to be often used by them in the future, and it is noticeable that Radical candidates for the next Parliament are very generally pledging themselves to a repeal of the obnoxious statutes.

There remains the greatest of all the religious changes—the disestablishment and disendowment of the English, Welsh, and Scotch Churches: the public national confession that henceforward the State will concern itself only with the conduct and no longer with the speculations of its citizens. The disestablishment of the Churches will be easily enough effected; the English and Welsh bishops will disappear from the House of Lords as quietly as did their Irish brethren, to the advantage of that House, by the removal of a special obstructiveness, and, let us hope, to the advantage of those dioceses to which their attention will thenceforth be more completely confined. The disendowment clauses of the Bill will present far more difficulty, not only from the vast wealth with which they will deal, but also from the complexity of the interests concerned. The cry of "Sacrilege" and of "Robbery" is sure to be raised when Parliament lays its hands on "Church property". Those who use such epithets will have to be reminded that an enormous part of the Church's wealth is drawn from lands given to the Roman Catholic Church by pious Papists, and that if it be theft for the State to divert to new ends property given to a corporation within its limits, then the first theft was made when Henry VIII. by Act of Parliament severed the Church in England from

---

[1] "The Laws relating to Blasphemy and Heresy." By Charles Bradlaugh. P. 31.

the Papal obedience, and it does not lie with the receiver of stolen goods to complain of robbery when the goods are again removed. Every one knows that many fellowships of the Universities of Oxford and Cambridge were charged with the payment of masses for the souls of the defunct donors; Protestants who regard masses for the dead as "dangerous deceits" have gaily pocketed the Papists' money, and have left their souls unprayed and unpaid for. The Church as by law established has been quite content to fatten on the spoils of its Roman predecessor, and it is with but a bad grace that it commences to pose as the injured innocent, when a second transfer of the cash is proposed. The ground which we should take in dealing with Church funds is a simple one; the State cannot allow the hands of long-mouldered corpses to determine the disposition of wealth now in its midst, and is itself the supreme arbiter in dispensing huge accumulations made by the generations of its dead. Funds which are annually voted to the Church can be stopped by omission of the votes; the rest must be dealt with by the Bill. It is earnestly to be hoped that the State will retain in its own hands all the glebe lands. Their rental will then form a source of national income and will go to lighten the general burden of taxation. The rental of the ecclesiastical buildings to bodies desiring to use them for religious worship, lectures, etc., will form another large item on the credit side of the national balance-sheet. Some provision out of these funds will have to be made for the aged beneficed clergy, as it would be cruel to turn them out helpless into the world. The clergy of the future will have to be supported by their own congregations, as Dissenting ministers are supported now, and "Church people" will no longer be religious paupers, with their souls fed and clothed at the expense of their neighbors.

Changes in the Tenure of Land, vaster than any hitherto attempted, will probably be made by the Reformed Parliament. The huge masses of agricultural laborers now dowered with the vote have been wearing the agricultural shoe long enough to know where it pinches, and they are likely to prove energetic shoemakers. The changes to be made will be radical changes, involving the substitution of a rational system of land-holding for the quasi-feudal one now existing. The new system will be based on the recognition of the principle that land, being the sole fundamental means of existence for all, cannot expediently be regarded as the private property of individuals. Since men can only live by virtue of what they obtain from land, so long as land belongs to a set of individuals in a nation the remainder of the nation must work for these at whatever wages they will give, and freedom of contract between those who hold the means of existence and those who need them becomes a meaningless phrase. Hence, unearned accumulations of wealth for the privileged class, and continual struggle for existence for the unprivileged, with an ever-widening gulf between the unjustly rich and unjustly poor. The substitution of the new system for the old implies too vast a change to be wrought at once; but it is essential that every alteration made in the present tenure of land shall be an alteration tending towards the goal of nationalisation, and not a mere tinkering of abuses on the present basis. The more drastic of the proposals put forward by the Land Law Reform League should be transformed into law by the new Parliament. (I omit the suggested reforms on which all Liberals are agreed, such as cheap transfer, security for improvements, etc.) Thus: cultivable land kept uncultivated and not used for public purposes should be forfeit to the State, "with payment to the dispossessed landowner of say twenty years' purchase at the average annual value of the land for the seven years prior to the" dispossession. "Annual value" is to be understood as meaning any amount really obtained from actual produce: in many shameful cases this is only a few head of game. "Payment to be made by bonds of the State, bearing the same interest as the consolidated debt." "*The land to be State property*, and to be let to actual tenant cultivators. . . . The amount paid as rent to the State to be applied to the payment of the interest [on the bonds], and to form a sinking fund for the liquidation of the principal." The words I have italicised are of vital importance; this forfeited land is not to be sold; it is to be let by the State. Thus the State will become a landholder on a large scale, and a huge step towards nationalisation will be made. The glebe lands above spoken of will add another great slice to the national estate, and no acre of land acquired by the State must ever again be sold to an individual. The breaking up of large estates and the further acquisition of land by the State will be brought about by the imposition of a graduated land tax, "say, the normal tax on the first 5,000 acres, a double tax on the second 5,000 acres, again doubled on the next 10,000 acres," and so on. As the amount thus imposed as tax would soon exceed the value of the land, unduly large estates would be made untenable, and the owners would be forced to sell. "Re-valuation of lands for the more equitable imposition of the land tax" is another matter of pressing importance, the nominal tax of 4s. in the £ being in many cases now a real tax of $\frac{3}{4}$d., 1d., or 1$\frac{1}{2}$d. If the land-tax were levied on the present value of land, instead of on the value it had nearly 200 years ago, it would amount to about £50,000,000 a year, and this fourth part of the income from land would go into the Exchequer of the State, instead of into the ever-gaping pockets of the privileged class.

Before very long, also, Parliament must take into consideration cases like those of the Dukes of Portland, Bedford, and Westminster, whose predecessors let out land on building leases, and who come into possession, as the leases fall in, of houses to the building of which they have not contributed a penny. This shameful confiscation of other people's property should be stopped and that speedily, or else we may hereafter be called on to compensate these all-swallowers for depriving them of property to which they have not the smallest title, and which they should not be allowed to acquire.

The Education of the young will, I hope, receive at the hands of the Reformed Parliaments wide extension and development. The State schools will probably become entirely secular, religious education being left to the various religious sects and to teachers selected by the parents. Compulsion will be enacted by the law of the land, instead of by bye-laws as at present. School fees paid by the parent, already avoidable by the very poor, will be entirely abolished, and the whole cost of education will be charged on the rates, instead of the greater part only, as at present. The abolition of these will relieve the teachers from much heavy clerical work, now imposed on them; will do away with all the machinery for enquiry which now exists to deal with cases in which the remission of fees is asked; and will reduce to a minimum the prosecutions for non-attendance, and the cost of the army of officials now needed to enforce it. Thus will the work of 1870 and 1876 be completed, and we shall have a system of National Education, secular, compulsory, and rate-supported.

What shall be included in this education is a question too wide for discussion at the close of this paper. I look forward to a time when every child shall receive in the national schools the elements of a literary, scientific, artistic, and technical education; when neither boy nor girl shall leave the school ignorant of the glories of our literature, of the wonders of science, of the delight in beauty, of some definite means of bread-winning. Be it tailoring, or dress-making, or cookery, or carpentering, or any one of the many trades needed in a civilised society, every pair of hands should be able to do at least some one thing well, by which a living may be honestly earned. The maturity that follows a youth spent in such training will be useful to the State, and enjoyable to the individual; and such a maturity it should be the object of educational laws to make possible for every citizen.

The lines here sketched are not likely to be followed out in any one Parliament, however great the impulse for improvement, but it is along these lines that the reforming energy will travel, if the study of the past shed any light upon the future of Reform.

THE TRADES UNION MOVEMENT.

BY

ANNIE BESANT.

LONDON:
FREETHOUGHT PUBLISHING COMPANY,
63 FLEET STREET, E.C.

1890.

LONDON:
PRINTED BY CHARLES BRADLAUGH AND ANNIE BESANT,
63 FLEET STREET, E.C.

THE TRADES UNION MOVEMENT.

It is now well-nigh a truism to say that to understand the phænomena of the present we must trace them to their roots in the past. Institutions which surround us to-day, complicated and seeming-unreasonable in much, become easy of comprehension as we study their origin and trace their growth; puzzling and apparently meaningless excrescences then take their place as rudimentary organs; provoking absurdities are seen in their true light as inevitable expedients to meet pressing difficulties; startling anachronisms are recognised as survivals from a past condition, and become luminous landmarks instead of aggravating stupidities. In the light of historical evolution all institutions justify their existence, and, with systems as with individuals, to understand all is to pardon all.

Regarded from this standpoint, the Trades Union movement is but a part, and a small part, of that vast onward movement of Labor which begins in Slavery and will end in the transformation of Class Society into a Brotherhood of equal Workers. At its noblest, it shows that willingness to subordinate the one to the all, to use strength for mutual support and not for mutual destruction, which is the keynote of the higher social morality: at its worst, it shows the brutality which is the reverse side of oppression, the class-feeling which is the negation of brotherhood, the narrowness which is born of ignorance and limited outlook upon life. Trades Unionism can point, for its justification, to a long list of benefits to Labor wrested from reluctant Parliaments and from oppressive capitalists;

it can claim to have demonstrated the value of combination, the force of united action, the strength of self-reliance where the self is a union of many selves; and if sometimes it has forgotten that the cause of Labor is greater than Unionism, signs are not awanting that it is rising to a sense of the larger responsibilities which it should accept as the natural leader of the armies of skilled and unskilled labor, and is preparing its weapons for the final struggle between Industry and Capital, a struggle during which the present social system will go down and the New Order will be evolved.

As the workers, after countless centuries of slavery and serfage, began slowly to claim their rights as men and women, they found themselves fettered with a network of restrictive legislation which checked every movement, much as Gulliver, awaking from his slumber, found his limbs rendered incapable of motion by the countless cords wreathed round them by the inhabitants of Lilliput.

When the lords of the manor began to accept a money payment from their tenants in lieu of the rent paid in labor, it became necessary for them, in turn, to hire laborers to perform the duties erstwhile discharged by the bodily service of their tenantry. Hence arose wages in agricultural industry; and from the reign of Edward II onwards, this practice of hiring labor became more general.[1] When famines and plagues reduced the population, wages rose in a way that naturally annoyed the employing class, accustomed to exact bodily service to an extent measured by its own needs, and not by the comfort of those by whom it was rendered. And when the Black Death, in the reign of Edward III, swept away one third of the population, the ruling classes betook themselves to law to restrict the rising of wage. The struggle began by a royal mandate, forbidding the payment of wages higher than the customary; and this was followed by the Statute of Laborers (25 Edwd. III), fixing wage at the rate paid in 1347, and punishing those who paid and those who received a higher wage. In this statute we find the first legal recognition of the germ of the future Trades Unionism of England, under the uncomplimentary title of "the malice of servants in husbandry"; these malicious

---

[1] "Work and Wages." By J. E. Thorold Rogers. Small reprint, p. 4, ed. 1885.

servants combined to take higher wages than those set out in the royal proclamation, and succeeded generally, by hook or by crook, in obtaining more for their labor than the customary wage. This inchoate Trades Union, working in harmony with economic laws, scored its first success despite the Statute of Laborers. This statute, re-inforced and strengthened by various Parliaments, remained in force until the fifth year of Elizabeth, when it was formally repealed. Of this and similar enactments Hallam justly remarks :

"Such an enhancement in the price of labor, though founded on exactly the same principles as regulate the value of any other commodity, is too frequently treated as a sort of crime by law-givers, who seem to grudge the poor that transient amelioration of their lot, which the progress of population, or other analogous circumstances, will, without any interference, very rapidly take away ".[1]

The Statute of Laborers, of course, affected wages of all kinds, those of artizans as those of laborers; but the artizans were in a stronger position than their agricultural brethren. Without entering on the vexed question of the origin of Gilds, we may observe that from the time of Edward II, all traders, merchants, and master-workmen belonged to their respective Trade Gilds; but from these Gilds craftsmen were gradually excluded, and consequently began to form Crafts Gilds of their own. At one time the trader and the craftsman were united in one person; thus "the London tailors in the time of Edward III were the importers of the woollen cloth which they made up. With the increase of wealth and of population there also came a greater division of labor; the richer carried on trade, the poorer became craftsmen."[2] Into some Gilds men were only admissible when they had "foresworn their trade for a year and a day"; and inevitably, under these circumstances, the Craft Gild arose in opposition to the Trade Gild. It is within the Craft Gild that is to arise the Trade Union of the future.

These Craft Gilds were recognised by the law, and every craftsman was compelled to belong to a Gild; "the punish-

---

[1] "Europe during the Middle Ages." By Henry Hallam, p. 566, Ed. 1869.

[2] "The Conflicts of Capital and Labor." By George Howell, p. 25. Ed. 1878.

ment of refractory members was by fines, contributions of beer, wine, etc., for the Gild feasts; for more serious offences, exclusion from the Gild, which was equivalent to being deprived of the right to carry on the craft . . . . For enforcing the payment of these fees, contributions, dues, and fines, the old Craft Gilds resorted to rattening, that is, taking away the tools of their debtors, precisely as they do still in Sheffield sometimes ".[1]

After the Great Plague, the combinations of workmen grew apace, masons so distinguishing themselves that they had the honor of having a statute—34 Edward III, c. 9—directed especially against them, and we read of a royal mandate against "workmen who have withdrawn from the palace of Westminster", *i. e.* who had gone out on strike. In 1383, the authorities of the City of London forbade "all congregations, covins, and conspiracies of workmen in general"; and four years afterwards three bold journeymen cordwainers found themselves in Newgate for trying to found a fraternity under the protection of the Pope. From this time onwards we read of frequent suppressions of fraternities of journeymen, these combinations being formed within the Crafts Gilds, for the protection of the poorer members. As the Crafts Gilds decayed, these internal combinations came more and more to the front, and assumed more and more the character of the modern Trade Union.

It is noteworthy that combinations among the manual workers thus had their rise at a period when the agricultural and artizan population was in a condition of higher material prosperity and comfort that it enjoyed before or has enjoyed since. It was what Thorold Rogers calls "the golden age of the English laborer". Ordinary artizans earned 6d. a day, agricultural laborers 4d.; the cost of maintenance was reckoned, when board was given, at 6d. a week, the highest ever reckoned in this way being 1s. a week. Hallam, contrasting wages and prices in the reigns of Edward III and Henry VI, with wages and prices in the reign of Victoria, states that the laboring classes were better provided with the means of subsistence then than now; and after making various allowances, he concludes: "After every allowance of this kind, I should find it diffi-

[1] "The Conflicts of Capital and Labor." By George Howell, p. 48. Ed. 1878.

cult to resist the conclusion, that however the laborer has derived benefit from the cheapness of manufactured commodities, and from many inventions of common utility, he is much inferior in ability to support a family than were his ancestors four centuries ago ".[1]

The growing strength of the workmen's combinations, despite all attempts to suppress them, is shewn by the ferocious statute of Henry VI (3rd Henry VI, cap. 1) against such combinations. The preamble states that "Artificers, Handicraftsmen and Laborers have made confederacies and promises, and have sworn mutual oaths not only that they should not meddle with another's work and perform and finish that another hath begun, but also to constitute and appoint how much work they shall do in a day, and what hours and times they shall work, contrary to the laws and statutes of this realm, and to the great impoverishment of his Majesty's subjects ". It was therefore enacted that "if any artificers, workmen, or laborers, do conspire, covenant, or promise together, or make oath that they shall not make to do their work but at a certain price or rate, and not entertain to take upon them to finish that another hath begun, or shall do but a certain work in a day, or shall not work but at certain hours and times," they shall be guilty of felony, and be severely punished, the penalty for the third offence being the loss of the ears and infamy.

From this time forward the hand of Parliament weighed more and more heavily on the English workman, until it pressed him down into the position in which he lay at the beginning of the present century. The Gilds, long decaying, were crushed out, while the later combinations were branded as felony.

It is not possible in this brief survey to sketch the causes which led to the lamentable degradation of the workers—the enclosures of common lands, the eviction of cultivators to make large grazing farms, the vagabondage resulting from wars and the break-up of the great feudal houses, the debasing of the currency, etc. It must suffice to roughly outline the resulting legislation.

This legislation, at first, was harshest towards unskilled labor, the old customary protection of the Gilds still

---

[1] "Europe during the Middle Ages." Pp. 649, 650.

influencing some of the laws touching skilled labor, as the clauses in the Statute of Apprentices of Elizabeth, designed to prevent the overcrowding of handicrafts, to the advantage of the skilled artizan. On the landless and the craftless then, as now, fell the heavier hand of the law.

In 1494, by the 11 Henry VII, c. 2, able-bodied vagrants were rendered liable to the stocks and whipping; and this Act was reinforced in 1530, and again in 1535, when death was adjudged as penalty for a third offence. Seventy-two thousand vagrants were, according to Hollinshed, executed in the reign of Henry VIII.[1] In 1547, men and women were forced to hire themselves for "meat and drink" if they had been idle three days, under penalty of branding in the face; and a runaway might be enslaved for two years: if such a slave fled his employment he was branded and enslaved for life; and a third evasion was punished with death. Similar laws, yet more severe, were passed under Elizabeth and James; lack of employment, the curse of the worker's life, being thus judged as crime. Other legislation dealt with combinations, apprenticeship, and wages. By 2 and 3 Edward VI, c. 15, combinations of workmen "concerning their work or wages" were made punishable with fine or imprisonment for the first offence, fine or the pillory for the second, and fine, pillory, loss of one ear, and judicial infamy for the third. "This statute was confirmed by 22 and 23 Charles II, and was in force till the general repeal of all such prohibitions on the combinations of workmen, which took effect under 6 George IV, c. 129."[2] By the Statute of Apprentices, 5 Elizabeth c. 4, persons were forbidden to exercise any "art, mystery, or manual occupation" without an apprenticeship of seven years, thus still further shackling the unlucky unskilled worker; and the justices in Quarter Sessions were ordered to fix the rates of wage in husbandry and handicrafts. It is sometimes said that all attempts to fix wage by law are rendered nugatory by economic causes. As a matter of historical fact, this is not true. As Thorold Rogers explicitly says, dealing with the period that followed the passing of the Act: "The wages of labor do conform, notwithstanding

[1] See "Historical Basis of Socialism in England." By H. M. Hyndman. Pp. 40-43. Ed. 1883.

[2] "Work and Wages." Pp. 64, 65.

the continual increase in the price of the necessaries of life, to the assessments of the Quarter Sessions; and the system is continued under legal sanction till 1812, and by a sufficient understanding for long after that date ".[1] And this, although he goes on: "It seems that as long as the practice remained, under which the wages of the peasant were eked out by land allowances and commonable rights, he continued to subsist, though but poorly, under the system; but that when the enclosures of the eighteenth century began, and the full influence of the Corn Laws was felt, during the fourth quarter of that century and the first quarter of the nineteenth, it became necessary to supplement his wages by an allowance from the parish fund, and thus to indirectly qualify the assessment which the magistrate had established." The law of Parochial Settlement, 13 and 14 Car. II, c. 12, tied the people to the soil, though work might be unattainable there; and, if a man found work elsewhere, empowered the churchwardens and overseers of the parish into which he had gone, to obtain an order from two justices of the peace to remove him back to his own parish. The 8 and 9 William III, c. 30, permitted churchwardens and overseers to issue licences to migrate, provided that they admitted their liability to take the migrant and any family that he might have back to his original parish, if he became chargeable in the new. Thus the laborer became, as he has been well called, "a serf without land, the most portentous phænomenon in agriculture".[2]

The completing touch was put to the degraded helplessness of the worker by extending the law of conspiracy to enmesh all his combinations. This extension was the work of the lawyers, who construed the statutes of Edward and Elizabeth in this sense; until Parliament lightened their labor by passing, in 1799, the 39 Geo III, c. 106, which suppressed all workmen's trade associations, of whatever kind, and forbade them to accumulate common funds. "At the conclusion of the eighteenth century," says Thorold Rogers, "an Act of Parliament was carried which declares that all contracts, except between master and man, for obtaining advances of wages, altering the usual time of working, decreasing the quantity of work, and the

---

[1] "Work and Wages." Pp. 52, 53. [2] *Ib.* P. 97.

like, illegal. Workmen who enter into such illegal combinations are punishable by imprisonment, and a similar punishment is inflicted on those who enter into combinations to procure an advance of wages, or seek to prevent other workmen from hiring themselves, or procuring them to quit their employment. Meetings and combinations for effecting such purposes are punishable in like manner; and offenders who inform against their associates are to be indemnified."[1] This act followed various others, passed during the century, forbidding combinations in different trades—as 12 George I, c. 34, forbidding combinations of workmen employed in woollen manufactures—and summed up the restrictive legislation which placed the workman helpless in the hands of the capitalist. During the first thirty-five years of the nineteenth century the English worker reached the nadir of political and social degradation. He was voiceless in the State, a bondslave in industrial life. Gripped by the law of Settlement, his wages fixed by those who lived on his labor, forbidden to associate with his fellows for his own improvement, gagged if he tried to advise with his mates on the conditions of their labor, he was ringed round by laws that bruised him at his lightest movement. The Government was his tyrant, the law his worst enemy; no marvel that his one cry was to get rid of the interference of the State, that he panted for individual liberty.

While legislation thus fettered the worker, the economic revolution worsened all his life conditions. The invention of steam-machinery brought with it the replacement of home industries by factory production; the aggregations of population consequent on this brought about an overcrowding, a squalor, a mass of festering misery, unknown in the less complex life of simpler times; the rising of new trades, uncontrolled by the apprenticeship legislation, enabled untrained men, as well as women and children, to crowd into the industrial field; and between the dying protective legislation of the past and the yet unborn regulative legislation of modern times, came an interregnum of *laissez faire*, during which Capitalistic Industrialism exploited the workers at its will, while they, bound hand

---

[1] "Work and Wages." Pp. 66, 67.

and foot, were unable to resist, save by violence, the unendurable oppression under which they suffered.

As might be expected, secret combination took the place of the open associations forbidden by law; and riot in public and malicious injury in private were the only weapons left to the hapless workers. Some trades indeed combined under the guise of Friendly Societies; but these were practically useless for trade defence, since trade defence took their funds out of the protection of the law.

Riot from time to time broke out during the seventeenth century, as when the framework knitters in London and Westminster rose in revolt, smashed some hundred frames, and were driven by starvation into such oft-repeated violence that, in 1727, an act was passed punishing frame-breaking with death. Nor was this law inoperative, for, among other cases, we find loom-breakers in Spitalfields, in 1770, hanged in the front of the houses wherein the looms had been broken. In 1779 the rejection by the House of Commons of a Bill regulating this trade was followed by rioting in Nottingham, whither the trade had gone; and the whole district round Nottingham was for years in continual labor troubles; so that in 1811–12 we find Parliament again enacting the punishment of death for frame-breakers. In 1805, "the London Fire Insurance Companies received letters of caution from the workmen, wherein they declared that, as Parliament refused to protect their rights, they would do so themselves;"[1] and a factory on fire lent point to the warning. With the introduction of steam-machinery, the pressure on the workers was increased as machines took the place of men; while women and children also entered into competition with the male workers. All over the country rioting occurred. In Wiltshire and Somersetshire, in 1802, riots followed the introduction by the Master Clothiers of a machine for dressing cloth, called the Gig-Mill, by which one man and four children could do the work of thirty men. Organised bands of men, known as Luddites from the name of one of their leaders, destroyed machines in many parts of the country, until in 1810 and 1811 the whole land, well-nigh, was in a state of turmoil. During six years the Luddites carried on their work of destruction; and in one year, 1813, no less than

[1] "Capital and Labor." P. 94.

eighteen of them were hanged at York. Some thousand stocking frames and eighty lace frames were destroyed by them in Nottingham.

In Scotland, the struggle was carried on in even rougher fashion. In the evidence laid before a Parliamentary Committee in 1824, a lurid light is thrown on the results of a policy which, forbidding open agitation for the redressal of grievances, threw men back on secret violence. We read of the spinners in Glasgow and the surrounding district:

"In 1819, 1820, and 1823 a series of outrages was committed of the most brutal and atrocious character. A great number of threatening letters are quoted in the report, of which the following extract will give some idea:

'*August* 9th, 1823.

'We have given you long enough time to gether money to pay your expenses back agian to Belfast, therefore, we hope you will lave the wheels that you are on at presant to men that have a better right to them than you, on Monday first, and if you do not atten to this, will sarve you like Linzie Phillips.

'This we swaer by the living God.

'Signed by the Captain of the Blood Red Knights.'

(Then a representation of a hand holding a sword with a pierced heart, two pistols, a coffin, etc., with death's head and crossbones.)

"Another letter is signed 'Captain of the Vitriol Forces'. A third is dated 'nine miles below hell'. Others contain allusions to the judgment seat of Christ, and other sacred things, mingling the most disgusting profanity with the most revolting atrocity.

"Another is a demand by Mr. Houldsworth's operatives that, as Mr. Dyson and James Fisher are too vigilant, they shall be reprimanded before the men; and that Mr. Russell shall be discharged, 'being no judge of his business' and also that J. McKenzie Phillips may not be admitted in future. This Phillips was subsequently 'vitrioled', his face burnt in places to the bone, and the sight of one eye destroyed.

"Nor were others of these letters mere empty threats Several mills were set fire to; one manufacturer, writing in 1821 from Paisley, said that scarcely a night passed in Johnston without shots being discharged, and the lowest depths of cowardly brutality were reached, in vitriol-throwing and woman-beating. . . . . Tired of quarrelling with his men, one of the manufacturers hired women, and built a mill with machinery specially adapted to them; but the women were beaten, and one old woman so severely that she died three days afterwards. . . . . Alexander Fisher was shot at when in bed about one o'clock, Aug. 2nd., 1820: the shot lodged near the bed, and some of the glass was driven into the children's bed. He was again shot at on the 16th of September, about two o'clock in the morning. On the 29th of November, two men waylaid him on his way to work at six o'clock in the morning, and threw a quantity of vitriol over his face and breast, which burnt him dreadfully. On the 14th of December, he, having only just attempted to resume work, was again shot at while at the mill. On the 4th of January he was still without the use of his left eye."[1]

The strong language used in this report is not surprising, if the crimes are regarded apart from all circumstances connected with them. But those who realise the terrible position of these men, fighting for bare life against overwhelming odds, persecuted by the law, helpless in the capitalists' grip, will, while condemning the outrages, feel pity for, rather than wrath against the criminals. The beating of woman was shameful enough; but it should be remembered that the masters were using the women to starve out the men, and that the women — may be also driven by starvation — yielded themselves as weapons to stab their men comrades. In a fight for life, the gentlest often become cruel; and these men had been brutalised by a life-time of injustice, misery, and degradation. The Scotch laws were worse even than the English, and the consequent brutalisation greater. Slavery was still in existence in the last quarter of the eighteenth century, and Dr. Burton, writing of Fletcher of Saltoun (1653—1716), says:

"If Fletcher were not a slaveholder himself, he lived surrounded by slaveholders and their slaves. His paternal territory lay in that county of East Lothian, where the two classes of works labored by slaves—collieries and salt-works—had their oldest and still their chief establishment. The slaves went to those who bought or succeeded to the property of the works, and they could be sold, bartered, or pawned. What is peculiar and revolting in this institution is, that it was no relic of ancient serfdom, but a growth of the seventeenth century. The oldest trace we have of the bondage of the colliers and salt-workers is an Act of the year 1606, passed, as

[1] Trade Societies and Strikes; report of the Committee on Trade Societies, appointed by the National Association for the promotion of Social Science, 1860. Pp. 357, 358.

it would seem, to strengthen somewhat as to them the laws so common at the time for restricting the pursuit of all occupations to those embarked in them. By interpretation of this Act, but more by the tyrannous power of the strong owners of the soil over a weak and unfriended community, slavery had been as amply established in the community where Fletcher dwelt, as ever it had been in Rome, Sparta, or Virginia." [1]

With such a past lying immediately behind them, the wonder to me is that there was so little crime during these long years of desperate and apparently hopeless misery.

The Repeal of the Statute of Apprentices in 1814 did nothing to lessen, but, on the contrary, much to increase, the bitterness of the industrial conflict; the abolition of compulsory apprenticeship only served to intensify the terrible struggle for employment; and the abrogation of the assessment of wages at Quarter Sessions—which, instituted for the benefit of the master, had come to be a benefit to the workman, as interposing between his employer and himself—left him to the enforced acceptance of wages driven by unfettered competition below subsistence level. It is noteworthy that in this case, as in many others, laws initiated to help the employing class became, in the course of years, serviceable to the workers. The truth is that the condition of the workers deteriorated so rapidly that the minimum forced on them in the sixteenth century became the maximum they struggled to retain in the eighteenth. No more eloquent proof of their misery can be given than this one fact.

Continual prosecutions of workmen for transgressions of the iniquitous combination laws give the last touch of blackness to this gloomy picture. We read of men sent to gaol for the most harmless actions; of one linen weaver of Knaresborough suffering three months' imprisonment in 1805 for carrying a letter to York asking for assistance from other workmen. Of men fined and imprisoned for simple combination. Of a master using these laws to avoid payment of wages. Of a workman—who acted as chairman at a meeting at which two resolutions were passed—sentenced to a year's imprisonment, although his employer gave evidence that he himself had advised the passing of the resolutions; two other workmen, who acted as

[1] Quoted in an interesting article on Fletcher of Saltoun, by John M. Robertson, in *Our Corner* for February, 1888.

secretaries at the same meeting, suffered two years' imprisonment each. The sinful resolutions which brought such heavy punishment on these three men were: one that advised the acceptance of a proposed compromise between masters and men; the second, "That as it is in the power of the manufacturer to compel the weaver to weave out his work in the loom or on hand, he is advised in such case to obey the dictates of the law; yet no injunction is hereby laid upon him by this meeting, and he is left entirely to his own discretion; but he is not to bring any more work from any manufacturer under the proposed advance mentioned in the first resolution".

The long-continued political agitation, carried on side by side with the industrial revolts, and intensified by the troubles consequent on the Corn Laws, brought matters to such a point that, in 1817, the terrified Government suspended the Habeas Corpus Act, and in 1819 stained itself with the blood of Peterloo. But repression and yeomanry charges do not cure disaffection, which springs from substantial grievances; and in 1824, Joseph Hume, the Radical, with some other members of Parliament, obtained a Parliamentary Committee to enquire into the working of the laws affecting labor, and the state of the law "so far as relates to the combination of workmen and others to raise wages, or to regulate their wages". A mass of evidence was laid before this Committee, showing that, as a rule, through the strikes and disputes, the men had exhibited marvellous self-control.

On the report of this Committee, was brought in by Mr. Hume and passed the 5 George IV, c. 95, which repealed the statutes forbidding the combinations of workmen, and enacted that no workman should be liable to be indicted or prosecuted for conspiracy, or to any punishment, for entering into any combination for advancing or fixing wages, altering the hours of labor, and so on. The passing of the Act was followed by a large number of strikes; and in the following year another Act was passed —6 George IV, c. 122—which repealed 5 George IV, c. 95, and while re-enacting the section which repealed the combination laws, yet, in the words of Mr. Wallace, who introduced the Bill, made "all associations illegal, excepting those for the purpose of settling such amount of wages as would be a fair remuneration for the workmen".[1] It threw the workmen once more into the toils of the common law as to conspiracy, and limited any workmen's combination to raise wages to those present at the meeting at which the decision was come to. "All meetings or agreements whatever for the purpose of affecting the wages or hours of work of persons not present at the meeting, or parties to the agreement, were conspiracies. So were all agreements for controlling a master in the management of his business, in the persons he employed, or the machinery which he should use. So also were all agreements not to work in the company of any given person, or to persuade other persons to leave their employment, or not to engage themselves. In fact, there was scarcely an act performed by any workman as a member of a trade union which was not an act of conspiracy and a misdemeanor."[2] One would imagine that the framers of this Act agreed with Sir Archibald Alison, that "worse than plague, pestilence, and famine, combinations among workmen were the greatest social evil which, in a manufacturing or mining community, afflicts society".[3]

In the Report of the Commission on Trades Unions of 1867, the position of the Unions under this legislation is clearly laid down. "With regard to the legality of Trades Unions as at present constituted, we are advised and believe that prior to the Act 5 George IV, c. 95, any such concerted proceeding on the part of the workmen as a strike, would have been an unlawful combination punishable at common law by fine and imprisonment; and that a union or association of workmen for raising funds to support the men engaged in such a strike, would have been an unlawful association. The Act 5 George IV, c. 95, which exempted from punishment the parties to such a combination when not attended with violence, was itself repealed by the Act 6 George IV, c. 199. This Act had a much more limited operation than the Act which it repealed. It did not go further than to exempt from punishment, either by statute or at common law, persons meeting together for consulting upon and determining the rate of wages which *the persons present at the meeting or any of them* should demand for their

---

1 "Conflicts of Capital and Labor." P. 129.

2 *Id.* Pp. 133, 134.

3 "History of Europe," by Sir A. Alison, xx, 26.

work, or the hours during which they should work; and it contained a similar limited exemption with respect to persons entering into an agreement for the same pupose. With this limited exception it left the common law in force as before. No trades union, so far as our observation has extended, has attempted to give to the combination a wholly legal character by confining the application of its funds in support of men on strike to the limits within which alone combinations are legalised by the Act 6, Geo. IV, c. 129. Unions contemplate generally the application of their funds to the support of men engaged in a strike for the purpose of enforcing some decision come to by the union in what they deem to be the interests of trade. Many such strikes would therefore be unlawful combinations at common law, and would not be relieved by the statute."

The legal position of Trades Unions was thus eminently unsatisfactory, and agitation for legal recognition still went on. It was intensified by the persecution of those who were endeavoring to unite the workers. In 1834, six Dorchester laborers were sentenced to seven years' transportation, nominally for administering unlawful oaths, really for advocating association. George Howell says:

"This conviction was so manifestly unjust and the sentence so outrageously cruel, that some of the ablest, certainly the most independent, men of that day condemned both in no measured terms; and they demanded the remission of the sentence on these six poor men, and their immediate liberation. An immense demonstration took place in the Copenhagen Fields, on Monday, March 21st, 1834, attended, it is said, by about 400,000 persons: a procession between six and seven miles in length, consisting of nearly 50,000 workmen, proceeded to the official residence of Lord Melbourne for the purpose of presenting a petition with over 266,000 signatures, on behalf of the six convicted peasants. After a good deal of opposition on the part of the Whig ministry of the day, backed as it was by the major portion of the manufacturing classes, and after much delay, the men were 'pardoned', and ordered to be liberated."

Among the cottonspinners, during these years of trouble, the principle of organisation was rapidly making way. In 1829, there was a great strike at Manchester against a percentage reduction in wages as the number of spindles managed by one spinner increased. A spinner could manage 300 spindles, if he had four little children to help him as piecers, *i.e.* to piece together any threads broken in the spinning. It was found that many more spindles might be added to a machine, if the number of piecers was increased, and that a man could, at least for a time, work a machine carrying 1,000 spindles. The spinner was paid per lb. of twist produced, and the manufacturers objected to pay the full rate, as the machine was made to carry more spindles, although as the number of spindles increased the work grew more and more exhausting. They accordingly claimed to deduct from the wages earned a percentage as the number of spindles increased; and against this imposition the men struck, starved for six months, and went in beaten. In Glasgow a similar battle was fought in 1837, and after a four months struggle, ended in similar fashion. Undaunted, the men met failure with attempts at wider organisation, and enrolled over 100,000 spinners in England, Scotland and Ireland, in one association, in lieu of having a Union for each town—a step in the right direction, although not yet to be successful. A "National Association for the Protection of Labor", with a newspaper, *The Voice of the People*, was also started, with a view to federating all trades, but this also perished, born out of due time.[1]

On January 11th, 1838, five Glasgow cotton spinners were sentenced to seven years transportation for conspiracy and illegal combination; and once more the scandal of a great judicial iniquity forced the House of Commons into action. A Select Committee was ordered to enquire into the 6 Geo. IV, c. 129, and into trade unions and combinations in general, and took evidence plentifully, after the fashion of such committees. They found there was much combination and little, though some, violence; at Glasgow picketing was extensively employed, one man was murdered, one woman had vitriol thrown on her, and there were two attempts at incendiarism. The Committee of the Union had been tried on the charge of instigating these crimes, but a verdict of "not proven" had been returned. The Glasgow masters thought the Union promoted intemperance, and that the men lost in drink and in Union contributions as much as they gained in wage through it,

[1] See on all this Mr. Godfrey Lushington's abstract of the Evidence given before the Commission of 1838, prepared for the Social Science Association, 1860.

a view by no means endorsed by the men. In Ireland, also, deeds of violence occurred; but the Committee notes that they had steadily decreased in number since the repeal of the Combination Laws, and that the effect of this repeal "upon the conduct of strikes had been in general beneficial". The Committee further stated that "as a class, unionists were pronounced by the majority of masters to be more highly skilled operatives and more respectable men than others in the trade", and that "unionists, as a rule, were in the receipt of higher wages than non-unionists".[1]

From this period (1838) onwards to 1871, so far as Parliament was concerned, little improvement was made in the legal position of Trade Unions. Strikes were mostly accompanied by prosecutions of workmen; the law of conspiracy was used against them; being illegal associations, their funds were unprotected and their treasurers might swindle at will. In 1847 and 1848, prosecutions for conspiracy occurred, in one of which a man named Drury was sentenced at Sheffield, with some others, to ten years transportation; but the conviction was quashed, presumably on error. Very many other prosecutions kept the Unions always in a state of unrest, but they were only nerved thereby to fresh efforts. The "National Association of United Trades", founded in 1845, with its newspaper, *The Labour League*, had a vigorous life of fifteen years; and in 1850-1 the various branches of the engineering trade consolidated themselves into the Amalgamated Society of Engineers, now one of the largest and strongest labor organisations in the world. But the difficulties under which all this progress was made are well exemplified by a decision of Lord Chief Justice Cockburn in 1866, in the case of Hornby *v.* Close, in which a fraudulent official who had plundered a union was able to escape from punishmont. In 1867, the "leaders of the tailors' strike were declared guilty of 'conspiracy' for having combined to organise a system of pickets, who confined themselves to informing the workmen that such and such a shop was under strike. . . . . The reasons given for this decision increased its importance. The common law of England declares every engagement 'opposed to the

[1] See report of G. Lushington.

common weal' null and void: and the decisions of the Courts have settled that all combinations, either of masters or workmen, with the view of controlling the labor-market, are in restraint of trade and 'opposed to the common weal'."[1]

During these years of trial Parliament was liberal with Committees, if not with legislation. In 1856, in 1860, in 1865 and '66, Committees sat enquiring into the laws. The only mouse of legislation from this mountain of Committee-sitting, was the Masters and Servants Act of 1867, which abolished inequalities of penalty for breach of contract inflicted respectively on masters and men, and abolished some of the Georgian legislation.

As is too often the case in England, it was outrage that finally determined Parliament to action; and the struggle that ended in the conclusive victory of the Unions was initiated by what are known as "the Sheffield outrages". As George Howell well puts it, "Men who know that they are criminals by the mere object which they have in view, care little for the additional criminality involved in the means they adopt;" and in this sentence lies the real explanation of the outrages in Sheffield, Manchester, and Nottingham. Trade Unions were illegal associations, and, branded by the law, they became indifferent to the law. They were unable to bridle their wilder members, unable to enforce discipline, or effectively punish traitors. They saw their own mates helping the masters to make life harder and bitterer to the workers they were banded together to redeem: what wonder that sometimes righteous anger led to unrighteous violence, and that men used their physical strength to coerce renegades and paralyse oppression as against the legal persecution to which they were subjected?

In Sheffield, the chief theatre of the outrages, all the circumstances lent themselves to violence. Historically the cutlery trades, unhealthy and life-shortening, have been given to rough personal arguments, arguments *ad hominem* in a literal sense. The following verse from a song written during the strike of 1787 against a master who insisted on the "extortionate practice" of having

---

[1] "The Trades Unions of England." By the Comte de Paris. Pp. 27, 29, 30, ed. 1869.

thirteen knives to the dozen, suggests a certain lack of meekness: [1]

"That monster Oppression—behold how he stalks!
Keeps picking the bones of the poor as he walks.
There's not a mechanic throughout the whole land
But what more or less feels the weight of his hand.
That offspring of Tyranny, Baseness, and Pride,
Our rights hath invaded and almost destroyed.
May that man be banished who villany screens,
Or sides with big W—— and his thirteens.

CHORUS.

Then may the odd knife his great carcase dissect,
Lay open his vitals for men to inspect;
A heart full as black as the infernal gulf,
In that greedy, blood-sucking, bone-scraping wolf."

Throughout the century there were many strikes and trade disputes in Sheffield, and much deep distress. In 1842 the condition of the artisans was brought to the notice of the House of Lords; and relief to the casual poor, which had been £715 in 1837, had risen to over £15,000, some ten to fifteen thousand people being wholly destitute. Despite the efforts of the Trades Unionist leaders, some outrages occurred—"rattening (as the stealing of workmen's wheel bands, thus disabling their machines, is called) was frequent . . . . Incendiary fires occurred in more than one factory, and a wheel in Abbeydale was blown up by gunpowder." In 1843 the distress continued, and outrages "directed against unpopular manufacturers and non-unionist workmen" were frequent. At an important meeting in 1845, delegates from the unions urged the limitation of the working day and the restriction of the numbers employed in the trade. The joiners said that in 1841 two-thirds of their number were working on the roads, or taking parish relief; but by forming a union and limiting the hours of labor to eight a day they had found employment for all their men, and full employment for two-thirds of them. Other trades gave similar evidence. The state of trade shortly afterwards improved, and wages rose, and as trades unionism grew stronger and stronger the hatred of non-unionists increased. It was against them that violence was most often used. Thus, in June, 1854,

[1] See throughout Mr. F. Hill's paper on "Trade Combinations in Sheffield," Social Science Association, 1860.

one Mark Firth is warned, "unless you get shut of those knobstick grinders from your weel that we shall be obliged to try some Remedy of our own". In 1853 a man named Parker was shot and his horse hamstrung, and he was thus persuaded to join the Union. A manufacturer named Wilson refused, during fourteen years, to employ Union men; his house was partly blown up, and one of his workmen injured by gunpowder being placed in his glazing trough, so that it was fired by sparks from the glazer. It is stated, but the authority is not given and I doubt the veracity of the narrative, that it was the custom for the man who was to commit the outrage to be drawn by lot, and that only he who drew the lot (and in some cases the President) knew that it had fallen on him: that the payment for the crime was placed in a drawer, and was thence taken by the person by whom the outrage was to be performed.

It will be seen from this brief sketch that outrages were no new thing in Sheffield; and the Royal Commission of 1867, appointed to enquire into them, and generally into Trade Union organisations, was really face to face with normal illegal violence used by men whom the law had refused to recognise and protect. The Commission traced a number of outrages—shooting with air-guns, blowing up with gunpowder, etc.—to the instigation of Broadhead, the Secretary of the Saw Grinders' Union; and he confessed to having hired men to commit them, at a cost to the Union funds of some £200. Ginger beer bottles, filled with gunpowder and nails, with a lighted fuse attached, were used to cause explosions; gunpowder was put in the troughs of grinders, bellows and bands were cut, bricks destroyed, tools stolen, men beaten. Of the sixty trade unions in Sheffield, twelve were reported as having "promoted or encouraged outrages". In Manchester and its neighborhood, the outrages were chiefly among the brickmakers: non-unionists found needles and broken glass mixed with the tempered clay, their tools and barrows broken, and they were often seriously assaulted.[1]

Apart from the question of outrages, this Commission took an immense mass of evidence both from employers and employed, from unionists and non-unionists, on the

[1] See Reports of the Commission as laid before Parliament.

conduct of strikes, the effects of unionism, the organisation of unions, and other allied subjects. The Commission finally reported that there was no doubt that "Trades unions have had certain injurious effects on the character of the working men, as well as on the relations between them and their employers", but declined to pronounce authoritatively between the conflicting assertions of masters and men. It was much shocked at the "utter perversion of all sense of law and duty" which made unionists "regard workmen who stand aloof from the union with a feeling akin to that which defenders of their country have towards a citizen who deserts to the invaders for the sake of better pay". It reported that "no trades union" had preserved "a wholly legal character, for many of the strikes were unlawful combinations; and the unions themselves, by interfering with trade, became unlawful associations". It then recommended that the right to combine should be granted, there being "no ground of justice or policy for withholding such a right from the workmen"; and that facilities should be afforded for registration, where the Registering Officer found the rules and bye-laws of a Union unobjectionable. Other suggestions were made, as for the appointment of a Public Prosecutor, of Boards of Conciliation, etc. The final outcome of the Commission was the Acts of 1871 and 1875, and with that legal recognition of the existence and the objects of the Unions, outrages disappeared, and rational argument took the place of explosions. A knobstick or a blackleg may still, now and then, in times of great excitement, be threatened or even used with violence; but such incidents are rare, and rarest of all with the firmly organised Unions.

The Act of 1871 (34 and 35 Vict., c. 31) protected the funds of Trade Unions, if they were registered under the Act; and in 1876 (39 and 40 Vict. c. 22) this protection was rendered complete and thoroughly effective. But much more than this was wanted, ere Unionists could feel secure, for the Act of 1871, while first giving the sanction of law to Trade Unions, did not deliver them from the meshes of conspiracy at common law. Not only so, but the Criminal Law Amendment Act of 1871 (34 and 35 Vict. c. 32) punished with imprisonment certain acts, if intended to coerce either master or workman; even the refusal to work with a person was regarded as criminal, and was punishable with imprisonment, as was breach of contract by leaving work. Under the pretence of preventing intimidation, the most quiet picketting was punished with imprisonment. "Under the Criminal Law Amendment Act, a workman was sentenced at the Hammersmith Police Court to two months' imprisonment with hard labor for delivering handbills; he did not coerce, nor even persuade; it did not appear that he spoke to the complainant; all he did was to deliver a handbill which was neither offensive nor dictatorial. But the employers prosecuted and the man was sentenced. On appeal, the prosecution withdrew from the case, and the man escaped punishment. In other cases men were convicted for asking for contributions from members in arrears, and for speaking persuasively without molestation or obstruction."[1] In 1872 the London Gas Stokers were convicted under this Act. "The last of such cases was the Cabinet Makers', just before the repeal of the Act, which excited the sympathy of great numbers entirely outside the pale of the unions, and even of some who were opposed to them."[2] Once more, agitation led to reform, and in 1875 an Act was passed (38 and 39 Vict. c. 83) which enacts that "an agreement or combination by two or more persons to do any act in furtherance of a Trade dispute between employers or workmen, should not be indictable as a conspiracy, if such act committed by one person would not be punishable as a crime". Here was the shattering of the old wicked law, which had ever hung, as the sword of Damocles, over the head of every workman engaged in a struggle with his employer. The Act went on to declare that "The breach of contract between master and workman is to be dealt with as a civil and not as a criminal act, except in the case of the person employed in the supply of water, or gas, breaking his contract with his employer, or in the case where the breaking of contract of service would endanger human life or expose valuable property to destruction".

With this group of laws ends the breaking off of the fetters of restrictive legislation from the limbs of the work-

[1] "Conflicts of Capital and Labor." Pp. 340, 341.
[2] Ibid. P. 341.

man. He was left free to combine, to agitate, to accumulate funds, to protect himself, always within the bounds which limit the freedom of every citizen in a civilised community—that he must not use his own liberty to infringe on the equal liberty of his neighbor. While the laws of the oppressive past were thus cancelled, a new law raised the workman to the rank of a citizen. The Reform Act of 1867 gave the Franchise to the town artisan, while that of 1885 gave it to the agricultural laborer. At the beginning of the century the workman was bound by oppressive laws in the making of which he had no voice, and which he could only oppose by violence; at the close of the century, he stands politically master of the country, if he would only realise his strength and would combine with his fellows to use it.

In estimating the value of Trades Unionism to the cause of Labor, apart from the utility of the discipline and habits of co-operation involved in it, it is difficult, if not impossible, to disentangle from the complicated effects those which are specifically due to Unionism as a cause. So far as wages are concerned, it is certain that the power ascribed to Unions of driving wage up, or of resisting its fall, has been very greatly over-estimated. Their ability in this respect is restricted within very narrow limits. When prices are rising, a strong Union can—by threatening a strike—obtain an increase of wage more quickly than could isolated workers; but wages rise and fall irrespective of Unions and are not controllable by them, except in so far as an exceptionally circumstanced Union, consisting of highly skilled workmen, in some branch of production in which apprenticeship is enforced, may be able to limit the supply of labor in its trade, and by limiting the supply increase its selling price. Or again, where the wage paid in a trade is, in consequence of the ignorance and helplessness of the workers, below the average wage at that time and place, the formation of a Union and the threat of a strike may raise the wage to the current level. But apart from such exceptional circumstances, the old idea of the value of Unions, under this head, must be given up, although probably few Unionists would endorse the view of the Commission of 1867, that it was "doubtful whether the net earnings of the workmen connected with unions have not, on the whole, been diminished rather than increased through the agency of the unions".

The great field of victory of the Unions has been the improvement of the conditions under which the workmen labor; here none can challenge the services they have rendered. The miners' unions obtained the Act of 1850, enforcing inspection in mines, after petitioning as to ventilation, etc., in 1830, '34, '35, '42, and onwards to 1850, and twice obtaining Committees on the question; in 1842 they obtained an Act excluding young children from mines, and again for stopping the underground labor of women. Dissatisfied with the Act of 1850, they still petitioned and agitated, and after two more Committees in 1852 and 1853, a better Act was obtained in 1855. Still, owing to the bitter opposition of mine-owners, conditions of safety were not sufficiently stringent, and five more years of struggle won the Act of 1860. Since that date, Act after Act has been passed to ensure safety, to throw responsibility for accidents on employers, and generally to improve the conditions amid which labor is performed.

The miners' unions carried on an equally persistent fight for the extension of education, declaring in 1854 that the men unanimously desired "that a certain sum, say not exceeding 2d. per week, should be stopped out of their wages for school purposes, provided that the men are fairly represented on the committee which manages the particular school to which their contributions are applied"[1] And this, be it remembered, was said sixteen years before the passing of Mr. Foster's Education Act. In 1860, within eight days, 50,000 adult miners signed a petition that this educational tax should be levied on themselves.

With regard to the length of the working day, the Unions have done good work. Before the seventeenth century, an average ten hour day was worked, taking summer and winter together, but this day was lengthened gradually, until the child-labor of our factories became the scandal of our civilisation. The factory legislation which commenced feebly in 1801, but became fairly efficient in 1833, and finally successful in 1847, was throughout

---

[1] See Alexander Macdonald's evidence before the Commission of 1867.

strongly supported by the workmen's organisations, aided well by Robert Owen, the great and noble Socialist, outside Parliament, and by Lord Ashley (Lord Shaftesbury) within it. By limiting the hours of labor for women and children, the Factory Acts indirectly limited the hours of the men whose labor was dependent on theirs. In trades in which men only are employed, the working day has been shortened by the clumsier and more painful process of strikes; thus the builders reduced their day to ten hours, but an attempt in 1859 to reduce it to nine was met with a lock-out. Printers work nine hours; many of the miners eight hours. But in some trades the reduction is a farce, and means only that hours over the fixed day-limit shall be paid for as overtime at higher rates.

The Unions are much divided on the question of enforcing by law an eight hour day. The figures of the late votings on the subject are challenged, it being believed that the antagonism of the older leaders has led to some misrepresentation of the returns. It has been remarked that a Trade Council voting against Parliamentary action was credited with the whole voting strength of the unions represented on it, while a Trade Council voting for it was only credited with the number of individuals composing the Council. It is probably near the truth to say that the younger members are, as a rule, in favor of using their political power to obtain labor reforms, while the older ones—with all their memories of legal oppressions, and the suspicion of State interference inwrought into their very natures by the bitter experiences of their long struggles to be delivered from it—cling to extra-Parliamentary modes of action.

In this division lies really the essential difference between the old Unionism and the new. The old is still dominated by the anachronistic idea that the State is set over against the People, whereas in the modern Democracy the People *are* the State. Parliament is no longer a class, making laws for a Nation; but it is the Nation in its legislative activity. The New Unionism will recognise this fact, and when it desires change it will use the ballot-box instead of the strike; it will vote instead of starving women and children.

This New Unionism has doubtless been influenced indirectly, but I think not at all directly, by the theories which have set the Continent throbbing with new life. The old Unionism looks askance at Internationalism, and prides itself on being British to the core. With the brief interlude of the "International", in which men like Lucraft and George Odgers took active part, British Trades Unionism has been hostile to, and suspicious of, "the foreigner". This anti-fraternal spirit is still strong in the Trades Unionism which has Mr. Broadhurst as its type, and which refused this year to even circulate the invitations to an International Labor Congress at Paris. But the new Unionism is being leavened by a strong Socialist party, which, international in its hopes and its ideals, is yet distinctively British enough to influence the younger generation of Unionists. Many of the most active Socialists are prominent members of Trades Unions, and are bringing into them the spirit which seeks to transform society, and not only to increase wage, to shorten the hours of work, and to improve the conditions of labor, while leaving it still in subjection to capital.

This new spirit is seen in the attitude lately assumed by Trades Unions towards women workers and unskilled laborers, the two unorganised mobs which have hung round the disciplined army of unionists, and have lost them many a fight. Comprising but a small minority of the working class, the Unions have ever been hampered by the crowding ranks of cheap, because unskilled, untrained, and unorganised labor, and they have tried to exclude as enemies those whom they should have welcomed as allies. Now Trades Unionism is spreading among women, and large and powerful unions are springing up among unskilled laborers; so that there is hope that at last all workers will be enrolled in disciplined hosts, and there will be no stragglers from the army of labor.

When each Trade Union comprises the majority of the workers in its Trade, and when these unions are united in a National Trade Federation, then will come the time for the International Federation, which will mean the triumph of labor and the freedom of the workers everywhere. But that International Federation can only come when the Socialist leaven, already working in the Trades Unions, shall have leavened the whole lump. And then, when labor is triumphant, and when its forces are spent for human service and not wasted in the struggle for existence and the struggle against oppression, then the workman, no longer exploited for another's profit, shall once more take joy in the work of his hands and pride in the beauty he creates. Then shall rise from the sepulchre wherein Commercialism has entombed her, the spirit of the old craftsman, to whom work was a pleasure and creation was a delight, to whom craft and art were one and indivisible, and who deemed that a man's true life was to inbreathe the natural and to outbreathe the art. But that resurrection waits for the dawning, and we are yet in the shadows of the night; content if, amid the shadows, we can trace the path towards the sunrising; joyous if, on the far-off horizon, we catch a glimmer that shall brighten into day.

SECTION II

THE

POLITICAL STATUS

OF

WOMEN.

BY

ANNIE BESANT.

[THIRD EDITION.]

LONDON:
FREETHOUGHT PUBLISHING COMPANY,
28, STONECUTTER STREET, E.C.

PRICE TWOPENCE.

LONDON:
PRINTED BY ANNIE BESANT AND CHARLES BRADLAUGH,
28, STONECUTTER STREET, E.C.

POLITICAL STATUS OF WOMEN.

Various arguments are advanced by the opponents of woman suffrage, which require to be met by those who maintain that the political status of women should be the same as the political status of men. Of these the principal—apart from party arguments, such as those which regard the momentary strengthening of Tory, Whig, or Radical, by the female vote—are as follows :—

Why should the political incompetency of women receive so much attention when more pressing wrongs require a remedy ?

Women are naturally unfit for the proper exercise of the franchise.

They are indifferent about the matter.

They are sufficiently represented as it is.

Political power would withdraw them from their proper sphere, and would be a source of domestic annoyance.

It can scarcely be necessary for me to clear my way by proving to you that there are such things as *rights*. "Every great truth," it has been said, "must travel through three stages of public opinion: men will say of it, first, that it is not true; secondly, that it is contrary to religion; lastly, that every one knew it already." The "rights of man" have battled through these first two stages, and have reached the third; they have been denounced as a lie, subversive of all government; they have been anathematised as a heresy, to be abhorred of all faithful Christians; but now every one has always known that men have rights, it is a perfect truism. These rights do not rest on the charter of a higher authority; they are not privileges held at the favour of a superior; they have their root in the nature of man; they are his by "divine"—that is to say, by *natural*—right. Kings, presidents, governments, draw their authority from the will of the people; the people draw their authority from themselves.

It is quite a new light to the general public that women have any rights at all; duties? ay, plenty of them, with sharp penalties for their non-fulfilment. Wrongs? ay, plenty of them, too—wrongs which will not be borne much longer. Privileges? yes, if we will take them as privileges, and own that we hold them at the will of our masters; but *rights?* The assertion was at first met with laughter that was only not indignant, because it was too contemptuous. Our truth is as yet in its infancy—first, it is not true; secondly, it is contrary to religion. The matter is taken a little more seriously now; men begin to fancy that these absurd women are really in earnest, and they condescend to use a little argument, and to administer a little "soothing-syrup" to these fractious children. Gentle remonstrance takes the place of laughter, and thus we arrive at my first head—surely there are more pressing female wrongs to attend to than the question of political incapacity.

It is perfectly true that the want of representation in Parliament is not, *in itself*, a grave injury. In itself, I say, it is of secondary importance; its gravity consists in what it involves. You do not value money for its own sake—those little yellow counters are not intrinsically beautiful, nor are they in themselves worth toil, and trouble, and danger; but you value them for what they represent; and thus we value a vote, as means to an end. In a free country, a vote means power. When a man is a voter, his wishes must be taken into consideration; he counts as one in an election—his opinion influences the return. When the working-classes wished to alter laws which pressed hardly on them, they agitated for Parliamentary reform. What folly! what waste of time! what throwing away of strength and energy! how unpractical! Why agitate for an extension of the franchise, when so many social burdens required to be lightened? Why? Because they knew that when they won the franchise they could trust to themselves to remedy these social anomalies—when they had votes, they could make these questions the test of the fitness or unfitness of a candidate for Parliament. Non-voters, they could only *ask* for reform; voters, they could *command* it. And this is the answer of women to those who urge on them that they should turn their attention to practical matters, and leave off this agitation about the franchise. We shall do nothing so foolish. True, certain laws press hardly on us; but we are not going now to agitate for the repeal of these laws one by one. We might agitate for a very long time before we gained attention. We prefer going to the root of the matter at once. We will win the right of representation in Parliament, and when we have won that, *these laws will be altered.* Ten years after women become voters, there will be some erasures in the Statute Book. There will no longer be a law that women, on marriage, become paupers, unless steps are taken beforehand to prevent it; marriage will have ceased to bring with it these disabilities. There will no longer be a law which gives to the father despotic authority over the fate of the child; which enables the father to take the child from the mother's arms, and give it into the charge of some other woman; which makes even the dead father able to withhold the child from the living mother. There will be no longer be a law which sanctions the consignment of thousands of women to misery and despair, in order that men's lives may be made more safely luxurious, and their homes, when they choose to make them, kept more pure. The laws whose action is more and more driving women (in the large towns especially) to prefer unlegalised marriages to the bonds of legal matrimony, will have vanished, to the purifying of society and the increased happiness of both men and women. The possession of a vote, by giving women a share in the power of the State, will also make them more respected. Hitherto, law, declaring women to be weak, has carefully put all advantages into the hands of those who are already the powerful. Instead of guarding and strengthening the feeble, it has bound them hand and foot, and laid them helpless at the feet of the strong. To him that hath, it has indeed been given; and from her that hath not, has been taken away even the protection she might have had.

"Women are naturally unfit for the proper exercise of the franchise." It has been remarked, more than once, that, in this contest about the voting of women, men and women have exchanged their characteristics. Women appeal to reason, men to instincts; women rely on logic, men on assumptions; women are swayed by facts, men by prejudices. To all our arguments, to all our reasoning, men answer, "It is unfeminine—it is contrary to nature." If we press them, How and why? we are only met with a re-assertion of the maxim. I am afraid that we women sadly lack the power of seeing differences. It is unfeminine to be a doctor, but feminine to be a nurse. It is unfeminine to mix drugs, but feminine to administer them. It is unfeminine to study political economy, but feminine to train the future Statesmen. It is unfeminine to study sanitary laws, but feminine to regulate the atmosphere of the nursery, whose wholesomeness depends on those laws. It is unfeminine to mingle with men at the polling-booth, but feminine to labour among them in the field and the factories. In a word, it is unfeminine to know how to do a thing, and to do it comprehendingly, wisely, and well; it is feminine to do things of whose laws and principles we know absolutely nothing, and to do them ignorantly, foolishly, and badly. We do not see things in this light. I suppose it is because we, as women, have "the poetical power of seeing resemblances," but lack the "philosophical power of seeing differences." We must, however, analyse this natural inferiority of women; it is shown, we are told, in their mental weakness, their susceptibility to influence, their unbusiness-like habits. If this natural mental inferiority of woman be a fact, one cannot but wonder how nature has managed to make so many mistakes. Mary Somerville, Mrs. Lewis (better known as George Eliot), Frances Power Cobbe, Harriet Martineau, were made, I suppose when nature was asleep. They certainly show no signs of the properly-constituted feminine intellect. But, allowing that these women *are* inferior in mental power to the uneducated artisan and petty farmer, may I ask why that should be a *political* disqualification? I never remember hearing it urged that the franchise should only be conferred on men of genius, or of great intellectual attainments. Even the idea of an educational franchise was sneered at, low as was the proposed standard of education. When a law is made which restricts the franchise to those who rise above a certain mental level, the talk about mental inferiority will become reasonable and pertinent; but, when that law is passed, I fear that nature will not be found to have been sufficiently careful of the male interest to have placed all men above the level, and all women below it. Susceptibility to influence is an argument that also goes too far. I am afraid that many people's opinions are but rarely "opinions" at all. They are simply their neighbours' thoughts covered over with a film of personal prejudice. It is, however, a new idea in England that a class liable to be unduly influenced should be disfranchised; the Ballot

Act lately passed was, I always understood, specially designed to protect the weak from the pressure of the strong. Oliver Cromwell said that it was unjust to deprive any one of a natural right on the plea that, were it given, it would be abused. Not so; "when he hath abused it, judge." Business incapacity may, or may not, exist on the part of women; it is difficult to judge what power a person may have when he is never permitted to exercise it. Tie up a man's hands, and then sneer that he has no aptitude for writing; or chain his feet, and show his natural incapacity for walking. John Stuart Mill has remarked: "The ladies of reigning families are the only women who are allowed the same range of interests and freedom of development as men, and it is precisely in their case that there is not found to be any inferiority. Exactly where and in proportion as woman's capacities for government have been tried, in that proportion have they been found adequate." In France, at the present day, the women rule business matters more than do the men, and the business capacity of French-women is a matter of notoriety. Lastly, I would urge on those who believe in women's *natural* inferiority, why, in the name of common sense, are you so terribly afraid of putting your theory to the proof? Open to women the learned professions; unlock the gates which bar her out from your mental strifes; give her no favour, no special advantages; let her race you on even terms. She *must* fail, if nature be against her; she *must* be beaten, if nature has incapacitated her for the struggle. Why do you fear to let her challenge you, if she is weighted not only with the transmitted effects of long centuries of inferiority, but is also bound with nature's iron chain? Try. If you are so sure about nature's verdict, do not fear her arbitration; but if you shrink from our rivalry, we *must* believe that you feel our equality, and, to cover your own doubts of your superiority, you prattle about our feebleness.

"Women are indifferent about the possession of the franchise." If this is altogether true, it is very odd that there should be so much agitation going on upon the subject. But I am quite willing to grant that the mass of women are indifferent about the matter. Alas! it has always been so. Those who stand up to champion an oppressed class do not look for gratitude from those for whom they labour. It is the bitterest curse of oppression that it crushes out in the breast of the oppressed the very wish to be free. A man once spent long years in the Bastille; shut up in his youth, old age found him still in his dungeon. The people assailed the prison, and, among others, this prisoner was set free; but the sunshine was agony to the eyes long accustomed to the darkness, and the fresh stir of life was as thunder to the ears accustomed to the silence of the dungeon; the prisoner pleaded to be kept a prisoner still. Was his action a proof that freedom is not fair? The slaves, after generations of bondage, were willing to remain slaves where their masters were kind and good. Is this a proof that liberty is not the birthright of a man? And this rule holds good in all, and not only in the extreme, cases I have cited. Habit, custom, make hard things easy. If a woman is educated to regard man as her natural lord, she will do so. If the man to whom her lot falls is kind to her, she will be contented; if he is unkind, she will be unhappy; but, unless she be an exceptional character, she will not think of resistance. But women *are* now beginning to think of resistance; a deep, low, murmuring is going on, suppressed as yet, but daily growing in intensity; and such a murmur has always been the herald of revolt. Further, do men think of what they are doing when they taunt the present agitators with the indifference shown by women? They are, in effect, telling us that, if we are in earnest in this matter, we must *force* it on their attention; we must agitate till every home in England rings with the subject; we must agitate till mass meetings in every town compel them to hear us; we must agitate till every woman has our arguments at her fingers' ends. Ah! you are not wise to throw in our teeth the indifference of women. You are stinging us into a determination that this indifference shall not last; you are nerving us to a struggle which will be fiercer than you dream; you are forcing us into an agitation which will convulse the State. You dare to make indifference a plea for injustice? Very well; then the indifference shall soon be a thing of the past. You have as yet the frivolous, the childish, the thoughtless, on your side; but the cream of womanhood is against you. We will educate women to reason and to think, and then the mass will only want a leader.

"Women are sufficiently represented as it is." By whom? *by those whose interests lie in keeping them in subjection.* So the masters told the workmen: "*We* represent you; *we* take care of your interests." The workmen answered: "We prefer to represent ourselves: we like to have our interests guarded by our own hands." And such is our answer to our "representatives." We don't agree with some of your views; we don't like some of your laws; we object to some of your theories for us. You do not really represent *us* at all; what you represent is your own interests, which, in many cases, touch ours. The laws you pass are passed in the interests of men, and not of women; and naturally so, for you are made legislators by men, and not by women. There are few cases where men are really the representatives of women. John Stuart Mill—now dead, alas!—noblest and most candid of philosophers and Statesmen; Professor Fawcett, a future leader; Jacob Bright, our steadfast friend: these, and a few others, might fairly be called representatives of women in Parliament. Outside the House, too, we have a few gallant champions, pre-eminent among whom is Moncure Conway, whose voice is always raised on the side of freedom and justice. But what we demand is the right to choose our own representatives, so that our voice may have its share in making the laws which we are bound to obey. We share the duty of supporting the State, and we claim the right of helping to guide it. Taxation and representation run side by side, and if you will not allow us to be represented, you have no right to tax us. I may suggest here, in reference to the contest about married women having votes, that this point is altogether foreign to the discussion. The *right* to a vote and the *qualification for* a vote, are two distinct things, and come under different laws. The one is settled by Act of Parliament, the other by the revising barrister. A blunder was lately made by putting into a Bill a special disqualification of married women. Such a clause is absurdly out of place. We are contending to remove from a whole sex a legal disability; the details come later, and must be arranged when the principle is secured. A man has the right to vote because he is a man; but he must possess certain qualifications before he can exercise his right. Let womanhood, as such, cease to be a disqualification; that is the main point. Let the discussion on qualifications follow. Further, if it be urged that women are represented by their husbands, what are we to say about those who have none? In 1861, fifteen years ago, there were three and a half millions of women in England working for their livelihood—two and a half millions of these were unmarried, and were, therefore, unrepresented. Is there no pathos in these figures? Two and a half millions struggling honestly to live, but mute to tell of their wants or their wrongs. Mute, I say, for not one in a thousand has the power of the pen. And this is not the worst. Oh, friends! below these, pressed down there by the terrible struggle for existence, there is a lower depth yet, tenanted by thousands of whom it is not here my province to speak, thousands, from whom a bitter wail goes up, to which men's ears are deaf. Surely, women need representation—surely, there are grievances and wrongs of women which can only be done away by those whom women send to Parliament as their representatives. It is natural that men should not desire that many of these laws should be altered. In the first place, it is impossible they should understand how hardly they press on women; only those who wear it, says the proverb, "know where the shoe pinches." And, in the second place, the holders of a monopoly generally object to have their monopoly interfered with. They can't imagine what in the world these outsiders want pressing in upon their social domains. The nobleman cannot understand why the peasant should object to the Game Laws; it *is* so unreasonable of him. The farmer cannot make out why the labourer should not attend quietly to his hedging and ditching, instead of making all this fuss about a union. The capitalist cannot see the sense of the artisan banding himself with his brethren, instead of going on with his duty, and working hard. Men can't conceive why women do not attend to their household duties instead of fussing about Parliament. Unfortunately, each of these tiresome classes cares very little whether those to whom they are opposed can or cannot understand *why* they agitate. We may be told continually that we are sufficiently represented; we say that we do *not* think so, but that we mean to be.

"Political power would withdraw women from their proper sphere, and would be a source of domestic annoyance." Their proper sphere—*i.e.*, the home. This allegation is a very odd one. Men are lawyers, doctors, merchants; every hour of the day is pledged, engrossing speculations stretch the brain, deep questions absorb the mind, great ideas swell in the intellect. Yet men vote. If occupation be a fatal disqualification, let us pass a law that only idle people shall have votes. You will withdraw workers from their various spheres of work, if you allow them to take an interest in politics. For heaven's sake, do not go and take the merchant from the desk, the doctor from the hospital, the lawyer from the court; you will disorganise society—you will withdraw the workers. Do you say it is not so—that the delivery of a vote takes up a very short time at considerable intervals? that a man must have some leisure, and may very well expend it, if he please, in studying politics? that a change of thought is very good for the weary brain? that the alteration of employment is a positive and most valuable relaxation? You are quite right; outside interests are healthy, and prevent private affairs from becoming morbidly engrossing. The study of large problems checks the natural tendency to be absorbed in narrower questions. A man is stronger, healthier, nobler, when, in working hard in trade or in profession for his home, he does not forget he is a citizen of a mighty nation. I can think of few things more likely to do women real good than anything which would urge them to extend their interests beyond the narrow circle of their homes. Why, men complain that women are bigoted, narrow-minded, prejudiced, impracticable. Wider interests would do much to remedy these defects. If you want your wife to be your toy, or your drudge, you do perhaps wisely in shutting up her ideas within the four walls of your house; but if you want one who will stand at your side through life, in evil report as well as in good, a strong, large-hearted woman, fit to be your comfort in trouble, your counsellor in difficulty, your support in danger, worthy to be the mother of your children, the wise guardian and trainer of your sons and your daughters, then seek to widen women's intellects, and to enlarge their hearts, by sharing with them your grander plans of life, your deeper thoughts, your keener hopes. Do not keep your brains and intellects for the strife of politics and the conflicts for success, and give to your homes and to your wives nothing but your condescending carelessness and your thoughtless love. Further, do you look on women as your natural enemies, and suppose they are on the look out for every chance of running away from their homes and their children? It says very little for you if you hope only to keep women's hearts by chaining their minds, or limiting their range of action. What is it really worth, this compelled submission—this enforced devotion? Do you acknowledge that you make home-life so dull, so wearisome, that you dare not throw open the cage-door, lest the captive should escape? Do you confess that your service is so hard a one that she you call your friend is only longing to be free? You do yourselves an injustice, friends; you shame your own characters—you discredit your homes. A happy home, the centre of hopes and fears, the cherished resting-place from life's troubles, the sure haven from life's conflicts, the paradise brightened by children's prattle and children's laughter—this home is not a place where women must be chained down lest they should run away. Admitting, however, for argument's sake, the absurd idea that women would neglect their homes if they possessed the franchise, may I ask by what right men restrict women's action to the home? I can understand that, in Eastern lands, where the husband rules his wives with despotic authority, and woman is but the plaything and the slave of man, woman's sphere *is* the home, for the very simple reason that she cannot get outside it. So, in this sense, in the Zoological Gardens, is the den the sphere of the lion, and the cage of the eagle. Shut any living creature up, and its prison becomes its sphere. But if the prisoner becomes restless—if nature beats strongly at the captive's heart—if he yearns for the free air and the golden sunshine, you may, indeed, keep him in the sphere you have built for him; but he will break his heart, and will die in your hands. Many women now, educated more highly than they used to be—women with strong brains and loving hearts—are being driven into bitterness and into angry opposition, because their ambition is thwarted at every step, and their eager longings for a fuller life are forced back and crushed. A tree *will* grow, however you may try to stunt it. You may disfigure it, you may force it into awkward shapes, but grow it will. One would fain hope that it is in thoughtlessness and in ignorance that men try to push women back. Surely they do not appreciate the injury they are doing, both to themselves and to women, if they turn their homes into prison-houses, and the little children into incumbrances. In the strong, true, woman there is a tender motherhood which weaker natures cannot reach; but if these women are to be told that domestic cares only are to fill their brains, and the prattle of children to be the only satisfaction of their intellect, you run a terrible risk of making them break free from home and child. Allow them to grow freely, to develop as nature bids them, and they will find room for home-cares in their minds, and the warmest nestling-place in their bosom will be the haven of the little child. But if you check, and fret, and carp at them, you will not succeed in keeping them back, but you will succeed in souring them, and in making them hard and bitter. Oh, for the sake of English home life—for the sake of the tender ties of motherhood—for the sake of the common happiness, do not turn into bitter opponents the women who are still anxious to be your friends and your fellow-workers. This is no imaginary danger; it is a thunder-cloud brooding over many English homes. I can scarcely believe that men and women would be so unreasonable as to make the power of voting into a domestic annoyance. Of course, if a married couple want to quarrel, there are sure to be plenty of differences of opinion between them which will give them the proper opportunity. But why should *political* disagreement be specially fatal to domestic peace? Theology is now a fruitful source of disagreement. If the husband is the free-thinker, he does not suffer, because he does not allow his wife to worry him too far; but if the free-thinking is on the side of the wife, matters are apt to become uncomfortable. There is only one way to remedy this difficulty. Let the husband feel, as the wife now does, that between two grown-up people control of one by the other is an absurdity. Bitterness arises now from disagreement, because the wife who forms her opinion for herself is regarded as a rebel to lawful authority. Remove the authority, which is a tyranny, and people will readily "agree to differ." There will possibly be a little more care before marriage about the opinions of the lady wooed than there is now, when the man fancies that he can mould the docile girl into what shape he pleases, and the future happiness of both is marred if the woman happens to be made of bright steel, instead of plastic clay. In any case, Parliament is scarcely bound to treat one half of England with injustice, lest the other half should find its authority curtailed.

One by one I have faced the only arguments against the extension of the franchise to women with which I am acquainted. You yourselves must judge how far these arguments are valid, and on which side right and justice rest. I would add that I feel sure that, when the matter is fairly placed before them, most men will sympathise with, and assist our cause. Some noble and brave men have come forward to join our ranks already, and speak boldly for woman's cause, and work faithfully for its triumph. The mass of men only need to study our claims in order to accept them. They have been reared to regard themselves as our natural superiors; small blame to them that they take the upper seats. Kind and gentle as many of them are, working hard for wife and children, thinking much of women and loving them well, it cannot be expected that they should readily understand that their relations to the weaker sex are founded on an injustice. But if they want to see how false is their idea of peace, and how misled they are when they think women's position satisfactory, let them go out and see what the laws are where the power they give is wielded by brutality and tyranny. Let them try to imagine what women suffer who are too weak and timid to resist the strength under whose remorseless exercise they writhe in vain; let them try to appreciate the sharper agony of those whose bolder hearts and stronger natures defy their tyrants, and break, at whatever cost, their chains. Laws must be tested by their working; these laws which make the woman the helpless servant of man are not enforced in happy homes; but they exist, and elsewhere they are used.

Injustice is never good; it is never even safe. There is a higher life before us, a nobler ideal of marriage union, a fairer development of individual natures, a surer hope of wider happiness. Liberty for every human being, equality before the law for all in public and in private, fraternity of men and women in peaceful friendship, these are the promise of the dawning day. Co-workers in every noble labour, co-partners in every righteous project, co-soldiers in every just cause, men and women in the time to come shall labour, think, and struggle side by side. The man shall bring his greater strength and more sustained determination, the woman her quicker judgment and purer heart, till man shall grow tenderer, and woman stronger, man more pure, and woman more brave and free. Till at last, generations hence, the race shall develop into a strength and a beauty at present unimagined, and men and women shall walk this fair earth hand-in-hand, diverse, yet truly one, set each to each—

"As perfect music unto noble words."

THE LEGALISATION

OF

FEMALE SLAVERY IN ENGLAND.

By ANNIE BESANT.

[Reprinted from the *National Reformer*, June 4, 1876.]

THE first annual meeting of the "British, Continental, and General Federation for the Abolition of Government Regulation of Prostitution" was lately held at the Westminster Palace Hotel, and was largely attended by friends of the movement from all parts of England, from France, and from Switzerland. M. Loyson, better known as Father Hyacinthe, was to have been present, but a severe attack of bronchitis chained him to his room; M. de Pressensé, another well-known French speaker, was, however, there to take his place, together with M. Aimé Humbert, a gentleman whose talent appears to lie in organisation and in work more than in speech. The long-sustained labor of the Society for the Repeal of the Contagious Diseases Acts is well-known to our readers; many of them may not, however, be aware of the late extension of the sphere of their work, consequent on the thought and toil of their noble-hearted missionary, Mrs. Josephine E. Butler. The narrative of her crusade through Europe in the bitter cold, through France, into Italy, into Switzerland, over the Jura in the depth of winter, now lies before us, and is the record of a heroism equalled by few women, or by few men either. (The title of the book is "The New Abolitionists", price half-a-crown, and it well deserves careful perusal.) Undaunted by failure, unwearied by defeat, loyal in spite of taunts, brave in spite of threats, gallant-hearted in face of a misery and an evil which might well drive the boldest to despair, Mrs. Butler sets us all an example by which we should strive to profit. Societies have been formed in all directions in France, Switzerland, and Italy, and these are now federated together into one body, sworn to destroy the recognition and encouragement of prostitution by the State.

Reaction from Christian cant upon this subject, and the rightful recognition of the sacredness and dignity of human nature, physical as well as mental, have to a great extent prejudiced many of the Secular party against the society agitating for repeal; the unwise and indelicate proceeding of scattering wholesale—so that they fell into the hands of the youth of both sexes—a number of tracts and leaflets dealing with medical details and with terrible crimes, the perusal of which by young girls and boys is about as wholesome as the reading of the *Police News*, roused a feeling of bitter indignation against those whose names appeared as leaders of the repeal movement, although they were very likely utterly ignorant of the follies perpetrated by unwise coadjutors. This phase fortunately seems to have disappeared; and it is hardly necessary to say that there is nothing in the speeches made at the meetings of the society to which the most prudish could object, unless, indeed, they object to the question being dealt with at all. Should this position be taken, surely it is then well to remind such that the discussions to which they object only become necessary through the existence of the evil attacked, and that the lack of modesty lies in the commission of the evil, and not in the endeavor to rescue the victims of it. When men of the world angrily object to women touching such a subject, they should remember that if they really respected the modesty and purity of women no such subject would be in existence, and that to those who gain nothing by the perpetuation of prostitution their loud indignation looks very much like the angry dread of a slave-owner who fears that the abolitionist preacher may possibly, sooner or later, deprive him of the services of his human property. I assert that the Secular party, as a whole, has a duty with regard to this subject, which it somewhat fails to discharge; a duty towards the promotion of national morality, of national health; and a duty also of asserting the sacredness of the individual liberty of women as well as of men, the inalienable rights of each over his or her own person.

It is perfectly true that marriage is different as regarded from the Secularist and from the Christian point of view. The Secularist reverences marriage, but he regards marriage as something far higher than a union "blessed" by a minister; he considers, also, that marriage should be terminable, like any other contract, when it fails in its object, and becomes injurious instead of beneficial; he does not despise human passion, or pretend that he has no body; on the contrary, reverencing nature, he regards physical union as perfecting the union of heart and mind, and sees in the complete unity of marriage the possibility of a far higher and nobler humanity than either man or woman can attain in a state of celibacy. But, surely, in proportion to our admiration for this true marriage, and our reverence for the home which it builds up, and which forms the healthy and pure nursery for the next generation of citizens, must be our pain and our regret when we come face to face with prosti-

ution. By prostitution I mean simply and solely physical union
old by one sex and bought by the other, with no love, no respect,
o reverence on either side. Of this, physical degradation and mental
legradation are the invariable accompaniments: just as intoxication
nay be sometimes indulged in without leaving perceptible and per-
nanent bad effects, but, persisted in, destroys body and brain, so
nay sexual irregularity be practised for a time with little apparent
njury, but, persisted in, destroys as fatally as intoxication. This is
o matter of theory, it is simply a matter of observation ; individuals
vhose lives are irregular, nations where prostitution is widespread,
ose stamina, virility, physical development, the whole type becoming
legraded. It is urged that "man's physical wants must be satisfied,
nd therefore prostitution is a necessity". Why *therefore*? It might
s well be argued, man's hunger must be appeased, and therefore
heft of food is a necessity. The two things have no necessary con-
exion with each other. Does prostitution promote the national
ealth? If so, why this necessity for legislation to check the spread
f contagious diseases? Those diseases spring from sexual irregu-
arities, and are an outraged Nature's protest against the assertion
hat prostitution is the right method of providing for the sexual
ecessities of man. As surely as typhoid results from filth and
eglect, so does the scourge of syphilis follow in the wake of prosti-
ution. These unfortunate women who are offered up as victims of
nan's pleasure, these poor white slaves sold for man's use, these
ecome their own avengers, repaying the degradation inflicted on
hem, and spreading ruin and disease among those for whose wants
hey exist as a class. Mrs. Butler truly writes: "You can under-
tand how the men who have riveted the slavery of women for such
legrading ends become, in a generation or two, themselves the greater
laves; not only the slaves of their own enfeebled and corrupted
atures, but of the women whom they have maddened, hardened, and
tamped under foot. Bowing down before the unrestrained dictates
f their own lusts, they now bow down also before the tortured and
iendish womanhood *which they have created*. . . . They plot and
lan in vain for their own physical safety. Possessed at times with
sort of stampede of terror, they rush to International Congresses,
nd forge together more chains for the dreaded wild beast they have
o carefully trained, and in their pitiful panic build up fresh barri-
ades between themselves and that womanhood which they proclaim
o be a 'permanent source of sanitary danger'." Mrs. Butler was
vriting from Paris, where the system is carried out which we have in
England in only a few towns. If any one doubts the reality of this
atural retribution, let him go and watch the streets where many of
hese poor ruined creatures may be found, and there see what women
re when transformed into prostitutes—a source of disease instead of
ealth, of vice instead of purity. Each one might have been the
entre of a happy home, the mother of brave men and women who
vould have served the Fatherland, and we have made them *this*.

National morality and national health go hand-in-hand; a vicious
ation will be a weak nation, and when a government begins to deli-

berately license women for the purposes of prostitution, it has taken the first step towards the ruin of the nation it administers. Louis Napoleon made Paris a sink of impurity; when the struggle came, the working-classes only—whose circumstances preserved them from gross excesses—were fit to fight for France. When the license system has had a fair trial, and the danger spreads and spreads, the government finds itself burdened with a class of women it has formed and certificated; and despairing of repressing disease by simple licensing, it begins to gather the women into houses, licensed also by itself; abroad, in England's colonies, these houses are licensed by England's rulers, and in France, in Italy, and elsewhere, they are found in most cities. Thus government becomes saddled with the supervision of a vast and organised system of prostitution, and struggles vainly against the evils resulting from it. In Italy, the government draws money from this source, and the shame of Italy's daughters and the profligacy of her sons are made a source of national revenue. And what is the result? simply that these houses become *foci* of vice, demoralising the youth of the country. "Pastor Borel testified to having seen schoolboys entering these haunts of patented vice, with their satchels on their backs." Well might we ask, with the old Roman Consul, Postumius: "Can ye think that such youths are fit to be made soldiers? That wretches brought out of the temple of obscenity could be trusted with arms? That those contaminated with such debaucheries could be the champions for the chastity of the wives and children of the Roman people?" Profligates can never be made into sturdy citizens; muscles enervated by the embraces of purchased women will never be strung to heroism; a vicious nation will never be a nation of freemen. Then, in the name of the liberty we have won, of the glory of England, in the hope of the coming Republic, we are surely bound to protest against the introduction of a system among us that has degraded every nation in which it has been tried, which has only got, as yet, one foot upon our shores, and which, if we were true to our duty, we might easily drive from our English soil before it has time to sap the strength of our men and to destroy the honor of our name.

It still remains to see how this legislation is consonant with individual liberty; how it is touched by the question of a standing army; and how the evil of prostitution may be met and overcome.

I have already urged that no repressive Acts will destroy disease in a community where prostitution is encouraged, and that the wide prevalence of prostitution is ruinous to the physique of a nation; the admitted failure of regulation abroad, and the more and more complete control demanded for the police over the unfortunate women sacrificed to the "necessities of men", prove, beyond the possibility of denial, that no eradication of disease is to be hoped for unless the registered women be given over thoroughly to continual supervision, and be literally made slaves, equally obedient to the call of the doctor who heals and to that of the man who infects, holding their bodies at the hourly order of each class, with no right of self-possession, no power of self-rule permitted to them. I challenge this claim, made in the name of the State, over one class of its citizens, and I assert that the sacred right of individual liberty is grossly and shamefully outraged by this interference of government, and that, therefore, every soldier of liberty is bound to rise in protest against the insult offered to her. No more inalienable right exists than the right of the individual to the custody of his own person; in a free country none can be deprived of this right save by a sentence given in open court, after a jury of his peers has found him guilty of a crime which, by the laws under which he lives, is punished by restriction of that liberty; so jealously is this right guarded, however, even in the criminal whose full exercise of it is temporarily suspended, that the limits within which it may be touched are carefully drawn; even in the prison-cell the felon has not lost all right over himself, and his personal liberty is only restricted on the points where the law has suspended it. No official may dare to compel a criminal to labor, for instance, unless compulsion to labor is part of the judicial sentence. Firm and strong lies the foundation stone of liberty. *No citizen's personal liberty may be interfered with, unless proof of guilt justifying that interference be tendered in open court, and every citizen has a right to demand that open trial if he be arrested by any officer of the law.* This is the foundation stone which is rudely upset by the Contagious Diseases Acts. Under them women are arrested, condemned, and sentenced to a terrible punishment, without any open accusation or public trial; by simple brute force they are compelled to submit, despite their pleading, their cries, their struggles; they have no redress, no assistance; they are degraded both in their own sight and in the sight of all who deal with them; a free woman is deprived by force of the custody of her own body, and all human right is outraged in her person—and for what? in order that men may more safely degrade her in the future, and may use her for their own amusement with less danger to themselves. A number of citizens are deprived of their natural rights in order that other citizens may profit by their loss; and the State, the incarnation of justice, the protector of the rights of all, dares thus to sacrifice the rights of some of its members to the pleasure of others. It is idle to urge that these women are too degraded to have any rights; the argument is too dangerous for men to use; for if the women are too degraded, the men who make and keep them what they are are partners of their degradation; if the women are brutalised, only brutalised men can take pleasure in their society; every harsh word cast at these poor victims recoils with trebled force on the head of those who not only seek their companionship, but actually pay for the privilege of consorting with them.

But not only is liberty outraged by this intrusion on individual self-possession, but it is still further trampled under foot by the injustice perpetrated. Two citizens commit a certain act; the law punishes one by seizure, imprisonment, disgrace; it leaves the other perfectly free. No registration of women would be necessary if the other sex left women to themselves; no disease could be spread except by the co-operation of men. By what sort of justice, then, does the law seize one only of two participators in a given action? If it be pleaded that individual liberty may be overborne by social necessities—an argument which does not really admit of being used in this matter—then the "good of society" demands the arrest, imprisonment, and examination of both parties; it can serve no useful purpose to allow unhealthy men to propagate disease among healthy women. If men have the right to demand the protection of the law, why should women be deprived of that same protection? If so necessary for the safety of men, why not necessary for the safety of women? Is it not, really, far more needed among the men, for, if a married man should contract disease, he may infect his innocent wife and his unborn children? Surely the State should interfere for the protection of these; and any man found in a house of ill-fame, or consorting with a prostitute, should be at once arrested, be compelled to prove that he is not married, and has no intention of being so; and, failing such proof, should be examined, and kept in hospital, if need be, until perfectly cured. The Acts would be very rapidly repealed in St. Stephen's if all their provisions were carried out justly, on both sexes alike. "Men would not submit to it." Of course they would not, if one gleam of manhood remained in them; and neither would women, with any sense of womanhood, submit to it, if they were not bound hand and foot by the triple cord of ignorance, weakness, and starvation. Poor, pitiful sufferers, trampled on by all, till the sweet flower of womanhood is crushed out for evermore, and only some faint breath of its natural fragrance now and then arises to show how sweet it might have been if left to grow unbruised. In the name, then, of Liberty outraged, in the name of Equality disregarded, we claim the repeal of these one-sided Acts, even if the bond of Fraternity prove too weak to hold men back from this cruelty inflicted on their sisters.

But, it is urged, with a celibate standing army, prostitution is a physical necessity. Then, if an institution lead to disease, deterioration of physique, and moral and mental injury, destroy the institution which breeds these miseries, instead of trying to kill its offspring one by one. A large standing army is unnecessary; the enforcement of celibacy is a crime. Of course, if a number of young and healthy men are taken away from home, kept in idleness, and deprived of all female society, immorality must necessarily result from such an unnatural state of things. The enforcement of celibacy on vigorous men always results in libertinage, whether among celibate priests or celibate soldiers. But the natural desires of these men are not rightfully met by the State supplying them with a number of licensed women; to do that is to treat them simply like brutes, and thereby to degrade them; it is to teach them that there is nothing holy in love, nothing sacred in womanhood; it is to change the sacrament of humanity into an orgie, and to pollute the consecration of the future home with the remembrance of a parody of love. With a celibate standing army prostitution *is* a necessity, and I know of no reason why we should look at facts as we should like them to be, instead of facts as they are; but a celibate standing army is *not* a necessity. The true safeguard of a free nation is not a large standing army; rather is it a well-organised militia, regularly drilled and trained, whose home-ties and home-interests will, in case of honorable war, nerve each arm with double strength, and string each muscle with the remembrance of the home that is threatened by the foe. The hero-armies of history are not the armies which idle in peace, and have nought in common with the citizens; such armies are the pet toys of aristocratic generals, and are easily turned against the people by tyrants and by ambitious soldiers; but the hero-armies are the armies of citizens, less dainty in dress, less exact in marching, less finished in evolutions, but men who fight for home and wife, who draw sword in a just quarrel, but to please no prince's whim; men like Cromwell's Ironsides, and like Hampden's yeomen; men who are terrible in war because lovers of peace; men who can never be defeated while living; men who know how to die, but not how to yield.

What remedy is there for prostitution other than that attendant upon a celibate standing army? So far as the women are concerned, the real remedy for prostitution is to give women opportunities of gaining fairly paid employment. By far the greater number of prostitutes are such *for a living*. Men are immoral for their amusement; women are immoral for bread. Ladies in the upper classes have no conception of the stress of agony that drives many a forlorn girl "on the streets". If some of them would try what life is like when it consists of making shirts at three halfpence each (cotton not provided), and starving on the money earned, they would perhaps learn to speak more gently of "those horrid women". Lack of bread makes many a girl sell herself, and, once fallen, she is doomed. On the one side are self-respect, incessant toil, starvation; on the other side prostitution, amusement, plenty. We may reverence the heroic virtue that resists, but we can scarcely dare to speak harshly of the frailty that submits. Remunerative employment would half empty the streets; pay women, for the same work, the same wage that men receive; let sex be no disqualification; let women be trained to labor, and educated for self-support;. then the greatest of all remedies will be applied to the cure of prostitution, and women will cease to sell their bodies when they are able to sell their labor.

The second great remedy, as regards the women, is that society should make recovery more possible to them. Many a young and loving girl is betrayed through her love and her trust; having "fallen" she is looked down upon by all; deserted, she is aided by none; everybody pushes her away, and she is driven on the streets, and in despair, reckless, hopeless, she becomes what all around call her, and drearily sinks to the level assigned her by the world. Meanwhile her seducer passes unrebuked, and in the families where she would not be admitted as scullery-maid he is welcomed as fit husband for the daughter of the house. That which has ruined her and many others is only being "a little wild" in the circles where he moves. A public opinion which should be just is sorely needed. The act so venial in the man cannot be a crime in the woman, and if, as it is said, men *must* be immoral, then those who are necessary to them ought not to be looked down upon for their usefulness. We ask for justice equal to both sexes; punishment for both, if their intercourse be a crime against society;

immunity for both, if it be a necessary weakness. We hold up one standard of purity for both, and urge the nobility of sexual morality on man and woman alike.

More reasonable marriage laws would also tend to lessen prostitution. Much secret immorality is caused by making the marriage tie so unfairly stringent as it is to-day; people who are physically and mentally antagonistic to each other are bound together for life, instead of being able to gain a divorce without dishonor, and to be set free, to find in a more congenial union the happiness they have failed to find with each other. Reasonable facility of divorce would tend to morality, and would strengthen the bond of union between those who really loved, who would then feel that their true unity lay in themselves more than in the marriage ceremony, and was a willing, ever renewed mutual dedication instead of a hard compulsion.

But at the root of all reform lies the inculcation of a higher morality than at present prevails. We need to learn a deeper reverence for nature, and therefore a sharper repugnance for all disregard of physical and moral law. Young men need to learn reverence for themselves and for the physical powers they possess, powers which tend to happiness when rightly exercised, to misery and degradation when abused. They need also to learn reverence for the humanity in those around them, and the duty of guarding in every woman everything which they honor in mother, wife, and daughter. If a man realised that in buying a prostitute he was buying the womanhood of those he loved at home, he would shrink back from such sacrilege as from the touch of a leper. Woman should be man's inspiration, not his degradation; woman's love should be his prize for noble effort, not his purchased toy; the touch of a woman's lips should breathe of love and not of money, and the clasp of the wife should tell of passionate devotion and supremest loyalty, and never be mingled in thought with the memory of arms which were bought by a bribe, of caress that was paid for in gold.

ONE PENNY.

Printed by ANNIE BESANT and CHARLES BRADLAUGH, 63, Fleet Street, London, E.C.—1885.

THE

LAW OF POPULATION:

ITS CONSEQUENCES,

AND

Its Bearing upon Human Conduct and Morals.

BY

ANNIE BESANT

[ONE HUNDRED AND SEVENTY-FIFTH THOUSAND.]

LONDON:
FREETHOUGHT PUBLISHING COMPANY.
SOLD BY R. FORDER, 28 STONECUTTER STREET, E.C.,
AND W. H. REYNOLDS, CAMPLIN HOUSE,
HATCHAM PARK, S.E.
1891.

PRICE SIXPENCE

LONDON:
PRINTED BY A. BONNER,
34 BOUVERIE ST., FLEET ST., E.C.
Jan., 1891.

PREFACE TO THE 155TH THOUSAND.

THIS little tract has enjoyed so wide a circulation that a prefatory word would not be needed, were it not for the changed position of the population question in the public mind, from that it occupied in 1877. The doctrines which were so bitterly attacked but a few short years ago are now preached from many different quarters; clergy of the Church of England, out of their personal parish experiences, come forward and declare that limitation of the family should be plainly taught; last year some important conferences were held on the subject, and many of those attending them clearly and emphatically proclaimed the necessity for such teaching as is contained in this pamphlet. Mr. Lant Carpenter has actually lectured on the subject, and has stated that limitation of the family is right and necessary. In Australia, where a prosecution was initiated against this tract as obscene, Mr. W. W. Collins bravely assumed the responsibility of publishing it, was condemned by an ignorant magistrate, carried the case to the superior court, and was rewarded by the quashing of the conviction, Mr. Justice Windeyer declaring that "like all attempted persecutions of thinkers" that one would fail in its object, and that "truth, like a torch, 'the more it's shook it shines'". In England, we are never likely to have another prosecution, and the responsibility of parentage, the duty of safe-guarding every life called into being by a voluntary action, is being recognised more and more as an essential part of morality.

In Chapter IV.—"Objections considered"—I have, in this edition, dealt with the objections raised by some of my Socialist comrades to the teaching contained in this tract. Myself a Socialist, I am none the less a neo-Malthusian, and as the objections raised by my Socialist fellow-workers are more likely to have weight with those I specially desire to reach than objections put forward from any other quarter, I have thought it right to deal with them.

ANNIE BESANT.

LONDON, *Jan.*, 1890.

THE LAW OF POPULATION.

CHAPTER I.

THE LAW OF POPULATION.

THE law of population first laid down in this country by the Rev. T. R. Malthus in his great work entitled "The Principle of Population", has long been known to every student, and accepted by every thinker. It is, however, but very recently that this question has become ventilated among the many, instead of being discussed only by the few. Acknowledged as an axiom by the naturalist and by the political economist, the law of population has never been appreciated by the mass of the people. The free press pioneers of the last generation, Richard Carlile, James Watson, Robert Dale Owen—these men had seen its importance and had endeavored, by cheap publications dealing with it from its practical side, to arouse attention and to instruct those for whom they worked. But the lesson fell on stony ground and passed almost unheeded; it would, perhaps, be fairer to say that the fierce political conflicts of the time threw all other questions into a comparative shade; nor must the strong prejudice against Malthus be forgotten—the prejudice which regarded him as a hard, cold theorist, who wrote in the interest of the richer classes, and would deny to the poor man the comfort of wife and home. The books issued at this period—such as Carlile's "Every Woman's Book", Knowlton's "Fruits of Philosophy", R. D. Owen's "Moral Physiology"—passed unchallenged by authority, but obtained only a limited circulation; here and there they did their work, and the result was seen in the greater comfort and respectability of the families who took advantage of their teachings: but the great mass of the people went on in their ignorance and their ever-increasing poverty, conscious that mouths multiply more rapidly than wages, but dimly supposing that Providence was the responsible agent, and that where "God sends mouths" he ought to "send meat". One or two recognised advocates of the people did not forget the social side of the work which they had inherited; men like Austin Holyoake and Charles Bradlaugh, carrying on the struggle of Carlile and Watson, were not careless of this vital portion of it, and Mr. Holyoake's "Large and Small Families", and Mr. Bradlaugh's declaration that the *National Reformer* was to be "Malthusian" in its political economy, proved that these two, at least, were sound on this scarcely regarded branch of social science.

Now, all has changed; over-population has become one of the "burning questions" of the day, and a low-priced work on the subject has become a necessity. Our paternal authorities, like their predecessors, entertain a horror of cheap knowledge, but they will have to assent to the circulation of cheap information on social science, as those who went before them were compelled to tacitly assent to cheap information touching kings and priests.

The law of population, tersely stated, is—"there is a tendency in all animated existence to increase faster than the means of subsistence". Nature produces more life than she can support, and the superabundant life is kept down by the want of food. Malthus put the law as "the constant tendency in all animated life to increase beyond the nourishment prepared for it". "It is observed by Dr. Franklin," he writes, "that there is no bound to the prolific nature of plants or animals but what is made by their crowding and interfering with each other's means of subsistence. . . . . Throughout the animal and vegetable kingdoms, nature has scattered the seeds of life abroad with the most profuse and liberal hand; but has been comparatively sparing in the room and the nourishment necessary to rear them." "Population," Malthus teaches, "when unchecked, goes on doubling itself every twenty-five years"; "in the northern States of America, where the means of subsistence have been more ample, the manners of the people more pure, and the checks to early marriages fewer than in any of the modern States of Europe, the population has been found to double itself, for above a century-and-a-half successively, in less than twenty-five years. . . . . In the back settlements, where the sole employment is agriculture, and vicious customs and unwholesome occupations are little known, the population has been found to double itself in fifteen years. Even this extraordinary rate of increase is probably short of the utmost power of population."

The "power of increase" of the human species, according to John Stuart Mill, "is indefinite, and the actual multiplication would be extraordinarily rapid, if the power were exercised to the utmost. It never is exercised to the utmost, and yet, in the most favorable circumstances known to exist, which are those of a fertile region colonised from an industrious and civilised community, population has continued for several generations, independently of fresh immigration, to double itself in not much more than twenty years. . . . . It is a very low estimate of the capacity of increase, if we only assume that in a good sanitary condition of the people, each generation may be double the number of the generation which preceded it." James Mill wrote: "That population therefore has such a tendency to increase as would enable it to double itself in a small number of years, is a proposition resting on the strongest evidence, which nothing that deserves the name of evidence has been brought on the other side to oppose".

Mr. McCulloch tells us that "it has been established beyond all question that the population of some of the States of North America, after making due allowance for immigration, has continued to double for a century past in so short a period as twenty, or at most five-and-twenty, years". M. Moreau de Jonnés gives us the following table of the time in which the population of each of the under-mentioned countries would double itself:—

Turkey	would take	..	..	555	years.
Switzerland	„	..	..	227	„
France	„	..	..	138	„
Spain	„	..	..	106	„
Holland	„	..	..	100	„
Germany	„	..	..	76	„
Russia	„	..	..	43	„
England	„	..	..	43	„
United States	„	..	..	25	„

(Without reckoning immigrants.)

We shall take but a narrow view of the law of population if we confine ourselves exclusively to human beings. Man is but the highest in the animal kingdom, not a creature apart from it, and the law of population runs through the animal and vegetable worlds. To take the commonest illustration: the horse is but a slowly breeding animal, producing but one at a birth, and that at considerable intervals of time; yet how small a proportion of the horses of a country are either stallions or brood mares; the reproductive organs of the colt are destroyed in the enormous majority of those born, and, nevertheless, our production of horses suffices for the vast needs of our commercial and luxurious classes. Darwin, in his "Origin of Species", writes :—"There is no exception to the rule that every organic being naturally increases at so high a rate that, if not destroyed, the earth would soon be covered by the progeny of a single pair. Even slow-breeding man has doubled in twenty-five years, and at this rate, in a few thousand years, there would literally not be room for his progeny. Linnæus has calculated that if an annual plant produced only two seeds—and there is no plant so unproductive as this—and their seedlings next year produced two, and so on, then in twenty years there would be a million plants. The elephant is reckoned the slowest breeder of all known animals, and I have taken some pains to estimate its probable minimum rate of natural increase; it will be under the mark to assume that it breeds when thirty years old, and goes on breeding till ninety years old, bringing forth three pair of young in this interval; if this be so, at the end of the fifth century there would be alive 15,000,000 elephants, descended from the first pair. But we have better evidence on this subject than mere theoretical calculations, namely, the numerous recorded cases of the astonishingly rapid increase of various animals in a state of nature, when circumstances have been favorable to them during two or three following seasons. Still more striking is the evidence from our domestic animals of many kinds which have run wild in many parts of the world; if the statements of the rate of increase of slow-breeding cattle and horses in South America, and latterly in Australia, had not been well authenticated, they would have been incredible. So it is with plants; cases could be given of introduced plants which have become common throughout whole islands in a period of less than ten years. Several of the plants, such as the cardoon and a tall thistle, now most numerous over the wide plains of La Plata, clothing square leagues of surface almost to the exclusion of all other plants, have been introduced from Europe; and there are plants which now range in India, as I hear from Dr. Falconer, from Cape Comorin to the Himalayas, which have been imported from America since its discovery. In such cases, and endless instances could be given, no one supposes that the fertility of these animals or plants has been suddenly and temporarily increased in any sensible degree. The obvious explanation is that the conditions of life have been very favorable, and that there has consequently been less destruction of the old and young, and that nearly all the young have been enabled to breed. In such cases the geometrical ratio of increase, the result of which never fails to be surprising, simply explains the extraordinarily rapid increase and wide diffusion of naturalised productions in their new homes. In a state of nature almost every plant produces seed, and amongst animals there are very few which do not annually pair. Hence, we may confidently assert that all plants and animals are tending to increase at a geometrical ratio, that all would most rapidly stock every station in which they could anyhow exist, and that the geometrical tendency to increase must be checked by destruction at some period of life."

Mr. John Stuart Mill also remarks: "The power of multiplication inherent in all organic life may be regarded as *infinite*. There is no species of vegetable or animal, which, if the earth were entirely abandoned to it, and to the things on which it feeds, would not in a small number of years overspread every region of the globe of which the climate was compatible with its existence."

The rapid multiplication of rabbits in Australia has lately given a startling instance of reproductive power. A number of rabbits were taken over and let loose; the district was thinly peopled, so they were not shot down to any great extent; their natural enemies, the hawks, weasels, etc., that prey on their young in England, were not taken over with them; food was abundant, and there was no check to keep them back; the consequence was that whole districts were overrun by them, and the farmers were at their wits' end to save their crops from the swarming rodents. In France, again, owing to the wholesale destruction of small birds, there was a perfect plague of insects, and the inhabitants of many districts have striven to import birds, so as to prevent the insects from practically destroying the vegetation.

While in the vegetable and animal kingdoms the rapidity of the increase is generally far greater than in the human race, we have yet seen how rapidly man has been found to increase where the circumstances surrounding him were favorable to vigorous life. We have never yet, however, seen the full power of reproduction among mankind; the increase of population in America "falls very far short", says the author of "The Elements of Social Science", "of the possible rate of increase, as is seen by the short average of life in America, and by the large amount of the reproductive power which, even in that country, is lost from celibacy and prostitution. . . . . The capacity of increase in the human race, as in all other organised beings, is, in fact, boundless and immeasurable."

But while animated existence increases thus rapidly, no such swift multiplication can be secured of the means of subsistence. The means of subsistence of vegetable life are strictly limited in quantity; the amount obtainable from the soil may be increased by manure, by careful tillage, by rotation of crops, by improved methods of husbandry, but none the less is this amount limitable, while there is no limit to the power of life-production; if the soil and air and light could be indefinitely stretched, vegetable life would still suffice without effort to clothe the increased surface. But since the size of the globe inexorably limits the amount of vegetable produce possible of growth, the limited vegetable produce must, in its turn, limit the amount of animal life which can be sustained. While increased knowledge, skill, and care, may augment the means of subsistence obtainable from the earth, yet animal life multiplies more rapidly than can its food. As is truly said by the author just quoted: "From a consideration of the law of agricultural industry, and an estimate of the rate at which the means of subsistence could be increased in old countries, even under the most favorable circumstances, it may be inferred with certainty that these means of subsistence could not possibly be increased so fast as to permit population to increase at its natural rate. . . . . Let us apply the American rate of increase to the population of this country. Is it conceivably possible that the population of England or any old country should double itself every twenty-five years? In Great Britain there are now" (the book was written many years ago) "about twenty-one millions; is it conceivable that the means of subsistence could be so rapidly increased as to allow these twenty-one millions to swell to forty-two millions in the first twenty-five years; to eighty-four millions in the next; 168 millions in the next, etc? The supposition is evidently absurd.

Even the rate of increase of the last fifty-three years (in which time the population has doubled) cannot possibly be long continued. If it were it would increase our population in three centuries to about 1,300 millions; or, in other words, to more than the total population of the globe, which is estimated at about 1,000 millions."

Wherever, then, we look throughout Nature, we find proofs of the truth of the law, that "there is a tendency in all animated existence to increase faster than the means of subsistence". This is the law of which Miss Martineau said that it could be no more upset than a law of arithmetic; this is the law which John Stuart Mill regarded "as axiomatic"; this is the law which Lord Chief Justice Cockburn, in the trial of the Queen *v.* Bradlaugh and Besant, designated "an irrefragable truth". Controversialists may quarrel as to its consequences, and may differ as to man's duty in regard to them; but no controversy can arise among thinkers on the law itself, any more than on the sphericity of the earth.

CHAPTER II.

ITS CONSEQUENCES.

It is abundantly clear, from experience, that population does not, as a general rule, increase at anything like the rate spoken of in the preceding chapter. The earth would, long ere this, have become unable to support her offspring if they had multiplied at the pace which the naturalist tells us is possible—if, for instance, all rabbits had increased in the same ratio as those taken over to Australia and naturalised there. Some cause must therefore be at work checking the increase and preventing over-rapid multiplication, holding the balance, in fact, roughly even between the means of subsistence and the living creatures who consume them. In the vegetable kingdom the checks to increase are not difficult to find. Every plant needs for its development suitable soil, moisture, air, and light; these are its means of subsistence. The amount of these is limited, while the power of multiplication in the vegetable is unlimited. What is the necessary consequence? That of the myriad seeds produced only a few will develop into seed-bearing plants; each seed needs a certain proportion of soil, moisture, air light; if they fall round the parent stem and sprout into seedlings they so crowd each other that the weaker perish; every gardener knows that his seedlings need thinning if any are to grow into useful plants, that his plantations must be thinned out if any tree is to have full development; an over-crowded plantation, an over-crowded garden-bed, gives a crop of dwarfed, stunted, weak, and useless plants. These facts are so commonplace that they pass continually before our eyes, and the simple inference from them is unregarded. There is another check of a severe character on vegetable increase. Birds eat the seeds; animals browse on the plants; man uses many kinds for his own support; the wheat sown in one year not only produces the seed-corn for the ensuing season, but also affords so vast a multiplication as to supply the world with bread; the animal world preys on the vegetable, and so is made a check which destroys the mature, as well as the check of want of room and nourishment which destroys the infant, growth. Out of 357 seedlings of English weeds, carefully watched by Mr. Darwin, 295 were destroyed. On some heaths near Farnham, in the portions enclosed during ten years previously, self-sown firs were observed by him springing up so closely that all could not live, while in the unenclosed portions not one young tree was to be seen. On close examination Mr. Darwin found in one square yard thirty-two little trees no higher than the heather, one with twenty-six rings of growth; the check here was the browsing of cattle over the open part of the heath. In the animal kingdom the same class of checks is found; the rabbit which in Australia has become an intolerable plague, is kept down to a fair level in England, not because he multiplies less rapidly, but because the check of destruction is brought to bear upon him; food is scarcer in the more cultivated land; guns and traps send him to the market in millions; hawks, weasels, cats, prey upon his young; he produces life rapidly, but the check of death waits upon him and keeps him down. The swift increase of plants and animals under favorable circumstances, dealt with in Chapter I., shows the enormous power of the destructive checks which generally keep in subjection the life-producing force. Once more turning to Mr. Darwin, we read:—

"Of the many individuals of any species which are periodically born, but a small number can survive. . . . . A struggle for existence inevitably follows from the high rate at which all organic beings tend to increase. Every being, which during its natural lifetime produces several eggs or seeds, must suffer destruction during some period of its life, and during some season or occasional year, otherwise, on the principle of geometrical increase, its numbers would quickly become so inordinately great that no country could support the product. Hence, as more individuals are produced than can possibly survive, there must in every case be a struggle for existence, either one individual with another of the same species, or with the individuals of distinct species, or with the physical conditions of life. It is the doctrine of Malthus applied with manifold force to the whole animal and vegetable kingdoms; for in this case there can be no artificial increase of food, and no prudential restraint from marriage. Although some species may be now increasing more or less rapidly in numbers, all cannot do so, for the world would not hold them. . . . . . Our familiarity with the larger domestic animals tends, I think, to mislead us: we see no great destruction falling on them, and we forget that thousands are annually slaughtered for food, and that in a state of nature an equal number would have somehow to be disposed of. . . . . In looking at nature, it is most necessary to keep the foregoing considerations always in mind—never to forget that every single organic being around us may be said to be striving to the utmost to increase in numbers; that each lives by a struggle at some period of its life; that heavy destruction inevitably falls either on the young or old during each generation or at recurrent intervals. Lighten any check, mitigate the destruction ever so little, and the number of the species will almost instantaneously increase to any amount."

If there be such vast destruction of life throughout the vegetable and animal kingdoms, necessarily consequent on the superabundance of life produced, is man exempt from the same law?

Malthus laid down the three following propositions, propositions of which his book is only an amplification:—

"1. Population is necessarily limited by the means of subsistence.

"2. Population invariably increases where the means of subsistence increase, unless prevented by some very powerful and obvious checks.

"3. These checks, and the checks which repress the

superior power of population, and keep its effects on a level with the means of subsistence, are all resolvable into moral restraint, vice, and misery.

"The ultimate check to population appears to be a want of food, arising necessarily from the different ratios according to which population and food increase. But this ultimate check is never the immediate check, except in cases of actual famine. The immediate check may be stated to consist in all those customs and all those diseases, which seem to be generated by a scarcity of the means of subsistence; and all those causes, independent of this scarcity, whether of a moral or physical nature, which tend prematurely to weaken and destroy the human frame." These causes which retard the growth of population by killing human beings, either slowly or rapidly, are all classed together by Malthus under the head of "positive" checks; they are the "natural" checks to population, common alike to vegetables, to animals, to man; they are all checks of suffering, of want, of disease; they are life-destroying, anti-human, brutal, irrational.

These checks are, as might be imagined, more striking, more openly repulsive, more thorough, among savage than among civilised nations. War, infanticide, hardship, famine, disease, murder of the aged, all these are among the positive checks which keep down the increase of population among savage tribes. War carries off the young men, full of vigor, the warriors in their prime of life, the strongest, the most robust, the most fiery—those in fact, who from their physical strength and energy would be most likely to add largely to the number of the tribe. Infanticide, most prevalent where means of existence are most restricted, is largely practised among barbarous nations, the custom being due, to a great extent, to the difficulty of providing food for a large family. Hardship carries away many a child in savage life: "Women," says Malthus, "obliged, by their habits of living, to a constant change of places, and compelled to an unremitting drudgery for their husbands, appear to be absolutely incapable of bringing up two or three children nearly of the same age. If another child be born before the one above it can shift for itself, and follow its mother on foot, one of the two must almost necessarily perish from want of care." Famine, so easily caused among a primitive community, sweeps off young and old together; epidemics carry away almost a whole tribe at one swoop; the aged are often slain, or left to perish, when their feebleness no longer permits them to add to the productive force of the community.

All these miseries are the positive and natural checks to population among uncivilised beings; among the more civilised the checks are the same in kind although more decently veiled. But the moment we come among civilised nations a new factor is introduced into the problem which complicates it very considerably. Hitherto we have seen Nature—apart from man—going her own way, producing and destroying without let or hindrance. But when we examine civilised nations we find a new agent at work; Nature's grandest product, the brain of man, now comes into play, and a new set of circumstances arises. Men, women, and children, who would be doomed to death in the savage state, have their lives prolonged by civilisation; the sickly, whom the hardships of the savage struggle for existence would kill off, are carefully tended in hospitals, and saved by medical skill; the parents, whose thread of life would be cut short, are cherished on into prolonged old age; the feeble, who would be left to starve, are tenderly shielded from hardship, and life's road is made the smoother for the lame; the average of life is lengthened, and more and more thought is brought to bear on the causes of preventible disease; better drainage, better homes, better food, better clothing, all these, among the more comfortable classes, remove many of the natural checks to population. Among these nations wars become less frequent and less bloody: famines, owing to improved means of inter-communication, become for a time almost impossible; epidemics no longer depopulate whole districts. In England, in A.D. 1258, no less than 15,000 people were starved to death in London alone; in France, in A.D. 1348, one-third of the whole population perished from the same cause; in Rome, from A.D. 250-265, a plague raged, that, for some time, carried off daily 5,000 persons; in England, in A.D. 1506 and 1517, the sweating sickness slew half the inhabitants of the large towns and depopulated Oxford; in London, in A.D. 1603-4, the plague killed 30,578 persons, and in A.D. 1664-5 it destroyed 68,596; in Naples, in A.D. 1656, 400,000 died, and in Egypt, A.D. 1792 above 800,000. These terrible epidemics and famines have ceased to sweep over Europe, but for how long? This decrease of natural checks to population, consequent on advancing civilisation, has, unfortunately, a very dark side. Darwin has remarked: "Lighten any check, mitigate the destruction ever so little, and the number of the species will almost instantaneously increase to any amount". A signal instance of the truth of this remark is now being given to us in our Indian empire by the introduction there of Western civilisation. Lord Derby says: "We have established there order and peace; we have done away with local wars; we have lessened the ravages of pestilence, and we do what we can—and, in ordinary seasons, we do it with success—to mitigate the effects of destitution. The result is, naturally and necessarily, a vast increase in population; and, if present appearances can be trusted, we shall have in every generation a larger aggregate of human beings relying upon us for help in those periods of distress which must, from time to time, occur in a country wholly agricultural and liable to droughts." So that it appears that our civilisation in India, taking away the ordinary natural checks to population, *and introducing no others in their stead*, brings about a famine which has already destroyed more than 500,000 people in one Presidency alone, and has thrown about one-and-a-half million more on charity. From this point of view civilisation can scarcely be regarded as an unmixed blessing, and it must not be forgotten that what is happening in India now must, sooner or later, happen in every country where science destroys the balance of nature.

Turning to England, we find that our population is growing rapidly enough to cause anxiety; although there are some severe checks, with which we shall deal presently, England has more than doubled her population during the last seventy years. While it is true that the abolition of private property in land and capital, would lead to a better distribution of population: while it is true that many country districts are as much underpopulated as the towns are overcrowded: while it is true that under a saner social system, England could support in comfort a larger population than it has at present: it is none the less true that, dealing with the birth-rate, we must adopt our *immediate* policy to England as it is, not to England as it will be. Further, under any social system, the law of population holds good; it can never safely be ignored. (This question will be more fully considered in Chapter IV.) In 1810 the population of England and Wales was about

10,000,000, and in 1881 it was 25,974,439. "At the present time", writes Professor Fawcett, "it is growing at the rate of 200,000 every year, which is almost equivalent to the population of the county of Northampton. If in fifty years the descendants of one million become two millions, it is obvious that in 100 years the two millions will have become four millions, so that if the population of England were eight millions in 1810 it would be eighty millions in 1960." Forty years hence, if we maintain the rate of increase which we have kept up since the commencement of this century, some forty millions of people will be crowded into our little island. So long as our present system is maintained, Professor Fawcett is justified in saying: "Every trade and every profession is overcrowded; for every vacant clerkship there are hundreds of applications. Difficult as it is for men to obtain a livelihood, it is ten times more difficult for women to do so; partly on account of unjust laws, and partly because of the tyranny of society, they are shut out from many employments. All that has just been stated is admitted by common consent —it is the topic of daily conversation, and of daily complaint—and yet with the utmost complacency we observe 200,000 added to our population every year, and we often congratulate ourselves upon this addition to our numbers, as if it were an unerring sign of advancing prosperity. But viewed in relation to the facts just mentioned, what does this addition to our numbers indicate? To this question only one reply can be given—that in ten years' time, where there are a hundred now seeking employment, there will then be a hundred and twenty. This will not apply simply to one industry, but will be the case throughout the whole country. It will also further happen that in ten years' time, for every hundred who now require food, fuel, and clothing, a similar provision will have to be made for one hundred and twenty. It therefore follows that, low as the general average standard of living now is, it cannot by any means be maintained, unless in ten years' time the supply of all the commodities of ordinary consumption can be increased by 20 per cent., without their becoming more costly."

One of the earliest signs of population increasing too rapidly for its accommodation is the overcrowding of the poor. Just as the overcrowded seedlings spoil each other's growth, so do the overcrowded poor injure each other morally, mentally, and physically. Whether we study town or country the result of our enquiries is the same—the houses are too small and the families are too large. Take, as illustrating this, the terrible instances given by Mr. George Godwin, in his essay on "Overcrowding in London". In Lincoln Court he states that: "In the majority of the houses the rooms are small and the staircases are narrow and without ventilation. In two of them it was admitted that more than thirty-five persons lived in each; but it would probably be nearer the truth to say that each house of eight rooms contains on an average, including children, forty-five persons." "A child was found dead in Brownlow Street, and on enquiry it was learnt that the mother, a widow, and six children slept in one bed in a small room. The death of the child was attributed to the bedclothes." "In a model lodging house for families, a father, who with his wife and one child occupies one room, has accommodated six of his nine other children the crossway on two camp bedsteads, while three elder girls, one sixteen years old, sleep on a small bedstead near." "In a respectable house not far from the last, occupied by steady artisans and others, I found that nine persons slept in one of the rooms (12 feet by 14 feet), a father, mother, and seven children. Eleven shoemakers worked in the attics; and in each of the other five rooms there was a separate family. I could quote scores of such cases of overcrowding in what would seem to be decent houses." "Hundreds of modern houses, built in decent suburban neighborhoods, as if for one family only, are made to contain several. The neat external appearance of many of them gives no suggestion of the dangerously-crowded state of the houses. A description of one of them in Bemerton Street, Caledonian Road, will be more truthful. The basement below the level of the street contains in the front room an old man and his wife; in the back room, two lodgers; in the parlors there are a man and his wife and eight children. On the first floor, a man and his wife and infant; two girls, sixteen and eighteen years of age, and occasionally their mother—all in the front room; and in the small back room, two women, a girl, and two young children. On the second floor, a father, mother, two grown-up sons, an infant, and a brood of rabbits. Two women and two boys in the back room make the whole population of the house thirty-four. In the next there were thirty-three persons similarly divided." "In one small house, with staircase in the centre, there were in the four small rooms on each side of it forty persons in the daytime. How many there may be at night I cannot say. The atmosphere on the staircase was sickening." Who can wonder that the death-rate is so high in large cities, and that the difference in the death-rate between the rich and poor sections of the same city is appalling? In Glasgow the death-rate in the Blythswood division was 19; that in the Bridgegate and Wynds division 52½. Dr. Drysdale, in the "Report of Industrial Remuneration Conference", 1885, says: "At present the average age at death among the nobility, gentry, and professional classes in England and Wales was 55 years; but among the artisan classes of Lambeth it only amounted to 29 years; and whilst the infantile death-rate among the well-to-do classes was such that only 8 children died in the first year of life out of 100 born, as many as 30 per cent. succumbed at that age among the children of the poor in some districts of our large cities. The only real cause of this enormous difference in the position of the rich and poor with respect to their chances of existence lay in the fact that at the bottom of society wages were so low that food and other requisites of health were obtained with too great difficulty." Many of the deaths in the richer districts might be prevented by better sanitary arrangements and wider sanitary knowledge; the excess in the poorer districts is clearly preventible with our present knowledge, and preventible death is manslaughter. As might be expected, the rate of infant mortality is very high in these over-crowded districts; where 200 children under the age of five years die among the rich, 600 die among the poor; a young child is easily killed, and the bad air and unwholesome food rapidly murder the little ones; again quoting from the Glasgow report: "A large number of the deaths, bearing the relation of 13½ per cent. to the total births, were those of children under one year". In addition to the actual deaths caused by overcrowding, we must add to the mass of misery accruing from it, the non-fatal diseases and the general debility and lack of vigorous life so common in our large centres of industry. "Overcrowding", says Mr. Godwin, 'means want of pure air, and want of pure air means debility, continued fever, death, widowhood, orphanage, pauperism, and money loss to the living"

Epidemics are most fatal in overcrowded districts, not only because they pass so rapidly from one to another, but also because the people dwelling in those districts have less vitality, less vigor of resistance, than those more fortunately circumstanced. "The great reason", said Dr. Drysdale in the Knowlton trial in the Court of Queen's Bench, "that typhus fever is so terrible a disease is that people are crowded. It is impossible to have health with large crowded families." Here then is one of the commonest checks to population in all great cities. Nor must the results to morality be omitted in this imperfect summary of the evils which grow out of over-crowding. What modesty, what decency, what self-respect are possible to these men and women, boys and girls, herded together, seven, ten, fourteen in a room? Only the absence of these virtues could make the life endurable for four-and-twenty hours; no delicacy of feeling can exist there, and we cannot wonder at Dr. Drysdale's sad answer in the above trial: "They do not know what modesty is".

Can there be any doubt that it is the large families so common among the English poor that are at the root of this over-crowding? For not only would the "model-lodging-house" spoken of above have been less crowded if the parents, instead of having ten children, had had only two, but with fewer children less money would be needed for food and clothing, and more could be spared for rent. The artisan with six children, forced to live in a stifling pair of rooms in a back street in London in order to be near his work, might, if he had only two, spare money enough to pay his rail to and from the suburbs, where the same rent would give him decent accommodation; and not only would he have a better home, but the two children would grow strong in the free air, where the six pine in the London street, and the two would have plenty of food and clothing, where the six lack both. Mr. Godwin recognises this fact; he says: "Amongst the causes which lead to the evil we are deploring we must not overlook the gradual increase of children, while in the case of the laboring man the income mostly remains the same. . . . As the children increase in number the wife is prevented from adding by her earnings to the income, and many years must elapse before the children can be put to work." "Ought to be put to work" would be a truer phrase, for the age at which young children are forced to help in winning their daily bread is one of the disgraces of our civilisation.

Overcrowding in country districts is, naturally, not so injurious to health as it is in the towns; the daily work in the open air, the fresh breeze blowing round the cottage, and cleansing, to some extent, the atmosphere within, the fields and lanes where the children can play, all these things may do much to neutralise the harm to health wrought by overcrowding at night. The injury to health caused by large families among the agricultural poor arises more from other causes than from over-crowding; the low wage cannot pay for a house sufficiently good, and the cheap ill-built cottage, damp, draughty, badly-drained, brings to those who live in it the fever and the ague and the rheumatism so sadly common among these laboring classes. But the moral effect of over-crowding is, as the late Bishop of Manchester said — when serving as the Rev. J. Fraser in the Royal Commission on the employment of children, young persons, and women in agriculture —"fearful to contemplate". "Modesty", he goes on, "must be an unknown virtue, decency an unimaginable thing, where, in one small chamber, with the beds lying as thickly as they can be packed, father, mother, young men, lads, grown and growing-up girls—two and sometimes three generations—are herded promiscuously; where every operation of the toilette and of nature—dressings, undressings, births, deaths—is performed by each within the sight or hearing of all; where children of both sexes, to as high an age as twelve or fourteen, or even more, occupy the same bed; where the whole atmosphere is sensual, and human nature is degraded something below the level of the swine."

The too early putting of the children to work is one of the consequences of over-large families under the pressure of our present system. In the country the children working in gangs in the fields learn evil speech and evil act at an age when they should be innocent, at school and at play. In town, in the factory and in the workroom, the seeds of disease are sown in the child-laborers. "Children in big families", says Dr. Drysdale, "are taken out to work very early, and premature exertion often injures them for life. . . . . Children are not fit to do very much work so long as they are half developed, and early death is often the consequence." Children should not work for their bread; the frame is not fit for toil, the brain is not ready for the effort of long attention; those who give the life should support and protect it until the tenderness of childhood is passed away, and the young body is firm-knit and strong, prepared to take its share of the battle, and bear the burden and heat of the day.

Baby-farming has only too justly been called the "hideous social phænomenon of the 19th century". It is the direct result of the pressure of over-large families, and is simply a veiled form of infanticide. Mr. Benson Baker, one of the medical officers of Marylebone, has written a sad notice of baby-farming. He speaks of a notorious case: "One of the stock from that model baby-farm is now under my care. This child, three years old, was employed by the proprietress as a gaffer or ganger over the younger babies. His duties were to sit up in the middle of the bed with eight other babies round him, and, the moment any one of them awoke, to put the bottle to their mouth. He was also to keep them quiet, and generally to superintend them." A vast number of children are slowly murdered annually in this way, and the death-rate is also very high in every place where many infants are kept together, whether it be in workhouse, hospital, or crèche.

Another consequence of large families which must not be overlooked is the physical injury caused to the mothers. Among the poor, cases of *prolapsus uteri*, or falling of the womb, are only too common. *Prolapsus uteri* results frequently from "getting about" to rapidly after child-birth, it being impossible for the mother of the increasing family to lie by for that period of rest which nature absolutely enjoins. "Women", says Dr. Drysdale, "ought never to get up from confinement for some weeks after the child is born; but these poor women are so utterly unable to do without work that they are compelled to get up in a day or two. The womb, being full of blood, falls down and produces infirmity for life." The doctor also says of this disease: "It is extremely common. Indeed, when I was obstetrical assistant at Edinburgh, it was one of the commonest diseases among women—the principal one, in fact." "Prolapsus, or falling of the womb", says Dr. Graily Hewett, "is an affection to which women are in one form or other exceedingly liable, and it is one which is not unfrequently productive of very much inconvenience and distress". The reason of the disease is not far to seek.

The womb, in its unimpregnated state, is from two and a half to three inches long, an inch and a half wide, more or less, at its largest part, and about an inch thick. During the nine months of pregnancy this organ is stretched more and more, until, at the end of nine months, it is capable of containing the fully-developed infant. During these nine months the muscular substance of the womb increases in thickness, while the whole organ enlarges. At birth the muscular fibres begin to contract, and the womb ought to return to almost its original size. But in order that it may so return, the horizontal position is absolutely necessary for some days, and much rest for some weeks, until the muscles connected with the womb have regained something of their natural elasticity. If the mother be forced to leave her bed too early, if she be compelled to exert herself in housekeeping cares, to stand over the wash-tub, to bend over the fire, what happens? The womb, so long distended, has no chance of healthy contraction; the muscles which support it in its proper position have not recovered from the long strain; the womb itself is heavy with the blood flowing from the vessels yet unclosed, and it naturally falls and "produces infirmity for life". Too frequent pregnancy is another cause of *prolapsus uteri*, and of many other diseases of the womb. "We frequently find that the uterus becomes diseased from the fact that the pregnancies rapidly succeed each other, the uterus not having recovered its natural size when it becomes again occupied by an ovum" (Dr. Graily Hewett). The womb is too constantly put on the stretch, and is not allowed sufficient rest to recover its original vigor and elasticity. It takes about two months for the womb to thoroughly reconstruct itself after the delivery of a child; a new mucous membrane develops, and a degeneration and reconstruction of the muscles takes place, technically known as "the involution of the uterus". During pregnancy, the uterine muscles "increase very considerably in size. Their texture becomes much more distinctly granular, and their outlines more strongly marked. . . . . The entire walls of the uterus, at the time of delivery, are composed of such muscular fibres, arranged in circular, oblique, and longitudinal bundles. About the end of the first week after delivery, these fibres begin to undergo a fatty degeneration. . . . . The muscular fibres which have become altered by the fatty deposit, are afterwards gradually absorbed and disappear, their place being subsequently taken by other fibres of new formation, which already begin to make their appearance before the old ones have been completely destroyed. As this process goes on, it results finally in a complete renovation of the muscular substance of the uterus. The organ becomes again reduced in size, compact in tissue, and of a pale ruddy hue, as in the ordinary unimpregnated condition. This entire renewal or reconstruction of the uterus is completed, according to Heschl, about the end of the second month after delivery." (Dr. Dalton). No words can add strength to this statement, proving the absolute right of women to complete repose from sexual disturbance during this slow recovery of the normal condition of the womb. Many a woman in fairly comfortable circumstances suffers from lack of knowledge of physical laws, and from the reckless English disregard of all conjugal prudence. Short of absolute displacement of the womb, and of grave uterine diseases, various disorders result from weakness of the over-taxed generative organs. Leucorrhea is one of the commonest of these, producing general debility, pain in the back, indigestion, etc. It is not right, it is not moral, that mothers of families should thus ruin their health, causing suffering to themselves and misery to those around them; it is only a perverted moral sense which leads men and women to shut their eyes to these sad consequences of over-large families, and causes them thus to disregard the plainest laws of health. Sexual intemperance, the over-procreation of children, is as immoral as intemperance in drink.

Among the melancholy consequences of the suffering caused by the felt pressure of over-large families, we must not omit the foolish and sometimes criminal attempts made by ignorant people to limit the family; the foolish attempt is the prevalent habit of over-lactation, arising from the mistaken idea that conception is impossible during the nursing of a child; the criminal attempt is the procuring of abortion by means of drugs or by the use of instruments. Too often, indeed, do these come under the head of the positive, the life-destroying, checks.

To turn to a different, and more immediately life-destroying class of checks, that of war cannot, of course, be left out of this melancholy picture. Great famines are positive checks on a still more frightful scale. Lord Derby says as to India: "If present appearances can be trusted, we shall have in every generation a larger aggregate of human beings relying upon us for help in those periods of distress which must from time to time occur in a country wholly agricultural and liable to droughts". But what a confession of helplessness! Is it possible to sit down with folded hands and calmly contemplate the recurrence at regular intervals of such a famine as lately slew its tens of thousands? Yet the law of population is "an irrefragable truth", and these people are starved to death according to natural law; early marriages, large families, these are the premises; famine and disease, these are the conclusions. The same consequences will, sooner or later, —sooner in an agricultural country, dependent on its crops, later in a manufacturing country, commanding large foreign supplies, but always inexorably—produce the same fearful results.

One more melancholy positive check must be added, the last to which we shall here refer. It is absolute child-murder by desertion or by more violent means: Dr. Lankester said that "there were in London alone 16,000 women who had murdered their offspring". Dr. Attwood lately stated of Macclesfield that the doctors in that town often had moral, though not legal, proof that children were "put away", and that Macclesfield was "no worse than any other manufacturing town".

Such are some of the consequences of the law of population: the power of production is held in check by the continual destruction, the number of births is balanced by the number of deaths. Population struggles to increase, but the want of the means of existence beats it back, and men, women, and children perish in the terrible struggle. The more civilisation advances the more hopeless becomes the outlook. The checks imposed by "nature and providence", in which Sir Hardinge Giffard trusts for the prevention of over-population, are being removed, one by one, by science and by civilisation. War will be replaced by arbitration, and those who would have fallen victims to it will become fathers of families; sanitary knowledge will bring sanitary improvement, and typhus fever and small-pox will disappear as the plague and black death have done; children will not die in their infancy, and the average length of human life will increase. The life-destroying checks of "nature and providence" will be met with the life-preserving attempts of science and of reason, and population will increase more and more rapidly. What will be the result? Simply this: India to-day is a microcosm of the world of the future, and the statesman of that time will re-echo the words of the present Foreign Secretary with a wider application. Ought we then to encourage positive checks so as to avert this final catastrophe? Ought we to stir up war? Ought we to prevent sanitary improvements? Ought we to leave the sickly to die? Ought we to permit infants to perish unaided? Ought we to refuse help to the starving? These checks may be "natural", but they are not human; they may be "providential", but they are not rational. Has science no help for us in our extremity? has reason no solution to this problem? has thought no message of salvation to the poor?

CHAPTER III.

ITS BEARING UPON HUMAN CONDUCT AND MORALS.

To the question that closes the last chapter there *is* an answer; all thinkers have seen that since population increases more rapidly than the means of subsistence, the human brain should be called in to devise a restriction of the population, and so relieve man from the pressure of the struggle for existence. The lower animals are helpless, and must needs suffer, and strive, and die; but man, whose brain raises him above the rest of animated existence, man rational, thoughtful, civilised, he is not condemned to share in the brute struggle, and to permit lower nature to destroy his happiness and his ever-growing rapidity of progress. In dealing with the law of population, as with every other natural law which presses on him unpleasantly, civilised man seeks so to alter the conditions which surround him as to produce a happier result. Thinkers have, therefore, studied the law and its consequences, and have suggested various views of its bearing on human conduct and morals. It was acknowledged that under any social system the only way of escape from ultimate poverty and from the misery occasioned by positive checks, was in the limitation of the population within the available means of subsistence, and the problem to be solved was—How shall this be done? Malthus proposed that preventive, or birth-restricting, should be substituted for positive, or life-destroying, checks, and that "moral restraint" should supersede "misery and vice". He lays it down as a principle of duty, that no one "is to bring beings into the world for whom he cannot find the means of support". This obligation, he says, is a "duty intelligible to the humblest capacity". But the duty being admitted on all sides, the crucial point is—How is this duty to be fulfilled? Malthus answers:—By delay of marriage. We are bound "not to marry till we have a fair prospect of being able to support our children"; in a right state of society "no man, whose earnings were only sufficient to maintain two children, would put himself in a situation in which he might have to maintain four or five"; a man should "defer marrying, till, by industry and economy, he is in a capacity to support the children that he may reasonably expect from his marriage". Thus marriage—if ever possible to the poor—would be delayed until the middle of life, and the birth-rate would be decreased by a general abstention from marriage until a comparatively late age.

This preventive check would doubtless be an effectual one, but it is open to grave and fatal objections, and would only replace one set of evils by another. If late marriage were generally practised the most melancholy results would follow. The more marriage is delayed, the more prostitution spreads. It is necessary to gravely remind all advocates of late marriage that men do not and will not live single; and all women, and all men who honor women, should protest against a teaching which would inevitably make permanent that terrible social evil which is the curse of civilisation, and which condemns numbers of unhappy creatures to a disgraceful and revolting calling. Prostitution is an evil which we should strive to eradicate not to perpetuate, and late marriage, generally adopted, would most certainly perpetuate it. The state of the streets of our large towns at nightfall is the result of deferred marriage, and marriage is deferred owing to the ever-increasing difficulty of maintaining a large family in anything like comfort.

Mr. Montagu Cookson, writing in the *Fortnightly Review*, says: "If, indeed, we could all become perfect beings, the rule of life deduced by Malthus from the unalterable law of population would be both practicable and safe; as it is, it has a direct tendency to promote the cardinal vice of cities—that of unchastity. The number of women in England who ply the loathsome trade of prostitution is already large enough to people a county, and, as our great thoroughfares show at nightfall, is certainly not diminishing. Their chief supporters justify themselves by the very plea which Malthus uses to enforce the duty of continence, namely, that they are not well enough off to maintain a wife and family. If they could be sure that they could limit the number of their children, so as to make it commensurate with their income, not only would the plea be generally groundless, but I believe it would not be urged, and the so-called social evil would be stormed in its strongest fortress."

The evils resulting from late marriage to those who remain really celibate must not be overlooked in weighing this recommendation of it as a cure for the evils of over-population. Celibacy is not natural to men or to women: all bodily needs require their legitimate satisfaction, and celibacy is a disregard of natural law. The asceticism which despises the body is a contempt of nature, and a revolt against her; the morality which upholds virginity as the type of womanly perfection is unnatural; to be in harmony with nature, men and women should be husbands and wives, fathers and mothers, and until nature evolves a neuter sex celibacy will ever be a mark of imperfection. Very clearly has nature marked celibacy with disapproval; the average life of the unmarried is shorter than the average life of the married; the unmarried have a less vigorous physique, are more withered, more rapidly aged, more peevish, more fanciful; "the disordered emotions of persons of both sexes who pass lives of voluntary or enforced celibacy", says Dr. Drysdale in his essay on Prostitution, "is a fact of every-day observation. Their bad temper, fretfulness and excitability are proverbial." We quote from the same tractate the following opinions: "M. Villamay, in his 'Dictionnaire des Sciences Médicales', says: 'It is assuredly true that absolute and involuntary abstinence is the most common cause of hysteria'. Again, at a meeting of the Medico-Chirurgical Society, reported in the *Lancet* of February 14th, 1859, Mr. Holmes Coote is reported to have said: 'No doubt incontinence was a great sin; but the evils connected with continence were productive of far greater misery to society. Any person could bear witness to this, who had had experience in the wards of lunatic asylums.' Again, Sir Benjamin Brodie, at the Birmingham Social Science Meeting, is reported to have said, in a discussion on prostitution, that 'the evils of celibacy were so great that he would not mention them; but that they quite equalled those of prostitution'." M. Block informs us that in France, out of 100 male lunatics, 65·72 are celibate, 5·61 are widowers, and only 28·67 are married; of 100 female lunatics, 58·16 are celibate; 12·48 are widows, and 29·36 are married. M. Bertillon, dealing with France, Holland, and Belgium, states that men who live celibate lives after twenty have, on an average, six years less of life than those who marry. The same fact holds good as regards married and unmarried women. A long train of formidable diseases results from celibacy—such as spermatorrhœa in the male, chlorosis and hysteria in the female—and no one who desires society to be happy and healthy should recommend late marriage as a cure for the social evils around us. Early marriage is best, both physically and morally; it guards purity, softens the affections, trains the heart, and preserves physical health; it teaches thought for others, gentleness and self-control; it makes men gentler and women braver from the contact of their differing natures. The children that spring from such marriages—where not following each other too rapidly—are more vigorous and healthy than those born of middle-aged parents, and in the ordinary course of nature the parents of such children live long enough to see them make their start in life, to aid, strengthen, and counsel them at the beginning of their career.

Fortunately, late marriage will never be generally practised in any community; the majority of men and women will never consent to remain single during the brightness of youth, when passion is strongest and feelings most powerful, and to marry only when life is half over and its bloom and its beauty have faded into middle age. But it is important that late marriage should not even be regarded as desirable, for if it become an accepted doctrine among the thoughtful that late marriage is the only escape from over-population, a serious difficulty would arise; the best of the people, the most careful, the most provident, the most intelligent, would remain celibate and barren, while the careless, thoughtless, thriftless ones would marry and produce large families. This evil is found to prevail to some extent even now; the more thoughtful, seeing the misery resulting from large families on low wage, often abstain from marriage, and have to pay heavy poor-rates for the support of the thoughtless and their families. The preventive check used by Malthus must therefore be rejected, and a wiser solution of the problem must be sought.

Later thinkers, recognising at once the evils of over-population and the evils of late marriage, have striven to find a path which shall avoid both Scylla and Charybdis, and have advocated early marriages and small families. John Stuart Mill has been one of the most earnest of these true friends of the people; in his "Political Economy" he writes: "In a very backward state of society, like that of Europe in the Middle Ages, and many parts of Asia at present, population is kept down by actual starvation. . . . In a more improved state, few, even among the poorest of the people, are limited to actual necessaries, and to a bare sufficiency of those; and the increase is kept within bounds, not by excess of deaths, but by limitation of births. The limitation is brought about in various ways. In some countries, it is the result of prudent or conscientious self-restraint. There is a condition to which the laboring people are habituated; they perceive that by having too numerous families they must sink below that condition, or fail to submit it to their children; and this they do not choose to submit to. The countries in which, so far as is known, a great degree of voluntary prudence has been longest practised on this subject are Norway and parts of Switzerland . . . . In both these countries the increase of population is very slow; and what checks it is not multitude of deaths, but fewness of births. Both the births and the deaths are remarkably few in proportion to the population; the average duration of life is the longest in Europe; the population contains fewer children, and a greater proportional number of persons in the vigor of life than is known to be the case in any other part of the world. The paucity of births tends directly to prolong life by keeping the people in comfortable circumstances." Clearly and pointedly Mill teaches "conjugal prudence"; he quotes with approval the words of Sismondi, who was "among the most benevolent of his time, and the happiness of whose married life has been celebrated": "When dangerous prejudices have not become accredited, when a morality contrary to our true duties towards others, and especially towards those to whom we have given life, is not inculcated in the name of the most sacred authority, no prudent man contracts matrimony before he is in a condition which gives him an assured means of living and no married man has a greater number of children than he can properly bring up." Many other eminent men and women have spoken in the same sense; Professor Leone Levi advocates "prudence as regards the increase of our families". Mrs. Fawcett writes: "Those who deal with this question of pauperism should remember that it is not to be remedied by cheap food, by reductions of taxation, or by economical administration in the departments, or by new forms of government. Nothing will permanently affect pauperism while the present reckless increase of population continues." Mr. Montagu Cookson says that some may think "prudential restraint after marriage wilder than anything Malthus ever dreamt", but urges that "the numbers of children born after marriage should be limited", and that "such limitation is as much the duty of married persons as the observance of chastity is the duty of those that are unmarried".

It remains, then, to ask how is this duty to be performed? It is clearly useless to preach the limitation of the family and to conceal the means whereby such limitation may be effected. If the limitation be a duty, it cannot be wrong to afford such information as shall enable people to discharge it.

There are various prudential checks which have been suggested, but further investigation of this intricate subject is sorely needed, and it is much to be wished that more medical men would devote themselves to the study of this important branch of physiology. The main difficulty in the way is the absurd notion that prudential checks are obscene, and very few doctors have the courage to face the odium that would arise from a frank treatment of the subject. Some medical men do, at the present time, recommmend the use of checks to their female patients, but even these would hesitate ere they openly dealt with the subject. The consequence of this unfortunate state of things is that much doubt hangs over the efficacy of the checks proposed, and all that can be done is to state what these checks are, adding a word of recommendation on those which have proved most successful in practice.

The complete ignorance of their own bodies, which is supposed to be a necessary part of "female modesty", makes necessary a preliminary word on the mechanism of the womb and the process of fertilisation. The passage leading from the exterior of the body to the mouth of the womb varies from four to five inches. At its upper end, projecting into it, is the mouth of the womb, which is normally closed by two thick lips; so that the womb may be regarded as a bag with its mouth kept shut by an india-rubber ring. Now, fertilisation depends on the active element, the spermatozoa, from the male reaching the ova (eggs) of the female, and this can only occur by the spermatozoa making their way through the mouth of the womb into its interior cavity. This mouth opens slightly from time to time during sexual excitement, and thus makes it possible for the spermatozoa to work their way in. If then the mouth of the womb can be kept closed, or in any way guarded, no fertilisation can take place. Further, nothing which is used for this purpose can pass into the womb, the mouth being closed, except as above stated, and the opening under excitement being very slight.

Under these circumstances the most reliable checks are those which close the passage into the womb. Of these there are three useful kinds; the soluble pessary, the india-rubber pessary, and the sponge. The first can be obtained from Mr. Rendell at the address given on his advertisement, and this is the one which, from a very wide experience, I recommend as at once the most certain and the least inconvenient; the second from Mr. Rendell or from Messrs. Lambert and Son (see advertisements); the third from any chemist. A piece of very fine sponge, about the size of a large walnut when fairly dry, should be soaked in a solution of alum, or a solution of Dr. Palfrey's powder (see p. 33); a piece of very narrow tape can be tied round the sponge to facilitate its withdrawal; this sponge should be slipped up the passage to the womb as far as it will go, and it need not be removed until the following morning. There is no difficulty in the use of any one of these three checks: and they have the enormous advantage of being entirely in the hands of the woman and of being absolutely unobtrusive.

The use of quinine in connexion with the last two of

these checks is recommended by many. Quinine kills the spermatozoa, and it is the active agent in Mr. Rendell's soluble pessaries. A compound of quinine, vaseline and cacao - nut butter, used with the india-rubber pessary according to the directions supplied with it, gives, if possible, added security against conception. If the sponge be preferred, there is no better solution to soak it in than one consisting of twenty grains of quinine to a pint of water. In every case, it is wise to syringe with a solution of quinine (ten grains to a pint of water) in the morning before removing the pessary.

Mr. H. A. Allbutt, M.R.C.P. (Edin.), in "The Wife's Handbook", says: "A kind of artificial sponge or vaginal Tampon, containing in its centre a friable capsule filled with slightly acidulated quinine solution, would, I believe, make a very good and cheap preventive. All that the woman would have to do before intercourse would be to take one of the Tampons, and squeeze it, which would break the capsule, setting free the solution, which would then permeate the whole sponge. She would then insert it into the vagina as far as possible. It would be better to have a string attached, so as to be able to withdraw it easily." These Tampons have not, so far as I know, been yet tried, but the principle of their action is the same as that of the pessaries.

The preventive check advocated by Dr. Knowlton was the use of the ordinary syringe *immediately after intercourse*, a solution of alum, or one of sulphate of zinc, being used instead of water. This check is said to have frequently failed, and the modification of it proposed by the late Dr. Palfrey, one of the most eminent physicians in London, has not proved uniformly successful, although effective in the great majority of cases. Dr. Palfrey wrote the following note for a previous edition of this work: "I must point out that the ordinary Higginson's syringe fitted with the common female tube is perforated at the extremity of the tube, and therefore is not to be trusted. The tube should be perforated with holes at the *sides only*, and so perforated as absolutely to secure a stream flowing in the reverse (backward) direction only. 'Higginson's syphon syringe with reverse current' is what should be asked for. These syringes may be obtained of all respectable chemists or druggists, and their price is from 3s. 6d. to 5s. each. Instead of a solution of alum or of sulphate of zinc being used, in the manner mentioned in the text, a dessert spoonful of a powder—composed of sulpho-carbolate of zinc, and dried sulphate of zinc, of each 1 ounce, alum 4 ounces—is recommended. Care must be taken that these drugs be reduced to a *perfectly fine powder*. The better plan is to dissolve the quantity of the powder just named in a few ounces of boiling water to ensure its perfect solution, to pour this solution when cool in a bottle, and keep it ready for use, adding the solution to a pint of tepid, or in hot weather cold, water at the time of using the syringe, and this is the quantity to be used on each occasion. As a matter of caution the solution must be kept from the reach of children or curious persons, and it is wise to label the bottle in which the solution is kept, '*Poison*'."

Dr. Palfrey informed me that in his own practice he continually recommended the use of this check to married women, and that it had been very largely and very successfully adopted.

The solution of quinine with twenty grains to a pint of water may be used with the syringe instead of the solution of alum, of sulphate of zinc, or of Dr. Palfrey's powder. But there is much uncertainty attending the use of all these injections. If the spermatozoa have entered the womb before the injection is used, conception may occur, and though many women have found this check satisfactory, there are also many failures marked against it. There are also many obvious disadvantages attending its use.

There are two other checks which are very widely used, but which cannot be regarded as so satisfactory as those which depend on closing the entrance to the womb. In France the check most generally used is that of withdrawal, but many doctors regard this action on the part of the man as injurious to the nervous system. The use of a sheath by the man is also common.

Mr. Montagu Cookson, in the essay before mentioned, says that the family may be limited by "obedience to natural laws which all may discover and verify if they will". The "natural laws" to which Mr. Cookson refers, would be, we imagine, the results of observation on the comparative fertility of women at some periods over others. It is well known that the menstrual discharge, or the Catamenia, recurs in normal cases at monthly intervals, during the whole of the fertile period of female life; a woman does not bear children before menstruation has commenced, nor after it has ceased. There are cases on record where women have borne children but have never menstruated, but these are rare exceptions to the general rule; menstruation is the sign of capability of conception as its cessation is the sign of future disability to conceive. Recent investigators have collected many cases in which "the menstrual period was evidently connected with the maturation and discharge of ova" (Carpenter). "The essential part of the female generative system," says Dr. Carpenter, "is that in which the ova (eggs) are prepared. . . . . In the higher animals, as in the human female, the substance of the ovarium is firm and compact. . . . . As development proceeds the cells. . . . . multiply, and single cells or groups of cells, round, ovoid, or tubular, come to be enclosed in the tissue of the ovary by delicate vascular processes which shoot forth from the stroma. These cells constitute the primordial ova." These ova gradually mature, and are then discharged from the ovary and pass into the uterus, and on the fertilisation of one of them conception depends. Dr. Kirke writes: "It has long been known that in the so-called oviparous animals the separation of ova from the ovary may take place independently of impregnation by the male, or even of sexual union. And it is now established that a like maturation and discharge of ova, independently of coition, occurs in mammalia, the periods at which the matured ova are separated from the ovaries and received into the Follopian tubes being indicated in the lower mammalia by the phænomena of *heat* or *rut*; in the human female by the phænomena of *menstruation*. . . . . It may therefore, be concluded that the two states, heat and menstruation, are analogous, and that the essential accompaniment of both is the maturation and extrusion of ova." Seeing, then, that the ova are discharged at the menstrual period, and that conception depends on the fertilisation of the ova by the male, it is obvious that conception will most readily take place immediately before or after menstruation. "It is quite certain that there is a greater aptitude for conception immediately before and after that epoch than there is at any intermediate period" (Carpenter). A woman "is more apt to conceive soon after menstruation than at any other time" (Chavasse). So much is this fact recognised by the medical profession, that in cases of sterility a husband is often recommended only to visit his wife immediately after the cessation of the Catemenia. Since women conceive more easily at this period, the avoidance of sexual intercourse during the few days before and after menstruation has been recommended as a preventive check. Dr. Tyler Smith writes. "In the middle of the interval between the periods, there is little chance of impregnation taking place. The same kind of knowledge is of use, by way of caution, to women who menstruate during lactation, in whom there is a great aptitude to conceive; pregnancy, under such circumstances, would be injurious to the health of the fœtus, the child at the breast, and the mother herself, and therefore should be avoided, if possible." The most serious objection to reliance on this check is that it is not certain. M. Raciborski says that only six or seven per cent. of conceptions take place during this interval, but the six or seven exceptions to the general rule prevent recommendation of the check as thoroughly reliable; we can scarcely say more than that women are far less likely to conceive midway between the menstrual periods than either immediately before or after them.

There is a preventive check attempted by many poor women which is most detrimental to health, and should therefore never be employed, namely the too-long persistence in nursing one baby, in the hope of thereby preventing the conception of another. *Nursing does not prevent conception.* A child should not be nursed, according to Dr. Chavasse, for longer than nine months; and he quotes Dr. Farr, as follows: "It is generally recognised that the healthiest children are those weaned at nine months complete. Prolonged nursing hurts both child and mother: in the child, causing a tendency to brain disease, probably through disordered digestion and nutrition; in the mother, causing a strong tendency to deafness and blindness." Dr. Chavasse adds: "If he be suckled after he be twelve months old, he is generally pale, flabby, unhealthy, and rickety; and the mother usually nervous, emaciated, and hysterical . . . . A child nursed beyond twelve months is very apt, if he should live, to be knock-kneed, and bow-legged, and weak-ankled, to be narrow-chested, and chicken-breasted." If pregnancy occur, and the mother be nursing, the consequences affect alike the mother, the babe, and the unborn child. To nurse under these circumstances, says Dr. Chavasse, "is highly improper, and it not only injures her own health, and may bring on a miscarriage, but it is also prejudicial to her babe, and may produce delicacy of constitution from which he might never recover".

Another class of checks is punishable by law, *i.e.*, the procuring of abortion. Various drugs are taken by women with this intent, and too often their use results in death, or in dangerous sickness. Dr. Fleetwood Churchill gives various methods of inducing labor prematurely, and argues, justly, that where the delivery of a living child at the full term is impossible, it is better to bring on labor than be compelled to perform later either craniotomy or the Cæsarian section. But he goes further: "There are cases where the distortion [of the pelvis] is so great as to render the passage of a seven months' child impossible, and others still worse, where no reduction of the viable child's bulk will enable it to pass. I do not see why abortion should not be induced at an early stage in such cases." And Dr. Churchill quotes Mr. Ingleby as saying: "Premature labor may with great propriety be proposed on pregnancy recurring, assuming the delivery of a living child at term to have already proved impracticable". If there is a chance for the child's life, this is sound advice, but if the delivery of a living child has been proved to be impossible, surely the prevention of conception is far better than the procuring of abortion. The destruction of the fœtus is destruction of life, and it is immoral, where a woman cannot bear a living child, that she should conceive at all.

CHAPTER IV.

OBJECTIONS CONSIDERED.

Many people, perfectly good-hearted, but somewhat narrow-minded, object strongly to the idea of conjugal prudence, and regard scientific checks to population as "a violation of nature's laws, and a frustration of nature's ends". Such people, a hundred years ago, would have applauded the priest who objected to lightning conductors as being an interference with the bolts of Deity; they exist in every age, the rejoicers over past successes, and the timid disapprovers of new discoveries. Let us analyse the argument. "A violation of nature's laws"; this objection is couched in somewhat unscientific phrase;

nature's "laws" are but the observed sequences of events; man cannot violate them; he may disregard them, and suffer in consequence; he may observe them, and regulate his conduct so as to be in harmony with them. Man's prerogative is that by the use of his reason he is able to study nature outside himself, and by observation may so control nature as to make her add to his happiness instead of bringing him misery. To limit the family is no more a violation of nature's laws than to preserve the sick by medical skill; the restriction of the birth-rate does not violate nature's laws more than does the restriction of the death-rate. Science strives to diminish the positive checks; science should also discover the best preventive checks. "The frustration of nature's ends." Why should we worship nature's ends? Nature flings lightning at our houses; we frustrate her ends by the lightning conductor. Nature divides us by seas and by rivers; we frustrate her ends by sailing over the seas and by bridging the rivers. Nature sends typhus fever and ague to slay us; we frustrate her ends by purifying the air and by draining the marshes. Oh! it is answered, you only do this by using other natural powers. Yes, we answer, and we only teach conjugal prudence by balancing one natural force against another. Such study of nature, and such balancing of natural forces, is civilisation.

It is next objected that preventive checks are "unnatural" and "immoral". "Unnatural" they are not: for the human brain is nature's highest product, and all improvements on irrational nature are most purely natural: preventive checks are no more unnatural than every other custom of civilisation. Raw meat, nakedness, living in caves, these are the *irrational* natural habits; cooked food, clothes, houses, these are the *rational* natural customs. Production of offspring recklessly, carelessly, lustfully, this is irrational nature, and every brute can here outdo us; production of offspring with forethought, earnestness, providence, this is rational nature, where man stands alone. But "immoral". What is morality? It is the greatest good of the greatest number. It is immoral to give life where you cannot support it. It is immoral to bring children into the world when you cannot clothe, feed, and educate them. It is immoral to crowd new life into already over-crowded houses, and to give birth to children wholesale, who never have a chance of healthy life. Conjugal prudence is most highly moral, and "those who endeavor to vilify and degrade these means in the eyes of the public, and who speak of them as 'immoral' and 'disgusting', are little aware of the moral responsibility they incur thereby. As already shown, to reject preventive intercourse is in reality to choose the other three true population checks—poverty, prostitution, and celibacy. So far from meriting reprobation, the endeavor to spread the knowledge of the preventive methods, of the great law of nature which renders them necessary, is in my opinion the very greatest service which can at present be done to mankind" (Elements of Social Science").

But the knowledge of these scientific checks would, it is argued, make vice bolder, and would increase unchastity among women by making it safe. Suppose that this were so, it might save some broken hearts and some deserted children; men ruin women and go scatheless, and then bitterly object that their victims escape something of public shame. And if so, are all to suffer, so that one or two already corrupt in heart may be preserved from becoming corrupt in act? Are mothers to die slowly that impure women may be held back, and wives to be sacrificed, that the unchaste may be curbed? As well say that no knives must be used because throats may be cut with them; no matches sold because incendiarism may result from them; no pistols allowed because murders may be committed by them. Blank ignorance has some advantages in the way of safety, and if all men's eyes were put out none would ever be tempted to seduce a woman for her beauty. Let us bring for our women the veil to cover and the eunuch to guard, and so be at least consistent in our folly and our distrust! But this knowledge would *not* increase unchastity; the women who could thus use it would be solely those who only lack opportunity, not will, to go astray; the means suggested all imply deliberation and forethought. Are these generally the handmaids of unchastity? English women are not yet sunk so low that they preserve their loyalty to one only from fear of the possible consequences of disloyalty; their purity, their pride, their honor, their womanhood, these are the guardians of their virtue, and never from English women's heart will fade the maiden and matronly dignity which makes them shield their love from all taint of impurity, and bid them only surrender themselves where the surrender of heart and of pledged faith have led the way. Shame on those who slander England's wives and maidens with the foul thoughts that can only spring from the minds and lips of the profligate!

Another class of objectors appears—those who argue that there is no need to limit the population, at any rate for a long while to come. Some of these say that there is food enough in the world for all, and point out that the valley of the Mississippi would grow corn enough to feed the present population of the globe. They forget that the *available* means of subsistence are those with which we have to deal. Corn in Nebraska and starving mouths in Lancashire are not much use to each other. When the cost of carriage exceeds the money-power of the would-be buyer, the corn-fields might be in the moon for all the good they are to him. If means can be discovered of bringing corn and mouths together, well and good; but until they are discovered undue production of mouths here is unwise, because their owners will starve while the corn is still on the other side of the sea.

But if the corn can't be brought to the mouths, may not the mouths go to the corn? Why not emigrate? Because emigration is impracticable to the extent needed for the relief of the labor market. Emigration caused by starvation pressure is not a healthy outlet for labor. Men with £300 or £400 of capital may find more profitable investment for it in the West in America, or in our colonies, than at home; but their outgoing will not much relieve the labor market. Emigration for penniless agricultural laborers and for artisans means only starvation abroad instead of at home. And it is starvation under worse conditions than they had left in the mother-country. They have to face vicissitudes of climate for which they are utterly unprepared, extremes of heat and of cold which try even vigorous constitutions, and simply kill off underfed, half-clothed, and ill-housed new comers. Nor is work always to be had in the New World. No better proof of the foolishness of emigration to the United States can be given than the fact that at the present time contractors in England are in treaty with American workmen with the object of bringing them over here. Unskilled labor does not improve its chances by going abroad. Nor is skilled labor in a better position, for here the German emigrant undersells the British; he can live harder and cheaper, and has had a better technical education than has fallen to the lot of his British rival. One great evil connected with emigration is the disproportion it causes between men and women both in the old country and in the new, those who emigrate being chiefly males. Nor must it be forgotten that when England colonised most, her population was far smaller than it is at the present time. Physical vigor is necessary for successful colonising, and the physical vigor of our laboring poor deteriorates under their present conditions. As the Canadian roughly said at the meeting of the British Association at Plymouth; "The colonies don't want the children of your rickety paupers". Colonisation needs the pick of a nation, if it is to succeed, not the poor who are driven from home in search of the necessaries of life. John Stuart Mill points out how inadequate emigration is as a continued relief to population, useful as it is as a sudden effort to lighten pressure. He remarks that the great distance of the fields of emigration prevents them from being a sufficient outlet for surplus laborers; "it still remains to be shown by experience," he says, "whether a permanent stream of emigration can be kept up sufficient to take off, as in America, all that portion of the annual increase (when proceeding at its greatest rapidity) which being in excess of the progress made during the same short period in the arts of life, tends to render living more difficult for every averagely situated individual in the community. And unless this can be done, emigration cannot, even in an economical point of view, dispense with the necessity of checks to population." 1,173 infants are born in the United Kingdom every day, and to equalise matters about 1,000 emigrants should leave our shores daily. Careful calculations are sometimes entered into by anti-Malthusians as to the acreage of Great Britain as compared with its population, and it is said that the land would support many more than the present number of inhabitants; quite so; there is a very large quantity of land used for deer, game, and pleasure, that, if put under cultivation, would enormously increase the food-supply. But to know this does not remedy the pressing and immediate evils of over-large families; what service is it to the family crowded into a St. Giles' cellar to tell them that there are large uninhabited tracts of land in Perthshire? In the first place they can't get to them, and if they could, they would be taken up for trespassing. Such information is but mockery. By all means let Parliament give power to the County

Councils to at once take over all uncultivated lands, and let it then proceed to the total abolition of private land-owning; but meanwhile let a woman with five children refuse to introduce a sixth into the narrow home, and the husband will be none the worse agitator for social change because he has not one more child to feed out of his scanty wage.

An extraordinary confusion exists in some minds between preventive checks and infanticide. People speak as though prevention were the same as destruction. But no life is destroyed by the prevention of conception, any more than by abstention from marriage; if it is infanticide for every man and woman not to produce as many children as possible during the fertile period of life, if every person in a state of celibacy commits infanticide because of the potential life he prevents, then, of course, the prevention of conception by married persons is also infanticide; the two things are on exactly the same level. Before conception no life exists to be destroyed; the seminal fluid is simply a secretion of the body; its fertilising power is not a living thing, the non-use of which destroys life; the spermatozoa, the active fertilising agents, are not living existences, and "they have been erroneously considered as proper animalculæ" (Carpenter). The living being does not exist until the male and female elements are united, and if this is prevented, either by abstention from intercourse among the unmarried, or by preventive intercourse among the married, life is not destroyed, because the life is not yet in existence.

Mr. Darwin puts forward an argument against scientific checks which must not be omitted here; he says: "The enhancement of the welfare of mankind is a most intricate problem; all ought to refrain from marriage who cannot avoid abject poverty for their children, for poverty is not only a great evil, but tends to its own increase by leading to recklessness in marriage. On the other hand, as Mr. Galton has remarked, if the prudent avoid marriage, whilst the reckless marry, the inferior members tend to supplant the better members of society. Man, like every other animal, has no doubt advanced to his present high condition through a struggle for existence, consequent on his rapid multiplication, and if he is to advance still higher it is to be feared that he must remain subject to a severe struggle; otherwise he would sink into indolence, and the more gifted men would not be more successful in the battle of life than the less gifted. Hence our natural rate of increase, though leading to many and obvious evils, must not be greatly diminished by any means."

If the struggle for existence among mankind were waged under the same conditions as among animals, then Mr. Darwin's argument would have great force, terrible as would be the amount of human misery caused by it. Then the strongest, cleverest, craftiest, would survive, and would transmit their qualities to their offspring. But Mr. Darwin forgets that men have qualities which the brutes have not, such as compassion, justice, respect for the rights of others —and all these, man's highest virtues, are absolutely incompatible with the brute struggle for existence. Where the lion would leave his parents to starve, man would feed his; where the stag would kill the sickly one, man would carry him to the hospital and nurse him back to health. The feeble, the deformed, the helpless, are killed out in brute nature; in human nature they are guarded, tended, nourished, and they hand on to their offspring their own disabilities. Scientific checks to population would just do for man what the struggle for existence does for the brutes; they enable man to control the production of new human beings; those who suffer from hereditary diseases, who have consumption or insanity in the family, might marry, if they so wished, but would preserve the race from the deterioration which results from propagating disease. The whole British race would gain in vigor, in health, in longevity, in beauty, if only healthy parents gave birth to children. At present there is many a sickly family, because sickly persons marry; they revolt against forbiddance of marriage, celibacy being unnatural, and they are taught that "the natural consequences of marriage" must follow. Let them understand that one set of "consequences" results naturally from one set of conditions, another set from different conditions, and let them know that *laisser aller* in marriage is no wiser than in other paths of life.

During the last few years the exaggerations of Neo-Malthusians, as though the application of the Law of Population would suffice to banish *national* poverty, has led to an exaggeration on the Socialist side, as though poverty could be avoided without the application of the law. It is argued that the wage-fund theory, on which was based the simple view that wages rose and fell exactly according to the number of laborers seeking employment, has been proved to be false. This is so: the wage-fund theory is not now held by competent economists. John Stuart Mill, after saying that he had himself accepted the theory without the necessary qualifications and limitations, says: "There is supposed to be, at any given instant a mine of wealth, which is unconditionally devoted to the payment of wages of labor. . . More than that amount it is assumed that the wages-receiving class cannot possibly divide among them; that amount, and no less, they cannot but obtain. So that, the sum to be divided being fixed, the wages of each depend solely on the divisor, the number of participants. In this doctrine it is by implication affirmed, that the demand for labor not only increases with the cheapness, but increases in exact proportion to it, the same aggregate sum being paid for labor, whatever its price may be. But is this a true representation of the matter of fact? Does the employer require more labor, or do fresh employers of labor make their appearance, merely because it can be bought cheaper? Assuredly no." (Dissertations and Discussions, vol. iv., p. 43.) A practical proof also of the falseness of the theory may be seen in the condition of the French workers, strictly as they limit their families, wherever they are divorced from the soil. The French artisan, or miner, with his family of two, works for lower wage and longer hours than the English artisan, with his family of six. So long as the means of production are owned by one class and used by another, the one that uses them will obtain only subsistence wage; and if his average expenses fall, his average wage will fall with them. If the French peasantry had not seized the land, in addition to limiting their families, they would be no better off than the French urban population. Besides, no limitation of the family could lead to a general rise of wages in any case, unless immigration were prevented; on any shewing, nothing could be gained by checking home-grown population, if the labor market is to be swamped by foreigners. Even prevention of immigration would not suffice: if capitalists found wages rising here, they would—as many are now doing—manufacture abroad instead of in England, and fill the market with cheap foreign goods. Protection would be the next step necessary to lessen national poverty, and that would be as futile as the rest. So far, the Socialists are right; the application of the Law of Population will not lift a nation, as such, out of poverty. The workers must control the material whereon they work, the tools wherewith they work, and the finished product of their work, ere poverty can disappear. Nay more: it is very likely that the drones got rid of, shooting grounds turned into pasture and arable lands, uncultivated land fully cultivated, our islands might support in comfort a far larger population than they now support in poverty. A certain density of population is necessary for full productivity in manufactures, and division of labor requires many laborers. None the less, is it obvious, that granted all this, the comfort of the people, and ultimately their safety from poverty, must depend on the proportion between the mouths that consume without producing and the arms that produce. Under all social conditions disregard of the Law of Population must finally result in catastrophe.

More immediately vital is it for Socialists to remember that, with a fixed wage, the large or small family means all the difference between privation and fair comfort. The man with 30s. a week, or with £100 a year, will be always struggling with six children, while he can scrape along with two. And so long as the present system lasts, he has no right to bring six children into the world to starve on means barely sufficient to maintain two. If he does so, he not only commits a crime against them, but he delays social change; with his brain always racked with anxiety, he cannot do his duty in spreading the light; half-fed, miserably-clothed children cannot grow up into citizens of sound mind and sound body, fit for the Social Commonwealth. While we work with all our might for social regeneration, it is of vital importance to *at once* adopt the principle of limiting the family. The huge mass of helpless non-combatants handicaps the workers in their struggle with the capitalists; and, as the children grow up, they swell the vast "fringe" of unorganised surplus labor, by the aid of which the capitalist can almost always crush the workmen in a prolonged strike. The Trade Unions know the importance of limiting the number of apprentices in a skilled trade, but they seem to miss the application of their practice in society, and recklessly crowd the competitors for entrance into all trades, competitors who, shut out from each, must swell the number of the unskilled, the most hopeless class of all.

Earnestly, then, I plead to my Socialist comrades not to oppose the immediate palliative while striving after the more distant good. We shall serve Socialism the better, and not the worse, by lightening the strain on our at present meagre resources. Against the foes with whom we combat, we must use every weapon on which we can lay our hands, and a very useful weapon is the limitation of the family, by which we deprive the capitalist of that crowded labor-market by which he partly makes his gains. If every family were limited, and every worker in his or her Trade Union, the Army of Labor would be in better case for the combat. Ultimate victory is sure, but the time of the victory depends on our prudence as well as on our courage. We work for the redemption of the poor, for the salvation of the wretched; the cause of the people is the sacredest of all causes, and is the one which is the most certain to triumph, however sharp may be the struggle for the victory.

MARRIAGE,

AS IT WAS, AS IT IS, AND AS IT SHOULD BE:

A Plea for Reform.

BY

ANNIE BESANT.

[SECOND EDITION.]

LONDON:
FREETHOUGHT PUBLISHING COMPANY,
28, STONECUTTER STREET, E.C.
1882.

LONDON:
PRINTED BY ANNIE BESANT AND CHARLES BRADLAUGH,
28, STONECUTTER STREET, E.C.

MARRIAGE:

AS IT WAS, AS IT IS, AND AS IT SHOULD BE.

"Either all human beings have equal rights, or none have any."—CONDORCET.

THE recognition of human rights may be said to be of modern growth, and even yet they are but very imperfectly understood. Liberty used to be regarded as a privilege bestowed, instead of as an inherent right; rights of classes have often been claimed: right to rule, right to tax, right to punish, all these have been argued for and maintained by force; but these are not rights, they are only wrongs veiled as legal rights. Jean Jacques Rousseau struck a new note when he cried: "Men are born free;" free by birthright was a new thought, when declared as a universal inheritance, and this "gospel of Jean Jacques Rousseau" dawned on the world as the sun-rising of a glorious day—a day of human liberty, unrestrained by class. In 1789 the doctrine of the "Rights of Man" received its first European sanction by law; in the August of that year the National Assembly of France proclaimed: "Men are born, and remain, free and equal in rights . . . . The aim of political association is the conservation of the natural and imprescriptible rights of man; these rights are—liberty, property, safety, and resistance of tyranny." During savage and semi-civilised ages these "imprescriptible rights" are never dreamed of as existing; brute force is king; might is the only right, and the strong arm is the only argument whose logic meets with general recognition. In warlike tribes fair equality is found, and the chief is only *primus inter pares;* but when the nomadic tribe settles down into an agricultural community, when the habit of bearing arms ceases to be universal, when wealth begins to accumulate, and the village or town offers attractions for pillage, then strength becomes at once a terror and a possible defence. The weak obey some powerful neighbour partly because they cannot resist, and partly because they desire, by their submission, to gain a strong protection against their enemies. They submit to the exactions of one that they may be shielded from the tyranny of many, and yield up their natural liberty to some extent to preserve themselves from being entirely enslaved. Very slowly do they learn that the union of many individually feeble is stronger than a few powerful, isolated tyrants, and gradually law takes the place of despotic will; gradually the feeling of self-respect, of independence, of love of liberty, grows, until at last man claims freedom as of right, and denies the authority of any to rule him without his own consent.

Thus the Rights of Man have become an accepted doctrine, but, unfortunately, they are only rights of *man*, in the exclusive sense of the word. They are sexual, and not human rights, and until they become human rights, society will never rest on a sure, because just, foundation. Women, as well as men, "are born and remain free and equal in rights:" women, as well as men, have "natural and imprescriptible rights;" for women, as well as for men, "these rights are—liberty, property, safety, and resistance of tyranny." Of these rights only crime should deprive them, just as by crime men also are deprived of them; to deny these rights to women, is either to deny them to humanity *quâ* humanity, or to deny that women form a part of humanity; if women's rights are denied, men's rights have no logical basis, no claim to respect; then tyranny ceases to be a crime, slavery is no longer a scandal; "either all human beings have equal rights, or none have any."

Naturally, in the savage state, women shared the fate of the physically weak, not only because, as a rule, they are smaller-framed and less muscular than their male comrades, but also because the bearing and suckling of children is a drain on their physical resources from which men are exempt. Hence she has suffered from "the right of the strongest," even more than has man, and her exclusion from all political life has prevented the redressal which man has wrought out for himself; while claiming freedom for himself he has not loosened her chains, and while striking down his own tyrants, he has maintained his personal tyranny in the home. Nor has this generally been done by deliberate intention: it is rather the survival of the old system, which has only been abolished so slowly as regards men. Mrs. Mill writes: "That those who were physically weaker should have been made legally inferior, is quite conformable to the mode in which the world has been governed. Until very lately, the rule of physical strength was the general law of human affairs. Throughout history, the nations, races, classes, which found themselves strongest, either in muscles, in riches, or in military discipline, have conquered and held in subjection the rest. If, even in the most improved nations, the law of the sword is at last discountenanced as unworthy, it is only since the calumniated eighteenth century. Wars of conquest have only ceased since democratic revolutions began. The world is very young, and has only just begun to cast off injustice. It is only now getting rid of negro slavery. It is only now getting rid of monarchical despotism. It is only now getting rid of hereditary feudal nobility. It is only now getting rid of disabilities on the ground of religion. It is only beginning to treat any *men* as citizens, except the rich and a favoured portion of the middle class. Can we wonder that it has not yet done as much for women?" ("Enfranchisement of Women," Mrs. Mill. In J. S. Mill's "Discussions and Dissertations," Vol. II., page 421.) The difference between men and women in all civil rights is, however, with few, although important, exceptions, confined to married women; *i.e.*, women in relation with men. Unmarried women of all ages suffer under comparatively few disabilities; it is marriage which brings with it the weight of injustice and of legal degradation.

In savage times marriage was a matter either of force, fraud, or purchase. Women were merchandise, by the sale of whom their male relatives profited, or they were captives in war, the spoil of the conqueror, or they were stolen away from the paternal home. In all cases, however, the possession once obtained, they became the property of the men who married them, and the husband was their "lord," their "master." In the old Hebrew books—still accounted sacred by Jews and Christians—the wife is regarded as the property of her husband. A man may "sell his daughter to be a maidservant;" *i.e.*, a concubine, as is shown by the following verse (Ex. xxi. 7), and Jacob served seven years for each of his wives, Leah and Rachel; his other two wives were his by gift, and were rather concubines than recognised wives, their children counting to their mistresses. If a Hebrew conquered his enemies, and saw "among the captives a beautiful woman, and hast a desire unto her, that thou wouldst have her to thy wife," he might take her home, and become her husband, "and she shall be thy wife" (Deut. xxi. 10-14). After the destruction of Benjamin, as related in Judges xx., it was arranged that the survivors should possess themselves of women as wives by force and fraud: "Lie in wait in the vineyards, and see and behold if the daughters of Shiloh come out to dance in dances, then come ye out of the vineyards, and catch you every man his wife.... And the children of Benjamin did so, and took their wives according to their number, of them that danced, whom they caught" (Judges xxi. 20, 21, 23). The same plan was adopted by the Romans in their earliest days, when they needed wives. Romulus invited the people of the Sabines and the neighbouring towns to see some public games, and in the midst of the show the Romans rushed in and carried off all the marriageable maidens they could lay hands on (Liddell's "History of Rome," p. 20). These instances may be objected to as legendary, but they are faithful pictures of the rough wooing of early times. Among some barbarous nations the winning of a bride is still harsher: the bridegroom rushes into the father's house knocks the maiden down, picks up her senseless body, flings it over his shoulder, and runs for his life; he is pursued by the youth of the village, pelted with stones, sticks, &c., and has to win his wife by sheer strength and swiftness. In some tribes this is a mere marriage ceremony, a survival from the time when the fight was a real one, and amongst ourselves the slipper thrown after the departing bridegroom and bride is a direct descendant of the heavier missiles thrown with deadly intent thousands of years ago by our remote ancestors. Amongst many semi-barbarous nations the wives are still bought; in some parts of Africa the wooer pays a certain number of cows for his bride; in other places, money or goods are given in exchange. The point to be noted is that the wife is literally taken by force, or bought; she is not free to choose her husband; she does not give herself to him; she is a piece of property, handed over by her original owner—her father—to her new owner—her husband—in exchange for certain solid money or money's worth; hence she becomes the property of the man who has paid for her.

In an admirable article in the *Westminster Review* for April, 1876, the following striking passage is to be found:

"As Aristotle long since remarked, among savages women and slaves hold the same rank. Women are bought primarily as slaves, to drudge and toil for their masters, whilst their function as wives is secondary and subordinate. It is more right to say of polygamous people that their slaves are also their wives, than to say that their wives are slaves. They are purchased as slaves, they work as slaves, and they live as slaves. 'The history of uncultivated nations,' it has been said, 'uniformly represents the women as in a state of abject slavery, from which they slowly emerge as civilisation advances.' In Canada a strap, a kettle, and a faggot are placed in the new bride's cabin, to indicate that it will be henceforth her duty to carry burdens, dress food, and procure wood for her husband. In Circassia it is the women who till and manure the ground, and in parts of China they follow the plough. A Moorish wife digs and sows and reaps the corn, and an Arabian wife feeds and cleans and saddles her master's horse. Indeed, the sole business of Bedouin wives is to cook and work, and perform all the menial offices connected with tent-life. . . . From the absolute power of a savage over his slaves flow all those rights over a woman from which the marital rights of our own time are the genealogical descendants. . . . A trace of it [purchase] is found in the following customs of old English law:—'The woman at the church-door was given of her father, or some other man of the next of her kin, into the hands of her husband, and he laid down gold and silver for her upon the book, as though he did buy her.'" This custom is still maintained in the Church ritual; the priest asks: "Who giveth this woman to be married to this man?" and when the man gives the ring to the priest, he gives money with it, receiving back the ring to give the woman, but the money remaining, a survival of the time when wives were literally bought.

By the old Roman laws, the married woman had no personal rights; she was but the head slave in her husband's house, absolutely subject in all things to her lord. As the Romans became civilised, these disabilities were gradually removed. It is important to remember these facts, as these are the origin of our own marriage laws, and our common law really grows out of them.

One other point must be noticed, before dealing immediately with the English marriage laws, and that is the influence exerted over them by ecclesiastical Christianity

The Old Testament expressly sanctions polygamy; but while the New Testament does not proscribe it—except in the case of bishops and deacons—ecclesiastical Christianity has generally been in favour of monogamy; at the same time, both the New Testament and the Church have insisted on the inferiority of the female sex; "the husband is the head of the wife" (Eph. v. 23); "wives, submit yourselves unto your own husbands" (Col. iii. 18); "your women . . . are commanded to be under obedience" (1 Cor. xiv. 34); "ye wives, be in subjection to your own husbands . . . even as Sara obeyed Abraham, calling him lord, whose daughters ye are as long as ye do well" (1 Pet. iii. 1, 6). The common law of England is quite in accordance with this ancient Eastern teaching, and regards men as superior to women; "Among the children of the purchaser, males take before females, or, as our male lawgivers have expressed it, the worthiest of blood shall be preferred" ("Comm. on the Laws of England," J. Stephen, 7th ed. vol. i. p. 402).

The feudal system did much, of course, to perpetuate the subjection of women, it being to the interest of the lord paramount that the fiefs should descend in the male line: in those rough ages, when wars and civil feuds were almost perpetual, it was inevitable that the sex with the biggest body and strongest sinews should have the upper hand; the pity is that English gentlemen to-day are content to allow the law to remain unaltered, when the whole face of society has changed.

Let us now turn to the disabilities imposed upon women by marriage.

Blackstone lays down, in his world-famous "Commentaries on the Laws of England," that the first of the "absolute rights of every Englishman" is "the legal and uninterrupted enjoyment of his life, his limbs, his body, his health, and his reputation" (9th ed., bk. 1, p. 129). The second right is personal liberty, and he says: "the confinement of a person in anywise is an imprisonment. So that the keeping a man against his will in a private house. . . . is an imprisonment" (Ibid, 136). The third is property, "which consists in the free use and enjoyment of all his acquisitions, without any control or diminution, save only by the laws of the land" (Ibid, 138). A subordinate right, necessary for the enforcement of the others, is "that of applying to the courts of justice for redress of injuries." I shall proceed to show that a married woman is deprived of these rights by the mere fact of her marriage.

In the first place, by marriage a woman loses her legal existence; the law does not recognize her, excepting in some few cases, when it becomes conscious of her existence in order to punish her for some crime or misdemeanour. Blackstone says—and no subsequent legislation has in any way modified his dictum: "By marriage the husband and wife are one person in law; that is, the very being or legal existence of the woman is suspended during the marriage, or at least is incorporated or consolidated into that of the husband; under whose wing, protection, and *cover*, she performs every thing; and is therefore called in our law-French a *feme covert*" (p. 442). "Husband and wife are one person in law" (Comyn's Digest, 5th ed., vol. ii., p. 208), and from this it follows that "by no conveyance at the common law could the husband give an estate to his wife;" that "a husband cannot covenant or contract with his wife," even for her own advantage, and that any prenuptial contract made with her as to money she shall enjoy for her separate use after marriage, becomes void as soon as she is married. All covenants for the wife's benefit must be made with some one else, and the husband must covenant with some other man or unmarried woman who acts as trustee for the wife. This is the fundamental wrong from which all the others flow: "'Husband and wife are one person,' and that one is the husband." The wife's body, her reputation, are no longer her own. She can gain no legal redress for injury, for the law does not recognize her existence except under cover of her husband's suit. In some cases more modern legislation has so far become conscious of her, as to protect her against her husband, and if this protection separates her from him, it leaves her the more utterly at the mercy of the world.

Various curious results flow, in criminal law, from this supposition that husband and wife are only one person. They are incompetent—except in a few special instances—to give evidence for or against each other in criminal cases; if a woman's husband be one of several defendants indicted together, the woman cannot give evidence either for or against any of them. Where the wife of an accomplice is the only person to confirm her husband's statement, the statement falls to the ground, as, in practice, confirmation thereof is required; in the case of Rex *v.* Neal (7 C. and P.

168), Justice Park said: "Confirmation by the wife is, in this case, really no confirmation at all. The wife and the accomplice must be taken as one for this purpose. The prisoners must be acquitted." They may, however, be severally called as witnesses by the prosecution and the defence, in order that they may contradict each other. Where the wife has suffered personal violence from her husband she is permitted to swear the peace against him, and in divorce suits husband and wife are both admissible as witnesses. A wife who sets fire to her husband's house may escape punishment, as in the case of Rex. *v.* March: "March and his wife had lived separate for about two years; and, previous to the act, when she applied for the candle with which it was done, she said it was to set her husband's house on fire, because she wanted to burn him to death. Upon a case reserved upon the question whether it was an offence within the 7 and 8 George IV., cap. 30, sec. 2, for a wife to set fire to her husband's house for the purpose of doing him a personal injury, the conviction was held wrong, the learned judges thinking that to constitute the offence, it was essential that there should be an intent to injure or defraud some third person, not one identified with herself" (Ibid, p. 899). Identification with one's beloved may be delightful in theory, but when, in practice, it comes to being burned at pleasure, surely the greatest stickler for the "twain being one" must feel some twinges of doubt. The identity of husband and wife is often by no means advantageous to the husband, for he thereby becomes responsible, to a great extent, for his wife's misdoings. "For slanderous words spoken by the wife, libel published by her alone, trespass, assault and battery, &c., he is liable to be so sued, whether the act was committed with or without his sanction or knowledge. . . . . And wherever the action is grounded on a tort, committed by the wife, it no way affects the necessity of joining the husband, that the parties are living apart, nor even that they are divorced *a mensâ et thoro*, or that the wife is living in adultery" (Lush's "Common Law Practice," 2nd ed., p. 156). Pleasant position for a man whose wife may have left him, to be suddenly dragged before a court of justice for some misdeed of hers, of which he may never have heard until he finds himself summoned to answer for it! A large amount of injustice arises from this absurd fiction that two are one; it sometimes injures, sometimes protects the married woman, and it often shields those who have wronged her; but whether it injure or whether it protect, it is equally vicious; it is *unjust*, and injustice is a radical injury to a community, and by destroying the reasonableness and the certainty of the law, it saps that reverence for it which is one of the safeguards of society.

Let us now take Blackstone's "rights of every Englishman," and see what rights the common law allowed to a married Englishwoman. A married woman is not protected by the law in the "uninterrupted enjoyment of" her "limbs," her "body," or her "reputation." On the contrary: "If a wife be injured in her person, or her property, she can bring no action for redress without her husband's concurrence, and in his name as well as her own" (Blackstone, p. 443). If in a railway accident a married woman has her leg broken, she cannot sue the railway company for damages; she is not a damaged *person*; in the eye of the law, she is a piece of damaged *property*, and the compensation is to be made to her owner. If she is attacked and beaten she cannot at law sue her assailant; her master suffers loss and inconvenience by the assault on his housekeeper, and his action is necessary to obtain redress. If she is libelled, she cannot protect her good name, for she is incapable by herself of maintaining an action. In fact, it is not even needful that her name should appear at all in the matter: "the husband may sue alone for loss of his wife's society by injury done to her, or for damage to her reputation" (Comyn's Digest, under "Baron and Feme"). The following curious statement of the law on this head is given in Broom's "Commentaries:" "Injuries which may be offered to a person, considered as a husband, and which are cognizable in a court of common law, are principally three: 1, abduction, or taking away a man's wife; 2, beating her; 3, indirectly causing her some personal hurt, by negligence or otherwise. 1. As to the first sort, abduction, or taking her away, this may either be by fraud and persuasion, or open violence; though the law in both cases supposes force and constraint, the wife having no power to consent, and therefore gives a remedy by action of trespass; and the husband is also entitled to recover damages in an action on the case against such as persuade and entice the wife to live separate from him without a sufficient cause. . . . 2, 3. The second and third injuries above mentioned are constituted by beating a man's wife, or otherwise ill-using her; or causing hurt to her by negligence. For a common assault upon, or battery, or imprisonment, of the wife, the law gives the usual remedy to recover damages, by action of trespass, which must be brought in the names of the husband and wife jointly: but if the beating or other maltreatment be so enormous, that thereby the husband is deprived for any time of the company and assistance of his wife, the law then gives him a separate remedy by action for this ill-usage, *per quod consortium amisit*, in which he may recover a satisfaction in damages. By a provision of the C. L. Proc. Act, 1852, s. 40, in an action by husband and wife jointly for an injury to the wife, the husband is now allowed to add a claim in his own right—as for the loss of the wife's society—or where a joint trespass and assault have been committed on the husband and his wife" (vol. iii., pp. 149, 150). So far is recognised the husband's complete claim over his wife's person, that anyone who receives a married woman into his house and gives her shelter there after having received notice from her husband that he is not to permit her to remain under his roof, actually becomes liable in damages to the husband. The husband cannot sue for damages if he has turned his wife out of doors, or if he has lost his right of control by cruelty or adultery; short of this, he may obtain damages against any friend or relative of the woman who gives her shelter. The wife has no such remedy against anyone who may induce the husband to live apart, or who may give him house-room at his own wish. The reason for the law being as we find it, is stated by Broom without the smallest compunction: "We may observe that in these relative injuries notice is only taken of the wrong done to the superior of the parties related, by the breach and dissolution of either the relation itself, or at least the advantage accruing therefrom: while the loss of the inferior by such injuries is, except where the death of a parent has been caused by negligence, unregarded. One reason for which may be, that the inferior has no kind of property in the company, care, or assistance of the superior, as the superior is held to have in that of the inferior; and therefore the inferior can, in contemplation of law, suffer no loss consequential on a wrongful act done to his superior. The wife cannot recover damages for the beating of her husband. The child has no property in his father or guardian. And the servant, whose master is disabled, does not thereby lose his maintenance or wages" (Ibid, p. 153). A man may recover damages equally for the injury done to his servant or to his wife; in both cases he loses their services, and the law recompenses him. A peculiarly disgusting phase of this claim is where a husband claims damages against a co-respondent in the divorce court; if a wife be unfaithful, the husband can not only get a divorce, but can also claim a money payment from the seducer to make up for the damage he has sustained by losing his wife's services. An unmarried girl, under age, is regarded as the property of her father, and the father may bring an action against her seducer for the loss of his daughter's services. It is not the woman who is injured, or who has any redress; it is her male owner who can recover damages for the injury done to his property.

If a wife be separated from her husband, either by deed or by judicial decree, she has no remedy for injury or for libel, unless by the doubtful plan of using her husband's name without his consent. On this injustice Lord Lyndhurst, speaking in the House of Lords in 1856, said: "A wife is separated from her husband by a decree of the Ecclesiastical Court, the reason for that decree being the husband's misconduct—his cruelty, it may be, or his adultery. From that moment the wife is almost in a state of outlawry. She may not enter into a contract, or if she do, she has no means of enforcing it. The law, so far from protecting, oppresses her. She is homeless, helpless, hopeless, and almost wholly destitute of civil rights. She is liable to all manner of injustice, whether by plot or by violence. She may be wronged in all possible ways, and her character may be mercilessly defamed; yet she has no redress. She is at the mercy of her enemies. Is that fair? Is that honest? Can it be vindicated upon any principle of justice, of mercy or of common humanity?"

A married woman loses control over her own body; it belongs to her owner, not to herself; no force, no violence, on the husband's part in conjugal relations is regarded as possible by the law; she may be suffering, ill, it matters not; force or constraint is recognised by the law as rape, in all cases save that of marriage; the law "holds it to be felony to force even a concubine or harlot" (Broom's "Commentaries," vol. iv., p. 255), but no rape can be committed by a husband on a wife; the consent given in marriage is held to cover the life, and if—as sometimes occurs—a miscarriage or premature confinement be brought on by the husband's selfish passions, no offence is committed in the eye of the law, for the wife is the husband's property, and by marriage she has lost the right of control over her own body. The English marriage law sweeps away all the tenderness, all the grace, all the generosity of love, and transforms conjugal affection into a hard and brutal legal right.

By the common law the husband has a right to inflict corporal punishment on his wife, and although this right is now much restricted, the effect of the law is seen in the brutal treatment of wives among the rougher classes, and the light—sometimes no—punishment inflicted on wife-beaters. The common law is thus given by Blackstone: "The husband also (by the old law) might give his wife moderate correction. For as he is to answer for her misbehaviour, the law thought it reasonable to entrust him with this power of restraining her, by domestic chastisement, in the same moderation that a man is allowed to correct his apprentices or children. The lower rank of people, who were always fond of the old common law, still claim and exert their ancient privilege." Blackstone grimly adds, after saying this is all for woman's protection: "So great a favourite is the female sex of the laws of England" (444 and 445). This "ancient privilege" is very commonly exercised at the present time. A man who dragged his wife out of bed (1877), and, pulling off her nightdress, roasted her in front of the fire, was punished (?) by being bound over to keep the peace for a short period. Men who knock their wives down, who dance on them, who drag them about by the hair, &c., are condemned to brief terms of imprisonment, and are then allowed to resume their marital authority, and commence a new course of ill-treatment. In dealing later with the changes I shall recommend in the marriage laws, this point will come under discussion.

Coming to the second "right," of "personal liberty," we find that a married woman has no such right. Blackstone says, as we have seen: "the confinement of a person in any wise is an imprisonment. So that the keeping a man against his will in a private house . . . is an imprisonment" (p. 136). But a husband may legally act as his wife's gaoler; "the courts of law will still permit a husband to restrain his wife of her liberty, in case of any gross misbehaviour" (Blackstone, p. 445). "If the wife squanders his estate, or goes into lewd company, he may deprive her of liberty" (Comyn's Digest, under "Baron and Feme"). Broom says that at the present time "there can be no question respecting the common-law right of a husband to restrain his wife of her personal liberty, with a view to prevent her going into society of which he disapproves, or otherwise disobeying his rightful authority; such right must not, however, be exercised unnecessarily, or with undue severity: and the moment that the wife by returning to her conjugal duties, makes restraint of her person unnecessary, such restraint becomes unlawful" (vol. i, p. 547). In the year 1877 a publican at Spilsby chained up his wife to the wall from one day to the afternoon of the following one, in order, he said, to keep her from drink; the magistrates dismissed him without punishment. It may be argued that a woman should not get drunk, go into bad company, &c. Quite so; neither should a man. But would men admit, that under similar circumstances, a wife should have legal power to deprive her husband of liberty? If not, there is no reason in justice why the husband should be permitted to exercise it. Offences known to the law should be punished by the law, and by the law alone; offences which the law cannot touch should entail no punishment on an adult at the hands of a private individual. Public disapproval may brand them, but no personal chastisement should be inflicted by arbitrary and irresponsible power.

The third right, of "property," has also no existence for married women. Unmarried women have here no ground for complaint: "A *feme sole,* before her marriage, may do all acts for disposition, etc., of her lands or goods which any man in the same circumstances may do" (Comyn's Digest, under "Baron and Feme"). The disabilities which affect women as women do not touch property; a *feme sole* may own real or personal estate, buy, sell, give, contract, sue, and be sued, just as though she were of the "worthier blood;" it is marriage that, like felony and insanity, destroys her capability as proprietor. According to the common law—with which we will deal first—the following results accrued from marriage:—

"Whatever personal property belonged to the wife before marriage, is by marriage absolutely vested in the husband. . . . in chattel interests, the sole and absolute property vests in the husband, to be disposed of at his pleasure, if he chooses to take possession of them" (Blackstone, book ii. 443). If he takes possession, they do not, at his death, revert to the wife, but go to his heirs or to anyone he chooses by will. "If a woman be seized of an estate of inheritance, and marries, her husband shall be seized of in her right" (Comyn's Digest, under "Baron and Feme"). If a woman own land in her own right, all rents and profits are not hers, but her husband's; even arrears of rents due before coverture become his; he may make a lease of her land, commencing after his own death, and she is barred, although she survive him; he may dispose of his wife's interest; it may be forfeited by his crime, seized for his debt; she only regains it if she survives him and he has not disposed of it. If a woman, before marriage, lets her land on a lease, the rental, after marriage, becomes her husband's, and her receipt is not a good discharge. If a wife grants a rent-charge out of her own lands (or, rather, what should be her own) without the husband's consent, it is void. All personal goods that "the wife has in possession in her own right, are vested in her husband by the marriage" (Ibid); gifts to her become his; if he sues for a debt due to his wife, and recovers it, it is his; if a legacy be left her, it goes to him; after his death, all that was her personal property originally, goes to his executors and administrators, and does not revert to her; so absolutely is all she may become possessed of his by law that if, after a divorce *a mensâ et thoro*, the wife should sue another woman for adultery with her husband, and should be awarded her costs, the husband can release the woman from payment.

If a woman own land and lease it, then if, during marriage, the husband reduce it into possession, "as where rent accruing on a lease granted by the wife *dum sola* is received by a person appointed for that purpose during the husband's life," under such circumstances the husband's "executors, not his widow, must sue the agent" (Lush's "Common Law Practice," 2nd. ed., p. 27). In a case where "certain leasehold property was conveyed to trustees upon trust to permit the wife to receive the rents thereof to her sole and separate use, and she after marriage deposited with her trustees part of such rents and died; it was held that her husband might recover the same in an action in his own right. Such money, so deposited, was not a *chose in action* belonging to the wife, but money belonging to the husband, the trust having been discharged in the payment of the rents to the wife" (Ibid, p. 97). Marriage, to a man, is regarded as a kind of lucrative business: "The next method of acquiring property in goods and chattels is by marriage; whereby those chattels, which belonged formerly to the wife, are by act of law vested in the husband, with the same degree of property, and with the same powers, as the wife, when sole, had over them . . . A distinction is taken between chattels real and chattels personal, and of chattels personal, whether in possession or reversion, or in action. A chattel real vests in the husband, not absolutely, but *sub modo.* As, in case of a lease for years, the husband shall receive all the rents and profits of it, and may, if he pleases, sell, surrender, or dispose of it during the coverture; if he be outlawed or attainted, it shall be forfeited to the king; it is liable to execution for his debts; and if he survives his wife, it is to all intents and purposes his own. Yet, if he has made no disposition thereof in his lifetime, and dies before his wife, he cannot dispose of it by will: for, the husband having made no alteration in the property during his life, it never was transferred from the wife; but after his death she shall remain in her ancient possession, and it shall not go to his executors. If, however, the wife die in the husband's lifetime, the chattel real survives to him. As to chattels personal (or choses) in action, as debts upon bonds, contracts, and the like, these the husband may have if he pleases; that is, if he reduces them into possession by receiving or recovering them at law. And upon such receipt or recovery they are absolutely and entirely his own; and shall go to his executors or administrators, or as he shall bequeath them by will, and shall not revest in the wife. But, if he dies before he has recovered or reduced them into possession, so that, at his death, they still continue choses in action, they shall survive to the wife; for the husband never exerted the power he had of obtaining an exclusive property in them. If the wife die before the husband has reduced choses in action into possession, he does not become entitled by survivorship; nevertheless, he may, by becoming her administrator, gain a title. Chattels in possession, such as ready money and the like, vest absolutely in the husband, and he may deal with them, either whilst living, or by his will, as he pleases. Where the interest of the wife is reversionary, the husband's power is but small; unless it falls into possession during the marriage, his contracts or engagements do not bind it" ("Comm. on the Laws of England," Broom and Hadley, vol. ii., pp. 618, 619). So highly does the law value the claims of a husband that it recognizes them as existing even before marriage; for if a woman who has contracted an engagement to marry dispose of her property privately, settle it on herself, or on her children, without the cognizance of the man to whom she is engaged, such settlement or disposition may be set aside by the husband as a fraud.

So cruel, as regards property, was felt to be the action of the common law, that the wealthy devised means to escape from it, and women of property were protected on their marriage by "marriage settlements," whereby they were contracted out of the law. A woman's property was by this means, "settled on herself;" it was necessary to treat her as incapable, so her property was not in her own power but was vested in trustees for her separate use; thus the principal, or the estate, was protected, but the whole interest or rental, as before, could be taken by the husband the moment it was received by the wife; her signature became necessary to draw it, but the moment it came into her possession it ceased to be hers. The next step was an attempt to protect women's money in their own hands; terrible cases of wrong were continually arising: men who deserted their wives, and left them to maintain the burden of a family, came back after the wife had accumulated a little property, sold the furniture, pocketed the proceeds, and departed, leaving the wife to recommence her labours. Orders of protection were given by magistrates, but these were not found sufficient. At last, parliamentary interference was called for with an urgency that could no longer be resisted, and a Bill to amend the laws relating to married women's property was introduced into the House of Commons. How sore was the need of such amendment may be seen from the following extracts :—

Mr. Russell Gurney, in moving (April 14, 1869) the second reading of the Bill, observed : "It is now proposed that, for the first time in our history, the property of one half of the married people of this country should receive the protection of the law. Up to this time the property of a wife has had no protection from the law, or rather, he should say, in the eye of the law it has had no existence. From the moment of her marriage the wife, in fact, possesses no property; whatever she may up to that time have possessed, by the very act of marriage passes from her, and any gift or bequest made to her becomes at once the property of the husband. Nay, even that which one might suppose to be her inalienable right, the fruit of her mental or bodily toil, is denied her. She may be gifted with powers which enable her to earn an ample fortune, but the moment it is earned, it is not hers, it is her husband's. In fact, from the time of her entering into what is described as an honourable estate, the law pronounces her unfit to hold any property whatever."

Mr. Jessel (now Master of the Rolls) in seconding the motion, in the course of an able and impassioned speech, said: "The existing law is a relic of slavery, and the House is now asked to abolish the last remains of slavery in England. In considering what ought to be the nature of the law, we cannot deny that no one should be deprived of the power of disposition, unless on proof of unfitness to exercise that power; and it is not intelligible on what principle a woman should be considered incapable of contracting immediately after she has, with the sanction of the law, entered into the most important contract conceivable. The slavery laws of antiquity are the origin of the common law on this subject. The Roman law originally regarded the position of a wife as similar to that of a daughter who had no property, and might be sold into slavery at the will of her father. When the Roman law became that of a civilised people, the position of the wife was altogether changed. . . . The ancient Germans—from whom our law is derived—put the woman into the power of her husband in the same sense as the ancient Roman law did. She became his slave. The law of slavery—whether Roman or English—for we once had slaves and slave-laws in England—gave to the master of a slave the two important rights of flogging and imprisoning him. A slave could not possess property of his own, and could not make contracts except for his master's benefit, and the master alone could sue for an injury to the slave; while the only liability of the master was that he must not let his slave starve. This is exactly the position of the wife under the English law; the husband has the right of flogging and imprisoning her, as may be seen by those who read Blackstone's chapter on the relations of husband and wife. She cannot possess property—she cannot contract, except it is as his agent; and he alone can sue if she is libelled or suffers a personal injury; while all the husband is compellable to do for her is to pay for necessaries. It is astonishing that a law founded on such principles should have survived to the nineteenth century."

A quotation from a later debate finds its fit place here: Mr. Hinde Palmer, in moving (February 19, 1873) the second reading of the Married Woman's Property Act

(1870) Amendment Bill, pointed out that the common law was, that by marriage "the whole of a woman's personal property was immediately vested in her husband, and placed entirely at his disposal. By contracting marriage, a woman forfeited all her property. In 1868, the Chancellor of the Exchequer, Mr. Lowe, said: 'Show me what crime there is in matrimony that it should be visited by the same punishment as high treason—namely, confiscation, for that is really the fact.' Mr. Mill, too, speaking on that question, said that a large portion of the inhabitants of this country were in the anomalous position of having imposed on them, without having done anything to deserve it, what we inflicted on the worst criminals as a penalty: like felons, they were incapable of holding property."

Some great and beneficial changes were made by the Acts of 1870 and 1873, although much yet remains to be done. By the Act of 1870, the wages and earnings of married women were protected; they were made capable of depositing money in the savings' banks in their own names; they might hold property in the Funds in their own names, and have the dividends paid to them; they might hold fully-paid up shares, or stock, to which no liability was attached; property in societies might be retained by them; money coming to a married woman as the next-of-kin, or one of the next-of-kin to an intestate, or by deed or will, was made her own, provided that such money did not exceed £200; the rents and profits of freehold, copyhold, or customary-hold property inherited by a married woman were to be her own; a married woman might insure her own or her husband's life; might, under some circumstances, maintain an action in her own name; married women were made liable for the maintenance of their husbands and children. The Act of 1873 relates entirely to the recovery of debts contracted by the woman before marriage. It will be perceived that these Acts are very inadequate as regards placing married women in a just position towards their property, but they are certainly a step in the right direction. The Acts only apply to those women who have been married subsequently to their passing.

One great omission in them will have to be promptly remedied, both for the sake of married women and for the sake of their creditors: while a married woman now may, under some circumstances, sue, no machinery is provided whereby she may be sued—without joining her husband.

In an admirable letter to the *Times* of March 14, 1878, Mrs. Ursule Bright, alluding to the "obscurity and uncertainty of the law," points out

"The effect of that obscurity upon the credit of respectable married women earning their own and their children's bread, in any employment or business carried on separately from their husband; the inconvenience and risk to their creditors is, as you have most ably pointed out, great; but the injury to honest wives is far greater. It puts them at a considerable disadvantage in the labour market and in business. A married woman, for instance, keeping a little shop, may sue for debts due to her, but has no corresponding liability to be sued. If the whereabouts of the husband is not very clearly defined, it is evident she may have some difficulty in obtaining credit.

"Again, what employer of labour can with any security engage the services of a married woman? She may leave her work at the mill at an hour's notice unfinished, and her employer has no remedy against her for breach of contract, as a married woman can make no contract which is legally binding. There is no question that such a state of the law must operate as a restriction upon her power to support herself and family.

"The state of muddle of the present law is almost inconceivable. Even now a woman need not pay her debts contracted before marriage out of earnings made after marriage. Suppose an artist or a literary woman to marry when burdened with debts and having no property; should she be earning £1,000 or £10,000 a year by her profession after marriage, these earnings could not be made liable for her debts contracted before marriage."

It cannot too plainly be repeated that non-liability to be sued means non-existence of credit.

The law, as it stands at present, is the old Common Law, modified by the Acts of 1870 and 1873. Archbold says—dealing with indictments for theft—"Where the person named as owner appears to be a married woman, the defendant must, unless the indictment is amended, be acquitted . . . because in law the goods are the property of the husband; even though she be living apart from her husband upon an income arising from property vested in trustees for her separate use, because the goods cannot be the property of the trustees; and, in law, a married woman has no property" (Archbold's "Criminal Cases," p. 43). Archbold gives as exceptions to this general rule, where a judicial separation has taken place, where the wife has obtained a protection order, or where the property is such as is covered by the Married Women's Property Act, 1870. "Where a married woman lived apart from her husband, upon an income arising from property vested in trustees for her separate use, the judges held that a house which she lived in was properly described as her husband's dwelling-house, though she paid the rent out of her separate property, and the husband had never been in it. R. *v.* French, R. *v.* R., 491" (Ibid, p. 521). If a burglary be committed in a house belonging to a married woman, the house must be said to be the dwelling-house of her husband, or the burglar will be acquitted; if she be living separate from her husband, paying her own rent out of money secured for her separate use, it makes no difference; it was decided, in the case of Rex *v.* French, that a married woman could own no property, and that the house must, therefore, belong to the husband. If a married woman picks up a purse in the road and is robbed of it, the property vests in the husband: "Where goods are in the possession of the wife, they must be laid as the goods of her husband; thus, if A is indicted for stealing the goods of B, and it appears that B was a *feme covert* at the time, A must be acquitted. And even if the wife have only received money as the agent of another person, and she is robbed of that money before her husband receives it into his possession, still it is well laid as his money in an indictment for larceny. An indictment charging the stealing of a £5 Bank of England note, the property of E. Wall, averring, in the usual way, that the money secured by the note was due and payable to E. Wall; it appeared that E. Wall's wife had been employed to sell sheep belonging to her father, of or in which her husband never had either possession or any interest, and she received the note in payment for the sheep, and it was stolen from her before she left the place where she received it. It was objected that the note never was the property of E. Wall, either actually or constructively; the money secured by it was not his, and he had no qualified property in it, as it never was in his possession; but it was held that the property was properly laid" (Russell on Crimes, 5th ed., vol. ii., pp. 243, 244). Yet even a child, in the eye of the law, has property, and if his clothes are stolen, it is safer to allege them to be the child's property. The main principle of English law remains unaltered by recent legislation, that "a married woman has no property." Married women share incapacity to manage property with minors and lunatics; minors, lunatics, and married women are taken care of by trustees; minors become of age, lunatics often recover, married women remain incapable during the whole of their married life.

Being incapable of holding property, a married woman is, of course, incapable of making a will. Here, also, the Common Law may be checkmated. She may make a will "by virtue of a power reserved to her, or of a marriage settlement, or with her husband's assent, or it may be made by her to carry her separate estate; and the court in determining whether or not such will is entitled to probate, will not go minutely into the question, but will only require that the testatrix had a power reserved to her, or was entitled to separate estate, and will, if so satisfied, grant probate to her executor, leaving it to the Court of Chancery, as the court of construction, to say what portion of her estate, if any, will pass under such will. In this case the husband, though he may not be entitled to take probate of his wife's will, may administer to such of her effects as do not pass under the will" ("Comm. on the Laws of England," Broom and Hadley, vol. iii., pp. 427, 428). Thus we see that a husband may will away from his wife her own original property, but a wife may not even will away her own, unless the right be specially reserved to her before marriage. And yet it is urged that women have no need of votes, their interests being so well looked after by their fathers, husbands, and brothers!

We have thus seen that the "rights of every Englishman" are destroyed in women by marriage; one would imagine that matrimony was a crime for which a woman deserved punishment, and that confiscation and outlawry were the fit rewards of her misdeed.

From these three great fundamental wrongs flow a large number of legal disabilities. Take the case of a prisoner accused of misdemeanour; he is often set free on his own recognizances; but a married woman cannot be so released, for she is incapable of becoming bail or of giving her own recognizances; she is here again placed in bad company: "no person who has been convicted of any crime by which he has become infamous is allowed to be surety for any person charged or suspected of an indictable offence. Nor can a married woman, or an infant, or a prisoner in custody, be bail" (Archbold, p. 88). Let us now suppose that a woman be accused of some misdemeanour, and be committed for trial: she desires to have her case tried by a higher court than the usual one, and wishes to remove the indictment by writ of *certiorari:* she finds that the advantage is denied her, because, as a married woman, she has no property, and she cannot therefore enter into the necessary recognizances to pay costs in the case of a conviction. Thus a married woman finds herself placed at a cruel disadvantage as compared with an unmarried woman or with men.

In matters of business, difficulties arise on every hand: a married woman is incapable of making a contract; if she takes a house without her husband's knowledge and without stating that she is married, the landlord may repudiate the contract; if she states that she is married, the landlord knows that she is unable to make a legal contract, and refuses to let or lease to her, without heavy security. If she buys things she cannot be sued for non-payment without making the husband a defendant, and she consequently finds that she has no credit. If she is cheated, she cannot sue, except in cases covered by the recent Acts, without joining her husband, and so she has often to submit to be wronged. "A *feme covert* cannot sue without her husband being joined as co-plaintiff, so long as the relation of marriage subsists. It matters not that he is an alien, and has left the country; or that, being a subject, he has absconded from the realm as a bankrupt or for other purpose; or that he has become permanently resident abroad; or that they are living apart under a deed of separation; or have been divorced *a mensâ et thoro;* for none of these events dissolve or work a suspension of the marriage contract, and so long as that endures, the wife is unable to sue alone, whatever the cause of action may be. This disability results from the rule of law which vests in the husband not only all the goods and chattels which belonged to the wife at the time of the marriage, but also all which she acquires afterwards" (Lush's "Common Law Practice," 2nd ed., pp. 33, 34). The same principle governs all suits against a married woman; the husband must be sued with her: "In all actions brought against a *feme covert* while the relation of marriage subsists, the husband must be joined for conformity, it being an inflexible rule of law that a wife shall not be sued without her husband. . . . If therefore a wife enters into a bond jointly with her husband, or makes a bill of exchange, promissory note, or any other contract, she cannot be sued thereon, but the action should be brought against, and the bond, bill, &c., alleged to have been made by, the husband" (Ibid, p. 75).

The thoughtful author of the "Rights of Women" remarks that the incapacity to sue is "traceable to the time when disputes were settled by the judgment of arms. A man represents his wife at law now, because in the days of the judicial combat he was her champion-at-arms, and she is unable to sue now, because she was unable to fight then" (p. 22). The explanation is a very reasonable one, and is only an additional proof of the need of alteration in the law; our marriage laws are, as has been shown above, the survival of barbarism, and we only ask that modern civilisation will alter and improve them as it does everything else: trial by combat has been destroyed; ought not its remains to be buried out of sight? The consequence of these business disabilities is that a married woman finds herself thwarted at every turn, and if she be trying to gain a livelihood, and be separated from her husband, she is constantly pained and annoyed by the marriage-fetter, which hinders her activity and checks her efforts to make her way. The notion that irresponsibility is an advantage is an entirely mistaken one; an irresponsible person cannot be dealt with in business matters, and is shut out of all the usual independent ways of obtaining a livelihood. Authorship and servitude are the only paths really open to married women; in every other career they find humiliating obstacles which it needs both courage and perseverance to surmount.

Married women rank among the "persons in subjection to the power of others;" they thus come among those who in many cases are not criminally liable; "infants under the age of discretion," persons who are *non compotes mentis* (not of sound mind), and persons acting under coercion, are not criminally liable for their misdeeds. A married woman is presumed to act under her husband's coercion, unless the contrary be proved, and she may thus escape punishment for her wrongdoings: "Constraint of a superior is sometimes allowed as an excuse for criminal misconduct, by reason of the matrimonial subjection of the wife to her husband; but neither a son, nor a servant is excused for the commission of any crime by the command or coercion of the parent or master. Thus, if a woman commit theft, or burglary, by the coercion of her husband, or even in his company, which the law *primâ facie* construes a coercion, she is dispunishable, being considered to have acted by compulsion, and not of her own will" ("Comm. on the Laws of England," Broom and Hadley, vol. iv., p. 27). "A *feme covert* is so much favoured in respect of that power and authority which her husband has over her, that she shall not suffer any punishment for committing a bare theft, or even a burglary, by the coercion of her husband, or in his company, which the law construes a coercion" (Russell "On Crimes," vol. i., p. 139). "Where the wife is to be considered merely as the servant of the husband, she will not be answerable for the consequences of his breach of duty, however fatal, though she may be privy to his conduct. C. Squire and his wife were indicted for the murder of a boy;" he had been cruelly treated by both, and died "from debility and want of proper food and nourishment;" "Lawrence, J., directed the jury, that as the wife was the servant of the husband, it was not her duty to provide the apprentice with sufficient food and nourishment, and that she was not guilty of any breach of duty in neglecting to do so; though, if the husband had allowed her sufficient food for the apprentice, and she had wilfully withholden it from him, then she would have been guilty. But that here the fact was otherwise; and therefore, though *in foro conscientiæ* the wife was equally guilty with the husband, yet in point of law she could not be said to be guilty of not providing the apprentice with sufficient food and nourishment" (Ibid., pp. 144, 145). It is hard to see what advantage society gains by this curious fashion of reckoning married women as children or lunatics. Some advantages, however, flow to a criminal husband: a wife is not punishable for concealing her husband from justice, knowing that he has committed felony; a husband may not conceal his wife under analogous circumstances: "So strict is the law where a felony is actually complete, in order to do effectual justice, that the nearest relations are not suffered to aid or receive one another. If the parent assists his child, or the child his parent, if the brother receives the brother, the master his servant, or the servant his master, or even if the husband receives his wife, having any of them committed a felony, the receiver becomes an accessory *ex post facto*. But a *feme covert* cannot become an accessory by the receipt and concealment of her husband; for she is presumed to act under his coercion, and therefore she is not bound, neither ought she, to discover her lord" (Ibid., p. 38). The wife of a blind husband must not, however, regard her coverture as in all cases a protection, for it has been held that if stolen goods were in her possession, her husband's blindness preventing him from knowing of them, her coverture did not avail to shelter her.

Any advantage which married women may possess through

the supposition that they are acting under the coercion of their husbands ought to be summarily taken away from them. It is not for the safety of society that criminals should escape punishment simply because they happen to be married women; a criminal husband becomes much more dangerous to the community if he is to have an irresponsible fellow-conspirator beside him; two people—although the law regards them as one—can often commit a crime that a single person could not accomplish, and it is not even impossible that an unscrupulous woman, desiring to get rid easily for awhile of an unpleasant husband, might actually be the secret prompter of an offence, in the commission of which she might share, but in the punishment of which she would have no part. For the sake of wives, as well as of husbands, this irresponsibility should be put an end to, for if a husband is to be held accountable for his wife's misdeeds and debts, it is impossible for the law to refuse him control over her actions; freedom and responsibility must go hand in hand, and women who obtain the rights of freedom must accept the duties of responsibility.

A woman has a legal claim on her husband for the necessaries of life, and a man may be compelled to support his wife. But her claim is a very narrow one, as may be seen by the following case:—A man named Plummer was indicted for the manslaughter of his wife; he had been separated from her for several years, and paid her an allowance of 2s. 6d. a week; the last payment was made on a Sunday, and she was turned out of her lodgings on the Tuesday following; she was suffering from diarrhœa, and on the Wednesday was very ill. Plummer was told of her condition, but refused to give her shelter; the evening was wet, and a constable meeting her wandering about took her to her husband's lodgings, but he would not admit her; on Thursday he paid for a bed for her at a public-house, and on Friday she died. Baron Gurney told the jury that the prisoner could not be charged with having caused her death from want of food, since he made her an allowance, and under ordinary circumstances he might have refused to do anything more; the only question was whether the refusal as to shelter had hastened her death. The man was acquitted. A wife has also some limited rights over her husband's property after his death; she may claim dower, her wearing apparel, a bed, and some few other things, including her personal jewellery. Her husband's power to deprive her of her personal ornaments ceases with his life.

To redress the whole of the wrongs as to property, and to enable justice to be done, it is only necessary to pass a short Act of Parliament, ordaining that marriage shall in no fashion alter the civil status of a woman, that she shall have over property the same rights as though she were unmarried, and shall, in all civil and criminal matters, be held as responsible as though she were a *feme sole*. In short, marriage ought no more to affect a woman's position than it does a man's, and should carry with it no kind of legal disability; "marital control" should cease to exist, and marriage should be regarded as a contract between equals, and not as a bond between master and servant.

Those who are entirely opposed to the idea that a woman should not forfeit her property on marriage, raise a number of theoretical difficulties as to household expenses, ownership of furniture, &c., &c. Practically these would very seldom occur, if we may judge by the experience of countries whose marriage laws do not entail forfeiture on the woman who becomes a wife. In the "Rights of Women," quoted from above, a very useful summary is given of the laws as to property in various countries; in Germany these laws vary considerably in the different states; one system, known as "Gütergemeinschaft" (community of goods) is a great advance towards equality, although it is not by any means the best resolution of the problem; under this system there is no separate property, it is all merged in the common stock, and "the husband, as such, has no more right over the common fund than the wife, nor the wife than the husband" (p. 26); the husband administers as "representative of the community, and not as husband. He is merely head partner, as it were, and has no personal rights beyond that;" he may be dispossessed of even this limited authority if he is wasteful; "he cannot alienate or mortgage any of the common lands or rights without her consent—a privilege, it must be remembered, which belongs to her, not only over lands brought by herself, but also over those brought by her husband to the marriage. And this control of the wife over the immovables has, for parts of Prussia, been extended by a law of April 16th, 1850, over movables as well; for the husband has been forbidden to dispose not only of immovables, but of the whole or part of the movable property, without the consent of his wife. Nor can the husband by himself make donations *mortis causa;* such arrangements take the form of mutual agreements between the two respecting their claims of inheritance to one another" (p. 27). In Austria, married couples are more independent of each other; the wives retain their rights over their own property, and can dispose of it "as they like, and sue or be sued in respect of it, without marital authorisation or control; and just as they have the free disposition of their property, so they can contract with others as they please. A husband is unable to alienate any of his wife's property in her name, or to lend or mortgage it, or to receive any money, institute any law-suits, or make any arrangements in respect of it, unless he has her special mandate. . . . If no stipulation is made at the marriage, each spouse retains his or her separate property, and neither has a claim to anything gained or in any way received by the other during the marriage" (p. 50). In the New York code (U.S.A.), "beyond the claim of mutual support, neither [husband nor wife] has any interest whatever in the property of the other. Hence either may into any enter engagement or transaction with the other or with a stranger with respect to property, just as they might do if they continued unmarried" (p. 95). The apportionment of household expenses must necessarily be left for the private arrangement of the married pair; where the woman has property, or where she earns her livelihood it would be her duty to contribute to the support of the common home; where the couple are poor, and the care of the house falls directly on the shoulders of the wife, her personal toil would be her fair contribution; this matter should be arranged in the marriage contract, just as similar matters are now dealt with in the marriage settlements of the wealthy. As means of livelihood become more accessible to women the question will be more and more easily arranged; it will no longer be the fashion in homes of professional men that the husband shall over-work himself in earning the means of support, while the wife over rests herself in spending them, but a more evenly-divided duty shall strengthen the husband's health by more leisure, and the wife's by more work. Recovery of debts incurred for household expenses should be by suit against husband and wife jointly, just as in a partnership the firm may now be sued; recovery of personal debts should be by suits against the person who had contracted them. Many a man's life is now rendered harder than it ought to be, by the waste and extravagance of a wife who can pledge his name and his credit, and even ruin him before he knows his danger;

would not the lives of such men be the happier and the less toilsome if their wives were responsible for their own debts, and limited by their own means? Many a woman's home is broken up, and her children beggared, by the reckless spendthrift who wastes her fortune or her earnings: would not the lives of such women be less hopeless, if marriage left their property in their own hands, and did not give them a master as well as a husband? Women, under these circumstances, would, of course, become liable for the support of their children, equally with their husbands—a liability which is, indeed, recognized by the Married Women's Property Act (1870), s. 14.

It is sometimes further urged by those who like "a man to be master in his own house," that unless women forfeited their property in marriage, there would be constant discord in the home. Surely the contrary effect would be produced. Mrs. Mill well says, in the Essay before quoted from: "The highest order of durable and happy attachments would be a hundred times more frequent than they are, if the affection which the two sexes sought from one another were that genuine friendship which only exists between equals in privileges as in faculties." Nothing is so likely to cause unhappiness as the tendency to tyrannize, generated in the man by authority, and the tendency to rebel, generated in the woman by enforced submission. No grown person should be under the arbitrary power of another; dependence is touching in the infant because of its helplessness; it is revolting in the grown man or woman because with maturity of power should come dignity of self-support.

In a brilliant article in the *Westminster Review* (July, 1874) the writer well says: "Would it not, to begin with, be well to instruct girls that weakness, cowardice, and ignorance, cannot constitute at once the perfection of womankind and the imperfection of mankind?" It is time to do away with the oak and ivy ideal, and to teach each plant to grow strong and self-supporting. Perfect equality would, under this system, be found in the home, and mutual respect and deference would replace the alternate coaxing and commandment now too often seen. Equal rights would abolish both tyranny and rebellion; there would be more courtesy in the husband, more straightforwardness in the wife. Then, indeed, would there be some hope of generally happy marriages, but, as has been eloquently said by the writer just quoted, "till absolute social and legal equality is the basis of the sacred partnership of marriage (the division of labours and duties in the family, by free agreement, implying no sort of inequality), till no superiority is recognized on either side but that of individual character and capacity, till marriage is no longer legally surrounded with penalties on the woman who enters into it as though she were a criminal —till then the truest love, the truest sympathy, the truest happiness in it, will be the exception rather than the rule, and the real value of this relation, domestic and social, will be fatally missed." That some marriages are happy, in spite of the evil law, no one will deny; but these are the exception, not the rule. The law, as it is, directly tends to promote unhappiness, and its whole influence on the relations of the sexes is injurious. To quote Mrs. Mill once more: "The influence of the position tends eminently to promote selfishness. The most insignificant of men, the man who can obtain influence or consideration nowhere else, finds one place where he is chief and head. There is one person, often greatly his superior in understanding, who is obliged to consult him, and whom he is not obliged to consult. He is judge, magistrate, ruler, over their joint concerns; arbiter of all differences between them. . . . His is now the only tribunal, in civilized life, in which the same person is judge and party. A generous mind in such a situation makes the balance incline against its own side, and gives the other not less, but more, than a fair equality, and thus the weaker side may be enabled to turn the very fact of dependence into an instrument of power, and in default of justice, take an ungenerous advantage of generosity; rendering the unjust power, to those who make an unselfish use of it, a torment and a burthen. But how is it when average men are invested with this power, without reciprocity and without responsibility? Give such a man the idea that he is first in law and in opinion—that to will is his part, and hers to submit—it is absurd to suppose that this idea merely glides over his mind, without sinking into it, or having any effect on his feelings and practice. If there is any self-will in the man, he becomes either the conscious or unconscious despot of his household. The wife, indeed, often succeeds in gaining her objects, but it is by some of the many various forms of indirectness and management." When marriage is as it should be, there will be no superior and inferior by right of position; but men and women, whether married or unmarried, will retain intact the natural rights "belonging to every Englishman."

In dealing with the wrongs of the wife, according to the present English marriage laws, the wrongs of the mother must not be omitted. The unmarried mother has a right to her child; the married mother has none: "A father is entitled to the custody of his child until it attains the age of sixteen, unless there be some sufficient reason to the contrary" (Russell "On Crimes," vol. i., p. 898). The "sufficient reason" is hard to find in most cases, as the inclination of the Courts is to make excuses for male delinquencies, and to uphold every privilege which male Parliaments have conferred on husbands and fathers. In Shelley's case the father was deprived of the custody of his children, but here religious and political heresy caused a strong bias against the poet. The father's right to the custody of legitimate children is complete; the mother has no right over them as against his; he may take them away from her, and place them in the care of another woman, and she has no redress; she may apply to Chancery for access to them at stated times, but even this is matter of favour, not of right. The father may appoint a guardian in his will, and the mother, although the sole surviving parent, has no right over her children as against the stranger appointed by the dead father. If the parents differ in religion, the children are to be brought up in that of the father, whatever agreement may have been made respecting them before marriage; if the father dies without leaving any directions, the children will be educated in his religion; he can, if he chooses, allow his wife to bring them up in her creed, but she can only do so by virtue of his permission. Thus the married mother has no rights over her own children; she bears them, nurses them, toils for them, watches over them, and may then have them torn from her by no fault of her own, and given into the care of a stranger. People talk of maternal love, and of woman's sphere, of her duty in the home, of her work for her babes, but the law has no reverence for the tie between mother and child, and ignores every claim of the mother who is also a wife. The unmarried mother is far better off; she has an absolute right to the custody of her own children; none can step in and deprive her of her little ones, for the law respects the maternal tie when no marriage ceremony has "legitimated" it. Motherhood is only sacred in the eye of the law when no legal contract exists between the parents of the child.

Looking at a woman's position both as wife and mother, it is impossible not to recognise the fact that marriage is a direct disadvantage to her. In an unlegalised union the woman retains possession of all her natural rights; she is mistress of her own actions, of her body, of her property; she is able to legally defend herself against attack; all the Courts are open to protect her; she forfeits none of her rights as an Englishwoman; she keeps intact her liberty and her independence; she has no master; she owes obedience to the laws alone. If she have a child, the law acknowledges her rights over it, and no man can use her love for it as an engine of torture to force her into compliance with his will. Two disadvantages, however, attach to unlegalised unions; first, the woman has to face social disapprobation, although of late years, as women have been coming more to the front, this difficulty has been very much decreased, for women have begun to recognise the extreme injustice of the laws, and both men and women of advanced views have advocated great changes in the marriage contract. The second disadvantage is of a more serious character: the children proceeding from an unlegalised union have not the same rights as those born in legal wedlock, do not inherit as of right, and have no legal name. These injustices can be prevented by care in making testamentary dispositions protecting them, and by registering the surname, but the fact of the original unfairness still remains, and any carelessness on the parents' part will result in real injury to the child. It must also be remembered that the father, in such a case, has no rights over his children, and this is as unfair to him as the reverse is to the mother. As the law now is, both legal and illegal unions have disadvantages connected with them, and there is only a choice between evils; these evils are, however, overwhelmingly greater on the side of legal unions, as may be seen by the foregoing sketch of the disabilities imposed on women by marriage. So great are these that a wise and self-respecting woman may well hesitate to enter into a contract of marriage while the laws remain as they are, and a man who really honours a woman must reluctantly subject her to the disadvantages imposed on the English wife, when he asks her to take him as literally her master and owner. The relative position is as dishonouring to the man as it is insulting to the woman, and good men revolt against it as hotly as do the most high-spirited women. In happy marriages all these laws are ignored, and it is only at rare intervals that the married pair become conscious of their existence. Some argue that this being so, small practical harm results from the legal injustice; it would be as sensible to argue that as honest people do not want to thieve, it would not be injurious to public morality to have laws on the statute book legalising garotting. Laws are made to prevent injustice being committed with impunity, and it is a curious reversal of every principle of legislation to make laws which protect wrong-doing, and which can only be defended on the ground that they are not generally enforced. If the English marriage laws were universally carried out, marriage would not last for a month in England; as it is, vast numbers of women suffer in silence, thousands rebel and break their chains, and on every side men and women settle down into a mutual tolerance which is simply an easy-going indifference, accepted as the only possible substitute for the wedded happiness which they once dreamed of in youth, but have failed to realise in their maturity.

Things being as they are, what is the best action for those to take who desire to see a healthier and purer sexual morality—a morality founded upon equal rights and diverse duties harmoniously discharged? The first step is to agitate for a reform of the marriage laws by the passing of such an Act of Parliament as is alluded to above. It would be well for some of those who desire to see such a legislative change to meet and confer together on the steps to be taken to introduce such a Bill into the House of Commons. If thought necessary, a Marriage Reform League might be established, to organize the agitation and petitioning which are *de rigueur*, in endeavouring to get a bill passed through the popular House. Side by side with this effort to reform marriage abuses, should go the determination not to contract a legal marriage while the laws remain as immoral as they are. It is well known that the Quakers persistently refused to go through the legal English form of marriage, and quietly made their declarations according to their own conscience, submitting to the disadvantages entailed on them by the illegality, until the legislature formally recognised the Quaker declaration as a legal form of marriage. Why should not we take a leaf out of the Quakers' book, and substitute for the present legal forms of marriage a simple declaration publicly made? We should differ from the Quakers in this, that we should not desire that such declaration should be legalised while the marriage laws remain as they are; but as soon as the laws are moralised, and wives are regarded as self-possessing human beings, instead of as property, then the declaration may, with advantage, seek the sanction of the law. It is not necessary that the declaration should be couched in any special form of words; the conditions of the contract ought to be left to the contracting parties. What is necessary is that it should be a definite contract, and it is highly advisable that it should be a contract in writing—a deed of partnership, in fact, which should — when the law permits—be duly stamped and registered. The law, while it does not dictate the conditions of the contract, should enforce those conditions so long as the contract exists; that is, it should interfere just as far as it does in other contracts, and no further; the law has no right to dictate the terms of the marriage contract; it is for the contracting parties to arrange their own affairs as they will. While, however, the province of the law should be thus limited in respect to the contracting parties, it has a clear right to interfere in defence of the interests of any children who may be born of the marriage, and to compel the parents to clothe, feed, house, and educate them properly: this duty should, if need be, be enforced on both parents alike, and the law should recognise and impose the full discharge of the responsibilities of parents towards those to whom they have given life. No marriage contract should be recognised by the law which is entered into by minors; in this, as in other legal deeds, there should be no capability to contract until the contracting parties are of full age. A marriage is a partnership, and should be so regarded by the law, and it should be the aim of those who are endeavouring to reform marriage, to substitute for the present semi-barbarous laws a scheme which shall be sober, dignified, and practicable, and which shall recognise the vital interest of the community in the union of those who are to be the parents of the next generation.

Such a deed as I propose would have no legal force at the present time; and here arises a difficulty: might not a libertine take advantage of this fact to desert his wife and possibly leave her with a child, or children, on her hands, to the cold mercy of society which would not even recognize her as a married woman? Men who, under the present state of the law, seduce women and then desert them, would probably do the same if they had gone through a form of marriage which had no legally binding force; but such men are, fortunately, the exception, not the rule, and there is no reason to apprehend an increase of their number, owing to the proposed action on the part of a number of thoughtful men and women who are dissatisfied with the present state of the law, but who have no wish to plunge into debauchery. I freely acknowledge that it is to be desired that marriage should be legally binding, and that a father should be compelled to do his share towards supporting his children; but while English law imposes such a weight of disability on a married woman, and leaves her utterly in the power of her husband, however unprincipled, oppressive, and wicked he may be—short of legal crime—I take leave to think that women have a fairer chance of happiness and comfort in an unlegalised than in a legal marriage. There is many an unhappy woman who would be only too glad if the libertine who has legally married her would desert her, and leave her, even with the burden of a family, to make for herself and her children, by her own toil, a home which should at least be pure, peaceful, and respectable.

Let me, in concluding this branch of the subject, say a word to those who, agreeing with Marriage Reform in principle, fear to openly put their theory into practice. Some of these earnestly hope for change, but do not dare to advocate it openly. Reforms have never been accomplished by Reformers who had not the courage of their opinions. If all the men and women who disapprove of the present immoral laws would sturdily *and openly* oppose them; if those who desire to unite their lives, but are determined not to submit to the English marriage laws, would publicly join hands, making such a declaration as is here suggested, the social odium would soon pass away, and the unlegalised marriage would be recognised as a dignified and civilized substitute for the old brutal and savage traditions. Most valuable work might here be done by men and women who—happy in their own marriages—yet feel the immorality of the law, and desire to see it changed. Such married people might support and strengthen by their open countenance and friendship those who enter into the unlegalised public unions here advocated; and they can do what no one else can do so well: they can prove to English society—the most bigoted and conservative society in the world—that advocacy of change in the marriage laws does not mean the abolition of the home. The value of such co-operation will be simply inestimable, and will do more than anything else to render the reform practicable. Courage and quiet resolution are needed, but, with these, this great social change may safely and speedily be accomplished.

II.

DIVORCE.

ANY proposed reforms in the marriage laws of England would be extremely imperfect, unless they dealt with the question of divorce. Marriage differs from all ordinary contracts in the extreme difficulty of dissolving it—a difficulty arising from the ecclesiastical character which has been imposed upon it, and from the fact that it has been looked upon as a religious bond instead of as a civil contract. Until the time of the Reformation, marriage was regarded as a sacrament by all Christian people, and it is so regarded by the majority of them up to the present day. When the Reformers advocated divorce, it was considered as part of their general heresy, and as proof of the immoral tendency of their doctrines. Among Roman Catholics the sacramental—and therefore the indissoluble—character of marriage is still maintained, but among Protestants divorce is admitted, the laws regulating it varying much in different countries.

In England—owing to the extreme conservatism of the English in all domestic matters—the Protestant view of marriage made its way very slowly. Divorce remained within the jurisdiction of ecclesiastical courts, and these granted only divorces *a mensâ et thoro* in cases where cruelty or adultery was pleaded as rendering conjugal life impossible. These courts never granted divorces *a vinculo matrimonii*, which permit either—or both—of the divorced persons to contract a fresh marriage, except in cases where the marriage was annulled as having been void from the beginning; they would only grant a separation "from bed and board," and imposed celibacy on the divorced couple until one of them died, and so set the other free. There was indeed a report drawn up by a commission, under the authority of 3 and 4 Edward VI., c. ii., which was intended as a basis for the re-modelling of the marriage laws, but the death of the king prevented the proposed reform; the ecclesiastical courts remained as they were, and absolute divorce was unattainable. Natural impatience of a law which separated unhappy married people only to impose celibacy on them, caused occasional applications to be made to Parliament for relief, and a few marriages were thus dissolved under exceptional circumstances. In 1701, a bill was obtained, enabling a petitioner to re-marry, and in 1798, Lord Loughborough's "Orders" were passed. "By these orders, no petition could be presented to the House, unless an official copy of the proceedings, and of a definitive sentence of divorce, *a mensâ et thoro*, in the ecclesiastical courts, was delivered on oath at the bar of the House at the same time" (Broom's "Comm.," vol. iii. p. 396). After explaining the procedure of the ecclesiastical court, Broom goes on: "A definitive sentence of divorce *a mensâ et thoro* being thus obtained, the petitioner proceeded to lay his case before the House of Lords in accordance with the Standing Orders before adverted to, and, subject to his proving the case, he obtained a bill divorcing him from the bonds of matrimony, and allowing him to marry again. The provisions of the bill, which was very short, were generally these:—1. The marriage was dissolved. 2. The husband was empowered to marry again. 3. He was given the rights of a husband as to any property of an after-taken wife. 4. The divorced wife was deprived of any right she might have as his widow. 5. Her after-acquired property was secured to her as against the husband from whom she was divorced. In the case of the wife obtaining the bill, similar provisions were made in her favour" (p. 398). In 1857, an Act was passed establishing a Court for Divorce and Matrimonial Causes, and thus a great step forward was taken: this court was empowered to grant a judicial separation—equivalent to the old divorce *a mensâ et thoro*—in cases of cruelty, desertion for two years and upwards, or adultery on the part of the husband; it was further empowered to grant an absolute divorce with right of re-marriage—equivalent to the old divorce *a vinculo matrimonii*—in cases of adultery on the part of the wife, or of, on the part of the husband, "incestuous adultery, or of bigamy with adultery, or of rape, or an unnatural crime, or of adultery coupled with such cruelty as would formerly have entitled her to a divorce *a mensâ et thoro*, or of adultery coupled with desertion, without reasonable excuse, for two years or upwards"

(Broom, vol. i., p. 542). The other powers held by the court need not now be specially dwelt upon.

The first reform here needed is that husband and wife should be placed on a perfect equality in asking for a divorce: at present if husband and wife be living apart, no amount of adultery on the husband's part can release the wife; if they be living together, a husband may keep as many mistresses as he will, and, provided that he carefully avoid any roughness which can be construed into legal cruelty, he is perfectly safe from any suit for dissolution of marriage. Adultery alone, when committed by the husband, is not ground for a dissolution of marriage; it must be coupled with some additional offence before the wife can obtain her freedom. But the husband can obtain a dissolution of marriage for adultery committed by the wife, and he can further obtain money damages from the co-respondent, as a *solatium* to his wounded feelings. Divorce should be absolutely equal as between husband and wife: adultery on either side should be sufficient, and if it be thought necessary to join a male co-respondent when the husband is the injured party, then it should also be necessary to join a female co-respondent where the wife brings the suit. The principle, then, which should be laid down as governing all cases of divorce, is that no difference should be made in favour of either side; whatever is sufficient to break the marriage in the one case should be sufficient to break it in the other.

Next, the system of judicial separation should be entirely swept away. Wherever divorce is granted at all, the divorce should be absolute. No useful end is gained by divorcing people practically and regarding them as married legally. A technical tie is kept up, which retains on the wife the mass of disabilities which flow from marriage, while depriving her of all the privileges, and which widows both man and woman, exiling them from home-life and debarring them from love. Judicial separation is a direct incentive to licentiousness and secret sexual intercourse; the partially divorced husband, refused any recognised companion, either indulges in promiscuous lust, to the ruin of his body and mind, or privately lives with some woman whom the law forbids him to marry and whom he is ashamed to openly acknowledge. Meanwhile the semi-divorced wife can obtain no relief, and is compelled to live on, without the freedom of the spinster or the widow, or the social consideration of the married woman. She can only obtain freedom by committing what the law and society brand as adultery; if she has any scruples on this head, she must remain alone, unloved and without home, living a sad, solitary life until death, more merciful than the law, sets her free.

It is hard to see what object there can be in separating a married couple, in breaking up the home, dividing the children, and yet maintaining the fact of marriage just so far as shall prevent the separated couple from forming new ties; the position of those who regard divorce as altogether sinful, is intelligible, however mistaken; but the position of those who advocate divorce, but object to the divorced couple having the right of contracting a new marriage, is wholly incomprehensible. No one profits by such divorce, while the separated couple are left in a dubious and most unsatisfactory condition; they are neither married nor unmarried; they can never shake themselves free from the links of the broken chain; they carry about with them the perpetual mark of their misfortune, and can never escape from the blunder committed in their youth. They would be the happier, and society would be the healthier, if the divorce of life and of interests were also a divorce which should set them free to seek happiness, if they will, in other unions—free technically as well as really, free in law as well as in fact.

If it be admitted that all divorce should be absolute, the question arises: What should be the ground of divorce? First, adultery, because breach of faith on either side should void the contract which implies loyalty to each other; the legal costs of both should fall on the breaker of the contract, but no damages should be recoverable against a third party. Next, cruelty, because where the weaker party suffers from the abuse of power of the stronger, there the law should, when appealed to, step in to annul the contract, which is thus a source of injury to one of the contracting parties; if a man be brought up before the magistrate charged with wife-beating or violence of any kind towards his wife, and be convicted and sentenced, the Divorce Court should, on the demand of the wife, the record being submitted to it, pronounce a sentence of divorce; in the rare case of violence committed by a wife on her husband, the same result should accrue; the custody of the children should be awarded to the innocent party, since neither a man nor a woman convicted of doing bodily harm to another is fit to be trusted with the guardianship of a child.* The next distinct ground of divorce should be habitual drunkenness; drunkenness causes misery to the sober partner, and is ruinous in its effect, both on the *physique* and on the character of the children proceeding from the marriage. Here, of course, the custody of the children should be committed entirely to the innocent parent.

At present, the usual unfairness presides over the arrangements as to access to the children by the parents: "In the case of a mother who is proved guilty of adultery, she is usually debarred from such access, though it has not been the practice to treat the offending father with the same rigour" (Broom's "Comm.," vol. iii., p. 404). In all cases of divorce the interests of the children should be carefully guarded; both parents should be compelled to contribute to their support, whether the guardianship be confided to the father or to the mother.

These glaring reasons for granting a divorce will be admitted by everyone who recognises the reasonableness of divorce at all, but there will be more diversity of opinion as to the advisability of making divorce far more easily attainable. The French Convention of 1792 set an example that has been only too little followed; for the first time in French history divorce was legalised in France. It was obtainable "on the application of either party [to the marriage] alleging simply as a cause, incompatibility of humour or character. The female children were to be entirely confided to the care of the mother, as well as the males, to the age of seven years, when the latter were again to be re-committed to the superintendence of the father; provided only, that by mutual agreement any other arrangement might take place with respect to the disposal of the children; or arbitrators might be chosen by the nearest of kin to determine on the subject. The parents were to contribute equally to the maintenance of the children, in proportion to their property, whether under the care of the father or mother. Family arbitrators were to be chosen to direct with respect to the partition of the property, or the alimentary pension to be allowed to the party divorced. Neither of the parties

* Since these lines were published in the *National Reformer*, a clause has been inserted in a bill now before Parliament, empowering magistrates to grant an order of separation to a wife, if it is proved that she has been cruelly ill-used by her husband, and further compelling the husband, in such a case, to contribute a weekly sum towards her maintenance. This will be a great improvement on the present state of things, but absolute divorce would be better than mere separation.

could contract a new marriage for the space of one year" ("Impartial History of the Late Revolution," vol. ii., pp. 179, 180). This beneficial law was swept away, with many other useful changes, when tyranny came back to France. At the present time the only countries where divorce is easily obtainable are some of the states of Germany and of America. It has been held in at least one American state that proved incompatibility of temper was sufficient ground for separation. And reasonably so; if two people enter into a contract for their mutual comfort and advantage, and the contract issues in mutual misery and loss, why should not the contract be dissolved? It is urged that marriage would be dishonoured if divorce were easily attainable; surely marriage is far more dishonoured by making it a chain to tie together two people who have for each other neither affection nor respect. For the sake of everyone concerned an unhappy marriage should be easily dissoluble; the married couple would be the happier and the better for the separation; their children—if they have any—would be saved from the evil effect of continual family jars, and from the loss of respect for their parents caused by the spectacle of constant bickering; the household would be spared the evil example of the quarrels of its heads; society would see less vice and fewer scandalous divorce suits. In all cases of contract, save that of marriage, those who make can, by mutual consent, unmake; why should those who make the most important contract of all be deprived of the same right?

Mr. John Stuart Mill, dealing very briefly with the marriage contract in his essay "On Liberty," points out that the fulfilment of obligations incurred by marriage must not be forgotten when the contract is dissolved, since these "must be greatly affected by the continuance or disruption of the relation between the original parties to the contract." But he goes on to say: "It does not follow, nor can I admit, that these obligations extend to requiring the fulfilment of the contract at all costs to the happiness of the reluctant party; but they are a necessary element in the question; and even if, as Von Humboldt maintains, they ought to make no difference in the *legal* freedom of the parties to release themselves from the engagement (and I also hold that they ought not to make *much* difference), they necessarily make a great difference in the *moral* freedom. A person is bound to take all these circumstances into account before resolving on a step which may affect such important interests of others; and if he does not allow proper weight to those interests, he is morally responsible for the wrong. I have made these obvious remarks for the better illustration of the general principle of liberty, and not because they are at all needed on the particular question, which, on the contrary, is usually discussed as if the interest of children was everything, and that of grown persons nothing" (p. 61). The essay of Von Humboldt, referred to by Mr. Mill, is that on the "Sphere and Duties of Government;" Von Humboldt argues that "even where there is nothing to be objected to the validity of a contract, the State should have the power of lessening the restrictions which men impose on one another, even with their own consent, and (by facilitating the release from such engagements) of preventing a moment's decision from hindering their freedom of action for too long a period of life" (p. 134, of Coulthard's translation). After pointing out that contracts relating to the transfer of *things* should be binding, Von Humboldt proceeds: "With contracts which render personal performance a duty, or still more with those which produce proper personal relations, the case is wholly different. With these coercion operates hurtfully on man's noblest powers; and since the success of the pursuit itself which is to be conducted in accordance with the contract, is more or less dependent on the continuing consent of the parties, a limitation of such a kind is in them productive of less serious injury. When, therefore, such a personal relation arises from the contract as not only to require certain single actions, but, in the strictest sense, to affect the person, and influence the whole manner of his existence; where that which is done, or left undone, is in the closest dependence on internal sensations, the option of separation should always remain open, and the step itself should not require any extenuating reasons. Thus it is with matrimony" (pp. 134, 135).

Robert Dale Owen—the virtuous and justly revered author of "Moral Physiology;" a man so respected in his adopted country, the United States of America, that he was elected as one of its senators, and was appointed American ambassador at the Court of Naples—Robert Dale Owen, in a letter to Thomas Whittemore, editor of the Boston *Trumpet*, May, 1831, deals as follows with the contract of marriage:—

"I do not think it virtuous or rational in a man and woman solemnly to swear that they will love and honour each other until death part them. First, because if affection or esteem on either side should afterwards cease (as, alas! we often see it cease), the person who took the marriage-oath has perjured himself; secondly, because I have observed that such an oath, being substituted for the noble and elevating principle of moral obligation, has a tendency to weaken that principle.

"You will probably ask me whether I should equally object to a solemn promise to live together during life whatever happens. I do not think this *equally* objectionable, because it is an explicit promise possible to be kept; whereas the oath to love until death, may become impossible of fulfilment. But still I do not approve even this possible promise; and I will give you the reasons why I do not.

"That a man and woman should occupy the same house, and daily enjoy each other's society, so long as such an association gives birth to virtuous feelings, to kindness, to mutual forbearance, to courtesy, to disinterested affection, I consider right and proper. That they should continue to inhabit the same house and to meet daily, in case such intercourse should give birth to vicious feelings, to dislike, to ill temper, to scolding, to a carelessness of each other's comfort and a want of respect for each other's feelings,—this I consider, *when the two individuals alone are concerned*, neither right nor proper; neither conducive to good order nor to virtue. I do not think it well, therefore, to promise, at all hazards, to live together for life.

"Such a view may be offensive to orthodoxy, but surely, surely it is approved by common sense. Ask yourself, sir, who is—who can be the gainer—the man, the woman, or society at large—by two persons living in discord rather than parting in peace, as Abram and Lot did when their herdsmen could not agree. We have temptations enough already to ill humour in the world, without expressly creating them for ourselves; and of all temptations to that worst of petty vices, domestic bickering, can we suppose one more stronger or more continually active than a forced association in which the heart has no share? Do not the interests of virtue and good order, then, imperiously demand (as the immortal author of 'Paradise Lost' argued, in his celebrated work 'On Divorce,') that the law should abstain from perpetuating any association, after it has become a daily source of vice?

"If children's welfare is concerned, and that they will be injured by a separation, the case is different. Those who impart existence to sentient beings are, in my view, responsible to them for as much happiness as it is in their power to bestow. The parent voluntarily assumes this greatest of responsibilities; and he who, having so assumed it, trifles with his child's best interests for his own selfish gratification, is, in my eyes, utterly devoid of moral principle; or, at the least, utterly blind to the most sacred duty which a human being can be called to perform. If, therefore, the well-being and future prosperity of the children are to be sacrificed by a separation of the parents, then I would positively object to the separation, however grievous the evil effects of a continued connection might be to the dissentient couple.

"Whether the welfare of children is ever promoted by the continuation of an ill-assorted union, is another question; as also in what way they ought to be provided for, where a separation actually takes place.

"But to regard, for the moment, the case of the adults alone. You will remark, that it is no question for us to determine whether it is better or more proper that affection, once conceived, should last through life. We might as well sit down to decree whether the sun should shine or be hid under a cloud, or whether the wind should blow a storm or a gentle breeze. We may rejoice when it does so last, and grieve when it does not; but as to legislating about the matter, it is the idlest of absurdities.

"But we *can* determine by law the matter of living together. We may compel a man and woman, though they hate each other as cordially as any of Byron's heroes, to have one common name, one common interest, and (nominally) one common bed and board. We may invest them with the legal appearance of the closest friends while they are the bitterest enemies. It seems to me that mankind have seldom considered what are the actual advantages of such a proceeding to the individuals and to society. I confess that I do not see what is gained in so unfortunate a situation, by keeping up the appearance when the reality is gone.

"I do see the necessity, in such a case, if the man and woman separate, of dividing what property they may possess equally between them; and (while the present monopoly of profitable occupations by men lasts) I also see the expediency, in case the property so divided be not sufficient for the woman's comfortable support, of causing the man to continue to contribute a fair proportion of his earnings towards it. I also see the impropriety, as I said before, that the children, if any there be, should suffer. But I cannot see who is the gainer by obliging two persons to continue in each other's society, when heart-burnings, bickerings, and other vicious results, are to be the consequence.

"There are cases when affection ceases on one side and remains on the other. No one can deny that this is an evil, often a grievous one; but I cannot perceive how the law can remedy it, or soften its bitterness, any more than it can legislate away the pain caused by unreturned friendship between persons of the same sex.

"You will ask me, perhaps, whether I do not believe that, but for the law, there would be a continual and selfish change indulged, without regard to the feelings or welfare of others. What there might be in the world, viciously trained and circumstanced as so many human beings now are, I know not, though I doubt whether things *could* be much worse than they are now; besides that no human power can legislate for the heart. But if men and women were trained (as they so easily might!) to be even decently regardful of each other's feelings, may we not assert positively, that no such result could possibly happen? Let me ask each one of your readers, and let each answer to his or her own heart: 'Are you indeed bound to those you profess to love and honour by the law *alone?*' Alas! for your chance of happiness, if the answer be 'Yes!'"

The fact is, as Mr. Owen justly says, that a promise to "love . . . until death us do part" is an immoral promise, because its performance is beyond the power of those who give the promise. To love, or not to love, is not a matter of the will; Love in chains loses his life, and only leaves a corpse in his captive's hand. Love is, of its very nature, voluntary, freely given, drawing together by an irresistible sympathy those whose natures are adapted to each other. Shelley well says, in one of the notes on Queen Mab: "Love is inevitably consequent on the perception of loveliness. Love withers under constraint; its very essence is liberty; it is compatible neither with obedience, jealousy, nor fear; it is there most pure, perfect and unlimited, where its votaries live in confidence, equality, and unreserve." To say this, is not to say that higher duty may not come between the lovers, may not, for a time, keep them apart, may not even render their union impossible; it is only to recognize a fact that no thoughtful person can deny, and to show how utterly wrong and foolish it is to promise for life that which can never be controlled by the will.

But marriage, it is said, would be too lightly entered into if it were so easily dissoluble. Why? People do not rush into endless partnerships because they are dissoluble at pleasure; on the contrary, such partnerships last just so long as they are beneficial to the contracting parties. In the same way, marriage would last exactly so long as its continuance was beneficial, and no longer: when it became hurtful, it would be dissolved. "How long then," asks Shelley, "ought the sexual connection to last? what law ought to specify the extent of the grievances which should limit its duration? A husband and wife ought to continue so long united as they love each other; any law which should bind them to cohabitation for one moment after the decay of their affection, would be a most intolerable tyranny, and the most unworthy of toleration. How odious a usurpation of the right of private judgment should that law be considered which should make the ties of friendship indissoluble, in spite of the caprices, the inconstancy, the fallibility and capacity for improvement of the human mind. And by so much would the fetters of love be heavier and more unendurable than those of friendship, as love is more vehement and capricious, more dependent on those delicate peculiarities of imagination, and less capable of reduction to the ostensible merits of the object. . . . The connection of the sexes is so long sacred as it contributes to the comfort of the parties, and is naturally dissolved when its evils are greater than its benefits. There is nothing immoral in this separation" (Notes on "Queen Mab"). In spite of this facility of divorce, marriage would be the most enduring of all partnerships; not only is there between married couples the tie of sexual affection, but around them grows up a hedge of common thoughts, common interests, common memories, that, as years go on, makes the idea of separation more and more repulsive. It would only be where the distaste had grown strong enough to break through all these, that divorce would take place, and in such cases the misery of the enforced common life would be removed without harm to any one. Of course, this facility of divorce will entirely sweep away those odious suits for "restitution of conjugal rights" which occasionally disgrace our courts. If a husband and wife are living apart, without legal sanction, it is now open to either of them to bring a suit for restitution of conjugal rights. "The decree of restitution pronounces for the marriage, admonishes the respondent to take the petitioner home and treat him or her as husband or wife, and to render him or her conjugal rights; and, further, to certify to the court, within a certain time, that he or she had done so; in default of which, an attachment for contempt of court will be issued against the offending party" (Broom's "Comm.," vol. iii., p. 400). It is difficult to understand how any man or woman, endued with the most rudimentary sense of decency, can bring such a suit, and, after having succeeded, can enforce the decision. We may hope that, as sexual morality becomes more generally recognised, it will be seen that the essence of prostitution lies in the union of the sexes without mutual love; when a woman marries for rank, for title, for wealth, she sells herself as veritably as her poorer and more unfortunate sister; love alone makes the true marriage, love which is loyal to the beloved, and is swayed by no baser motive than passionate devotion to its object. When no such love exists the union which is marriage by law is nothing higher than legalised prostitution: the enforcement on an unwilling man or woman of conjugal rights is something even still lower, it is legalised rape.

It may be hoped that when divorce is more easily obtainable, the majority of marriages will be far happier than they are now. Half the unhappiness of married life arises from the too great feeling of security which grows out of the indissoluble character of the tie. The husband is very different from the lover; the wife from the betrothed; the ready attention, the desire to please, the eager courtesy, which characterised the lover disappear when possession has become certain; the daintiness, the gaiety, the attractiveness which marked the betrothed, are no longer to be seen in the wife whose position is secure; in society a lover may be known by his attention to his betrothed, a husband by his indifference to his wife. If divorce were the result of jarring at home, married life would very rapidly change; hard words, harshness, petulance, would be checked where those who had won the love desired to keep it, and attractiveness would no longer be dropped on the threshold of the home. Here, too, Shelley's words are well worth weighing: "The present system of restraint does no more, in the majority of instances, than make hypocrites or open enemies. Persons of delicacy and virtue, unhappily united to those whom they find it impossible to love, spend the loveliest season of their life in unproductive efforts to appear otherwise than they are, for the sake of the feelings of their partner, or the welfare of their mutual offspring; those of less generosity and refinement openly avow their disappointment, and linger out the remnant of that union, which only death can dissolve, in a state of incurable bickering and hostility. The early education of the children takes its colour from the squabbles of the parents; they are nursed in a systematic school of ill-humour, violence and falsehood. Had they been suffered to part at the moment when indifference rendered their union irksome, they would have been spared many years of misery: they would have connected themselves more suitably, and would have found that happiness in the society of more congenial partners which is for ever denied them by the despotism of marriage. They would have been separately useful and happy members of society, who, whilst united, were miserable, and rendered misanthropical by misery. The conviction that wedlock is indissoluble, holds out the strongest of all temptations to the perverse; they indulge without restraint in acrimony, and all the little tyrannies of domestic life, when they know that their victim is without appeal. If this conviction were put on a rational basis, each would be assured that habitual ill-temper would terminate in separation, and would check this vicious and dangerous propensity" (Notes on "Queen Mab"). To those who had thought over the subject carefully, it was no surprise to hear Mr. Moncure Conway say—in a debate on marriage at the Dialectical Society—that in Illinois, U.S.A., where there is great facility of divorce, the marriages were exceptionally happy. The reason was not far to seek.

Dealing elsewhere with this same injurious effect of over-certainty on the relations of married people to each other, Mr. Moncure Conway writes as follows:—"In England we smilingly walk our halls of Eblis, covering the fatal wound; but our neighbours across the Channel are frank. Their moralists cannot blot out the proverb that 'Marriage is the suicide of love.' Is it any truer here than there that, as a general thing, the courtesies of the courtship survive in the marriage? 'Who is that domino walking with George?' asks Grisette No. 1, as reported by *Charivari*. 'Why,' returns Grisette No. 2, 'do you not walk behind tnem, and listen to what they say?' 'I have done so, and they do not say a word.' 'Ah, it is his wife.' But what might be George's feeling if he knew his wife might leave him some morning? 'If conserve of roses be frequently eaten,' they say in Persia, 'it will produce a surfeit.' The thousands of husbands and wives yawning in each other's faces at this moment need not go so far for their proverb. If it be well, as it seems to me to be, that this most intimate relation between man and woman should be made as durable as the object for which it is formed will admit, surely the bond should be real to the last, a bond of kindliness, thoughtfulness, actual helpfulness. So long as the strength of the bond lies simply in the disagreeable concomitants of breaking it, so long as it is protected by the very iron hardness which makes it gall and oppress, what need is there of the reinforcement of it by the cultivation of minds, the preservation of good temper, and considerate behaviour? Love is not quite willing to accept the judge's mace for his arrow. When the law no longer supplies husband or wife with a cage, each must look to find and make available what resources he or she has for holding what has been won. We may then look for sober second thoughts both before and after marriage. Love, from so long having bandaged eyes, will be all eye. Every real attraction will be stimulated when all depends upon real attraction. When the conserve becomes fatiguing, it will be refreshed by a new flavour, not by a certificate. From the hour when a thought of obligation influences either party to it, the marriage becomes a prostitution." ("The Earthward Pilgrimage," pp. 289, 290, 291).

A remarkable instance of the permanence of unions dissoluble at pleasure is to be found related by Robert Dale Owen, in an article entitled "Marriage and Placement," which appeared in the *Free Inquirer* of May 28, 1831. It deals with the unions between the sexes in the Haytian Republic, and the facts therein related are well worthy of serious attention. Mr. Owen writes:—

"Legal marriage is common in St. Domingo as elsewhere. Prostitution, too, exists there as in other countries. But this institution of *placement* is found nowhere, that I know of, but among the Haytians.

"Those who choose to marry, are united, as in other countries, by a priest or magistrate. Those who do not choose to marry, and who equally shrink from the mercenary embrace of prostitution, are (in the phraseology of the island) *placés*: that is, literally translated, *placed.*

"The difference between *placement* and marriage is, that the former is entered into without any prescribed form, the latter with the usual ceremonies: the former is dissoluble at a day's warning, the latter is indissoluble except by the vexatious and degrading formalities of divorce; the former is a tacit social compact, the latter a legal compulsory one; in the former the woman gives up her name and her property; in the latter, she retains both.

"Marriage and placement are, in Hayti, equally respectable, or, if there be a difference, it is in favour of placement; and in effect ten placements take place in the island for one marriage. *Pétion*, the Jefferson of Hayti,* sanctioned the custom by his approval and example. *Boyer*, his successor, the president, did the same;† and by far the largest portion of the respectable inhabitants have imitated their presidents, and are *placed*, not married. The children of the placed have, in every particular, the same legal rights and the same standing as those born in wedlock.

"I imagine I hear from the clerical supporters of orthodoxy one general burst of indignation at this sample of national profligacy; at this contemning of the laws of God and man; at this escape from the Church's ceremonies and the ecclesiastical blessing. I imagine I hear the question sneeringly put, how long these same *respectable* connections commonly last, and how many dozen times they are changed in the course of a year.

"Gently, my reverend friends! it is natural you should find it wrong that men and women dispense with your services and curtail your fees in this matter. But it is neither just nor proper, that because no prayers are said, and no fees paid, you should denounce the custom as a profligate one. Learn (as I did the other day from an intelligent French

* "It may suffice, in illustration of Pétion's character, to quote the touching inscription found on his tomb—'Here lies Pétion, who enjoyed for twelve years absolute power, and during that period never caused one tear to flow.'"

† "Boyer's resolution in this matter is the more remarkable, as he has been urged and pestered to submit to the forms of marriage. Grégoire, archbishop of Blois, and who is well known for the perseverance and benevolence with which he has, for a long series of years, advocated the cause of the African race, wrote to the president of Hayti in the most urgent terms, pressing upon him the virtue—the necessity, for his salvation—of conforming to the sacrament of marriage. To such a degree did the good old archbishop carry his intermeddling officiousness, that when Boyer mildly but firmly declined availing himself of his grace's advice, a rupture was the consequence, greatly to the sorrow of the president, who had ever entertained the greatest respect and affection for his ecclesiastical friend."

gentleman who had remained some time on the island)—learn, that *although there are ten times as many placed as married, yet there are actually fewer separations among the former than divorces among the latter.* If constancy, then, is to be the criterion of morality, these same profligate unions—that is, unions unprayed-for by the priest and unpaid for to him—are ten times as moral as the religion-sanctioned institution of marriage.

"But this is not all. It is a fact notorious in Hayti, that libertinism is far more common among the married than among the placed. The explanatory cause is easily found. A placement secures to the consenting couple no *legal* right over one another. They remain together, as it were, on good behaviour. Not only positive tyranny or downright viragoism, but petulant peevishness or selfish ill humour, are sufficient causes of separation. As such, they are avoided with sedulous care. The natural consequence is, that the unions are usually happy, and that each being comfortable at home, is not on the search for excitement abroad. In indissoluble marriage, on the contrary, if the parties should happen to disagree, their first jarrings are unchecked by considerations of conquences. A husband may be as tyrannical as to him seems good; he remains a lord and master still; a wife may be as pettish as she pleases; she does not thereby forfeit the rights and privileges of a wife. Thus, ill humour is encouraged by being legalized, and the natural results ensue, alienation of the heart, and sundering of the affections. The wife seeks relief in fashionable dissipation; the husband, perhaps, in the brutalities of a brothel.

"But, aside from all explanatory theories, the FACT is, as I have stated it, viz.: that (taking the proportion of each into account) *there are ten legal separations of the married, for one voluntary separation of the placed.* If anyone doubts it, let him inquire for himself, and he will doubt no longer.

"What say you to that fact, my reverend friends? How consorts it with your favourite theory, that man is a profligate animal, a desperately wicked creature? that, but for your prayers and blessings, the earth would be a scene of licentiousness and excess? that human beings remain together, only because you have helped to tie them? that there is no medium between priestly marriage and unseemly prostitution?

"Does this fact open your eyes a little on the real state of things to which we heterodox spirits venture to look forward? Does it assist in explaining to you how it is that we are so much more willing than you to entrust the most sacred duties to moral rather than legal keeping?

"You cannot imagine that a man and a woman, finding themselves suited to each other, should agree, without your interference, to become companions; that he should remove to her plantation, or she to his, as they found it most convenient; that the connection should become known to their friends without the agency of banns, and be respected, even though not ostentatiously announced in a newspaper. Yet all this happens in Hayti, without any breach of propriety, without any increase of vice; but, on the contrary, much to the benefit of morality, and the discouragement of prostitution. It happens among the white as well as the coloured population; and the president of the country gives it his sanction, in his own person.

"Do you still ask me—accustomed as you are to consider virtue the offspring of restrictions—do you still ask me, what the checks are that produce and preserve such a state of things? I reply, good feeling and public opinion. Continual change is held to be disreputable; where sincere and well-founded affection exists, it is not desired; and as there is no pecuniary inducement in forming a placement, these voluntary unions are seldom ill-assorted."

Where social anarchy is feared, facts like these are worth pages of argument. If the Haytians are civilised enough for this more moral kind of marriage, why should Europeans be on a lower level? For it should not be forgotten that the experiment was tried in St. Domingo under great disadvantages, and these unlegalised unions have yet proved more permanent than those tied with all due formality and tightness.

It may be urged: if divorce is to be so easily attainable, why should there be a marriage contract at all? Both as regards the pair immediately concerned, and as regards the children who may result from the union, a clear and definite contract seems to me to be eminently desirable. It is not to be wished that the union of those on whom depends the next generation should be carelessly and lightly entered into; the dignity and self-recollection which a definite compact implies are by no means to be despised, when it is remembered how grave and weighty are the responsibilities assumed by those who are to give to the State new citizens, and to Humanity new lives, which must be either a blessing or a curse. But the dignity of such a course is not its only, nor, indeed, its main, recommendation. More important is the absolute necessity that the conditions of the union of the two adult lives should be clearly and thoroughly understood between them. No wise people enter into engagements of an important and durable character without a written agreement; a definite contract excludes all chance of disagreement as to the arrangements made, and prevents misunderstandings from arising. A verbal contract may be misunderstood by either party; lapse of time may bring about partial forgetfulness; slight disagreements may result in grave quarrels. If the contract be a written one, it speaks for itself, and no doubt can arise which cannot be reasonably settled. All this is readily seen where ordinary business partnerships are concerned, but some—unconsciously rebounding from the present immoral system, and plunging into the opposite extreme—consider that the union in marriage of man and woman is too tender and sacred a thing to be thus dealt with as from a business point of view. But it must be remembered that while love is essential to true and holy marriage, marriage implies more than love; it implies also a number of new relations to the outside world which—while men and women live in the world—cannot be wholly disregarded. Questions of house, of money, of credit, &c., necessarily arise in connection with the dual home, and these cannot be ignored by sensible men and women. The contract does not touch with rude hands the sensitive plant of love; it concerns itself only with the garden in which the plant grows, and two people can no more live on love alone than a plant can grow without earth around its roots. A contract which removes occasions of disagreement in business matters shelters and protects the love from receiving many a rude shock. "Society will ere long," said Mr. Conway, "be glad enough to assimilate contracts between man and woman to contracts between partners in business. Then love will dispense alike with the bandage on its eyes and the constable's aid." Some pre-nuptial arrangement seems necessary which shall decide as to the right of inheritance of the survivor of the married pair. As common property will grow up during the union, such property should pass to the survivor and the children, and until some law be made which shall prevent parents from alienating from their children the whole of their property, a provision guarding their inheritance should find its place in the proposed deed. A definite marriage contract is also desirable for the sake of the children who may proceed from the union. Society has a right to demand from those who bring new members into it, some contract which shall enable it to compel them to discharge their responsibilities, if they endeavour to avoid them. If all men and women were perfect, no contract would be necessary, any more than it would be necessary to have laws against murder and theft; but while men and women are as they are, some compulsive power against evil-doers must be held in reserve by the law. Society is bound to guard the interests of the helpless children, and this can only be done by a clear and definite arrangement which makes both father and mother responsible for the lives they have brought into existence, and which shows the parentage in a fashion which could go into a law-court should any dispute arise. Again, if there were no contract, in whom would the guardianship of the children be vested, in case of wrong-doing of either parent, of death, or of separation? Suppose a brutal father: his wife leaves him and takes the children with her; how is she to keep them if he claims and takes them? If she has the legal remedy of divorce, the Court awards her the guardianship and she is safe from molestation. If a wife elope, taking the children with her, is the father to have no right to the guardianship of his sons and daughters, but to remain passive while they pass under the authority of another man? Application for divorce would guard him from such a wrong. If the parents separate, and both desire to have the children, how can such contest be decided, save by appeal to an impartial law? Marriage, as before urged, is a partnership, and where common duties, common interests, and common responsibilities grow up, there it is necessary that either party shall have some legal means of redress in case of the wrong-doing of the other.

To those who, on the other hand, object to facility of divorce being granted at all, it may fairly be asked that they should not forget that to place divorce within the reach of people, is not the same as compelling them to submit to it. Those who prefer to regard marriage as indissoluble could as readily maintain the indissolubility of their own wedded tie under a law which permitted divorce, as they can do at the present time. But those who think otherwise, and are unhappy in their marriages, would then be able to set themselves free. No happy marriage would be affected by the change, for the attainability of divorce would only be welcomed by those whose marriage was a source of misery and of discord; the contented would be no less content, while the unhappy would be relieved of their unhappiness; thus the change would injure no one, while it would benefit many.

It is a pity that there is no way of obtaining the general feminine view of the subject of marriage and divorce; women who study, who form independent opinions are—so far as my experience goes—unanimous in their desire to see the English laws altered; advanced thinkers of both sexes are generally, one might say universally, in favour of change. To those who think that women, if polled to-morrow, would vote for a continuance of the present state of things, may be recommended the following passage from Mrs. Mill: "Women, it is said, do not desire, do not seek what is called their emancipation. On the contrary, they generally disown such claims when made in their behalf, and fall with *acharnement* upon any one of themselves who identifies herself with their common cause. Supposing the fact to be true in the fullest extent ever asserted, if it proves that European women ought to remain as they are, it proves exactly the same with respect to Asiatic women; for they too, instead of murmuring at their seclusion, and at the restraint imposed upon them, pride themselves on it, and are astonished at the effrontery of women who receive visits from male acquaintances, and are seen in the streets unveiled. Habits of submission make men as well as women servile-minded. The vast population of Asia do not desire or value, probably would not accept, political liberty, nor the savages of the forest, civilization; which does not prove that either of those things is undesirable for them, or that they will not, at some future time, enjoy it. Custom hardens human beings to any kind of degradation, by deadening the part of their nature which would resist it. And the case of women is, in this respect, even a peculiar one, for no other inferior caste that we have heard of have been taught to regard their degradation as their honour." Mr. Conway considers that changed circumstances would rapidly cause women to be favourable to the proposed alteration: "Am I told," he remarks, "that woman dreads the easy divorce? Naturally, for the prejudices and arrangements of society have not been adapted to the easy divorce. Let her know that, under the changed sentiment which shall follow changed law, she will meet with sympathy where now she would encounter suspicion; let her know that she will, if divorced from one she loves not, have only her fair share of the burdens entailed by the original mistake; and she who of all persons suffers most if the home be false will welcome the freer marriage" ("The Earthward Pilgrimage," p. 289).

Both in theory and in practice advanced thinkers have claimed facility of divorce. John Milton, in his essay on "Divorce," complains that "the misinterpreting of Scripture . . . hath changed the blessing of matrimony not seldom into a familiar and co-inhabiting mischiefe; at least into a drooping and disconsolate household captivitie, without refuge or redemption" (p. 2), and in his Puritan fashion he remarks that because of this "doubtles by the policy of the devill that gracious ordinance becomes insupportable," so that men avoid it and plunge into debauchery. Arguing that marriage is not to be regarded merely as a legitimate kind of sexual intercourse, but rather as a union of mind and feeling, Milton says: "That indisposition, unfitness, or contrariety of mind, arising from a cause in nature unchangable, hindring and ever likely to hinder the main benefits of conjugall society, which are solace and peace, is a greater reason of divorce than natural frigidity, especially if there be no children, and that there be mutual consent" (p. 5). Luther, before Milton, held the same liberal views. Mary Wolstonecraft acted on the same theory in her own life, and her daughter was united to the poet Shelley while Shelley's first wife was living, no legal divorce having severed the original marriage. Richard Carlile's second marriage was equally illegal. In our own days the union of George Henry Lewes and George Eliot has struck the key-note of the really moral marriage. Mary Wolstonecraft was unhappy in her choice, but in all the other cases the happiest results accrued. It needs considerable assurance to brand these great names with immorality, as all those must do who denounce as immoral unions which are at present illegal.

In the whole of the arguments put forward in the above pages there is not one word which is aimed at real marriage, at the faithful and durable union of two individuals of opposite sexes—a union originated in and maintained by love alone. Rather, to quote Milton once more, is reverence for marriage the root of the reform I urge: he who "thinks it better to part than to live sadly and injuriously to that cherfull covnant (for not to be belov'd and yet retain'd, is the greatest injury to a gentle spirit), he I say who therefore seeks to part, is one who highly honours the married life, and would not stain it; and the reasons which now move him to divorce, are equall to the best of those that could first warrant him to marry" (p. 10). In the advocacy of such views marriage is elevated, not degraded; no countenance is given to those who would fain destroy the idea of the durable union between one man and one woman. Monogamy appears to me to be the result of civilization, of personal dignity, of cultured feeling; loyalty of one man to one woman is, to me, the highest sexual ideal. The more civilized the nature the more durable and exclusive does the marriage union become; in the lower ranges of animal life difference of sex is enough to excite passion: there is no individuality of of choice. Among savages it is much the same: it is the female, not the woman, who is loved, although the savage rises higher than the lower brutes, and is attracted by individual beauty. The civilised man and woman need more than sex-difference and beauty of form; they seek satisfaction for mind, heart, and tastes as well as for body; each portion the complex nature requires its answer in its mate. Hence it arises that true marriage is exclusive, and that prostitution is revolting to the noble of both sexes, since in prostitution love is shorn of his fairest attributes, and passion, which is only his wings, is made the sole representative of the divinity. The fleeting connections supposed by some Free Love theorists are steps backward and not forward; they offer no possibility of home, no education of the character, no guarantee for the training of the children. The culture both of father and of mother, of the two natures of which its own is the resultant, is necessary to the healthy development of the child; it cannot be deprived of either without injury to its full and perfect growth.

But just as true marriage is invaluable, so is unreal marriage deteriorating in its effects on all concerned: therefore, where mistake has been made, it is important to the gravest interests of society that such mistake should be readily remediable, without injury to the character of either of those concerned in it. Freed from the union which injures both, the man and woman may seek for their fit helpmeets, and in happy marriages may become joyful servants of humanity, worthy parents of the citizens of to-morrow. Men and women must know conjugal, before they can know true parental, love; each must see in the child the features of the beloved ere the perfect circle of love can be complete. Husband and wife bound in closest, most durable and yet most eager union, children springing as flowers from the dual stem of love, home where the creators train the lives they have given—such will be the marriage of the future. The loathsome details of the Divorce Court will no longer pollute our papers; the public will no longer be called in to gloat over the ruins of desecrated love; society will be purified from sexual vice; men and women will rise to the full royalty of their humanity, and hand in hand tread life's pathways, trustful instead of suspicious, free instead of enslaved, bound by love instead of by law.

Printed by ANNIE BESANT and CHARLES BRADLAUGH, 28, Stonecutter Street, London, E.C.

THE SOCIAL ASPECTS OF MALTHUSIANISM.

By ANNIE BESANT.

Perhaps scarcely sufficient regard is had, as a rule, to the social effects which would follow a general adoption of Malthusian views. Yet the question of "Large or Small Families," is one of an essentially social character, and we may well ask how would society be affected if conjugal prudence became the rule instead of the exception.

Small families, I venture to assert, are best for the interests of society as a whole, as well as best for the family and for the individual. It would be for the happiness of each and of all if the home were gladdened with two or three children, instead of being overcrowded with ten or twelve. To gain, however, all the advantages possible, small families must run side by side with early marriages. Late marriage is bad, politically, socially, and individually. Politically it would, if universally adopted, be injurious, because it would weaken the physique of the race, not only by the less robust health which long maintained celibacy would inflict upon the parents, but also because the children of those who marry late in life are not as strong and as vigorous as those which spring from parents in the full flush of their youth and strength. A race, healthy and powerful physically, forms a nation capable of self defence, and of active initiative, and early marriage gives this race to the State. Socially late marriage is bad, because it implies a number of dwarfed and isolated lives, instead of a number of happy homes, radiating brightness around them on every side. And since late marriage does not, and never will, imply celibacy, it is the source of endless social corruption, degrading love into lust, and ruining thousands of helpless women, outcasts from all pure affection and respect, at once the children and the scourgers of man's vice. Early marriage saves both men and women from prostitution, and by purifying society, makes it more stable and more happy.

Individually late marriage is bad, physically, mentally, and morally. Prolonged celibacy shortens the term of life; the unmarried die, on an average, at an earlier age than do the married. It tends also to inflict injury on the mind, as may be seen by a slight examination into the statistics of lunatic asylums. Morally, it deteriorates both men and women; it makes men harder, more cynical, more selfish, more sceptical of human virtue; it makes women more frivolous, more narrow-minded, more sour. The home is the best school both for man and for woman; there they learn patience, gentleness, thought for others, selflessness, tenderness, and charity. There are no teachers of these virtues like the little children, and these added to courage, strength, endurance, intellectual effort, make up nobility of chararacter in both sexes alike.

The only reason why marriage is delayed, or avoided, in the majority of cases, is the dread of a burden of a family too large to be supported on the available means. This dread removed hundreds would form happy homes who now live discontentedly in solitary lodgings. Early marriage to the non-Malthusian, means the almost certainity of a large family, with the necessary accompaniments among those who are straitened in means, of endless toil for the man, endless drudgery for the woman. The spectre of poverty scares people back from marriage, and this great social mischief would entirely pass away if Malthusian views were generally adopted by the people.

But it is not only in respect of early marriage that the social aspects of Malthusianism are attractive. Not only does Malthusianism make early marriage possible, but it also makes it healthier and happier.

And first with regard to health. How many women are annually sacrificed to constant child-bearing. Let anyone call to mind some merry girl, married at the age of twenty, and a mother at twenty-one; as each year passes it brings another child; the mother becomes paler and weaker with each successive birth; the children become more fragile as they too quickly succeed one another. Ten years pass away; the mother at thirty is a worn-out shadow of her former self; she is aged, weak, weary, too happy if she have escaped actual disease. It cannot be too often stated that over-rapid child-bearing is ruinous to woman's health, and that that teaching is immoral and mischievous which sacrifices the strength and happiness and usefulness of a women's life to the Moloch of an imagined duty. In a fashionable journal, a week or two ago, it was stated that a late Duchess, married young, brought her husband twelve children in twelve years, and died in giving birth to a thirteenth child. No wonder; but the journal seemed to think it quite a matter of course that the woman should thus suffer what it was pleased to call "maternal martyrdom." Martyrdom is only admirable when suffered in a good cause; sacrifice for home or for country is glorious and noble, but what benefit did the home or the country derive from the martyrdom that gave to both twelve little lords and ladies, while it deprived the home of the wife and mother? Society would have been none the worse for a smaller invasion of new citizens, and the children would have been much the better had the mother's life been cherished instead of being thrown away. And even where the actual life of the mother is not sacrificed, the home suffers where the over-rapid child bearing destroys the mother's vigorous strength. It is a wrong to a little child of a year old that it should be thrust out of the exclusive right to mother-care by a new-comer whose still tenderer youth claims still more constant cherishing. And where the mother's strength is failing under the never ceasing drain made upon it, she is unable to exert the vigorous and steady over-looking on which the future of her children depends.

The happiness of every home must rest chiefly on the wife and mother. Where the mother's health is sacrificed, the happiness of the home must suffer. Narrowing for a moment our views of women's duties to those which she discharges as wife and as mother, the perfection of such discharge must depend, to a great extent upon her health. The happiness of many a middle-class home is marred by the ill health of the wife; her children run wild, the household is irregular, the absence of guidance and control causes constant discomfort; the husband is over-weighted and consequently ill-tempered, and draws an unfavourable contrast between the active girl he wedded and the languid woman who is his wife. Aye, but the girl had not had the spring of activity destroyed by the constantly repeated physical strain, and who is to blame for the change, save the husband and wife themselves for their lack of conjugal prudence, and the Society which frowns on the limitation of the family, and bids every married pair increase and multiply without the smallest regard to consequences?

If for no higher reason, yet for their personal comfort and happiness, English husbands and fathers should take a lesson from their French brethren. The vivid sympathy which grows out of united interests can never thoroughly arise where the wife's ill-health prevents her from sharing the husband's more vigorous life. It is easy for a man to complain that he does not find a companion in his wife, and that she takes no interest in the larger life outside the house, and does not feel the throb of intellectual movement of the age; if the man were in the woman's place, if he were in constant weariness of body, if he had to care for, and watch, and tend half a dozen young children, while his own condition needed physical rest rather than physical exertion, perhaps he also might be indifferent to the strife of opinion, and be too much taken up with the problems of bab es to care to solve the problems of sociology. Intellectual sympathy will never be thorough between husband and wife, while the wife is over-burdened and over-harassed by the care of a family too large for one woman to tend.

But is woman to be regarded only as wife, as mother, as nurse, as housekeeper? Is she never to be thought of as an individual, but always in relation to somebody else? Has a woman no right as an independent human being? We do not regard a man only as a husband and father: why should we regard a women only as a wife and mother? To think of a man as a citizen, as an orator, as a statesman, as a philosopher, is not thought to throw contempt on the sacredness of his life as husband and as father; why should it be thought, then, to imply indifference to the beauty of wifehood and motherhood, when we say that woman's life does not consist of these alone? It is the radically false notion of "woman's sphere," which twists men's views of these questions. Woman is not only for man; she also has a right to her own life, and to condemn her to constant child-bearing, to consume the prime of her life in continual illness and recovery, is an injustice to herself and a grave injury to society. Regarded as wife and as mother, she will be more useful in proportion as these duties take a share of, but do not absorb the whole of the best part of her life; regarded in her completeness as woman, she will be nobler and more beautiful when her intellectual life is fuller and stronger, when she recognises her duty to the world as well as her duty to the home. When this step forward has been made then will true social reform become possible. Man alone can never base on a just and secure foundation a society formed of women as well as of men. The two together must work for the common good, and by joint effort build up the happiness of all.

The woman, however, is not the only one who will benefit socially from the general adoption of Malthusianism. The benefit to the husband will be as great as to the wife, for in a country in which—as in France—small families are the rule the proportion of producers to non-productive consumers is changed, and thus the burden of toil laid on the producers is lightened. A short time since an advertisement appeared in one of our daily papers, asking that public charity should be extended to the family of a man who had just died, leaving his widow and children penniless; the advertisement stated that the dead man had been the sole support of his wife, nine children, and two female relatives; one poor brain and one pair of arms were required to maintain their owner and twelve other people! The burden pressed this man out of life; how many men are not actually murdered in this fashion, but have all youth, and spring and joy crushed out of them under a similar weight. Where the proportion of children to grown people is as great as it is in England, the grown people have to work too hard, and life is made one long toil. A man may be able to feed and clothe and house and educate two children who will be a joy and a delight to him, but may be unable to do the same justice to ten, and may wear out his life in a hopeless struggle after the impossible. Thus fatherhood is made a terror instead of a blessing, and men are compelled to remain childless, lest a family they are unable to support should be crowded on their hands. When conjugal prudence is recognised as the highest morality, the bread winner's life will be gladdened and lightened; he will have leisure, comfort, rest in his home—a home musical with the laughter of happy well cared children, instead of discordant with quarrelling and petulance which grow out of poverty and neglect.

Passing from the home to the State, what effect will result from the general adoption of Malthusian views? When Malthusianism is thoroughly understood and believed in, the great principle will be recognised: "it is a crime for a man and woman to bring into the world more children than they are able to feed, clothe, and educate." A crime as towards the children, and as towards each other, for the reasons given above; a crime towards society, as I now propose to shew.

Let us take a very common case. A young man is earning

as an agricultural labourer 12s. a week in winter and 15s. in summer; he falls in love with a young woman, as is natural—marries her, and the new home is bright, though the poverty is great. A child is born, and its coming is welcomed, and the narrow wage is stretched to cover the new claimant. A second year passes, and brings another child; the rejoicing is less, for the mouths are growing while the food remains stationary; years go by, and each year adds another life to the household, husband and wife are young and strong, the country air is pure and invigorating, the children thrive, though the later-born lack the full strength and sturdiness of the elder. At the end of a dozen years, eight little children sit round the cottage board, and the mother works daily in the field and nightly at the needle, striving to win bread and clothing for the eight hungry mouths and the eight growing bodies. And her old beauty has gone, and she is pale and worn, and coarsened by ceaseless toil, and her voice has grown sharp and her temper harsh. And when the ninth child is born and the mother is idle, no resource remains but—the parish. So the parish doctor is called in, and some out-door relief is asked for and obtained, and parish loaves appear on the cottage table. And henceforth, whenever sickness comes the family falls back on parish aid, and the squire's lady and the parson's wife send odds and ends of food and clothing to "that poor Mrs. Jones with her nine children to keep on such small earnings." And so the habit of dependence is formed and self reliance and self respect gradually dwindle away before the pressing need for food. Week after week parish aid is given. But what is the "parish?" It is the other members of the community in which Mrs. Jones lives, so that the large family of Mr. and Mrs. Jones, is fed by her neighbours, and the prudent and the temperate are taxed to fill the mouths created by the thoughtless and the improvident. Thus do we encourage temperance among our English workers! Is a man thoughtful, saving, and provident? Tax him to support the family of his reckless, thoughtless neighbour. And then we complain the rates are heavy. They are likely to become heavier, until we teach everywhere the doctrine that no one has a right to possess a larger family than he and his wife can themselves support. We have no more right to compel other people to feed and clothe our children, than we have to steal their purses; the one is as much robbery as is the other. We do not urge only that the limitation of the family is not immoral: we say that the immorality is in the non-limitation, and that conjugal prudence is a duty imperative on all.

Let every man and woman remember that if their neighbours have a larger family than they can support, those neighbours take so much out of the mouths and off the backs of their own children. Let it be looked upon as a sin against society when a large family comes upon the rates. Let it be regarded as disloyalty to duty when too many are thrown into the labour market and thus reduce the wages of labour. So shall public opinion condemn reckless multiplication, and the greatest social reform of the century shall raise the masses from the poverty in which they are now plunged.

THE MALTHUSIAN LEAGUE.

28, Stonecutter Street, Farringdon Street, E.C.

President: C. R. Drysdale, M.D., M.R.C.P., Lond., F.R.C.S. Eng. Consulting Physician to the Farringdon General Dispensary; Physician to the North London Consumption Hospital; Lock Hospital, &c., &c.

Hon. Secretaries: W. H. Reynolds & J. Page.

This society was formed in 1877 to spread among the people, by all practicable means, a knowledge of the law of population, of its consequences, and of its bearing upon human conduct and morals, and also to agitate for the abolition of all legal penalties upon the public discussion of the question.

PRINCIPLES.

1. "That population has a constant tendency to increase beyond the means of subsistence.

2. That the checks with counteract this tendency are resolvable into positive or life destroying, and prudential or birth restricting.

3. That the positive or life-destroying checks comprehend the premature death of children and adults by disease, starvation, war and infanticide.

4. That the prudential or birth-restricting checks consist of the limitation of offspring by abstention from marriage, or by prudence after marriage.

5. That prolonged abstention from marriage—as advocated by Malthus—is productive of many diseases and of much sexual vice; early marriage, on the contrary, tends to ensure sexual purity, domestic comfort, social happiness, and indvidual health; but it is a grave social offence for men and women to bring into the world more children than they can adequately house, feed, clothe, and educate.

6. That over-population is the most fruitful source of pauperism, ignorance, crime and disease.

7. That the full and open discussion of the Population Question is a matter of vital moment to society, and such discussion should be absolutely unfettered by fear of legal penalties.

MEMBERSHIP.

That the condition of Membership be the payment of an entrance fee of 6d. (which shall be taken to imply adhesion to the rules of the League), an annual subscription of 1s., or, to constitute life-membership, a single payment of one guinea.

PUBLICATIONS OF THE MALTHUSIAN LEAGUE.

The MALTHUSIAN, a Monthly Journal, the official organ of the League, Published on the First of every month. Price 1d., by post 1½d. Office—28, Stonecutter Street, E.C. Also of E. TRUELOVE, 256, High Holborn, and HAINES, 212, Mile End Road, E.C.

TRACTS.

1. The Principle of Population. ½d.
2. The Struggle for Enjoyable Existence. 1d.
3. The Limitation of Families. 1d.
4. Evils produced by Over Child-bearing and Excessive Lactation. ½d.
5. Great is Truth, and it will prevail. ½d.
6. The Presidential Address 1878. 1d.
7. The Bondsmen of these Our Days. 1d.
8. The Cause of Poverty. ½d.
9. Large Families and Over Population, being the Presidential Address 1879. 1d.
10. The Social Aspects of Malthusianism. 1d.

LEAFLETS.

(Intended for gratuitous Distribution).

J. S. MILL on Small Families.

Low Wages and Over Population. (Extracted from the late Professor CAIRNES, great work.)

Mr. MATTHEW ARNOLD on the French Peasant.

Low Wages and Dear Food, an Address to Working People.

The Propriety of not having more children than we can keep.

The Half-penny tracts can be had by members of the League at 50 for 1s., postage additional; the Penny ones at 25 for 1s. The Leaflets ar sent gratuitously on receipt of stamped and directed wrapper; but no notice can be taken of communications which do not fulfil this condition.

Printed and Published by the MALTHUSIAN LEAGUE, 28, Stonecutter Street, London, E.C.

Price 1d. In Packets of 25 (to members only) 1s.

SECTION III

THE

STORY OF AFGHANISTAN;

OR,

WHY THE TORY GOVERNMENT GAGS THE INDIAN PRESS.

A PLEA FOR THE WEAK AGAINST THE STRONG.

BY

ANNIE BESANT.

LONDON:
FREETHOUGHT PUBLISHING COMPANY,
28, STONECUTTER STREET, E.C.

PRICE TWOPENCE.
1879.

LONDON:

PRINTED BY ANNIE BESANT AND CHARLES BRADLAUGH,

28, STONECUTTER STREET, E.C.

THE STORY OF AFGHANISTAN;

OR,

WHY THE TORY GOVERNMENT GAGS THE INDIAN PRESS.

A PLEA FOR THE WEAK AGAINST THE STRONG

AMONG the many grave charges to be brought against the Tory Government when at last—forced by the inevitable hand of Time—it is compelled to face its master, the people of Great Britain; among the crimes to be alleged against it at the bar of public opinion; among the counts of the indictment which is there to be presented against it, one weighty, one most fatal impeachment will come from the smouldering villages, the fire-blackened homes, the trampled harvests, the murdered men, the frozen women and children of the far-off Afghan land.

The history of English policy in Afghanistan is one which each citizen of Britain is now bound to study. No adult individual in a nation is free from responsibility of national policy—only some have votes, but all have influence. To-day the hands of the citizens are in so far clean that when this Tory Government was placed in power, it was placed there for inaction, for rest, for quietude. None voted that it should embroil us in Europe, in Asia, in Africa. None chose it that it should waste our savings and embarrass our finances. None raised it that it should pour out our money as dross, nor shed human blood as water in three of the four continents of the globe. To-morrow, if England vote Tory, on England, and not on the Ministry, will rest the crimes of the last six years. England's the dishonor in South Eastern Europe if she endorse the war-with-disgrace-treaty of Berlin. England's the shame if she condone the murder of women and children in cold blood in South Africa, the slaughter of the helpless by dynamite as they crouched for shelter in the caves. England's the disgrace—and the rapidly advancing Nemesis—if she approve our broken treaties, our dishonored promises, our inhuman cruelties, touching the wronged, the betrayed, the crushed races of the mountains and valleys of Afghanistan.

On behalf of the latter alone I raise my voice to-day. It is said to be unpatriotic to blame one's country. But not so have I read the history of England's noblest patriots. Love of England does not mean approval and endorsement of the policy of some Oriental adventurer whom chance and personal ability and unscrupulousness have raised to power. Love of England means reverence for her past, work for her future; it means sympathy with all that is noble and great in her history, and endeavor to render her yet more noble, yet more great; it means triumph in her victories over oppression, delight in her growing freedom, glory in her encouragement of all nations struggling towards liberty; it means pride in her pure name, in her fair faith, in her unsoiled honor, in her loyal word; it means condemnation of her bullying, boasting, cruel imperialism since Lord Beaconsfield seduced her from her purity, and regretful remorseful turning back to the old paths of duty, of honor, and of faith.

Therefore this plea of mine for "the weak against the strong" is not an unpatriotic attack on our own beloved land, but rather the loving effort of a child to save a mother whose honor and whose life are threatened by unscrupulous betrayers.

In 1838 we first interfered in Afghan politics. An Afghan ruler, Shah Soojah, had ceded some of his realm to Runjeet Singh, "the Lion of the Punjaub," and had been, therefore, driven into exile by his indignant countrymen. Dost Mahommed succeeded to the vacant throne, and Shah Soojah appealed to Lord Auckland, Governor General of India, for aid against the selected of the Afghan people. He raised the ghost of Russian influence; he played on the unworthy fear of Russia that from time to time discredits English courage; he spoke of Russian spies, Russian designs, Russian intrigues, until Lord Auckland, panic-struck, rushed to meet the imagined danger, took up Shah Soojah's cause, placed an army at his virtual disposal, overran Afghanistan, entered Cabul, and propped up Shah Soojah on his throne with the sharp points of British bayonets. The seat was an uneasy one. In 1841 it gave way. Afghanistan rose. The hill tribes blocked the passes. From the 6th to the 13th January (1842), the English army of occupation strove to cut its way back to India. Food failed it. Snow blocked its path. Bitter cold destroyed its weaklings. Sharp swords cut down its loiterers. Out of 16,000 troops and camp followers one exhausted, starving, fainting, fugitive fell still living within the gates of Jellalabad.

Il va sans dire that massacre revenged massacre. By sword and fire Britain punished the Afghan uprising, and then—wise at length—withdrew her troops, recognised Dost Mahommed, practically admitted her blunder, and left Afghanistan free and independent, mistress of herself.

In 1849 we annexed the Punjaub, and so advanced our border until it marched with that of Afghanistan. Dost Mahommed had no will to break himself against British power; he recognised the position of affairs, and in 1855 entered into a definite treaty with the British Government of India. In this treaty were two important pledges. One on the part of England promised that we would "never interfere" within the possessions of the Ameer. The other pledged the Ameer to be "friend of our friends, and enemy of our enemies." The phrase "never interfere" had a peculiar and important signification. For some fifty years English annexation in Hindustan had been remarkably rapid. This annexation ran through a well-defined cycle. First—an English Resident; then, advice urgently pressed; then, complaint of misgovernment constantly published; then, interference; then, compulsion; then, open annexation. The free and turbulent Afghan people saw this play repeated over and over again on the other side of the Suleiman range. Hence arose a jealous fear of the like fate. Hence a keen dread of British interference. Hence an ineradicable distrust of British officers and a determination not to open the flood gates of subjugation by admittance of a British Resident. Therefore when the treaty of 1855 was signed, the promise of Afghan friendship was made to depend on the promise of England not to interfere within Afghanistan, not to send British Resident or Envoy to the Ameer's court.

In 1857 another treaty was made with Dost Mahommed. We were at war with Persia and subsidised the Ameer as our ally. By this treaty British officers were admitted to Cabul, Candahar, and Balkh to supervise the expenditure of our money in defence of Afghanistan. But in this very treaty their functions were carefully limited to "all military and political matters connected with the war." It was further agreed that "whenever the subsidy should cease, the British officers were to be withdrawn from the Ameer's country" (Art. 7), and that the British Government might appoint a Vakil (Agent) at Cabul, provided that such agent should not be "a European officer." Such was the clear and well-defined position of the British Government towards Afghanistan. Dost Mahommed lived till 1863, and the promise on either side was carefully performed. In the war of succession which followed, England's faith was preserved untouched. Sir John Lawrence, her representative, permitted no interference, but simply recognised as Ameer the chosen of the Afghan people. We were safe, at peace, free from peril. Afghanistan was a bar between Russia and ourselves, and was a friendly Power, jealous of her own independence, but trustful in our faithfully-kept pledge of non-interference within her borders.

Governments in England changed, but our policy towards Afghanistan did not alter. Sir John Lawrence who, as Chief Commissioner of the Punjaub, had negotiated the treaty of 1855, became, in 1863, Governor-General of India. Naturally, as Governor-General, he pursued the policy he had advocated as Chief Commissioner. When, in 1867, Ufzul Khan triumphed at Cabul, he sent, under the 7th Article of the Treaty of 1857, a "Mahommedan gentleman of rank and character" as agent to the then Ameer, and when, in 1868, Shere Ali again conquered, the same ties were maintained.

In 1867 Sir Stafford Northcote, then Secretary of State for India, frankly recognised that the Russian advances in Central Asia were likely to continue. He declared that they afforded "no reason for any uneasiness or for any jealousy," and that the conquests of Russia were "the natural result of the circumstances in which she finds herself placed." Sir Stafford Northcote was not then the mere tool of Mr. Disraeli, as he now is of Lord Beaconsfield. He had then a character for discretion and for good sense; he was yet not bitten by the mad dog, Imperialism. Sir Henry Rawlinson, in 1868, in vain tried to alarm the Indian Secretary. Sir Stafford refused to be led away, and kept his head cool and clear. It is important to remember that the most rapid advances made by the Russians were made before 1869; that they had then established themselves in Bokhara, and had thus become the immediate neighbors of Afghanistan. Lord Mayo succeeded Sir John Lawrence in 1869, and followed the same line of policy. Shere Ali was very anxious to obtain from England a pledge of future assistance in securing his family on the throne. This pledge Lord Mayo refused to give, but in March, 1869, he met the Ameer in Conference at Umballa. Writing home on March 10th, Lord Mayo declared: "We want no Resident at Cabul, or political influence in his kingdom," and with these views he went into the Conference. The Ameer complained somewhat bitterly that the Treaty of 1855 was one-sided, but Lord Mayo steadfastly declined to involve England in the local disputes of Afghanistan; he gave Shere Ali some money, some arms, and a distinct reiteration of the pledge that "no European officers should be placed as Residents in his cities," and so smoothed over the necessary refusal to actively support his throne. Of Lord Mayo's promise there can be no doubt. He himself writes on June 3rd: "The only pledges given were, that we would not interfere in his affairs; that we would support his independence; that we would not force European officers or Residents upon him against his wish."

It is worthy of notice that ordinary communication between Russia and Afghanistan has not, until lately, been regarded as a matter of complaint. In 1870 General Kaufmann wrote to Shere Ali a letter which was communicated by Prince Gortshakoff to the British Ambassador at St. Petersburg. In this letter General Kaufmann warned the Ameer not to interfere with Bokhara; the letter was laid before Lord Mayo, who, instead of objecting to the communication, expressed his approval of it. Other letters passed between General Kaufmann and the Ameer, and no word of complaint was ever heard from the English government. Friendly communications were never objected to until Lord Beaconsfield's craven fear of Russia cast a green light of jealousy over all her actions.

In 1872 Lord Mayo was unfortunately assassinated, and was succeeded by Lord Northbrook. The Seistan arbitration, owing to the dissatisfaction of the Ameer, led to the conferences at Simla in 1873. Lord Northbrook suggested that a British officer should interview the Ameer at Cabul, or some other Afghan town; but Shere Ali said he would prefer to send into India one of his own ministers, and Lord Northbrook, mindful of our pledges, at once accepted the offer. Here again arms were given to the Ameer, but he declined the money offered to him, and remained somewhat sulky, refusing to allow a British officer to inspect his northern frontiers with a view to their defence in case of need. He would not even permit Mr. Forsyth to pass through Afghanistan on his return from Yarkand. In spite of all this discontent on Shere Ali's part, the good faith and tact of Lord Northbrook again restored him to his former cordial relationship with us.

The evil genius alike of Hindustan and of South Africa now appeared on the scene. Sir Bartle Frere, in January 1875, wrote to the government that it was advisable to occupy Quettah, and to establish British officers in Afghanistan. Sir Bartle Frere, with his customary immoral disregard of good faith towards the weak, ignored our repeated pledges not to so establish them, and he sarcastically mocked the notion—a mockery somewhat lurid in the glare of the fate of Sir Louis Cavagnari—that they would be in any risk of life from Afghan jealousy. Sir Bartle Frere is wont to advise others to go into peril "with a light heart," but history recordeth no case of his putting his advice personally into effect.

Immediately on the receipt of this letter Lord Salisbury, as Secretary of State for India, wrote to Lord Northbrook, directing him to obtain the assent of the Ameer to the establishment of British officers at Herat and then at Candahar, alleging that if the Ameer's "intentions are still loyal, it is not possible that he will make any serious difficulty now." With astounding ignorance, or want of honesty, Lord Salisbury ignored the repeated pledges given by England that she would not send European agents into Afghanistan. With the same recklessness Lord Salisbury averred at Manchester that Afghanistan was the only country in which we were not represented, when he ought to have known that we had an accredited, though not European, agent at Cabul. Lord Northbrook on receiving this despatch, most honorably hesitated to obey it. He asked if discretion were allowed him, or if he were compelled to obey. He was directed to consult Sir Richard Pollock, Mr. Thornton and Mr. Girdlestone, and after some delay Lord Northbrook wrote home (June 7, 1875), urging that we were bound by our pledges, and had no reason, no ground for departing from them.

The unhappy policy of the Tory Government in Europe now began to cast its fatal blight over our policy in Asia.

The Russophobia diligently cultured by Lords Beaconsfield and Salisbury drove wild a large part of the British people, and the two Earls now felt that the time had come when they might venture to disregard all good faith, pleading in excuse "*La patrie en danger*." In November, 1875, Lord Salisbury penned the infamous command to "induce him [the Ameer] to receive a temporary Embassy in his capital. It need not be publicly connected with the establishment of a permanent Mission within his dominions. There would be many advantages in ostensibly directing it to some object of smaller political interest, which it will not be difficult for your Excellency to find, or, if need be, to create." Every decent English citizen must feel his cheeks burn with shame when he reads of one of his Ministers condescending to treachery so mean as well as so wicked.

Lord Northbrook—being an Englishman and a gentleman—declined to "find" or to "create" an "ostensible pretext," under cover of which he might disregard the treaties and promises made by England. Refusing to act as Lord Salisbury's tool, he was compelled to resign, and a more supple Viceroy was appointed in the person of Lord Lytton (1876).

The Tory Goverment instructed Lord Lytton to demand from the Ameer for their Agents "undisputed access to the frontier positions" of his kingdom, and to insist that these agents would expect "becoming attention to their friendly counsels." Sir Lewis Pelly—who had just destroyed the native Government of Baroda—was chosen as the messenger to convey these peremptory demands, and no permission was, as usual, asked from the Ameer as to sending the Envoy, but he was requested simply to say where he would receive him. "The ostensible pretext" "created" by Lord Lytton was his own assumption of the Viceroyalty, and the new title of Empress so foolishly allowed to the Queen by Parliament. The Ameer—with the courtesy of suspicion—"gushed" in reply, but suggested that there was no need for the coming of any new Envoy, as the existing relations were sufficiently defined by former agreements.

As the lamb declined to be coaxed into offering himself for dinner, the wolf began to growl. Shere Ali was told that he would incur "grave responsibility" by his refusal, and as this veiled menace had no effect he was sharply informed that England might make an arrangement with

Russia "which might have the effect of wiping Afghanistan out of the map altogether;" that he was "an earthen pipkin between two iron pots;" and that "the British Government is able to pour an overwhelming force into Afghanistan, which could spread round him like a ring of iron, but if he became our enemy, it could break him as a reed." Wise and conciliatory language if we desired a good understanding! Nevertheless, it was well chosen if we sought "to create" an "ostensible pretext" for a declaration of war.

Meantime Lord Lytton was preparing for the invasion of Afghanistan. While messengers were passing backwards and forwards to Cabul, the Viceroy was arranging for permanent barracks at Quettah, massing soldiers there and building a bridge across the Indus ready for the passage of troops (November, 1876). Stores were gathered, troops collected, and the Maharajah of Cashmere stirred up to attack tribes subject to Shere Ali. Threatened by word and act the Ameer gave way, consented to send an envoy to meet Sir Louis Pelly and nominated Noor Mahommed Khan, his Prime Minister, as his agent at the proposed Conference. Foiled in his first attempt to make war, the Viceroy was compelled to stand by his own proposition and to send Sir Louis Pelly to meet the Ameer's envoy. Sir Louis was supplied with two treaties, a public and a private one, the private one so narrowing down and guarding the promises made in the public one that they were rendered almost nugatory. The Envoys met at Peshawur in January, 1877. The account of the interview can only be read with shame. Noor Mahommed asked, what "if this Viceroy should make an agreement and a successor should say 'I am not bound by it?'" Again: were "all the agreements and treaties from the time of Sir John Lawrence and the late Ameer up to the time of Lord Northbrook and the present Ameer, invalid and annulled?" Sir Louis Pelly fenced and equivocated, but no answer was possible to the sad, straightforward challenge of the Afghan Envoy. Noor Mahommed then made a long and elaborate statement, recalling the former pledges of the English Government, and concluding with a prayer not to urge the establishment of British officers and so "abrogate the former treaties and agreements." A month later Sir Louis Pelly gave his answer, under written instructions from Lord Lytton. This melancholy State Document asserts that the 7th article of the Treaty of 1857 had "nothing whatever to do with the matters now under consideration" (!) and that all treaties existing between us and Afghanistan being old, they "afforded no basis for further negotiation." When we remember that the Tory Government posed as upholders of the treaty obligations of 1856 in Europe, it is interesting to learn that treaty obligations of 1855 and 1857 in Asia were too old to be of any binding force. It was next alleged that the "utterances" of previous Viceroys had not "the force of a Treaty"; yet surely the promises of England's highest Asian representatives ought to be held sacred. But Sir Louis Pelly actually stated: "His Excellency the Viceroy instructs me to inform your Excellency plainly that the British Government neither recognises nor has recognised, the obligation of these promises." Alas for our national honor! Alas for our lost good faith! What more could the most treacherous nation do than repudiate all pledges given by its representatives? The whole tone of the answer was rough, menacing, provocative, and Noor Mahommed, long ill, died in the hopeless attempt to reason with the peremptory Envoy of England. The Ameer, anxious at all risks to preserve our friendship, hearing of Noor Mahommed's serious illness, despatched another Envoy to Peshawur with instructions to yield to any demand that might be made. But submission was not what Lord Lytton desired. He telegraphed to Sir Louis Pelly to close the Conference, adding that if any new Envoy had arrived, all negotiations with him were to be refused. At the same time Lord Lytton recalled our agent in Cabul, and broke off all diplomatic communication with the Ameer. And this was deliberately done in order to forestall the undesired submission of Shere Ali to our unjustifiable demands.

Meanwhile in Europe our antagonism to Russia had been plainly shewn. We had made a grant of six millions to thwart her; we had summoned troops from India to fight her; we had called out our Reserves. Russia probably thought that if Indian troops were to fight in Europe, she might as well find them employment nearer home, and—very probably to embarrass us, or to feel her way—she despatched a mission to Cabul. Not very willingly, apparently, Shere Ali received the Russian Mission; but the "earthen pipkin" may have thought it wise to make friends with one of the "iron pots," as the other was threatening to break him. Whether he desired friendship with Russia or not matters little, for the Treaty of Berlin was signed, and the Russian mission immediately withdrew. While the Russians were at Cabul, a message arrived from Lord Lytton, stating that Sir Neville Chamberlain would "immediately" visit the Ameer; the messenger arrived to find the Ameer mourning the death of his best loved son and heir, Abdoolah Jan. Reckless of the father's pain, Lord Lytton declared that any delay in receiving the British Mission would be regarded as "open hostility." The Russian Envoy left Cabul on August 25th. Abdoolah Jan had died on August 17th, and as the Russians had left before Lord Lytton's first letter reached Cabul, there was no need to worry the unhappy Ameer during the forty days of mourning required by the custom of his country. But, cruelly pressed as he was, the Ameer did not, as has been pretended, refuse to receive the Mission. He only pleaded for the delay of a decent interval, and for outward courtesy. "I do not agree" he said "to the Mission arriving in this manner. It is as if they wish to disgrace me. I am a friend as before, and entertain no ill-will. The Russian envcy has come, and has come with my permission. I am still afflicted with grief at the loss of my son, and have had no time to think over the matter." He declared that he would send for the Mission, that he believed a personal interview would be useful, and only asked that the decent delay during the mourning might be granted him, and that the mission might not seem to come by force, without his consent. Our own messenger, Gulam Hussein Khan, even sent word from Cabul that if the "Mission will await Ameer's permission, everything will be arranged. . . . . If the Mission starts on 18th without waiting for the Ameer's permission, there would be no hope left for the renewal of friendship or communication." But Lord Lytton meant war, and did not desire to grant time for arrangement, so the Mission advanced to Ali Musjid before the forty days of mourning were expired, and was there stopped. It has been pretended that the Mission was repulsed with insult, but Major Cavagnari himself reported that the Afghan officer behaved "in a most courteous manner, and very favorably impressed both Colonel Jenkins and myself." Shere Ali wrote, complaining of the "hard words, repugnant to courtesy and politeness" used publicly to himself and to his chiefs. But complaint was useless. An "ostensible pretext" had been created for war, and war was declared.

Public opinion at home had, meanwhile, been sedulously misled. The Gagging Act had silenced the Indian Press; the telegraphs were in the hands of the Government; news was sent home that the Afghans had fired on our Mission and had insulted our flag. The fiction set aflame the hot English pride, and the now admitted falsehood served its intended purpose. Our troops—prepared beforehand by Lord Lytton—advanced rapidly, the hill-tribes were bribed, and we marched triumphantly forward, overrunning Afghanistan.

It might have at least been supposed that a war begun avowedly to protect our interests would have been carried on with some regard to humanity. We loudly proclaimed that we had no quarrel with the Afghan nation; yet we burned their villages, destroyed their crops, stole their cattle, looted their homes, hanged their men as "rebels" if they resisted, while we drove out their women and children to perish in the snow. If thus we treat those with whom we have no quarrel, what distinction do we draw between our friends and our foes?

All the world knows how we hunted out Shere Ali to perish broken-hearted. How we raised a puppet Ameer in his stead. How against all warning, all prayer, we established our Mission. How our Envoy perished—as Shere Ali had predicted—and how Yakoob Khan was driven out as traitor to his own people. All the world has heard also of our revenge. How we marched into Afghanistan murdering as "rebels" all who loved their country and their freedom well enough to face us. How we hanged by the hundred the wicked "traitors" who defended their own homes. How we refused quarter to the flying, and "cut up" the stragglers who had been vile enough to resist the invaders. These horrors have been committed under the pretence that the Afghans were "rebels." Rebels to whom? Where there is no rightful claim to authority there can be no rebellion in resistance. Resistance to the invader is a duty that each man owes to his fatherland, and the war of self-defence, of defence of wife and child, of hearth and home, is a righteous—aye, the only righteous—war. In such war every soldier is a patriot; in such war every death is a martyrdom. The defence of the road to Cabul, the battle of Charasiab, were episodes in such a war, and not in a rebellion. They were carried on by the regular Afghan army, led by its own officers, fighting honorably and gallantly. The Afghans were defeated, and contrary to the rules of civilised warfare, all quarter was refused, all "prisoners taken in fight" were shot. Then General Roberts issued a proclamation offering rewards "for any person who has fought against British troops since Sept. 3rd; larger rewards offered for rebel officers of Afghan army." Again: "Amnesty not extended to soldiers or civilians . . . who were guilty of instigating the troops and people to oppose the British troops. Such persons will be treated without mercy as rebels." Under this bloodthirsty proclamation the religious leaders of the people have been pitilessly murdered; the military leaders when found have shared the same fate. The *Statesman* gives the crimes of some of those who were thus killed:—

"Muhammad Aslam Khan, chief magistrate of Cabul, issued a proclamation calling upon all true Muhammadans to go out and fight the British.

"Sultan Aziz, a Barukzye of the Royal blood, bore a standard at Kharasiab.

"Kwaja Nazir, a city moola, gave his followers a standard to be borne as a sign of a holy war."

An unknown number of prisoners—reckoned by hundreds—have been found guilty of defending their country and have been hanged. Well may Frederic Harrison cry aloud in burning indignation: "Let the old watch words be erased from all English flags: *Dieu et mon droit*—*Honi soit*—and the rest, are stale enough. We will have a new imperial standard for the new Empress of Asia, and emblazon on it—*Imperium et Barbaries*."

In dealing with these executions, the *Daily News* has a letter so horrible, so forcibly in contrast with the humanity for which it is honorably remarkable, that one can only imagine that it is written by one of General Roberts's staff officers, and printed by the *Daily News* to show the spirit prevailing in our Afghan army. The correspondent first tells how some villages were ransacked, and all disbanded Afghan soldiers were seized, and how on one occasion eighty-nine were brought in. Of these forty were released, as they were able to show that they had not been engaged against the British troops, but any who had been at Cabul during the outbreak, or who had "returned later to fight against us," were hanged, and forty-nine were thus murdered in cold blood on November 10, 11, and 12. The letter then goes on:—

> "Our great regret is that, while we are sending the rank and file to the gallows, the ringleaders are still at large. Such poor specimens of humanity as these marched daily to execution are of but little account in our sight, and will not be missed in a country like this; whereas the execution of leading men—as Kushdil Khan, Nek Mahomed, or Mahomed Jan—would have a wholesome effect on the whole tribe of intriguers who have brought Yakoob Khan so low. Unfortunately we have not these sirdars in our hands; they are still living, and capable of further evil-doing."

It seems impossible to believe that these words were written by an English soldier. Mahomed Jan is the gallant leader of the Afghan resistance; he is a soldier who has fought bravely and honorably against us. In the old days such a foe, when defeated, would have been treated with the respect due to a brave man, but the wild beasts who dishonor English manhood in Afghanistan long for the moment when defeat shall enable them to strangle him. The result of this butchery is seen in the now general rising in Afghanistan, and it is not likely that the Afghans, driven to madness by our murder of prisoners, will show any more mercy to our wounded or to any prisoners who may fall into their hands than we have shown to them.

If our conduct towards men defending their country has been criminal, what shall we say of our conduct towards the non-combatants? These, at least, are held sacred in wars carried on by civilised powers. But the word "civilised" is forgotten by our army in Afghanistan, and non-combatants share the fate of other rebels. Sword and halter are not enough—the torch is also called in to assist in the march of civilisation. By the light of flaming villages may be traced the blessings of the Empress of India's advancing rule. While the combatants dangle in the air from the gallows, the non-combatants freeze to death on the ground We have burned villages when the thermometer registered 20° below freezing point, and, while we carefully sheltered our soldiers in thick tents, we have driven out women and children, houseless and foodless, to perish in the awful cold. Nine villages were thus destroyed in a single day. In this way do we discharge, to use Lord Lytton's words, "our high duties to God and man as the greatest civilizing Power:" in this way do Bishops in our House of Lords vote for the spreading of the Gospel of Christ.

General Roberts may well lay claim to the succession of the title of "Butcher," borne by the Duke of Cumberland of Scotch renown, and when he returns to his welcome at Windsor, her Imperial Majesty might bestow on him, with his other decorations, a new coat of arms, emblazoned with a drumhead and halter, crest a scull, supporters a frozen woman clasping a child, and a strangled Mahommedan mollah.

Well may General Roberts silence all independent correspondence. Well may Lord Lytton gag the Indian Press, and manipulate Indian telegrams. Yet even in the few facts that creep out from time to time England is learning how her name is being soiled, her honor tarnished by bloodthirsty cruelty, by stony-hearted recklessness of human pain. From out the darkness that veils Afghanistan moans of suffering reach us, and we shrink in horror from the work which is being done in our name. These frozen women cry aloud against us. These starved babes wail out our condemnation. These stiffened corpses, these fire-blackened districts, these snow-covered, blood-stained plains, appeal to Humanity to curse us. Englishmen, with wives nestled warm in your bosoms, remember these Afghan husbands, maddened by their wrongs. Englishwomen, with babes smiling on your breasts, think of these sister-women, bereft of their little ones. The Afghan loves wife and child as ye do. He also is husband and father. He also has his love, his pain, and his despair. To him also the home is happy, the hearth is sacred. To you he cries from his desolated fireside, from his ravaged land. In your hands is his cause. You only can deliver him. And his deliverance can come only through the ballot-box Peace can return only when the "wicked earl" has fallen. The message that carries the news of the defeat of the Tory Government will carry peace, liberty, and hope to South Africa, to India, and to Afghanistau. Will England be loyal to her love of truth and her hatred of oppression, or has she began to tread the path of disregard of all duty, of contempt for all morality, the path that inevitably leads to national decay?

THE TRANSVAAL.

By ANNIE BESANT.

At the meeting of the Executive of the National Secular Society on February 23rd, it was decided to formally protest against the violation of public faith in proclaiming the annexation of the South African Republic, and the disregard of public morals shown in persisting in the path of wrong-doing. As one of the vice-presidents of the N. S. S. I sketch here an outline of British policy towards the Dutch South African Republic, thinking that it may be well to place in the hands of our branches facts which they may find it impossible to collect for themselves.

It is well known to every reader of history that the Dutch settled in Southern Africa before the English founded any colonies therein; the English, however, after awhile got the upper hand, and those Dutch who cared for independence retreated before them from time to time. The Cape of Good Hope and the Colony of Natal thus passed beneath British rule, many Dutch remaining as colonists, many "trekking" to live elsewhere in freedom. The Orange Free State was founded by some of these liberty-loving Dutch, and still exists independently, with a President at its head. Others of the travellers crossed the Vaal river, into a country which was uninhabited in some districts, and in others sparsely habited by various native tribes. The Rev. G. Blencowe writes to the Earl of Kimberley under date May 24th, 1880 (South Africa: Further Correspondence, C. 2740. 1881. No. 3, p. 5):—

"When the Boers entered the Transvaal, the Wakkerstroom, the Heidelburg, the Pretoria and the Potchefstroom districts were without any of the original inhabitants; while the Southern half of the Rustenburg, the southern two-thirds of the Middleburg, and the like proportion of the Lydenburgh districts were also unoccupied. Thus the greater part of the present Transvaal territory was free for occupation, and the Boers did not remove any natives in actual possession of the parts in which they had originally settled."

It is clear that the Boers were here doing wrong to no man; they were settling on free land, land without occupants. They established a Republican form of Government, increased and prospered. From time to time this Government made grants of farms outside the uninhabited districts first colonised, and the Boers came into contact with the natives. Mr. Blencowe says on this:

"Those Boers who had obtained grants of farms in these parts, and who only occupied them for winter grazing, have for many years paid a tax to the natives of two heifers or two oxen per annum per farm."

This testimony is important as showing that the Dutch settlers were not oblivious of native rights when they came into contact with the original owners of the soil, and the same honorable fact is borne witness to by the Rev. A. Merensky, superintendent of the Berlin Missionary Society, a twenty years' resident in the Transvaal, in a letter to Sir W. O. Lanyon, dated August 10th, 1880 (*loc. cit.*, p. 19, Enclosure 2 in No. 52); he is speaking of the North Transvaal, in which the Boers ruled over the natives, and says:—

"The fact is that when they arrived they could do with the natives almost what they pleased, as the latter were not in possession of guns. . . . . Although the natives were entirely left to the mercy of the Boers, and considered themselves their subjects in the first years after the arrival of the latter, they soon augmented in numbers, accumulated wealth, and came into the possession of guns, by means of which single tribes managed to hold their own against the Boers in the quarrels which arose."

Sir W. O. Lanyon, writing to the Earl of Kimberley, on August 20th, 1880 (*loc. cit.*, p. 28), also notes the same fact, stating that while the Transvaal was independent

"many of the settlers had to pay black mail to the native chiefs in order to occupy their farms in peace."

We, of course, object to paying "black mail," *i.e.*, rent for the land we take. In Ireland we pass Coercion Bills to make starving tenants pay rent, and in the Transvaal we stigmatise rent as black mail. But then we receive in the one case, and ought to pay it in the other, and all candid persons will admit that this makes a great difference.

In 1852 a definite arrangement was made between the South African Republic and the British Government. Commissioners from her Majesty met the deputies of the "Emigrant Boers," at a farm, Sandriver, to settle the boundaries between the Cape Colony and the Dutch territory; on the 16th of January, 1852, the following convention was agreed to (Transvaal Dispatches, C. 2794, p. 4.)

"1. The Assistant Commissioners guarantee in the fullest manner, on the part of the British Government, to the emigrant farmers beyond the Vaal River the right to manage their own affairs, and to govern themselves according to their own laws, without any interference on behalf of the British Government; and that no encroachment shall be made by the said Government on the territory beyond to the north of the Vaal River, with the further assurance that the warmest wish of the British Government is to promote peace, free trade, and friendly intercourse with the emigrant farmers now inhabiting, or who hereafter may inhabit, that country; it being understood that this system of non-interference is binding upon both parties."

Various other engagements were made which do not touch on the main question. By this convention, the British Government distinctly pledged itself to respect the independence of the Dutch Republic, and for some time all went well. The Republic was acknowledged not only by England, but by France, America, Prussia, Portugal, Belgium, and Holland. The services rendered by the Boers to the colonists of Natal at a critical moment were formally acknowledged by the Legislative Assembly of Natal, and no point in the convention was violated by the Dutch. The next point of interest is the way in which England redeemed her word not to interfere to the North of the Vaal River.

In 1877 the Government of Jingoism was in power in England, and Lord Carnarvon hit upon the notable plan of forcing confederation on the various colonies and states in South Africa. The Government cast greedy eyes at the little Republic across the Vaal, and made up its mind to annex it. Sir Theophilus Shepstone was appointed Commissioner, and was empowered to proclaim her Majesty's authority over the Transvaal on obtaining the consent of the Volksraad (Parliament of the Republic). But the Volksraad would give no consent, and on April 9th, 1877, Sir T. Shepstone wrote to the Executive Council of the Republic, saying that he was going at once to proclaim British sovereignty over the Transvaal. In answer, the Executive Council, on April 11th, resolved that her Majesty's Government had no right to disregard the convention of 1852, that the people of the Republic had by a large majority shown their dislike to the destruction of their independence, and concluded their resolutions as follows (Despatches No. 2.):—

"The Government most strongly protests against the action of Her Majesty's Special Commissioner, resolving further to despatch immediately a commission of representatives to Europe and America with power and instructions to add to itself, if necessary, a third person, to try in the first instance to appeal to Her Majesty's Government, and if this should have no result, which the Government should regret and can as yet not believe, then to try and invoke the friendly help and assistance of other powers, foremost of those who have acknowledged the independence of this country."

Sir Theophilus Shepstone, however, pursued his way, and in defiance of treaty and of justice, he proclaimed in the Queen's name the annexation of the Transvaal, on April 12, 1877. The President of the Republic thereupon issued the following document:—

"PROCLAMATION.

"Whereas Her British Majesty's Special Commissioner, Sir Theophilus Shepstone, notwithstanding my solemn protest of yesterday entered against his purposes, communicated to me by his letter of 9th April, has been pleased to execute his designs, and has this day proclaimed Her British Majesty's Government over the South African Republic; and whereas the Government has decided to acquiesce for the present, under protest, for the purpose of despatching meanwhile a deputation to Europe and America, in the persons of Messrs. S. J. P. Kruger and E. P. Jorrisen, for the purpose there to defend the rights of the people, and to try to obtain a *peaceful* solution of the case;

"So it is that I, Thomas Francois Burgers, State President of the South African Republic, proclaim and make hereby known, with consent and advice of the Executive Council, to all officials, citizens, and inhabitants, to abstain from every word or deed calculated to frustrate the work of the mission.

"And I admonish all burghers and inhabitants to help carry out this decision of the Government for the preservation of order and the avoidance of bloodshed.

"THOMAS BURGERS,
"State President.

"Government Office, Prétoria,
12th April, 1877."

The protest could scarcely be more dignified and more moderate. The Republic was small, the oppressor was mighty, and, in addition to this disparity of strength, we note all through the desire of the Boers to avoid a conflict which might result in a war of black against white throughout Southern Africa. In 1877 and 1878 deputations were sent to England, but the Tory Government would not give way. Representatives from 4,000 burghers assembled in camp were sent to meet Sir Bartle Frere, and while this gentleman accepted their memorial to the Queen, and deceived them with professions of friendship, he wrote home expressing his regret that he had not artillery enough to destroy their camp. No answer was ever given to the memorial; the patience of the Boers was misinterpreted into submission, their payment of taxes into acceptance of British authority, and at last a general meeting of the people was held (December 10—17, 1879), and it was decided to call together the Volksraad.

Small excuse has ever been made for the high-handed violence of England towards the little Republic. It has been alleged that the Boers kept slaves, and although slavery amongst them consisted of indenturing natives for terms of service, it has been fairly argued that to indenture for years those who could not resist, was really to enslave them. I admit it. But the fact does not justify us in abolishing the Boer Republic. We have no right to annex Spain because the Spaniards hold slaves in Cuba. And the less have we the right in South Africa, since we follow the same abominable custom, and indenture helpless natives just as did the Boers. Mr. J. N. P. de Villiers, Civil Commissioner, writes as follows to the Secretary for Native Affairs, Cape Town, on August 18, 1880 (Further Correspondence, C 2740, Enc. 4 in No. 33):—

"The prisoners of both sexes sent hither from Koegas in November, 1878 (the adults being principally women), were indentured by me during the period from December, 1878, to November, 1879 (both months inclusive), to persons of known respectability. . . . With the exception of those apprentices who have since absconded (and these form, I believe, a large portion of their number), the natives before mentioned are still in service; the shortest terms stipulated under the regulations, that for adults, being three years . . . . Many of these [natives coming into the colony from outlying districts—A.B.] now appear to have been the reputed fathers and husbands of those under contracts of service who readily found their way to them; and it is to this circumstance that the numerous instances of desertion above alluded to must be attributed."

At Koegas a massacre of natives had occurred, women and children being shot by the gallant colonists. The murderers were not punished, and the women and children who escaped were indentured. That is, helpless prisoners were turned into slaves. It is instructive to note that many "absconded," and that "reputed husbands and fathers" were wicked enough to try and free the female slaves related to them. Mr. Villiers asks that some check shall be put on the arrival of free natives in the district, as they disturb the happy apprentices with their kind masters of "known respectability." The same gentleman writes, under date December 8th, 1879 (*loc. cit.*, Enc. 5 in No. 33):—

"About 99 natives, being 46 adults and 53 children, have been placed under contracts of service between the 4th of December,

1878, and the 17th of November, 1879. . . . In pursuance of the approval which you were pleased to give to my suggestion previously made, parents and their younger children were kept together as far as possible when indentured."

And when not possible, Mr. Villiers? Looking at the list of these 99 natives, we observe that one is indentured only for six months, the rest for 3, 4, 5, 6, 9, 10, 11, 12, 13 or 15 years. Most of them are indentured to Dutchmen, so that while indenturing to Dutchmen by Dutchmen is a crime justifying annexation of the offenders, indenturing to Dutchmen by Englishmen is a highly moral action. Two slaves were sold—I beg pardon, two apprentices were indentured—to Mr. C. J. Esterhingen; the man absconded, the woman was "reported to have been found dead on the farm of Mr. Esterhingen." Unfortunate, very. On the whole, perhaps we had better not say too much regarding "indenturing" in the Boer Republic. It is right to add that I do not know whether the allegation that the Boers countenance this modified form of slavery is true or not. But one thing is certain: under the Boers the natives multiplied and grew wealthy (see *ante*), while we are constantly troubled with native revolts.

Since April 12th, 1879, the Transvaal had been in a state of suppressed excitement, fondly awaiting the news that the Home authorities had reversed the iniquitous acts of their colonial representatives. The downfall of the Jingo Government and the accession to power of Mr. Gladstone seemed to carry message to the oppressed and injured Dutch that at length right should be done. They waited. The meeting of the Volksraad, decided on in December, 1879, did not take place until December, 1880, no good news having reached the patient petitioners for justice. At last it met, and on December 13th, 1880, it appointed Messrs. Kruger, Pretorius and Joubert as a triumvirate, to take more vigorous steps for the attaining of the righteous wish of the people. These gentlemen republished the Sandriver Convention, adding to it a pathetic declaration of the good faith kept by the Republic, and saying that the

"Government and people of the Republic have not then made use of their right to take up arms, being convinced that her Majesty's Government, better informed, would disapprove of the action of her official, and as the threats of that official made them fear that armed resistance would cause a civil war amongst the Colonists in South Africa, and war of extermination between the white and black race. The Government of the South African Republic has allowed this act of violence to be committed under protest, and the people have kept quiet in obedience to the lawful authority."

Sir O. Lanyon, on December 18th, proclaimed the Boers as rebels, but they indignantly replied, that "The people of the South African Republic have never been subjects of her Majesty and never will be." They declare that they are ready to confederate with the colonies and states of Southern Africa, and will accept a general native policy decided on by representatives of the various powers.

The declaration of independence seems to have come as a surprise on the Colonial Government. I find Mr. George Hudson, Colonial Secretary, writing to Sir O. Lanyon on November 26, 1880:—

"I do not think the Boers will take the initiative, but I do think they will resist any present action taken to arrest the men for whom warrants are out."

[The Boers, finding that their honest payment of taxes pending negotiations was used to show that they assented to annexation, had declined to pay, and warrants had been issued.]

On December 5th, 1880, Sir O. Lanyon wrote to the Earl of Kimberley, touching these men who so plainly and distinctly demanded the restoration of their independence:—

"Neither the leaders nor the people know what they want, further than that they object to pay taxes, or to be subordinate to the laws of the State. . . . . I still do not think there is much cause for anxiety."

This was written on December 5th. On December 16th the flag of the Republic was hoisted.

On this same December 16th a patrol of eight Boers ride into Potchefstroom to carry the proclamation to the printing office. The English soldiers in Potchefstroom fire on them —war not having been proclaimed. The Boers retort, and the English bombard the town. On the same day the Boers send their demands to Sir O. Lanyon, allowing forty-eight hours for reply, and saying that any advance of troops will be regarded as a declaration of war. On the 17th they write to Sir G. Colley, to send him their proclamation, but dryly add as a postscript: "We are unable to send your Excellency the proclamation, as coming into Potchefstroom to have it printed, our patrol was fired upon by the troops." On the 18th Sir O. Lanyon proclaims the Boers as rebels, and they receive his answer on December 19th. On December 20th a detachment of English troops advances from Lydenburg towards Pretoria, and is attacked and defeated by the Boers. In England cries of "treachery" and "massacre" are raised, but the authorities in South Africa state that the Boers warned them that any advance of troops would be resisted; and the Colonel Commanding reports: "I have warned them [the soldiers] to expect attack." So far from behaving with cruelty, as pretended, the Boers sent the wounded men on to their friends in Pretoria, and Major General Sir G. Colley reports: "They have acted with courtesy and humanity in the matter of our wounded," and have "released most of the prisoners taken from us." In the proclamation issued by the Republic on January 13th, 1881, respectful mention is made of the courage of the British troops, who "promptly went into laager, and proceeded to battle with the band playing." This proclamation charges Sir O. Lanyon:

> "(1) With having commenced war without notice; (2) with carrying on this war against all rules of civilised warfare; and (3) particularly with the barbarous cruelties at Potchefstroom, bombarding an exposed town without warning."

Here the official information ends, and we await with keen anxiety the decision of the Ministry.

We ask that the South African Republic may be left undisturbed in freedom and independence. We ask that the three and a-half years' patient forbearance of the Boers may meet with its just reward. We ask that the English name may not be dishonored by the endorsement of the unrighteous act of an unscrupulous official. The Boers are weak; England is strong. So much the more reason that those who cannot be compelled by force should feel compelled by duty to do the right. We, who have not, like Sir Bartle Frere, "deep religious feelings;" we, who do not believe in God, but who do believe in justice, in truth, and in righteous dealing; we, who maintain that the prestige of a nation depends on its honor and its virtue and not on its armies and its navies; we plead that the right may be done by our Liberal leaders, and if they persist in wrong and in disregard of justice, we then dissever ourselves from, and publicly protest against, a policy which makes strength the excuse for oppression, and past error a plea for present wrong.

PRICE ONE PENNY.

London: Printed by ANNIE BESANT and CHARLES BRADLAUGH,
28, Stonecutter Street, E.C.

EGYPT.

By ANNIE BESANT.

In the general election of 1880, the nation pronounced a distinct vote of censure on the foreign policy of Lord Beaconsfield. That policy was a policy of aggression on weak countries, under pretence of safe-guarding British interests, a policy of endeavoring to control the government of semi-barbarous States for our own advantage, and for the supposed protection of India. For this Lord Beaconsfield invaded Afghanistan; for this he stole Cyprus; for this he brought Indian troops to the Mediterranean. Fortunately for England, the Liberals were then in opposition, and every Liberal platform rang with denunciations of "the Jingo policy." The immorality, the folly, the waste of money—all these were fertile themes for Liberal eloquence, and so well was its work performed that the nation hurled Lord Beaconsfield from power, and placed at its head the man whose policy was one of peace, of righteousness, and of respect for the rights of others. The new Cabinet performed well a large part of the duty entrusted to it. It withdrew our troops from Afghanistan; after some delay and vaccillation, it restored the Transvaal to independence; it is now engaged in trying to undo the mischief wrought in Zululand. On one portion only of the foreign policy of Lord Beaconsfield has the Cabinet failed in fulfilling the mission it received from the nation. His policy in Egypt was not repudiated by them. They allowed themselves—probably influenced by Mr. Goschen—to sanction by silence the responsibilities he had created, and the injustices his interference had wrought; the consequence of this dereliction from duty is the war in which we are involved, a war whose end the wisest cannot foresee.

I propose to briefly sketch the events which have led up to this war,[1] and to urge the application to Egypt, as to

[1] The statement of facts is given on the authority of Parliamentary papers, and is drawn partly from the original documents, partly from Mr. J. Seymour Keay's "Spoiling the Egyptians," a pamphlet all should read.

Afghanistan and to the Transvaal,[1] of those principles of morality without which no progress is possible for nations, any more than for individuals. I have not yet reached that height of party spirit attained by Mr. Guinness Rogers and his friends, of whom he says that "they judge the Ministerial decision very differently from what they would have done, had it been shaped by politicians under the inspiration of Lord Salisbury." To me a war of aggression is wrong, even though—alas! that it should be so—it is covered by the justly-revered name of William Ewart Gladstone. I admit that the war is part of the fatal legacy of mischief left by Lord Beaconsfield to the nation, but I think that in this, as in other matters, Mr. Gladstone should have reversed, not continued, that policy. The nation condemned the policy, and Mr. Gladstone was not placed in power to continue it. To the historical sketch I propose to add brief answers to the arguments advanced in defence of the English policy in Egypt.

Mr. Keay justly begins his full account of the events which led to the present war with the loans raised by the Khedive (Ismail) in 1862, 1864, 1866, and 1868, but as his list is not quite complete, I take the one printed by Mr. Bradlaugh in 1876 (*N. R.*, Feb. 6th):—

Borrowed—	1862, at 7 per cent.	...	...	£3,292,800
,,	1864 ,, ,,	...	...	5,704,200
,,	1866 ,, ,,	...	...	3,000,000
,,	,, ,, ,,	...	...	3,387,700
,,	1867, at 9 ,,	...	...	2,080,000
,,	1868, at 7 ,,	...	...	11,890,000
,,	1870 ,, ,,	...	...	7,142,000
,,	1873 ,, ,,	...	...	32,000,000
,,	1874 ,, ,,	...	...	5,000,000
				£73,496,700

(The above rates of interest are only on the nominal amounts of the loans; the real rates would depend on the amounts actually paid over by the contractors.)

The loan of £3,000,000 (1866) was repaid, but there was a floating debt of between £15,000,000 and £20,000,000. Less than £50,000,000 in cash appear to have been received by

[1] See "Afghanistan" and "The Transvaal," by the writer.

the Khedive, although Egypt was saddled with the full amount stated. Of the money received £10,000,000 were said to have been used to pay the debts of one of his predecessors, and £16,000,000 for the Suez Canal. The way in which the speculators robbed their reckless borrower may be judged from the fact that in one case a loan of £9,000,000 was paid into the Treasury in bonds of Egyptian floating debt, the bonds being purchased by the speculators "sometimes at a price as low as 65 per cent, and paid into the Treasury at 93 per cent," the speculators thus quietly pocketing an immediate profit of 28 per cent. The taxes were used to pay the interest on this debt, an interest admittedly varying from 12½ to 26 per cent, and in many cases enormously higher; and when Mr. Stephen Cave went out to Egypt in 1875, to investigate the position of affairs, "he found that a floating debt to the extent of £18,000,000 had been incurred, chiefly to pay the half-yearly interest, and that this floating debt was being renewed from time to time at the ruinous rate of 25 per cent. per annum." Mr. Cave reported that "a sum of £34,898,000 had been paid away as interest in ten years, and yet the principal of the debt was greater than ever." The total revenue of Egypt from all sources was £8,500,000; and as the interest on debt came annually to £5,700,000, only £2,800,000 were left for carrying on the State. The result was that the Egyptian ruler, with the charming facility of an Eastern potentate, collected taxes before they fell due, made forced loans, and finally issued the "Law of Moukabala," by which the landowners were allowed to redeem half the annual rent due to the State, by paying down a capital sum equal to six years' rental. The rent of land—or, as we should call it, land-tax—amounted to one half of the revenue of the State; and this arrangement, while affording a slight immediate relief, permanently increased the difficulties of Egyptian finance.

The mission of Mr. Cave was the first blunder of our Government; the Khedive asked for the help of two English accountants to help in setting right his entangled finances "under the direction and orders of his own Minister of Finance." Instead of sending these, Lord Derby sent Mr. Stephen Cave to make—I quote Mr. Henry Richards—"a thorough inquisition into the finances of Egypt." "But,"

Mr. Richards continues, "in sending him Lord Derby evidently had some foreboding that they might be entering on a perilous path; therefore, in the instructions he gave to Mr. Cave, he earnestly impressed upon that gentleman 'to be careful not to commit the Government to any course of proceeding, by advice or otherwise, which might be taken to imply a desire to exercise any undue influence on the internal affairs of Egypt.'"

After Mr. Cave's return it was suggested that "an International Commission," supported by the English and French governments, should be formed to manage Egyptian finances. This was refused by Lord Derby, so the holders of Egyptian stock sent out Messrs. Goschen and Joubert in October, 1876, Mr. Goschen having been engaged in floating the two first loans. The bondholders, having failed to entangle Lord Derby directly, now essayed to use British influence indirectly, and our Consul at Alexandria was induced to "unofficially" press Mr. Goschen's advice on the Khedive. Mr. Goschen soon picked a quarrel with the Khedive's Finance Minister, and this unlucky opponent of European usurers was exiled "to the White Nile," a place from which, as the Consul afterwards remarks placidly, "few prisoners ever return." In another week Mr. Goschen had triumphed over all difficulties, and the Khedive agreed to appoint "two European comptrollers to receive and audit the whole revenues of the State," and "European commissioners of the Public Debt, who were to see to the payment of the interest to the bondholders;" but Lord Derby still obstinately and wisely refused to take part in these proceedings. The comptrollers, however, went gaily on their way; and, on January 15th, 1877, £2,301,000 were paid as interest, the Consul stating "that, under the extreme pressure put upon the authorities, the taxes are being collected in some districts for six months in advance." Meanwhile Europeans were swarming into Egypt to take office under the new Control, and the salaries of one set of Europeans, who arrived in Alexandria on March 2nd, 1877, "alone amounted to £33,500 a year." While the unhappy fellahs were being ruined by taxation to pay interest on the Khedive's loans, large salaries were being freely paid to unnecessary European functionaries. A second payment of interest, amounting to £2,094,975, fell due on July 15th, and was made under the threats of our Consul, who remarked that "the creditors ought not to suffer for a deplorable state of things for which they were in no way responsible." But even this Consul admitted that he feared that "the European Administration may be unconsciously sanctioning the utter ruin of the peasant-creators of the wealth of the country," and suggested that "the revenues of Egypt might be greatly increased, without imposing further sacrifices upon the already over-taxed cultivators, by correcting abuses connected with smuggling by Europeans, and compelling them to contribute fairly towards the resources of the country." He pointed out that European vessels, "notoriously full of contraband goods," were protected from search, and that when the goods were once landed and stored "in the house of some European" the Egyptian authorities dared not touch them. In addition to thus cheating the revenue, the resident Europeans were exempted from taxation, and as the number of these was about 100,000 a very serious loss fell on the crippled revenue. This position of privilege so long enjoyed by foreigners yields a very simple explanation of the hostility now shown by the natives towards all Europeans.

By November, 1877, the condition of the Egyptians had become desperate; the soldiers' pay was months in arrear, and many of the civil servants (Egyptian) of the Khedive were in a state of starvation. The poorer classes of the peasantry had been squeezed dry, and the Khedive urged on the comptrollers that from these "the taxes can only be wrung by sale of their lands and cattle." Of the £9,543,000 raised as revenue in 1877, £7,473,000 went to the bondholders, £1,000,000 as tribute and interest on the Suez Canal Shares, leaving, according to the statement of the European officials, "only £1,070,000 for the necessary expenses of the Government."

Lord Salisbury had now come into power, and the prudent policy of Lord Derby was laid aside. Hitherto, in spite of the ruin which was being wrought in Egypt for the sake of the bondholders, the Government might plead that they were not directly responsible; but, in December, 1877, and March, 1878, the Consul was directed that he might speak officially to the Khedive in the name of his Government to obtain another Commission. After long resistance, the Khedive consented to the Commission, and

Mr. Rivers Wilson was appointed its head. It summoned the Minister of Foreign Affairs before it, and on his refusal compelled him to resign. It forced the Khedive to give up more than half the Crown Lands, and a little later seized the remainder, assigning him a Civil List, and having placed two of its number in the Cabinet, it compelled him to sign a decree making ministers responsible and himself a cipher. It then began to dismiss the Egyptian officials by the hundred, replacing them by Europeans. Mr. Richard draws attention to the way in which Europeans ousted Egyptians from all posts in their own country. He says: "At the beginning of the year 1879 only 744 Europeans were in the pay of the Government of Egypt, and these, it must be remembered, already filled all the offices both in the Courts, Railways, Telegraphs, Port Trusts, etc., where foreigners were naturally required, or had been employed under the Consular Convention of 1870. But at the close of 1879, 208 had been added to that number, with salaries aggregating £60,000 a year. In 1880, 250 more were appointed, with emoluments of £62,000 a year; and again in 1881, a further batch of 122 Europeans was introduced, drawing £26,016 a year. The total number actually receiving pay in March, 1882, was 1325; and the total pay was £373,000 a year, which is about one-twelfth part of the entire available revenue of the country." In February, 1879, 2,500 officers of the army were placed on half-pay, "without receiving the heavy arrears due to them;" their money was wanted to pay the bondholders. Mr. Rivers Wilson and his Cabinet next issued a decree whereby "large numbers of fellahs [belonging to a higher class] hitherto exempt from forced labor became liable to it;" and so money was squeezed from them to purchase exemption. A Commission was sent out to inquire into the terms on which the peasantry held their lands; a proposal was made to raise the land-tax. Meanwhile the miserable lower-class fellahs were in the most terrible state of destitution; the Consul reported, a little later, that it was "impossible adequately to describe the wretched state of the poor persons, driven with their cattle to the market, and followed by their families;" that they were "severely and cruelly treated, the whip and bastinado being the necessary concomitants of every demand for the payment of taxes," and that they were "very severely whipped" to extort money. On the whole, perhaps, it is not extraordinary that the Egyptians failed to see our action in its proper light, and did not understand that it was all for their good when the subordinates of the European Control flogged them to wring from them money for the bondholders. A national movement against the foreigners began.

This movement soon made itself felt. A deputation of Sheikhs came from the ruined provinces to protest against any more "pressure"—*i.e.*, whip and bastinado—for taxes; "a certain amount of fermentation in the country" became apparent. Mr. Rivers Wilson was dragged from his carriage by a crowd headed by some of the officers he had ruined, and was saved by the personal exertions of the Khedive, whose power he had usurped, and whom he promptly rewarded by excluding him from the Cabinet, on the ground that his action had shown that he possessed independent power. The announcement of the intention of the Europeans to "force the Government of Egypt to pay the bondholders' coupon in full," crowned the excitement. Notables and Ulemas took the lead of the agitation, and "addresses against the designs of the European Ministers were also presented to the Khedive by sixty-two delegations of the clergy and the high functionaries, seventy-three civil and military officers, forty-one merchants and notables, and sixty members of the Chamber of Delegates." So great and so general was the movement that the Khedive was forced into choosing between a revolt against his European tyrants and the loss of his throne; he resumed his authority and dismissed the Comptrollers from his Cabinet. Lord Salisbury remonstrated, protested, and finally threatened, but the Khedive was compelled by his Ministers to stand firm; Lord Salisbury and the French Government then put pressure on the Porte, and Ismail was deposed and his son Tewfik was appointed in his place, to act as the tool of the foreigner in Egypt. A new European Commission was appointed, which on July 17, 1880, issued a report in which the interest on the bondholders' claim was fixed at £3,870,000 yearly, and the Law of Moukabala (see p. 3) was repealed, "thereby confiscating both the £17,000,000 which the cultivators had paid, and the valuable right which they had thereby purchased to a reduction in perpetuity of 50 per cent. in the rentals of their lands from the year 1885. Consequently, not only have the landholders lost their £17,000,000, but a confiscatory tax on land, amounting to £1,700,000 sterling every year, is raised from 1,000,000 cultivators and paid over to the bondholders." These unhappy, plundered landowners were awarded by the Commission £150,000 a year—to be divided among 1,000,000 persons—for 50 years, as compensation for the robbery inflicted on them.

This report of the Commission should obviously have been considered by the new Liberal Government, and the latter should have disavowed and repudiated all further dabbling in Egyptian finance on behalf of the speculators of the Stock Exchange. Above all, it should have declared that the plundering of the fellahs and the landowners should no longer be carried on under English supervision, and that the Joint Control should at once be put an end to. What the Government may have done we do not know, as a blank of a year and a half occurs at this point in the Parliamentary papers; but it is clear that it did not disentangle British honor from the network of complicity in the oppression and fraud going on in Egypt. It is certain, further, that the national movement against the foreign interlopers continued, for in February, 1881, some officers who had petitioned for reform were arrested by the pliable Khedive, and forcibly released, a few hours later, by their soldiers. From this time forward the army plays a prominent part. Enormous reductions had been made in it by the Europeans (see p. 6), and further reductions were meditated; large arrears of pay were due to officers and men alike; the mass of impoverished Egyptians looked on the army as the only means of deliverance from their European oppressors. On Sept. 9, 1881, the first serious outbreak took place, and the soldiers, under Colonel Arabi Bey, besieged the palace, and "demanded—1st, the dismissal of the ministry, 'which had sold the country to the English;' 2nd, the convocation of a representative chamber; and 3rd, the raising of the army to 18,000 men." The first two demands were above criticism, the third was the number fixed by the Firmans; and Arabi told the English Comptroller to his face, that he came "to secure by arms the liberties of the Egyptian people;" our Consul, hostile as he had showed himself throughout to

Egyptian interests, reports that Arabi appealed to England, to "whose efforts for the liberation of slaves he alluded, as showing that she ought, to sympathise with the Egyptians in their attempt to obtain liberty." Alas! the appeal fell on deaf ears; England might move for Bulgarian Christians suffering under Mahommedan despotism; she had no sympathy for the Egyptian Moslems, starving, fainting, dying, under the lash wielded by Christian Comptrollers.

A gleam of light appeared in the Egyptian sky in the appointment of Cherif Pasha as head of the ministry, Arabi Bey professing "to have full confidence in" him, and the old Chamber of Notables offering him their support. A fresh difficulty, however, arose as to the calling of a new Chamber, the Europeans desiring that it should be summoned under the old law of 1866, and Arabi Bey insisting "upon the adoption of a law giving a much wider scope to the powers of the Chamber, which had been elaborated during the last days of the reign of Ismail Pasha." After some struggle Arabi gave way, and matters were again progressing more smoothly, when the whole position was suddenly aggravated by England and France despatching two ironclads to Alexandria as "refuges in case of disturbance," no disturbances being threatened. Cherif Pasha is reported by the Consul as "very anxious about it [the news of the despatch of the ships], as it will revive agitation, cause distrust in him, and weaken his authority." Lord Dufferin, from Constantinople, telegraphed a remonstrance addressed to him by the Sultan, urging that "such a demonstration is not based on any treaty rights. It implies danger for Alexandria and Jeddah. It is calculated to cause agitation and disturbance among the whole Arab population, and it is not improbable that it may lead to a general revolution. . . . . Perfect order exists in Egypt." The Sultan, in answer, was insolently told that if he would recall certain envoys he had sent to Egypt—Egypt being part of his own dominions—the French and English governments would recall their ships of war. Under these disquieting circumstances the decree summoning the new Chamber of Notables was issued on Oct. 4, the meeting being fixed for Dec. 23. Having so far succeeded in his wish to give the Egyptians a voice in the management of their own affairs, Arabi Bey left Cairo, but before quitting it "made a speech in which he spoke of the

Khedive with the greatest respect." He said to the soldiers: "You have power in your hands, and united are invincible. But this power must only be used for the general good. You are at once the protectors of the weak and of the powerful, but you should only aid the latter while they remain within the limits of right and of justice." These words, with his other addresses to the troops, given in C. 3161 of the "Correspondence respecting the Affairs of Egypt," do not seem to me those of a mere "military adventurer," but rather of a thoughtful and earnest patriot.

Shortly before the meeting of the new Chamber, we find M. Gambetta very uneasy about it. He informed Lord Lyons that it was advisable "to make the Porte feel that any undue interference on its part would not be tolerated," and that "the time was come when the two Governments should consider the matter in common, in order to be prepared for united and immediate action in case of need." The very idea that the Egyptian people would soon have found a voice seems to have terrified the supporters of the unjust "European Control." It would be difficult to convince the world that the Control existed for the benefit of Egypt, if the Egyptians themselves spoke out clearly through a representative Chamber. Meanwhile a difficulty had arisen between the Control and the Egyptian Ministry on the subject of the Budget of the Minister of War. Mahmoud Pasha Sami, the War Minister, demanded an increase on his Budget of £280,000, afterwards reducing the amount asked for to £120,000. The Comptrollers declined to consent to this increase, and the Consul remarked that such action would "create a breach between the Government and the Control." They sent to the Council of Ministers a note stating that "The Firmans authorise, it is true, the Egyptian Government to keep up an army of a maximum effective force of 18,000 men, but the Comptrollers-General cannot advise the raising of the army to this figure, except in the event of the resources of the Budget enabling all the expenses to be met." The expenses could not be met without an increase in the War vote, and against this the Comptrollers set their faces. On the 5th January, 1882, Colonel Arabi Bey was appointed Under-Secretary of State for War, and on the 10th the Consul telegraphed that the Chamber claimed the right of voting on the half of the Budget dealing with revenues not "assigned to the Public Debt." It did not claim to touch the revenues managed by the European Control, but only to distribute those supposed to be left to Egypt in the way the Notables considered most advantageous for their own country. The claim was a reasonable one, but the Comptrollers took alarm. If the Chamber once began to discuss financial matters, the European locusts might not be permitted to devour so freely as heretofore. On January 20th the Consul telegraphed to Lord Granville that "armed intervention will become a necessity if we adhere to the refusal to allow the Budget to be voted by the Chamber." Sir A. Colvin and M. de Blignières, the Comptrollers, had, on the 17th, complained that the Chamber was "certainly disposed to eliminate all the European element from the administration of the country, and it puts forward a claim to interfere in all the details of the administration." Such claims on the part of a representative Chamber were clearly an attack on the supreme rights of the foreigners to govern Egypt for their own benefit, and the Comptrollers and the Consul preferred war to the concession to the Egyptians of the right to rule themselves.

While this contest was going on in Cairo considerable uneasiness was manifested in the country. At Damietta "a little child" called the French Vice-Consul "a Christian dog in the streets, and the child's father, on the complaint of the Vice-Consul, was imprisoned for 24 hours."

On February 5th a new Ministry was constituted, in which Arabi Bey was nominated Minister of War, and the new Cabinet declared that an organic law would at once be issued, which "will respect all rights and all obligations of a private or international character, as well as all engagements relative to the Public Debt and to the charges which the latter impose on the Budget of the State." This law was approved by the Khedive, and decreed on February 8th, and on the same day the Minister of Foreign Affairs, Moustapha Fehmy, wrote that, "The foreign governments never ceased protesting in this respect that it was their formal intention not to mix themselves up in the internal administration of Egypt," that the Budget, "containing the credits necessary for the service of the Public Debt," was withheld "in an absolute manner from the vote of the Chamber," and asked: "Can it [the Government] fairly be blamed for admitting the taxpayers to examine the use of the public funds devoted to administrative expenses? Is it not a right common to all countries, a primordial right which cannot seriously be denied to the Government of his Highness the Khedive?" It is this promising attempt at government by the representatives of the people that England, so proud of its own representative system, has trampled out in blood in Egypt.

An excuse for forcible interference was still wanting, but was soon found in a quarrel between the Khedive and his Ministers, a quarrel instigated, fomented and embittered by our Consul, who laid stress on the fact that "the present Ministry is distinctly hitherto bent upon diminishing the Anglo-French protection." A conspiracy of some Circassian officers to murder Arabi Bey was discovered, the conspirators were arrested, brought before a court-martial, convicted, and condemned to exile to the White Nile. The sentence was in due course laid before the Khedive for his signature. Sir E. Malet advised him to refuse to sign it, and a rupture occurred between the Khedive and his Ministry. Hereupon Sir E. Malet telegraphed home, on May 11th, that "the guarantee given by the Ministers of the safety of the Khedive and of Europeans can hardly be relied upon as a solid one," and on the same day Lord Granville intimated to the French Government that England was "willing to send two ironclads to Alexandria to protect Europeans." Sir E. Malet telegraphed that he thought that the appearance of the ships of war would be so politically advantageous "as to outweigh any danger it might be to Europeans in Egypt." He threatened Arabi that he would be held personally responsible for any disturbance of order; but Arabi answered "that he would guarantee public order and the safety of his Highness the Khedive as long as he remained Minister, but that in the event of an Anglo-French squadron arriving he could not guarantee public safety." In spite of this, and in spite of the fact telegraphed home by Sir E. Malet that "Perfect tranquillity reigns in Cairo," the squadron went on its mischievous errand. Meanwhile the Ministers had submitted to the Khedive, and the aspect of affairs was for a moment less menacing. The men of war arrived at Alexandria on the 20th May, and their presence apparently emboldened the Europeans to strike directly at their great foe, Arabi

Pasha. Sir E. Malet and his French colleague coolly suggested that Arabi Pasha and three others should leave the country, and persuaded Sultan Pasha, the President of the Chamber, to support them in this outrageous request; as at last distinctly formulated on May 25, their demands were:—

(1) The temporary retirement from Egypt of his Excellency Arabi Pasha with the maintenance of his rank and pay;

(2) The retirement into the interior of Egypt of Ali Fehmy Pasha and Abdoullah Pasha, who will also retain their rank and pay;

(3) The resignation of the present Ministry.

This action, taken while the guns of the Fleet menaced Alexandria, could have but one result. The Ministers handed their resignations to the Khedive on the 26th, protesting against the foreign interference which had led to their fall. The army rose in anger at the insult offered to their favorite leader, but declared their willingness to await "the decision of the Porte." The people saw in Arabi's fall the death of their hoped-for liberty and the re-instalment of the European tyranny under which they groaned. Egypt was ripe for revolt against the foreign yoke, and against the Khedive, so skilfully used as a tool.

On the 28th of May "the Chiefs of Religion, including the Patriarch and the chief Rabbi, all the Deputies, Ulemas and others, wait on the Khedive and ask him to re-instate Arabi as Minister of War." On the 29th the Egyptians are busy throwing up earthworks to defend Alexandria. On June 1 the Khedive states that he is informed that the army intend to depose him, and Sir B. Seymour telegraphs that the earthworks are progressing. Continued communications take place without any result, until on June 11 a riot occurs in Alexandria "between Arabs and Europeans," and is quelled by the Egyptian troops, who patrol the town "day and night" to maintain the peace. With the constant menace of the foreign fleet in front of Alexandria the Egyptians, not unnaturally, continue their defensive works; Admiral Seymour demands that they shall leave their town defenceless against his guns, and on their persistence in their work of fortification, he bombards the city. "The Egyptians," he reports, "fought with determined bravery, replying to the hot fire poured into their forts from our heavy guns until they must have been quite decimated." When they had done their best to defend their homes they retreated, and the town, already fired by the English shell, was plundered by the Arabs the moment the troops, who had hitherto protected it, were driven out by the overwhelming force of our artillery. Since that day, July 11, 1882, Arabi has maintained his ground (I write on August 30th) ; but the contest he wages so gallantly is hopeless, against the crushing might of England. Egypt is fighting against us for its national life and liberty, as Afghanistan, as Zululand, as the Transvaal fought. It will fail, as they failed; but it will fail with honor, while we conquer in shame.

Let us glance at the excuses made for this iniquitous war, excuses similar in character to those made in defence of Lord Beaconfield's aggressions, and as futile as they.

It was said (1) that Arabi Pasha is "an unscrupulous and savage adventurer," and that "in vindicating the rights of its own subjects against a bandit chief, Great Britain is only discharging a duty of police to which the Khedive was unequal and which the Sultan refused to undertake" (J. Guinness Rogers). So far as we have evidence, Arabi Pasha has acted with moderation, courage and patriotism. He has been supported by all the chiefs of his own religion, by the representative chamber of his country, by the army, and by the people. One man cannot intimidate a nation, and Arabi is strong because he incarnates Egyptian nationality. He is now proclaimed a rebel, but the proclamation was made only when the Khedive was a helpless prisoner in our hands, and when his life and throne depended on his obedience to his foreign masters. The long struggle of the Sultan shows how his own lawful sovereign regards Arabi, and to speak of him as a rebel is merely to insult a gallant enemy in the most cowardly and unworthy fashion. But suppose that Arabi were all that his foes call him, by what right do we interfere? Who made us the "police" of Egypt? Until we can govern Ireland decently, the less we say about misgovernment abroad the better. Suppose Egypt claimed to discharge the "duty of police to which the Queen was unequal" in Ireland, what should we say? And if not

Egypt in Ireland, why we in Egypt? Of course, the answer is that we have the strength on our side, but we scarcely expected to hear the Beaconsfield theory that "might is right" from the lips of William Ewart Gladstone.

It is said (2) that Egypt must not "claim a right to close" the Suez Canal (J. G. Rogers). But when has Egypt made any such claim, or attempted to close the Canal? The only closure of the Canal has been made by the English military authorities, they having broken through the rule of non-interference with the passage which has been kept by the "bandit chief," although he might have increased his chances of safety by wholly destroying the great engineering work.

It is said (3), still by Mr. Rogers, that the "bondholders are the creditors of the Egyptian Khedive and his people." True, although the Khedive who incurred the debt, was a reckless spendthrift, encouraged by the speculators, and the people gained nought by the millions which they are called upon to repay. But when did the English people engage to force the payment of high interest at the point of the bayonet? When did England promise to make good rotten security with the blood of her children? Are English wives to be made widows, and English babes to be rendered fatherless, in order that greedy gamblers in foreign stocks may play with dice loaded with English lives? If we are to fight to fill brokers' purses in Egypt, we had better send troops to Chili, to Peru, to Bolivia, to Spain, to every bankrupt State where greed of high interest has accepted bad security.

It is said (4) that we are acting in self-defence. Mr. Henry Richard has well answered this monstrous plea:—

"But perhaps the hardiest, I may almost say the most audacious plea put forward is that the bombardment of Alexandria was a strict act of self-defence. Now, look at that plea for a moment. You send your fleet to the waters of a foreign nation, which nobody pretends had up to that time attacked or molested us in any way. You send it avowedly in a menacing attitude, and with hostile purpose, and when the Government and people of that country take some precautions to fortify their coasts against this invading force, that is treated as an affront, and you pour your infernal fire upon them 'in strict self-defence.' I find a man prowling about my house with obviously felonious purpose. I hasten to get locks and bars, and to barricade my windows. He says that is an insult and threat to him, and he batters down my doors and declares that he does so only as an act of strict self-defence."

It is said (5) that we are strengthening the authority of the Khedive. Do we strengthen the Khedive's position by forcing him into the most odious of all positions, that of the monarch who crushes out the legitimate aspirations of his people in obedience to foreign dictation? And even suppose that we hold Tewfik on his throne by our troops, as Napoleon III. held the Pope on his against the will of his subjects. Why? and for how long? We sent no troops to reinstate Bomba—but then we had not learned that it was the duty of a great nation to become bailiffs to enforce a judgment-summons taken out by usurers.

In this invasion of Egypt the most sacred principles of Liberalism have been trampled under foot. We have commenced a war to enforce a foreign yoke on a people striving to break it; to crush back into slavery a nation trying to shake it off; to stifle the aspirations of a race awaking into national life; to re-establish a despotism over a community endeavoring to create a system of self-government. Sure am I that the English people who rose in righteous protest against the wrongs inflicted on Afghanistan, on Zululand, and on the Transvaal, will rise again to repeat that protest against the wrongs inflicted on Egypt, and to recall Mr. Gladstone to those principles of national righteousness which he proclaimed so boldly and so effectually in his magnificent stand against Tory Jingoism.

PRICE TWOPENCE.

London: Printed by ANNIE BESANT and CHARLES BRADLAUGH, 28, Stonecutter Street, E.C.
1882.

The Atheistic Platform.

V.

THE STORY OF THE SOUDAN.

BY

ANNIE BESANT.

[TENTH THOUSAND.]

LONDON:
FREETHOUGHT PUBLISHING COMPANY,
63, FLEET STREET, E.C.
1885.

PRICE ONE PENNY.

THE STORY OF THE SOUDAN.

(*Told from the Parliamentary Papers.*)

FRIENDS,—The thoughts of England have been turned much during these latter weeks to the Soudan, and as there is the profoundest and most widespread ignorance concerning that vast country, it may, I think, be helpful at the present crisis if I take it as the subject of my lecture this morning, and try to throw some light on that dim strange land.

The country now named the Soudan embraces the whole of Nubia, as well as Kordofan and Darfour. It stretches from Assouan on the first cataract on the Nile southwards as far as the equator; on the east it is bounded by the Red Sea, the kingdom of Abyssinia, and the districts inhabited by the Caffre and Galla tribes; on the South stretch vast deserts inhabited by Gallas, Somalis, and others, who "do not encourage travellers", and which are "practically almost quite unknown". ("Report on the Soudan", by Lieutenant-Colonel Stewart, p. 7 Parliamentary paper, "Egypt, No. 11, 1883". This document will henceforth be referred to simply as Report.) On the west is the Libyan desert inhabited by Bedouin Arabs, and the boundaries are undefined, but run between the 22nd and 30th parallels of longitude. In length about 1,650 miles, and at its broadest part from 1,200 to 1,400 miles, it forms a country, according to General Gordon, covering an area larger than that of France, Germany, and Spain put together, or larger than our Indian Empire.

In this enormous district there are naturally vast differences of race, soil, and climate. "Between Assouan and Khartoum, beyond the narrow strip of cultivation along the Nile, the country is almost a desert, and inhabited by nomads belonging, it is said, to aboriginal tribes. A low range of broken and barren hills separates the Nile valley from the coast. Another low range to the west shuts out the Nile from the Desert of Bayuda. The climate is dry and enervating. The summer heat is excessive . . . . To the country west of the White Nile, between the parallels of Khartoum and Kaka (about 11° latitude) the general appearance is that of a vast steppe, covered with low thorny trees (mimosa, gum-trees, etc.) and prickly grass. Occasionally low groups of bare hills are met with. The villages and the patches of cultivated ground are few and far between. Water is scarce, and stored in wells and trunks of baobab trees. In the extreme west of the Darfour Province the country greatly improves in appearance. The hills are more lofty and continuous, and the cultivation is luxuriant. In summer the heat is excessive. From September to May the climate is dry, with no rain. The rainy season lasts from about the middle of May to the end of September . . . . East of the White Nile, and for some degrees south of the parallel of Khartoum, the country is a well-cultivated and a well-watered plain . . . . From the parallel of Kaka (11° north) to that of Gondokoro (5° north), the country is a perfectly level plain, with huge marshes on both banks of the Nile and the Bahr Ghazelle. South of the Gondokoro to the equator the country becomes more and more mountainous. The forests are everywhere very extensive, and with a large variety of trees, fruit-trees, etc. Water is everywhere abundant, and owing to it the climate to the west of the Nile is unhealthy. The heat is very great" (Report, pp. 7, 8).

Taking this description as accurate, we cannot wonder at General Gordon's estimate of the Soudan as a whole: "The Soudan is a useless possession, ever was so, and ever will be so . . . . No one who has lived in the Soudan can escape the reflexion, 'What a useless possession is this land'. Few men also can stand its fearful monotony and deadly climate" (Parliamentary paper, Egypt, No. 7, 1884, pp. 2, 3).

Turning to the history of the Soudan, we find that Arabs, crossing the Red Sea from Arabia, settled there in 700 and 800 A.D. These intermarried with the native negroes, and became "known collectively under the name of Fung", and the Fung kingdom spread far and wide. The pure-blooded negroes were constantly attacked by the more warrior mixed race, and were carried captive into slavery; these settled in villages and cultivated the ground, while the Fung tribes were mostly nomadic, their wealth consisting in these slaves, cattle, camels, and horses. In

1786 this Fung kindom perished by intestine wars, and general anarchy prevailed, tribe fighting with tribe for the supremacy. In 1819 Mehemet Ali, then ruler of Egypt, "wishing to introduce the benefits of a regular government, of civilisation, and *at the same time to occupy his troops* (the italics are mine), ordered his son Ismaël, with a numerous army of regulars and irregulars, with many learned men and artisans, to invade the country" (Report p. 4). Ismaël was murdered, in revenge for his barbarities, but from that time forth the Soudan was claimed as subject to Egypt, and the former anarchy continued, with such additional disorder as was imported by the Egyptian governors. In 1874 Colonel (now General) Gordon was appointed by the Khedive Governor-General of the Equatorial Provinces. Two years later he was raised to the Governor-Generalship of the Soudan.

In August, 1881, a remarkable personage appeared on the scene, Mahomet Achmet, the Mahdi. He proclaimed himself sent from God as the foretold prophet, to raise Islam, and to drive the infidels before him. The people were superstitious and credited his mission; they were miserable, and hoped it was true. To understand the welcome given to him, you must listen to what Colonel Stewart tells us of the administration of "justice", and of taxation under the Egyptian rule. In each province there is a chief town, and here was established a court, consisting of a president and eight members. At Khartoum was a Court of Appeal, and all very serious cases were carried to Cairo. Both the Court of First Instance and Court of Appeal might only inflict imprisonment up to a certain maximum. But "although these courts are thus tied down as to the amount of imprisonment they may award, there is no limit as to the length of time to which they can keep a case pending, so that practically an accused person can be kept in prison awaiting trial for a period perhaps considerably exceeding that to which he could be legally sentenced if guilty of the crime of which he is accused . . . With reference to this point, there are now in the Istinaff Court seven cases pending, and in the Malhalla Court (of Khartoum) eighteen to twenty-one. The oldest of these cases dates back twelve years. It is presumably worse in the provinces." Colonel Stewart alleges "General ignorance of the president and members . . . . The members being unpaid, and having other business to attend to, are with difficulty induced to attend in sufficient numbers to form a court . . . . Their decisions are liable to be biassed by their enmities and friendships. Probably bribery and corruption exert a considerable influence." He further speaks of "the ease and facility with which false testimony can be procured" (Report, pp. 11, 12). The *raison d'être* of a government being to administer justice, I consider that the utter failure of the Egyptian rulers on this head justified the Soudanese in revolt. When invaders seize and cannot administer, surely the invaded may throw off the forcibly imposed yoke.

But this was not all. The governors who could not govern could tax, and used their power to wring the very last piastre from the burdened and suffering people. One instance given by Colonel Stewart is eloquent of the system. Jaafar Pasha, Governor-General, fixed a certain tax at 500 piastres. "This officer stated openly that he was quite aware the tax was excessive, but that he had fixed it at that rate in order to see how much the peasant would really pay, and that he hoped after three years' trial to be able to arrive at a just mean." He was, however, removed long before his three years were over, and his successors, either through ignorance or indifference, allowed the tax to continue. In the Report just quoted a melancholy account is given of the ruin this excessive taxation brought on the country. Many were reduced to destitution, others had to emigrate, and so much land went out of cultivation that in 1881, in the Province of Berber, "there were 1,442 abandoned sakiyes (waterwheels) and in Dongola 613" (Report, p. 14). This is not wonderful when we learn that a commission found on examining "two sakiyes irrigating fair average land . . . . that the net returns, exclusive of taxes, were for one sakiye 391 piastres, and for the other 201" (Report, p. 15). As Jaafar Pasha had put a tax of 500 piastres on each sakiye, and as in addition to this there were other taxes raising the taxation to 607 piastres per sakiye, it is hardly surprising that the people found it cheaper to abandon them, and with this abandonment necessarily went the non-cultivation of the ground.

In a despatch forwarded home on January 20th, 1883, Colonel Stewart says: "The chief means of oppression is through the tax-gatherer. All over the country is a class of small officials, on salaries from 200 to 400 piastres, who have the very responsible duty of collecting the taxes. These officials are irregular soldiers (Bashi-Bazouks),

Turks, Tunisians, Dongolauroi, etc., the former race perhaps predominating. As there can be but little supervision over such an immense area, these men have it pretty much their own way, and squeeze the people to their hearts' content. I have heard of instances where the Bashi-Bazouk on his small salary maintains twelve horses, twenty servants, and a number of women, and this in places where the payment for the water for his cattle alone would have cost more than three times his salary. It is no uncommon thing for a peasant to have to pay his taxes four or five times over, without the treasury being any the richer" (Egypt, No. 13, 1883, p. 4). "One octroi farmer actually defended himself on the ground that for every piastre he took others stole dollars; that he robbed the poor, but did not meddle with the wealthy; that I showed great ingratitude in finding fault with him, after his hospitable reception. . . . . I think there can be no doubt that the whole local government is in league to rob and plunder" (Egypt, No. 22, 1883, p. 7). "They (the Bashi-Bazouks) appear to consider themselves in a conquered country, and that they have a right to take anything they choose" (p. 9).

It was to these people, oppressed and burdened, high-spirited and smarting with a sense of wrong, hating and despising their Egyptian rulers, and longing for the return of their old freedom, that the Mahdi appeared as a messenger of deliverance and of independence. Little wonder that they crowded to his standard and hoped that the disorder and civil war in Egypt might facilitate their own struggle for freedom. Lord Dufferin on April 2nd, 1883, wrote to Lord Granville his belief "that the recent disturbances were mainly to be attributed to the misgovernment and cruel exactions of the local Egyptian authorities at Khartoum, and that, whatever might be the pretensions of the Mahdi to a divine mission, his chief strength was derived from the despair and misery of the native population" (Egypt, No. 13, 1883, p. 54). So also Colonel Stewart said that "the real cause of the rebellion was misgovernment and oppression, and that all the Mahdi did was to apply a lighted match to the fully prepared tinder" (Egypt, No. 22, 1883, p. 6).

During 1882 almost constant conflict seems to have been going on in the Soudan; the various towns garrisoned by the Egyptian troops became more and more imperilled; "rebels" appeared and disappeared, cutting off stragglers, fighting when fighting at advantage was possible, vanishing when hardly pressed. Colonel Stewart on January 5th, 1883, described their tactics: "I am constantly hearing of small fights and of the slaughter of a few rebels. The rebels attack, are driven back, and disperse to reassemble on the following day" (Egypt, No. 13, p. 9). So troublesome was the aspect of affairs that on October 2nd, 1882, Sir E. Malet forwarded to Earl Granville a memorandum from Sir Charles Wilson stating that "it would be advisable to send two English officers to the Soudan to report on the state of the country and the steps which will be necessary to insure its pacification"; to this Sir E. Malet added: "I do not think we can possibly be in a position to form a correct opinion as to the state of affairs in the Soudan unless we obtain information from agents of our own, and I therefore beg to recommend Sir Charles Wilson's suggestion of sending officers to your lordship's favorable consideration" (Egypt, No. 1, 1883, p. 31). Lord Granville assented to the proposition, giving permission to "send Captain Stewart to the Soudan to report of the state of that district" (p. 35). He was, however, careful to guard against the idea that England had any responsibility for the state of affairs in the Soudan, and on November 3rd he wrote to Lord Dufferin (p. 48): "Her Majesty's Government are not prepared to undertake any expedition into the Soudan", and again on November 7th to Sir E. Malet (p. 50): "I have to inform you that Her Majesty's Government are unwilling to take any responsibility for the proposed expedition or military operations in that district. They assent to Colonel Stewart and the two other officers named proceeding thither to make enquiries, but it must be distinctly understood that these gentlemen shall under no circumstances assume to act in any military capacity."

But why, under these circumstances, send English officers into the Soudan at all? Why make enquiries which were to lead to no results? The time was not suitable for enquiries of merely historical interest, and what was the sense of sending English officers into a district where fighting was going on, if England had there no responsibility? Confusion was rendered the more likely, and misconception the more probable, by the presence of other English officers in the Soudan who were fighting in the Egyptian army. Was it likely that these officers, some fighting as Egyptians, others surveying operations as

Englishmen, would hold no communications with each other? Was it likely that they would miss so fine an opportunity of dragging England into the *mêlée* on the side of their adopted country?

That which happened was exactly what might have been expected. On December 10th, 1882, Colonel Stewart had reached Berber, and telegraphed to Sir E. Malet that a reinforcement of 800 men had reached Khartoum and that all was safe (p. 91). He continued to send home detailed reports on military matters as well as on the causes of Soudanese discontent. On March 2nd, after a long report on military affairs, he remarked: "I expect Colonel Hicks to arrive either to-morrow or the day following" (Egypt, No. 13, 1883, p. 54), and he telegraphed on the 10th from Khartoum: "General Hicks arrived here on the 2nd inst." (p. 25). Colonel Hicks during March—he is called Colonel and General indifferently—telegraphed to Lord Dufferin accounts of his proceedings at Khartoum, as though Lord Dufferin were his employer, and Lord Dufferin sent on the telegrams to Lord Granville. At last Lord Granville took alarm, and though he had hitherto accepted copies of Colonel Hicks' telegrams without protest, he wrote on May 7th the following letter to Mr. Cartwright: "I notice that in your despatch of the 10th ultimo you inclose a telegram from General Hicks to Sir E. Malet, on the subject of the military operations in the Soudan. I understand the whole of that telegram, with the exception of the first sentence, to be a message from General Hicks to General Baker, and I presume that it was addressed to Sir E. Malet because General Hicks found it convenient to forward it through Colonel Stewart. But it is unnecessary for me to repeat that Her Majesty's Government are in no way responsible for the operations in the Soudan, which have been undertaken under the authority of the Egyptian Government, or for the appointment or actions of General Hicks" (p. 65).

But the situation was becoming complicated; English General Hicks, General Baker, General Wood were irresponsible; English Colonel Stewart and Sir E. Malet were responsible; General Hicks, irresponsible, "found it convenient" to telegraph to General Baker, irresponsible, viâ Sir E. Malet, responsible, and with the help of Colonel Stewart, responsible. No wonder the position of the English became rather difficult to understand. Lord Dufferin's position complicated matters even more, for General Hicks telegraphed to Lord Dufferin on May 3rd about his victory on April 29th, and his intentions, and asked Lord Dufferin to "communicate to Baker Pasha and ask him to send to War Office" (Egypt, No. 22, 1883, p. 1). Ten days later he telegraphed again, and Lord Dufferin having left Cairo, Sir E. Malet forwarded the telegram to Cherif Pasha, saying that "although General Hicks finds it convenient to communicate with Lord Dufferin or with me, it must not be supposed that we indorse in any way the contents of his telegrams. It is, I am sure, unnecessary for me to repeat to your Excellency, that Her Majesty's Government are in no way responsible for the operations in the Soudan which have been undertaken under the authority of His Highness' Government, or for the appointment or actions of General Hicks" (p. 27). Nevertheless, on June 5th, Sir E. Malet telegraphed to Lord Granville, sending on a telegram he had received from the General, in which the latter asked what troops could be sent to him by the Egyptian Government, and Sir E. Malet in forwarding this told Lord Granville that it was "impossible for the Egyptian Government to supply the funds demanded for the Soudan," and remarked that "a question arises as to whether General Hicks should be instructed" to narrow the sphere of his operations (p. 27). Here, again, if "Her Majesty's Government are in no way responsible for the operations in the Soudan", why should Her Majesty's officials accept telegrams on military details, and take into consideration the giving of instructions to the commanding officer?

On August, 1883, the East Soudan joined in the insurrectionary movement, and "Osman Digna, the Vizier of the Mahdi", summoned the sheiks to follow him in the war (Egypt No. 1, 1884, p. 13). In this district Tewfik Bey was holding Sincat, and defending it with remarkable courage and ability. Meanwhile things were going from bad to worse. Captain Moncrieff, British Consul at Suakin, left his post at the end of October, with 500 Egyptian soldiers, who were endeavoring to relieve Tokar. Sir E. Baring, on the ground that he could not "do any good, whilst he may do harm, by joining the Egyption troops," telegraphed to his superior officer to instruct Captain Moncrieff to "return to his post at Suakin, and remain there" (p. 83), an English ship being sent to Suakin to protect British subjects. Unfortunately, Captain Moncrieff's rashness proved fatal to him; before the message of recall could reach him, the Egyptian troops whom he had so injudiciously and improperly accompanied, had been attacked by the Arabs near Tokar, and Captain Moncrieff fell in the battle.

During October and November no news from General Hicks reached Cairo. On November 19th, Sir E. Baring telegraphed home that great anxiety was felt as to the general's fate, and added: "I think that it is not at all improbable that the Egyptian Government will request Her Majesty's Government to send English or Indian troops"; to this Lord Granville promptly replied: "We cannot lend English or Indian troops. If consulted, recommend abandonment of the Soudan within certain limits" (p. 93). On November 22nd, news arrived: "A fight took place at Kuz, between rebels and Egyptian troops; rebels in great numbers. During two first days rebels suffered great loss; Mahdi, seeing this, advanced with his regular troops from Obeid, all well armed. Fighting continued from 2nd to 5th November, when Hicks' whole army was destroyed" (p. 94).

If the Government had now remained true to their declarations that they would accept no responsibility for General Hicks, all might yet have been well. The Arabs would have driven the Egyptians out of the Soudan, and would have regained their freedom. Unhappily Lord Granville hesitated. On November 1st he had instructed Sir E. Baring that the English force in Egypt was to be reduced, and only 3,000 men were to be left in Alexandria (p. 19), the duty of preserving civil order being remitted into the hands of the constabulary under General Baker. But at the request of the Egyptian Government, after General Hicks' defeat, although he had refused to lend English troops, he practically did so by countermanding the order for withdrawal (Nov. 25th), thus setting free the Egyptian forces to carry on the iniquitous war. At the very same time that this help was given, the parrot-phrase was repeated: "Her Majesty's Government can do nothing in the matter which would throw upon them the responsibility of operations in the Soudan" (p. 98).

> "And saying she will ne'er consent,
> Consented."

Lord Granville next bent his efforts towards forcing the Egyptian Government to surrender the Soudan. At first, as we see above, he only directed Sir E. Baring to recommend that course "if consulted". On December 13th, he no longer awaited consultation, but wrote: "Her Majesty's

Government recommend the Ministers of the Khedive to come to an early decision to abandon all territory south of Assouan, or at least of Wady Halfa" (p. 131). Cherif Pasha, however, declined to adopt this course: "His Highness' Government could not adopt the decision to abandon territory which they regarded necessary for the safety and even existence of Egypt' (p. 146). Accordingly Cherif Pasha made vigorous efforts to send forth another army. Zebehr Pasha was communicated with, and directed to raise some negro regiments, with which to proceed to Suakin; Sir E. Baring, fearing that "the employment of Zebehr Pasha may not improbably attract attention in England", very justly urged: "Up to the present time [Dec. 9th] the whole responsibility for the conduct of the affairs in the Soudan has been left to the Egyptian Government. It appeared to me that, under present circumstances, it would not have been just, whilst leaving all responsibility to the Egyptian Government, to have objected to that Government using its own discretion on such a point as the appointment of Zebehr Pasha" (p. 137). Baker Pasha was also called on for aid, Zebehr being placed under his orders, and on December 17th, he was nominated "to take command of the operations which have for their object the pacification of the region lying between Berber and Suakin" (p. 161).

Lord Granville, however, remained resolute against these proposed measures. On January 4th, 1884, he wrote to Sir E. Baring that the English Government "see no reason to modify their conclusions", and at last he claimed on behalf of England the absolute right to dictate the Egyptian policy, declaring that it was "indispensable" that the "advice" tendered by England "should be followed", and declared that, in view of "the responsibility which for the time rests on England", the Government must "insist on the adoption of the policy which they recommend, and that it will be necessary that those ministers and governors who do not follow this course should cease to hold their offices" (pp. 175, 176). Rather a change this from the repudiation of responsibility, and the advice which was to be tendered "if consulted".

On this the Cherif Pasha Ministry resigned, and the more flexible Nubar Pasha accepted office, entirely concurring "in the wisdom of abandoning the Soudan" (p. 181).

Meanwhile Baker Pasha had reached Suakin, and on

the 18th January he left Suakin to endeavor to relieve Tokar. His troops were of the most wretched description; many were carried in irons on board the steamers in which they were embarked, weeping and praying to be left in peace at home. With such troops, undrilled, half-armed, filled with fear of the Soudan and its wild tribes, the failure of his expedition was fore-doomed. On February 5th, Sir W. Hewett telegraphed from Suakin that the Egyptian army under Baker Pasha had been defeated, and that he intended to land "men to take charge of town and allay panic" (Navy, Egypt, c. 3890). Upon this all the "non-responsibility" was suddenly dropped, and all the previous policy reversed. Lord Northbrook telegraphed to Sir W. Hewett to ask how many men were wanted to relieve Sinkat and Tokar by arms (p. 8); Sinkat fell on February 12th and on the same day Sir W. Hewett was ordered to "try by native messenger, at any expense, to tell garrison [of Tokar] they will be relieved by British troops before end of month" (p. 9). On the same day the Adjutant-General telegraphed to the general officer commanding in Egypt: "Force to be collected at Suakin with the object, if possible, of relieving Tokar garrison", and desiring "the greatest publicity to be given to the determination to relieve Tokar by British soldiers" (c. 3889, p. 314). Tokar, however, surrendered before we reached it.

Why this sudden, this extraordinary change? Why should British troops have been sent to relieve Tokar, after they had been so long and so steadily refused? Was it done to pacify the factitious cry raised by the idlers in the London clubs, the loudly proclaimed sympathy with Pashas Hicks, Baker, and other English adventurers in Egypt? It was said that England should step in to avenge Hicks and to save the others. Why? Free-lances, who hire themselves out to foreign Governments and degrade themselves by leading savages against savages in brutal and barbarous warfare, should be left to the companions they have deliberately chosen. The hired bravos should lose all rights of English citizenship, and should take the risks with the gains of their ignoble trade.

It is not necessary to trace in detail the brief and shameful campaign. As we invaded without reason, so we slew without ruth. In two frightful battles some 6,000 Arabs were killed and some 18,000 wounded; Arabs fighting on their own soil, in defence of their own land, fighting with dauntless bravery, with splendid self-devotion, but, to quote from a war-correspondent: "they never reached our square; they were mown down in layers as they came". Who is answerable to humanity for that awful slaughter? at whose door flows that river of uselessly shed human blood? We penetrated into the wilds as far as the chief village of Osman Digna; the women and children had wisely fled, and only mud-huts remained, "not worth a lucifer match". These were burned "to show we had put our foot there"—beautiful mark of English civilisation—careless that, while not worth a match to us, they were the homes of the natives of the land, and dear to them as ours to us. When we had performed all these horrors, we left the Soudan again, having quenched many brave lives, broken many hearts, left many maimed for life, and beyond this—Nothing. Our retreat was as inexplicable as our advance. Having protested we would not go, why did we go? Having gone, why did we return with nothing settled?

While all these events were passing in East Soudan a most curious tale, the *dénoûment* of which is still unreached, was being told in the central part of the country—the mission of General Gordon.

On December 1st, 1883, Lord Granville telegraphed to Sir E. Baring: "If General Gordon were willing to go to Egypt would he be of any use to you or to the Egyptian Government, and if so, in what capacity?". The reply came promptly: "The Egyptian Government is very much averse to employing General Gordon, mainly on the ground that the movement in the Soudan being religious, the appointment of a Christian in high command would probably alienate the tribes who remain faithful". On January 10th, 1884, Lord Granville again telegraphed: "Would General Charles Gordon or Sir C. Wilson be of assistance, under altered circumstances, in Egypt?". The Egyptian Government again refused. On the 15th Lord Granville tried again, and on the 16th the Egyptian Government gave way, and "would feel greatly obliged if her Majesty's Government would select a well-qualified British officer to go to Khartoum". On this Gordon was appointed (Egypt, No. 2, 1884, pp. 1, 2). His instructions were to report "on the military situation in the Soudan, and on the measures which it may be advisable to take for the security of the Egyptian garrisons still holding positions in that country, and for the safety of the European population in Khartoum. You are also desired to consider and report upon the best means of effecting the evacuation of the interior of the Soudan", and "you will consider yourself authorised and instructed to perform such other duties as the Egyptian Government may desire to intrust to you" (pp. 2, 3). A most extraordinary mission, in which an Englishman is to try to serve two masters, and is to receive orders from London and Cairo indifferently.

General Gordon's view of the situation had at least the merit of clearness: "My idea is that the restoration of the country should be made to the different petty Sultans who existed at the time of Mehemet Ali's conquest, and whose families still exist; that the Mahdi should be left altogether out of the calculation as regards the handing over the country; and that it should be optional with the Sultans to accept his supremacy or not . . . . the arsenals . . . . should be handed over to the Sultans of the states in which they are placed . . . . Her Majesty's Government will now leave them as God has placed them; they are not forced to fight among themselves" (Egypt, No. 7, 1884, pp. 2, 3).

Why, with such a policy accepted by the Government, we should have tried to destroy Osman Digna, a man of one of these ruling families, and why we should call those rebels in East Soudan to whom in Central Soudan Gordon, our accredited agent, was proclaiming freedom from the Egyptian yoke, it is impossible to say. If the Government understands its own policy, it is a pity it does not explain it, for most certainly no one else can see any coherency or consistency in it.

General Gordon arrived at Khartoum on February 18th, and one of his first acts was to recognise the slave trade. He issued the following proclamation: "To all the people; my sincerest desire is to adopt a course of action which shall lead to public tranquillity, and knowing your regret at severe measures taken by government for suppression of slave traffic, and seizure and punishment of all concerned according to Convention and Decrees, I confer upon you these rights, that henceforth none shall interfere with your property; whoever has slaves shall have full right to their services, and full control over them".

General Gordon at the same time proclaimed Mahomet Achmet, the Mahdi, as Sultan of Kordofan, and telegraphed (still on Feb. 18th) to Sir E. Baring recommending Zebehr Pasha as his own successor at Khartoum: "As for the man, her Majesty's Government should select one above all others, namely, Zebehr. He alone has the ability to rule the Soudan, and would be universally accepted by the Soudan" (Egypt, No. 12, 1884, p. 72). Sir E. Baring endorsed the recommendation: "I believe Zebehr Pasha to be the only possible man" (p. 73). To this Lord Granville replied that "The public opinion of this country would not tolerate the appointment of Zebehr Pasha" (p. 95); Gordon shortly answered: "That settles question for me. I cannot suggest any other. Mahdi's agents active in all directions" (p. 115). Sir E. Baring, in forwarding this telegram to Lord Granville, urged strongly that some clear policy should be adopted; two courses were possible, he argued: to evacuate the Soudan and leave it to anarchy; or to set up a capable governor acceptable to the Soudanese and able to hold his own as Sultan independently: "Whatever may be said to the contrary, Her Majesty's Government must in reality be responsible for any arrangements which are now devised for the Soudan, and I do not think it is possible to shake off that responsibility. If, however, Her Majesty's Government are unwilling to assume any responsibility in the matter, then I think they should give full liberty of action to General Gordon and the Khedive's Government to do what seems best to them. I have no doubt as to the most advisable course of action. Zebehr Pasha should be permitted to succeed General Gordon. . . I think General Gordon is quite right when he says that Zebehr Pasha is the only possible man. I can suggest none other, and Nubar Pasha is strongly in favor of him. It is for Her Majesty's Government to judge of the importance to be attached to public opinion in England, but I venture to think that any attempt to settle Egyptian questions by the light of English popular feeling is sure to be productive of harm, and in this, as in other cases, it would be preferable to follow the advice of the responsible authorities on the spot" (pp. 114, 115). Colonel Stewart advanced the same opinion (p. 137). General Gordon repeatedly telegraphed, pleading and urging that Zebehr should be sent: "I tell you plainly it is impossible to get Cairo employés out of Khartoum, unless the Government helps in the way I told you. They refuse Zebehr, and are quite right (may be) to do so, but it was the only chance" (March 1st, p. 152). "The sending of Zebehr means the extrication of the Cairo employés from Khartoum, and the garrisons from Senaar and Kassala. I can see no possible way to do so except through him" (March 8th, p. 145). The

General was evidently intensely depressed by the refusal of the Government to follow his advice; on March 9th and 10th, he sent telegram after telegram, begging for definite instructions, urging that there was no use in holding out at Khartoum if nothing was to be done, that all the roads were being closed; "you must give a prompt reply" (p. 161). Leave Khartoum he would not till the safety of those surrounding him was secured; "how could I look the world in the face if I abandoned them and fled?" (p. 156). At last he seems to despair; he will send all the white troops and employés to Berber with Colonel Stewart, and will "ask her Majesty's Government to accept the resignation of my commission, and I would take all steamers and stores up to the Equatorial and Bahr Gazelle Provinces, and consider those provinces as under the King of the Belgians" (p. 161). The last telegram from him was dated April 8th, and of this Sir E. Baring says: "he evidently thinks he is to be abandoned, and is very indignant". Apparently, however, General Gordon does not at present regard himself as in immediate danger; his chief difficulty is that he sees no prospect of improvement. At last, on April 23rd, Lord Granville appears to have realised that it was the duty of the Government to ensure General Gordon's safe retreat from Khartoum, and telegraphed asking what force was "necessary in order to secure his removal" (Egypt, No. 13, 1884, p. 15).

That he should be removed is clear. Gordon went to Khartoum as an English agent, and whatever blunder was committed in sending him, England's honor would be stained by allowing him to perish at his post. And his rescue should be effected as rapidly as possible, and so an end put to the weary vacillations of our policy. We ought never to have interfered, and the sooner we cease interfering the better. Enough blood has been shed; enough ruin has been wrought. Nothing that Lord Beaconsfield ever did was worse than our bloody incursion into East Soudan, and well may Radicals blush for the conduct denounced in Opposition and practised in Government. The least that can now be done is to prevent further mischief, leaving the Story of the Soudan to take its place in history with those of the Transvaal, of Zululand, and of Afghanistan.

Printed by Annie Besant and Charles Bradlaugh, at 63, Fleet Street, London, E.C.—1885.

GORDON

JUDGED OUT OF HIS OWN MOUTH.

BY

ANNIE BESANT.

LONDON:
FREETHOUGHT PUBLISHING COMPANY,
63, FLEET STREET, E.C.
1885.

PRICE TWOPENCE.

LONDON:
PRINTED BY ANNIE BESANT AND CHARLES BRADLAUGH,
63, FLEET STREET, E.C.

GORDON JUDGED OUT OF HIS OWN MOUTH.

"SAVE me from my friends!" has been a proverbial saying, and never had man more reason to cry for such salvation than the man whom unwise friends have exalted into a modern martyr and saint—the late General Gordon. A straightforward, brave, soldier of fortune; a sharp man of business, with an "eye to the main chance"; by no means heroic, and making no pretence to heroism; laughing rather at the humbug of friends at home who desired to gild his work with some thin coating of philanthropy, and describing it honestly as hateful work that he was sick of, cruel and unjust to the highest degree. A man worthy neither of very high praise nor of very severe blame; trying to do his duty to the tyrant who hired him, while often disgusted with the acts entailed by that duty; fearless, hot-tempered, variable, inconsistent, often violent and unjust, but on the whole endeavoring to do the best he could under conditions which rendered right action impossible; possessed of arbitrary authority and often exercising it recklessly, but on the whole not misusing it as much as many might have done; fanatical in his religion, but tolerant of the various forms of religious belief around him, and tempering his own fanaticism with a shrewd common-sense when it interfered with his work; genial at times, with a vein of humor in him, sometimes grim, sometimes mocking; a canny Scotch Covenanter, with a sturdy faith in God and a strenuous belief that his own will was identical with the divine—such was General Gordon, as drawn, not by the pencil of his admirers, but by himself in his own letters home, sketched unconsciously in his narration of his doings in letters not intended for publication, and given to the world under the title of "General Gordon in Central Africa, 1874—1879." On the whole, a far more likable and sensible human being than the impossible hybrid of heroism, saintliness, St. Michael-and-the-dragonism, and pietism that has been held up for the homage—or the derision—of the world.

The editor of these letters, Dr. G. Birkbeck Hill, speaks of General Gordon in the fashionable hyperbolical style: "Rarely . . . has so great a hero told his own story in words so great. Where could the like of Gordon be found—where in the pages of history or romance? In Spenser's 'Faerie Queen', in 'Cromwell's Letters', in 'George Fox's Journal', in 'Bunyan's Pilgrim's Progress', in 'Robinson Crusoe', in the story of the Israelites, in the Gospel story, he may be seen; but in his letters alone are gathered together the parts that have gone to the making up of this one glorious man. . . . Who can be said to put us in mind of Gordon? Who that is alive now? Who that has ever lived?" Dr. Butler, the Dean of Gloucester, preaching in the Chapel Royal, St. James's, used similar words of high-flown eulogy:

"It is no exaggeration to say that the great and good man who has just been snatched away speaks like a prophet of Christ to the men of this generation. The last week has been a week of Mission in this vast diocese. And then, just as these special services began, and the prayers of thousands were rising to God that he would lift them out of their worldliness, and teach them the lessons of the manger and the cross, suddenly there flashed across deserts and seas the tidings of the lonely martyrdom of one who stood out before the world as the very symbol of unworldliness and self-sacrifice; a man who cared absolutely nothing for wealth, or honor, or comforts of any kind; who lived for others, prayed for others, and was at any moment ready to die for them;

Who, doomed to go in company with Pain,
And Fear and Bloodshed, miserable train,
Turned his necessity to glorious gain;

a man who was never so much in his element as when ministering, at home or abroad, to misery and want; whose conception of life was drawn straight from the Bible, and that faithful mirror of one aspect of the Bible, the famous 'Imitation of Christ'; a man who had for years trodden with unfaltering feet what that high-toned book describes as 'the King's highway of the Holy Cross', and had accepted and, as it were, drunk in with every fibre of his being, that most sublime of Christian truisms—'Go where thou wilt, seek whatsoever thou wilt, thou shalt not find a higher way above, nor a safer way below, than the way of the holy cross'. During the solemn week that has just closed, while every preacher and missioner in London was seeking to impress once more this ideal first on himself and then on those to whom he ministered, was it nothing to know that the most conspicuously Christ-like man of his day had just crowned a Christ-like life with a Christ-like death? Was there any appeal at such a time to compare with his example? Was there any voice so eloquent as the hushed voice of the dead?

Therefore in an age of boundless self-indulgence, when comfort in every form, and avoidance of effort, physical and intellectual, spread their snares so wide and so fatally, let us give thanks for this illustrious spectacle of heroic and saintly self-sacrifice.

Let his great example stand,
Colossal, seen of every land,
And keep the soldier firm, the statesman pure."

Curious indeed is it to read such words and then to read his own view of his work: "Some philanthropic people write to me about 'noble work', 'poor blacks', etc. I have, I think, stopped their writing by acknowledging ourselves to be a pillaging horde of brigands, and proposing to them to leave their comfortable homes, and come out to their favorite 'poor blacks'! or to give up their wine and devote the proceeds to sending out *real* missions. . . . 'We do not want your beads; we do not want your cloth;' of the poor Moogies rings in my ears. 'We want you to go away.' They know well enough the little benefits that would ever accrue from our occupation" (p. 143). (All the quotations are from the fourth edition of the book named above.) Again: "We derided the poor blacks who fought for their independence, and now God gave them the victory, and I declare, in spite of the expressions you may note in my letters, I truly sympathise with them. They say, 'We do not want your cloth and your beads; you go your way and we will go ours; we do not want to see your chief.' This they have said over and over again, but we cannot leave them on our flank, and it is indispensable that they shall be subjected. They have said, 'This land is ours, and you shall not have it, neither its bread nor its flocks.' Poor fellows! . . . Just this moment I see four sheep upon our long island where I was to-day. I expect the poor inhabitants want peace, and (D. V.) I will go and reassure them to-morrow. It is such a fine island, about three miles long, and with such fine trees. A station there would command all the country" (pp. 114, 115). "I can quite enter into these poor people's misery at their impotency. 'We do not want beads; we do not want to see the Pasha;' (I am sure I do not want to see them!) 'we want our own lands, and you to go away.' Their poor minds never conceived such a trial as this before. Rain was their only care before, now *civilisation* (?) is to begin with them; they are to be brought into the family of nations" (p. 120). "How cordially glad I shall be when the whole relations between us cease! I cannot help it, but I have taken such a dislike to these blacks that I cannot bear their sight. I do not mean the natives, but these soldiers. They are nothing but a set of pillagers, and are about as likely to civilise these parts as they are to civilise the moon" (p. 139). So far was he from feeling any philanthropic yearnings towards the people he was conquering and ruling that he wrote: "Cowardly, lying, effeminate brutes these Arabs and Soudanese! without any good point about them that I can see. It is degrading to call these leaders and these men officers and soldiers—I wish they had one neck and someone would squeeze it! When not obliged, I keep as far as I can from them, out of earshot of their voices" (p. 77). "As for the Arabs, with one exception, they are lazy, effeminate, shirking, and only seeking a hole to hide in. As for the Soudanese, they are idle, only thinking of their own comfort, and shirking" (p. 127). "I cannot say I shall ever take a great interest in the black tribes. They are to me all alike; whether one has a bunch of leaves or a scrap of calico does not make much difference to my mind; they are all black, they shave their heads, and they look all alike, male and female" (p. 47). Rather a contrast, this expression by Gordon of his own view about his work, to that of Dr. Butler! The preacher sees him "ministering" "to misery and want"; he sees himself as the chief of "a set of pillagers", rendering miserable savages who were happy before he invaded their land. His own account of these tribes was: "They would seem to get on well without any regular laws, and to live out their span in comparative quiet. . . . . No country presents such a field to a philosopher as this country does, with its dense population quite innocent of the least civilisation. I should say that they are singularly free from vice; their wars are generally very harmless affairs, and seldom cause bloodshed" (pp. 99, 100). "The people are quite quiet and inoffensive, and a man of some intellect would soon gain an immense influence over them" (p. 82). If Gordon took such a view of his work, it may fairly be asked, why did he do it? His reasons were simple enough, but certainly not heroic. He bargained for £2,000 a year pay, and says at the outset: "I took the opportunity of asking him [Shereef Pasha] to express to the Khedive my ideas of giving up the affair if it did not pay" (p. 1). He states that if he be dismissed he will not care much, as the work is hard and the gain not large: "At the end of two years, say £2,000; at the end of three, say £3,500 at the outside" (p. 93). Then again he liked the freedom of the wild life: "I felt too independent to serve, with my views, at Malta or in the corps, and perhaps I felt I had in me something that, if God willed, might benefit these lands, for he has given me great energy and health and some little common sense" (p. 59). "I am quite independent of the Khedive for money, and have heaps of stores of all sorts, ammunition, etc. In fact, I am semi-independent. In a year he has had £48,000 from the province, and I have spent say £20,000 at the outside, and have £60,000 worth of ivory here" (p. 117). He thought that on the whole his own rule was better than that of an Egyptian pasha: "If they are to be put down, it is better I should do it than an exterminating pasha who would have no mercy" (p. 105). A saint and a hero ought scarcely to have embraced evil work because he would be less cruel in the doing it than would an unredeemed ruffian, but then Gordon did not pretend to be either the one or the other. He took a very common-sense view of the situation: "Remember that no one is ever obliged to enter the service of one of these States, and that if he does he has to blame himself and not the Oriental State. If the Oriental State is well-governed, then it is very sure he will never be wanted. The rottenness of the State is his *raison d'être*; and it is absurd for him to be surprised at things not being as they ought to be according to his ideas" (pp. 351, 352).

Passing from his opinion of his work and from the ludicrous misrepresentations of it by press and preachers, let us see what instructions he took from the Khedive, and what the nature of his work really was.

It seems from the "Abstract of the Khedive's final Instructions to Colonel Gordon" (pp. xxxi.—xxxiii.) that the province to which Gordon was sent had never really belonged to Egypt at all. Factories were established there by "lawless adventurers", who traded in slaves and ivory. The Egyptian Government "took the factories into their own hands, paying the owners an indemnification"; but some of the men were allowed to carry on trade "under a promise that they would not deal in slaves," and they were "placed under the control of the Governor of the Soudan". As this Governor had no means of controlling his new subjects, they went on in their own way; the

Khedive, according to his own account, "resolved to form them into a separate government, and to claim as a monopoly of the State the whole of the trade with the outside world"; he declared that he was moved to this by his desire to make clear "even in those remote parts, that a mere difference of color does not turn men into wares, and that life and liberty are sacred things". This admirable sentiment loses much of its force when we learn something of the real motives actuating the Khedive (Ismail Pasha). It seems that adventurers of various nationalities opened up the way towards the Equator, and that they fortified stations as they went, raiding for slaves and ivory. "About the year 1860 the scandal became so great that the Europeans had to get rid of their stations. They sold them to their Arab agents, who paid a rental for them to the Egyptian Government" (p. xxxvi.). Dr. Hill tells us that these Arabs were supplied with arms and ammunition by the Egyptian Government, and that the Khedive's sudden anxiety to put down the slave-hunters was caused "not by pity for the countless sufferers, but by the dread of the growth of a rival power". The slave-dealers "refused to the Government the rental that had been agreed on", and when the Khedive no longer shared the plunder he became alive to the fact that "life and liberty are sacred things". Colonel Gordon wrote "how anxious, how terribly anxious, the Khedive is to put down the slave-trade, which threatens his supremacy" (p. xl.), and Colonel Gordon's work was, as we shall see, not to put down slavery, but to destroy the power of the slave-hunters who were acquiring wealth in a country which the Khedive desired to annex to his own dominions. The action was a purely aggressive one on the part of Egypt, prompted by the desire to monopolise the lucrative Nile trade in ivory and cattle, and we shall see that Gordon served his employer well.

Colonel Gordon began his work as soon as he reached Khartoum: "I have issued a stinging decree, declaring the Government monopoly of the ivory trade, and prohibiting the import of arms and powder, the levying of armed bands by private people, and the entry of any one without passports—in fact I have put the district under martial law, *i.e.*, the will of the General" (p. 6). This "will" was somewhat imperious and unjust at times, by his own confession; "I am quite well, but my temper is very, very short, and it is a bad time for those who come across me the wrong way" (p. 41). "I have worked them up well here the last two days, and hope the severe examples will brighten them up" (p. 84). He met a lad with a gang of slaves. "I asked the lad in charge of the gang to whom they belonged. As he hesitated, I gave him a cut across the face with my whip, which was cruel and cowardly; but I was enraged to see the poor women and children so utterly forlorn, and could not help it" (p. 288). One instance may serve as an example of his rough and ready "justice" (?), and may show the kind of work he did. There was a sheikh named Bedden, and "as he occupied a tract of land too near me to be comfortable, [!] and as he lately attacked a sheikh who had always been very friendly" (p. 69), Gordon after some hesitation resolved to make a raid on his cattle. The cattle at night are shut up in seribas (enclosures) with only one entrance, and if this entrance is seized the cattle are secured. Gordon started off with friendly natives, attracted by the prospect of plunder, and "we got the cows. We rewarded, with what was not our own, the 'friendlys', and came back . . . . . We got altogether 2,600 head" (p. 72). On the next day "we got 500 cows" (p. 73), and "I hope Bedden and Lococo will both submit before many days are over. I do most cordially hate this work; but the question is, what are you to do?" (p. 73). The sequel of the story is interesting; Gordon discovered "I had unwittingly carried off the cows of a friendly chief when I made my raid on Bedden" (p. 76), so he restored those, and a little later he met Bedden and found him to be a poor old man, partially blind (p. 78). He then "gave him twenty of the stolen cows, a coil of copper and a pair of scissors . . . These twenty cows are nothing to give for me, for we took 2,000, and I have everything to gain by such conduct" (p. 79). Not very heroic work, this, yet this was Gordon's work, done by him for years, although he continually protests that he dislikes it. "These are their maxims: if the natives do not act after the most civilised manner, then punish them for not so acting; but, if it comes to be a question of our action, then follow the customs of the natives, viz., recognise plunder as no offence whatever. Such is the reasoning of these creatures" (p. 80). But Gordon led "these creatures" and acted on their system.

Gordon raised his revenue by "taxation", *i.e.*, by raiding

for cattle, selecting for this purpose the tribes who did not welcome his invasion. "The taxgatherers are out, and there is an immense amount of excitement among the natives on the other side. . . . . The results of the expedition are not great—200 cows and 1,500 sheep. The natives did not know of the expedition and were taken by surprise" (p. 119). "Another tribe close here to the south shows hostility—they are to be taxed to-night. . . . . The party have come back with no cows, but with a heap of things used by the natives. . . . . How I hate this country and all the work" (pp. 123, 124, 125). Mere looting expeditions were these, bare, indefensible robbery. "Yesterday we moved on the Moogie tribe, but it was a failure as regards the capture of cows. . . . . Made another attack on the Moogie, and took 1,500 cows" (p. 147). Such extracts might be multiplied indefinitely.

Cow-lifting, however, was not the only means by which Gordon raised his revenue; he made large captures of ivory, seizing all that he found in the hands of traders, for he had "decreed the monopoly of ivory and commerce" for the State, and he confiscated all the ivory he found. To use his own description of his position: "I am quite independent, raise my own revenue and administer it, and send the residue to Cairo" (p. 118).

The traders who brought down slaves generally brought with them cows and ivory; these Gordon seized, and generally stripped the dealers, flogged them, and turned them loose. Thus we read: "Everyone took from them what they liked, till they were despoiled. They were then beaten and dismissed" (pp. 341, 342). "I gave the captured slave-dealer a good flogging, and let him go" (p. 365). "We have captured a great deal of ivory" (p. 358), he writes in narrating his stoppage of several slave-raiders' caravans. "I heard from my German that there were slaves on board, so I sent him to see, and he found stowed away in the wood some 105 of them; so I confiscated them and the ivory. . . . The ivory confiscated is worth £2,000" (pp. 36, 37). "In a year he [the Khedive] has had £48,000 from the province, and I have spent say £20,000 at the outside, and have £60,000 worth of ivory here" (p. 117). On the whole the Khedive profited largely by his determination to show that "life and liberty are sacred things". "I shall confiscate the 2,000 cows, for I cannot give them back to the far-away tribes from whom they were stolen" (p. 19). "Nassar has at least 300 slaves with him and 2,000 cows . . . so I shall wait here for the cows, and then start up for the slaves up the Saubat River. If I miss them I shall hear if they have passed; if they have I shall confiscate all the property of the slavers here and elsewhere in the province" (pp. 23, 24). As might be guessed by anyone who knew anything of Egyptian rule, the objections of the Khedive to the slave-trade were purely business-like, and Gordon carried out his instructions faithfully, and endorsed slavery wherever it did not injure his employer's interests.

Gordon's attitude towards slavery has been so grossly misrepresented in this country, that it is necessary to define clearly his course of action, and to prove by his own words how far he was out of sympathy with those who urge our Government to persevere in their invasion of the Soudan with the view of putting down slavery. It will be convenient to take separately his actions during his first stay in Central Africa, as Governor of the Equatorial Provinces from 1873—1876, and his policy from 1877—1879, as active Governor-General of the Soudan. (He retained the office for some time after he left Africa.)

1873—1876.—So far from disapproving the buying and selling of slaves, Colonel Gordon himself shared in such practices. "One of the men brought me over his two children, twelve and nine years old, because he could not keep them, and sold them to me for a small basketful of dhoora. I gave one of them to ——, and the other to a German" (p. 17). "I have bought another lad to-day, sold by his brother for a small basket of dhoora" (p. 20). Perhaps his views are best put in the following passage: "I think that the slavers' wars, made for the purpose of taking slaves, are detestable; but if a father or mother, of their own free will, and with the will of the child, sells that child, I do not see the objection to it. It was and is the wholesale depopulation of districts which makes slavery such a curse, and the numbers killed, or who perish, in the collection of slaves" (pp. 24, 25). As to family affecttion and the sufferings caused by separation in buying and selling slaves, Colonel Gordon treated these with contempt. "The father", he writes, alluding to his above-named purchase of two children, "did not even take leave of them; and though he has been over since, has never noticed them or spoken to them" (p. 17). A man with two children had stolen a cow; "I happened to go round, and passing the hut saw only one child. 'Where was the other?' I asked of the mother. 'Oh, it had been given to the man from whom the cow had been stolen.' This was said with a cheerful smile by the mother. 'But', I said, 'are you not sorry?' 'Oh no! we would rather have the cow.' 'But', said I, 'you have eaten the cow, and the pleasure is over.' 'Oh, but all the same, we would sooner have had the cow!'. This is perfectly true. The other child of twelve years old, like her parents, did not care a bit. A lamb taken from a flock would bleat, while here you see not the very slightest vestige of feeling. Is it not very odd? If the mother had expressed the slightest wish, I would have rescued the child again; but it was evidently a matter of rejoicing, and she did not care as much as if she had lost a handful of dhoora" (pp. 19, 20). "In spite of what Livingstone says, I do not myself, about here, find that any affection exists between the parents and the children; there is a mutual pleasure in parting with one another" (p. 24).

When Colonel Gordon came under the influence of English feeling he wrote in very different fashion. In a letter to the *Times*, March 23, 1881, he writes: "I appeal to my countrymen who have wives and families, and who can realise to some degree the bitterness of parting with them—to God—what it must be for those poor black peoples to have their happy households rent asunder for an effete, alien, set, like the pashas of Egypt and Turkey" (p. 346, note). Happy households rent asunder? There is a mutual pleasure in parting with one another! I do not think that Gordon was consciously dishonest in his letter to the *Times*; he was a variable, impressionable creature, reflecting the circumstances around him. In 1874 he saw the blacks would sell their children for a trifle, and he reflected them; in 1881 he was surrounded by people who objected to slavery and imported their own ideas into the blacks' heads, and he reflected them.

1877–1879.—As Governor-General of the Soudan, Gordon tried hard to put down slave-raiding, but bought slaves for his army, and when he captured a slave-gang he distributed the slaves as he best could. "A party of seven slave-dealers with twenty-three slaves were captured and brought to me. . . . The men and boys were put in the ranks; the women were told off to be wives (!) of the soldiers" (p. 345). (The note of exclamation is Gordon's, not mine.) "Just as I wrote this I heard a very great tumult going on among the Arabs, and I feared a fight. However, it turned out to be caused by the division of the slaves among the tribes; and now the country is covered by strings of slaves, going off in all directions with their new owners. . . . . It appears that the slaves were not divided, but were scrambled for. It is a horrid idea, for of course families get separated, but I cannot help it, and the slaves seem to be perfectly indifferent to anything whatsoever" (p. 359). "I gave the captured slave-dealer a good flogging and let him go, and gave the six slaves to a tribe near the spot" (p. 365). He defended his action by necessity: "The 25,000 black troops I have here are either captured slaves or bought slaves. How are we to recruit if the slave-trade ceases?" (p. 351). "Of course I must let time soften down the ill effects of what is written against me in the papers, on account of my purchasing the slaves now in possession of individuals in order to obtain the troops necessary to put down slavery. I need troops—how am I to get them but thus? . . . I want you to understand this, for I doubt not people will write and say—1. Colonel Gordon buys slaves for the Government. 2. Colonel Gordon lets the Gallabats take slaves. To No. 1 I say: 'True, for I need the purchased slaves to put down the slave-dealers, and to break up their semi-independent bands.' To No. 2 I say: 'True, for I dare not stop it to any extent, for fear of adding to my enemies, before I have broken up the nest of slave-dealers at Shaka'" (pp. 254, 255). "One thing troubles me. What am I to do with the three or four thousand slaves, women and children, that are now at Shaka, if we take it? I cannot take them back to their own country; I cannot feed them. Solve this problem for me. I must let them be taken by my auxiliaries, or by my soldiers, or by the merchants" (p. 256). He protests hotly against the injustice of blaming him because he allows slavery: "Would you shoot them all? [slave-dealers] Have they no rights? Are they not to be considered? Had the planters no rights? Did not our Government once allow slave trading? Do you know that cargoes of slaves came into Bristol Harbour in the time of our fathers? I would have given £500 to have had you and the Anti-slavery Society in Dara during the three days of doubt whether the slave-dealers would fight or not . . . . I do not believe in you all. You say this and that, and you do not do it; you give your money and you have done your duty; you praise one another, etc. . . . . Now understand me. If it suits me I will buy slaves. I will let captured slaves go down to Egypt and not molest them, and I will do what I like, and what God in his mercy may direct me to do about domestic slaves; but I will break the neck of slave-raids even if it cost me my life. I will buy slaves for my army; for this purpose I will make soldiers against their will to enable me to prevent raids. I will do this in the light of day and defy your resolutions and your actions" (pp. 279, 280).

Egypt had entered into a treaty to liberate her slaves in 1884 and those in her dependencies in 1889, but Colonel Gordon did not look on the matter as hopeful. "When you have got the ink which has soaked into blotting-paper out of it, then slavery will cease in these lands" (p. 285). "The people are bent on slave-traffic . . . . I declare I see no human way to stop it" (p. 289). "If the liberation of slaves takes place in 1884, and the present system of government goes on, there cannot fail to be a revolt of the whole country. . . . . Seven-eighths of the population of the Soudan are slaves, and the loss of revenue in 1889 will be more than two-thirds, if it is ever carried out" (p. 351).

Gordon was not in favor of European meddling in Egyptian affairs, either on behalf of the slaves or of anything else. "Europe wants to wash them—they do not want to be washed. . . . . Let us keep clear of interfering with their internal affairs; let us leave reforms to them and their peoples" (pp. 352, 353). "I put aside, in the first place, the fact that God has made the people of Egypt what they are; that it is by His will the Khedive is their ruler; and go on to say, that, after European ideas, the Egyptian people are a servile race, as foretold they should be; and that, not only do they not deserve a better government than they have, but they would not be content under a better government" (p. 435). "To remedy the state of these Oriental countries . . . . there are two ways: either for European nations to annex *in toto*, or exterminate their populations—there is no middle route; the first is a bad speculation; the second is impossible; and the best way is to let them alone, and not be philanthropic to those who do not need it" (p. 436).

Any judgment of Gordon's character which left out of

sight his religion would be a very imperfect one. He had a curious strain of mysticism in him, and was by no means an orthodox Christian: "Have you read *Modern Christianity a civilised Heathenism?* I had those views long before I read the book" (p. 282). Christian missionaries were not to his mind. "How refreshing it is to hear of the missionary efforts made in these countries! —— wrote me word, 'Three mission parties leave shortly for the East Coast. One under Mr. —— takes a steam launch for Lake Nyassa, and "down",—— says, "he will run the first slave nuggar he meets on the lake"'. Of course it not signifying a jot who is on board. This reminds one so forcibly of the mission labors of St. Paul, and of the spirit of St. John. —— wrote and asked me if a missionary could get along with Mtesa [a chief]. You see that a missionary likes to deal with Cæsars, and not with the herd of common mortals" (p. 81). From living so long among Mussulmans he had imbibed much of their fatalism, and with it the indifferent courage which fears no peril, convinced that the hour of death is pre-ordained, and can neither be hurried nor retarded. "I do nothing of this—I am a chisel which cuts the wood; the carpenter directs it" (p. 175). "You are a machine, though allowed to feel as if you had the power of action" (p. 152). "The events of the future are all written, and are mapped out in all their detail for each one of us. The Negro, the Arab, and the Bedouin's course —their meeting with me, etc., is decreed" (p. 213). "Everything that happens to-day, good or evil, is settled and fixed, and it is no use fretting over it" (p. 26). "No comfort is equal to that which he has who has God for his stay; who believes, not in words but in fact, that *all* things are ordained to happen and must happen" (p. 42). His German servant lost his rifle: "I said, 'You are a born idiot of three years old! How dare you touch my rifle?' However, as it was ordained to be lost, I soon got over it" (p. 48). "I feel compelled to say either 'I hope', or 'I trust'—is it the presage of evil or what, or is it my liver? It is, however, all written, and is only unrolling" (p. 117). The courage which has been so much talked of was the result of this fatalism, and Gordon shared it with his Mussulman comrades.

He carried out his belief in God's directing influence to the fullest extent, and when in doubt was wont to decide his own actions by tossing, evidently not agreeing with

Thomas Gataker, who in 1619 in his book on "The Nature and Use of Lots", said that to expect God's interference "by an immediate and extraordinarie worke is no more lawfull here than elsewhere, yea, is indeed mere superstition". "I am quite well, and think things promise, with God's help, to work out all right. Tossing up about difficult questions relieves me of much anxiety. Two servants who were useless were brought in, and the question whether they went on or not decided by a toss in their presence. It went for them once; however, afterwards they were sent away—they exasperated me dreadfully" (p. 6). The last *naïve* confession is delightful. God decided that the servants should go, so Gordon took them, but—a touch of shrewdness tempering the superstition—he sent them away again when his view of their usefulness did not coincide with the divine. Be sure he did not toss when his mind was made up.

The superstition which was ingrained in his character came out strongly from time to time. Some African magicians practised some incantations against him, and soon afterwards his men were defeated: "Did I not mention the incantations made against us by the magicians on the other side, and how somehow, from the earnestness that they made them with, I had some thought of misgiving on account of them? It was odd this repulse was so soon to follow. These prayers were earnest prayers for celestial aid in which the Prayer knew he would need help from some unknown power to avert a danger. That the native knows not the true God is true, but God knows him, and moved him to pray and answered his prayer". (p. 117).

Such is Gordon's character as limned by himself. As the glamor-mist which enwraps him dissolves away, his figure, now magnified to the heroic, will be seen in its true human proportions. He will be recognised as soldier of fortune, honest and loyal to his employers, instead of as the ideal warrior-saint of modern Christianity. His death will no longer be styled a martyrdom, but the natural outcome of his fanatical imprudence and self-will; and England will then rejoice that the rebuking voices of her workers checked the statesmen and the pressmen who were using his name as the fiery cross to gather an army of revenge.

FORCE NO REMEDY.

By ANNIE BESANT.

There is excessive difficulty in dealing with the Irish question at the present moment; Tories are howling for revenge on a whole nation as answer to the crime committed by a few; Whigs are swelling the outcry; many Radicals are swept away by the current, and, feeling that "something must be done," they endorse the Government action, forgetting to ask whether the "something" proposed is the wisest thing. A few stand firm, but they are very few; too few to prevent the Coercion Bill from passing into law. But few though we be, who lift up voice of protest against the wrong which we are powerless to prevent, we may yet do much to make the new Act of brief duration, by so rousing public opinion as to bring about its early repeal. When the measure is understood by the public half the battle will be won; it is accepted at the moment from faith in the Government; it will be rejected when its true character is grasped.

The murders which have given birth to this repressive measure came with a shock upon the country, which was the more terrible from the sudden change from gladness and hope to darkness and despair. The new policy was welcomed so joyfully; the messenger of the new policy was slain ere yet the pen was dry which had signed the orders of mercy and of liberty. Small wonder that cry of horror should be followed by measure of vengeance; but the murders were the work of a few criminals, while the measure of vengeance strikes the whole of the Irish people. I plead against the panic which confounds political agitation and political redressal of wrong with crime and its punishment. The Government measure gags every mouth in Ireland, and puts, as we shall see, all political effort at the mercy of the Lord Lieutenant, the magistracy, and the police.

The point round which rages the whole of the struggle in Ireland is the land. The absence of manufactures—destroyed by past English legislation—has thrown the people wholly on the soil. From this arises the fierce competition which has forced rents up to figures impossible to pay; from this the terrible truth that "a sentence of eviction is a sentence of death;" from this the despair of the Irishman turned off the land, and the revenge born of the despair striking down the author and the messengers of the ejection. What the rack-renting has been is proved by the wholesale reduction of rents made by the Land Commissioners. In his best times the rent was only paid by the Connaught peasant by leading starvation life; in his worst, he was pushed over the famine-precipice on the brink of which he was always tottering. Men who see the life slowly drained out of their dearest by the pressure of the landlord—who have seen aged mother, or wife with the new-born babe at her breast, die on the turf whereon they were laid by the bailiff who unroofed the cabin—such men lose all thought of the sanctity of human life when the lives of the dearest are reckoned as less worth than the shillings of overdue rack-rental, and either catch up the rifle to revenge their own pain, or stand with folded arms in sullen indifference when landlord or agent falls dead under bullet, with a dim feeling that the crime in some poor fashion makes more level the balance of misery, and that the pain in the mud-cabin has in some sort reacted in the anguish thus caused in the hall.

Let the report of Mr. Fox, "On the Condition of the Peasantry of the County of Mayo," in 1880, speak of the misery which preceded the present "social revolution:"—

> "I do not believe that tongue, or pen, however eloquent, could truly depict the awful destitution of some of those hovels. The children are often nearly naked. Bedding there is none, everything of that kind having long since gone to the pawn-office, as proved to me by numerous tickets placed in my hands for inspection in well-nigh every hovel. A layer of old straw covered by the dirty sacks which conveyed the seed potatoes and artificial manure in the spring is the sole provision of thousands —with this exception, that little babies in wooden boxes are occasionally indulged with a bit of thin, old flannel stitched on to the sacking. Sometimes even charity itself had failed, and the mother of the tender young family was found absent, begging for the loan of some Indian meal from other recipients of charitable relief—the father being in almost every instance away in England laboring to make out some provision for the coming winter. Men, women, and children sleep under a roof and within walls dripping with wet, while the floor is saturated with damp, not uncommonly oozing out of it in little pools. The construction and dimensions of their hovels are, as abodes of human beings, probably unique. On the uplands they are mostly built of common stone walls without plaster, and are often totally devoid of the ordinary means of exit for the smoke, as it may also be almost said they are devoid of anything in the shape of furniture. On the low-lying lands, on the other hand, they may be briefly described as bog holes, though by a merciful dispensation of the architect these are undoubtedly rendered somewhat warmer by their very construction out of the solidified

peat and mud. Their dimensions are even more extraordinary still, varying from 12 feet by 15 feet down to one half that limited space. Yet all of them are inhabited by large families of children, numbers of whom sleep on a little straw spread on the bare ground, with nothing to cover them save the rags and tatters worn during the day. I invariably found them on the occasion of my visits crouching around the semblance of a fire, lighted on the open hearth. And this at midsummer, shewing how terribly low must be the vitality amongst them . . . .

"We visited more than thirty hovels of the poor, principally in the townlands of Culmore and Cashel, in which I beheld scenes of wretchedness and misery wholly indescribable. In some of those hovels evicted families had lately taken refuge, so that the overcrowding added to the other horrors of the situation. In one hovel, in the townland of Cashel, we found a little child, three years old, one of a family of six, apparently very ill, with no person more competent to watch it than an idiot sister of eighteen; while the mother was absent begging committee relief, the father being in England. In another an aged mother, also very ill, lying alone, with nothing to eat save long-cooked Indian meal, which she was unable to swallow. In another, in the townland of Culmore, there were four young children, one of whom was in a desperate condition for want of its natural food—milk—without which it was no longer capable of eating the Indian meal stirabout, or even retaining anything whatever on its stomach. I took off my glove to feel its emaciated little face, calm and livid as in death, which I found to be stone cold. My companion gently stirred its limbs, and after a while it opened its eyes, though only for a moment, again relapsing into a state of coma, apparently. It lay on a wallet of dirty straw, with shreds and tatters of sacking and other things covering it. The mother was in Foxford begging for relief, the father being in England in this case also. In no Christian country in the world probably would so barbarous a spectacle be tolerated, except in Ireland."

Mr. Fox further remarks on the absence of crime, borne witness to by the police themselves; on the action of absentee landlords, one of whom, an Irish peer, was "drawing £30,000 a year out of the country, whose tenants are everywhere living upon the Indian meal which we have had so much labor in collecting from the four quarters of the globe." Even Mr. Forster admitted that the "normal condition" of the peasantry and small tenant farmers was one predisposing to fever—famine fever.

The Land League was founded by Michael Davitt to win such a change in the tenure of land as should prevent the "normal condition" of the people in the future being such as was described by Mr. Forster. The organisation was, at least, an enormous advance on previous attempts at settling the question, and its tendency was to lead the people to look to public and open agitation for a remedy, instead of to secret conspiracy and armed redress. That outrages resulting from misery and longing for vengeance should continue side by side with the healthier movement was not wonderful, but Michael Davitt—alone among the leaders of the Land League—strove with strenuous effort to raise the new movement out of the old ruts in which Irish agitation had run so long, and would probably have succeeded had not the Government silenced him, and helped the outragemongers by throwing him into Portland Prison. His imprisonment became the answer to those who urged that peaceful agitation was the best road whereby to win redressal of wrong, and the old secret societies gathered new force and wider immunity, when the gaol held the founder of the Land League, and the Coercion Act—to quote Lord Cowper—drove discontent "under the surface."

The complete failure of the Coercion Act as a repressor of outrages is now so generally recognised that it would be idle to dwell upon it. Mr. Gladstone himself, in the debate on the second reading, described it as "a bill of an invidious and offensive character." (In passing, I wonder with what adjectives Mr. Gladstone will describe the new Coercion Act a year hence.) The Goverment determined that it should become a dead letter, and that a policy of redressal of wrong and relief of misery should take the place of coercive legislation. This decision being carried out shortly after the murders of Mr. Herbert and of Mrs. Smythe, a plainer declaration could scarcely have been made that suspension of constitutional liberty did not touch crime. The murders of Lord Frederick Cavendish and of Mr. Burke followed, and on this Mr. Gladstone stated that these had forced the Government to "recast their policy." The new Coercion Bill is the recasting. But the question is inevitable: "If it was right to reverse a policy of coercion after the murders of Mr. Herbert and Mrs. Smythe, why is it also right to return again to the policy of coercion after the murders of Lord F. Cavendish and Mr. Burke?" It is impossible to avoid seeing in the present proposal of the Government the result of personal feeling and personal pain; that the feeling is natural all must admit; that the murder of a colleague and a relative should make deeper impression than the murder of a stranger is not marvellous; but the treatment of a nation should not be swayed by such feelings, and if two murders were followed by the lightening of coercive pressure, two others ought not to be followed by the increase of the same pressure. The plain fact is that the murderers have succeeded. They saw in the new policy the reconciliation of England and Ireland; they knew that friendship would follow justice, and that the two countries, for the first time in history, would clasp hands. To prevent this they dug a new gulf, which they hoped the English nation would not span; they sent a river of blood across the road of friendship, and they flung two corpses to bar the newly-opened gate of reconciliation and peace. They have succeeded.

The new Act will not prevent crime, but it will still further alienate the Irish people. The daily life of each citizen is put under the most aggravating restrictions, and under a constant menace, while criminals will easily slip through the clumsy meshes of the new Act. Secret societies are said to be aimed at; but never yet was secret society destroyed by repressive legislation. Secret societies are only destroyed by the destruction of the social wrongs in which they strike their roots. In Russia we have a standing example of what repressive legislation can do against a secret society: its Czar is shivering in Gatskina, and dares not even to publicly assume his diadem. Yet repression there is carried on with a brutality and a thoroughness which public opinion in England would not tolerate, even in Ireland. If measure after measure of growing cruelty is to be levelled against secret societies within these realms, we may yet come to a period when an English Prime Minister will be trembling in a new Gatskina, and the rulers of free England, encircled by police and by soldiery, will be degraded to the level of the agents of continental tyranny.

Let us examine the Bill, dividing it into the clauses that give new judicial powers, and those which deal with "offences." Part I.: Power is given to the Lord Lieutenant to issue a Special Commission, forming a court to try persons accused of certain crimes. The court is to consist of three judges, who shall try prisoners without a jury, the prisoner, if convicted, to have the right of appeal to a court consisting of not less than five judges, none of whom must have sat in the first court. This part of the Act is met by a protest from the Irish judges, who object to the new duties forced upon them, and, if passed, will therefore be administered by a reluctant Bench. The abolition of trial by jury is, I venture to submit, both unwise and useless. It would be better, if any change be made, either to take the verdict of a majority, as in Scotland, or to legalise the transference of trials for certain offences to England, where a jury composed of Irishmen living in England would not be in terror of their lives. But really it is not a question of justice failing because of the failure of juries to convict; the difficulties in Ireland do not lie with the juries; the difficulties are the non-finding of the criminals, and the failure of witnesses to give evidence, the first being by far the greater. In the returns of agrarian offences for January, February and March of the present year, this important fact is very clearly shown. In January 479 outrages were committed (of these 290 were only threatening letters and notices and 46 more "intimidation otherwise than by threatening letters and notices"); for these 31 persons only were rendered "amenable to justice;" of these 12 were convicted, 16 were not convicted, and 3 are awaiting trial; in 448 cases out of the 479 no persons were brought to justice. In February, out of 407 cases, only 23 persons were charged; 7 of these are awaiting trial, and 4 were convicted. In March 531 outrages, and only 46 persons charged; 18 are awaiting trial, 5 have been convicted. No details are given as to the convictions in January, the 12 in February, or the 23 in March, so we cannot judge whether in these the jury or the witnesses broke down. Now how will the new Court help us? They cannot try in the cases where no persons are charged; they cannot convict without evidence if the persons are charged; and even supposing that they convict every person brought before them, with or without evidence, they will make very small impression on the roll of outrages. If such a Court had existed during January, February and March, and had condemned every prisoner brought before it, out of 1417 outrages, 1317 would have remained unpunished, 28 persons would be awaiting trial, while only 72 would have been condemned. It is hardly worth while to abolish trial by jury for such small results, and it must be remembered that even judges sitting without jury must have some evidence before they can convict.

The "Court of Summary Jurisdiction," erected by the Bill, is even more objectional than the Special Commission Court. It is formed of one police magistrate in Dublin, and two resident magistrates elsewhere. "Any offence against this Act" may be dealt with by this Court, and from its decision there is no appeal. So that while the decision of three judges may be appealed against, the decision of one or of two petty magistrates stands above all revision. When we remember the woful abuses of magisterial authority in Ireland (see "Coercion in Ireland and its Results"), we may well stand aghast in considering the tremendous powers vested in them under this Act. For let us see what the "offences" are. Some are crimes of violence and assaults which need no statute to become punishable offences. But a new one is "intimidation," defined as "any word spoken or act done calculated to put any person in fear of any injury or danger to himself . . . . business, or means of living." Under this clause a Major Clifford Lloyd and a friend may send to gaol for six months any person who uses any sort of argument to his neighbor to persuade him to, or dissuade him from, any course of action. Any suspicion, any private spite, may cause two magistrates to see in the most harmless discussion an attempt at "intimidation," and against their abuse of authority there is no appeal.

Another offence is taking part in an "unlawful assembly." Such an assembly may be construed as consisting of any number of persons over three; and the Lord Lieutenant has power to forbid any proposed assembly if he considers it "dangerous to the public peace or the public safety." What political leader will dare to call a public meeting in Ireland when the new Act is in force? Every person present at such meeting, if it be forbidden, comes at once under the power of the court of summary jurisdiction, and even idle curiosity becomes punishable with six months' imprisonment. The great political question there is the question of the land; the agrarian outrages arise because of the evil system of land-tenure; any political meeting called to ask for the redressal of grievances connected with the land will most certainly be regarded as "dangerous to the public peace;" and the people, denied all open expression of their grievances, will be more than ever thrown back on violent means.

Not only is liberty of meeting taken away, but liberty of the press is also annulled. The Lord Lieutenant may confiscate any newspaper which "appears" to him "to contain matter inciting to the commission of treason, or of any act of violence or intimidation"—intimidation being as before defined. The publisher of such forfeited newspaper is to be made to give security to the extent of £200 not to repeat the offence, and if he has not given this within fourteen days, any paper he issues is to be seized, whether it be mischievous or not. So that if a paper is wicked enough to complain of Major Clifford Lloyd's destruction of huts sent to shelter from the weather the miserable victims of landlord cruelty, the paper will be forfeited, and the publisher's journalistic career cut short.

Liberty of person follows liberty of meeting and of press. Any person criminal enough to be out of doors (in a proclaimed district) one hour later than sunset or before sunrise, may be arrested by "any constable" who chooses to consider the circumstances "suspicious," while any stranger may be similarly arrested at any hour. It is very certain that the victims of police vigilance will not be the intending committers of outrages, who will always be provided with some ostensible reason for their walk, but silly, harmless, nervous people, terrified out of their wits by the sudden arrest. No quiet evening strolls for Irishmen and Irishwomen during the long cool summer evenings; no saunterings of man and maid side by side; what court of summary jurisdiction will believe that Pat, loitering near a stile, is only peeping over the hedge to watch for Bridget's coming? Love-making will be too dangerous a pastime to indulge in for the next three years on Irish soil.

Right of search at any hour of the day or night is also to be a power granted by the Lord Lieutenant, and this right is one which may be very easily made intolerable. The Alien Act is to be revived, and the cost of extra police and of compensation for injury is to be levied on the district where outrages take place. This last enactment is the only rational one in the Act.

To sum up: When this Act passes, trial by jury, right of public meeting, liberty of press, sanctity of house, will one and all be held at the will of the Lord Lieutenant, the irresponsible autocrat of Ireland, while liberty of person will lie at the mercy of every constable. Such is England's way of governing Ireland in the year 1882. And this is supposed to be a Bill for the "repression of crime;" it will strike at the personal comfort and dignity of everyone living in Ireland for the next three years, but will leave criminals absolutely untouched. Such a law, administered by a Mr. James Lowther, as it may very likely be, will cause more crime and more bloodshed in Ireland than any measure passed during this generation, and it will turn passive alienation from law into active, and perhaps violent, hostility.

It may be fairly asked of me: Would you, then, do nothing? No; I would do something, but the something should be levelled against criminals only. Instead of keeping thousands of soldiers concentrated in large bodies, I would draft off infantry enough to hold headquarters not too far apart in each district where outrages took place: to these headquarters I would send cavalry. and a part of the cavalry each night should be divided into small bodies of six or eight men each, well mounted and lightly armed, who should patrol the district from end to end. Every isolated farmhouse should be regularly visited, and should be further provided with signal lights or rockets, to be used in case of attack. The knowledge that aid was within reach would give courage to the inmates of any attacked house to hold out for a short time against their assailants. These patrolling parties should have orders, if they came across any attacking party, to take every man prisoner, alive or dead. And in case of attack, where help came after the criminals had escaped, or of murder where the body was found after the disappearance of the assassins, or of wounding when the assailants had vanished, I should be inclined to put a muzzled bloodhound on their track, and literally hunt them down. Men caught in the act of committing outrage, or found with blackened faces and armed, should be sent straight to Dublin for speedy trial, and penalties on all crimes of violence should be increased. Firing at a person or firing into a house should be classed as murder, and punished as such. The measures would be severe, but their severity would fall wholly on criminals. Innocent men do not attack houses, nor wander about armed at night with blackened faces, and the man who fires into a house, and whose bullet may strike the child in its cot or the mother with babe in her bosom, is a murderer in will and should be treated as a murderer. No innocent man or woman would run the smallest chance of suffering by such laws, and for the scoundrels who make Ireland's name a shame throughout the world no mercy need be shown nor felt.

PRICE ONE PENNY.

London: Printed by ANNIE BESANT and CHARLES BRADLAUGH, 28, Stonecutter Street, E.C.—1882.

COERCION IN IRELAND
AND ITS RESULTS.

A Plea for Justice.

By ANNIE BESANT.

On the 24th of January, 1881, Mr. Forster, Chief Secretary for Ireland, asked leave to introduce a Bill entrusting the Irish Executive with power to arrest and keep imprisoned any person "suspected of treasonable practices," and any person "suspected of agrarian crime in any proclaimed district." Mr. Forster explained that the proposed Act was not directed against fair agitation for redressal of grievances, but was intended to strike only at those concerned in agrarian outrages. The classes against whom it was to be directed were three in number: 1st. Those who belonged to the old secret societies; 2nd. Those who belonged to new secret societies; 3rd. "Village ruffians." It was alleged that the actors in crimes were often known, but that such was the terror inspired by the outrages that it was impossible to obtain evidence sufficient to lead to their conviction. In the discussions which took place during the debates on the Bill, re-iterated assurances were given that these classes were those really aimed at, that the number of arrests would be small, and that the most scrupulous care should be taken to avoid abuse of the powers asked for. Mr. Bradlaugh spoke strongly against the Bill on its first reading; he said in the course of his speech:—

"No member of the House would, he thought, be found to deny the fact that all kinds of illegal proceedings should be strongly reprobated. The Government, through the right hon. gentleman, said they could make no terms with lawlessness (hear, hear); aye! but while in Ireland criminals were few, the sufferers were many. And they proposed to suspend the constitutional rights of all. Were they sure they were not about to make terms with fear and panic? Terms with the landlord influence and injustice, which had made the misery of the people, out of which the crime spoken of had grown? It was not asserted that the ordinary law was insufficient for all purposes; what was asserted was that men injured would not prosecute, that evidence could not be obtained to support prosecutions, and that jurymen could not be found to convict. But what did that show? It showed that the national feeling was with the crime (hear, hear) —that is, with one kind of crime, not with all crime; for it was admitted that in respect of non-agrarian crime Ireland stood higher than England did. Why was it that there was one class of crime sheltered by the people of Ireland? It was because the people had come by experience to think that the Government gave them no protection, and that the law afforded them no remedy. They were now, however, instead of being subject to remedial legislation, to be subjected to eighteen months' imprisonment for any crime charged against them, not before a court of law, but before a magistrate, and which charge was sustained by the word of any petty constable. (Hear, hear.) He believed that the right hon. gentleman would take all the precautions in his power in applying this law, but what effectual precautions against wrong-doing could be taken when arbitrary power was brought to bear upon individual liberty? Neither the right hon. gentleman, nor the noble lord at the head of the Irish Government, could personally examine the details of every case. They must trust to others, and these in turn to others, until at last perhaps private malice might strike the one whom this House has stripped of his constitutional right."

Leave was given to introduce the Bill by 164 votes against 19, the minority being smaller than it ought to have been, in consequence of the vote being taken suddenly, while some English Radicals were away for a brief space of rest, after sitting sixteen hours continuously.

When the second reading of the Coercion Bill was moved, Mr. Bradlaugh moved its rejection; he urged:

"Many members of that House were old enough to remember the time when the landlords, encumbered with debt, encouraged resistance to civil law when it was set in motion against themselves. (Hear, hear.) These landlords, who to-day asked for extraordinary powers, had themselves left a bad example to the unfortunate and miserable men who to-day threatened and repeated the bad acts of their superiors. The right hon. gentleman had said that the effect of this terrorism was to prevent injured persons from prosecuting, witnesses from giving evidence, and juries from convicting; but the measure now brought forward would not ensure that persons should prosecute, that witnesses should testify, or juries convict. All it would do would be to give to the Government or to the unfortunate gentleman—and unfortunate indeed would be his position, charged with this duty—who had the right of arresting, to give to him the duty of superseding the conscience of the prosecutor and the evidence of witnesses; to take the place of all juries, and, on suspicion, to have the power to imprison the person whom he arrested for eighteen months. . . . . The right hon. gentleman had told them that the terror was occasioned by two classes—men from the old secret societies, and men belonging to the new ones. Would the House pardon him if he pointed out why the old secret societies existed? They existed because the landlords extorted unjust rents, and compelled their tenants to pay an enormous price for rooms—it was a shame to call them rooms, for he had seen hovels in which hon. members would not kennel their dogs nor stable their horses—rent which it was impossible for them to pay. These unfortunate people had no law to appeal to, nor could they appeal to Parliament, for Parliament was deaf to their appeals. This was not an evil created to-day or by the Land League; it was an evil to which years ago the right hon. gentleman at the head of the Government had directed his attention, and tried to grapple with, but which had baffled him, because his generous efforts had been crippled by the very landlord class now asking for protection by coercive law. What was the result? These men could not appeal to the law; for them the statute had no relief, so they made their own laws and, the courts being shut to them, established their own secret tribunals, secret because illegal. The Prime Minister had made several attempts to remedy this state of things, but the rights of land were valued in another place at a higher rate than the rights of life, and so those efforts had proved useless. . . . . It was said that the Act was directed against treason. Was there treason now? From the words that had fallen from the right hon. gentleman there was ground to fear that he thought such to be the case. But, then, Parliament could not act upon what the right hon. gentleman thought. If such was really the case, the evidence ought to be there. He trusted the right hon. gentleman and the Government in every way that a representative could do, but no representative should entrust the constitutional liberties of his fellow-citizens to any Government, except the strongest evidence was placed before him. The Chief Secretary for Ireland had told them that there was matter which it was impossible he could explain—matter possibly of wanton malice, matter, it might be, of actual treason, but for all that matter certainly growing out of wrongs endured."

Unhappily the Coercion Bill passed into law, and has been in action for the last twelve months. Under it, up to last week, no less than 918 persons have been deprived of their liberty, and 511 were still in custody on April 1. The "reasonable suspicions," on the ground of which they are or have been detained, are of very various character; of the 511 still in jail 31 are detained on suspicion of having committed murder, most of them as principals. Now the charge of murder is not one which should be kept hanging over a man's head; clearly, suspected murderers should be publicly tried, and either convicted or acquitted. Are these supposed murderers to be let loose on society in September next, never, if guilty, to be punished, and never, if innocent of the horrible crime, to have a chance of proving their innocence, and purging themselves of so fearful a suspicion? Reasonable suspicion of having attempted to murder, or to do grievous bodily harm, or of having committed assaults, is charged against fifty-seven persons, while several others are charged with firing into or attacking dwelling-houses. There are a few cases of arson, and two or three of maiming cattle. But the vast majority are detained on reasonable suspicion of having been concerned in intimidation, no less than 344 persons being kept in jail on this very vague charge. Mr. Parnell is one of this number, but he is also suspected of having "been guilty, as principal, of treasonable practices." Mr. O'Kelly is detained on the same ground, but Mr. Dillon is only charged with intimidation. If Mr. Parnell and Mr. O'Kelly have been guilty of treasonable practices, why are they not put on their trial? Putting on one side for the moment the people suspected of intimidation, the whole of the other prisoners have a right to demand that they shall at once be tried for the offences alleged against them. To imprison men on a vague charge of suspicion of intimidation is to commit a cruel injustice; if there is solid evidence that they have committed this offence, let them be tried. If there is none, let them be set free. Four hundred and seven persons have been arrested under this Act and have been liberated. Were they guilty or not of any crime? If yes, why are they set free untried? If no, why has a heavy punishment been inflicted on them? They have been torn from their homes, their farms have in many cases remained untilled, for to till the farm of a "suspect" was to incur suspicion; their businesses have in some cases been ruined by their absence. These heavy penalties should be inflicted on no one without open trial, without public judgment. Can Mr. Forster be sure that every one of the 918 persons arrested is a criminal? If one of them should be innocent, should be a victim of private malice, of false witness boldly given because secrecy ensured safety to the liar—if only one of these be wrongly suspected, is not a very terrible crime being committed in the punishment inflicted, and are not bad citizens being made by wrong committed under sanction of the law?

Do the men lying in jail come within the classes specified as those against which the Act was to be directed? Mr. Parnell, Mr. Dillon, Mr. O'Kelly, cannot fairly be described as "village ruffians," and if two of them have been guilty of treasonable practices no Coercion Act was needed for their arrest. If Englishmen read that in Russia, in Turkey, in Spain, 918 persons had been arrested during twelve months on suspicion, that the Government neither put them on their trial nor released them, a very torrent of righteous indignation would be poured on the head of the peccant rulers. Even in Russia they at least try their Nihilists; they do not punish them "on suspicion" without trial. However abandoned the criminal, he should have justice. If some foreign State shut up our citizens on some suspicion of crime, refusing to try them, refusing to release them, Englishmen would go mad with fury, and no minister would keep his place for a month who did not insist on justice being done. Unhappily, English people are very quick to see the wrongfulness of their neighbors' tyranny, but are remarkably dense as to the wickedness of their own.

Putting aside the bad nature of the Coercion Act, it may be well to note that it has been a most complete failure. Murder is far more frequent than it was; the most odious and revolting outrages are committed; neither man nor woman, rich nor poor, is safe from the blow of the assassin. The "village ruffians" appear to have multiplied, and the criminals, who are making the name of Ireland shameful in the eyes of the world, go on their way unscathed.

The Coercion Act is not the only coercive measure now being largely used in Ireland. By 34 Edw. III., c. 1, justices of the peace are empowered to "bind over to the good behavior" "all them that be not of good fame." This statute is being utilised in the most cruel way in Ireland, more especially against women. If the accused person is unable, or refuses to enter into recognisances, the justices can imprison. Now, it must be remembered that the justices belong to the landlord class, that the persons arraigned before them belong to the class now struggling to gain the right to live, and the "justice" meted out will be readily understood. Thus, the other day, they ordered a married woman, Mrs. Moore, to enter into recognisances, and committed her in default. A married woman is legally incapable of entering into recognisances, and Mrs. Moore was imprisoned because her legal incapacity made it impossible for her to give the required sureties. Miss Reynolds was the first lady imprisoned under this most evil law, which, in Ireland, puts the liberty of the workers at the mercy of persecuting landlords. She was prosecuted for advising a man not to pay his rent. I am informed that the following are the facts of the case: Patrick Murphy lived in a cottage bought by his father from the man who built it; it stood on a plot of grass in the middle of cross-roads, and no rent and no taxes were paid for it during the more than twenty-one years since it came into the Murphys' hands. Rent for three years for this cottage was suddenly claimed by a landlord from whom Murphy held other land, and to whom he was in debt. Murphy was advised that if he paid it, he would lose the right acquired by his long and undisturbed possession. Miss Reynolds apparently counselled him not to pay under these circumstances; she was sent to jail, and Murphy was turned out of his house.

Miss O'Carroll and Miss Curtis were sent to prison for a month, charged with belonging to an illegal association, the Ladies' Land League. This conviction was quashed on an informality on the day that their sentence expired.

Miss McCormick was sentenced by Major Lloyd—on the evidence of a policeman that he believed she had been going about inciting the people to discontent—to three months imprisonment in default of bail. The judges, on application, held that Miss McCormick's admission that she was a member of the Ladies' Land League was a proof of the truth of the charges. My informant complains that "in Ireland the fact of her being a member of the Ladies' Land League was held to be a proof of her criminality, while in England, in the House of Commons, the Attorney-General cited the fact of her imprisonment as a proof of the criminality of the League."

Eugene Sullivan was accused by an "Emergency man" of putting pins in his potatoes; Sullivan was arrested, but there was no proof of the charge offered; the man then said he went in fear of his life, the only reason therefor being that when he met Sullivan the latter used to grin and say "Three cheers for Parnell." For this crime Sullivan was bound over in bail so heavy that he had to go to jail (for six months).

Miss O'Connor is now in prison at Mullingar. This young lady—the sister of Mr. T. P. O'Connor, M.P.—is only twenty years of age, and suffers from weakness of the lungs.

She is imprisoned on the evidence of a constable, who swore that he heard her tell the people to pay no rent until the suspects were released. On cross-examination, however, he swore that she told them to come to a settlement with the landlord if he would take what was a fair rent; that she had strongly denounced outrages, quoting O'Connell's words, that "he who commits a crime gives strength to the enemy." Surely this poor young delicate girl, so young, moved by the misery around her to protest, and trying to restrain the starving from desperate deeds, ought not to be left in jail. What sort of Government is it in Ireland that needs such acts as these to be done in its support?

Imprisonment under this vile statute of Edward III. is of a far more cruel character than under the Coercion Act. The prisoners spend twenty-two hours out of the twenty-four in their cells, and during the two hours' exercise are not allowed to speak to each other. Imprisonment can be avoided by entering into heavy recognisances, but the difficulty is that the same justices who condemn on suspicion, estreat the recognisances on suspicion.

I have spoken of one class of outrages committed in Ireland, but the outrages committed by the landlord order must also come in for condemnation. During the quarter ending March 31st, 7,020 persons have been evicted. Of these, 3,050 persons have been re-admitted as care-takers, that is, they can be turned out again at any moment, and seventy-eight have been re-admitted as tenants. Thus, during the last three months, the landlords have finally turned out from their homes, 3,892 persons. The number of evictions in comparatively peaceful Ulster is higher than in the other provinces. I never shrink from denouncing the horrible murders and mutilations committed in Ireland, but horror of crime should not deter us from seeking its cause. The evictions are the seeds which grow up into agrarian outrages, and justice will lay on the head of Irish landlords the heavier share of the guilt of Irish crimes.

Is it hopeless to appeal to the Government to return to the paths of constitutional liberty in Ireland? Let them try their prisoners, and deal out justice; Ireland asks no more. She does not desire that murders should go unpunished; bring to open trial the men now imprisoned on suspicion of having committed murder. She does not approve of midnight assault, brutal injury, atrocious wounding, malicious arson; bring out the men charged with these wicked deeds; try them and condemn them to heaviest legal punishment if their guilt be proved. Set free the 344 charged with intimidation only; in such a struggle as that between the landlords and the tenants of Ireland, the intimidation is not all on one side, and unless the landlords are put on their trial for their share of it, those who took the tenants' side may well go free. The working of the Land Act has revealed some of the cruel wrongs done by the landlords, the exorbitant rents wrung by threat from the helpless and often starving tenants; surely some latitude should be allowed to men fighting before the Land Act against the wickedness which the Land Act is trying to prevent. For the "treasonable practices"—judgment is harder; I suppose every Government has the right of defending itself against treason, but the English are always very lenient in their judgment of foreign political offenders, nay, even honor them as heroes when stirred to their treason by tyranny. The misery of Ireland is the cause of her disaffection. Let England be generous, and let the remedial measure have fair play, by giving bill of indemnity for the past, and "starting clear." Mr. Parnell's treasonable practices cannot be so terribly dangerous to the State, when he is let out on parole for a fortnight to attend a funeral. But no chance is given for the healing measures to cure the sore of Irish disaffection, until not only are the prisoners in Ireland set at liberty, but until brave, unfortunate Michael Davitt stands once more a free man on Irish soil.

PRICE ONE PENNY.

London: Printed by Annie Besant and Charles Bradlaugh,
28, Stonecutter Street, E.C.
1882.

England's Jubilee Gift to Ireland.

BY ANNIE BESANT.

Jubilee gifts, Jubilee testimonials, Jubilee memorials, are on every hand. It is not, therefore, an unsuitable time for the presentation by England to Ireland of a Jubilee gift, and with a fine sense of the fitness of things she presents her with a Coercion Act. It would be impossible to choose a more appropriate gift, one that could better crown the fifty years of her Majesty's Irish reign. Mr. Mulhall, in his "Fifty Years of National Progress", says of Ireland:

"The present reign has been the most disastrous since that of Elizabeth, as the following statistics show: Died of famine, 1,225,000; persons evicted, 3,668,000; number of emigrants, 4,186,000. Evictions were more numerous immediately after the famine, the landlords availing themselves of the period of greatest calamity to enforce their 'rights'. Official returns give the number of families, and these averaging seven persons, we ascertain the actual number of persons evicted:

Years.	Families.	Persons.
1849–51	263,000	1,841,000
1852–60	110,000	770,000
1861–70	47,000	329,000
1871–86	104,000	728,000
Total	524,000	3,668,000

The number of persons evicted is equal to 75 per cent. of the actual population. No country, either in Europe or elsewhere, has suffered such wholesale extermination."

There is a curious sameness in Irish history. Landlord aggression and tyranny gave birth to the Whiteboys, and the Whiteboy Acts were passed to put them down. Landlord aggression and tyranny have in our own times given birth to the Moonlighters, and the Whiteboy Acts are utilised by the present Government to put them down. In the State Trials of 1843, '44, '48, '49, '59, Catholics were excluded from juries, and packed Protestant juries were empanelled. In the trial of John Dillon and his comrades similar tactics were employed. The impossibility of getting verdicts from fairly chosen juries in agrarian cases has long been matter of complaint; the present Bill abolishes trial by jury in the most commonly occurring cases in order to avoid the difficulty. Yet Englishmen from their own struggle for liberty ought to be familiar with the way in which juries have stood between technically guilty but morally praiseworthy prisoners and the penalty oppressors longed to wreak on them. Many a man in the struggle for English freedom has been saved from a prison by the verdict of a jury, which has acquitted the accused in face of proven facts. But in England when it is seen that the conscience of the people rejects a law, the law is changed. In Ireland, when the conscience of the people revolts against a law, the law is enforced from outside.

Without going beyond the fifty years of Queen Victoria's reign it is easy to see how the agrarian rebellion has been brought about by the landlords, and I can scarcely be said to be appealing to ancient history if I confine myself to the events of the present reign. The famine of 1845 onwards was an artificial famine manufactured by the Irish landlords, who drained the country of its agricultural produce and left the people who raised the produce to starve. The exorbitant demands of this odious class drove the people to exist on poorer and poorer kinds of food, until they became dependent almost wholly on potatoes, and when the blight destroyed these nought was left. In 1845 the oat crop was exceptionally good, but it was exported to pay rent, although the potato blight had appeared. From September to Christmas, 1845, five hundred and fifteen deaths from starvation were registered, and three million two hundred and fifty thousand quarters of wheat, besides herds of cattle, were shipped to England during the same time. After a while, the country having been drained of its own food supply, Indian meal was sent to it as charity. In 1847, the value of the agricultural produce was £44,958,120; during 1847, 21,770 persons died of starvation, and 250,000 of fever consequent on starvation.

During and after the famine the landlords used their power of eviction remorselessly against this starving and patient tenantry. Hundreds of thousands were driven from the land of their birth, and left Ireland with a burning hatred in their hearts against their oppressors and against the England that enabled them to carry out their tyrannical will. The result of this famine caused wholesale emigration, and was the building up of an Ireland beyond the seas, a New Ireland which gazed ever lovingly and longingly on the Old, ever wrathfully and revengefully on England. At first the Irish emigrants sent money across the Atlantic to their relatives at home for the payment of the landlords' exactions, and the landlords lived for awhile on the funds supplied by the American Irish.

Yearly, also, some of the home Irish crossed St. George's Channel into England, and by work here earned enough to pay for the right to live in their own land. Rent as paid in Ireland was in no sense economic rent; rent was paid for land which produced no rent, and the landowners lived on tribute levied by force from the peasantry and provided by their own or by their relatives' toil in other lands. Still rents rose, and ever all succor sent home by successful emigrants went to swell the absentee landlords' bankers' accounts. At last the Irish both at home and abroad grew weary of the continual drain, and those abroad more especially began to question whether they might not utilise their hard-earned money better by helping their friends at home to resist the landlords' exactions than by continually filling the pockets of Ireland's worst enemies. The struggle in Ireland against unjust rents began, and the American Irish contributions began to swell the receipts of the Land League instead of the rent-roll of the landlords. At once they were assailed with every slander, with every term of abuse, which the landlords and a landlord-loving press could devise. Outrages wrought in despairing anger against intolerable oppression were laid at their door; and the wild talk of a few, maddened by a remembrance of wrongs suffered at England's hands, was ascribed to the whole body of American Irish. The funds for the Parliamentary and Land League agitations were provided chiefly by the successful Irish emigrants, and a compact body of members was built up in Parliament, to carry on there the struggle which was being also waged in Ireland itself. Some grievances were got rid of; the Irish Establishment fell; improvements in the Land Laws were made. But still the landlord pressure continued, and, weighing on a people who for the first time had been touched by Hope, it was borne with ever increasing impatience. In 1880 Gladstone sought, by a short Bill, to check evictions during the approaching winter of 1880–81, but the landlords' House gaily threw out a Bill pressed on it by the Prime Minister of England on the plea that it was necessary to prevent civil war in Ireland.

The civil war broke out. Not open warfare; for that Ireland was too weak. But underground warfare, dangerous as smothered combustion, and waged by underground means. Most unhappily, Gladstone met it by coercion, coercion that I am free to blame to-day, as I denounced it when it was before Parliament in 1881. Hundreds of men were imprisoned, many a gross act of injustice was done, and Ireland remained, of course, as hostile as ever, only learning wisdom in the choice of the weapons she employed. The suppressed Land League rose again as the National League, stronger than ever and more unassailable; and at last Gladstone, not too proud to learn from experience, proposed to give Ireland freedom and to permit her to cure her diseases in her own way. He fell in the attempt to use conciliation instead of force as remedy, and Lords Salisbury and Randolph Churchill reigned in his stead.

With the succession to power of the landlord party came the renewal of the struggle. Lord Randolph Churchill, as Leader of the House of Commons, pledged the whole power of the State to the support of the landlords in their exaction of rents, and the landlords, at once inspirited and revengeful, gave full play to their hatred of the Irish tenantry. Preparations were made for wholesale evictions; landlordism was triumphant at last. Then to meet the threatened evictions and to save the people from outrages that would madden them into reprisals, a wise and gentle man formulated the famous Plan of Campaign. By the adoption of this the whole tenantry on an estate was bound together; the rich tenants made common cause with the poor; a fair rent was always to be tendered to the landlord, and only on his refusal to accept it was to be lodged in the hands of trustees. A few "good landlords" voluntarily made reductions; many bad ones were driven into making them by the fear that if they did not yield some they would lose all; some bad ones held out. Prominent among these was Lord Clanricarde, a typical absentee landlord. Unknown by face to the tenantry on whose labor he lived; harsh and exacting in his demands; taking everything and giving nothing; deaf to every appeal for mercy and for pity; how can such a one be forced into decency save by some such plan as that adopted by his tenants? Under the old method a bullet would have been sent through his agent, and Lord Clanricarde would have been none the worse. Under the new plan not a hair of his agent's head was harmed, but Lord Clanricarde found his money bags unfilled. He was touched in his only vulnerable spot, his trousers pocket, and his tenants did well.

Naturally the landlords, helpless before this new development, cried to their own Government for aid. The first attack on the Plan of Campaign failed ignominiously. And then, as the ordinary law proved impotent to check it, it was determined once more to resort to coercion, and to rivet the landlord chain by unconstitutional means since constitutional means had failed. As the people on the whole remained very quiet, despite the terrible provocations of barbarously cruel evictions carried out remorselessly through the months of an exceptionally severe autumn and winter, it was impossible to bring forth in support of the new Coercion Bill such a list of outrages as that whereby Mr. Gladstone thought that he justified his own measure. It was therefore necessary to manufacture them, and terrible accounts appeared of committed outrages, which however familiar in London press circles were wholly unknown in the localities in which they occurred. This wicked local ignorance was, however, of little importance. It took time to investigate and contradict, and meanwhile the lie went on its way rejoicing, and was circulated from habitation to habitation of the Primrose League, and repeated in circles never reached by the contradiction. Thus merrily went on the conspiracy, and at last the Government felt the time was ripe for the introduction of its Bill.

It would be interesting to know how many of those who are in favor of the Coercion Bill are acquainted with its provisions, and realise the position in which Ireland will be placed by its passing. An analysis of it may fitly then find its place here.

The first clause authorises an enquiry on oath in any case in which "the Attorney-General for Ireland believes (!) that any offence to which this section applies has been committed in a proclaimed district", although no person may be accused thereof; a witness examined under this clause "shall not be excused from answering any question on the ground that the answer thereto may criminate or tend to criminate himself". This odious clause is defended on the ground that Scotch law contains a similar provision; the fact that it does contain so unfair an engine for concocting evidence on suspicion may be a very good reason for amending Scotch law, but is certainly no reason for importing an unjust rule into Ireland. Besides, it is admitted that the power has not been put in force in Scotland within the legal experience of the law officers of the Crown, and that it is historically only known to have been used, and that rarely, in cases of murder. The present Bill authorises this inquisition in cases not only of felony and misdemeanor, but also of any manufactured "offence punishable under this Act".

In clause 2 a list of these offences is given, and they are brought within the punitive authority of the courts of summary jurisdiction, the punishment awardable by the court being six months' imprisonment, with or without hard labor (clause 11). The offences are:

"(1) Any person who shall take part in any criminal conspiracy to compel or induce any person or persons either not to fulfil his or their legal obligations, or not to let, hire, use, or occupy any land, or not to deal with, or work for, or hire any person or persons in the ordinary course of trade, business, or occupation; or to interfere with the administration of the law. (2) Any person who shall wrongfully and without legal authority use violence or intimidation" to make anyone do or abstain from doing, or to punish anyone for having done or having abstained from doing, any legal act. "(3)—(*a*) Any person who shall take part in any riot or unlawful assembly, or (*b*) within twelve months after the execution of any writ of possession of any house or land shall wrongfully take or hold forcible possession of such house or land or any part thereof; or (*c*) shall assault, or wilfully and unlawfully resist or obstruct, any sheriff, constable, bailiff, process server, or other minister of the law, while in the execution of his duty, or shall assault him in consequence of such execution. (4) Any person who shall commit any offence punishable under the Whiteboy Acts as defined by this Act. (5) Any person who, by words or acts, shall incite, solicit, encourage, or persuade any other person to commit any of the offences herein-before mentioned."

These make boycotting into a criminal offence, and as "intimidation" is defined (clause 19) to include "any words or acts intended and calculated to put any person in fear of any injury or danger to himself, or to any member of his family, or to any person in his employment, or in fear of any injury to or loss of property, business, employment, or means of living", it seems doubtful whether any person, who pointed out to another the evils that might result to him from a certain course of conduct, would not run a risk of being imprisoned for six months with hard labor. The Plan of Campaign will have to be carried on secretly when this clause becomes law. (*b*) and (*c*), under (3) will delight the hearts of the existing landlords, for a man will be liable to six months' hard labor if he obstructs the sheriff's officer by locking his door against him. It ought to be made a crime for a man not to offer to carry out his own furniture when he is ejected from a cabin built by his own hands.

Clauses 3 and 4 give power to order a special jury or to change the *venue* to England, so as to enable the Crown to obtain verdicts against political prisoners from prejudiced juries.

Clause 5 gives power to the Lord Lieutenant to proclaim a district, and clause 6 authorises him to declare that the enactments of the Act against dangerous associations shall come into force; these "dangerous associations" are such as the Lord Lieutenant shall be pleased to consider "are (*a*) formed for the commission of crimes; or (*b*) carrying on operations for or by the commission of crimes; or (*c*) encouraging or aiding persons to commit crimes; or (*d*) promoting or inciting to acts of violence or intimidation; or (*e*) interfering with the administration of the law or disturbing the maintenance of law and order". It would have been shorter to have said, "any association formed for the purpose of protecting poor and helpless tenants against heartless and wicked robbery by tyrannical landlords". The law which throws out a young child to die in a pigstye is so admirable a thing that none ought to wish to interfere with it.

Clause 7 authorises the Lord Lieutenant to proclaim "any association which he believes to be a dangerous association", and anyone who assists in any way the proclaimed association becomes liable to six months' hard labor. By this monstrous clause the Lord Lieutenant is given the power to destroy any political association of which he disapproves; all liberty of combination vanishes, and secret conspiracy is left as the only weapon of the oppressed. What this clause may become in the hands of a Tory Lord Lieutenant, egged on by irate landlords, it is easy to conceive.

Clause 8 continues for five years Gladstone's most objectionable Coercion Bill. Clauses 9 and 10 regulate proceedings with special juries and change of *venue*. Clauses 11–19 deal with Punishment, Procedure, and Definitions. The court to which is awarded the power of imprisoning for six months with hard labor, is to consist in Dublin of a divisional justice, and elsewhere of two resident magistrates, *i.e.* of the bitter enemies of the persons who are to be tried. Thus shall "law and order" become admirable and lovable things in Ireland.

Remains the question, what can be done to prevent the Bill becoming law in face of the overwhelming majority in Parliament, and what can be done to resist it after it has become law? The Parliamentary opposition is in good hands, and it may be impertinence even to make a suggestion. But to a humble outsider like myself it seems as if every possible means should be adopted to delay the passage of the Bill. The more the closure is applied during the course of the debate the more obvious will it be that the Bill is being forced through the House against the will of a very large minority. The longer the question is kept in debate the more familiar will the English democracy become with the odious principles embodied in the Bill. The main thing now is to prepare for the reversal of the Tory policy at the next election, and prolonged Parliamentary debate is the best educative process now attainable.

In Ireland, when the Bill becomes law, matters will assume a graver aspect. No Liberal who justifies the English Revolutions of the seventeenth century can deny that the Irish might rightfully resist this confiscation of their constitutional liberties. But though they have right on their side they have not might, and to take up arms against England would be a heroic folly. All that a nation can do by passive resistance carried to extremest lengths, ought, however, to be done. Every Government official should be rigorously boycotted, and so should be every non-official who makes common cause with the officials. Every eviction should be passively obstructed in every possible way. Orderly meetings should be held in every proclaimed district. Combinations should be carried on, and the proclamations of the Lord Lieutenant quietly ignored. This policy, steadily adhered to, would make the Act unworkable, for prison accommodation is limited, and when the gaols are filled with political prisoners, what can the Government do? It will become ridiculous as well as detestable, and will find its boasted weapon blunted after the first few strokes. Of course, the condition of the success of such a policy is that there should be no violence; but the Irish people have lately shown so strong a self-control that it does not seem impossible that they may offer to the world the sublime spectacle of a small nation standing like a rock against the oppression of a large one, and guarding its rights with bruised but unstained hands.

One thing at least is gained by the protest going up day by day both from inside and outside Parliament. Ireland sees that the wrong inflicted on her is felt to be a wrong by large numbers on this side St. George's Channel, and therefore one thing at least this latest Coercion Bill shall not do: it shall not widen the gulf between the two democracies; it shall not deepen the wound which has been bleeding for centuries, but which now, at last, begins at the touch of loving hands to close.

ONE PENNY.

Printed by ANNIE BESANT and CHARLES BRADLAUGH, 63, Fleet St., E.C.—1887.

SECTION IV

WHY I AM A SOCIALIST.

By ANNIE BESANT.

"A Socialist! you don't mean to say you are a Socialist!" Such is the exclamation with which anyone who adopts the much-hated name of Socialist is sure to be greeted in "polite society". A Socialist is supposed to go about with his pocket full of bombs and his mind full of assassinations; he is a kind of wild beast, to be hunted down with soldiers if he lives under Bismarck, with sneers, abuse, and petty persecutions if he lives under Victoria. The very wildness of the epithets launched at him, however, shows how much there is of fear in the hatred with which he is regarded; and his opponents, by confining themselves to mere abuse, confess that they find themselves unable to cope with him intellectually. Prejudice and passion, not reasoned arguments, are the weapons relied on for his destruction. Once let the working classes understand what Socialism really is, and the present system is doomed; it is therefore of vital necessity that they shall be prevented from calmly studying its proposals, and shall be so deafened with the clamor against it that they shall be unable to hear the "still small voice" of reason. I do not challenge the effectiveness of the policy—for a time. It has been the policy of the governing classes against every movement that has been aimed against their privileges; Radicalism has been served in exactly similar fashion, and now that Radicalism has grown so strong that it can no longer be silenced by clamor, it is the turn of Socialism to pass through a like probation. There is always an ugly duckling in Society's brood; how else should be maintained the succession of swans?

With a not inconsiderable number of persons the prejudice against the name of Socialist is held to be a valid reason for not adopting it, and it is thought wiser to advocate the *thing* without affronting the antagonism aroused against the *name*. With such a policy I have ever had no sympathy. It seems to me the wiser, as well as the franker course, to boldly wear any name which expresses an opinion held, and live down the prejudice it may awaken. The name Socialist is in itself a fine name, connoting as it does the social union; it is the recognised label of the school which holds as its central doctrine that land and the means of production should be the property of the social union, and not of privileged individuals in it; it is the one name which is recognised all the world over as the name of those who are opposed to political, religious, and social tyranny in every land; of those who look with brotherly sympathy on the efforts of every nation which is struggling for its freedom; of those who are on the side of the poor and the toiling everywhere; of those who recognise no barriers of nationality, of class, or of creed, but who see a brother in every worker, a friend in every lover of the people. Every political name is of the country in which it is born; but the name Socialist, like the name Atheist, is of no one land; it is valid in every country; it is whispered on Russian steppe, in German field, in French city, in Italian vineyard; and wherever it is heard the chains of the captive for a moment seem lighter, for Hope has lifted them, and the careworn faces of the toilers brighten, as a gleam from a sunnier day gilds the tools over which they bow.

Pass we from the name to the thing, from "the outer and visible sign to the inward and spiritual grace". Within the compass of a brief paper it is not possible for me to give all the reasons which have made me a Socialist, but there are three main lines of thought along which I travelled towards Socialism, and along which I would fain persuade my readers to travel also, in the hope that they too may find that they lead to the same goal.

I. *I am a Socialist because I am a believer in Evolution.* The great truths that organisms are not isolated creations, but that they are all linked together as parts of one great tree of life; that the simple precedes the complex; that progress is a process of continued integrations, and ever-increasing differentiations; these truths applied to the physical animated world by Darwin, Huxley, Haeckel, Büchner, and their followers, have unravelled the tangles of existence, have illuminated the hidden recesses of Nature. But the service to be done to science by Evolution was not completed when natural history was made a coherent whole instead of a heterogeneous heap of irrelevant facts; its light next fell on the universe of mind, and traced the growth of mentality from the lowest organism that responds to a stimulus up to the creative brain of man. And still it had work to do, and next it reduced to order the jarring elements of the sphere of morals, and analysed duty and conscience, right and wrong, obligation and responsibity, until it rendered intelligible and consequent all that seemed supernatural and incoherent. And both in mind and in morals Spencer was the great servant of Evolution, illuminating the previous darkness by lucid exposition and by pregnant suggestion. But having done so much in the ordering of thought in every realm of study save one, it was not possible that Evolution should leave Sociology untouched, a mere chaos of unrelated facts, of warring opinions. Hither also came the light, and out of the chaos slowly grew a cosmos. Society was seen evolving from lowliest savagery, from the embryonic tate of barbarism, through nomad life to settled order, through ribes to nation, through feudalism to industrialism, through industrialism to —— Nowhither? Evolution complete? Further progress barred? Not so. For science, which cannot prophesy details of the future, can grasp tendencies of the present, and ecognising the conditions of the social growth of the past, can ee how the present has been moulded, and along which lines its urther development must inevitably pass. Now the progress of ociety has been from individualistic anarchy to associated order; rom universal unrestricted competition to competition regulated nd restrained by law, and even to partial co-operation in lieu hereof. Production from being individualistic has become co-operative; large bodies of workmen toiling together have re-laced the small groups of masters and apprentices; factory roduction has pushed aside cottage production, and industrial rmies are seen instead of industrial units. Laws for the egulation of industry—which failed when they were made by few for their own advantage, and were used in the vain effort keep down the majority—have been carried and applied suc-ssfully to some extent in defence of the liberty of the majority gainst the oppression of a privileged few. Since the partial lmission of the workers to the exercise of political power, ese laws for the regulation of industry have rapidly multiplied, d at the same time laws which hindered the free association the workers have been repealed. The State has interfered ith factories and workshops, to fix the hours of labor, to insist sanitary arrangements, to control the employment of the ung. Land Acts and Ground Game Acts, Education Acts and ipping Acts, Employers' Liability Acts and Artisans' Dwellings cts, crowd our Statute book. Everywhere the old ideas of free ntract, of non-interference, are being outraged by modern legislation. And it is not only Socialists who point to these reiterated interferences as signs of the tendencies of society. John Morley, in his "Life of Cobden", notes that England, where Socialism is supposed to have but small influence, has a body of Socialistic legislation greater than can found in any other country in the world.

II. *I am a Socialist because of the failure of our present civilisation.* In an article which appeared in the July number of the *Westminster Review*, after alluding to Professor Huxley's declaration that he would rather have been born a savage in one of the Fiji islands than have been born in a London slum, I put the following question, which I will venture to quote here. "Is it rational that the progress of society should be as lopsided as it is? Is it necessary that, while civilisation brings to some art, beauty, refinement—all that makes life fair and gracious—it should bring to others drudgery, misery, degradation, such as no uncivilised people know? and these emphasised and rendered the bitterer by the contrast of what life is to many, the dream of what it might be to all. For Professor Huxley is right. The savage has the forest and the open sea, the joy of physical strength, food easily won, leisure sweet after the excitement of the chase; the civilised toiler has the monotonous drudgery of the stuffy workshop, the hell of the gin-palace for his pleasure-ground, the pandemonium of reeking court and stifling alley for his lullaby; civilisation has robbed him of all natural beauty and physical joy, and has given him in exchange—the slum. It is little wonder that, under these circumstances, there are many who have but scant respect for our social fabric, and who are apt to think that any change cannot land them in a condition worse than that in which they already find themselves."

Now if this view should spread widely among the inhabitants of the slums, it is obvious that the present civilisation would stand in very considerable peril, and it would be likely to sink as feudalism sank in France, beneath the waves of a popular revolution. But such a revolution, sweeping from the slums over the happier parts of the towns, would not be a revolution set going by men of genius, directed by men of experience and of knowledge, as was the French Revolution of 1789. It would be a mad outburst of misery, of starvation, of recklessness which would for a brief space sweep everything before it, and behind it would leave a desolate wilderness. Walk at midnight through the streets near the Tower, along Shadwell High Street or about "Tiger Bay", and imagine what would happen if those drunken men and women, singing, shouting, fighting, in the streets, were to burst the barriers that hem them in, and were to surge westwards over London, wrecking the civilisation which had left them to putrefy in their misery, and had remained callous to their degradation. Is it not the part of a good citizen to try to change a social system which bears such products as these in every great city?

The slum population, however, is not wholly composed of such persons as I have spoken of. Large numbers of honest, temperate, industrious people are forced by poverty, and by the necessity of being near their work, into the dismal fate of living in the slums. And among them is spreading a discontent which is pregnant with change. Education is awakening in them desires and hopes which find no satisfaction in the slums. It is opening to them wider views of human life, and the penny newspaper tells them of enjoyments and luxuries of which they would have known nothing, pent in the dreary mill-round of their toiling lives, had ignorance kept them blind. Slowly is being formed that "educated proletariat" which shall work out its own salvation, and which shall refuse any longer to act as the basis on which is reared the pyramid of civilisation. The present civilisation rests on the degradation of the workers; in order that they may accept their lot they must be kept poor, ignorant, submissive; the culture of their superiors is paid for with their ignorance; the graceful leisure of the aristocrat is purchased by the rough toil of the plebeian; his dainty fingers are kept soft and white by the hardening and reddening of the poor man's hands; the workers are daily sacrificed that the idlers may enjoy. Such is modern civilisation. Brilliant and beautiful where it rises into the sunlight, its foundation is of human lives made rotten with suffering. Whited sepulchre in very truth, with its outer coating of princes and lords, of bankers and squires, and within filled with dead men's bones, the bones of the poor who builded it.

Most hopeful sign, perhaps, for the future is the fact that discontent with the present system is not confined to those who are in a special sense its victims. In every class of society are found men and women who look and work for a complete revolution in the method of the production and distribution of wealth. Among those who profit most by the present system are found the most eager workers against it, and many whose lot is cast among the "comfortable classes" are striving to undermine the very constitution which gives them the privileges they enjoy. In them sympathy has triumphed over selfishness, and their own rich wine of life tastes sour when they see the bitter water of poverty pressed to their brothers' lips. They are indignant that their own hands should be so full while others' hands are empty; and would fain lessen their own heap in order that the share of their neighbors may be made equal with their own.

At present the Socialist movement in England is far more a middle-class than a working-class one; the creed of Socialism is held as an intellectual conviction by the thoughtful and the studious, and is preached by them to the workers, who have everything to gain by accepting it, and some of whom have already embraced and are teaching it. Instead of being a class movement, it is a movement of men and women of all classes for a common end, and the Socialist army is composed of persons of various social ranks, who have renounced for themselves the class distinctions they are banded together to destroy.

III. *I am a Socialist because the poverty of the workers is, and must continue to be, an integral part of the present method of wealth-production and wealth-distribution.* Under that method land, capital, and labor, the three factors in wealth-production, are divorced from each other, and landless, capitalless labor—which must sell itself to live—lies at the mercy of the privileged classes. The owner of the land demands a share of the produce raised on or from it, and this share is claimed by him not because he helps in gaining the produce, but because he owns the raw material of the soil, and can prevent anyone from utilising it, if he so pleases. The land is his; for him the rain softens and the sunshine warms the soil; for him sweet Mother Nature bares her fragrant bosom, and pours out the treasures with which her arms are laden; for him she has been working through the silent centuries, growing her forests, carbonising her buried vegetable treasures, storing her vast unseen realms with gem and ore of metal, building through myriads of ages by life and death, by creation and destruction, by swift birth and slow decay. And all this toil of ages, wrought out by the mighty unseen forces, finds its end in my Lord Emptyhead, who stretches out his useless hands over the noble product, and cries to his countless brothers, "This is mine!". Then he bargains with them, and claims the right to tax their labor in exchange for permitting them to use what ought to be the common property, and to tax it, moreover, in proportion to its success. Thus Dukes of Westminster, of Bedford, and of Portland; Marquises of Londonderry, of Anglesey, and of Bute; Earls of Derby and of Dudley; with many another beside; all these grow ever and ever wealthier, not because they work, but because their ancestors by force or fraud got grip of the soil, and in days when the people were unrepresented made laws which secured to them and their descendants the monstrous monopoly of natural agents. As the people multiply and press ever more and more on the means of subsistence, they have to pay more and more to the owners thereof; and while private property in land is permitted to exist, so long will the landless lie at the landlord's mercy, and wealthy idler and poverty-stricken worker will form integral parts of our social, or rather anti-social, system.

Similarly is a share of the worker's product claimed by the class which holds as individual property the accumulated wealth made by generations of toilers, the present means of production; this wealth is obtained by forcing labor to accept as "wage" less than the value it creates; unless it will accept these terms it is not permitted to create any value at all, so that it has the choice between starvation and exploitation. The share of its own produce which it receives as wage varies from time to time; sometimes it is less, sometimes more; but it is always less than the value made by it. Only when there is a "profit" to be made—that is when the capitalist can get out of his "hands" more value than he returns to them as wage—will he employ them. The machines which have been invented by human genius, and which ought to lessen human labor, are used to make fortunes for a few. A skilful workman sees a possible improvement; his master reaps the profit of the improved machine, patenting it for his own enrichment. Huge fortunes rapidly made date from the invention of machinery, because only by the possession of machinery can a man utilise the labor of many for such swift gain. Possessing this, he is in a position of advantage which enables him to say to his fellow-men: "You shall use my machinery on condition that you are content with bare subsistence, and leave to me the wealth which flows from you and the machine". Thus machinery, which is one of the advantages of civilisation, gives wealth to its individual owner, and bare subsistence to the toilers who work with it. And so long as the possession of all the mechanical advantages is in the hands of individuals, so long will they be able to enslave and exploit those who have only their natural tools, and the machine-owner may lie at his ease and watch the growing piles of his wealth, as his bondmen heap it together, and gratefully accept the fraction of it which his higher servants fling to them as wage. Poverty will last so long as one class depends on another for "employment"; so long as one man must sell another man his labor at whatever rate the condition of the market may fix. Free men may associate their labor for a common end, and divide the common product; slaves are obliged to let their labor be at the direction of their master, and to accept subsistence in exchange.

Class distinctions will endure while men stand in the position of employer and employed; the one who holds the means of subsistence feels himself superior to the one who craves them. And this is not all. The life-surroundings of the rich fashion an organism easily distinguishable from the organism produced by the life-surroundings of the poor. Take two healthy week-old babies, one the child of a ploughman and the other the child of a duke; place them side by side, and the keenest eye will not be able to separate the aristocrat and the plebeian. But give to one the best education and to the other none, and place them side by side when each is grown to manhood, and the easy polished manner and soft speech of the one will be contrasted with the clumsy roughness and stumbling articulation of the other. Education, training, culture, these make class distinc-tinctions, and nothing can efface them save common education and equally refined life-surroundings. Such education and life-surroundings cannot be shared so long as some enjoy wealth they do not earn, and others are deprived of the wealth they do earn. Land and capital must be made common property, and then no man will be in a position to enslave his brother by placing before him the alternative of starvation or servitude. And because no system save that of Socialism claims that there shall be no individual monopoly of that on which the whole nation must depend, of the soil on which it is born and must subsist, of the capital accumulated by the labor of its innumerable children, living and dead; because no system save that of Socialism claims for the whole community control of its land and its capital; because no system save that of Socialism declares that wealth created by associated workers should be shared among those workers, and that no idlers should have a lien upon it; because no system save that of Socialism makes industry really free and the worker really independent, by substituting co-operation among workers for employed and employing classes; because of all this I am a Socialist. My Socialism is based on the recognition of economic facts, on the study of the results which flow inevitably from the present economic system. The pauper and the millionaire are alike its legitimate children; the evil tree brings forth its evil fruits.

PRICE ONE PENNY.

Printed by Annie Besant and Charles Bradlaugh, at 63, Fleet Street. London, E.C.—1886.

THE

EVOLUTION OF SOCIETY.

BY

ANNIE BESANT.

[Reprinted from *Our Corner*.]

LONDON:
FREETHOUGHT PUBLISHING COMPANY,
63, FLEET STREET, E.C.
1886.

PRICE THREEPENCE.

LONDON:
PRINTED BY ANNIE BESANT AND CHARLES BRADLAUGH,
63, FLEET STREET, E.C.

THE EVOLUTION OF SOCIETY.

THE recognition of Evolution in the physical world, of gradual progress from the simple to the complex, of reiterated integration as the steps of that progress, has led to the application of the same unifying principle to the psychical world, and to the suggestion of its application to the sociological. As the lowest forms of life consist of simple independent cells, as these cells become grouped, differentiated, integrated into tissues, as these tissues become more complex in arrangement, more co-ordinated, in the highest organisms, so, it is argued, do the individual human units become grouped into families and tribes, integrated into a social organism, of which the multiplicity of the composing elements is the measure of its adaptability, the unity and the correlation thereof the measure of its strength. If Society be thus regarded as an organism instead of as a bag of marbles, if it be conceded that the health of the whole depends upon the healthy functioning of every part, in correlation not in independence, then all that tends towards integration will be recognised as of life, all that tends towards disintegration as of death. Judging the future by the past we shall be prepared to look forward to the realisation of a fuller social unity than has yet been reached, and to recognise that by an inexorable necessity Society must either integrate yet further, or must begin a movement which will result in its resolution into its elements. The further integration may be regarded as an ideal to be embraced, or as a doom to be striven against, as a brotherhood to be rejoiced in or as a slavery to be abhorred;

but the believer in Evolution must acknowledge that if Society is to endure, this further integration is inevitable.

The object of this and of the following papers is to roughly outline this Evolution of Society, and to consider the type towards which it is working; and they will deal with: I. The Barbaric Period and its Survivals; II. The Industrial Period and its products; III. The Conflict between Social and Anti-Social Tendencies; IV. The Reconcilement of Diverging Interests.

I.—The Barbaric Period and its Survivals.

Association for the common weal is, as is well known, by no means confined to man. Many herbivorous animals live in herds, and in the pastures the females and the young graze in the centre, while the males form a protective ring, and sentinels, carefully posted, give warning cries of alarm if danger approaches. Wolves hunt in packs, and together pull down prey with which singly they could not cope. Bees and ants live in thickly populated communities, with their builders, food-gatherers, nurses, and in many cases soldiers, all working for the Society as a whole. Man's nearest congeners, the apes, are social animals and differ little in their qualities and morality from the lowest savages. And in all these one phænomenon is noteworthy: the submission of the individual to restraints for the general good. When a tribe of monkeys goes out on a predatory expedition—as to rob an orchard—the young ones are slapped if they are not silent and obedient. When a goat is discharging a sentinel's duty, he may not feed at ease on the tempting grass on which his comrades are luxuriating, confident in his vigilant loyalty. The working-bee must not keep the honey it gathers, but must carry it home for storing. Each member of the community yields up something of individual freedom, receiving in exchange the benefits of association, and it is among those who—like the bees and ants—have carried very far the subordination of the unit to the social organism that the most successful communities are found.

In the Barbaric Period of human society the virtues evolved are much the same as those which characterise the brute communities—courage, discipline of a rudimentary kind, loyalty to the head of the tribe. These are evolved because they are necessary to the success of the tribe, and those who are weak in them perish in the struggle for existence. They are evolved by the pressure of necessity, by the exigencies of the common life. As disputes can only be settled by war, the military chief is indispensable, and the strong and cunning man is made the head of the community. As social conditions become a little more settled, and the conventions which grew up from necessity become gradually crystallised into law, the hereditary principle creeps in, and the most capable adult member of a family —now recognised as royal—is selected to fill the throne; as law increases yet more in authority, the personal capacity of the sovereign becames a matter of less vital necessity, and the eldest son succeeds to his father's crown, whether he is major or minor; at last the time is reached, as with ourselves, in which a monarch is simply a survival, interesting—as are all rudimentary organs, because marks of an ancestral condition—but perfectly useless: a mere excrescence like the dew-claw of a St. Bernard dog. Essentially barbaric, it is an anachronism in a civilised society, and only endures by virtue of its inoffensiveness and of the public inertia.

Still keeping within the Barbaric Period, but passing out of the stage in which every man was a warrior, we come to the time in which Society was constituted of two classes: the fighting class, which consisted of king and nobles; the working class, which consisted of those who toiled on the land and of all engaged in commerce of any kind, whether by producing goods for sale or by selling them when produced. The fighting class had then its real utility; if the king and the nobles claimed the privilege of governing, they discharged the duty of protecting, and while they tyrannised and robbed at home to a considerable extent, they defended against foreign oppression the realm to which they belonged. Fighting animals they were, like the big-jawed soldiers of the Termites, but they were necessary while the nations had not emerged from barbarism. But these were not in the line of evolution; the evolving life of the nation was apart from them; they were the wall that protected, that encircled the life that was developing, and their descendants are but the crumbling ruins which mark where once the bastions and the ramparts frowned.

The life of the nation was in its workers, among whom the agriculturists claim our first attention. The villeins who tilled the soil under the feudal system were, in a very real sense, the chattels of their lord. They were bound to the soil, might be recovered by a legal suit if they left their lord's estate, were liable to seizure of all their property by their lord at his mere will, might be imprisoned or assaulted by him, and in many cases the lord held over them a power of life and death. These feudal privileges of the lord gradually disappeared in England during the Middle Ages; many villeins fled their native soil, hired themselves out in other parts of the country, and were never recovered by their lords; residence for a year and a day in a walled town made a villein free: relaxations of servitude made by an indulgent lord became customary: villeins became transformed into copyholders in many cases, and in one way or another the peasantry emerged from nominal slavery.

In trying to realise the lot of the villein and to compare it with that of his modern descendant, the agricultural laborer, it is not sufficient to study only the conditions of his servitude, the extreme roughness and poorness of his house, his ignorance, the frequent scarcity and general coarseness of his food. It must be remembered that if his lord was his owner he was also his protector, and that the landowner's feeling of duty to his tenants and the tenants' feeling of dependence and claim for assistance on the landowner which still exist in some old-world parts of England, are survivals of the old feudal tie which implied subjection without consciousness of degradation. Further, while the hut of the villein was of the poorest kind, the castle of the lord by no means realised our modern idea of a comfortable house: the villein had straw on his floor, but the lord had only rushes; and the general roughness of the time effected all alike. If the villein was ignorant, so was the lord, and if the lord tilted gaily with the lance, the villein broke heads as gaily with his staff. If the villein was sometimes sorely put to it to find bread, at other times he revelled in rough abundance, and the doles at the monastery gates often eked out his scanty supply when Nature was unkind. Speaking broadly, there was far less difference then in fashion of living between lord and villein than now between lord and laborer: less difference of taste, of amusements, of education, and therefore more comradeship: the baron's retainers then dined at the table of the lord without shocking any fastidious taste, while my lord marquis now would find his dinner much interfered with if his servants sat at it as of old. And since happiness is very much a matter of comparison, it may be doubted whether the villein was not happier than the agricultural laborer is now, and whether the lop-sided progress of Society, which has given so little to the toiler in comparison with what it has given to the idler, has been much of a blessing to the laboring agricultural class.

The growth of industries other than agricultural marked with unmistakable distinctness the evolution of society from barbarism. Handworkers in these tended to produce in groups, and soon associated themselves in towns, partly for convenience in production and distribution, partly for self-defence; divorced from the land, they were naturally less directly dependent on the landowners than were the agriculturists, and as the king's wish to plunder them was checked by the nobles, and the nobles' wish to plunder by the king, they gradually secured charters which protected them from both, and waxed free and prosperous. Each craft had its guild, and the apprentice entering to learn his trade worked his way step by step up to the position of a master craftsman. There were then no large aggregations of workers, as in our modern factories, but the lad placed in a workshop was one of a small group, and was trained as a member of a family rather than as a "hand". Entrance into the workshop of a famous master was eagerly sought for, and in consequence of the slight division of labor there was a pride in capable workmanship which is now almost impossible. Individual ability, under this system, was at once apparent and had scope for development, so that art and industry were more closely united than they have ever been since. The artist was largely a handicraftsman in the industrial sense, and the handicraftsman was largely an artist; and side by side with this mental development existed physical vigor, in consequence of the small size of the towns and the accessibility of the open country. In industrial pursuits, as in those of the countryside, the great division between classes which is now so grievous did not exist; the "master" worked with his men, eat with them, lived with them, and the "industrious apprentice" who "married his master's daughter" was not a poetic fiction, but an inspiring and realisable ideal. Certainly the amount of products turned out could not rival the vast quantities now produced, but the lives of the producers were healthier and more human than those of too many of the handicraftsmen of to-day.

Among the survivals from the Barbaric Period present in modern society, the monarch has already been mentioned. Perhaps no form of monarchy exposes its anachronistic character more completely than the "limited monarchy" of modern England. There is an exquisite absurdity in the man who *can* being changed into the man who can *not*.[1] The hereditary aristocracy is another survival from barbarism, and is a curious travesty of the scientific truth as to race. The analogy of a high-bred horse and a high-bred man is misleading, for the human breeding is a matter of name, not of qualities. There can be no doubt that a human aristocracy might be bred, by matching men and women who showed in marked degree the qualities which might be selected as admirable, but the aristocracy which proceeds from male idlers, profligate in their undisciplined youth and luxurious in their pampered maturity, matched with female idlers, whose uselessness, vanity, and extravagance are their chief recommendations, is not one which should bear rule in a strong and intellectual nation. To the barbaric Past it belongs, not to the semi-civilised Present, and the lease of its power will be determined when the workers realise the power which has now passed into their hands.

II.—The Industrial Period and its Products.

The Industrial Period may fairly be taken as beginning for all practical purposes with the invention of the Spinning Jenny by Hargreaves, a weaver, in 1764; of the Spinning Machine by Arkwright, a barber, in 1768; of the Mule, by Crompton, a weaver, 1776. If to these we add the virtual invention of the Steam Engine by Watt in 1765, we have within these twelve years, from 1764 to 1776, the vastest revolution in industry the world has known, the birth of a new Period in the Evolution of Society. As

[1] King, German *Konig*, has the same root as *Können*, to be able.

Green points out in his "History of the English People", the "handloom used in the Manchester cotton trade had until that time retained the primitive shape which is still found in the handlooms of India" (p. 768), and the conditions of labor were feudal, patriarchic, domestic, not industrial, in the modern sense of the word. The introduction of machinery (other than the simple kinds used in earlier times) revolutionised social life as well as industry, and the vast increase of man's power over nature not only affected the production of manufactured goods, but affected also the condition of the worker, the climate and aspect of the country, as also, with the most far-reaching results, the framework and tendencies of society. These all are the products of the Industrial Period, and these all must be taken into consideration if we would estimate fairly and fully the net result of good or of evil which remains.

It is obvious that the great value of machinery lies in the fact that it produces much with little labor; in the words of a Report: "One man in a cotton-mill superintends as much work as could have been done by two hundred, seventy years ago." The result of this should have been widespread comfort, general sufficiency of the necessaries of life, a great diminution of the hours of labor: the result of it has been the accumulation of vast fortunes by a comparatively few, the deadening and the brutalising of crowds of the handworkers. Whether we regard the immediate or the general results, we shall find them very different from the rosy hopes of those who gave to the world the outcome of their inventive genius.

The immediate result of the introduction of machinery was, as everyone knows, terrible suffering among handicraftsmen. Let us hear Green, an impartial witness. "Manufactures profited by the great discoveries of Watt and Arkwright; and the consumption of raw cotton in the mills of Lancashire rose during the same period from fifty to a hundred millions of pounds. The vast accumulation of capital, as well as the constant recurrence of bad seasons at this time, told upon the land, and forced agriculture into a feverish and unhealthy prosperity. Wheat rose to famine prices, and the value of land rose in proportion with the price of wheat. Inclosures went on with prodigious rapidity; the income of every landowner was doubled, while the farmers were able to introduce improvements into the processes of agriculture which changed the whole face of the country. But if the increase of wealth was enormous, its distribution was partial. During the fifteen years which preceded Waterloo, the number of the population rose from ten to thirteen millions, and this rapid increase kept down the rate of wages, which would naturally have advanced in a corresponding degree with the increase of the national wealth. Even manufactures, though destined in the long run to benefit the laboring classes, seemed at first rather to depress them. One of the earliest results of the introduction of machinery was the ruin of a number of small trades which were carried on at home, and the pauperisation of families who relied on them for support. In the winter of 1811 the terrible pressure of this transition from handicraft to machinery was seen in the Luddite, or machine-breaking, riots which broke out over the northern and midland counties, and which were only suppressed by military force. While labor was thus thrown out of its older grooves, and the rate of wages kept down at an artificially low figure by the rapid increase of population, the rise in the price of wheat, which brought wealth to the landowner and the farmer, brought famine and death to the poor, for England was cut off by the war from the vast cornfields of the Continent or of America, which nowadays redress from their abundance the results of a bad harvest. Scarcity was followed by a terrible pauperisation of the laboring classes. The amount of the poor-rate rose fifty per cent., and with the increase of poverty followed its inevitable result, the increase of crime" ("Hist. of the English People", pp. 805, 806).

It is noteworthy that where handworkers are concerned, no claim for compensation is ever put forward when they are deprived of their means of livelihood. If it is proposed to nationalise the land, it is at once alleged that the present owners must be bought out, on the ground that it would be unjust to deprive them of their incomes from land and to reduce them to poverty for the benefit of the community. But no one is so scrupulous, or so tender-hearted, when only laborers are ruined; no one ever proposed to compensate the handicraftsmen who were robbed of their means of existence by the introduction of machinery. Great stress is laid on the general benefit of the community, for which it appears it is right to sacrifice the worker, but wrong to sacrifice the idler. And further, if a starving laborer fall back on the poor-rate he is at once "pauperised", and everyone knows it is a disgrace to be a pauper—on the parish: but if a Duke of Marlborough, with huge estates, pockets a sum of £107,000 out of the taxes he is not "pauperised", and everyone knows it is no disgrace to be a pauper—on the nation.

The general result of the introduction of machinery has clearly been a great increase of comfort and wealth to the upper and middle classes, and to the upper stratum of the artisans; but great masses of the people are worse off absolutely, as well as relatively, in consequence of its introduction. They are more crowded together, the air they breathe is fouler, the food they eat is more unwholesome, the trades they live by are more ruinous to health, than they were in the time when towns were smaller, the open country more accessible, the air unpoisoned by factory chimneys and chemical works; the times when "master and man" slept in the same house, dined at the same table, worked in the same room.

Machinery has enormously increased the amount of goods produced, but it has not lightened the toil of the workers; it has sent down prices, but the laborer must work as long to gain his bare subsistence. The introduction of sewing-machines may serve as a typical instance. It was said that they would lighten the toil of the needlewoman, and enable her to earn a livelihood more easily. Nothing of the sort has happened; the needlewoman works for quite as many hours, and earns quite as meagre a subsistence; she makes three or four coats where before she made one, but her wages are not trebled or quadrupled; the profits of her employer are increased, and coats are sold at a lower price. The real value of machinery, again, may be seen when a sewing machine is introduced into a house where the needlework is done at home; there the toil *is* lightened; the necessary work is done in a fifth part of the time, and the workers have leisure instead of long hours of labor. The inference is irresistible; machinery is of enormous value in lessening human toil when it is owned by those who produce, and who produce for use, not for profit; it is not of value to those who work it for wages, for the wages depend, not on the worth of the goods produced, but on the competition in the labor-market and the cost of subsistence.

In dealing with the products of the Industrial Period, the human products are of the most extreme importance. How have the conditions of labor, the environment, and therefore the life of the laborer, been affected by the introduction of machinery? I say, without fear of contradiction, that the environment of the manufacturing laborers has altered for the worse, and that the result of that worsening may be seen in the physical deterioration of the great masses of the workers in factory towns. Compare the tall, upright, brown laborer of Lincolnshire with the short, bowed, pallid knife-grinder of Sheffield: compare the robust, stalwart Northumberland miner with the slender, pasty-cheeked lads who come trooping out of a Manchester cotton-mill; and you will soon see the physical difference caused by difference of labor-conditions. Sheffield workers die young, their lungs choked with the metal dust they inhale; cotton-factory "hands" die of the fibre-laden air they breathe. I grant that Sheffield goods are cheap, if by cheapness is meant that fewer coins are paid for them than would have been required ere they were made by machinery; but to me those things are not cheap which are rendered less in money-cost by destruction of human life. Hood once wrote of cheap shirts:

"O men with sisters dear,
O men with mothers and wives,
It is not linen you're wearing out,
But human creatures' lives!"

And to me there is many a "cheap" article which is dear by the price that has been paid for its cheapness, price of human health, price of human happiness, price of human life, making it costly beyond all reckoning, for it incarnates the misery of the poor.

I grant readily that things were worse before the Factory Acts were passed; but this truth only makes me desire their extension, and also a far greater insistence on sanitation than at present prevails. It is necessary that a large number of workers should co-operate in production by machinery; it is not necessary that they should be poisoned or wearied out with toil. The working-day should be short, because mechanical toil tends to stupefy; and every factory should have a recreation-ground, prettily laid out, with facilities for games, to which the workers might resort for the intervals between the hours of labor. Thorough ventilation should ensure the wholesomeness of the air within the factory, a task which would be greatly facilitated by each factory standing alone and being tree-surrounded.

The law should also promptly concern itself with the scandalous pollution of the atmosphere and of rivers by the smoke and refuse of factories. There is no reason why every factory should not consume its own smoke, and the law already existing on this matter should be sternly enforced, by imprisonment, not by fine. A man who poisons one person is punished; a man who poisons a whole neighborhood goes free. The thick cloud of black smoke hanging over a town like Sheffield or Manchester is a sickening sight; it blights the trees, destroys the flowers, soils every house, dirties every article of clothing. Who that has lived in Manchester can forget "Manchester blacks"? It is pitiable to go through the country and see exquisite landscapes destroyed by smoke and refuse; huge chimneys belching out black torrents; streams that should be dancing in the sunlight gleaming with phosphorescent scum, and rolling along thick and black with filth. What sort of England is the Industrial Period going to leave to its successors?

If there be any truth in the scientific doctrine that the environment modifies the organism, what can be the tendency of the modifications wrought by such an environment as the Black Country? What is there of refining, of elevating, of humanising influence in those endless piles of cinders, that ruined vegetation, that pall of smoke, lighted at night by the lurid glare of the furnaces? What kind of race will that be whose mothers work in the chain-fields till the children come to the birth, and who return thither sometimes on the very day on which they have given new lives to the world?

Many people, true products of the Industrial Period, are indifferent to natural beauty, and only see in a waterfall a source of power, in a woody glen a waste of productive soil. But if, again, the environment modifies the organism, beauty is useful in the highest degree. A high human type cannot be bred in a back slum, trained amid filth and ugliness and clangor, sent to labor ere maturity; it must be bred in pure air, trained amidst sights and sounds that are harmonious and beautiful, educated until mature; then let it turn to labor, and give back to the community the wealth of love and comfort which shielded its earlier years. On the faces of the lads and lasses who come tumbling out of factories and great warehouses at the close of every day, filling the streets with tumult and rough horseplay, is set the seal of the sordid conditions under which they live. The lack of beauty around them has made them unbeautiful, and their strident voices are fitted to pierce the din amid which they live.

In truth, in its effect on Society, the wealthy manufacturing class is far worse than the feudal nobility it is gradually pushing aside. The feudal lords lived among their tenantry, and there were ties of human sympathy between them which do not exist between the manufacturer and those whom he significantly calls his "hands". The manufacturers live away from the place in which their wealth is made, dwelling luxuriously in beautiful suburbs, and leaving the "hands" to stew in closely-packed dwellings under the shadow of the huge and unsightly factories. The division of classes becomes more and more marked; between the rich and the poor yawns an ever-widening gulf.

The tendency of Industrialism to produce castes should not be overlooked. Practical men have noted that when people have for generations lived by weaving, their children learn weaving far more easily than children who come from a mining district. If a trade becomes hereditary, the aptitude for the trade becomes marked in members of the family. And this is not well. It is a tendency to produce fixed castes of workers, instead of fully-developed various human beings. It means, if present forces go on working unrestrained, the dividing of society into castes, the formation of rigid lines of demarcation, the petrifaction which has befallen some older civilisations.

Over against those who laud the present state of Society with its unjustly rich and unjustly poor, with its palaces and its slums, its millionaires and its paupers, be it ours to proclaim that there is a higher ideal in life than that of being first in the race for wealth, most successful in the scramble for gold. Be it ours to declare steadfastly that health, comfort, leisure, culture, plenty for every individual, are far more desirable than breathless struggle for existence, furious trampling down of the weak by the strong, huge fortunes accumulated out of the toil of others, to be handed down to those who have done nothing to earn them. Be it ours to maintain that the greatness of a nation depends not on the number of its great proprietors, on the wealth of its great capitalists, on the splendor of its great nobles; but on the absence of poverty among its people, on the education of its masses, on the universality of enjoyment in life.

III.—The Conflict between Social and Anti-Social Tendencies.

The conflict between social and anti-social tendencies has existed as long as Society itself. It is the contest between the integrating and disintegrating forces, between the brute survival and the human evolution. The individual struggle for existence which had gone on through countless centuries over the whole world had become to some extent modified among the social animals, and savage man, as the highest of these, had also modified it within the limits of each community. As Society progressed slowly in civilisation, the contest went on between the surviving brutal, or savage, desire for personal accumulation and personal aggrandisement without regard for others, and the social desire for general prosperity and happiness with the readiness to subordinate the individual to the general good. It is the still-enduring conflict between these tendencies which now claims our attention. The openings for personal accumulation offered during the Industrial Period gave a great impetus to the anti-social tendencies; the codification of the laws of wealth-getting in Political Economy was seized upon for defence, as though Political Economy offered any law for the general guidance of human conduct, or held up any object as the aim of human life. In their eagerness to represent as right and useful their own greed of gain, members of the *laissez-faire* school sheltered themselves under philosophic names, and used Political Economy as though instead of laying down the conditions of wealth-getting, it had declared it to be the one duty of human beings to get wealth.

The anti-social tendencies seized on three sources of

wealth as especially promising: mines, factories, landed estates. So ruinous in each department proved their unrestricted play, that in each case law had to be called in to check their operation.

MINES.—In these the anti-social tendency of unrestricted accumulation, by competition with others, led to the employment of women and children in labor for which they were unfitted, at wages lower than those obtained by men. Women worked half-naked, with band round forehead dragging laden trucks up steep inclines. Children were born in the darkness, and grew up underground, never seeing the brightness of the sun. The most frightful demoralisation existed, and infants, sleeping at their trapdoors, were crushed beneath the hurrying truck. Manly decency, womanly modesty, childly weakness, all went down before the Juggernaut car of unrestricted competition, until the social tendency, in the guise of law, stepped in to curb the brutality of anti-social greed.

FACTORIES. — Here, again, the labor of women and children has been utilised in antagonism to the better-paid labor of men. And both women and children were scandalously overworked until law intervened to protect them. In *Our Corner* for March, 1885 (vol. v., pp. 158, 159), I gave some details of the labor imposed on children before the legislature interposed, and when we find such Acts as the Factory and Workshops Acts attacked by those who pretend to defend Liberty (see report of the 3rd annual meeting of the Liberty and Property Defence League, p. 10), we know that the liberty they defend is the liberty to plunder others unchecked, the liberty which the burglar might claim in annexing his neighbors' goods. At the present time the chain-works in Warwickshire and Worcestershire show us examples of overmuch liberty in dealing with other people's lives. Women there work semi-nude, dragging heavy chains. A young girl will be absent from her work one day, and reappearing on the morrow will excuse her languid work to the inspector on the ground: "I had a baby yesterday". Child-bearing girls, to the anti-social school, are only "hands" worth so much less in the labor market. These facts have to be faced. No vague talk of "general improvement" will avail us here. These people are suffering while we are discussing, and dilettante sympathy is of small use.

Landed Estates. Here, again, the anti-social tendencies have had full swing. Taxation, levied on land as the rent to the State for the privilege of holding it, has been shifted off the land on to the people, and the land has been claimed as private property instead of as public trust. Improvements made by the tenant have been confiscated, and then the improved condition of the land has been utilised as a reason for raising the rent of the tenant who improved it. Rents have been raised to an extent the tenant could not meet, until he has become hopelessly indebted to his landlord, and so bound to him, hand and foot. Game has been preserved until the crops of farmers have been ruined by it, and until wild animals luxuriated while human beings starved. When the anti-social tendency has had full play and when it has spread abroad sufficient misery for purblind eyes to recognise, then the social tendency has asserted itself, and has established Land Courts in Ireland to fix fair rents; has secured to the tenant the results of his own labor; has permitted the farmer to kill the ground game preying on his crops.

In towns the landlord has been even a greater curse than he has been in the country. Undrained, filthy, rotten hovels have been rented by him to the poor. The slums of all great cities testify to the results of the anti-social tendency, and warn us that the deepest and widest degradation will never touch men's hearts sufficiently to overbear the desire for personal gain.

Law, and law alone, can curb these anti-social tendencies. Granted that a time will come when men shall be too noble to profit by the misery of their fellows, that time is not yet. The anti-social tendencies ruin and degrade, and the few who recognise the evil while not personally experiencing it, aided by the many who suffer from it without fully understanding it, must carry legislation which shall fetter the savage inclination to prey on human beings.

So far we have considered the play of anti-social tendencies in modern society. Let us turn now to the social tendencies, to those which make for integration.

The first of these which we will note is the tendency to co-operation. Handicapped as it is by being compelled to make its way in a society based on competition, co-operation has yet done much to better the lot of the poor. How much it might do if everywhere it replaced competition, may be guessed at from what it has done despite the evil atmosphere which has surrounded it. Anyone who goes over the stores of the Rochdale Pioneers, who sees the great library it has gathered there, who knows the educational agencies centred there, must recognise the enormous good done by even partial co-operation under uncongenial circumstances. That productive co-operation has not succeeded as well as distributive is due partly to the fact that the co-operative workers have sought too eagerly and paid too highly for "influential names" to "float" their companies; and partly to the fact that production, under the present system, needs a larger capital to withstand trade crises than workers are able to command. Many promising enterprises have been ruined by straining after large profits, while working with an undue proportion of borrowed money, money which, in times of panic, has been suddenly withdrawn.

The social tendency is shown in the assignment of public money for educational purposes, the passing of the Education Acts, the pressure of public feeling in favor of rate-supported schools, of higher education for all at the public expense. It is shown in the demand for shorter hours of labor; the insistence that all should work; the attempts —at present only by agitation—to enact limits to the accumulation by individuals of land and capital.

And above all the social tendency is shown in the inclination to resort to law for the effecting of the desired changes; in the recognition that social, not individual effort is necessary for the reform of the social system; in the feeling that the continuance of vice and misery side by side with civilisation is intolerable, and that some means must be found to put an end to them.

The problem now set before us is how to eradicate the anti-social, and to cultivate the social, instincts in men and women. Much would be gained if once it were generally recognised that the desire for huge personal accumulation is essentially anti-social, is a survival from the brute. At the present time this desire is veiled under less offensive names, such as "business ability", "sharpness", "energy", etc., etc., but when the veil is stripped away it stands forth in its repulsive nudity. To desire sufficiency, sufficiency for health and pleasure now, and for the time when work-power has failed, that is natural and reasonable; to desire superfluity, superfluity for ostentation and waste, that is barbaric.

Enough for each of work, of leisure, of joy; too little for none; too much for none; such is the Social Ideal. Better to strive after it worthily, and fail, than to die without striving for it at all.

IV.—The Reconcilement of Diverging Interests.

Wherever a school of thought has succeeded in gaining many adherents, and in holding its ground for a considerable period, it is probable that it possesses some truth, or part of some truth, valuable to humanity. Very often it may see only one side of the truth, and so may present a half as though it were the whole; and the bitterest combats are generally waged between those who hold separately the two halves which, united, would form the perfect whole. Truths which are complementary to each other are held as though they were mutually destructive, and those who should be brothers in a common strife turn their weapons against each other's breasts. Such has been the conflict between the "Individualistic" and the "Socialistic" schools; each holds a truth and does well to cling to it, for neither truth could be lost without injury to Society; the whole truth is to be found by joining the twain, for there is needed for the highest humanity the perfecting of the Individual within a highly organised Society.

Looking back for a moment at our Industrial Period, which may be taken as incarnated in the "Manchester School", we shall find that it has given to the world some important information touching production. It has proved that the productiveness of labor can be enormously increased by co-operation and the division of labor; that individual production of the ordinary necessaries of life is a mistake; that it is cheaper to weave cotton goods by machinery than to leave each housekeeper to do her own spinning and weaving. The Manchester School has for ever rendered it impossible that we shall return to general production by "cottage industries": it has proved that large numbers should co-operate in production; that labor should be economised by much division; that machine-made goods should supersede hand-made in large departments of industry; these are the contributions of the Manchester School to progress. With these truths which it taught were bound up errors which raised against it a widespread revolt. Its system appeared as though it were based on the assumption that, while labor was to be co-operative, the profits arising from the associated labor were to go to the enrichment of an individual. It deified competition, and consecrated as its patterns those who could best outwit their rivals and outstrip them in the race for wealth. Its maxim, "buy in the cheapest market and sell in the dearest", while admirable as counsel for money-making, did not always conduce in practice to perfect honesty, and is scarcely sufficient as the end of life. "Get money; by fair means if thou canst, but by all means get money", was a somewhat brutally frank way of putting "business" morality. It tended to regard men too much as mechanical instruments of production, significantly calling men, women, and children "hands", instead of human beings. This school it was of which I spoke on p. 15 as having misused Political Economy, and as having taught as though the laws of Political Economy said "Get rich", instead of stating the conditions of getting rich; they have used it as the science of Mechanics might be used, if instead of teaching by it how a weight may be lifted with least exertion of muscular strength, it were appealed to as declaring that everyone should lift weights.

Turning to the Socialistic School, we find that it enshrines the truth that man is a social animal, and that his progress must lie in the direction of closer social union. Within this school again we find three camps, the Collectivist, the Communistic, and the Anarchist, the latter of which is really tenanted by extreme Individualists, who are separated from the ordinary Individualistic School by their desire to overturn the present social system, and to destroy the "rights of property"

The Socialists have learned from the Manchester School the conditions of wealth-production on a large scale, and seeing that industry as now conducted leads to the enriching of a few and the hopeless poverty of the many, it lays hands on the raw material and the means of production and claims these as collective property. There is, perhaps, among many of us who belong to this school too great an inclination to think that the environment is everything, and to ignore the reaction of the organism on the environment. There is too much forgetfulness of the worse types of men and women, results of the Industrial Period, who would not be suddenly changed even if their environment could be suddenly transformed; there is too reckless a desire to overturn, without asking what curb would be kept, in the general overturning, on the degraded and criminal products of our present civilisation.

The Individualistic School, whether it is carried to the extreme Anarchist position, or maintains the sufficiency of reform along the broad lines of the present social state, brings into prominence the right of individual liberty, and the value of individual initiative. One outside, and one inside, nominal Socialism, each is the result of a dread of, a recoil against, over-much State regulation and State interference. Each lays down the vital truth that free play for human faculties, encouragement not discouragement of variations, are necessary to human progress. Each points out that a perfect State is only possible by the perfecting of individual citizens, and each is apt to lay so much stress on the organism as to overlook the immense importance of the environment. There is, of course, as I have said above, the fundamental difference between the Anarchists and those generally recognised as Individualists, that the former appear to negate, while the latter maintain, the right of private property. I have only put them together as alike in one thing, that they assert the right of the Individual against the State, while the Collectivist Socialist asserts the right of the State as against the Individual.

Pressed on the matter, however, both Individualist and Socialist are found to hold a common object; the Individualist admits that the claims of the unit must yield if they come into conflict with those of Society: the Socialist admits that he is working for a higher social state in order that each individual may have room and opportunity to develop to the highest point of which he is capable. Is there not here a possible reconcilement? Is not the ideal of all good and earnest reformers practically the same, although seen by them from different sides? True, the Individualist is not generally in favor of nationalising the means of production, and herein differs in his method from the Socialist; but is this difference any reason for their posing as antagonists? The difference is not greater than that between the Socialist who secures to the worker the private property he has himself earned, and the Communist who would have all property common; or between the Collectivist and the Anarchist schools. Yet these can work together for common objects, while differing in much; and so should work the Socialist and the Radical Individualist against the common foe, the idle class that lives as parasite on Society.

The first matter on which all agree is that the environment must be largely modified by law. The Socialist will carry this modifying process further than will the Individualist, but here again it is a question between them of degree. Speaking as a Socialist, I desire to see laws passed which will render education tax-supported, compulsory, and secular, so that all the children of the community may receive a common education; which will fix a normal working day; which will render factory inspection more efficient, and extend inspection to shops and rooms of every kind in which employees work; which will enforce sanitary inspection and prevent it from being the farce it now is; which will enable the building of healthy houses, and provide plenty of recreation ground in every town. All these measures are imperatively necessary now, and immediately necessary, in order that the environment may be changed sufficiently for the development of healthier organisms. After a while most of them will not be needed; when all have felt the benefit of education, compulsion to educate will become a dead letter; when labor is better organised, when the words employer and employee shall no longer have any facts answering to them, when all production is for use, not for profit, there will be no need of a law limiting the working day, for none will be driven to over-long labor by the awful pressure of starvation and of fear of future distress. Factory inspection will be a very easy task when there are no longer over-greedy owners trying to wring every possible penny out of their "hands"; and the need for sanitary inspection will pass when there are no slums, and when every householder understands the conditions of health.

The organism, born into and growing up in a healthier environment, will be more vigorous and therefore more capable of evolving a higher individuality, a more marked personality. The evolution of individuality is now checked, in some by poverty and over-hard and prolonged toil, in some by the strict conventions of fashion, in some by the unsuitability of their work to their capacities, in some by a narrow and superstitious education, in all by the unhealthy social atmosphere they are compelled to breathe. The loss to the community by waste of power, due to the crushing out of all individuality among hundreds upon hundreds of thousands, is a loss simply incalculable. When all are fully educated through childhood and youth, the faculties of each developed and trained, then each individual will be able to evolve along his own line, and the full value of each personality will enrich Society. It is often argued that a wide and thorough education will unfit people for the drudgery necessary for supporting the existence of Society, and that "some one"—never the speaker, of course!—must do the "dirty work". There are two lines of answer to the objection. First, education does *not* unfit people for doing any necessary work; it is the ignorant, superficial, "genteel" person who fears that the veneer of polish may rub off in use. The educated brain, brought to bear on manual work, economises labor and minimises drudgery. General education will certainly bring about the substitution of machinery for men and women wherever possible, for doing really unpleasant labor; and ingenuity will be exerted in the invention of labor-saving machinery when educated people find themselves face to face with repulsive kinds of toil. At present they shove off all the unpleasant work on to others: then, all being educated and there being no helot class, means will be found to avoid most of the really disagreeable work. If any such remains, which cannot be done by machinery, those who by doing it serve Society will be honored, not looked down on as they are now; or possibly some minute fraction of it will fall to the lot of each. Secondly, if it were as true as it is false that education unfitted people for "menial" work, no class has the right to keep another class in ignorance and degradation, in order that its own fingers may not be soiled. The answer to the querulous argument: "Who is to light our fires and cook our dinners, when the servants are as good as their masters?" is the very plain one: "You yourself, if you want the things done, and cannot find anyone willing to do those services for you, in exchange for services you are able to do for them." In the coming times everyone will have to do something, and to do some one thing well. We shall not all have to light fires, for the principle of division of labor will come in, but the one who lights the fire will be a free and independent human being, not a drudge. There is no doubt that domestic labor will be very much lessened, when those who enjoy the results can no longer put off all the toil which produces them on some one else. Even now, the work of a house can be wonderfully diminished if a little intelligence be brought to bear upon it, although domestic labor-saving machines are still in their infancy. The great "servant problem" will be solved by the disappearance of servants, the wide introduction of machinery, and the division among the members of each domestic commonwealth of the various necessary duties. The prospect is really not so very terrible when quietly surveyed.

Whither is Society evolving? It is evolving towards a more highly developed individuality of its units, and towards their closer co-ordination. It is evolving towards a more generous brotherhood, a more real equality, a fuller liberty. It is evolving towards that Golden Age which poets have chanted, which dreamers have visioned, which martyrs have died for: towards that new Republic of Man, which exists now in our hope and our faith, and shall exist in reality on earth.

THE

SOCIALIST MOVEMENT.

BY

ANNIE BESANT.

[REPRINTED FROM THE "WESTMINSTER REVIEW".]

LONDON:
FREETHOUGHT PUBLISHING COMPANY,
63, FLEET STREET, E.C.
1887.

PRICE THREEPENCE.

LONDON:
PRINTED BY ANNIE BESANT AND CHARLES BRADLAUGH,
63, FLEET STREET, E.C.

THE SOCIALIST MOVEMENT.

Some good-hearted people must have felt an uncomfortable thrill when they heard Professor Huxley declare that he would rather have been born a savage in one of the Fiji Islands than have been born in a London slum. The advantages of civilisation, from the slum point of view, must appear somewhat doubtful; and as a considerable part of the population of every large city live in the slums, the slum view has an importance of its own as a factor in the future social evolution. For it must be remembered that the slum population is not wholly composed of criminals and ne'er-do-weels—the "good-for-nothings" of Herbert Spencer. The honest workman and struggling seamstress live there cheek by jowl with the thief and and the harlot; and with the spread of education has arisen an inclination to question whether, after all, everything has been arranged quite as well as it might be in this best of all possible worlds. The question, Whether on the whole civilisation has been an advantage? has been a theme of academical discussion since Rousseau won the prize for an essay on "Has the restoration of the Sciences contributed to purify or to corrupt Manners?" and laid down the audacious thesis that riches gave birth to luxury and idleness, and from luxury sprang the arts, from idleness the sciences. But it has now changed its form, and has entered the arena of practical life: men are asking now, Is it rational that the progress of society should be as lopsided as it is? Is it necessary that, while civilisation brings to some art, beauty, refinement—all that makes life fair and gracious—it should bring to others drudgery, misery, degradation, such as no uncivilised people know; and these emphasised and rendered the bitterer by the contrast of what life is to many, the dream of what it might be to all? For Professor Huxley is right. The savage has the forest and the open sea, the joy of physical strength, food easily won, leisure sweet after the excitement of the chase; the civilised toiler has the monotonous drudgery of the stuffy workshop, the hell of the gin-palace for his pleasure-ground, the pandemonium of reeking court and stifling alley for his lullaby: civilisation has robbed him of all natural beauty and physical joy, and has given him in exchange—the slum. It is little wonder that, under these circumstances, there are many who have but scant respect for our social fabric, and who are apt to think that any change cannot land them in a condition worse than that in which they already find themselves.

The tendency to think of complete social change as a possible occurrence has come down to the present generation as an inheritance of the past. Old men still dwell fondly on the hopes of the "social missionaries" who were preaching when the men now of middle-age were born. Some even remember the experiments of Robert Owen and of his personal disciples, the hopes raised by New Lanark and Arbiston, the chill disappointment of New Harmony. The dream that glorified their youth has remained a sacred memory, and they have told how all might have been different had society been prepared in Owen's time for the fundamental change. And the great and far-reaching co-operative movement, born of Owen's Socialism, has kept "his memory green", and has prepared men to think of a possible future in which co-operation should wholly replace competition, and Owen's dream of universal brotherhood become a living reality. Such part of the energy of the Owenite Socialists as was not merged in co-operative activity was swamped in the sudden rush of prosperity that followed the repeal of the Corn Laws and the English triumph of Free Trade. Now that that rush is long over, and the old misery is on the workers once more, their minds turn back to the old schemes, and they listen readily to suggestions of a new social order.

The abnormally rapid multiplication characteristic of the very poor is at once constantly rendering the problem to be solved more difficult and more imperatively pressing.

Unhealthy conditions force the young into premature nubility; marriage takes place between mere lads and lasses; parenthood comes while father and mother are themselves legally infants; and the dwarfed, peaky little mortals, with baby frames and wizened faces, that tumble over each other in the gutters of the slums, are the unwholesome and unlovely products of the forcing-house of extreme poverty.

The spread of education and of religious scepticism has added the last touch necessary to make the poor ripe for social change. Ignorance is a necessary condition for prolonged submission to remediable misery. The School Boards are teaching the children the beauty of order, cleanliness, and decency, and are waking up in them desire for knowledge, hopes, and aspirations—plants unsuited for cultivation in the slums. They are sowing the seeds of a noble discontent with unworthy conditions, while at the same time they are developing and training the intelligence, and are converting aimless, sullen grumbling into a rational determination to understand the Why of the present, and to discover the How of change. Lastly, religious scepticism has enormously increased the value put upon the life which is. So long as men believed that the present life was the mere vestibule of an endless future, it was possible to bribe them into quiescence in misery by representing poverty as a blessing which should hereafter bring in its train the "kingdom of heaven". But now that many look on the idea of a life beyond the grave with doubt, and even with disbelief, this life has taken giant proportions in their eyes, and the human longing for happiness, which erstwhile fed on hopes of heaven, has fastened itself with passionate intensity on the things of earth.

Such is the soil, ploughed by misery, fertilised by education and scepticism, ready to receive and nourish the seed of social change.

While the soil has been thus preparing, the sowers who are to scatter the seed have been fashioning. Thoughtful persons have noted the regular cycle of alternate depression and inflation trodden by industrialism during the last century. At one time industry progresses "by leaps and bounds", employment is plentiful, wages high (as wages go), prices of coal and iron high, profits increase, and fortunes are rapidly built up. This inflation after a while passes away, and is succeeded by depression; "short time" is worked, wages are reduced, profits diminish, the "market is overstocked". This in its turn passes away, and temporary prosperity returns, to be after a while succeeded by another depression, and that by another inflation. But it is noticeable that the depressions become more acute and more prolonged as they return time after time, and that there is less elasticity of revival after each. The position of England in the world's markets becomes yearly one of diminished advantage; other nations raise their own coal and their own iron instead of buying from us, and as the competition of nations becomes keener, English trade can no longer monopolise the custom of the world. The radical weakness of our industrial system is thus becoming patent —no longer veiled, as it was during the first half of the century, by a monopoly which brought such enormous gains that the drain of wealth into a few hands was comparatively little felt. Now that there is so much less to divide, the unfairness of the method of division is becoming obvious.

Nor can we overlook, in tracing the fashioning of those who are to sow the seeds of change, the effect on English thought of the greatly increased communication with foreign countries, and especially with Germany. English religious thought has been largely influenced by the works of Strauss and Feuerbach; philosophic thought by those of Hegel, Kant, and Schopenhauer; scientific by the speculations of Goethe, the practical labors of Vogt, Büchner, and Haeckel. English insularity has been broken down in every domain of theoretical and speculative thought; it was inevitable that it should also be broken down in the domain of practical sociology, and that German proposals for social change should win the attention of English students of social problems. The works of Marx, Bebel, Liebknecht, and Engels have not reached any large number of English people; neither have those of Strauss, Hegel, and Kant. None the less in each case have they exercised a profoundly modifying influence on religious, philosophical, and sociological thought respectively; for, reaching a small band only, that band has in its turn influenced thought in the direction taken by itself, and has modified the views of very many who are unconscious of the change thus wrought in their own attitude towards progress. At the same time the German graft has been itself modified by the English stock, and English Socialism is beginning to take its own distinctive color; it is influenced by English traditions, race, habit, and methods of public procedure. It shows, at its best, the influence of the open-air of English political life, the tolerance of diversity of thought which is bred of free speech; it is less arrogant, less intolerant, than it is with Germans, or with those English who are most directly under German influence. In Germany the intolerance of oppression has caused intolerance of revolt; here the very power of the democracy has a tendency to sober its speech, and to make it take its own way in the quiet consciousness of its resistless strength. This peculiarity of English life must modify Socialism, and incline it to resort to methods of legislation rather than to methods of dynamite.

Nor has the effect of foreign thought been confined to the influence exerted by thinkers over thinkers, through the medium of the press. A potent worker for the internationalisation of thought has been silently busy for many years past. At first insular prejudices were broken down only for the wealthy and the nobles, when the "grand tour" was a necessary part of the education of the fine gentleman. Then the capitalist broke down national fences for his own gain, feeling himself nearer in blood to his foreign colleagues than to the workers in his own land; for, after all, common interests lie at the root of all fellow-feeling. And the capitalist abolished nationalism for himself: he hired Germans and Frenchmen for his counting-house work, finding them cheaper and better educated than English clerks; when his English wage-workers struck for better wages he brought over foreigners to take their place, so that he might live on cheap foreign labor while he starved the English into submission. The effect of foreign immigration and of foreign importation has not in the long run turned wholly to the advantage of the capitalist; for his foreign clerks and his foreign workers have fraternised with the English they were brought over to displace. They have taken part in club discussions; they have spread their own views; they have popularised in England the ideas current among workers on the Continent; they have made numbers of Englishmen acquainted with the solutions suggested abroad for social problems. Thus, the internationalism of the luxurious idle and of the wealthy capitalist has paved the way for the internationalism of the future—the internationalism of the proletariat, the internationalism of Socialism.

From this preliminary sketch of the conditions which make for a Socialist movement in England at the present time we must turn to an examination of the doctrines held and taught by the modern school, which claims to teach what is known as Scientific Socialism. The allegation, or even the proof, that modern civilisation is to a large extent a failure, is obviously not sufficient ground for a complete social revolution. Appeals to the emotions by means of word-pictures of the sufferings and degradation of the industrious poor, may rouse sympathy, and may even excite to riot, but can never bring about fundamental changes in society. The intellect must be convinced ere we can look for any wise movement in the direction of organic improvement; and while the passion of the ignorant has its revolutionary value, it is on the wisdom and foresight of the instructed that we must rely for the work of social reconstitution.

The first thing to realise is that the Socialist movement is an economic one. Despite all whirling words, and revolution fire, and poetic glamor, and passionate appeal, this one dry fact is the central one—Socialism rejects the present industrial system and proposes an exceedingly different one. No mere abuse can shake the Socialist; no mere calling of names can move him. He holds a definite economic theory—a theory which should neither be rejected without examination, nor accepted without study.

The preliminary stock objection which is often held to be sufficient to wave Socialism out of court is the statement that it is "against the laws of political economy". No statement could be more erroneous; though it may be pleaded in extenuation that the abuse levelled by ignorant Socialists at political economy has given excuse for supposing that it is in antagonism to Socialism. With political economy, as the science which deals with the nature, the production, and the distribution of wealth, Socialism can have no quarrel. Its quarrel is with the present industrial system, not with the science which points out the ascertained sequence of events under that system. Suppose a *régime* of avowed slavery: political economy, dealing with the production of wealth in such a state, would lay down how slaves might be worked to the best advantage—how most might be got out of them with least expenditure. But it would be irrational to attack political economy as brutal under such conditions; it would be the slave system which would be brutal, and blame of the science which merely dealt with the existent facts would be idle. The work of political economy is to discern and expound for any type of social system the best methods of producing and distributing wealth *under that system*; and it can as easily study and develop those methods under a *régime* of universal co-operation such as Socialism, as under a *régime* of universal competition such as the present. Socialism is in antagonism to the present system, and seeks to overthrow it; but only the ignorant and the thoughtless confound in their hatred the system itself, and the science that deals with its phænomena.

In truth, Socialism founds part of its disapproval of the present industrial system on the very facts pointed out by orthodox economists. It accepts Ricardo's "iron law of wages", and, recognising that wages tend to fall to the minimum on which the laborer can exist, it declares against the system of the hiring of workers for a fixed wage, and the appropriation of their produce by the hirer. It accepts Ricardo's theory of rent, with such modifications as are adopted by all modern economists. It assents to, and indeed insists on, the facts that all wealth is the result of labor applied to natural agents, that capital is the result of labor and abstinence, that in all save the most primitive forms of industry capital and labor—that is, the unconsumed result of past labor and present labor—are both necessary factors in the production of wealth.

Nor does Socialism challenge the accuracy of the deductions from the "laws of political economy" in a competitive system drawn by the trading community. That a man who desires wealth should buy in the cheapest market and sell in the dearest; that he should drive the hardest possible bargains; that in selling he should be guided by the maxim, *caveat emptor*; that in buying he should take advantage of the ignorance or the necessities of the seller; that the weakest should go the wall; that feeling should not interfere with business; that labor should be bought at the lowest possible price, and as much got out of it as may be; that trade morality differs from the morality of private life—all these maxims the Socialist regards as the evil fruits of the perpetuation among men of the struggle for existence; a struggle which, however inevitable among brutes, is from his point of view unworthy of human civilisation.

Recognising thus the unsatisfactory results which flow naturally and inevitably from the present system, Socialism proceeds to analyse the way in which wealth is produced and accumulated under it, to seek for the causes of the extreme wealth and extreme poverty which are its most salient characteristics.

Applying ourselves, then, to the study of the production of wealth, we find taking part therein three things—natural agents, capital, and labor. These, under the present system, are represented in England by three types—the landlord, the capitalist, and the proletarian. The transitional organisms need not detain us: the landlord who tills his land with his own hands, the capitalist who works in his own mill—these are exceptions; and we are concerned with the normal types. Abroad, the landlord pure and simple is comparatively rare. Of these three, the landlord owns the natural agents; no wealth can be produced without his consent. John Stuart Mill ("Principles of Political Economy", bk. ii., ch. xvi., sec. 1) remarks that "the only person, besides the laborer and the capitalist, whose consent is necessary to production, and who can claim a share of the produce as the price of that consent, is the person who, by the arrangements of society, possesses exclusive power over some natural agent". Given a person who, by possession of the natural agents from which wealth can be produced, can prevent the production of wealth by withholding the raw material, and you have a person who can successfully claim part of the wealth to be produced as a condition of allowing production to take place. He gains, by virtue of his position, wealth which one less fortunately placed can only acquire by prolonged labor. Nay, more; since many capitalists will compete for the raw material when it is advantageously situated, he will be able to obtain an ever higher price from the most eager bidder; as towns increase and trade develops, competition will drive the price up still higher; and this ever-mounting "rent", paid to the owner of the natural agents, will enrich the lucky possessor, however idle, ignorant, or useless he may be. Thus is produced a class which has a vested right to tax industry, and which taxes it in proportion to its success. Not an improvement can be effected, nor a railway constructed, nor a road made, without toll being first paid to the owner of the soil. The whole nation is at the mercy of a comparatively small class, so long as it consents to admit that this class has a right to own the ground on which the nation lives. Here is a point at which Socialism finds itself in direct antagonism to the present system of society. Socialism declares that natural agents ought not to be private property, and that no idle class should be permitted to stand between land and labor, and demand payment of a tax before it will permit the production of wealth. Socialism holds that the soil on which a nation is born and lives ought to belong to the nation as a whole, and not to a class within the nation; that the soil should be cultivated by individuals, or by co-operative groups, holding directly under the State—the "State" here meaning central organising body or district organising body, according as the organisation is communal or centralised. And here, among different Socialist schools, difference in detail manifests itself. All agree that the soil must in some fashion be controlled by the community, and the benefits derivable from it spread over the community. But some Socialists would have each commune practically independent, with the soil on which it lives vested in each; the agriculturists of the commune would form an organised body for cultivating the soil, and the agricultural products would be collected in the communal store, and thence distributed as each member of the commune had need of them. Nothing would here be recognised as "rent", since the total produce would pass under communal control. Other Socialists favor a system of more centralised management. But all agree that individual property in land must disappear, and that in the future land must not be used as an investment which is to bring in a profit in the shape of rent to some speculator or idler, but must be used for purposes of production for the general good, yielding food and raw materials for clothing and other necessaries of life, but profit in the shape of rent to no individual.

The extreme Radical school of politicians accepts the Socialist theory of land, and denounces private property in the soil as vigorously as does the Socialist. In fact, the Radical is a half-fledged Socialist—indignant as many would be at the description: he is in favor of the State being the landowner, but he boggles at the idea of the State being the capitalist. His attitude to the land is, however, an important factor in the Socialist movement, for it familiarises the national mind with the idea of the State absorbing the functions hitherto belonging to a class. The establishment of Land Courts, the fixing of judicial rents, the legal restrictions put on the "rights" of landlords—all these make for Socialism. M. Agathon de Potter, a well-known Continental writer, rejoices over the introduction of Mr. Charles Bradlaugh's Bill for expropriating landlords who keep cultivable land uncultivated, and for vesting the forfeited lands in the State, as a direct step towards Socialism. The shrinking of English politicians from the name does not prevent their advance towards the thing, and the Liberty and Property Defence League is justified in its view that politics are drifting steadily in a Socialist direction.

Pass we from the landlord who holds the natural agents to the capitalist who holds the means of production. What is capital, and how has it come into existence? Capital is any wealth which is employed for profit. On this there is no dispute. As Senior says: "Economists are agreed that *whatever* gives a profit is properly called capital". Now, as all wealth is the result of labor applied to natural agents, capital, being wealth, must have been so produced. But another factor has been at work; as Marshall says: it is "the result of labor *and abstinence*". Wherever there is capital there has been labor, and there has also been abstinence from consumption. But in studying the origin and the accumulation of capital, this remarkable historical fact stares us in the face—that capital is not found in the hands of the laborious and the abstemious, but is obtained by a process of confiscation of the results of labor and the imposition of privation on the laborious. On this John Stuart Mill has the following pregnant passage:

> "In a rude and violent state of society it continually happens that the person who has capital is not the very person who has saved it, but someone who, being stronger, or belonging to a more powerful community, has possessed himself of it by plunder. And even in a state of things in which property was protected, the increase of capital has usually been, for a long time, mainly derived from privations which, though essentially the same with saving, are not generally called by that name, because not voluntary. The actual producers have been slaves, compelled to produce as much as force could extort from them, and to consume as little as the self-interest or the usually very slender humanity of their taskmasters would permit. ("Principles of Political Economy", bk. i., ch. v., sec. 5).

Capital always has been, and it always must be, obtained by the partial confiscation of the results of labor; that is, it must be accumulated by labor which is not paid for, or by labor of which the payment is deferred. In slave communities the slave-owner becomes a great capitalist by appropriating the total results of his slaves' toil, and returning to them only such small portion of it as suffices to keep the wealth-producers in capable working order. That is, the wealth produced *minus* the amount consumed by the producers, goes to the owner, and that part of it which he does not consume is laid by to be employed as capital. And it is worth noting that no considerable accumulation of capital was made, and no rapid progress in civilisation was possible, until slavery was introduced. In a low stage of evolution men will not deny themselves present for the sake of future enjoyment, nor incur present toil for the sake of future ease. But when, as was neatly said to me, the barbarian discovered that he could utilise his conquered enemy to much greater advantage by making him work than by merely eating him, civilisation had a chance. Slavery was, in truth, a necessary stage in social evolution; only by forced toil and forced privation was it possible to accumulate capital, and without capital no forms of complex industry are realisable. At the present time that which was done frankly and unblushingly in the slave *régime* is done under a veil of fine phrases, among which free contract, free laborer, and the like, play a striking part. But in reality the "free laborer" only obtains as wage such portion of the results of his labor as enables him to exist at the standard of living current for his class at the time, and the remainder of his produce goes to his employer. And too often this portion of his is not sufficient to keep him in capable working order, as is shown by the sombre fact that the average age of the hand-workers at death is far less than that of the idlers. For in truth the slave of the past had this advantage over the wage-worker of the present—that it was to his master's interest to keep the slave in high physical condition, and to prolong his working life; whereas it is to the modern employer's interest to get as much work out of the "free laborer" as is possible in a short time, and then to fling him aside as he begins to flag, and hire in his place a younger and more vigorous competitor, to be in his turn wrung dry and thrown away.

Before considering what Socialism would do with the capitalist, we must turn to the proletarian, his necessary correlative. A proletarian is a person who is possessed of labor-force, and of nothing else. He is the incarnation of the "labor" necessary for the production of wealth, the third factor in our trio. This type, in our modern society, is numerous, and is rapidly increasing. He is the very antithesis of the really free laborer, who works on his own raw material with his own instruments of production, and produces for his own subsistence. In the country the proletarian is born on somebody else's land, and as he grows up he finds himself owner of nothing except his own body. The raw material around him is owned by the landlord; the instruments of production are owned by the capitalist farmers. As he cannot live on his own labor force, which can only become productive in conjunction with raw material and means of production (capital), he must either sell it or starve. Nominally he may be free; in reality he is no more free than is the slave. The slave is free to refuse to work, and to take in exchange the lash, the prison, the grave; and such freedom only has the present proletarian. If he refuses to work, he must take the lash of hunger, the prison of the workhouse, and, on continued refusal, the actual gaol. Nor can he put his own price on this solitary property of his, his body—he must sell it at the market rate; and in some agricultural counties of England at the present time the market rate is from 7s. to 9s. a week. It is most significant of the bearing of the propertyless condition of the proletarian that many farmers object to the very slight improvement made in the laborer's position by his being permitted to rent at a high price a small allotment which he cultivates *for himself*. The ground of the farmer's objection is that even such small portion of freedom makes the laborer "too independent", and thereby drives up wages. To get the full advantage out of him, the proletarian must be wholly dependent for subsistence on the wages he earns. The town proletarian is in a similar position—neither land nor instrument of production is his; but he also has his labor force, and this he must sell, or he must starve.

We have arrived at the citadel of the Socialist position. Here is this unpropertied class, this naked proletariat, face to face with landlord and capitalist, who hold in their grip the means of subsistence. It must reach those means of subsistence or starve. The terms laid down for its acceptance are clear and decisive: "We will place within your hands the means of existence if you will produce sufficient to support us as well as yourselves, and if you will consent that the whole of your produce, over that which is sufficient to support you in a hardy, frugal life, shall be the property of us and of our children. If you are very thrifty, very self-denying, and very lucky, you may be able to save enough out of your small share of your produce to feed yourself in your old age, and so avoid falling back on us. Your children will tread the same mill-round, and we hope you will remain contented with the position in which Providence has placed you, and not envy those born to a higher lot." Needless to say, the terms are accepted by a proletariat ignorant of its own strength, and the way to profit is open to landlord and capitalist. The landlord, as we have seen, obtains his share of the gains by taxing the capitalist through raising his rent. The capitalist finds his profit in the difference between the wage he pays and the value of the produce of his hired workers. The wage is fixed by the competition for employment in the labor market, and limited in its downward tendency by the standard of living. The minimum wage is that on which the worker can exist, however hardly. For less than this he will not work. Every shilling above this is fought over, and wage rises and falls by competition. At every stage of their relationship there is contest between employer and employed. If the wage is paid for a fixed day's work—as in nearly every trade—the employer tries to lengthen the day, the employed to shorten it; the longer the day, the greater the production of "surplus value"—*i.e.*, of the difference between the wage paid and the value produced. The employer tries to increase surplus value by pressing the workers to exertion; they lessen exertion in order not to hasten the time of their discharge. The employer tries still to increase surplus value by supplanting male labor with female and child labor at lower wages. The men resist such introduction, knowing that the ultimate result is to increase the amount taken by capital and to lessen that obtained by labor.

Now the Socialist alleges that these antithetical interests can never be reconciled while capital and labor are the possessions of two distinct classes. He points to the results brought about by the capitalist class while it was left unshackled by the State. The triumph of capitalism, and of *laisser-faire* between employers and employed, was from 1764 to 1833. During that time not only adults but young children were worked from fifteen to sixteen hours a day, and the production of surplus value was enormous. The huge fortunes of the Lancashire "cotton-princes" were built up by these overtasked, quickly worn-out workers. The invention of machinery centupled man's productive power, and its benefits were monopolised by a comparatively small class; while those who made the wealth festered in closely crowded courts, those who appropriated the wealth luxuriated in country seats; one side of industrialism is seen in the Lancashire mansions, pleasure-grounds, and hothouses; the other in the reeking slums within the sound of the factory bells. Under a saner system of production, the introduction of machinery would have lightened toil, shortened the hours of necessary labor, and spread abundance where there was want. Under capitalistic industrialism it has built up huge fortunes for a few, and has reduced thousands to conditions of insanitary living and dreary degradation, worse than anything the world has hitherto known. It has poisoned our rivers, polluted our atmosphere, marred the beauty of our country's face, bestialised large numbers of our people. Improvements in machinery, which should be hailed with joy, are regarded with dread by large classes of workers, because they will throw numbers out of work, and reduce men, who were skilled laborers with the old machinery, into the ranks of the unskilled. True, the result of the introduction of machinery has been to cheapen—in consequence of competition among capitalists—many commodities, especially articles of clothing. But this effect is little felt among the laboring classes. They can buy perhaps three coats where they used to buy one, but the easily worn-out shoddy, thought good enough for clothes sold in poor quarters, is but a poor exchange for the solid hand-made stuffs worn by their ancestors.

What, then, is the remedy proposed by Socialism? It is to deal with capital as it deals with land; to abolish the capitalist as well as the landlord, and to bring the means of production, as well as the natural agents on which they are used, under the control of the community.

Capital is, as we have seen, the result of unpaid labor; in a complex system like our own it is the result of co-operative—that is, of socialised—labor. It has been found by experience that division of labor increases productive ability, and in all forms of industry numbers now co-operate to turn out the finished product. In each commodity is embodied the labor of many workers, and the socialisation of labor has reached a very advanced stage. But while industrialism has been socialised in its aspect of labor, it has remained individualistic in its aspect of capital; and the results of the combined efforts of many are appropriated to the advantage of one, and when the one has exhausted his power of consumption he retains the remaining results, and employs them for the further enslavement and exploitation of labor. Thus labor constantly adds new links to the chain which fetters it, and is ever increasing the capital which, let out at interest by its owners, becomes ever a heavier tax upon itself. Socialism contends that these unconsumed results of socialised labor ought not to pass into the hands of individuals to be used by them for their own profit; but should pass either into the industrial funds of the several trades that produce them, or into a central industrial exchequer. In either case, these funds created by past labor would be used for the facilitation of present and future labor. They would be available for the introduction of improved machinery, for the opening up of new industries, for the improvement of means of communication, and for similar undertakings. Thus, in a very real sense, capital would become only the deferred payment of labor, and the whole results of toil would be constantly flowing back upon the toilers. Under such conditions, fixed capital or plant would, like land, be held for purposes of use by the workers who used it. Its replacement would be a constant charge on the commodities it helped to produce. A machine represents so much human labor; that embodied labor takes part in producing the finished commodity as much as does the palpable labor of the human worker who superintends the machine; that worker does not produce the whole value added in the factory to the material brought into it, and has no claim to that whole value. The wear and tear of the machine is an offset, and must be charged on the products, so that when the machine is worn out there may be no difficulty in its replacement. Under such conditions also the distinction between employers and employed would disappear. All would be members of industrial communities, and the necessary foremen, superintendents, organisers, and officers of every kind, would be elected as the officers of trades unions are elected at the present time.

Poverty will never cease so long as any class or any individuals have an interest in the exploitation of others. While individuals hold capital, and other individuals cannot exist unless that capital is used for their employment, the first class will prey upon the second. The capitalists will not employ unless they can "make a profit" out of those they hire to work for them; that is, unless they pay them less than the value of the work produced. But if one man is to have value for which he has not worked, another must have less than the value of his work; and while one class grows wealthy on unpaid labor, another must remain poor, giving labor without return. Socialism would give to each return for labor done, but it recognises no claim in the idle to grow fat on the produce of the industrious.

Interest on capital, paid to individuals, has—as is obvious from the foregoing—no place in Socialism. Strongly as Socialism protests against the whole system of which landlords and capitalists form an integral part, it reserves its uttermost reprobation for the theory which justifies a class of the latter in living solely on money drawn as interest on investments. If a man possesses three or four thousand pounds he can invest them, and live all his life long on the interest without ever doing a stroke of honest work, and can then bequeath to some one else the right to live in idleness; and so on in perpetuity. Money in the capitalist system is like the miraculous oil in the widow's cruse—it can always be spent and never exhausted. A man in sixty years will have received in interest at five per cent. three times his original fortune, and although he may have spent the interest, and thus have spent every penny of his fortune three times over, he will yet possess his fortune as large as it was when he began. He has consumed in commodities three times the sum originally owned, and yet is not one penny the worse. Other people have labored for him, fed him, clothed him, housed him, and he has done nothing in exchange. The Socialist argument against this form of interest lies in a nutshell: a man earns £5; he gives labor for which he receives in exchange a power of possession over £5 worth of commodities; he desires only to consume £1 worth now, and to defer the consumption of the remaining £4. He buys his £1 worth of commodities, and considers himself repaid for the fifth portion of his work by possessing and consuming these. But he expects to put out his saved £4 at interest, and would consider himself hardly used if, fourteen years hence, when he desired to exercise his power of consumption, deferred for his own convenience, that power had not increased although he had done nothing to increase it. Yet it can only be increased by other people's labor being left unpaid for, while he is paid twice over for his; and this arrangement the Socialist stamps as unjust. So long as capital remains in the hands of individuals, interest will be demanded by them for its use, and will be perforce paid; and so long also will exist an idle class, which will consume without producing, and will remain a burden on the industrious, who must labor to support these as well as themselves, and must produce sufficient for all.

Now, Socialism aims at rendering impossible the existence of an idle class. No healthy adult but will have to work in exchange for the things he requires. For the young, freedom from labor; they have to prepare for life's work. For the aged, freedom from labor: they have worked, and at eventide should come rest. For the sick also, freedom from labor; and open hospitals for all, without distinction of class, where tendance and all that skill can do shall be at the service of each. But for the strong and the mature, no bread of idleness, no sponging upon other people. With division of labor will come also division of leisure; the disappearance of the languid lady, full of *ennui* from sheer idleness, will entail the disappearance of the overworked slavey, exhausted from unending toil; and there will be two healthy women performing necessary work, and enjoying full leisure for study, for art, for recreation, where now are the over-lazy and the over-driven.

In thus condemning the existence of an idle class, Socialism does not assail all the individuals who now compose it. These are not to blame for the social conditions into which they have been born; and it is one of the most hopeful signs of the present Socialist movement, that many who are working in it belong to the very classes which will be abolished by the triumph of Socialist principles. The man who has inherited a fortune, and has embraced Socialism, would do no good by throwing it away and plunging into the present competitive struggle; all he can do is to live simply, to utilise his position of advantage as a pedestal on which to place his advocacy of Socialism, and to employ his money in Socialist propaganda.

It is feared by some that the success of the Socialist movement would bring about the crushing of individualism and an undue restriction of liberty. But the Socialist contends that the present terrible struggle for existence is the worst enemy of individualism, and that for the vast majority individuality is a mere phrase. Exhausting toil and ever-growing anxiety, these crush out individuality, and turn the eager promising lad into the harassed drudge of middle age. How many capable brains are wasted, how many original geniuses lost to the nations they might illuminate, by the strife for mere livelihood? The artist fritters away his genius in "pot-boilers"; the dramatist writes down to the piece that will "pay", and harnesses his delicate fancy into coarse burlesque full of wretched witticisms; in the stress of the struggle to live, patient study and straining after a great ideal become impossible. Individualism will only develop fully when Socialism has lifted off all shoulders the heavy burden of care, and has given to all leisure to think and to endeavor.

Nor is the fear of undue restriction of liberty better founded than that of the crushing out of individualism. One kind of liberty, indeed, will be restricted—the liberty to oppress and to enslave other people. But with this exception liberty will be increased. Only the very wealthy are now free. The great majority of people must work, and their choice of work is very limited. The poor must take what work they can get, and their complaint is not that they are compelled to work, but that they often cannot get work to do. In satisfying the complex wants of the civilised human being there is room for all the most diverse capacities of work; and if it be said that there are unpleasant kinds of work that must be done, which none would willingly undertake, it may be answered that those kinds of work have to be done now, and that the compulsion of the community would not be a greater restriction of personal liberty than the present compulsion of hunger; and further, that it would be easy to make a short period of unpleasant toil balance a long period of pleasant; and that it would be far better to have such tasks divided among a number, so that they would press very lightly upon each, than have them, as now, pushed on to a comparatively few, whose whole lives are brutalised by the pressure. The very strictest organisation of labor by the community that can be imagined, would be to the great majority far less oppressive than the present system, for at the worst, it would but control an extremely small portion of each working day, and would leave the whole of the rest of the existence free, to be used at the pleasure of the individual, untrammelled by anxiety and harassing care for the mere necessaries of life. The pride in skill, the stimulus of honorable ambition, the pleasure of success, all these would be present, as they are to-day; but instead of being the privilege of the few, they would brighten the life of all.

A profound moral impulse really underlies the whole of the Socialist movement. It is a revolt against the callous indifference of the majority in the "comfortable classes" to the woful condition of large numbers of the workers. It is an outburst of unselfish brotherhood, which cannot bear to sit at ease while others suffer, which claims to share the common human lot, and to bear part of the burden now pressing with crushing weight on the shoulders of the poor. It detests the theory that there must always be hewers of wood and drawers of water for a luxurious class, and proclaims that human degradation lies in idle living, not in earnest work. It would have all work, that all may have leisure, and would so distribute the necessary work of the world that none may be crushed by it, but that all may be disciplined. And this very outburst of human brotherhood is in itself a proof that society is evolving Socialismwards, and that the evolution of humanity is reaching a stage in which sympathy is triumphing over selfishness, and the desire for equality of happiness is becoming a potent factor in human conduct. The Socialist ideal is one which could not meet with wide acceptance if humanity were not marching towards its realisation.

On one matter the Socialist movement, both abroad and at home, has set itself in opposition to science and to right reason—*e.g.*, on the law of population. It is easy to see how this opposition has arisen, and it may be hoped that when Socialists in general disentangle the scientific statement of facts from Malthus' unwise applications of them, Socialism and prudential restraint will be seen to be indissolubly united. Malthus accurately pointed out that population has a tendency to increase beyond the means of subsistence; that as it presses on the available means, suffering is caused; and that it is kept within them by what he termed "positive checks"—*i.e*, a high death-rate, especially among the children of the poor, premature death from disease, underfeeding, etc. The accuracy of his statement has been proved up to the hilt by Charles Darwin, who describes with abundant illustrations the struggle for existence—a struggle which is the direct result of the fact stated in the law of population, of the tendency of all animated things to increase beyond their food supply; this has led, and still leads, to the survival of those who are fittest for the conditions of the struggle. Unhappily, Malthus added to his scientific exposition some most unfortunate practical advice; he advised the poor not to marry until, practically, they had reached middle life. The poor felt, with natural indignation, that in addition to all their other deprivations they were summoned by Malthus to give up the chief of the few pleasures left to them, to surrender marriage, to live in joyless celibacy through the passion-season of life, to crush out all the impulses of love until by long repression these would be practically destroyed. Under such circumstances it is little wonder that "Malthusianism" became a word hated by the poor and denounced by those who sympathised with them. It is true that the advice of Malthus as to the putting off of marriage has been and is very widely followed by the middle classes; but it is perfectly well known that the putting off of marriage does not with them mean the observance of celibacy, and the shocking prostitution which is the curse of every Christian city is the result of the following of the advice of Malthus so far as marriage is concerned. It is obvious that Malthus ignored the strength of the sexual instinct, and that the only possible result of the wide acceptance of his teaching would be the increase of prostitution, an evil more terrible than that of poverty. But the objection rightly raised to the practical teaching of Malthus ought not to take the form of assailing the perfectly impregnable law of population, nor is it valid against the teachings of Neo-Malthusians, who advise early marriage and limitation of the family within the means of existence.

The acceptance of this doctrine is absolutely essential to the success of Socialism. Under a system in which children are forced to labor, they may begin to "keep themselves" at a very early age; but under a Socialist system, where education will occupy childhood and youth, and where old age is to be free from toil, it will soon be found that the adult working members will not permit an unlimited increase of the mouths which they have to fill. Facilitate production as we may, it will always take more hours to produce the necessaries of life for families of ten or twelve than for families of three or four. The practical enforcement of the question will probably come from the women; highly educated women, full of interest in public work and taking their share in public duty, will not consent to spend year after year of their prime in nothing but expecting babies, bearing babies, and suckling babies. They will rebel against the constant infliction of physical discomfort and pain, and will insist on the limitation of the family as a condition of marriage. The sooner this is recognised by Socialists the better, for at present they waste much strength by attacking a doctrine which they must sooner or later accept.

A glance backward over the history of our own country, since the Reform Bill of 1832 opened the gate of political power to those outside the sacred circle of the aristocracy, will tell how an unconscious movement towards Socialism has been steadily growing in strength. Our Factory Acts, our Mines Regulation Acts, our Education Acts, our Employers' Liability Acts, our Land Acts—all show the set of the current. The idea of the State as an outside power is fading, and the idea of the State as an organised community is coming into prominence. In the womb of time the new organism is growing: shall the new birth come in peace or in revolution, heralded by patient endeavor or by roar of cannon? Who can tell? But this one thing I know, that come it will, whether men work for it or hinder; for all the mighty, silent forces of evolution make for Socialism, for the establishment of the Brotherhood of Man.

RADICALISM AND SOCIALISM.

BY

ANNIE BESANT.

[Reprinted from "Our Corner".]

LONDON:
FREETHOUGHT PUBLISHING COMPANY,
63, FLEET STREET, E.C.
1887.

PRICE THREEPENCE.

LONDON
PRINTED BY CHARLES BRADLAUGH AND ANNIE BESANT,
63, FLEET STREET, E.C.

RADICALISM AND SOCIALISM.

AMONG the various features of public life in England at the present time there is none which appears to me to be more regrettable, or more fruitful of evil consequences in the near future, than the antagonism between Radicalism and Socialism—or rather between Radicals and Socialists—which is so strongly marked on the platform and in the press. As a Socialist, it is with much regret that I am forced to acknowledge that the first provocation came from the Socialist side, and that it was the uncalled-for and unscrupulous abuse poured out on Radical leaders and workers which stirred up the anger of the Radicals, and caused reprisals as bitter as the attacks. The taunts and sneers levelled at working men's Radical organisations; the description of some of their most active and trusted officials as "fifth-rate political hacks"; the insolent contempt expressed by bran-new "leaders" for men who had been toiling for the popular cause for more years of service than they could themselves count months; all these things alienated the more self-reliant and thoughtful of the workers, and made them look with coldness, deeply tinged with dislike, on any idea which was presented to them under the guise of Socialism. The whole mischief has been done by a very small and very narrow-minded clique, the members of which have nothing but abuse for everyone who does not meekly follow in their wake, and who appear to be moved by a furious jealousy against everyone, Socialist or non-Socialist, who is able to serve the cause of the workers, and is regarded by them with trust and with love. It is time that it should be clearly seen that these few Socialists who are constantly attacking Radicals speak only for themselves, and not for English Socialists in general, but that, on the contrary, most of the latter desire earnestly to work with their Radical brethren for all objects which both parties regard as desirable; and that while they hold up steadily as their object the complete Socialisation of the State, they will gladly welcome the companionship of the Radicals over that portion of the road which the Radicals are ready to travel. No worse mischief can be done to the cause of labor, no more serious harm can be done to progress, than by setting Radicals and Socialists in antagonism, instead of binding them together; than by putting in opposite camps those who ought to be banded against the common foe; than by using wild and bitter words to drive apart those whose earnest desire is for the common good, and so, by dividing the army of progress, to render it easier for the privileged classes to defend their citadel of idleness and monopoly. The position that I desire to advance is that Socialism is the outcome, the legitimate and necessary outcome, of Radicalism; that the main current of Radical legislation, despite little eddies and backwaters, sets towards Socialism; and that just as Evolution, taking up the chaos of biological facts, set them forth as an intelligible and correlated order, so Socialism, dealing with the chaos of sociological facts, brings a unifying principle, which turns Radicalism from a mere empirical system into a reasoned, coherent, and scientific whole. Socialism is a far vaster thing than a changed system for the production and distribution of wealth, great as that economical change would be; it means the substitution, as method, of co-operation for competition in every department of human life; it means the substitution, as aim, of the common good for the personal profit of the individual; it means the placing of the production and distribution of wealth, as well as of all public affairs in which men and women are associated, under the control of bodies elected by and responsible to those who are concerned in them, whether as workers or as citizens, instead of leaving them, as so many of them now are, under individual authority.

Now it is impossible to realise what Socialism means, and to study the history of our own times with intelligence and insight, without recognising the vast revolution which has been going on during the present century, and without seeing that the changes which are being wrought are on the road of which Socialism is the natural and inevitable end. Radical legislation in removing privilege, in placing public affairs in the hands of the populace, in assailing landlord monopoly, in regulating the relations between employer and employed, is penetrated by the Socialist spirit, and has already leavened the community with Socialist ideas. At the beginning of the century there was little Socialism in our legislation; there was no interference on the part of the State between employers and employed, save in the way of tying down the employed and of preventing them from associating together for their common good. Of restrictions on the workers for the benefit of the exploiting classes there had been enough and to spare; but of legislation to equalise conditions, to check the strong in his oppression of the weak, to utilise the powers arising from the social union for the common benefit, of this there had been nothing. All that the commercial classes asked for was to be left alone by the State; they were willing to destroy laws which favored the landlord interest—as the Corn Laws—but they demanded for themselves merely a free hand; strong in their position of advantage, holding in their hands the means of subsistence of the population which seethed below them, they only required to be left "free" in order to gain their ends; free, that was, to use starvation as a whip with which to coerce the workers if they turned restive under their burdens, to buy them in the labor-market as "hands" to drive their machines, to pile up the riches made by the toiling myriads, flinging back to them as "wage" a fraction of the wealth they created. There were then no laws to regulate the conditions of labor; any man, who had the power to do so, might build up a fortune by the overwork of men, women, and children. At that time the democracy had no share in the Government; the workers were voiceless in the great Council of England, and were therefore wholly at the mercy of their employers. It was not until the degradation of the working population, the absolute physical ruin of hundreds and of thousands of the people, had become so patent that it could no longer be denied, that the State stepped in between the employer and the children he was murdering by over-work, and limited the hours during which, and the conditions under which, the children should be permitted to labor. Since that first interference with so-called "freedom of contract" there have been many others, some of which touched the "Rights of Property"; such as the Factory Acts which limited the hours of labor, and insisted on proper sanitary conditions, the Shipping, Irish Land, Agricultural Holdings, Employer's Liability, and Education Acts—all cases in which the State interfered with individual "rights" for the sake of effecting the common good. Thick-and-thin opponents of Socialism have been quick to notice this Socialist tendency of legislation, since the working classes have been able to influence Parliament. The Liberty and Property Defence League remarks that "every fresh curtailment of individual liberty, or substitution of collective for individual action in the assumed interest of the community, is a step in the direction of State Socialism", and it issues from time to time a list of the proposed measures which tend in this direction. Lord Pembroke complains that "Land Acts, Shipping Acts, Education Acts, Factory and Workshops Acts, Water Company Acts, and all the rest of them", are regarded "as exceptions that are justified by the circumstances of the particular case" by people who are not Socialists, whereas "each one that is added to the list weakens popular belief in the principles of freedom, and inclines it towards those of Socialism". Lord Wemyss, in a speech delivered in the House of Lords on July 31st, 1885, enumerated seven Acts and eight Bills between 1870 and 1885 that assumed "the right of the State to regulate the management of or to confiscate real property—steps in the direction of substituting 'land nationalisation' for individual ownership"; there were four Bills affecting corporate bodies in 1885, two of which dealt with Water Companies, and were "attempts to subject the chartered rights of private enterprise in water supply to municipal monopolies, by first reducing the value of the companies' property by harassing legislation"; then nine Acts affecting ships, and six affecting mines, which regulated "private enterprise and individual management"; nine Acts and three Bills regulating manufactures and trades, and six Railway Acts, "encroachments by the Board of Trade upon the self-government of private enterprise in railways". Passing over twenty Acts and six Bills about the Liquor Traffic, we come to sixteen Acts and three Bills which "embody the principle that it is the duty of the State to provide dwellings, private gardens, and other conveniences for the working classes, and assume its right to appropriate land for these purposes". Then thirteen Acts and four Bills on Education and Recreation, many of which "provide those things that ought to be left to the instincts and affections of the parents". "While on the Continent", said Lord Wemyss, "people are thinking and vaporing about Socialism, we in this country are adopting it in our legislation. Louise Michel, the French Communist, epitomised the matter very effectively when she said 'that whereas in France Socialists stand in the dock, in England they sit in the House of Commons'." Herbert Spencer in his "Man *versus* the State" summarises the legislation of the last twenty-five years, in order to show the increase of State interference which has taken place "during periods of Liberal ascendancy". Despite its length, I quote it here, so important is the testimony borne in it to the soundness of my position:

"To bring the illustrations within compass, let us commence with 1860, under the second administration of Lord Palmerston. In that year the restrictions of the Factories Act were extended to bleaching and dyeing works; authority was given to provide analysts of food and drink, to be paid out of local rates; there was an Act providing for inspection of gasworks, as well as for fixing quality of gas and limiting price; there was the Act which, in addition to further mine inspection, made it penal to employ boys under twelve not attending school, and unable to read and write. In 1861 occurred an extension of the compulsory provisions of the Factories Act to lace-works; power was given to poor-law guardians, etc., to enforce vaccination; local boards were authorised to fix rates of hire—horses, ponies, mules, asses, and boats—and certain locally-formed bodies had given to them powers of taxing the locality for rural drainage and irrigation works, and for supplying water to cattle. In 1862 an Act was passed for restricting the employment of women and children in open-air bleaching; and an Act for making illegal a coal-mine with a single shaft, or with shafts separated by less than a specified space, as well as an Act giving the Council of Medical Education the exclusive right to publish a Pharmacopœia, the price of which is to be fixed by the Treasury. In 1863 came the extension of compulsory vaccination to Scotland, and also to Ireland; there came the empowering of certain boards to borrow money repayable from the local rates, to employ and pay those out of work; there came the authorising of town authorities to take possession of neglected ornamental spaces, and rate the inhabitants for their support; there came the Bakehouses Regulation Act, which, besides specifying minimum age of employees occupied between certain hours, prescribed periodical lime-washing, three coats of paint when painted, and cleaning with hot water and soap at least once in six months; and there came also an Act giving a magistrate authority to decide on the wholesomeness or unwholesomeness of food brought before him by an inspector. Of compulsory legislation dating from 1864, may be named an extension of the Factories Act to various additional trades, including regulations for cleansing and ventilation, and specifying of certain employees in match-works, that they might not take meals on the premises, except in the wood-cutting places. Also, there were passed a Chimney-Sweepers Act; an Act for further regulating the sale of beer in Ireland; an Act for compulsory testing of cables and anchors; an Act extending the Public Works Act of 1863, and the Contagious Diseases Act, which last gave the police, in specified places, powers which, in respect of certain classes of women, abolished sundry of those safeguards to individual freedom established in past times. The year 1865 witnessed further provision for the reception and temporary relief of wanderers at the cost of ratepayers; another public-house closing Act; and an Act making compulsory regulations for extinguishing fires in London. Then, under the ministry of Lord John Russell in 1866, have to be named an Act to regulate cattle-sheds, etc., in Scotland, giving local authorities powers to inspect sanitary conditions, and fix the numbers of cattle; an Act forcing hop-growers to label their bags with the year and place of growth, and the true weight, and giving police powers of search; an Act to facilitate the building of lodging-houses in Ireland, and providing for regulation of the inmates; a Public Health Act, under which there is registration of lodging-houses and limitation of occupants, with inspection and directions for lime-washing, etc., and a Public Libraries Act, giving local powers by which a majority can tax a minority for their books.

"Passing now to the legislation under the first ministry of Mr. Gladstone, we have, in 1869, the establishment of State telegraphy with the accompanying interdict on telegraphing through any other agency; we have the empowering a Secretary of State to regulate hired conveyances in London; we have further and more stringent regulations to prevent cattle diseases from spreading, another Beer-house Regulation Act, and a Sea Birds Preservation Act (ensuring greater mortality of fish). In 1870 we had a law authorising the Board of Public Works to make advances for landlords' improvements and for purchase by tenants; we have the Act, which enables the Education

Department to form school boards which shall purchase sites for schools, and may provide free schools supported by local rates, and enabling school-boards to pay a child's fees; to compel parents to send their children, etc., etc.; we have a further Factories and Workshops Act, making, among other restrictions, some on the employment of women and children in fruit-preserving and fish-curing works. In 1871 we meet with an amended Merchant Shipping Act, directing officers of the Board of Trade to record the draught of sea-going vessels leaving port; there is another Factory and Workshops Act, making further restrictions; there is a Pedlar's Act, inflicting penalties for hawking without a certificate, and limiting the district within which the certificate holds, as well as giving the police power to search pedlars' packs; and there are further measures for enforcing vaccination. The year 1872 had, among other Acts, one which makes it illegal to take for hire more than one child to nurse, unless in a house registered by the authorities, who prescribe the number of infants to be received; it had a Licensing Act, interdicting sale of spirits to those apparently under sixteen; and it had another Merchant Shipping Act, establishing an annual survey of passenger steamers. Then, in 1873, was passed by the Agricultural Children's Act, which makes it penal for a farmer to employ a child who has neither certificate of elementary education nor of certain prescribed school-attendances, and there was passed a Merchant Shipping Act, requiring on each vessel a scale showing draught, and giving the Board of Trade power to fix the numbers of boats and life-saving appliances to be carried out.

"Turn now to Liberal law-making under the present Ministry. We have, in 1880, a law which forbids conditional advance-notes in payment of sailors' wages; also a law which dictates certain arrangements for the safe carriage of grain cargoes; also a law increasing local coercion over parents to send their children to school. In 1881 comes legislation to prevent trawling over clam-beds and bait-beds, and an interdict making it impossible to buy a glass of beer on Sunday in Wales. In 1882 the Board of Trade was authorised to grant licenses to generate and sell electricity; and municipal bodies were enabled to levy rates for electric-lighting; further, exactions from ratepayers were authorised for facilitating more accessible baths and washhouses, and local authorities were empowered to make bye-laws for securing the decent lodging of persons engaged in picking fruit and vegetables. Of such legislation during 1883 may be named the Cheap Trains Act, which, partly by taxing the nation to the extent of £100,000 a year (in the shape of relinquished passenger duty), and partly at the cost of railway proprietors, still further cheapens travelling for workmen; the Board of Trade, through the Railway Commissioners, being empowered to ensure sufficiently good and frequent accommodation. Again, there is the Act which, under penalty of £10 for disobedience, forbids the payment of wages to workmen at or within public-houses; there is another Factory and Workshop Act, commanding inspection of white-lead works (to see that they are provided with overalls, respirators, baths, acidulated drinks, etc.) and of bakehouses, regulating times of employment of both, and prescribing in detail some constructions for the last, which are to be kept in a condition satisfactory to the inspectors" (pp. 9–12).

After carefully following out the results of this policy, Herbert Spencer asks whither these changes "with the accompanying current of ideas" are carrying us, and he finally answers: "Thus influences of various kinds conspire to increase corporate action and decrease individual action. And the change is being on all sides aided by schemers, each of whom thinks only of his pet project, and not at all of the general reorganisation which his, joined with others such, are working out. It is said that the French Revolution devoured its own children. Here an analogous catastrophe seems not unlikely. The numerous Socialistic changes made by Act of Parliament, joined with the numerous others presently to be made, will by-and-bye be merged in State Socialism—swallowed in the vast wave which they have little by little raised" (pp. 26, 33, 34).

Now in all these separate steps towards Socialism, Radicals have advocated the particular measure on the ground of its individual usefulness, but they have not grasped the underlying tendency of the whole body of allied changes. The main difference between Radicals and Socialists in dealing with these practical questions is that Radicals take the steps towards Socialism without recognising whither they are going; while the Socialists see the goal as well as the steps, and recognise the general tendency of legislation as well as the separate Acts of Parliament. They have risen from empiricism to science. But in this difference lies no reason for quarrel, no cause for antagonism. There is, however, a cause of disagreement that might well arise between Radicals and Socialists as politicians, due to the fact that Socialists scrutinise the tendency of legislation as well as its immediate results. For instance peasant proprietorship, as distinguished from peasant tenancy, of land has many advocates among Radicals; to any legislation in this direction Socialists would offer an uncompromising resistance, as being retrograde in tendency, and as increasing the difficulty of bringing all land under the control of the community. But such disagreement on an isolated measure would not prevent full and cordial co-operation in matters on which both parties were agreed. And in order to dispose Radicals to such co-operation I point them to the legislation of our own generation, and I challenge them to disprove the assertion that this body of legislation tends to substitute collective control for individual independence, to limit private rights of property, to interfere in the name of the community between employer and employed, between parent and child, and to take over important branches of national enterprise into the hands of the State.

It is not only in legislation that the spirit of Socialism is making itself felt, but we see it again in the growing inclination of municipalities to extend the sphere of their activity, and to undertake the supply of important necessaries of life over the district they are elected to administer. The substitution of Socialism for individualism in matters affecting the citizens of any locality, is the substitution of the action of an elected body for private enterprise in supplying the wants of the community, and the consequent regarding of all excess of receipts over expenditure as being funds belonging to the community, and not to the individuals who have superintended the business out of which they may have arisen. I may take as a convenient illustration of the change from individualism to Socialism in the supply of one necessary of life, the methods in which a community may obtain its water. Each might buy as much water as he wanted from a private trader at a charge fixed by competition; or he might sink a well in his own back garden, and if he were very energetic and enterprising he might sink it deeper than the wells of his neighbors, and so obtain more water than he wanted for his own use, while their wells ran dry; in either of these cases, the water-supply of the town would be left to individual enterprise. Another individualistic method would consist in a body of men voluntarily associating themselves into a company for the supply of water; such a company would obtain an Act of Parliament giving it certain rights and privileges, and would levy a water-rate on the inhabitants of the district it supplied; the profits made would be pocketed by the company, and divided among the shareholders. But the water supply might be undertaken by the municipality elected by the community; the rate would then be fixed at a figure estimated to cover the cost, and if any profit should arise the profit would go into the town exchequer, and would be used for the benefit of the community. This would be Socialism, applied to the supply of water. Some few towns have already taken this step, and have found as result that the water-supply is better and cheaper when controlled by the municipality than when managed for the individuals. The supply of gas, again, is being undertaken by municipalities with very satisfactory results. In some cases gas is supplied at a cheaper rate than when it was in the hands of a private company, and at the same time there has been an excess of receipts over expenditure which has gone to the lessening of the rates. So blind are many to the real character of the changes taking place before their eyes, that while they would denounce the supply of milk or bread by the municipality as sheer Socialism, they regard with approval the supply by it of gas and water. Really each such step, placing the distribution of a necessary of life in the hands of an elected body, which trades in it for the advantage of a community electing it, is a step towards Socialism, and this growth of municipal Socialism, fostered and encouraged by the Radicals, shows how far unconscious Socialism has spread. It has already been proposed that the liquor trade shall be undertaken by the municipality, and Mr. Chamberlain has been a warm advocate of this (the Gothenburg) scheme. It is not so very far from this to the establishment of municipal stores, stores that would soon become popular from the purity of their goods and the lowness of their prices.

Now this growth of municipal Socialism, visible on all hands, cannot continue without a corresponding growth over a wider area, the area of the State. Already in the Post Office there is the beginning of the Socialism of the State; here the State has taken upon itself the functions of collecting and distributing the letters of the whole community; similarly it has taken in hand the business of telegraphing, and is taking that of conveying parcels; the superior certainty and celerity of the State carriage of parcels are being widely recognised, and the business is rapidly growing. Who now hesitates, if he wants to send a small parcel from London to Dundee, between the means of conveyance directed by the State, and those controlled by "private enterprise"? Nor is it, as has been suggested, any argument against the Socialist character of the Post Office that the charge made varies with the weight carried; Socialism estimates the value of a thing by the amount of human labor required to produce it, and those who require the expenditure of more human labor for their service must in exchange give more of their own labor, that is, of the results thereof. Socialism implies the equal exchange of equal amounts of labor, and only forbids that a third party who adds nothing should make a profit out of the exchange. It does not mean the distribution of everything in equal proportions, without any regard to what each one does. Nor is it necessary to Socialism that all the details of a business concern with many branches should be arranged from a single State centre. The Post Office, which is a State institution, is not governed in its minute details from St. Martin's-le-Grand. From the centre come certain laws and regulations which all must observe; but it is not the State which chooses the country postmen; it is not the State which controls the minutiæ of the work of the individual letter-carrier. He takes his order from the postmaster of his district, and not from the Postmaster-General. And so, in all kinds of business, under Socialism, there will be group after group, co-ordinate with each other, each being related to the wider group next above it; and the individual laborer would come into contact with his own group, not with the central executive. But we can see in the Post Office organisation the enormous gain of a central unifying power. When a great political speech is to be delivered, to telegraph which over the country would utterly overtax a local staff, then the central body steps in to supply the sudden demand, and affords the help necessary for the due discharge of the public service. While industry is under individual control, we have industrial anarchy; in one place there are too many workers, in another too few, and equilibrium is only attained after much friction and much suffering, to be again overthrown by the next fluctuation. But with a central regulative body, supply may be made to meet demand, and what is now done by the Post Office in a single branch would be done in all departments of industry. Then labor would be organised without waste and without excess, and while laborers would be as free as Post Office clerks are now, all profits made would come back to the nation as a whole; so that instead of individualistic gain there would be corporate good and corporate advantage everywhere. Radicals recognise the utility of the State collection and distribution of one kind of article—letters. Is there any difference *in principle* between the State collecting the letters of a district and collecting the goods manufactured in it? between distributing the letters and distributing the goods? In the latter case it would not need to do as much as it does with the letters; it delivers them at individual houses; it would only need to deliver the goods at district stores. Under such conditions, there would be no more fruit rotting in Yorkshire because its sale would not pay the cost of carriage, while high prices were being paid for similar fruit in London; no more exorbitant railway charges and middleman's profits eating up the whole price paid by the consumer.

Radicals, again, are to a great extent in favor of placing all the means of communication under State control. Many Radicals demand that all tramcars, omnibuses, and hackney carriages plying in a town shall be transferred to the municipality of the town, and that the railways shall be acquired by the State. Here once more Radicals desire that representative bodies shall acquire property and administer it for the general advantage; that any gains accruing shall go into the general exchequer; that public good, not private gain, shall be sought. But every step which substitutes agents of the community for men working for individual gain is a step towards Socialism; and when Radicals have taken all the steps the Socialist State will exist.

If we pass from these general questions of administration to the economic question of the production and distribution of wealth, we shall find that many Radicals go half-way to Socialism. And here let me point out that my friend Mr. Bradlaugh is attacking a very crude presentment of Socialism when he defines it as "the theory and the scheme which denies all individual property, which denounces individual effort for individual gain, and affirms that society organised as the State should own all wealth, protect all labor, and compel the equal distribution of all produce. A Socialistic State would be a State in which everything would be held in common, in which the labor of each individual would be protected and controlled by the State, to which would belong all results of such labor." Socialism does not deny "all individual property"; it would leave a man in full possession of his share of the value he and his fellow-laborers had produced. It denounces "individual effort for individual gain" when the individual utilises other people's efforts for his individual gain; and it points out that when many co-operate to produce no one man should claim the common product as his. It does not affirm that the State should "own all wealth", but that it should own the raw material and the means of production. It does affirm that the State should protect all labor, and it affirms further that the present State performs that primary function extremely badly. It does not affirm that the State should compel the equal distribution of all produce, nor of any produce, but seeks to secure to the worker the value he creates, leaves him free to exchange the results of his labor as he will. Nor does the Socialist ask that "everything should be held in common", but that those things only shall be held in common the possession of which by individuals enables them to enslave their fellows, and to force others to work for their advantage. To say that Socialists desire to destroy all property because they would vest the ownership of land and capital in the community, is as misleading as it would be to say that Radicals desire to destroy all order because they say that legislative power should be vested in the representatives of the people and not in an autocratic sovereign. Take the numerous suggestions put forward by representative Socialists, such as Bebel, that men should be paid for their work by labor-notes, or by some symbol of exchange, representing the labor given by the individual. Those labor-notes would represent so much time given to labor. The recipient would own these notes; he might save them, spend them, waste them; one thing only he would not be able to do with them—force men to sell themselves to him and annex their labor for his own profit.

I have already pointed out that we do not propose that the labor of every individual citizen should be directed by a central body; but even were it true that such were our proposal, I fail to see that the liberty of the worker would be narrower then than it is now. Why would it be worse to have one's labor controlled by the State than to have it controlled by the individual employer? A workman does not control his labor now; he must sell it for what he can get for it. His labor is controlled by the individual manufacturer, who controls it for his own advantage; whereas the State would control it for the corporate advantage in which the worker would share. But it is, of course, not practicable that the State, as a whole, should direct and control the labor of each individual. For what is the State? It is the people, organised as a community. As a whole, the State could not control the labor of each citizen; but when the people are organised in groups of workers, each group can very well control its own labor, and elect its own superintendents, as well as elect such representatives as might be necessary to constitute boards of management to keep group in touch with group. The Trades Unions have in them the germs of the necessary organisation. If every miner were in the Miners' Union, then that union, with its branches in every coal district, would be the body which would immediately control the production of coal in a Socialist State. Can Radicals, who have fostered Trades Unions and urged the workers to combine, oppose a development of them? Can they, who have so preached self-reliance and self-government, maintain that men must always work for masters, and that they are not competent to control their own labor and to regulate their own production?

Again, the Socialist declaration that private property in land should be abolished is endorsed by the majority of Radicals in principle, however much some may falter in carrying it into practice. The evils that result to the community from the soil on which it lives being owned by a class are patent even to careless observation. We see the increase of a town population drive up rents, and the owners of the soil growing wealthier and wealthier without any exertion of theirs contributing to their swelling revenues. They are able to levy a cumulative tax on industry, and to grow fat in idleness while others grow lean in toil. And if we seek the reason why some should be placed in a position of such huge advantage, we often find that it is because they are at the end of a long line, at the beginning of which stands a man who got the land by force or fraud. And seeking further, we find that the laws protecting the monopoly are laws which were made by the people who profited by it, so that the laws by which landlords hold the land are laws made by landlords. It is as though a minority of thieves, getting the upper hand, made laws legalising robbery; and it is time that the people, now that legislative power is theirs, should repeal the laws which legalise wrong, and should assume the collective ownership of the soil. The State should be the only landowner.

It does not, however, follow from State ownership that the whole land of a country should be controlled from its metropolis. It would be better that municipalities should hold the land in towns, and local boards in agricultural districts, than that the State for landholding purposes should be concentrated too much, centralised too severely. If a municipality held the land on which a town was built, all rents would go into the municipal exchequer, and they would be used for the benefit of the town instead of for the enrichment of an idle landlord. Now, a good many Radicals are at one with Socialists on this point, and in what position is the Radical who is in favor of the State being the only landlord? He is a long way on the road to Socialism, half-way towards it at least, since Socialism demands the abolition of private property in land *and capital.* If the Radical already goes so far as to desire the abolition of private property in land, it is not wonderful that Socialists should look forward to his taking the other step, the abolition of private property in capital.

For the reasons which lead the Socialists to desire the abolition of private property in capital are cogent, and are such as must appeal to the unpropertied classes of the community. A man who does not inherit land or capital can only live by the sale of his labor, and he must sell his labor for what it will fetch. The price he can get for it depends on population—the number competing for work—and on the cost of living. If a man can earn a bare subsistence by the sale of his labor, he will sell it. Competition among employers may drive up the rate of wages for a while, for the profit made out of men's labor may be so great that it becomes worth while to "throw away a herring to catch a whale". But wage ever tends to fall to the cost of living, and will continue to do so as long as there are employers and employed. The amount of a man's wage is not fixed by the value he produces by his labor; the same value may be produced by each of two workers, and the wage paid may differ considerably. The boot and shoe trade in Northamptonshire offers an apt illustration of this bearing of the cost of living on wage. It is complained in the town of Northampton that much of the boot-and-shoe-making for which the district is famous is now being carried on in the villages round, because the goods can be produced there more cheaply than in the town. Now it is clear that the goods produced in the villages are as valuable as those produced in the town: the same amount of labor is put into them, and the same price obtained for them. If the value of men's work influenced their wage, the country workers would receive a wage equal to that paid in the town. But the wage varies with the cost of living. Rent is lower in the country, and living is cheaper, so a man will take less money for his labor, the wage duly sinking to subsistence level. And much above that level it can never permanently rise.

Going a step further, we can see that the production by the laborer of a much greater value than he receives as wage is the condition of his employment. The employer does not hire a man for his amusement; he hires him that he may make something out of him. The employers are often spoken of as the benefactors of labor, but this view is a decidedly topsy-turvey one. Is it not the laborer who benefits the employer, rather than the employer the laborer? The laborer works hard all his life for wage, and deems himself lucky if he saves enough to keep himself out of the workhouse in his old age and to bury him decently. The employer builds his grand house, and his stables, and his hothouses, and leaves a fortune made in trade to his heirs. On which side is the benefit? Which is the benefactor? Is it not labor which benefits the employer? labor which makes bare subsistence for itself and heaps up wealth for another. If one man is to make a profit, another man must make a loss. Wealth is only made by hard human labor, and the profit made by the employer is the measure of the loss suffered by the workmen. Granted that wages may be forced up a little by combination, yet so long as a profit is made out of the worker so long will he have less than he ought to have. It is said that employers work, and in so far as the employer contributes to the value of the product just so far has he also a right to share in the total value produced. Working employers have a right to remuneration, but the remuneration should be based on the value they add to the product, and should not consist of profit made by annexing part of the value made by others. As a matter of fact, a large number of the owners of capital do not work at all: they invest their capital, or have it invested for them, and they live on the interest they draw from it—mere idlers existing on the work of others. As long as one class can prey upon another, so long will it prey; and the propertied classes will live on the unpropertied for just so long as the latter will submit to the burden. Capital is made by labor, by associated labor, and can only exist where men co-operate for a common end; surely it is not unreasonable to demand that that which is produced by common labor shall be under common control. No individual should have the right to monopolise the result of associated labor for his own personal advantage, for his own personal gain. Under the system proposed by Socialism, in which the means of production would be under common control—that is, in which each trade would own for use the machinery needed in the trade—under that system only can be stopped the constant war between capital and labor, for under it co-operating, self-ruling workers would be substituted for masters and men.

I have already suggested that under Socialism each trade would form a Trade Union, each such Union controlling its own industry. These Unions will need to be kept in touch with each other by a central Industrial Board, to which each will elect a representative. A step has been taken towards making such a Board possible by the establishment, on Charles Bradlaugh's initiative, of a Labor Bureau, which will collate the statistics relating to the various trades, and will so render possible a regulation of industry where at present we have blind and aimless competition.

It is said that any regulation of industry means slavery; that the State will say to a man, go and do so and so. Not so. There is no reason why, under Socialism, a man should not be as free to choose his work as he is now. If there were too many in one particular trade then, as now, some would have to choose another. There might be a rush to one industry, and some would have to take other work; but the advantage would lie in the central Board, able to say where labor was wanted, so doing away with the heart-breaking tramp after work which is the lot of so many to-day.

Socialism is no wild scheme, no Utopia impossible of realisation. It is a carefully-reasoned scheme of production, distribution, and administration, which it is contended is better than the monopoly system of to-day. It would put an end to the war of classes, for it would substitute a community of workers for the present gradations of social rank. It would bid all healthy adults work, but it would also give to each leisure to enjoy. And since of all the political parties it is the Radicals only who claim liberty and equality for all, who admit no hereditary rights, who demand from all discharge of social duty, who base society on justice, not on privilege, who look to reason as guide, and not to authority, therefore it is to them that the Socialists must naturally turn for alliance, seeking to march with them against the common foe.

Socialism:

FOR AND AGAINST.

BY

CHARLES BRADLAUGH AND ANNIE BESANT.

LONDON

FREETHOUGHT PUBLISHING COMPANY,

63, FLEET STREET, E.C.

1887.

PRICE FOURPENCE.

LONDON:
PRINTED BY ANNIE BESANT AND CHARLES BRADLAUGH,
63, FLEET STREET, E.C.

SOCIALISM: FOR AND AGAINST.

SOCIALISM: ITS FALLACIES AND DANGERS.

My greatest difficulty in treating this subject is in discovering any general agreement as to what is now meant in England by the word "Socialism". There are so many grades and shades of diverse opinion loosely included in, and attacked, or defended, as Socialism, that—in default of any authoritative, or official, or even generally accepted definition—I will at any rate make clear what it is that I attack as Socialism, and will endeavor at least to show that even if I am in error, I have been misled by Socialist writers, and have not invented the definition, or arbitrarily framed a formula, or built up a man of straw, for the mere purpose of attack. I understand and define Socialism as (1) denying, or destroying, all individual private property; and (2) as affirming that Society organised as the State should own all wealth, direct all labor, and compel the equal distribution of all produce. I understand a Socialistic State to be (3) that State in which everything would be common as to its user, and in which all labor would be controlled by the State, which from the common stock would maintain the laborer, and would take all the produce of the labor. That is (4), I identify Socialism with Communism.

This was substantially the definition of Socialism put forward by me in the debate with Mr. Hyndman[1] (pp. 14, 15), and as I then reminded him (p. 37) my definition was

[1] "Will Socialism Benefit the English People?"

never denied, and though language sometimes inconsistent with it was used, no other definition was put in its place. The point that Socialism "denies all individual private property" was referred to in that debate by Mr. Hyndman (p. 23), but so far from repudiating the doctrine, he justified it as to the moneys in savings banks and "paltry building allotments" (p. 24). Mr. J. L. Joynes clearly includes in his view of Socialism the cancelment of all private interest in the National Debt, for, having calculated the average share therein of the 2,309,225 members of Friendly Societies, at 2s. per head, he justifies the confiscation of this private property on the ground that "It does not require a very high standard of intelligence to enable a man to perceive that Socialists, who intend to deprive him of these 2s., and at the same time to secure to him the full value of his work, are proposing, not to diminish his income, but, on the contrary, to raise it in a very high degree" (*Our Corner*, 1884, vol. iii., p. 335). Believing Mr. Joynes to be an earnest, truthful man, it is difficult to quite understand how he confined himself to this illustration of confiscation out of the many similar ones presented to his notice, and which I propose to carefully re-state in the course of this paper. Messrs. William Morris and E. Belfort Bax say: "The land, the capital, the machinery, factories, workshops, stores, means of transit, mines, banking, all means of production and distribution of wealth, must be declared and treated as the common property of all" ("Manifesto of the Socialist League", p. 6); and that there may be no misapprehension as to what this means Mr. Bax writes: "That for which the working classes have to strive is nothing less than for Communism or a collectivist Socialism, understanding by this the assumption by the people, in other words the concentration in the hands of a democratic State, of land, raw material, instruments of production, funded capital, etc." ("Religion of Socialism", p. 78); and, again, the same writer says: "Socialism has been well described as a new conception of the world presenting itself in industry as co-operative Communism" (p. 81). It is true that Messrs. Hyndman, Morris, and Joynes say, denying that they are rightfully charged with attacking private property, "We only attack that private property for a few thousand loiterers and slave drivers, which renders all property in the fruit of their own labor impossible for millions" ("Socialism Made Plain", p. 7); but it is also true that Messrs. Hyndman, Morris, Bax, and Joynes declare that "idlers who eat enormously and produce not at all form the majority of the population" ("Principles of Socialism", p. 48), so that it would be at any rate the private property of the majority they attack. Prince Kropotkin, who is advertised in England as a Socialist publicist, puts the case in its harshest form: "A feeble minority lays claim to the bulk of the national wealth, has town and country houses built for itself, and accumulates in banks the coin, notes, and documents of all sorts which represent the wealth produced by labor. All this we must seize, and by one and the same blow we shall set free the unhappy peasant whose plot of ground is burdened by a mortgage, the small shopkeeper who lives in constant dread of bankruptcy, and a wretched crowd of persons who have not bread enough for the morrow" ("Expropriation", p. 5). "We must clearly see that private property is a conscious or an unconscious theft of that which belongs to all, and we must be prepared to seize all with alacrity for the common use and benefit" (p. 7). Mr. H. H. Sparling, a prominent writer in the *Commonweal*—which journal is described as "the official organ of the Socialist League"—says in the number for January, 1887:

"Under Socialism all things necessary to the production of wealth will be held and possessed in common; there will be no special prerogative to one or to the other whereby he may take or claim for himself the benefit accruing from any work done for the community; private property will have perished, and with it the power of extorting a revenue from those desiring access to any of the means of life."

And again, in the same article,

"Under Socialism, where each would produce as well as consume, the accumulation would be enormously magnified, but the resultant mass of wealth would be held socially for common objects, and no longer individually for personal profit."

Some of the English Socialists claim to base their theories more or less directly upon the doctrines of Karl Marx, yet the manifesto which he issued conjointly with Engels in 1847 was expressly Communistic. There is one passage of it which has been often quoted: "The Communists scorn to conceal their views and purposes. They declare openly that their aims can be attained only by a violent overthrow of the existing social order. Let the ruling classes tremble before a Communistic Revolution."

And the use of force is contemplated by an editorial writer in *Justice*, No. 157, who says:

"It is for us then to compel the Government by every means in our power—using the argument of words or the argument of force, just as it suits our purpose—to carry into effect these proposals of ours which will necessarily lead to the complete emancipation of the workers."

Whilst my identification of Socialism with Communism is admitted by some Socialist writers and speakers, it is as distinctly and even vehemently repudiated by others, and is clearly challenged by many whose views are entitled to respectful and thorough examination. A careful examination of the various utterances compels me, for reasons I shall set out, to adhere to my own definition. Many who describe themselves as Socialists I should describe as social reformers, and with these I am mostly in sympathy as to the evils they seek to redress, although I cannot accept the methods of remedy they propose. Mrs. Besant—of whose earnest devotion to the movement for alleviating human suffering it is impossible to speak too highly—thinks that she so defines Socialism as to clearly distinguish it from Communism. In her pamphlet "Modern Socialism" she says:

"Communism implies the complete abolition of private property and the supply of the wants of each individual from a common store, without regard to the contributions to that common store which may, or may not, have been made by the individual. Socialism merely implies that the raw material of the soil and the means of production shall not be the private property of individuals, but shall be under the control of the community; it leaves intact a man's control over himself and over the value of his work—subject to such general laws as are necessary in any community—but by socialising land and capital it deprives each of the power of enslaving his fellows and of living in idleness on the results of their labor instead of on the results of his own."

It is right to add that Mrs. Besant says most distinctly that "for man as he is Communism would mean the living of the idle on the toil of the laborious". It is unfortunate that on her own definition Socialism must—as I think can be made clear—if attempted in practice be Communism, or nothing but conflict and incoherence. It is clear, according to Mrs. Besant, that Socialism denies private property in land and capital. She defines capital as the accumulated unconsumed result of labor applied to raw material if devoted to purposes of profit. She endeavors to separate and distinguish capital from wealth. Wealth with her is the accumulated unconsumed result of labor applied to raw material, so long as it is not attempted to utilise such result for profit. Mrs. Besant would preserve private property in "wealth" in the hands of the laborer who created it. I do not think continuance of such private property possible under the terms of her own definition. There are many conceivable cases in which the surplus result of labor may fairly be reckoned as "means of production", and would then forthwith cease to be the private property of the laborer. It is clear that the "wealth" admitted to be private property would often be susceptible of user as "capital", and would then only remain private property while not utilised for increase.

The "wealth" which continued private property, whilst unproductive to anyone, would if converted, say, into the plant of a newspaper printing office, cease to be private property. There are some so-called Socialists, though I am not sure if Mrs. Besant would include herself with these, who would permit the ownership, as private property, of such wealth as would not enable the owner to avoid personal labor. In this description would come books, pictures, statuary, ornaments, household furniture, etc., though there is difference of opinion as to whether these descriptions of wealth may pass to others as private property by gift, inheritance, or bequest. It would be certainly in conflict with the definition that such chattels could be sold; as this must open the door to trading for profit, and it is difficult to imagine how any new articles of this kind are ever to be acquired by individuals if trade for profit is forbidden, as it would be when the thing if used for profit reverted to the State. Of course a great deal turns on what is meant by the "means of production" being "under the control of the community". At present machinery, plant, tools of the roughest and most minute and delicate character are manufactured, and stored to await purchasers, at the risk of those who, for possible profit, wait the convenience of the customer needing each article; but how is all this to be regulated when the means of production are under the control of the community? Under what conditions is the manufacture of means of production otherwise than for possible profit to be arranged; and how are such "means of production" to be placed at the service of the individual worker? Mrs. Besant complains that in our present complex system, a would-be-laborer "cannot get an instrument of production, and if he could he would have nothing to use it on; he has nothing but his labor-force, and he must either sell that to some one who wants it or he must die". This is not quite accurate. The laborer, if he would unite in co-operative combination with other laborers, could now in many departments of industry obtain instruments of production and many kinds of raw material. It is true that in all kinds of mining industry the landowner has over-weighted industry in very many instances with oppressive and almost prohibitive royalties. It is also true that the landlord has crippled agriculture, and often paralysed manufacture by rents and restrictive covenants. This may, and I hope will, be remedied by the legislature. The landowners' so-called rights are in these cases purely artificial creations. They are the result of law made by a class legislature, in which the landed interest was then all-powerful and labor was then unrepresented. But how under Socialism is the individual to obtain for his individual use and his individual advantage the means of production and raw material, both of which are the property of the State? Does Mrs. Besant mean that in every-day life each citizen should have equal right to require the local representative of the State to place at her or his sole and uncontrolled disposition, and for such period as the worker may please, such raw material and means of production as the worker is of opinion may be necessary to enable him to get the best value for his work? If yes, where is the control of the means of production by the State? If no, how can the scheme leave "intact a man's control over himself and over the value of his work"? Some Socialists certainly do not intend to "leave intact a man's control over himself", for in the pamphlet entitled "Socialism Made

Plain", signed by Herbert Burrows, H. H. Champion, H. M. Hyndman, and W. Morris, the "organisation of agricultural and industrial armies under State control" is advocated. Either this means that each individual must perform the labor task fixed for him by some State official or officials—much as in the army the soldier obeys his commanding officer—or it means nothing. Returning to Mrs. Besant's definition: How are the several officials having charge of raw material and of means of production to determine each individual's ability to utilise the special means or material demanded? Is the determination to be made by officials locally chosen to act in each locality or nationally chosen to act for the whole country? And how will it be possible to avoid favoritism and injustice in apportioning pleasant and easy employment as against unpleasant and difficult kinds of labor? May a man who thinks that he can make a watch or a delicate and costly machine insist on being furnished with the necessary means and material? How is the wilful damage or deterioration by an incapable worker of the material or means of production entrusted to him to be guarded against? How is the abandonment, involving perhaps enormous loss, of a difficult or unpleasant industry to be prevented? On what conditions, if any, are instruments of production to be furnished to the laborer? If more laborers demand at one time a kind of "means of production" than the State has at its immediate command, how is a selection to be made, and how are the laborers to be maintained who cannot work at the labor they have selected, and who will not work at any other? May the guardian of the means, or of the instruments, select which he shall furnish, or must they go "first come first served", without reference to fitness? In a word, can you have State control of industry and yet leave intact the freedom of the worker? When all raw material is the property of the State, and the added value of labor is the private property of the laborer, may the person who by his labor has added value to some portion take that portion away to a foreign market where he believes the highest value will be obtainable for the manufactured article? If yes, where is the guarantee that the sale value of the raw material will ever come back into this country? If the State is to control the sale of the finished article where is the worker's intact control of the value of his work? It is true that Messrs. Hyndman and Morris say "that exchange of produce should be social too and removed from the control of individual greed and individual profit". But exchange (that is, trade) has to be conducted with many foreign countries, from which we get raw material not producible here, and necessaries of food and medicine not grown within the limits of our own land. How is the great carrying trade of the country to be enterprised when the incitement of possible profit to the trader is erased?

"Socialism," says Mr. Hyndman ("Debate", p. 5), "is an endeavor to substitute for the anarchical struggle or fight for existence an organised co-operation for existence". While it is true that the struggle for existence has been far too bitter not only between employer and employed but also between the workers themselves, the brunt of the struggle being most severe on the poorest and weakest, the word "anarchical" is hardly explanatory as a word of description. The meaning of the definition depends on the translation of the words "organised co-operation". Voluntary co-operation is organised co-operation determinable—subject to the co-operative agreement—at the will of each co-operator, so far as he or she is concerned, but as each co-operator receives profit on his investment as well as his labor, and can withdraw his capital if he be not satisfied, this clearly is not what Mr. Hyndman meant, and when in debate he was pressed for explanation none was given. Mr. Joynes, commenting on this, rebuked the demand on the ground that "no scientific Socialist pretends to have any scheme or detailed plan of organisation". Surely to talk of organisation and yet to have no scheme is to waste words in the air. Mr. Hyndman did explain what he meant by anarchy. "There is, he said, "many a man who works as a skilled laborer to-day who if a machine is invented whereby man may benefit, will be turned out to compete against his fellows on the streets to-morrow. That is what I say is anarchy" ("Debate", p. 7); and he recommended as the cure for this "the collective ownership of land, capital, machinery, and credit by the complete ownership of the people". It is true that the introduction of each new labor-saving invention in machinery does deprive persons of methods of livelihood to which they have become accustomed. It is true that if the individual worker is advanced in life he will have great difficulty in adapting himself to new kinds of skilled employment. But it is not true that the introduction of machinery has permanently reduced the aggregate number of workers in the country where most machinery is used, nor is it true that the ratio of pauperism to population has, on the whole, increased in the countries where most machinery has been introduced. Mr. Hyndman's definition in the end means Communism or it means nothing. If the collective ownership of everything except labor, and the collective control of all the produce of labor for exchange, is not the total negation of private property, then words have no meaning.

Mrs. Besant says that "capital under our present industrial system is the result of unpaid labor". Most certainly this is not true of all capital: such capital as is now in the hands of the wage-paid laborer himself, or has been handed by him to others, can hardly come under this category. The illustrations may be given, say, in the 583,830 members of building societies, owning £52,611,198; 284,976 members of registered trade unions, owning £538,542; 572,610 members of co-operative societies, owning £8,209,722; 46,710 members of registered loan societies, owning £324,281; 1,582,474 savings bank depositors, owning £45,847,887 4s. 3d., this not including the 7,288 depositors in railway savings banks, owning £586,260; [1]2,300,000 members of friendly societies, owning £ ; members of industrial assurance societies registered as limited companies, owning £3,834,709. In the enormous number of small shareholders in home and foreign railways, in banks, in manufacturing concerns, small holders of consolidated stock, owners of small houses or plots of land not included in the building society statistics, small shopkeepers and the like, there must be an addition of capital which has been accumulated by the laborer out of payment received by him for his labor. Nor does the challenge to definition even stop at this point. The tailor sells to the laborer clothing cheaper than the laborer could make it; the clothing is necessary for the laborer; on each article of clothing a small profit is made by the tailor, and on the balance of

[1] The last returns are not made up; but the membership is now, I believe, over 2,500,000.

many such transactions, and after deducting the expenses of his business, there is a surplus "capital"; but it might well be that none of this "capital" was the result of unpaid labor. So of the baker, the butcher, the grocer, similar illustrations may be given. Even the capital of the great manufacturer who, employing hundreds or thousands of hands, grows rich in a brief space of years, is not always, or wholly, "the result of unpaid labor". A keen judgment which first utilises a new material as alpaca or alfa, or which initiates a fresh method of dealing with old material, or which discovers a market or employment of produce hitherto overlooked by others, may be rewarded by accumulated capital, which it is scarcely fair to describe as "the result of unpaid labor". Of course, all "wealth" originates with labor on raw material, but all capital is not the value of labor which has never been paid to the laborer.

Mrs. Besant—moved, and very properly moved intensely, by the suffering around her—is a little one-sided even in her coldest presentments. Take as illustration the following, vouched by her as "a statement of the facts as they are": "The worker produces a mass of commodities; the capitalist sells these commodities for what they will fetch in the market; . . . . the capitalist gives over to the producer sufficient of the results of the sale to enable the producer to exist, and pockets the remainder." Now this is not "the facts as they are" at all. The following corrected presentment would, I think, better represent the facts as they are: The worker, aided by the capitalist who furnishes raw material and means of production, produces a mass of commodities, and is paid by the capitalist a sum for his labor which seldom leaves a large margin over subsistence; the capitalist then sells these commodities for what they will fetch, recoups himself thereout for disbursements for raw material, working expenditure, and wages, pockets the remainder, if any, and bears the whole loss if the transaction should be unprofitable.

It is not that Mrs. Besant had herself overlooked the facts here restated; she gives them fairly enough at the top of the previous page of her own pamphlet ("Modern Socialism", p. 15).

Charles Bradlaugh.

SOCIALISM: ITS TRUTHS AND ITS HOPES.

A REPLY.

KNOWING, as I do, that the one aim of my friend and colleague, Charles Bradlaugh, in dealing with the social problem, is to seek the best possible solution of a vexed and difficult question, and knowing also that my own aim is identical with his, I accept the challenge to criticise his paper as frankly as it was given, trusting that the honest speech of two honest thinkers may be useful to the students of Sociology.

The difficulty felt by Mr. Bradlaugh "in discovering any general agreement as to what is now meant in England by 'Socialism'" is a difficulty felt by all who endeavor to define with scientific accuracy a rough-and-ready popular name. The suggested alternative, "Social Reformers", would be even less definitive than the name "Socialists", for I am not aware of a single principle on which all Social Reformers are agreed; and it would, for instance, classify me with men like Lord Brabazon and Mr. Arnold White, to whose proposals and methods I am vehemently opposed. Every name which is borne by a political party covers a wide variety of opinions, and is exclusive rather than inclusive; it suggests what is rejected rather than what is accepted. The Radical may be taken as a denier of the divine right of kings, but his party name does not tell if he be constitutional Monarchist or Republican. In every advanced party "there are so many grades and shades of diverse opinion"; this variety is the condition of progress. Only in parties which exist by repeating shibboleths of the past can uniformity of opinion be looked for. No political party includes more grades of diverse opinion than does the best of them all, the Radical, and this diversity is a proof of its vitality. The name Radical is worn by Land Nationalisers and by promoters of peasant proprietorship; by Local Optionists and by the supporters of free trade in drink; by advocates and opponents of compulsory vaccination; by Home Rulers and anti-Home Rulers; by men who would increase, and by men who would decrease, the sphere of the State. If a party is to be attacked *as a party*, it must be attacked on some principle on which it is agreed, and not on the principles on which its sections differ. While it is fair to attack any individual Radical writer for opinions put forward by him, it would not be fair to father all his individual eccentricities on Radicalism; and while it is just to attack any individual Socialist writer for the opinions he advances, it is not just to foist all his personal views on Socialism.

Mr. Bradlaugh, however, wisely defines Socialism before he assails it, and thus enables his readers to grasp the views he is attacking. He writes:

> "I understand and define Socialism as (1) denying, or destroying, all individual private property; and (2) as affirming that society organised as the State should own all wealth, direct all labor, and compel the equal distribution of all produce. I understand a Socialistic State to be (3) that State in which everything would be common as to its user, and in which all labor would be controlled by the State, which from the common stock would maintain the laborer, and would take all the produce of the labor. That is (4), I identify Socialism with Communism."

My first objection to this definition is that it excludes the vast majority of Socialists, if indeed it includes any, and it will be easy for me to show that the quotations by which Mr. Bradlaugh seeks to support it are insufficient for the task. (1) might possibly be accepted by the small group of Anarchists of whom, in England, Peter Kropotkin may be taken as a representative, but it is not accepted by the Collectivist school, which forms the great majority of the Socialist party in every civilised country. It is not accepted by Marx, Engels, Bebel, in Germany; by Schäffle, in Austria; by Colins, Agathon de Potter, in Belgium; by Gronlund in America; by the leading English Socialist writers. Marx and Engels say, in their famous "Manifesto to the Communists" of 1847: "When capital is converted into common property belonging to all members of society, personal property is not thereby changed into social property. . . . By no means do we want to abolish this personal appropriation of labor products for the support of life, an appropriation which leaves no surplus proceeds, no profit, and which can gain no control over other people's labor. . . . Communism deprives no one of the power to appropriate social products for his own use; it only deprives him of the power to subject others' labor by such appropriation" (pp. 14, 15). Bebel describes the worker as receiving "any kind of certificate, a printed piece of paper, gold, or brass", as a token of the time spent in labor, and this he can exchange for what he requires. "If he finds that his requirements are less than those covered by that which he receives for his work, he can work a correspondingly shorter time. If he prefers to give away his superfluity, no one can prevent him. . . . But no one can compel him to work for another, and no one can deprive him of a part of his claims for the work done" (Woman in the Past, Present, and Future," pp. 193, 194). Schäffle says that workmen are to be paid according to the quantity and the quality of the work they do (see *Fortnightly Review*, April, 1883, p. 556). Colins absolutely leaves untouched hereditary succession to property in the direct line, while vesting land and capital in the State (see *Ibid*, p. 555). Gronlund writes: "Instead of taking property away from everyone, it will enable everyone to acquire property. It will confirm the institution of individual ownership by placing property on an unimpeachable basis: that of being the result of the owner's exertions" ("Co-operative Commonwealth," p. 81). H. M. Hyndman, W. Morris, and J. L. Joynes, as Mr. Bradlaugh admits, deny that they attack private property, save that form of it which renders it impossible for millions, *i.e.*, as we shall see later, private property in the material of wealth-production. I submit, then, that these representative writers disprove that Socialism is that which it is affirmed to be in (1). (2) falls with (1), and it may be added that the "equal distribution of all produce" is no essential part of Socialism, as may be seen from the above citations. (3) appears to me to put forward a view impossible of realisation; how can "everything be common as to its user" when the necessity for individual use must imply individual possession? A pair of boots cannot be common as to the user, since the use of them by one person renders impossible their use by another. How would it be possible for the State—if by State is meant any central authority—to control and direct all labor, since for effective direction of labor the directors must be on the spot with the labor? How can there be a "common stock" for a whole nation? In what Socialist work can these, or similar proposals, be found? None of the quotations given by Mr. Bradlaugh justify such assumptions. In (4) we read: "I identify Socialism with Communism". But if discussion of controverted questions is to be instructive, of what use is it to identify arbitrarily two schools which claim to be distinct, and which are recognised as distinct by all Socialists and by most Individualists? There is a sense in which the word "Communism" is used by Collectivist writers such as Marx, to which I shall presently refer, but the Communism which is sketched in Mr. Bradlaugh's four propositions is not the Communism of Marx. Surely nothing would be gained if in arguing against Radicalism I used the word Liberalism to include the most stationary of old Whigs and the most progressive of modern Radicals, and then, stating that I identified Whiggism and Radicalism, went on to quote some of the most fossil utterances of the Duke of Argyll, alleging that in demolishing these I had demolished Radicalism? I do not fancy that such line of attack would convince many Radicals.

The quotations given by Mr. Bradlaugh to establish his case are sufficient to show the nature of the private property which is attacked by all Socialists, and the principle on which Socialists are agreed.

"Messrs. William Morris, and E. Belfort Bax say: 'The land, the capital, the machinery, factories, workshops, stores, means of transit, mines, banking, all means of production and distribution of wealth, must be declared and treated as the common property of all' (Manifesto of the Socialistic League', p. 6); and that there may be no misapprehension as to what this means Mr. Bax writes: 'That for which the working classes have to strive is nothing less than for Communism or a collectivist Socialism, understanding by this the assumption by the people, in other words the concentration in the hands of a democratic State, of land, raw material, instruments of production, funded capital, etc.' ('Religion of Socialism', p. 78); and, again, the same writer says: 'Socialism has been well described as a new conception of the world presenting itself in industry as co-operative Communism' (p. 81)."

There is no word here of the destruction of all private property; but there is the claim for the appropriation by the community of all material necessary for the production of wealth. And this is the fundamental position of Socialism; on other matters there may be diversity of opinion, but on this there is none. With regard to this material it is that the claim for "Communism" is made; Mr. Bax above defines Communism as "the concentration in the hands of a democratic State" of this material, not of all wealth. This, again, is the "Communism" advocated by Marx. When he has stated his objection to "that system of production and the appropriation of products which rests on the antagonism of classes—on the spoliation of the many by the few", he goes on: "*In this sense* (italics mine) the Communists can reduce their whole theory to one expression: the abolition of private property" (p. 13). He then proceeds to rebut the accusation that Communists "wish to destroy property which is the product of a man's labor—earned by his own work; that property, which forms the basis of all personal liberty, activity, and independence—personally earned, personally acquired property". And showing that the proletarian's work produces capital, "a species of property which plunders wage-labor", he states that it is this which is to be made "common property". Historically, Communism has implied a condition of things very different from that advocated by Marx, and a Communistic society, always small, has really had a "common stock". Such an arrangement is only possible in a small community, and would be utterly unworkable for a nation. It may well be questioned whether Marx was wise in using in a new sense a term already applied to a form of social organisation which he did not desire to establish; still, he showed plainly the sense in which he was using it, and it is only just to take terms with the definitions attached to them by those who use them. I have myself used the term Communism in the older sense, in my pamphlet "Modern Socialism", quoted by Mr. Bradlaugh, but Marx's use of the word must be taken with Marx's limitations.

I am not able to defend the position taken up by Peter Kropotkin, the Anarchist school being opposed to the Collectivist in all questions of method and organisation; but I would point out that he does not apparently mean to make everything quite common property, since he says: "Our opponents say to us, 'venture to touch the peasant's plot of ground or the mechanic's cottage, and see how they will receive you'. Very well! But we shall not interfere with the plot of ground nor with the cottage" ("Expropriation", p. 5). So far as I understand the Anarchist ideal of social reorganisation, it includes a system of federated communes, each commune to have a common stock; but I have not succeeded in obtaining any clear idea of the relations supposed to exist between the communes.

I come to Mr. Bradlaugh's criticism of my own position on pp. 11 and 12. I agree that Socialism denies that there should be private property in wealth-material. But the objection that I distinguish "wealth" and "capital" is, if valid against me, valid against every writer on political economy. I did not invent a new, but accepted the current, distinction. And the distinction is not wholly fictitious. If one man owned in a country the whole material necessary for the production of wealth, no wealth could be produced without his consent; if one man owned all the commodities in a country, but the people could reach the material needed for production, they could make the commodities they required. Private property in the first case means submission to the owner thereof or starvation; private property in the second case, however absurd in such an exaggerated form, leaves the people free to feed and clothe themselves with the new results of their own labor.

The whole of the next paragraph (line 23, p. 7—line 10, p. 10) appears to me to be based on a radical misconception of the change proposed by the "Scientific Socialists". They do not propose to make a number of laws: "A man shall not work for himself"; "A man shall not save up his wages, and let out his savings at interest"; any more than they propose to make a law, "A man who is going to swim across a river shall not handcuff his wrists together and tie a 20lb. weight to each foot". What the Scientific Socialist proposes to do is to take over the land and the total capital of the country (plant, means of transit, banks, etc.) into the hands of the community; those who want to earn a living, *i.e.*, all healthy adults, will have to utilise this material. Suppose the Northumberland Miners' Association desire to work the Northumberland mines, they would have to pay rent to the State (the whole community) for the right to work them; suppose the nail-makers of a town desired to utilise the factories in which they had warked as "hands", they would have to pay rent to the State for the use of land, factory, plant, etc. And now suppose that an individual nailmaker, dissatisfied with his work in the co-operative factory, determined to save some of his earnings and set up nailmaking on his own account. Need the State be convulsed, need his deserted fellow-workers of the factory cry out for a law to stop him? Not a bit of it. Unless the whole experience of the last century as to the advantages of division of labor and of large production over small be a delusion, the co-operative workers may look on at the individual capitalist with extreme serenity. If his nails cost ten, twenty, fifty, times as much as theirs to produce, who is going to be foolish enough to buy them, say at a shilling, when they can buy similar ones at a farthing? The capitalist now is the tyrant of the worker because he can say to him, "Work for me, or starve". The attempt of a man to be a capitalist under Socialism would be entertaining, but harmless. He could not compel any man to work for him by threat of starvation on refusal. The human desire to get as much as possible for as little labor as possible will very rapidly put an end to profit-mongering, not because none will be willing to make profits, but because none will be willing to be made a profit of by another, when starvation does not force him into submission. Once let monopoly in the material of wealth be destroyed, and the "natural forces" at work in society will settle the small matters without the interference of artificial laws.

Nor must it be supposed that I have devised this view of the subject merely to cut the ground from under the feet of Mr. Bradlaugh's objection. E. Belfort Bax, in his "Religion of Socialism", has dealt with a similar point in a similar manner:

"M. Leroy-Beaulien sneeringly complains that, under a Collectivist *régime*, no one would be allowed to mend his neighbor's trousers or shirt for a monetary consideration, inasmuch as he would then be employing his needle and thread for purposes of production, which would be a return to Individualism, and hence illegal. Let M. Leroy-Beaulien reassure himself. All those who desire to make a living by an individualistic mending of shirts and trousers will be allowed full liberty to satisfy their aspirations so far as any juridical coercion is concerned. We will not vouch for their being much patronised, for the probability of repairs of this character being executed better, more rapidly, and with less expenditure of labor in the communal workshop is great. But in any case, they would have their economic liberty to fatten on" (p. 41).

Looking over the details of the paragraph which I have subjected to the above sweeping criticism, some further points may be noted. Machinery, tools, etc., would be made when they were likely to be wanted, and stored till wanted, as now; it is hard to see where the difficulty here arises. The laborers now can unite in co-operative production to a small extent, but their attempts have failed, one of the chief reasons being that their command of capital is too small to enable them to compete with the big capitalist. I have above spoken of the individual worker starting on his own account, and so have partly answered Mr. Bradlaugh's question on this head; if he wants to get raw material and private means of production he will have to save up and purchase them from the community, and so buy the razor to cut his own foolish throat. No officer need trouble himself about the "individual's ability to utilise the special means or material demanded"; all he has to do is to receive from the applicant the value of that which he demands; the individual will have to judge his own ability, and if he blunders he will have only himself to blame. The difficulty of apportioning pleasant and unpleasant labor may be met in many ways; the unpleasant might be more highly paid, so that a short term of one might balance a longer term of another. Speaking generally, these matters will be settled by the law of supply and demand. As men's tastes differ, and technical education will have trained men for different forms of work, taste and education will play a large part in determining a man's work. Suppose a man is a weaver, and finds that there is no vacancy for a weaver in the factories of the town he is living in, he might apply at the municipal branch of the Labor Bureau—an establishment for which every Socialist must thank Charles Bradlaugh, and the full value of which will only be felt under Socialism—and learn in what town there are vacancies in his trade. If over the whole country there is no vacancy, he will have to accept temporary employment in some other industry, and he can leave his name on the books of the Bureau for the next vacancy. But are not all these questions based on the old idea that Socialism has a cast-iron scheme, with every detail mapped out on paper, and do they not rather imply that everyone is to be a perfect fool? We are not Utopian Socialists; we have no sudden cure-all for every ill which afflicts society; but we say that the private monopoly of the material of wealth means payment to idle individuals by the workers, and that any payment made by them for the use of this material should be made to the State, and used for the benefit of the community. The exact details of the working could only be given by one endowed with the spirit of prophecy, and many such matters will have to be solved by the common-sense and business experience of the administrators.

The worker's "control" over "the value of his work" does not mean that a man will have a right to "some portion" of a product to which he has added value. It means that where he has given so many hours of labor, and has received some symbol of exchange which represents their value, he may use that symbol of exchange as he pleases. Twenty workmen co-operate to produce a carved sideboard; it is not proposed that the workmen shall have the sideboard divided among them, so that one may carry his piece abroad (lines 34–40, p. 9), but that each shall receive a labor-note—or whatever the form of payment be—for the value given by work, and that each can use this as he pleases. The finished article might lie in the communal stores till wanted by an individual or a group who were prepared to pay for it as much labor as was required to produce it.

Mr. Bradlaugh, quoting Mr. Hyndman's proposal as to "collective ownership of land, capital, machinery, and credit", says:

> "Mr. Hyndman's definition in the end means Communism or it means nothing. If the collective ownership of everything except labor, and the collective control of all the produce of labor for exchange, is not the total negation of private property, then words have no meaning."

But is this so? Mr. Bradlaugh does not consider that the capitalist monopoly of "everything except labor", and the capitalist "control of all the produce of labor for exchange" is the "total negation of private property", although it implies the continued confiscation of the results of labor, and results in a condition of things in which 931 persons out of every 1,000 die "without property worth speaking of" (Mulhall's "Dictionary of Statistics", from Probate Duty Returns, p. 279). But if capitalist monopoly of the wealth-material be compatible with private property, why should not collective monopoly of the wealth-material be equally compatible therewith? In neither case does the laborer individually own it, but in the present system it is owned by a class, and part of the laborer's produce enriches the class; under the proposed system it would be owned by the community, and part of the laborer's produce would go to the community, and he, as one of the community, would benefit by the utilisation of this collective wealth.

Mr Bradlaugh is technically right in saying that my statement that capital "under our present industrial system is the result of unpaid labor" is too sweeping; I should have said, "capital, with trifling exceptions, is", etc. Taking Mr. Mulhall's figures, which are somewhat higher than Mr. Bradlaugh's, of the total capital of savings in trade societies, savings banks, and societies of every sort, we find it put at £156,000,000. This gives less than £6 per head to the members of the manual labor class, and this only on the incorrect assumption that all money in savings banks, etc., is put in by them. But everyone knows that, to take but one example, the savings banks are largely used by small gentry, shopkeepers, governesses, etc., and not exclusively by the manual labor class. In speaking of "capital under our present industrial system", I was thinking of capital in the bulk, rather than of the small savings made by some lucky workers. If the tailor and the others make "a profit", that is if they get out of the laborer more than the fair equivalent of the labor they have given in making or preparing their wares for his use, then the profit, being taken from the laborer without equivalent, is a confiscation of part of the results of his labor. As a matter of fact few working tailors, etc., do more than earn subsistence by their own labor; the capital is made by the tailor and others who employ wage-laborers, and who, by taking from each a little more than is returned to him as wage, *i.e.*, by not paying for all the labor, gradually or rapidly accumulate capital.

To the last paragraph, I do not think answer is needed. As Mr. Bradlaugh very fairly says, I analysed the facts on p. 15. I did not think it necessary to restate them on p. 16, in summarising the results as they bore on the question of Marx's three values.

I restate, in conclusion, my main objection to Mr. Bradlaugh's criticism of Socialism. He continually strikes at Utopian Socialism, not at Scientific. He never meets our main contention that private property in wealth-material must result theoretically in the servitude of the unpropertied to the propertied class, and practically does so result in every ancient and modern society; that it enables the idle to live on the industrious, by empowering them to charge the worker for the right to work; that it thus causes mischievous class distinctions, unjust acquirement of wealth without labor, equally unjust confiscation resulting in labor without wealth. He does not show us how these hitherto inevitable results of private property in wealth-material can be prevented. But until this central citadel can be carried, I and thousands more must remain Socialists.

ANNIE BESANT.

SOCIALISM: ITS FALLACIES AND DANGERS.

ROUGH NOTES BY WAY OF REJOINDER.

I NEED hardly say that I acknowledge to the very fullest extent the considerate tone of Mrs. Besant's criticisms, and though I have in everything to adhere to the propositions advanced in my original paper, I trust that I shall not depart from the friendly lines on which this presentation of antagonistic views on a most important subject has hitherto proceeded. I desire to repeat and emphasise my complete conviction that my always brave and loyal colleague has in the whole of this most important social movement been solely moved by her desire to alleviate the hard conditions of life of many workers, and to diminish the sum of human suffering. Where disagreeing with her most, and when expressing this disagreement, I desire that this may be fully remembered by my readers.

Mrs. Besant, admitting that I have by my definition made clear what it is I assail as Socialism, says that her first objection to my definition "is that it excludes the vast majority of Socialists, if indeed it includes any," and she goes to the length of asking me "in what Socialist work can these or similar proposals be found". I answer that until very recently they were to be found in the writings of almost every French, English, and American Socialist. This I have no doubt Mrs. Besant herself would admit, for she states that historically Communism meant something different from "that advocated by Marx", and the words Communism and Socialism were most certainly transposable equivalents with Robert Owen, Cabet, Fourier, Noyes, F. W. Evans, W. H. Hinds, and nearly all their American and French contemporaries. And this is not very ancient history; none of it dates back before the nineteenth century; much of it was in vigor in the lifetime of the present writer. The initial and vital point of difference between Mrs. Besant and myself—one which governs the whole controversy—is that I allege that, in express terms or in its practical working, Socialism must deny or destroy all individual private property. Mrs. Besant says this is not accepted by several Socialists she names, *e.g.*, Marx, Engels, and Bebel in Germany; yet she fairly enough quotes as follows from Marx: "In this sense the Communists can reduce their whole theory to one expression: the abolition of private property"; and saying that "it may well be questioned whether Marx was wise in using in a new sense" the term "Communism", Mrs. Besant gets over the definite "abolition of private property" by italicising the words "in this sense". That is, Mrs. Besant replies: Mr. Bradlaugh is wrong in attributing to Socialism identity with Communism; Mr. Bradlaugh is wrong in identifying Communism with abolition of private property—proof, Marx, a German Socialist of eminence, did not hold those views. True, Marx used the old word "Communism", but he so used it with a new meaning. True, Marx said he meant "abolition of private property" as a correct summary of his Communistic views, but he said so with a limitation of the sense in which he used the words, which totally changes their meaning. Mrs. Besant must pardon me if I venture to uphold Marx's ability to express himself clearly, and to express some doubt either of his straightforwardness or of her appreciation of his meaning on this point. I notice that Mrs. Besant omits all reference to French Socialistic authors, and takes Gronlund as if the representative of American Socialism, which I venture to think is hardly the case. Mrs. Besant, naming Colins, should, I think, have added that, though Colins is unquestionably very able and very earnest, his "rational Socialism" finds comparatively few adherents in the Socialistic ranks. M. Naville, writing on Cabet in *La Nouvelle Revue*, and criticising the various modern schools of French Socialists, "Collectivists", "Anarchists", "State Socialists", says: "Quels que soit les noms dont elles s'affublent et les procédés qu'elles préconisent, toutes ces doctrines partent d'un même principe, toutes visent au meme objectif: la transformation de l'etat social par la mise en commun des biens, par la creation d'une propriété universelle appartenant à tous et à chacun".

Mrs. Besant, objecting to my definition, asks: "How can there be a common stock for the whole nation?" and denies that this can be justified from any Socialist work; yet on the same page she requotes my extract from the Manifesto of the Socialist League that "land, capital, machinery, factories, workshops, stores, means of transit, mines, banking, all means of production and distribution of wealth, must be declared and treated as the common property of all". I am unable to distinguish between "common stock" and "common property", and fear that Mrs. Besant and myself are using words in such differing senses that useful discussion is impossible. Mrs. Besant says "the equal distribution of all produce is no essential part of Socialism". Unless there is some play on the word "equal", surely Mrs. Besant is here in direct conflict with the Socialist League and with the Social Democratic Federation. The organisation and control of distribution by the State and "the organisation of agricultural and industrial armies under State control" are both over and over again repeated as features in the programme. Mr. W. Morris says that "capital, including the land, machinery, factories, etc.," is to be put "into the hands of the community to be used for the good of all alike". A young man named Mahon, selected by the Socialist League to be one of its representatives amongst the miners lately on strike in Northumberland, in "A Plea for Socialism" addressed to those miners, and since published from the offices of the League, says: "*The Socialist proposal* is to take the land and capital from the private individuals who now unrighteously hold them, and put them under the control of the community, and use them for the benefit of the workers". Mrs. Besant refers to Colins and Agathon de Potter, but if I accurately appreciate Dr. Agathon de Potter he—for himself and for Colins —is the interpreter of what is called "Rational Socialism", which differs essentially from the Socialism taught by Mrs. Besant. Rational Socialism, to quote Agathon de Potter's own comment on Mrs. Besant, "maintains that a part of capital ought to rest in individual hands to constitute an individual personal estate to encourage wage labor. It neither suppresses capital nor interest on capital, but it renders both inoffensive by lowering the rate of interest *au minimum des circonstances* and in forbidding loans *plus que viagers*." That is, interest would be kept down to a minimum by the competition of the State as a lender, and every debt would be extinguished in a fixed term by a limited number of annual payments (A. de Potter, *La Société Nouvelle*, pp. 302, 305). Mr. Mahon, in the address I have just quoted, says "the taking of interest is wrong, no matter to what extent it may be carried".

Mrs. Besant, in her reply to me, in effect says that I do not understand Socialism, and that I consequently fail to accurately represent it in my criticisms. I quite admit that, if Socialism and Communism are not convertible words of equivalent meaning, Mrs. Besant's reply is well urged. Curiously enough, Mr. Tucker, an American Anarchist Socialist, in other words says almost this of Mrs. Besant, charging her with "stopping short of Communism in State Socialism", and therefore with failing "to give the public any complete and satisfactory idea" of what Socialism really is. At the outset of my first paper I admitted my difficulty in finding any general agreement amongst modern Socialists as to what was meant. I only pretended to make it clear what it was that I attacked under that name. Mrs. Besant says, "What the scientific Socialist proposes to do is to take over the land and total capital of the country". "Suppose the nailmakers of a town desired to utilise" any of this land or capital, "they would have to pay rent to the State". Suppose an individual nailmaker dissatisfied, he may, says Mrs. Besant, set up for himself when he has saved some of his earnings; "the co-operative workers may look on at the individual capitalist with great serenity". As I understand Mrs. Besant, Socialism says: "Capital is an evil, therefore it must be wholly taken away from the present possessors". I do not here discuss the possibility of so taking away all capital without a civil war, nor pause to comment on the terrible danger involved in the encouragement given to such a doctrine; but I suppose all capital taken away by the State from every individual capitalist. Then I understand Mrs. Besant to interpret Socialism as saying: we will not prevent an individual nailmaker from saving up his earnings and setting up as an individual capitalist nailmaker in competition with the co-operative factory, obtaining the uses of its materials of production by rental from the State. But supposing—which I cannot—that this can be reconciled with the organisation and direction of industrial armies by the State, does not this interpretation involve an utter abandonment of the principle that all private capital is an evil, and ought to be abolished? Mrs. Besant evidently does not think that there would be much reality in the permitted competition. She says: "The attempt of a man to be a capitalist under Socialism would be entertaining, but would be harmless"—meaning, probably, that she does not think that the individual already deprived of his previous savings would be readily able to even pay rent to the State, for the materials of production would only be attainable on hire from the State. But suppose that, in addition to being entertaining, the attempt really succeeded, and supposing that just as Robert Owen the poor mill hand did, by great thrift, individual energy, foresight, and enterprise, become Robert Owen the rich Socialist capitalist—some individual nailmaker did again acquire new capital in lieu of that of which he had been deprived—is he to be allowed to keep it? If not, to say that he may attempt is hardly serious. If yes, why destroy the present capitalists and yet permit the creation of new ones?

CHARLES BRADLAUGH.

A FEW WORDS IN FINAL REPLY.

ONE point at least has come out very clearly in the friendly controversy between Mr. Bradlaugh and myself. Namely, that what he attacks as "Socialism" is only one form of Socialism; and I think I may add, taking his list of names—Robert Owen, Cabet, Fourier, Noyes, F. W. Evans, W. H. Hinds—not the form of Socialism which is making its way in Europe and America to-day. It is true that none of these men date back beyond the present century, but in the science of sociology they are as much out of date as authorities as the early writers of the century on geology are in present-day geological science. Nothing perhaps has been more remarkable in the present century than the enormous advances made during it in all branches of science; a veritable gulf separates the thinkers of the early and of the later parts, and strictures levelled against the teachings of the older schools are pointless when turned against the doctrines of the new. Sociology has shared in the general advance, and has passed from a mere empiricism into a reasoned system. And most noteworthy is it that the leading thinkers in this young science—the birth of our own century—are, with the exception of Herbert Spencer, either tending towards Socialism or are declared Socialists, and that they are being more and more reinforced by the younger school of political economists. And these thinkers are influencing the course of political action, unconscious as are the politicians of the moulding force. Fifty years ago a Radical drafting a Bill for depriving non-cultivating landlords of uncultivated but cultivable land, would have parcelled out the land seized into small holdings which he would have sold to peasant *proprietors*; now-a-days, Mr. Bradlaugh, drafting his Bill, proposes to let the land to peasant *tenants*, paying rent to and holding from the State. The same sound Radical, attacking market rights and tolls in the hands of monopolising individuals and railway companies, proposes to abolish their charter rights, and to enable municipalities only to acquire authority over markets, so that rents and tolls paid shall go into the municipal exchequer instead of into the pockets of individuals. The same man is striving to prevent by law "free contracts" between employers and employed, in cases in which the employers use their position of advantage to make men take goods in lieu of money as wage, and to prevent them charging the men interest on money advanced before the agreed on pay-day. Truly, though Mr. Bradlaugh curses Socialism with his mouth, he is blessing it altogether in his legislation, and is making possible for us the way to the Promised Land.

In par. 3, is there not a little play on the word "stock"? I certainly understood "common stock" to mean common stock of commodities. I should not speak of a "stock" of "land, capital, machinery, factories", etc. The Socialist League sums up all these as "means of production and distribution of wealth", and claims these as common property. Again, in the quotations from W. Morris and J. L. Mahon, it is land and capital that are claimed as common property. I am not aware that the Socialist League, or the Social Democratic Federation, has declared in favor of "equal distribution of all produce", and the phrase in the Socialist League Manifesto that every man will "receive the full reward of his labor" seems to point in the other direction, since all men certainly do not labor equally.

I agree in the statement of the view taken by Colins and Agathon de Potter on capital; they would have the State part-holder only of the capital of the country, and would thus extinguish the worst evils of the present system, which flow from the constant exploitation of the worker by the capitalist; with the capital owned by the State available to the worker, he would no longer be at the mercy of a private employer, and would only work for the latter when he thought he could thus do better for himself than by setting up on his own account with capital borrowed from the State. Socialism carried to this extent would be an enormous improvement on the present system; and the moderate views of Colins and Agathon de Potter seem to me to be of special interest in the present controversy, as showing how far is the Belgian School of Socialism from occupying the position assailed by Mr. Bradlaugh.

Mr. Benjamin Tucker, as an Anarchist, would naturally charge me with not going far enough; in his eyes Collectivist Socialism is inconsistent and weak, Anarchism being the only logical and perfect system of thought. So Mr. Auberon Herbert, an extreme Individualist, regards Mr. Bradlaugh's Individualism as a very poor weak-backed kind of thing, since Mr. Bradlaugh thinks that a majority may rightly impose a tax for a common object, whereas individual liberty demands that a man shall be left free to pay a tax or not as he chooses. Everyone who does not go to the extreme length of every opinion held by some individual nominally belonging to his party must be prepared for reproaches of this kind. But I can support Mr. Benjamin Tucker's strictures with perfect equanimity, as doubtless can Mr. Bradlaugh any levelled at him by Mr. Auberon Herbert. And in truth Mr. Benjamin Tucker and Mr. Auberon Herbert are men of very much the same type, and are living examples of the truth of the adage that extremes meet.

Mr. Bradlaugh misunderstands me in thinking that I represent Socialism as saying that "capital is an evil". Capital is an essential factor in production, and is therefore most certainly not an evil. The evil arises when individuals, monopolising the capital made by many, and excluding those who made it from all control over it, employ it as an instrument to exploit those who have none, and to utilise them as hands to heap up wealth for themselves. Capital as a tyrant over labor is an evil; capital as fertiliser and servant of labor is a good.

My reason for thinking that the enterprising individual nailmaker would be making an entertaining and harmless experiment, was, I think, given in my original statement. First, if his individually-made nails cost more to produce than the nails made by co-operative labor—that is, if division of labor be an advantage in production—he would not be able to compete with the co-operative workers in the open market. Secondly, he could not accumulate by exploiting his neighbors, and no man can accumulate large capital by his own work alone. Robert Owen the mill-hand became Robert Owen the capitalist because, when he had saved a little out of his own earnings, he could hire others to work for him, and then by paying them back less than the value they give him in work, he was able to save out of *their* earnings, and so increase his capital; this increased capital enabled him to employ additional workers, and he then saved out of the earnings of a larger number of people, and so grew rich. Under the present system the workers are compelled either to submit to this continued appropriation of part of the results of their labor, or to remain unemployed, *i.e.*, to starve. Under Socialism no such compulsion would be upon them, and a man's natural objection to be exploited may be trusted to for the prevention of exploitation as soon as the compulsion to submit to it is removed. Hence the serenity with which any such private attempts might be regarded.

All I have sought to do in my brief criticisms of Mr. Bradlaugh's objections to Socialism has been to show that they do not go to the root of the question of Socialism, that they do not even touch the central position of Socialism. Looking out at the future of the workers in this country, pressed as they are by increasing foreign competition, I can see no hope for them save in their control of their own labor, and their possession of all which is necesssary for the production of wealth. As chattel-slavery and serfage so, I believe, must wage-slavery perish, and then shall man's dominion over man disappear, and liberty shall be a reality instead of a name.

ANNIE BESANT.

MODERN SOCIALISM.

BY

ANNIE BESANT.

[SECOND EDITION.]

LONDON:
FREETHOUGHT PUBLISHING COMPANY,
63 FLEET STREET, E.C.

1890.

LONDON:
PRINTED BY ANNIE BESANT AND CHARLES BRADLAUGH,
63 FLEET STREET, E.C.

MODERN SOCIALISM.

GREAT changes are long in the preparing, and every thought that meets ultimately with wide acceptance is lying inarticulate in many minds ere it is syllabled out by some articulate one, and stands forth a spoken Word. The *Zeitgeist* has its mouth in those of its children who have brain to understand, voice to proclaim, courage to stand alone. Some new Truth then peals out sonorous and far-sounding as the roll of the thunder, melodious to the ears attuned to the deep grand harmonies of Nature, but terrible to those accustomed only to the subdued lispings of artificial triflers, and the murmurs which float amid the hangings of courtly halls.

When such an event occurs a few hearken, study, and then rejoicingly accept the new Truth; these are its pioneers, its apostles, who go out to proclaim it to the as yet unbelieving world. They meet with ridicule, then with persecution; for ever the new Truth undermines some hoary Lie, which has its band of devoted adherents living on the spoils of its reign. Slowly, against custom and tradition, against selfishness and violence, even against indifference, deadliest foe of all, this band of devoted teachers makes its onward way. And the band grows and grows, and each convert becomes in his turn a pioneer; until at last the victory is won, and the minority has become the majority; and then the time comes for some new Truth once more, and the old struggle is gone over afresh, and so again and again; and thus the race makes progress, and humanity climbs ever upward towards the perfect life.

During the last century and a quarter the social problem has been pressing for solution on all who have brains to think, and hearts to feel. The coexistence of wealth and penury, of idle prodigality and laborious stint; the terrible fact that "progress and poverty" seem to march hand-in-hand; the growing slums in large towns; the huge fortunes and the starving poor; these things make content impossible, and force into prominence the question: "Must this state of things continue? Is there no possible change which will cure, not only palliate, the present evils?"

Great hopes have sprung into being from time to time, each in turn to be blighted. Machinery was to double production and diminish toil, to spread comfort and sufficiency everywhere. It made cotton-lords and merchant-princes with one hand, and with the other created a proletariat unlike aught the world had seen, poor in the midst of the wealth it created, miserable in the midst of luxury, ignorant in the midst of knowledge, savage in the midst of civilisation. When the repeal of the Corn Laws was striven for and accomplished, once more hope rose high. Cheap food was to put an end to starvation. Alas! in the streets of the wealthiest city in Christendom, men and women perish for lack of a loaf of bread.

Nor is this persistence of misery and of squalor the only sign which troubles the brain and the heart of the student of the social problem. He notes the recurring crises in industry, the inflations and depressions of trade. At one time all is prosperous; demand is brisk, and supply can scarce keep pace with it; wages rise, full time is worked, production is enormously increased. Then a change creeps over all; supply has overtaken, has surpassed demand; the market is glutted; the warehouses are filled with unsaleable goods; short time begins; wages fall; mills are closed; furnaces are damped out; many workers are discharged. Then the unemployed in the large towns increase in number; the poor-rate rises; distress spreads upwards. After a while the depression passes; trade improves; and the whole weary circle is trodden once more. Nor is this all; although there has been "over-production" there is want of the necessaries of life; there are unsaleable clothing goods in the warehouses, and half-naked people shivering outside; too many blankets, and children crying themselves to sleep for cold. This monstrous absurdity, of commodities a drug in the market, and human beings perishing for want of those very commodities, stares us ever in the face. Cannot human brain discover some means to put an end to this state of things, a state which would be ludicrous were it not for the horrible suffering involved in it? Some say, this must always be so; that the poor shall be for ever with us; that commercial crises are inevitable; that these evils are not susceptible of complete cure. If this indeed be true, then I know not that any better advice can be given to humanity than that given to Job by his wife, to "curse God and die". But I think not so meanly of human intelligence; I believe not that our present industrial system, little more than a century old, must needs be eternal; I believe that the present system, devised by man and founded in greed of gain, may by man be changed; and that man's growing power over external nature may be used to bring comfort and wealth to each, and not, as now, to enrich the few at the cost of the enslavement of the many.

Various attempts to bring about a better social state have been made by earnest and noble-hearted men during the last hundred years. I leave aside such systems as those of the Moravians, because they cannot be regarded as in any sense schemes for the reconstruction of society. They, like the monastic communities, were merely attempts to create oases, fenced in from the world's evils, where men might prepare for a future life. These efforts were but crude attempts at Communism, and were foredoomed to failure, economic evolution not having reached the point at which a scientific Communism will become possible. With these the name of Robert Owen will be for ever associated.

Owen's first experiment was made at New Lanark, in connexion with the cotton-mills established there by Mr. Dale, his father-in-law. He became the manager of these in 1797, and set himself to work to improve the condition of the operatives and their families. The success which attended his efforts, the changes wrought by education and by fair dealings, encouraged him to plan out a wider scheme of social amelioration. In 1817 he was asked to report on the causes of poverty to the Committee on the Poor Laws, and in this report he dwelt on the serious increase of pauperism which had followed the introduction of machinery, and urged that employment ought to be found for those who were in need of it. He "recommended that every union or county should provide a farm for the employment of their poor; when circumstances admitted of it, there should be a manufactory in connexion with it" ("Robert Owen," by A. J. Booth, p. 70). On the farm, buildings were to be built for housing the laborers, consisting of "a square, divided into two parallelograms by the erection of public buildings in the centre"; these would consist of "a kitchen, mess-room, school-rooms, library and lecture hall. The poor would enjoy every advantage that economy could suggest: the same roof would cover many dwellings: the same stove might warm every room: the food would be cooked at the same time, and on the same fire: the meals would be eaten from the same table, in the society of friends and fellow-workers. Sympathies now restricted to the family would be thus extended to a community: the union would be still further cemented by an equal participation in the profits, an equal share in the toil. . . . . Competition is the cause of many vices; association will be their corrective" (*Ibid*, pp. 70—72). Soon after this report, Mr. Owen published a letter, urging the reconstitution of "the whole of society on a similar basis"; the lowest class was to consist of paupers, to be drafted into the proposed establishments; the second of the "working class"; the third of laborers, artisans, and tradesmen, with property of from £100 to £2,000; the fourth of persons unable or unwilling to work, owning from £1,000 to £20,000; these were to employ the second class. The workman was to be supported by this class in comfort for seven years in exchange for his labor, and then was to be presented by it with £100, so that he might enter class three; if he remained as a worker for five years more he was to have £200.

A community of workers, as recommended by Owen, was started in 1825, under the management of Abraham Combe, at Orbiston, nine miles east of Glasgow, and it began well; but Combe died in 1827, and with his death the whole thing went to pieces. A few months before the settlement at Orbiston, Robert Owen sailed for America, and he purchased a property named Harmony, consisting of 30,000 acres in Indiana, from the Rappites, a religious communistic body. He advertised for inhabitants, and gathered together a mixed crowd; "there were some enthusiasts who had come, at great personal sacrifice, to face a rude life and to mix among rude men, who had no object but to work out the great problem of a New Society; there were others who fancied they could secure abundance with little labor, prepared to shirk their share in the toil, but not to forego their share in the reward" (*Ibid*, p. 106). In the following year, 1826, "New Harmony" inaugurated a system of complete Communism, much against Owen's judgment; a number of small independent communities were soon formed, eight of these having already broken off from New Harmony early in 1827, the difficulties attendant on widely extended common life being found insuperable. In 1828, Robert Owen was forced to confess that his efforts had failed, and that "families trained in the individual system" could not suddenly be plunged into pure Communism with success. It boots not to dwell here on his further efforts in England. Robert Owen's experiments failed, but out of his teaching arose the co-operative movement, and the impulse to seek some rational system of society has, since his time, never quite died out in England.

In America a large number of communities have been established, mostly religious in character. From the careful account given of them by Charles Nordhoff, the following brief details are taken (all numbers relate to 1874). The Amana community consists of 1,450 members; they have a property of 25,000 acres, and live in seven small towns; they are Germans, very pious and very prosperous; their head is a woman, who is directly inspired by God. The Harmony Society, Economy, near Pittsburg, consists of followers of Rapp, who founded the society in 1805. They are all Germans and number 110, in addition to about 100 hired laborers and some sixty children. They live in comfort, and have clearly done well unto themselves, owning now a very large amount of property. The Separatists of Zoar, Ohio, are, once more, Germans: they started in 1817, have now about 300 members, own 7,000 acres of land, and are prosperous exceedingly. The Shakers, established in 1792, are scattered over several States, number about 2,415, own about 100,000 acres of land, are divided into fifty-eight communities, and are wealthy and prosperous; the members are American and English. The Perfectionists of Oneida and Wallingford are American, and the first attempt by them at communal living took place in 1846. They number 521, and own 894 acres of land. They also are prosperous. The Aurora and Bethel Communes, in Oregon, are German, or "Pennsylvania Dutch"; they started in 1844, and now number some 600 persons: their property extends to 23,000 acres, and they live in much comfort. The Icarians, founded by Etienne Cabet in 1848, are nearly all French; they have hitherto been less fortunate than the preceding societies, in consequence of mismanagement at the start; a heavy debt was incurred early in the movement, and members fell off; but a few resolute men and women settled down steadily in Iowa, with 4,000 acres of land, and 20,000 dollars of debt; they had to give up the land to their creditors, but managed to redeem nearly half of it, and they are now 65 in number, own 1,936 acres, have no debts, and have acquired a large live stock. They still live very plainly, but are on their way to prosperity, having conquered all the difficulties amid which they started; their constitution is perfectly democratic and they are without religion. A Swedish community at Bishop Hill, Illinois, was formed by a pietist sect which emigrated to America to escape persecution in 1846-1848. They were terribly poor at first and lived in holes in the ground, with a tent for a church, but gradually acquired property; until in 1859 they owned 10,000 acres of land, worth 300,000 dollars, and some magnificent live stock. Unfortunately their piety led to such extreme dullness that the younger members of the society revolted: debt was incurred, individuality was advocated, the property was divided, and the community ceased to exist. Lastly, there are two small communities, founded in 1871 and 1874; the former, the Progressive Community, at Cedar Vale, consists partly of Russians; it possesses 320 acres of good land, and has only eight members, of whom one is a child. The second, the Social Freedom Community, consists of three adults and three lads, Americans, and has a farm of 333 acres.

The whole of these societies can only be regarded as in the nature of experiments, and as such they are extremely interesting; each community has succeeded in gaining comfort and independence, but these small bodies, living chiefly by agriculture in a thinly-populated country on virgin soil, while they show the advantages of associated labor, really offer no data for the solution of the problems which beset a complex society. They are a return to more primitive forms of living, not an onward social evolution, and they are only possible in a "new country". Further, while they are communistic so far as their own members are concerned, they are individualistic and competitive in their aspect to the outer world; each small group holds its own property, and transacts all its business on the old lines in its dealings with the rest of the nation. This is, of course, inevitable, since each is encircled by competition: but it must not be overlooked that all these organisations, like co-operative societies at home, are nothing more than enlarged families, and are essentially individualistic—winning sufficiency for their own narrow, isolated circles, but leaving untouched the question of national poverty. They are arks, rescuing their inmates from the deluge, but they do nothing to drain away the seething ocean of misery.

Modern Socialism has wider aims than the saving of a few, or the piecemeal reformation of society; it is an attempt to get at the root of the poverty which now prevails; to find out how fortunes are made; why commercial crises occur: what are the real relations of capital and labor at the present time.

In speaking of "fortunes", I do not here include fortunes made by gambling, as on the Stock Exchange. They fall under another category, for in gambling, whether on the Stock Exchange or on the card table, wealth is not really made: it only passes from one pocket to another. The gambler, or the burglar, may "make a fortune" so far as he is himself concerned; but it is not done by the creation of wealth, but only by transferring wealth already existing from the pocket of its temporory possessor into his own; in both businesses the profits are large because the risks are great, and the penalty for failure heavy for the moment.

Socialism, as an industrial system, is chiefly concerned with fortunes in the making, with the way in which the wealth created by associated labor passes into the hands of individuals who do little or nothing in exchange for it. These fortunes arise from the ownership of the instruments of production, or of the raw material out of which wealth is to be manufactured; from the ownership, that is, of capital or of land.

Production.

Let us take the case of the possessor of capital employed in manufacture. This man desires to obtain more wealth than he can produce alone, more than he can individually produce even with the help of machinery. He must consequently hire others, who, in exchange for a certain fixed sum to be paid to them by him, shall allow him to take over the whole results of their labor, and to pocket the difference between those results and the fixed sum paid by him. This fixed sum is known as wage, and is "the market price of labor". We have therefore here two classes face to face with each other: one is a class which is the owner of capital, that is which possesses the instruments of production; the other is a class which possesses the labor force, without which the instruments of production are useless, but which must perish if it cannot get hold of some of those instruments. (Behind the capitalists is a third-class, the land-owning, with which the capitalist has to come to terms: that will be dealt with afterwards.) This second class stands therefore at this disadvantage; that while the capitalist can, if he pleases, utilise his own labor-force for his own subsistence, it cannot subsist at all except with his consent and aid, being shut out from the raw material by the landowner, and from the instruments of production by himself. Put a naked man on fertile soil in a decent climate and he will subsist; he will live on fruits and berries while with his hands he fashions some rough tool, and with the help thereof makes him a better one; out of the raw material he will form an instrument of production with those original instruments of production given him by nature, his fingers and the muscles of his body; then with his instrument and the raw material at his feet he will labor and win his livelihood. But in our complex society this opening is not before him; the raw material is enclosed and trespassers are prosecuted; if he picks fruit for food, he is a thief; if he breaks off a bough to make a rough tool, he is arrested; he cannot get an instrument of production, and if he could he would have nothing to use it on; he has *nothing* but his labor-force, and he must either sell that to someone who wants it, or he must die. And the sale must be complete. His labor force is bought for so much down per week or per month; it no longer belongs to himself, it is owned by his master, and he has not any right over that which it produces; he has sold it, and if he wants to resume possession he must give notice of his wish to the owner thereof; having resumed possession it is of no use to him; he can only live by selling it to somebody else. He is "free", in so far that he is able to change his master: he is a slave in that he must sell the labor force in his body for food. The man whose labor-force has been sold to another for life is regarded by all as a slave; the man whose labor-force is sold for stated terms is regarded by most as free; yet in comparing the conditions of the two, it is well to bear in mind that the slave, in becoming a chattel, becomes of value to his master, and it is the interest of the latter to feed him well and to keep up his physical strength as long as is possible; also in old age he is fed and housed, and can die in peace amid his fellows. Whereas the wage earner has no such value, but it is his master's interest to get as much work out of him as is possible, without regard for his health, there being plenty to take his place when he is worn out; and when he is old, he is separated from wife and child and is left to die in the prison we call a workhouse. The slave is valuable, as the horse and the ox are valuable, to his owner: the wage-earner is valuable only as a garment, which is cast into the dusthole when it is worn out.

It may be answered that the wage-earner by good fortune, industry, and thrift, may be able so to save of his earnings that he may escape the workhouse, and may even himself become independent and an "employer of labor". True. So might a lucky slave become free. But the truth that some may rise out of their class does not render satisfactory the state of the class, and the very fact that such rising is held out as a reward and a stimulus is an admission that an escape from the proletariat must be the natural longing of every proletarian. The rising of a few does not benefit the proletariat as a whole, and it is the existence of this unpropertied proletariat which is the evil thing.

To this proletariat, waiting to sell its labor-force, the capitalist goes, for it is here that he will be able to obtain the wealth-making strength which he requires. The next question is: What determines the wage which he is to pay? That is: what fixes the market price of labor-force?

Putting on one side temporary and comparatively trivial causes which may slightly affect it one way or the other, there are two constant determinants: population, and standard of living. The market-price of labor-force will largely depend on the quantity of labor-force in the market; if the supply exceed the demand, the price will be low; if the demand exceed the supply, the price will go up. If an employer requires fifty laborers, and two hundred laborers compete with each other for the employment he offers, and if the employment stands between them and starvation, he will be able to beat down their price until it touches the lowest point at which they can subsist. The more rapid the multiplication of the proletariat, the better for the capitalist class.

The other determinant is the "standard of living" or "standard of comfort". Wage can never sink beyond the point at which a man and his family can temporarily exist thereon; this is the extreme limit of its fall, inasmuch as a man will not work unless he can exist on the results of his work. As a matter of fact, it does not often sink so low; the wage of an ordinary operative is more than barely suffices to keep him and his family alive, but large numbers of the laboring poor are habitually underfed, and are liable to the diseases brought on by low living, as well as to premature aging and death arising from the same cause. It is a significant fact that the deathrate of the poor is much higher than the deathrate of the rich. Wage is lower in countries in which the standard of living is low, than in those in which it is, by comparison, higher. Thus in parts of Scotland, where oatmeal is much used for food, and children run much barefoot, wage is normally lower than in England, where wheaten flour and shoes and stockings are expected. Any general lowering of the standard of living is therefore to be deprecated—as the wide substitution of cheap vegetable food-stuffs for more expensive articles of diet. The standard of living also (and chiefly, in any given country) affects wages through its effect on population. Mill points out ("Principles of Political Economy," Book II, chap. xi, sec. 2) that "wages do adapt themselves to the price of food", either (*a*) from children dying prematurely when food rises, and wages were before barely sufficient to maintain them, or (*b*) from voluntary restriction of the growth of population when the laborers refuse to sink below a certain standard of living. In each case the diminution of labor supply causes a rise of wage. "Mr. Ricardo", says Mill, "considers these two cases to comprehend all cases. He assumes that there is everywhere a minimum rate of wages: either the lowest with which it is physically possible to keep up the population, or the lowest with which the people will choose to do so. To this minimum he assumes that the general rate of wages always tends; that they can never be lower, beyond the length of time required for a diminished rate of increase to make itself felt, and can never long continue higher." This is the "iron law of wages", and it is the recognition of its truth which, among other reasons, sets Socialists against the wage-system of industry. [It must not be forgotten that the phrase "ordinary operative" does not include all the workers. There is a large class which obtains barely subsistence wage, and those who are not regularly employed are on the very verge of starvation. The hard lot of these must not be left out of sight in impeaching the present social state.]

The capitalist, then, buys as much labor-force as he desires, or as his means allow, at the market price, determined in the way we have seen. This labor-force he proposes to utilise for his own advantage; with some of his capital he buys it; some of his capital consists in machinery, and the labor-force set at work on this machinery is to produce wealth. The labor-force and the instruments of production are now brought together; they will now produce wealth, and both they and the wealth they produce are the property of the capitalist.

Our next inquiry is: Where does the capitalist look for his profit? He has bought machinery; he has bought labor-force; whence comes the gain he is seeking? The profit of the capitalist must arise from the difference between the price he pays for labor-force and the wealth produced by it; out of this difference must be paid his rent, the loss incurred by wear-and-tear, and the price of the raw material on which his machinery works; these provided for, the remainder of the difference is his "profit". The analysis of the way in which this profit arises is, then, the task that comes next.

In Karl Marx's "Das Capital" may be found a carefully

elaborated exposition of "surplus-value". The student will do well to read his seventh chapter, on the "production of use-value and surplus-value"; in reading, he must remember Marx's definitions of value and use-value, which of course govern the whole. Value is human labor incorporated in a commodity; use-value is that which in a commodity satisfies some human want. The "use-value" of Marx is identical with the "intrinsic natural worth" of Locke. Locke says: "The intrinsic natural worth of any thing consists in its fitness to supply the necessities, or serve the conveniences of human life". ("Considerations of the Lowering of Interest," etc, Locke's Works, vol. ii., p. 28, ed. 1777). As an instance of the production of surplus-value—that is of the difference between the capital which the capitalist expends in production and that which he possesses when the production is complete—Marx takes the case of the manufacture of ten pounds of thread. The capitalist buys ten pounds of cotton at 10s.; wear-and-tear of machinery in the spinning of the cotton into thread raises his expenditure to 12s.; further, six hours of work are necessary to turn the ten pounds of cotton into ten pounds of thread.

Now suppose that a man in six hours is able to produce sufficient to maintain himself for a day;—that is that he produces as much as might be exchanged for a day's consumption of the necessaries of life. Let us value this at 3s. in money. That 3s. which is the monetary equivalent of his six hours' labor must be added to the cost of production of the thread; its value has therefore risen finally to 15s. If the capitalist now sells his ten pounds of thread for 15s., he will only receive back as much as he has expended; he will have made no profit. But suppose the working day be of twelve hours instead of six, the wages paid will none the less be fixed at 3s. by the standard of living; but in that second six hours the operative can transform another ten pounds of cotton into another ten pounds of thread; as before, cotton and wear-and-tear will amount to 12s.; but these ten pounds of thread have a value of 15s. as had the previous ten pounds although they have only cost the capitalist 12s. Hence the final product of the day's labor has a value of 30s., but has cost the capitalist only 27s. The value added by the operative in the second six hours has brought *him* no equivalent; it is "surplus-value", value added by him over the value whose equivalent he receives in wage; this creation of surplus-value is the aim of the capitalist.

Now, without tying ourselves down to the exact figures and the phraseology of Marx, we may yet see by a little thought that his main position is essentially correct. If a capitalist buys £1 worth of raw material; if his machinery is depreciated say by the value of one shilling in working up the raw material; if he pays in wage 5s. for the labor-force expended on it; he will most certainly not be content with selling the finished product for 26s. He demands a "profit" on the transaction, and this profit can only be the difference between that which is paid to labor, and the value, in the ordinary sense of the word, which labor creates.

It is sometimes objected that nothing is gained by Marx's divisions of "value", "surplus value", and "exchange value", but that, on the contrary, they transport economics into a metaphysical region away from the solid ground of facts. It is urged that it is better to represent the conditions thus: that the worker produces a mass of commodities; that the capitalist sells these commodities for what they will fetch in the market, the price being fixed, not by the duration of the labor embodied in them, but by the relative utilities of money and commodity to buyer and seller; that the capitalist gives over to the producer sufficient of the results of the sale to enable the producer to exist, and pockets the remainder. This presentment is a statement of the facts as they are; Marx's "value" is a metaphysical abstraction corresponding to nothing existing at the present time, however true it would be under ideal conditions. The main point to grasp, however, is obvious, whichever of these presentments is thought preferable. Capital, under our present industrial system, is the result of unpaid labor—a matter to be further considered later in this essay. But it must be remembered that, as a matter of fact, the profit made by the capitalist is not a fixed quantity, as is the "surplus value" of Marx; but that the capitalist not only preys on the worker, but also on the necessities of the consumer, his profit rising and falling with the changes of demand and supply. The phrase "surplus value", if it is to be retained at all, might well be extended to cover the whole difference between the price paid to labor for the commodities it produces, and the price obtained for those commodities by the capitalist employer of labor. It is in this wide sense that the phrase is used in the following pages, not in the metaphysical sense of Marx.

We are now in a position to understand how large fortunes are made, and why Capital and Labor are ever at war.

Before the commencement of the Industrial Period—which may be fairly dated from the invention of the Spinning Jenny in 1764—it was not possible to accumulate great wealth by the employment of hired labor. By hand-work, or by the use of the very simple machines available prior to that date, a single operative was not able to produce sufficient to at once support himself and to largely enrich others. "Masters and men" consequently formed a community of workers, without the sharp divisions that now exist between capitalist and "hands"; and the employer would have been as much ashamed of *not* working deftly at his trade, as the son of a Lancashire cotton-lord would be ashamed if he were suspected of throwing a shuttle in one of his father's looms. Under these conditions there was very little surplus-value to be absorbed, and there were consequently no great aggregations of the purely industrial classes. The introduction of machinery multiplied enormously the productive power of the operative, while it did not increase the wage he received. A man receiving 3s. for a day of twelve hours, produced, we will say for the sake of illustration, surplus-value to the amount of 1s.; after the introduction of machinery he received the same wage and produced an enormously increased surplus-value. Thus the fortunes of the lucky possessors of the new machinery rose by "leaps and bounds"; lads who began at the loom were owners of palaces by middle age; even later on, after the first rush had spent itself, I have myself met Lancashire cotton-lords who were mill-hands in their youth; but most certainly their wealth had only been made by the results of the toil of many becoming concentrated in the hands of one.

Another step was taken to increase surplus-value. Depending, as it does, on the difference between the value produced by the worker and the amount paid to him as wage, it is obvious that if it be possible to obtain the same amount of produce from purchased labor-force while reducing the purchase-money, the surplus-value will become larger. This step was soon taken, for it was found that many machines could be superintended by a woman quite as effectively as by a man, while female labor-force was purchasable in the market at a lower rate. Hence the large introduction of female "hands" into cotton mills, and as married women were found more "docile" than unmarried—docility increasing with the number of mouths crying for bread at home—there came the double curse on the producers, of male labor being pushed aside by female labor at lower wage, and of untidy home and neglected children, bereft of mother's care. Yet another step. Child-labor was cheaper even than woman-labor, and by utilising children with their pitiful wage, surplus-value might be swollen to yet larger proportions; and as wives had fought with husbands for wage, so children now fought with fathers and mothers, until verily a man's foes in the labor-market were they of his own household.

There was, however, a way of increasing surplus-value apart from the amount of daily wage. The lengthening of the hours of labor has obviously the same result in this respect as the lowering of wage. The very zenith of the production of surplus-value, the most complete exploitation of the producers, the perfect triumph of the capitalist ideal of free contract and of *laissez-faire*, were reached when little children, at nominal wage, were worked from fifteen to sixteen hours a day, and princely fortunes were built up by human sacrifice to the devil of greed, in fashion that shall never, so help us tongue, and pen, and arm, be again possible in this fair English land.

We have at the present time no exact figures available which can enable us to judge of the precise amount of surplus value produced in the various departments of industry. In America, the Bureaus of Labor Statistics help us, and from these we learn some suggestive facts.

	Average wage paid to worker.		Extra net value produced by worker.			Average wage paid to worker.		Extra net value produced by worker.	
1850	£49	12	£41	16	1870	£62	0	£69	0
1860	58	8	65	10	1880	69	4	64	14

(Taken from Laurence Gronlund's quotation of these

returns in his "Co-operative Commonwealth", chap. i. The same figures, as regards total net produce and wages paid, have appeared in a capitalist work.) We have now in England a Labor Bureau somewhat similar to those now existing in the United States, but it is still too young to give us the figures we need. For this Bureau we have to thank Charles Bradlaugh, M.P., who succeeded in passing a resolution in favor of the official publication of similar statistics through the House of Commons. Among the many priceless services he has done to the workers, the obtaining of these is by no means the least. Exact knowledge of the present state of things is a necessary precedent of organic change, and the figures supplied by the Labor Bureau will give us the very weapons that we need.

The absolutely antithetical interests of Capital and Labor have necessitated—and must continue to necessitate while the present system lasts—a constant and embittered war. As Capital can only grow by surplus value, it strives to lengthen the working day and to decrease the daily wage. Labor struggles to shorten the hours of toil, and to wring from Capital a larger share of its own product in the form of higher wage. While Capital is the possession of one class, and Labor is the only property of the other, this strife must go on. There can never be industrial peace until this root of war be pulled up, and until Capital, under the control of the community, shall be used for the fertilisation, instead of for the oppression of Labor.

Since large fortunes are made by manufacturers, and there is no source of wealth save labor applied to natural objects, it is clear that these fortunes are due to the fact that the manufacturers are able to become the owners of the means of production and of labor-force; even these very means of production, with which the present labor-force works, are but past labor-force crystallised. The wage-earners must produce sufficient to maintain themselves from day to day and to increase the capital of the wage-payers, else they will not be employed. Hence arises another evil, the waste of productive force. Men are not employed because their labor-force, embodied in the necessaries of life, will spread sufficiency and comfort throughout the community. They are only employed when the articles produced can be *sold at a profit* by a third party; their products, fairly exchanged for the products of their fellow-laborers—woven cloth, say, for shoes—would clothe warmly the shivering population; but above the cloth produced by the one, and the shoes produced by the other, stand the capitalists, who demand profit for themselves ere the cloth shall be allowed to shield the naked back, or the shoes keep off the pavement the toes blued by the frost. If the employment fails, the wage-earner is out of food; but the erstwhile wage-payer has the capital made by the former to live upon, while its maker starves. The capitalist, truly, cannot increase his capital, unless he can buy labor-force; but he can live on his capital. On the other hand the labor-force must perish unless it can find a purchaser. Let us put the position plainly, for as the great majority of people think the arrangement a perfectly fair one, there is no need to cover it over with a veil of fine phrases and roundabout expressions. The owner of raw material and of the means of production faces the unpropertied proletarian, and says to him: "I hold in my hands the means of existence; unless you can obtain the means of existence you will die; but I will only let you have them on one condition. And that is that you shall labor for me as well as for yourself. For each hour that you spend in winning bread, you shall spend another in enriching me. I will give you the right to win a hard existence by your labor, if you will give me the right to take whatever you produce beyond that bare existence. You are perfectly free to choose; you can either accept my terms, and let me live on your work, or you can refuse my terms, and starve." Put so baldly, the proposition has a certain brutality in it. Yet when we Socialists argue that a system is bad which concentrates the means of existence in the hands of a propertied class, and leaves an unpropertied class under the hard condition of winning only the right to exist on such terms as may be granted by the propertied; when we urge this, we are told that we are incendiaries, thieves, idiots, or, at the mildest, that our hopes of freeing these enslaved ones are dreams, mere castles in the air.

We have now reached the foundation of modern Socialism. We say: As long as the industrial classes are divided into capitalists and proletarians, so long must continue the present strife, and the present extremes of wealth and of poverty. It is not a mere modification, but a complete revolution of the industrial system which is required. Capital must be controlled by labor, instead of controlling it. The producers must obtain possession of their own product, and must regulate their own labor. The present system has been weighed in the balances and found wanting, and on the wall of the capitalist banqueting-room is written by the finger of modern thought, dipped in the tears and in the bloody sweat of the over-tasked proletariat: "Man hath numbered thy kingdom and finished it. It is divided among the myriads thou hast wronged."

Competition.

Strife is the normal condition of the whole industrial world; Capital strives against Labor, and Labor against Capital, lock-outs and strikes being the pitched battles of the struggle; capitalists strive against capitalists for profits, and the list of the vanquished may be read in the bankruptcy court; workers strive against workers for wage, and injure their own order in the fratricidal combat. Everywhere the same struggle, causing distress, waste, hatred, in every direction; brothers wronging brothers for a trifling gain; the strong trampling down the weak in the frantic race for wealth. It is the struggle of the wild beasts of the forest transferred to the city; the horrible struggle for existence, only in its "civilised" form hearts are wrenched and torn instead of limbs.

It is constantly urged that competition is advantageous because it develops capacity, and by the struggle it causes it brings about the survival of the fittest. The allegation may be traversed on two grounds: granting that capacity is developed by struggle, it is yet developed at great cost of suffering, and it would be more worthy of reasoning beings to seek to bring about the capacity and to avoid the suffering; to borrow an illustration which suggests itself by the very word "struggle", we know that actual fighting develops muscle, endurance, readiness of resource, quickness of the senses; none the less do we regard war as a disgrace to a civilised people, and we find that the useful capacities developed by it may be equally well developed in the gymnasium and the playing-field, without the evils accompanying war. So may education take the place of competition in developing useful qualities. Further we deny that "the fittest" for social progress survive in the competitive struggle. The hardest, the keenest, the most unscrupulous survive, because such are the fittest for the brutal strife; but the generous, the magnanimous, the just, the tender, the thoughtful, the sympathetic, the very types in whose survival lies the hope of the race, are crushed out. In fact, competition *is* war, and the very reasons which move us to endeavor to substitute arbitration for war, should move us to endeavor to substitute co-operation for competition.

But it is urged, competition among capitalists is advantageous to the public, and it is shown that where two or three railway lines compete for custom, the public is better served than where there is only one. Granted. There is an old adage which says that "when thieves fall out, honest men come by their own"; none the less is it better to stop thieving, than to encourage it under the hope that the thieves may fall out, and some of the stolen goods be recovered. So long as capitalists are permitted to exploit labor, so long is it well that they should compete with each other and so have their profits lessened; but it would be still better to stop the exploitation. Accepting the railway instance, it may be rejoined that the German State railways have comfortable carriages that can hold their own against all comers, and that whereas a railway company, eager for dividends, can only be forced into providing decent carriages by fear of losing customers to a rival, a State railway is managed for the benefit of the public, and improvements are readily introduced. Our post-office system shows how improvements are made without any pressure of competition; it has given us cheaper postage, cheaper telegraphing, and is giving us cheaper parcel-delivery; so that we can send from London a letter to Wick for a penny, a telegram thither for sixpence, and a parcel for threepence. It is a matter of pride to the Postmaster-General of the day, as a public servant, to improve his department, although he is protected by law (save in case of parcels only just undertaken) from competition.

Even some economists who approve of competition see the need of limiting its excesses. Mr. R. S. Moffat, for instance, approves of it and thinks that "competition is not only the best, but the only practical means of meeting" "the conflicting natural conditions, between the exigencies of an unknown demand and the fluctuations of an uncertain supply", "that ever has been, or is ever likely to be discovered" ("The Economy of Consumption", p. 114, ed. 1878.) Yet Mr. Moffat points out that "the material cost of competition includes two items: first, superfluous production, or wasted labor; and secondly ill-balanced distribution, or misdirected labor" (p. 115); and he declares: "not content with promoting a healthful industry, it enforces tyrannous laws upon labor, and exacts from the free laborer an amount of toil which the hardest taskmaster never succeeded in wringing from the slave. It disturbs by its excesses the balance of industry which its moderation had established. In times of prosperous production it accumulates stocks till they become a nuisance and a source of the most serious embarrassment to producers, who do not know where to turn for employment to their productive resources; and in adverse times it gambles with them, and deprives consumption of their support at the very time for which they were provided" (pp. 116, 117). "It is upon laborers", he says, "not only as individuals, but as a class, that the great burden of over-production falls" (p. 190.)

I propose to consider I., the evils of competition; II., the remedy proposed by Socialism.

I.—The Evils.—Many of these lie on the surface; others become palpable on very slight investigation. They affect the capitalist manufacturer; the distributor; the consumer; and the producing classes.

An ingenious capitalist sees a want and devises an article to meet it; or he devises an article and sets to work to create the want. He places his article before the public, and a demand for it arises. The article either supplies a real want, or it becomes "the fashion", and the demand increases and outstrips the supply. Other capitalists rush in to compete for the profit which is to be made; capital flows rapidly into the particular industry concerned; high wages are offered; operatives flock to it; the supply swells until it overtops the demand. But when this point is touched, the supply is not at once lessened; so long as there is any hope of profit, the capitalists manufacture; wage is lessened to keep up the profit, but this expedient fails; short hours are worked; at last the market becomes thoroughly overstocked. Then distress follows, and while capital seeks new outlets, the operatives fall into the great army of unemployed; and very often the small capitalists, who went into the rush just when profit was at its highest, and who have not sufficient capital to hold out against the fall, and to await a rise, meet the fate of earthenware pots, carried down a torrent among iron ones. When this happens, the result of their speculative folly is held up as an example of the "risks run by capitalists". Nor is this the only way along which a small capitalist sometimes travels to the bankruptcy court. He often borrows money "to extend his business", and if the business shrinks instead of expanding, he becomes bankrupt. In the universal war, the big capitalist fish devour the small fry.

And, after all, even the "successful man" of our competitive society is not one whose lot is to be envied by the healthy human being. Not for him the pure joy in natural beauty, in simple amusements, in intellectual triumph, which is the dower of those unstained by the fight for gold. For the successful competitor in commercial war Nature has no laurel-crown. He has bartered himself for a mess of pottage, and his birthright of healthy humanity is gone from him for evermore. Well does Moffat write his fate: "The man who strives to make a fortune contemplates his own ease and enjoyment, not the good of society. He flatters himself that through his superior skill, tact, wisdom, energy, or whatever quality it is he thinks himself twice as strong in as his neighbors, he will be able to do in half a lifetime what it takes them their whole lives to do. For this he toils and sacrifices his health; for this he rushes upon reckless speculations, and hazards his character and reputation; for this he makes himself indifferent to the rights and callous to the feelings of others; for this he is sordid, mean, and parsimonious. All these are the means by which, according to different temperaments, the same end is pursued. And what is the end? An illusion, nay, worse, a dishonesty. The man who pursues a fortune is not qualifying himself for any other course of life besides that which he at present lives. He is merely striving to escape from duty into enjoyment. And the fever of the strife frequently becomes his whole existence; so that when he has obtained his object, he finds himself unable to do without the excitement of the struggle" (p. 220). Surely in judging the merits of a system it is fair to take into account the injuries it works to its most successful products. Its masterpieces are the withered and dehumanised; its victims are the paupers and the suicides.

Nor can we leave out of account in studying competitive production the waste of material, and of the time spent in working it up, which result from over-production. The accumulation of stock while the demand is lessening means the making and storing of unneeded wares. Some of these are forced into the market, some lie idly in the great warehouses. The retail dealers find themselves over-stocked, their shelves laden with unsaleable goods. These fade, and spoil, and rust away—so much good material wasted, so much human labor spent for nought, monuments of a senseless system, of the barbarous, uncalculating blindness of our productive force.

More heavily yet than on the capitalist does competition press on the distributor. A dozen traders compete for the custom which one could satisfactorily supply. The competition for shops in a thickly populated neighborhood drives up the rent, and so adds to the retailer's burden. He is compelled to spend large sums in advertising, striving by brilliancy of color or eccentricity of design to impress himself on the public mind. An army of commercial travellers sweeps over the country, each man with his hand against his neighbor in the same trade, pushing, haggling, puffing his own, depreciating his rival's wares. These agents push their goods on the retailer, often when no real demand for them is coming from the public, and then the retailer puffs them, to create a demand for his supply. Nor must we omit from notice the enormous waste of productive energy in this army of canvassers, advertisers, bill-posters, multiplied middlemen of every kind. The distributive work done by these is absurdly out of proportion to their number. We see several carriers' carts half-filled, instead of half the number filled; each carrier has to deliver goods over the whole of a wide area, so that a man may have to drive five miles to deliver a single parcel at a house a stone's throw from a rival office. Yet each man must receive his full day's wage, and must be paid for the hours he is compelled to waste, as well as for those he spends in useful work. It is the same thing in every business. Three or four carts of each trade go daily down each road, covering the same ground, supplying each one house here and one there, losing time, wearing out horses and traps, a foolish shameful waste. And all these unnecessary distributors are consumers when they might be producers, and are actually making unnecessary work for others as well as for themselves.

Short-sighted people ask: Would you add all these to the crowds of half-starving unemployed now competing for work? No, we answer. We would not add them to the *un*employed; it is only in a system of complete competitive anarchy that there could be unemployed labor on the one hand, and people clamoring for the necessaries of life on the other. We have already seen that under the present system men are only employed where some profit can be made out of them by the person who hires them. Under a saner system there would be none unemployed while the food and clothing supply was insufficient, and the turning of non-productive consumers into productive ones would only mean shorter hours of labor, since the labor necessary to supply the consumption of the population would be divided among a larger number than before. If wealth be the result of labor applied to raw material, poverty may come from the pressure of population on the raw material which limits the means of subsistence, but never from the greater part of the population working to produce wealth on raw material sufficient for their support.

On the consumer falls much of the needless additional expense of advertisements, canvassers, and the rest. The flaming advertisements we see on the walls we pay for in the price of the puffed articles we buy. The trader feels their burden, and tries to recoup himself by adding a fraction of it to the price of the goods he sells. If he is forced to lower his nominal prices in consequence of the pressure of competition with his rivals, yet by adulteration he can really raise, while he seems to lower, them. The nominal width of fabrics does not correspond with the real; woollen goods are sold of which the warp is cotton; tobacco is sold damped unfairly to increase its weight; sand is mixed with sugar; lard or dripping with butter;

chicory with coffee; sloe-leaves with tea; turnip with orange in marmalade; foreign meat is offered as home-grown; damaged flesh is chopped up for sausages; until, at last, as Moffat caustically remarks: "It is not rogues and vagabonds alone who have recourse in trade to expedients which could not be justified by a strict theoretical morality. When this incline is entered upon, there is no resting upon it. Morality itself becomes subject to competition; and the conventional standard of trade morality gets lower and lower, until the things done by respectable people can hardly be distinguished from those done by people who are not respectable, except by the respectability of the people who do them" (p. 154). And in all this adulteration the consumer suffers in health, comfort, and temper. Not only does he pay more than he should for what he buys, but he buys a good deal more than he pays for.

Heaviest of all is the burden on the operative classes, and they suffer in a double character, both as consumers and producers. As consumers, they share the general injury; as producers, their case is yet more serious. If they are in work, their wages are driven down by the competition for employment; they are the first to feel a lessening demand in lengthened hours, in lower wage; as the depression goes on, they are thrown out of work; illness not only incapacitates them for the time, but their place is filled up, while they lie helpless, by the eager waiters for hire; when they combine to strike for fairer treatment, the fringe of unemployed labor around is used against them by the employers; the lowest depth is reached by the crowd who at the dockyard gates at the East of London literally fight for a place in which the foreman's eye may fall on them, and out of the struggling hundreds units are taken on for the day at miserable wage for heavy exhausting work, to be turned out at night to undergo a similar struggle next morning.

The only classes who gain by competition are the big capitalists and the landlords. The big capitalists engaged in manufacture gain by the crushing out of their smaller rivals, and by their ability to hold over stocks produced when wages are low until prices are high. Capitalists who only lend out money on usury, and live on the interest thereby obtained, flourish when the demand for money is brisk. Most of all do landlords, who live on rent, profit by the struggle. In a growing neighborhood rents of commercial premises rise rapidly, and the shopkeeper finds himself heavily taxed by the landlord, who imposes on him practically a graduated income-tax for his own advantage. Thus the chief gainers by competition are the idlers who are permitted to hold the nation's soil, and who live in luxury on the toilers, laughing to see how the fratricidal struggles of those who labor turn to the advantage of those who lounge. And so the strain of living constantly increases for the one class, while the luxury and ostentation of those who levy tax on toil become ever greater, and more aggressive by the contrast.

II. The Remedy.—These evils can be radically cured only in one way; it is by the substitution of co-operation for competition, of organisation for anarchy in industry. The relation of employer and employed must disappear, and a brotherhood of workers, associated for facilitation of production for use, must replace the band of servants toiling for the enrichment of a master by profit. The full details of socialised industry cannot be drawn at length; but it is not difficult to see that the already existent co-operative societies offer a suggestive model, and the trades unions a sufficiently competent means for change. Probably each industry in each district will organise itself, and own, for use, all its means of production; thus the miners of Durham, for instance, organised in their lodges, with their central executive, would form the mining trade society of that district; all the mines of that district would be under their control, and they would elect their officers of all grades. So with all mining districts throughout the land. These separate trade societies would be federated, and a General Board elected by all. The elements of such a self-organised industry exist at the present time, and the more closely the miners can band themselves into district unions, and the unions into a national federation, the more prepared will they be to play their part in the great industrial revolution. It is probable that something of the nature of the royalties now paid to the individual mine-owners will be paid into the National Exchequer, in exchange for the right to work the national soil. A similar organisation would be needed for each productive industry, and probably representatives of each separate industry would form a central Industrial Board. But, I repeat, these details cannot now be laid down authoritatively, any more than the details of the present industrial competitive system could have been laid down before the Industrial Period. On these details Socialists would inevitably differ considerably at the present time, and no special scheme can be fairly stamped as "Socialist" to the exclusion of the rest. But on this main principle all Socialists are agreed: that the only rightful holders of capital are industrial groups, or one great industrial group —the State, *i.e.*, the organised community; that while individuals may hold private property for use, none should hold capital—that is *wealth employed in production*—for individual profit; that while each may have property to consume and to enjoy, none should be allowed to use property to enslave his neighbor, to force another to work for his advantage.

The revolution of distribution will be as great as that in production, and here again co-operation must take the place of competition. We already see the beginnings of a distributive change in the establishment of huge stores for the supply of all the necessaries of life, and the way in which these are crushing out the smaller retail shops. Housewives find it more convenient to go to the single building, than to trudge wearily from shop to shop. Goods bought in very large quantities can be sold more cheaply than if bought in small, and economy, as well as convenience, attract the purchaser to the store. At present these stores are founded by capitalists and compete for custom, but they are forerunners of a rational distributive system. The very enmity they create in the minds of the small traders they ruin is paving the way for the community to take them over for the general advantage. Under Socialism all goods manufactured by the producers would be distributed to the central store of each district; from this central store they would be distributed to the retail stores. Anyone who thinks such distribution impossible had better study the postal system now existing; we do not have post-offices jostling each other as do baker's and butcher's shops: there are sufficient of them for the requirements of the district, and no more. The letters for a town are delivered at the General Post Office; they are sorted out and delivered at the subordinate offices;

the distribution of the correspondence of millions is carried on by a Government Department, quietly, effectively, without waste of labor, with celerity and economy. But then in the Post Office co-operation has replaced competition, organisation has replaced anarchy. Such a system, one hundred years ago, would have been pronounced impossible as the Conservative minds of to-day pronounce impossible its extension to anything except letters and telegrams and parcels. I look for the time when the success of the Post Office will be repeated—and improved—in every department of distribution.

Capital.

We have already seen that Capital is accumulated by withholding from the producer a large part of the value he produces, and we have now to look more closely into the growth of Capital and the uses to which it is put. A glance over the historical Past, as well as the study of the Present, inform us that Capital has always been—as indeed it always must be—obtained from unpaid labor, or, if the phrase be preferred, by the partial confiscation of the results of labor. In communities the economic basis of which was slave-labor, this fact was obvious; the owner confiscated the whole products of his slaves' toil, and he became a capitalist by this process of continued confiscation; while the slave, fed, clothed, and housed out of the fruit of his own labor by his master, never owned anything as of right, nor had any property in that which he created. As civilisation advanced, serf-labor replaced slave-labor; here also the confiscation of the results of labor was obvious. The serf was bound to give so many days of work to his lord without payment; this service rendered, the remainder of his time was his own, to produce for his own subsistence; but the lord's capital increased by the confiscation of the results of the serf's labor during the days whereon he worked for his lord. In modern times "free labor" has replaced serf-labor, but in the present industrial system as truly as in slave and in serf communities, Capital results from unpaid labor, though now from the unpaid labor of the wage-earner. We may search the whole world over, and we shall find no source of wealth save labor applied to natural agents. Wealth is never rained down from heaven, nor is it ever a spontaneous growth; unless indeed wild fruits taken for food be counted wealth, and even to these must human labor be applied in the form of picking ere they can be used. It is the result of human labor; and if one man has more than he has produced, it necessarily follows that another man has less than he has produced. The gain of one must be the loss of another. There are but sixteen court cards in the fifty-two, and if by ingenious shuffling, packing, and dealing, all the court cards fall to one player, only the lower cards can remain for the others.

Separating "Capital" from "Wealth" we may conveniently define it as "wealth devoted to purposes of profit", and as "wealth is the result of labor applied to raw material", Capital becomes the result of labor devoted to purposes of profit. John Stuart Mill says the "accumulated stock of the produce of labor is termed Capital". Macleod: "Capital is any Economic Quantity used for the purpose of Profit". Senior: "Economists are agreed that *whatever* gives a profit is properly called Capital". Something more, however, than the activity of labor is implied in the existence of Capital. There must have been saving, as well as production. Hence Marshall speaks of Capital as "the result of labor and abstinence"; Mill of Capital as "the result of saving"; and so on. It is obvious that if the products of labor were consumed as fast as they were made, Capital could not exist. We have, therefore, reached this certainty when we contemplate Capital; someone has worked, and has not consumed all that he has produced.

Under these circumstances, we should expect to find Capital in the hands of industrious and abstinent producers. But as Mill very justly points out: "In a rude and violent state of society it continually happens that the person who has Capital is not the very person who has saved it, but some one who, being stronger, or belonging to a more powerful community, has possessed himself of it by plunder. And even in a state of things in which property was protected, the increase of Capital has usually been, for a long time, mainly derived from privations which, though essentially the same with saving, are not generally called by that name, because not voluntary. The actual producers have been slaves, compelled to produce as much as force could extort from them, and to consume as little as the self-interest or the usually very slender humanity of their task-masters would permit." How many of our great capitalists have produced and saved until they accumulated the fortunes they possess? These fortunes are greater than any human being could save out of his makings, even if he lived most abstemiously, instead of with the luxury and ostentation of a Rothschild or a Vanderbilt. But if they have not made and saved, how came they to possess? Mill gives the answer, though he did not mean it to be applied to modern industrialism. "In a rude and violent state of society" Capital is not in the hands of the producer and saver, but in the hands of those who possess themselves "of it by plunder"—legalised plunder, in our modern days. The "saving" is not voluntary; it is "derived from privations"; the "actual producers" are wage-earners, who are "compelled to produce as much as" pressure can extort from them, and to "consume as little" in the form of wage as they can be beaten down to by the competition of the labor-market. These men "have labored, and" others "have entered into their labors".

A very brief comparison of those who produce and save, and those who possess themselves of the results of labor and abstinence, will suffice to show the inequality which characterises the present system. The worker lives hardly and dies poor, bequeathing to his children the same necessity of toil: I do not forget that the more fortunate workers have shares in Building Societies, a few pounds in the Savings Bank, and even an interest in a Burial Club, so that the parish may not have the expense of burying them; but I say that these poor successes—vast indeed in the aggregate, but paltry when the share of the individual is looked at—bear no kind of reasonable proportion to the wealth created by the worker during his life-time. On the other hand the capitalist either starts with inherited wealth, grows richer, and bequeaths the increased wealth to his children; or he begins poor, saves a little, then makes others work for him, grows rich, and bequeaths his wealth. In the second generation, the capitalist can simply invest his wealth and live on the interest; and since all interest must be paid out of the results of labor, the workers not only lose a large proportion of their produce, but this very confiscated produce is made into a future burden for them, and while the fathers build up the capitalist, the children must toil to maintain his children in idleness.

Capital may also be accumulated by the ownership of raw material, since no wealth can be produced until labor can get at this. The question of rent will be considered under the head of Land; here we are only concerned with the fact that wealth appropriated in this way is investible, and on this also interest can be obtained.

Now the enormous burden placed on labor by the investment of money at interest, is not appreciated as it ought to be. The interest on the National Debt, including terminable annuities, amounted in 1884-5 to £28,883,672 12s.; how much is paid in dividends on railway, tram-car, and companies' shares, it would be difficult to discover. Mr. Giffen, in his "Progress of the Working Classes", estimates that the capitalist classes receive from capital—excluding "wages of superintendence" and salaries—some £400,000,000 a year. In 1881, the income-tax returns quoted by Mr. Giffen show that the income from capital was no less than £407,000,000, and in estimating those in Schedules B and D (Part I.) Mr. Giffen certainly takes care to make the gains on "idle capital" as small as he can. Mr. Giffen takes the aggregate income of the whole nation at about £1,200,000,000, so that according to his own figures Capital takes more than a third part of the national income. I should be prepared to contend that the burden on the producers is heavier than he makes out, but even taking his own calculations the result is bad enough. For all this money which goes to capitalists is money *not* earned by the receivers—mark that all which is in any sense earned, as wages of superintendence, etc., is excluded—and by all this is lessened the share of the produce of labor which goes to labor.

We have already dealt with the way in which the worker suffers injustice when capital is invested in machinery owned by private individuals; we have now to consider the portion of it used as loans, cases in which the capitalist takes no part in the management of any industrial concern, but merely lends his money at usury, living on the interest he receives. There is so much confusion of thought on this subject, so much idea that a man has "a right" to invest money at interest, that it necessary to try to get at the "bed-rock" of the question. Take the case of a man who earns 30s. in a week; suppose he spends 20s. and saves 10s. For the 20s. he spends he receives their equivalent in commodities, and these he consumes; he has had his "money's worth", and he is content, and if he requires more commodities he knows he must labor again to earn their equivalent in money. The 10s. he has saved, however, are to have a different fate; they represent, also, so much possibility of possession of their equivalent in commodities which he could consume; but he desires to defer this consumption to a future day, to defer it, perhaps, until he is too old to give labor in exchange for his needs. One might suppose that the equivalent of commodities for the 10s. would be as satisfactory as the equivalent of commodities for the 20s. But it is not so. He desires to invest his 10s. at interest; let us suppose he invests it at 5 per cent.; at the end of twenty years he will have received back his 10s. by instalments of 6d. a year, and will have exchanged it for 10s. worth of commodities; yet at the end of the twenty years he expects to receive back in addition his full 10s.; to have spent it all, and yet to find it undiminished; so that for his 10s. saved he expects to receive 20s. worth of commodities in twenty years, to have his labor paid for twice over. In the case of money only is it possible to eat your cake and have it, and after you have eaten it to pass it on as large as ever to your descendants, so that they may eat it and yet find it, like the widow's cruse, ever miraculously renewed.

Those who defend usury do so generally on its supposed collateral advantages, rather than on its central theory. It is argued that "*if a man gets no interest on his savings, he has no incitement to work*". To this it may be answered: (*a*) That there is clearly no incitement to work on the part of those who live on interest, since their money comes tumbling in whether they work or idle; it is the labor of others on which the interest-receiver lives. (*b*) That the incitement to work would be greater if the reward of work were not diminished by the imposition on it of a tax for the benefit of the idle; surely the abstraction of £400,000,000 annually for interest can hardly act as an incitement to those whose labor returns are diminished to that extent. (*c*) That the real incitement to work is the desire to possess the result of labor, and that the more completely that desire is satisfied, the greater will the incitement become. Would the incitement to tramcar employees be lessened, if the necessity of paying 10 per cent on shareholder's capital no longer kept down their wages? But, in truth, this argument as to incitement to workers is either ignorant, or disingenuous. The mainspring of the worker's toil is, as a matter of fact, compulsion, not the incitement of hope of reward. Had he control over the product of his own labor, then the desire to obtain more might incite him to work harder, as indeed, has been found to be the case with piece-work, and in co-operative undertakings: with his fixed wage it is to him a matter of indifference how much or how little he produces. The desire for interest is an incitement to the capitalist to press his wage-toilers to work harder, so that after he has satisfied his own power of consumption he may lay by all the surplus value he can squeeze out of them, and increase the capital he has out at interest. The higher the interest obtainable, the greater the compulsion to work put upon the producers. But this compulsion is clearly an evil, not a good, and in the case of the tramcar employees just cited, it is compulsion which forces them to accept the long hours of labor, and the compulsion is exercised in order to obtain interest for the shareholders.

"*The incitement to thrift will disappear.*" But (*a*) the interest obtainable by "thrift" is too small to serve as an incitement, for the savings of the industrious poor are not sufficient to give interest enough to subsist on. The Savings Banks are resorted to as a convenient place wherein to put money saved for future use; it is the safe keeping of the money "for a rainy day", not the trifling interest, which is the attraction to the anxious poor. The small amount permitted to an individual and the low interest are sufficient proofs of this assertion! no one must put in more than £30 in a year, the interest is only 2¼ per cent., and this is not paid yearly, but is added to the principal. And this future necessity is the real incitement to thrift. A man earns, say, sufficient this week to support himself for a fortnight; having satisfied his needs, he does not want to satisfy them twice over; he knows that some years hence his power of work will have disappeared, while his necessity of consumption will remain, and he defers his consumption of half the results of his labor till that time. Why should he look for added power of consumption as a reward for deferring his consumption for his own convenience? Without interest, thoughtful people would save, for the sake of comfort in their old age. It may, however, be conceded that the incitement to annex the results of the thrift of others —the only way in which big fortunes can be made—will disappear with the disappearance of interest, and the possibility of living idly by taxing the labor of others.

"*It will not be possible to get money for railroads, tramcars, etc., if interest on share capital disappears.*" But the indestructible reason for making railroads, tramways, etc., is the need for the conveniences they afford. And Socialism would place the making and carrying on of all means of transit in the hands of local bodies, municipalities, and so forth, who would raise the requisite funds from the community which is to enjoy the increased facilities. These funds would be used in remuneration of the labor expended on them, and none would have a right to levy a perpetual tax on the public on the pretence of having lent the money originally employed in the construction. Now a man claims the right to tax all future labors and all future consumers for the benefit of his posterity, as a reward for having transferred into his own pockets the results of his neighbor's toil. It is time that the immorality of this claim should be pointed out, and that people should be told that while they may rightly save and live on their savings, they ought not to use their savings for the enslavement and the taxing of other people. An effective step towards the abolition of interest might be taken by the closing of the sources of idle investment, the taking over by local bodies of the local means of transit, the gas and water supply, etc., while the central authority takes over the railways.

There is, however, one argument in favor of interest which brings conviction to many minds: an individual wants to perform a piece of productive work, but has no capital and is unable to do it; he borrows the capital and performs the work; since the man who lent the capital has facilitated the doing of the work, ought he not to share in the product, which would have had no existence but for his capital? Now it might be answered to this that if his capital is returned to him in full he has lost nothing by the transaction, but has, on the contrary, gained the advantage of having his money taken care of without trouble to himself, and returned to him uninjured at the time that he requires it. But the real answer is that interest is inevitable so long as Capital remains in private hands, so long as individuals are permitted to annex the results of the unpaid labor of others, and so manufacture a lien on all future industry. Interest will only be abolished when the results of the past unpaid labor of many are held by the many to facilitate the future labor of many. Now, industry can only be carried on with the permission and the assistance of those whose stores of wealth have been piled up for them by thousands of patient toilers; and that permission and assistance can only be gained by taxing labor for the enrichment of the lender. In future those vast stores will be used to carry on production, and while labor will constantly replace the capital it uses in production, it will not also be taxed for the benefit of individuals. Interest and private property in the means of production must stand and fall together. At the present time no law against usury could be passed, and even were the passing of such a law possible it would be a dead letter, so thoroughly is the present system built on the paying of interest. All Socialists can do for the moment is to expose the fundamental dishonesty and injustice of usury, and so pave the way for a better state of things.

Apart from the abuse of Capital here indicated Capital has a function which, of course, no Socialist ignores. Capital is necessary for all forms of industry, and its function is: to save labor, as by machinery; to facilitate it, by the introduction of improvements therein; to support it while it is employed in production, and until its products are exchanged. The true use of the savings of past labor is to lighten future labor, to fertilise production. But in order that it may be thus used, it must be in the hands of the community instead of in the hands of individuals. Being as it is, and must be, the result of unpaid labor, it should pass to the community to be used for the common good, instead of to individuals to enrich them to the common loss.

LAND.

Most Radicals are ready to admit that Land, *i.e.*, natural agents, ought not to be the private property of individuals. No absolute property in land is indeed recognised by the laws of this realm, but the proposition that land ought not to be private property goes, of course, much further than this legal doctrine. It declares that the soil on which a nation lives ought to belong to the nation; that those who cultivate it, or who mine in it, and who for practical purposes must have for the time the exclusive usufruct of portions of it, should pay into the national exchequer a duly-assessed sum, thus rendering an equivalent for the privilege they enjoy, and making the whole community sharers in the benefits derived from natural agents.

The present system of permitting private ownership of land has led to three great and increasing evils; the establishment of an idle class, which grows richer by increasingly taxing the industrious; the divorce of the really agricultural class from the soil; the exodus from the country districts into the towns.

Private ownership of natural agents must inevitably result in the first of these three evils. These natural agents are the basis of wealth; the very subsistence of the nation depends on their utilisation; yet a comparatively small class is permitted to claim them as private property, and to appropriate the rent to its private use. Hence, one of the first charges on the results of labor is rent, and rent, be it noted, not to the community, but to an individual who has acquired the legal right to stand between labor and land. Now just as wage is determined practically by the standard of living, so is rent determined by the same thing. The landlord exacts as rent the value of the produce minus the subsistence of the tenant, and in many cases, if the farmer's receipts sink and there is no corresponding lowering of rent, the farmer cannot even subsist, and becomes bankrupt. Hence, if a farmer improves the land and so obtains from it larger returns, the landlord steps in and raises his rent, claiming ever as his, produce minus subsistence, and confiscating for his own advantage the results of the labor and invested capital of the farmer. Thus also with the spread of commercial prosperity comes a rise in the tax levied by the landlords; as towns grow larger the land around them becomes more valuable, and thus the Stanleys grow wealthy by the growth of Liverpool, and the Grosvenors and Russells by that of London: competition drives up rents, and landlords may live in Italy or Turkey, and become ever wealthier by the growth of English trade, and the toil of English laborers. Moffat points out ("Economy of Consumpton," p. 142) that part of the retailer's profit, and possibly the larger part of it "is purely local, and which he could not carry away with him. It distinguishes the site of his business, and resolves itself into rent. If the retailer owns his own premises, he may be content with this part of his profits, and handing the business to another become a landlord. If they are owned by another, the owner, unless the retailer is able to find other suitable premises within a moderate distance, will be able to levy all the extra profit from him in the shape of rent. Hence the rapid rise of rents in the central localities of large towns." Socialists are accused of desiring to confiscate property, but the regular and uncensured confiscation of the property of busy people by idlers, the bloodsucking of the landlord leeches, passes unnoticed year by year, and Society honors the confiscators. The expropriation of small cultivators has been going on for the last 400 years, partly by big landlords buying up small ones, and partly by their thefts of common land. The story of Naboth's vineyard has been repeated in hundreds of country districts. The exorbitant rents demanded by landlords, with the pressure of American competition aided by capitalists on this side, have ruined the farming class, while the absorption of small holdings has turned into day-laborers at miserable wage the class that formerly were independent tillers of the soil. Attracted by the higher wage ruling in manufacturing towns this dislanded class has flocked into them, has crowded into unsuitable houses, increased the slums of our great cities, and, under most unwholesome condition has multiplied with terrible rapidity. The exodus has been further quickened by the letting of formerly arable land for sheep-pasture, and the consequent forced migration of the no longer needed tillers. And thus have come about the under-population of the agricultural districts, and the over-crowding of cities: too few engaged in agricultural, and too many competing for industrial, employment; until we find our own land undercultivated, and even in some districts going out of cultivation, while food is being imported to an alarming extent, and the unemployed are becoming a menace to public tranquillity. The effect on England of revolution abroad is apt to be overlooked in studying our own labor difficulties. A considerable portion of our imports represents rent and interest from estates abroad and foreign investments. This portion would suddenly stop as regards any country in which a revolution occurred, and foreign workmen were, in consequence, no longer subjected to exploitation for the benefit of English capitalists. Now this likelihood of foreign revolution is yearly increasing, and Europe is becoming more and more like a boiler with armed forces sitting on the safety valve.

The first attempt to move in the right direction was the Land Cultivation Bill introduced into the House of Commons in 1886 by Charles Bradlaugh. This proposes to expropriate landlords who hold cultivable land waste; to give them, as compensation, payment for twenty-five years equal in amount to the annual value of the produce obtained from the confiscated land—so that if there is no produce there will be no payment; to vest the land in the State, and to let it, not sell it, to cultivators. Thus, if the Bill passed, a large area of land would be nationalised early in the following year. Such an Act, followed up by others taking over all land let on building leases as they run out—probably paying to the present landlords, for life, the original ground-rents; making the Land Tax an adequate rent paid to the State; taking back without compensation all common lands that have been stolen; breaking up the big estates by crushing taxation; steps like these, if taken with sufficient rapidity, may effect a complete Land Revolution without violence, and establish Socialism so far as the ownership of natural agents is concerned.

It is of vital importance to progress in a Socialist direction that an uncomprising resistance should be offered to all schemes for the creation of new proprietors of the soil. Peasant cultivators, paying rent to the State, are good. Peasant proprietors are a mere bulwark, raised by landlords to guard their own big estates, and will delay the realisation of the true theory that the State should be the only landowner. It is also important that Socialists should popularise the idea of communal, or co-operative, farming. There can be no doubt that cereal crops can be raised most economically on large holdings, and such holdings should be rented from the body or bodies, representing the community, by groups of cultivators, so that both large and small farms should be found in agricultural districts. But it must be distinctly stated that the Socialisation of Land without the Socialisation of Capital will not solve the social problem. No replanting of the people in the soil, no improved balance of agricultural and industrial production, will by themselves free the wage-slaves of our towns. Means of production, as well as natural agents, must come under the control of the community, before the triumph of Socialism can be complete. The tendency of Radicals to aim only at the nationalisation of land has an effect, however, which will ultimately prove of service. It irritates the landlord class, and the landlords devote themselves to proving that there is no essential difference between property in Land and property in Capital. Just as they helped to pass the Factory Acts to restrain capitalists as a retort for the capitalist agitation against the Corn Laws, so they will be likely to help in nationalising Capital in revenge for the nationalisation of Land.

Education.

For the successful maintenance of a Socialist State a wide and thorough system of national education is an absolute necessity. A governed people may afford to be ignorant; a self-ruling community must be instructed, or it must perish. And the education contemplated by Socialism is a very different thing from the paltry modicum of knowledge deemed sufficient for the "masses" to-day. Under our present system education is a matter of class, and it is a misnomer to call it "national"; it is partly supported by the parents of the children who attend the Board Schools, and partly by the rates and taxes; it is limited to the mere elements of learning; the one object of the teachers is to cram the children so that they may pass stated examinations, and thus obtain a Government grant per head. Under Socialism the whole system will be revolutionised, as the one aim then will be to educate in such a way as will ensure the greatest possible healthy development of the young, with a view to their future position as members of a free community.

The foundations of complete social equality will be laid in the school. All the children will be educated in the communal schools, the only distinction being that of age. Boys and girls will not be separated as they are now, but a common education will prepare for common work. Every child will be led through a course, which will embrace a thorough training in the elements of the various sciences, so that in after life he may feel an intelligent interest in each, and if his taste so lead him, acquire later a fuller knowledge of any special branches. He—and "he" here includes "she"—will be instructed also in the elements of art, so that the sense of beauty may be developed and educated, and the refining influence of instructed taste may enrich both mind and manners. A knowledge of history, of literature, and of languages will widen sympathy and destroy narrowness and national prejudices. Nor will physical training be forgotten; gymnastics, dancing, riding, athletic games, will educate the senses and the limbs, and give vigor, quickness, dexterity, and robustness to the frame. To this will be superadded technical training, for these educated, cultured, graceful lads and lasses, are to be workers, every one of them. The foundations of this technical training will be the same for all; all will learn to cook and scrub, to dig and sew, and to render quick assistance in accidents; it is probable also that the light portions of household duties will form part of the training of every child. But as the child grows into the youth, natural capacities will suggest the special training which should be given, so as to secure for the community the full advantages which might accrue from the varied abilities of its members. No genius then will be dwarfed by early neglect, no rare ability then perish for lack of culture. Individuality will then at last find full expression, and none will need to trample on his brother in order to secure full scope for his own development. It is probable that each will learn more than a single trade—an easy task when brain acuteness and manual dexterity have been cultured—so as to promote the adaptability in the future industrial life.

Now to many, I fear to most, of my readers, this sketch of what education will be in a Socialist community will appear a mere Utopian dream. Yet is it not worth while for such to ask themselves: Why should not such an education be the natural lot of every child in a well-ordered community? Is there anything in it superfluous for the thorough development of the faculties of a human being? And if it be admitted that boys and girls thus educated would form nobler, completer, more many-sided human beings than are the men and women of to-day, is it not a rational thing to set up as an object to be worked for the realisation of an idea which would prove of incalculable benefit to the community?

It is hardly necessary to add that education in a Socialist State, would be "free"—*i.e.*, supported at the public cost, and compulsory. Free, because the education of the young is of vital importance to the community; because class distinctions can only be effaced by the training of children in common schools; because education is too important a matter to be left to the whims of individuals, and if it be removed from the parent's direction and supervision it is not just to compel him to pay for it. Compulsory, because the State cannot afford to leave its future citizens ignorant and helpless, and it is bound to protect its weak members against injustice and neglect.

Two objections are likely to be raised: the question of cost, and the question of unfitting persons for "the dirty work of the world, which someone must do".

As to cost. It must not be forgotten that this education is proposed for a Socialist community. In such a State there would be no idle adult class to be supported, but all would be workers, so that the wealth produced would be much greater than at the present time. Now according to the figures of anti-Socialist Mr. Giffen, the aggregate income of the people is at present about £1,200,000,000; of this the workers are assigned by him £620,000,000; deduct another £100,000,000 for return from investments abroad; this leaves £480,000,000 absorbed by the non-producing class. (It must be remembered, further, that a large number of the "workers" are unnecessary distributors, whose powers could be utilised to much better purpose than is done to-day.) The wealth producers have to bear the Church on their shoulders, and provide it with an income variously stated at from £6,000,000 to £10,000,000 a year. They have to bear the "landed interest", with its appropriation in rents, royalties, etc., of something like £260,000,000. They have to bear the ultimate weight of imperial and local taxation, estimated at about £120,000,000 for the present year. All these charges, by whomsoever nominally paid, have to come out of the wealth produced by the workers. Is it then to be pretended that when the idle class has disappeared there will not be wealth enough produced for the education of the children, or that their education will be as heavy a burden as the drones are to-day? Nor must it be forgotten that there are millions of acres of land that would produce wealth if labor were sent to them, and that plenty of our idlers will there find productive work which will enormously increase the national wealth. Nor also that the waste which results from luxurious idle living will be of the past, and that a simpler, manlier, rate of expenditure will have replaced the gluttony and intemperance now prevalent in the "higher circles of society".

But it will indeed be of vital importance that the proportion of workers to non-workers shall be considered, and that there shall not be in a Socialist community the over-large families which are a characteristic of the present system. Families of ten or a dozen children belong to the capitalist system, which requires for its success a numerous and struggling proletariat, propagating with extreme rapidity, so as to keep up a plentiful supply of men, women and children, for the labor market, as well as a supply of men for the army to be food for cannon, and women for the streets to be food for lust. Under a Socialist regime, the community will have something to say as to the numbers of the new members that are to be introduced into it, and for many years supported by it; and it will prefer a reasonable number of healthy, well-educated children, to a yearly huge increase which would overburden its industry. The limitation of the number in a family is a condition of Socialist success.

As to unfitting persons for work. So long as manual work is regarded as degrading, education, by increasing sensitiveness to public opinion, tends to make people shrink from it, at least if their sensitiveness is greater than their intelligence. But even now an educated person of strong will and clear judgment, who knows that all useful work is worthy of respect, finds that his education fits him to perform work more quickly and more intelligently than is possible to an ignorant person; and respecting himself in its thorough accomplishment he is conscious of no degradation. Weak persons, compelled to labor for their bread, and aware that manual work is considered to place the worker in a subordinate social class, feel ashamed of the inferior position assigned to them by public opinion; and knowing by experience that they will be snubbed if they treat their "superiors" as equals, they live down to their social rank, and long to raise their children into a class above their own. One consequence of the absurd artificial disadvantage attached to manual work, is that the children of the more successful workers crowd the inferior professional occupations, and a man prefers to be a clerk or a curate on £90 a year to being an artisan on £150. But in the Socialist State only idleness will be despised, and all useful work will be honored. There is nothing more intrinsically degrading in driving a plough than in driving a pen, although the ploughman is now relegated to the kitchen while the clerk is received in the drawing-room. The distinction is primarily a purely artificial one, but it is made real by educating the one type while the other is left ignorant, and by teaching the one to look on his work as work "fit for a gentleman", while the other is taught that his work is held in low social esteem. Each reflects the surrounding public opinion, and accepts the position assigned by it. In Socialism, both will be educated together as children; both will be taught to look on all work as equally honorable, if useful to the community; both will be cultured "gentlemen", following each his natural bent; the ploughman will be as used to his pen as the clerk; the clerk as ready to do heavy work as the ploughman; and as public opinion will regard them as equals and will hold them in equal honor, neither will feel any sense of superiority or inferiority, but they will meet on common ground as men, as members of a social unity. As to the physically unpleasant work—such as dealing with sewers, dung-heaps, etc.—much of that will probably be done by machinery, when there is no helpless class on whose shoulders it may be bound. Such as cannot be done by machinery, will probably be divided among a large number, each taking a small share thereof, and the amount done by each will thus become so insignificant, that it will be but slightly felt. In any case the profound selfishness, which would put all burden on a helot class, and rather see it brutalised by the crushing weight than bear a portion of the load on one of its fingers, must be taught that Socialism means equality, and that the divine right of idlers to live at ease on the labor of others and to be shielded by the bodies of the poor from all the unpleasantnesses of the world, is one of the notions against which Socialism wars, and which must follow the correlative superstition of the divine right of kings.

Justice.

The pretence that under the present system there is one law for rich and poor is so barefaced a piece of impudence, that it is hardly worth while to refute it. Everyone knows that a rich man is fined for an offence for which a poor man is sent to gaol; that no wise man goes to law unless he has plenty of money; that in a litigation between a rich and a poor man, the poor man practically stands no chance, for even if he at first succeeds the rich man can appeal, and, secure in the power of his money-bags, wear out his poor antagonist by costly delays and by going from court to court. The poor man cannot fee first-class counsel, seek out and bring up his witnesses from various parts of the country, and keep a stream of money continually running through his solicitor's hands. There might be the same law for him as for the rich man, if he could get it; but it is far away behind a golden gate, and he lacks the key which alone will fit the wards of the lock. Yet surely one of the primary duties of a State is to do justice among its members, and to prevent the oppression of the weak by the strong. In a civilised State justice should be dealt out without fee or reward; if a man gives up his inherent right to defend himself and to judge in his own quarrel, he ought not to be placed in a worse position than he would be in if society did not exist. Lawyers, like judges, should be officials paid by the State, and should have no pecuniary interest in winning the case in which they are engaged.

The administration of justice in a Socialist State will be a very much simpler matter than it is now. Most crimes arise from the desire to become rich, from poverty, and from ignorance. Under Socialism poverty and ignorance will have disappeared, and the desire to grow rich will have no *raison d'être* when everyone has sufficient for comfort, is free from anxiety as to his future, and sees above him no wealthy idlers whose luxury he desires to ape, and whose idleness is held up to him as a matter of envy, as the ideal state for man.

Amusement.

There is a curious inconsistency in the way in which people deal with the question of amusement at the present time. We should have an outcry about "pauperisation" and "interference with private enterprise", if anyone proposed that the theatres should be open to the public without charge. Yet Hyde Park is kept gorgeous with flowers, Rotten Row is carefully attended to, a whole staff of workers is employed, in order that the wealthy may have a fashionable and pleasant lounge; and all this is done at the national expense, without any expression of fear lest the wealthy should be pauperised by this expenditure on their behalf. Nor is complaint made of the public money spent on the other parks in London; the most that is suggested is that the money wanted ought to be taken from the London rates and not from the national taxes. No one proposes that the parks should be sold to the highest bidder, and that private enterprise should be encouraged by permitting some capitalist to buy them, and to make a charge at the gate for admission. It is significant that once anything gets under State control, the advantages are found to be so great that no one would dream of bringing it back under private exploitation. In some parks a band plays, and people are actually demoralised by listening to music for which they do not pay directly. Nay more; the British Museum, the National Gallery, the South Kensington Museum, are all open free, and no one's dignity is injured. But if the National Gallery be open free, why not the Royal Academy? If a band may be listened to in the open air without payment, why not in a concert room? And if a concert may be free, why not a theatre? Under the present system, the Royal Academy, the concert, the theatre, are all private speculations, and the public is exploited for the profit of the speculators. The National Gallery and the Museums are national property, and the nation enjoys the use of its own possessions. In a nation which has gone so far in the direction of providing intellectual amusement, it cannot be pretended that any principle is involved in the question whether or not it shall go further along the same road. A nation which collects the works of dead painters can hardly, on principle, refuse to show the works of living ones; and we Socialists may fairly urge the success of what has already been done in the way of catering for the public amusement as a reason for doing more.

As it is, with the exception of a few places, the poor, whose lives most need the light of amusement and of beauty, are relegated to the very lowest and coarsest forms of recreation. Unreal and intensely vulgar pictures of life are offered them at the theatres which specially cater for them; they never have the delight of seeing really graceful dancing, or noble acting, or of hearing exquisite music. Verily, the amusement of the wealthier leave much to be desired, and theatre and music-hall alike pander to a low and vulgar taste instead of educating and refining it; but still these are better than their analogues at the East End. Under Socialism, the theatre will become a great teacher instead of a catch-penny spectacle; and dramatists and actors alike will work for the honor of a noble art, instead of degrading their talents to catch the applause of the most numerous class of an uneducated people. Then an educated public will demand a higher art, and artists will find it worth while to study, when patient endeavor meets with public recognition, and crude impertinence suffers its due reproof. Theatres, concerts, parks, all places of public resort, will be communal property, open alike to all, and controlled by elected officers.

Conclusion.

It remains, in conclusion, to note the chief objections raised to Socialism by its opponents. Of these the most generally urged are three: that it will check individual initiative and energy; that it will destroy individuality; that it will unduly restrict personal liberty.

That it will check individual initiative and energy. This objection is founded on the idea that the impulse to initiative must always be desire for personal money gain. But this idea flies directly in the face of facts. Even under the individualistic system, no great discovery has ever been made and proclaimed merely from desire for personal money profit. The genius that invents is moved by an imperial necessity of its own nature, and wealth usually falls to the lot of the commonplace man who exploits the genius, and not to the genius itself. Even talent is moved more by joy in its own exercise, and in the public approval it wins, than by mere hope of money gain. Who would not rather be an Isaac Newton, a Shelley, or a Shakspere, than a mere Vanderbilt? And most of all are those of strong individual initiative moved by desire to serve their "larger self", which is Man. The majority of such choose the unpopular path, and by sheer strength and service gradually win over the majority. We see men and women who might have won wealth, position, power, by using their talents for personal gain in pursuits deemed honorable, cheerfully throw all aside to proclaim an unpopular truth, and to serve a cause they believe to be good and useful. And these motives will become far more powerful under Socialism than they are now. For the possession of money looms unduly large to-day in consequence of the horrible results of the want of it. The dread of hunger and of charity is the microscope which magnifies the value of wealth. But once let all men be secure of the necessaries and comforts of life, and all the finer motives of action will take their proper place. Energy will have its full scope under Socialism, and indeed when the value of a man's work is secured to him instead of the half being appropriated by someone else, it will receive a new impulse. How great will be the incentive to exertion when the discovery of some new force, or new application of a known force, means greater comfort for the discoverer *and* for all; none thrown out of work by it, none injured by it, but so much solid gain for each. It is interesting to notice, as bearing on this question, that even a partial sharing in profits by the workers stimulates invention and increases productive energy. Mr. Wordsworth Donisthorpe ("Labor Capitalisation", p. 97) quotes M. Godin as saying that the men in his "Familistère" are constantly making new inventions and improvements; and similar testimony has been borne by others who have given an interest in the business to the men they employ. In all such cases the man who invents or improves, enjoys the thanks and the praise of the community, as well as the material gain which he shares with his comrades. And let not the power of public opinion be undervalued as a stimulus to exertion. What Greek athlete would have sold his wreath of bay for its weight in gold? Only one kind of energy will be annihilated by Socialism—the energy that enslaves others for its own gain, and exploits its weaker brethren for its own profit. For this kind of energy there will be no room. The coarse purse-proud mediocrity who by sheer force of pushing brutality has trampled his way to the front, will have vanished. The man who grows rich by underpaying his employees, by being a "hard business man" will have passed away. Energy will have to find for itself paths of service instead of paths of oppression, and will be honored or reprobated according to the way in which it is used.

That it will destroy individuality. If this were true, the loss to progress would indeed be incalculable. But Socialism, instead of destroying individuality will cultivate and accentuate it, and indeed will make it possible for the first time in civilisation for the vast majority. For it needs, in order that individuality shall be developed, that the individual shall have his characteristics drawn out, and trained by education; it needs that he shall work, in maturity, at the work for which his natural abilities fit him; it needs that he shall not be exhausted by excessive toil, but shall go fresh and vigorous to his labor; it needs that he shall have leisure to continuously improve himself, to train his intellect and his taste. But such education, such choice of work, such short hours of labor, such leisure for self-culture, where are all these to-day for our laboring population? A tremendous individuality, joined to robust health, may make its way upward out of the ranks of the handworkers to-day; but all normal individuality is crushed out between the grinding-stones of the industrial mill. See the faces of the lads and lasses as they troop out of the factory, out of the great mercantile establishments; how alike they all are! They might almost have been turned out by the dozen. We Socialists demand that individuality shall be possible for all, and not only for the few who are too strong to crush.

That it will unduly restrict personal liberty. Socialism, as conceived by the non-student of it, is an iron system, in which the "State"—which is apparently separate from the citizens—shall rigidly assign to each his task, and deal out to each his subsistence. Even if this caricature were accurate, Socialism would give the great majority far more freedom than they enjoy to-day; for they would only be under the yoke for their brief hours of toil, and would have unfettered freedom, for the greater portion of their time. Contrast this compulsion with the compulsion exercised on the workers to-day by the sweater, the manager of the works or business, and above all the compulsion of hunger, that makes them bend to the yoke for the long hours of the working day, and often far into the night: and then say whether the "freedom" of Industrialism is not a heavier chain than the "tyranny" of the most bureaucratic Socialism imagined by our opponents. But the "tyranny of Socialism", however, would consist only in ordering—and enforcing the order if necessary—that every healthy adult should labor for his own subsistence. That is, it would protect the liberty of each by not allowing anyone to compel another person to work for him and by opening to all equal opportunities of working for themselves. The worker would choose his own work certainly as freely as he does now: at the present time, if one class of work has enough operatives employed at it, a man must take some other, and I do not see that Socialism could prevent this limitation of choice. At any rate, the limitation is not an argument against Socialism, since it exists at the present time.

Imagine the glorious freedom which would be the lot of each when, the task of social work complete, and done under healthy and pleasant conditions, the worker turned to science, literature, art, gymnastics, to what he would, for the joyous hours of leisure. For him all the treasures of knowledge and of beauty; for him all the delights of scenery and of art; for him all that only the wealthy enjoy to-day; all that comes from work flowing back to enrich the worker's life.

I know that our hope is said to be the dream of the enthusiast; I know that our message is derided, and that the gospel of man's redemption which we preach is scorned. Be it so. Our work shall answer the gibes of our opponents, and our faith in the future shall outlast their mockery. We know that however much man's ignorance may hinder our advance; however much his selfishness may block our path; that we shall yet win our way to the land we have seen but in our visions, and rear the temple of human happiness on the solid foundation stones of science and of truth. Above all sneer and taunt, above all laughter and bitter cries of hatred, rings out steadily our prophecy of the coming time:

"O nations undivided,
O single People, and free,
We dreamers, we derided,
We mad blind men that see,
We bear you witness ere ye come that ye shall be."

WHY I BECAME A THEOSOPHIST.

BY

ANNIE BESANT.

Fellow of the Theosophical Society.)

LONDON

FREETHOUGHT PUBLISHING COMPANY,

63 FLEET STREET, E.C.

1889.

PRICE FOURPENCE.

LONDON:
PRINTED BY ANNIE BESANT AND CHARLES BRADLAUGH,
63 FLEET STREET, E.C.

WHY I BECAME A THEOSOPHIST.

> Endurance is the crowning quality
> And patience all the passion of great hearts;
> These are their stay, and when the leaden world
> Sets its hard face against their fateful thought,
> And brute strength, like a scornful conqueror,
> Clangs his huge mace down in the other scale,
> The inspired soul but flings its patience in,
> And slowly that outweighs the ponderous globe.
> One faith against a whole world's unbelief,
> One soul against the flesh of all mankind.

Growth necessarily implies change, and, provided the change be sequential and of the nature of development, it is but the sign of intellectual life. No one blames the child because it has out-grown its baby-clothes, nor the man when his lad's raiment becomes too narrow for him; but if the mind grows as well as the body, and the intellectual garment of one decade is outgrown in the following, cries are raised of rebuke and of reproach by those who regard fossilisation as a proof of mental strength. Just now from some members of the Freethought party reproaches are being levelled at me because I have proclaimed myself a Theosophist. Yet of all people Freethinkers ought to be the very last to protest against change of opinion *per se*; for almost every one of them is a Freethinker by virtue of mental change, and the only hope of success for their propaganda in a Christian country is that they may persuade others to pass through a similar change. They are continually reproaching Christians in that their minds are not open to argument, will not listen to reason; and yet, if one of themselves sees a further truth and admits it, they object as much to the open mind of the Freethinker as to the closed mind of the Christian. To take up the position assumed by some of my critics is to set up a new infallibility, as indefensible, and less venerable, than that of Rome. It is to claim that the summit of human knowledge has been reached by them, and that all new knowledge is folly. It is to do what Churches in all ages have done, to set up their own petty fences round the field of truth, and in so doing to trace the limits of their own cemeteries. And for the Freethinker to do this is to be false to his creed, and to stain himself with the most flagrant inconsistency; he denounces the immovability of the Church as obstinacy, while he glorifies the immovability of the Freethinker as strength; he blames the one because it shuts its ears against *his* new truth, and then promptly shuts his own ears against new truth from some one else.

Let us distinguish: there is a vacillation of opinion which is a sign of mental weakness, a change which is a turning back. When all the available evidence for a doctrine has been examined, and the doctrine thereupon has been rejected, it shews a mental fault somewhere if that doctrine be again accepted, the evidence remaining the same. It does not, on the other hand, imply any mental weakness, if, on the bringing forward of new evidence which supplies the lacking demonstration, the doctrine previously rejected for lack of such evidence, be accepted. Nor does it imply mental weakness if a doctrine accepted on certain given evidence, be later given up on additions being made to knowledge. Only in this way is intellectual progress made; only thus, step by step, do we approach the far-off Truth. A Freethinker, who has become one by study and has painfully wrought out his freedom, discarding the various doctrines of Christianity, could not rebelieve them without confessing either that he had been hasty in his rejection or was insecure in his new adhesion: in either case he would have shewn intellectual weakness. But not to the Freethinker can be closed any new fields of mental discovery; not on his limbs shall be welded the fresh fetters of a new orthodoxy, after he has hewn off the links of the elder faith; not round his eyes, facing the sunshine, shall be bound the bandage of a cramping creed; not to him shall Atheism, any more than Theism, say: "Thus far shalt thou think, and no further". Atheism has been his deliverer; it must never be his gaoler: it has freed him; it must never tie him down.

Grateful for all it has saved him from, for all it has taught him, for the strength it has given, the energy it has inspired, the eager spirit of man yet rushes onward, crying: "The Light is beyond!"

I maintain, then, that the Freethinker is bound ever to keep open a window towards new light, and to refuse to pull down his mental blinds. Freethought, in fact, is an intellectual state, not a creed; a mental attitude, not a series of dogmas. No one turns his back on Freethought who subjects every new doctrine to the light of reason, who weighs its claims without prejudice, and accepts or rejects it out of loyalty to truth alone. It seems necessary to recall this fundamental truth about Freethought, in protest against the position taken up by some of my critics, who would fain identify a universal principle with a special phase of nineteenth century Materialism. The temple of Freethought is not identical with the particular niche in which they stand.

Nor is the Freethought platform so narrow a stage as Mr. Foote would make out in his recent attack on me. He accuses me of using the Freethought platform "in an unjustifiable manner", because I have lectured on Socialism from it, and he is afraid that I may lecture on Theosophy from it and "lead Freethinkers astray". I have hitherto regarded Freethinkers as persons competent to form their own judgment, not mere sheep to be led one way or the other. There is a curious clerical ring in the phrase, as though free ventilation of all opinions were not the very life-blood of Freethought. It is a new thing to seek to exclude from the Freethought platform any subject which concerns human progress. In his younger and broader days, Mr. Foote lectured from the Freethought platform on Monarchy, Republicanism, the Land Question, and Literature, and no one rebuked him for unjustifiable use of it; now he apparently desires to restrict it to attacks on theology alone. I protest against this new-fangled narrowing of the grand old platform, from which Carlile, Watson, Hetherington, and many another fought for the right of Free Speech on every subject that concerned human welfare, a noble tradition carried on in our own time by Charles Bradlaugh, who has always used the Freethought platform for political and social, as well as for anti-theological, work. I know that of late years Mr. Foote has narrowed his own advocacy, but that gives him no claim to enforce on others a similar narrowness, and to denounce their action as unjustifiable when they carry on the use of the platform which has always been customary. For my own part, I have so used it since I joined the Freethought party: I have lectured on Radicalism and on Socialism, on Science and on Literature, as well as on Theology, and I shall continue to do so. Of course if the National Secular Society should surrender its motto, "We seek for Truth", and declare, like any other sect, that it has the whole truth, there are many who would have to reconsider their position as members of it. If the National Secular Society should follow Mr. Foote's recent departure, and seek to exclude from the platform all non-theological subjects, it has the right to do so, though it ought then to drop the name of Secular and call itself merely the Anti-Theological Society; but until it does, I shall follow the course I have followed these fifteen years, of using the platform for lecturing on any subject that seems to me to be useful. When the National Secular Society excludes me from its platform I must of course submit, but no one person has a right to dictate to the Society what matters it shall discuss. A few weeks ago a Branch of the National Secular Society wrote asking me to lecture on Theosophy: was I to answer that the subject was not a suitable one for them to consider? Mr. Foote in one breath blames me for not explaining my position to the Freethought party, and in the next warns me off the platform from which the explanation can best be made. I had no paper in which I could give my reasons for becoming a Theosophist, and I am told that to use the platform is unjustifiable! Leaving this, I pass to the special subject of this paper, "Why I became a Theosophist".

Mr. Foote writes, with exceeding bitterness, that "amidst all her changes Mrs. Besant remains quite positive". What are all these changes? Like Mr. Foote and most of the rest of us, I passed from Christianity into Atheism. After fifteen years, I have passed into Pantheism. The first change I need not here defend; but I desire to say that in all I have written and said, as Atheist, against supernaturalism, I have nothing to regret, nothing to unsay. On the negative side Atheism seems to me to be unanswerable; its case against supernaturalism is complete. And for some years I found this enough: I was satisfied, and I have remained satisfied, that the universe is not explicable on supernatural lines. But I turned then to scientific work, and for ten years of patient and steadfast study I sought along the lines of Materialistic Science for answer to the questions on Life and Mind to which Atheism, as such, gave no answer. During those ten years I learned both at second hand from books and at first hand from nature, something of what was known of living organisms, of their evolution and their functions. Building on a sound knowledge of Biology I went on to Psychology, still striving to follow nature into her recesses and to wring some answer from the Eternal Sphinx. Everywhere I found collecting of facts, systematising of knowledge, tracing of sequences: nowhere one gleam of light on the question of questions: "What is Life? what is Thought?" Not only was Materialism unable to answer the question, but it declared pretty positively that no answer could ever be given. While claiming its own methods as the only sound ones, it declared that those methods could not solve the mystery. As Professor Lionel Beale says (quoted in "Secret Doctrine", vol. i, p. 540): "There is a mystery in life—a mystery which has never been fathomed, and which appears greater, the more deeply the phænomena of life are studied and contemplated. In living centres—far more central than the centres seen by the highest magnifying powers, in centres of living matter, where the eye cannot penetrate, but towards which the understanding may tend—proceed changes of the nature of which the most advanced physicists and chemists fail to afford us the conception: nor is there the slightest reason to think that the nature of these changes will ever be ascertained by physical investigation, inasmuch as they are certainly of an order or nature totally distinct from that to which any other phænomenon known to us can be relegated." Elsewhere he remarks: "Between the *living* state of matter and its *non-living* state there is an absolute and irreconcilable difference; that, so far from our being able to demonstrate that the *non-living* passes by gradations into, or gradually assumes the state or condition of, the *living*, the transition is sudden and abrupt; and that matter already in the living state may pass into the non-living condition in the same sudden and complete manner. . . .

The formation of bioplasm direct from non-living matter is impossible even in thought, except to one who sets absolutely at nought the facts of physics and chemistry" ("Bioplasm," pp. 3 and 13). Under these circumstances, it was no longer a matter of suspending judgment until knowledge made the judgment possible, but the positive assurance that no knowledge could be attained on the problem posited. The instrument was confessedly unsuitable, and it became a question of resigning all search into the essence of things, or finding some new road. It may be said: "Why seek to solve the insoluble?" But such phrase begs the question. Is it insoluble because one method will not solve it? Is light incomprehensible because instruments suitable for acoustics do not reveal its nature? If from the blind clash of atoms and the hurtling of forces there comes no explanation of Life and of Mind, if these remain *sui generis*, if they loom larger and larger as causes rather than as effects, who shall blame the searcher after Truth, when failing to find how Life can spring from force and matter, he seeks whether Life be not itself the Centre, and whether every form of matter may not be the garment wherewith veils itself an Eternal and Universal Life?

Riddles in Psychology.

No one, least of all those who have tried to understand something of the "riddle of this painful universe", will pretend that Materialism gives any answer to the question, "How do we think?", or throws any light on the nature of thought. It traces a correlation between living nervous matter and intellection; it demonstrates a parallelism between the growing complexity of the nervous system and the growing complexity of the phænomena of consciousness; it proves that intellectual manifestations may be interfered with, stimulated, checked, altogether stopped, by acting upon cerebral matter; it shows that certain cerebral activities normally accompany psychical activities. That is, it proves that on our globe, necessarily the only place in which its investigations have been carried on, there is a close connexion between living nervous matter and thought-processes.

As to the nature of that connexion knowledge is dumb, and even theory can suggest no hypothesis. Materialism regards thought as a function of the brain; "the brain secretes thought", says Carl Vogt, "as the liver secretes bile". It is a neat phrase, but what does it *mean*? In every other bodily activity organ and function are on the same plane. The liver has form, color, resistance, it is an object to the senses; its secretion approves itself to those same senses, as part of the Object World; the cells of the liver come in contact with the blood, take from it some substances, reject others, recombine those they have selected, pour them out as bile. It is all very wonderful, very beautiful; but the sequence is unbroken; matter is acted upon, analysed, synthesised afresh; it can be subjected at every step to mechanical processes, inspected, weighed; it is matter at the beginning, matter all through, matter at the end; we never leave the objective plane. But "the brain secretes thought"? We study the nerve-cells of the brain; we find molecular vibration; we are still in the Object World, amid form, color, resistance, motion. Suddenly there is a THOUGHT, and all is changed. We have passed into a new world, the Subject World; the thought is formless, colorless, intangible, imponderable; it is neither moving nor motionless; it occupies no space, it has no limits; no processes of the Object World can touch it, no instrument can inspect. It can be analysed, but only by Thought: it can be measured, weighed, tested, but only by its own peers in its own world. Between the Motion and the Thought, between the Object and the Subject, lies an unspanned gulf, and Vogt's words but darken counsel; they are misleading, a false analogy, pretending likeness where likeness there is none.

Many perhaps, as I have said, like myself, beginning with somewhat vague and loose ideas of physical processes, and then, on passing into careful study, dazzled by the radiance of physiological discoveries, have hoped to find the causal nexus, or have, at least, hoped that hereafter it might be found by following a road rendered glorious by so much new light. But I am bound to say, after the years of close and strenuous study both of physiology and psychology to which I have alluded, that the more I have learned of each the more thoroughly do I realise the impassibility of the gulf between material motion and mental process, that Body and Mind, however closely intermingled, are twain, not one.

Let us look a little further into the functions of Mind, as *e.g.*, Memory. How does the Materialist explain the phænomena of Memory? A cell, or group of cells, has been set vibrating; hence a thought. Similar vibrations are continually being set up, and every cell in the cerebrum must have been set vibrating millions of times during infancy, youth, and maturity. The man of fifty remembers a scene of his childhood; that is, a group of cells—every atom of which has been changed several times since the scene occurred—sets up a certain series of vibrations which reproduces the original series, or let us say the chief of the original series, and so gives rise to the remembrance, the vibration being prior in time, necessarily, to the remembrance. I will not press the further difficulty, as to the initiation of this motion and the complexities of "Association" in intensifying vibration so as to bring the thought above the threshold of consciousness. It will suffice to try and realise what is implied in the setting up of this series of vibrations, each cell vibrating in conjunction with its fellows as it vibrated forty years before, despite the myriad other combinations possible, each one of which would cause other thought. A well-stored memory contains thousands of "thought pictures"; each of these must have its vibratory cell-series in the human cerebrum. Is this possible, having regard to the laws of space and time, to which, be it remembered, cell-vibrations are subject?

But these difficulties are on the surface; let us go a step further. In dealing with psychology, we must study the abnormal as well as the normal. Normally, thought results from sense-impression; abnormally, sense-impression may result from thought. Thus, a young officer was told off to exhume the corpse of a person some time buried; as the coffin came into view the effluvium was so overpowering that he fainted. Opened, the coffin was found to be empty. It was the vivid imagination of the young man that had created the sense-impression, for which there was no objective cause. Again, a novelist, absorbed in his plot, in which one of his characters was killed by arsenic, showed symptoms of arsenical poisoning. Here the mouth, œsophagus and stomach were affected by a cause that existed only in the mind. I have failed to find any Materialist explanation of a large group of phænomena, of which these are types.

Take again the extraordinary keenness of perception found in some cases of disease. A patient suffering from one of certain disorders will hear words spoken at a distance far beyond that of ordinary audition. It seems as though the lowering of muscular power and of general vitality coincided with the intensifying of the perceptive faculties —a fact difficult to explain from the Materialist standpoint, though the explanation *saute aux yeux* from the Theosophical, as will be seen further on.

Or consider the phænomena of clairvoyance, clairaudience, and thought-transference. Here, if a person be thrown into an abnormal nerve condition, he can see and hear at distances which preclude normal vision and audition. A clairvoyant will read with eyes bandaged, or with a board interposed between reader and book. He will follow the closed or opened hand of the mesmeriser, and give its position and condition. Here, I do not give special instances, as the cases are legion and are easily accessible to anyone who desires to investigate. A large number of careful experiments have put cases of thought-transference beyond possibility of reasonable denial, and can be referred to by the student. I cannot burden this short pamphlet with them, especially as it is merely intended as a tracing of the road along which I have travelled, not as an exposition of the whole case against Materialism.

Mesmerism and hypnotism, again, suggest the existence in man of faculties which are normally latent. All sense-perception in the mesmerised is overcome by the will of the mesmeriser, who imposes on him "sense-perceptions" antagonistic to facts: *e.g.*, he will drink water with enjoyment as wine, with repugnance as vinegar, etc. The body is mastered by the mind of another, and responds as the operator wills. Experiments in hypnotism have yielded the most astounding results: actions commanded by the hypnotiser being performed by the person hypnotised, although the two were separated by distance, and though some time had elapsed since the hypnotic operation had been performed, and the person hypnotised restored apparently to the normal conditions. (See the experiments of Dr. Charcot and others.) So serious have been the results of these experiments that a society is now in course of formation in London, which seeks to restrict the practice of hypnotism to the medical profession and persons duly and legally qualified to practice it. "For this purpose", says the acting Secretary, "it is proposed to found a school of hypnotism in London, at which the science will be properly taught by the best exponents, scientifically demonstrated by lecture and experiment, and its beneficial uses correctly defined and expounded". Dr. Charcot has used hypnotism in the place of anæsthetics, and has successfully performed a dangerous operation on a hypnotised patient, whose heart was too weak to permit the use of chloroform. Dr. Grillot uses it for "moral cures", and hypnotises dishonest persons into honesty. A congress on the subject is sitting in Paris, while this pamphlet is passing through the press.

Allied to these are the phænomena of double-consciousness, many records of which are preserved in medical works; here, in some cases, a double life has been led, no memory of one state existing in the other, and each life on re-entering a state being taken up where it was dropped on leaving it. With only one brain to function, how can this duality of consciousness be explained? Hallucinations, visions of all kinds, again, do not seem to me to be reducible under any purely Materialist hypothesis: "matter and motion" do not solve these phænomena of the psychic world.

Another riddle in psychology is that of dreams. If thought be the result only of molecular vibration, how can dreams occur in which many successive events and prolonged arguments occupy but a moment of time? Vibrations, I again remind the reader, are subject to the conditions of space and time. Succession of thoughts must imply succession of vibrations on the Materialist hypothesis, and vibrations take time; yet thousands of these, which, waking, would occupy days and weeks, are compressed into a second in a dream.

Quite another class of phænomena is that in which abilities are manifested for which no sufficient cause can be discovered. Infant prodigies, like Hofmann and others, whence come they? We know what the brain of a very young child is like, and we find young Hofmann improvising with a scientific knowledge that he has not had time to acquire in the ordinary way. "Genius", we say, with our fashion of pretending to explain by using a word; but how can Materialism, which will have matter give birth to thought, find in the newly-made brain of this child the cerebral modifications necessary for producing his melodies? And when a servant in a farmhouse, ignorant in her waking hours, talks Hebrew in her sleep, how are we to regard her brain from the Materialist standpoint? Or when the calculating boy answers a complex calculation when the words are barely out of the questioner's mouth, how have the cells performed their duties? a problem that becomes the more puzzling when we find that the increase of circulation, etc., which normally accompany brain activity, have not, in his case, occurred.

These are only a few riddles out of many, but they are samples of the bulk. To some of us they are of overpowering interest, because they seem to suggest dimly new fields of thought, new possibilities of development, new heights which Humanity shall hereafter scale. We do not believe that the forces of Evolution are exhausted. We do not believe that the chapter of Progress is closed. When a new sense was developing in the past its reports at first must have been very blundering, often very misleading, doubtless very ridiculous at times, but none the less had it the promise of the future, and was the germ of a higher capacity. May not some new sense be developing to-day, of which the many abnormal manifestations around us are the outcome? Who, with the past behind him, shall dare to say, "It cannot be"? and who shall dare to blame those whose longing *to know* may be but the yearning of the Spirit of Humanity to rise to some higher plane?

The Theosophical Society.

Before showing the method suggested in Theosophical teachings for obtaining light on the above questions, or sketching the view of the universe given by occult science, it may be well to remove some misconceptions concerning the Theosophical Society, my adhesion to which has brought on my devoted head such voluminous upbraiding. I fear that the objects of the Society will come somewhat as an anti-climax after the denunciations. They are three in number, and any one who asks for admittance to the Society must approve the first of these:

1. To be the nucleus of a Universal Brotherhood.
2. To promote the study of Aryan and other Eastern literatures, religions, and sciences.
3. To investigate unexplained laws of nature and the psychical powers latent in man.

Nothing more! Not a word of any form of belief; no imposition of any special views as to the universe or man; nothing about Mahatmas, cycles, Karma or anything else. Atheist and Theist, Christian and Hindu, Mahommedan and Secularist, all can meet on this one broad platform, and none has the right to look askance at another.

The answer to the inquiry, "Why did you join the Society?" is very simple. There is sore need, it seems to me, in our unbrotherly, anti-social civilisation, of this distinct affirmation of a brotherhood as broad as Humanity itself. Granted that it is as yet but a beautiful Ideal, it is well that such an Ideal should be lifted up before the eyes of men. Not only so, but each who affirms that ideal, and tries to conform thereto his own life, does something, however little, to lift mankind towards its realisation, to hasten the coming of that Day of Man. Again, the third object is one that much attracts me. The desire for knowledge is wrought deep into the heart of every earnest student, and for many years the desire to search out the forces that lie latent in and around us has been very present to me. I can see in that desire nothing unworthy of a Freethinker, nothing to be ashamed of as a searcher after truth. "We seek for Truth" is the motto of the National Secular Society, and that motto, to me, has been no lip-phrase.

Beyond this, the membership of the Theosophical Society does not bind its Fellows. They can remain attached to any religious or non-religious views they may have previously held, without challenge or question from any. They may become students of Theosophy if they choose, and develop into Theosophists; but this is above and beyond the mere membership of the Society.

This fact, well known to all members of the Society, shows how unjust was the attack on Mdme. Blavatsky, accusing her of inconsistency because she said there was nothing to prevent Mr. Bradlaugh from joining the Theosophical Society. There is nothing in the objects to prevent anyone from joining who believes, as do all Atheists, I think, in the Brotherhood of Man.

While this pamphlet is passing through the press a curious judicial decision on the status of the Society reaches me from America. A Branch Society at St. Louis applied for a Decree of Incorporation, and in ordinary course the Report, based on sworn testimony, was delivered to the court by its own officer, and on this the decree was issued. The Report found that the Society was not a religious but an educational body; it "has no religious creed, and practises no worship". The Report then proceeded to deal with the Third Object of the Society, and found that among the phænomena investigated were "Spiritualism, mesmerism, clairvoyance, mind-healing, mind-reading, and the like. I took testimony on this question, and found that while a belief in any one of these sorts of manifestations and phænomena is not required, while each member of the Society is at liberty to hold his own opinion, yet such questions form topics of enquiry and discussion, and the members as a mass are probably believers individually in phænomena that are abnormal and in powers that are superhuman as far as science now knows." Perhaps those Secularists who have been so eager to credit me with beliefs that I have not dreamed of holding, will accept this deliverance of a court of justice, as they evidently refuse to take my word, as to the conditions of membership in the Theosophical Society. When, for instance, I find Mr. Foote in the *Freethinker* crediting me with belief in the "transmigration of souls", I can but suppose that he is moved rather by a desire to discredit me than by a desire for truth. Indeed, the headlong jumping at unfavorable conclusions, and the outcry raised against me, have been a most painful awakening from the belief that Freethinkers, as such, would be less bigoted and unjust than the ordinary Christian sectary. The Report proceeds: "The object of this Society, whether attainable or not, is undeniably laudable. Assuming that there are physical and psychical phænomena unexplained, Theosophy seeks to explain them. Assuming that there are human powers yet latent, it seeks to discover them. It may be that absurdities and impostures are in fact incident to the nascent stage of its development. As to an undertaking like Occultism, which asserts powers commonly thought superhuman, and phænomena commonly thought supernatural, it seemed to me that the Court, though not assuming to determine judicially the question of their verity, would, before granting to Occultism a franchise, enquire at least whether it had gained the position of being reputable, or whether its adherents were merely men of narrow intelligence, mean intellect, and omnivorous credulity. I accordingly took testimony on that point, and find that a number of gentlemen in different countries of Europe, and also in this country, eminent in science, are believers in Occultism. . . . . The late President Wayland, of Brown University, writing of abnormal mental operations as shown in clairvoyance, says: 'The subject seems to me well worthy of the most searching and candid examination. It is by no means deserving of ridicule, but demands the attention of the most philosophical enquiry.' Sir William Hamilton, probably the most acute, and undeniably the most learned of English metaphysicians that ever lived, said at least thirty years ago: 'However astonishing, it is now proved beyond all rational doubt, that in certain abnormal states of the nervous organism perceptions are possible through other than the ordinary channels of the senses.' By such testimony Theosophy is at least placed on the footing of respectability. Whether by further labor it can make partial truths complete truths, whether it can eliminate extravagances and purge itself of impurities, if there are any, are probably questions upon which the Court will not feel called upon to pass."

On this official Report the Charter of Incorporation was granted, and it may be that some, reading this gravely recorded opinion, will pause ere they join in the ignorant outcry of "superstition" raised against me for joining the Theosophical Society. Every new truth is born into the world amid yells of hatred, but it is not Freethinkers who should swell the outburst, nor ally themselves with the forces of obscurantism to revile investigation into nature.

THEOSOPHY.

It may, however, be granted that most of those who enter the Theosophical Society do so because they have some sympathy with the teachings of Theosophy, some hope of finding new light thrown on the problems that perplex them. Such members become students of Theosophy, and later many become Theosophists.

The first thing they learn is that every idea of the existence of the supernatural must be surrendered. Whatever forces may be latent in the Universe at large or in man in particular, they are wholly natural. *There is no such thing as miracle.* Phænomena may be met with that are strange, that seem inexplicable, but they are all within the realm of law, and it is only our ignorance that makes them marvellous. This repudiation of the supernatural lies at the very threshold of Theosophy: the supersensuous, the superhuman, Yes; the supernatural, No.

[I may here make a momentary digression to remark that some students quickly fall back disappointed because they have come to the study of Theosophy with conceptions drawn from theological religions of supernatural powers to be promptly acquired in some indefinite way. We shall see that Theosophy alleges the existence of powers greater than those normally exercised by man, and alleges further that these powers can be developed. But just because there is nothing miraculous, or supernatural, about them they cannot be suddenly obtained. A student of mathematics might as well expect to be able to work out a problem in the differential calculus as soon as he can struggle through a simple equation, as a student of Theosophy expect to exercise occult faculties when he has mastered a few pages of the "Secret Doctrine". A beginner may come into contact with someone whose ordinary life occasionally shows in a perfectly simple and natural way the possession of abnormal powers; but he must himself keep to his A B C for awhile, and possess his soul in patience.]

The next matter impressed on the student is the denial of a personal God, and hence, as Mme. Blavatsky has pointed out, Agnostics and Atheists more easily assimilate

Theosophic teachings than do believers in orthodox creeds. In theology, Theosophy is Pantheistic, "God is all and all is God". "It is that which is dissolved, or the illusionary dual aspect of That, the essence of which is eternally One, that we call eternal matter or substance, formless, sexless, inconceivable, even to our sixth sense, or mind, in which, therefore, we refuse to see that which Monotheists call a personal anthropomorphic God." ("Secret Doctrine", vol. i, p. 545.) The essential point is: "What lies at the root of things, 'blind force and matter', or an existence which manifests itself in 'intelligence' to use a very inadequate word? Is the universe built up by aggregation of matter acted on by unconscious forces, finally evolving mind as a function of matter: or is it the unfolding of a Divine Life, functioning in every form of living and non-living thing? Is Life or Non-life at the core of things? Is 'spirit' the flower of 'matter', or 'matter' the crystallisation of 'spirit'?" Theosophy accepts the second of these pairs of alternatives, and this, among other reasons, because Materialism gives no answer to the riddles in psychology, of which I gave some samples above, whereas Pantheism does; and the hypothesis which includes most facts under it has the greatest claim for acceptance. On the plane of matter, materialistic Science answers many questions and promises to answer more; on the plane of mind she breaks down, and continually murmurs "Insoluble, unknowable". On the other hand, assuming intelligence as primal, the developed and dawning faculties of the human mind fall into intelligible order, and can be studied with hope of comprehension. At any rate, where Materialism confesses itself incapable, no blame can be attached to the student if he seek other method for solving the problem, and if he test the methods offered to him by some who claim to have solved it, and who prove, by actual experiment, that their knowledge of natural laws in the domain of psychology, and outside it, is greater than his own. So far, however, as Theosophy is concerned in its acceptance of the Pantheistic hypothesis, it is not necessary to make any long defence. Pantheism, for which Bruno died and Spinoza argued, need not seek to justify its existence in the intellectual world.

The theory of the Universe which engages the attention of the student of Theosophy comes to him on the authority of certain individuals, as does every other similar theory, religious or scientific. But while all such theories are put forward by individuals, there is this broad difference between the tone of the priest and that of the scientific teacher: one claims to rest on authority outside verification; the other submits its authority to verification. One says: "Believe, or be damned; you must have faith." The other says: "Things are thus; I have investigated and proved them; many of my demonstrations are incomprehensible to you in your present state of ignorance, and I cannot even make them intelligible to you off-hand; but if you will study as I have studied, you can discover for yourself, and you can personally verify all my statements."

The Theosophical theory of the Universe comes into the latter category. The student is not even asked to accept it any faster than he can verify it. On the other hand, if he choose to be satisfied with the credentials of its teachers, pending the growth of his own capacity to investigate, he can accept the theory and guide his own life by it. In the latter case his progress will be more rapid than in the former, but the matter is in his own hands and his freedom is unfettered.

I have spoken of "its teachers", and it will be well to explain the phrase at the outset. These teachers belong to a Brotherhood, composed of men of various nationalities, who have devoted their lives to the study of Occultism and have developed certain faculties which are still latent in ordinary human beings. On such subjects as the constitution of man, they claim to speak with knowledge, as Huxley would speak on man's anatomy, and for the same reason, that they have analysed it. So again as to the existence of various types of living things, unknown to us: they allege that they see and know them, as we see and know the types by which we are surrounded. They say further that they can train other men and women, and show them how to acquire similar powers: they cannot *give* the powers, but can only help others in developing them, for they are a part of human nature, and must be evolved from within, not bestowed from without.

Now it is obvious that, while the teachings of Theosophy might simply stand before the world on their own feet, to meet with acceptance or rejection on their inherent merits and demerits, as they deal largely with questions of fact, they must depend on the evidence whereby they are supported, and, at the outset, very largely on the competence of the persons who give them to the world. The existence of these teachers, and their possession of powers beyond those exercised by ordinary persons, become then of crucial importance. Were the powers to be taken as miraculous, and were they apart from the subject matter of their teachings, I cannot see that they would be of any value as evidence in support of those teachings; but if they depend on the accuracy of the views enunciated and demonstrate those views, then they become relevant and evidential, as the experiments of a skilled electrician elucidate his views and demonstrate his theories.

We, therefore, are bound to ask, ere going any further: do these teachers exist? do they possess these (at present) exceptional powers?

The answers to these questions come from different classes of people with different weight. Those who have seen the Hindus among them in their own country, talked with them, been instructed by them, corresponded with them, have naturally no more doubt of their existence than they have of the existence of other persons whom they have met. Persons who are interested in the matter can see these people, cross-examine them, and form their own conclusions as to the value of their evidence. A large number of people, of whom I am one, believe in the existence of these teachers on secondhand evidence, that is, on the evidence of those who know them personally. And this evidence receives a collateral support when one meets with quiet matter-of-course exercise of abnormal faculties, in every day life, on the part of one alleged to be trained by these very men. A deception kept up for months with absolute consistency through all the small details of ordinary intercourse, without parade and without concealment, is not a defensible hypothesis. And it becomes ludicrous to anyone who, in familiar intercourse, has noted the quick, impulsive, open character of the much abused and little-known Mdme. Blavatsky, as frank as a child about herself, and speaking of her own experiences, her own blunders, her own adventures, with a *naïve abandon* that carries with it a conviction of her truth. (I am speaking of her, of course, among her friends; in face of strangers she can be silent and secret enough.) It should be added that personal proof of the existence of these teachers is given sooner or later to earnest students, just as, in studying any science, a student after awhile is able to obtain ocular demonstration of the facts he learns secondhand. On the other hand, those who feel that they have attained all possible knowledge and that nothing exists of which they are not aware, can deny the existence of these teachers and maintain, as stoutly as they please, that they are a dream, a fancy. "The Masters", as the students of Theosophy call them, are not anxious for an introduction, and they are not, like the orthodox God, angry with any who deny their existence. Shocking as it may seem to nineteenth century self-sufficiency, they are indifferent to its declaration that they are non-existent, and are in no wise eager to demonstrate to all and sundry that they live. Let it, however, be clearly understood that these teachers have nothing supernatural about them; they are men who have studied a particular subject and have become "masters" in it—Mahatmas, Great Souls, the Hindus call them—and who, because they know, can do things that ignorant people cannot do.

From these Masters then, say Theosophists, we derive our teachings, and you will find, if you examine them, that they throw light on the nature of man and guide him along the path to a higher life. Man, according to Theosophy, is a compound being, a spark of the Universal Spirit being prisoned in his body, as a flame in the lamp. The "higher Triad" in man consists of this spark of the Universal Spirit, its vehicle the human spirit, and the rational principle, the mind or intellectual powers. This is immortal, indestructible, using the lower Quaternary, the body, with its animal life, its passions and appetites, as its dwelling, its organ. Thus we reach the famous seven-fold division, or the "seven principles" in man: Atma, the Universal spirit; Buddhi, the human spirit; Manas, the rational soul; Kamarupa, the animal soul with its appetites and passions; Prana, the vitality, the principle of life; Linga Sharira, the vehicle of this life; Rupa, the physical body. Theosophy teaches that the higher Triad and lower Quaternary are not only separable at death, but may be temporarily separated during life, the intellectual part of man leaving the body and its attached principles, and appearing apart from them. This is the much talked of "astral appearance", and its reality can only be decided by evidence, like any other matter of fact. Those who know nothing about it will, of course, deride belief in it as superstition, as people like-minded with them derided in the past each newly discovered power in nature. Here again, after awhile, the student has ocular demonstration, and, when he reaches a certain stage, personal experience; but, if he is dissatisfied with second-hand evidence, no blame will fall on him for suspending his belief until he obtains personal proof.

Clairvoyance and allied phænomena become intelligible on this view of man, the projection of the human intelligence, while the body is in a state of trance, taking its place as one of the temporary separations alluded to. The Ego, thus freed, can exercise its faculties apart from the limitations of the physical senses, and has escaped from the time and space limits which are created by our normal consciousness. It is noteworthy that persons emerging from the mesmeric state have no memory of what has occurred during that state; *i.e.*, no impress has been left on the physical organism by the experiences passed through. But if the seeing or hearing is by the way of the external senses, this could not be, for the cerebral activity would have left its trace on the cerebral material.

If, on the other hand, the experiences have been supersensuous, there can be no reason to look for their record in the sense-centres; and the outcome of the experiment is merely the fact that, under these conditions, the Ego is powerless to impress on the physical frame the memory of its actions. So long, indeed, as the lower nature is more vigorous than the higher, this impotency of the Ego will continue; and it is only as the higher nature developes and takes the upper hand in the alliance, that the physical consciousness will become impressible by it. This stage has been reached by many, and then consciousness becomes unified, and higher and lower work in harmony under the control of the will.

The weakening of the body by disease sometimes brings about, but in an undesirable way, a temporary supremacy of the Higher Self, resulting in that keenness of perception referred to on page 11. To obtain such keenness normally, without injury to health, it would be necessary to refine and purify the physical organisation, and this, among other things, may be effected in due course.

On the existence of this separable and indestructible entity, the Ego, hinge the doctrines of Re-incarnation and Karma. Re-incarnation—ignorantly travestied as transmigration of souls—is the rebirth of the Ego, as above defined, to pass through another human life on earth. During its past incarnation it had acquired certain faculties, set in motion certain causes. The effects of these causes, and of causes set in motion in previous incarnations and not yet exhausted, are its Karma, and determine the conditions into which the Ego is reborn, the conditions being modified, however, by the national Karma, the outcome of the collective life. The faculties acquired in previous incarnations manifest themselves in the new life, and genius, abnormal capacities of any kind, possession of knowledge not acquired during the present existence, and so on, are explained by Theosophy on this theory of re-incarnation. Infant prodigies, calculating boys, *et hoc genus omne*, fall into order in quite natural fashion instead of remaining as inexplicable phænomena. From the point of view of Theosophy, nothing is lost in the Universe, no force is extinguished. Faculties and capacities painfully acquired during the long course of years do not perish at death. When, after long sleep, the time for rebirth comes, the Ego does not re-enter earth-life as a pauper; he returns with the fruits of his past victories, to make further progress upwards.

The only proof of this doctrine, apart from the explanation it gives of the otherwise inexplicable cases of genius, etc., and its inherent probability—given any intelligent purpose in human existence—must, in the nature of things, lie for us in the future if it exist at all; the Masters allege it on their personal knowledge, having reached the stage at which memory of past incarnations revives; the doctrine comes to us on their authority, and must be accepted or rejected by each as it approves itself to his reason.

Similarly the working of the law of Karma cannot be demonstrated as can a problem in mathematics. The law of Karma has been defined by Colonel Olcott as the law of ethical causation; Theosophists affirm that the harvest reaped by man is of his own sowing, and that, although not always immediately, yet inevitably, every act must work out its full results. We may argue to this law in the mental and moral worlds, by analogy from the physical. Each force on the physical plane has its own result, and where many forces interact, each has, none the less, its complete effect. On the higher planes, since the Universe is one, we may reasonably look for similar laws, and one of these laws is Karma. That it will be difficult to trace its exact working in any instance lies in the nature of the case. We may see a body rushing in a given direction, and we know that the line along which it is travelling is the resultant of all the forces that have impelled it; but that resultant may have been caused by any one of a thousand combinations, and in default of the knowledge of the whole history of its motion we cannot select one combination and say, such and such are the forces. How then can we expect to perform such a feat in the more complicated interplay of all the Karmic forces that ultimate in the character and environment of an individual? The general principle can be laid down; for the working out of a particular case in detail we have not the material.

One of my critics, Mr. G. W. Foote, asks me how I can reconcile Karma with Socialism, and he affirms that the Socialist, and "every social reformer, is fighting against Karma". Not so in any effective sense. To bring fresh forces to improve the present is not to deny the effects of past causes, but is only to introduce new causes which shall modify present effects and change the future. It may well be that the present poverty, misery, and disease spring inevitably from past evil, and this all scientific thinkers must admit, whether or not they use the word Karma; but that is no reason why we should not start forces of wisdom and love to change them, and create good Karma for the future instead of continuing to create bad. By every action we modify the present and mould the future; that the past has created so evil an heritage but makes the need the sorer for strenuous effort now. It must be remembered that Karma is not a personal Deity, against whose will it might be thought blasphemous to contend. It is simply a law, like any other law of nature, and we cannot violate it even if we would. But it no more prevents us from aiding our fellow-men than "the law of gravitation" prevents us from walking upstairs. We cannot prevent a man from suffering physical pain if he breaks his leg, but the law of nature that pain follows lesion of sensitive tissues does not hinder us from nursing the sufferer and alleviating the pain as much as possible. Neither can we save a man from the sway of Karmic law, but there is nothing to prevent us from trying to lighten his suffering, and above all from endeavoring to put an end to the causes which are continually generating such evil results. Does Mr. Foote deny that all around us is the outcome of past causes? or does he say that because there is causation we must sit with folded hands in face of evil? The true view, it seems to me, is that as present conditions are the results of past activities, so future conditions will be the results of present activities, and we had better bestir ourselves to the full extent of our powers to set going causes that will work out happier results.[1]

What belief in Karma does is to prevent mere idle and useless repining, and to teach a dignified and virile acceptance of inevitable suffering, while bracing the spirit to sustained endeavor to improve the present and thus inevitably improve the future. Nor must it be forgotten that courage to face pain, and love, and generous self-sacrifice for others, are all of them Karmic fruits, effects of past causes and themselves causes of future effects. The religionist, who hopes to escape from the consequences of his own misdeeds through some side-door of vicarious atonement, may shrink from the stern enunciation of the law of Karma, but the Secularist who believes in the reign of law can have no quarrel on this head with the Theosophist. Difference can only arise when the Theosophist says: "You must pay every farthing of the debt run up, either in this *or in some future incarnation*". The non-Theosophical Secularist would consider that death cancels all debts. To the Theosophist death merely suspends the payment, and the full undischarged account is presented to the dead man's successor, who is himself in a new dress.

Theosophy further teaches, in connexion with man,

---

[1] See an article, "Karma and Social Improvement", by the present writer, in *Lucifer* for August, 1889. The question is there more fully worked out.

that he may develope by suitable means not only the psychic qualities of which glimpses are given in the abnormal manifestations before alluded to, but power over matter far greater than he at present possesses, and psychic abilities in comparison with which those now looming before us are but as the capacities of infants to those of grown men. In the slow evolution of the human race these qualities will gradually unfold themselves; further, they may be, so to say, "forced" by any who choose to take the requisite means. And here comes in the asceticism to which Mr. Foote so vehemently objects; he declares that the acceptance of celibacy by an individual for a definite object implies that "Marriage is now a mere concession to human weakness. Celibacy is the counsel of perfection. The sacred names of husband and wife, father and mother, are to be deposed as usurpers. At the very best they are only to be tolerated. It is idle to reply that celibacy is only for the 'inner circle'. If it be the loftiest rule of life, it should be aimed at by all." With all due respect to Mr. Foote, his denunciation savors somewhat of clap-trap, though well calculated to appeal to the ordinary British Philistine of Mr. Matthew Arnold. No one wants to depose any names, sacred or otherwise, as usurpers. It sounds rather small after this tremendous objurgation, but all the Theosophist says is, if you want to obtain a certain thing you must use certain means; as who should say, if you want to swim across that swift current you must take off your coat. But if it be good, should not everyone try for it? Not necessarily. Music is very good, but I should be a fool to practise eight hours a day if I had but small talent for it; if I have great talent, and want to become a great artist, I must sacrifice for it many of the ordinary joys of life; but is that to say that every boy and girl must fling aside every duty of life and practise incessantly, without the slightest regard to anything else? Only one out of millions has the capacity for that swift development to which allusion is made, and celibacy is one of the smallest of the sacrifices it demands for its realisation. The spiritual genius, like other geniuses, will have its way, but Mr. Foote need not fear that it will become too common, and Theosophy does not advise celibacy to those not on fire with its flame.

I ought perhaps in passing to say a word as to the

power over matter spoken of above, because a good deal of fuss, quite out of proportion to their importance, has been made about the "phænomena" with which Mdme. Blavatsky's name has been associated, and many people assume that it is pretended that they are "miracles", or are a phase of "Spiritualistic manifestations". The bitter attacks made on Mdme. Blavatsky by Spiritualists ought to convince unprejudiced people that she has not much in common with them. As a matter of fact, her main object in the greater number of cases, as she said at the time, was to show that far more remarkable things than were done among Spiritualists by "spirits" in the dark, could be done in full daylight without any "spirits", merely by the utilisation of natural forces. All that she claimed was that she knew more about these forces than did the people about her, and could therefore do things which they could not. A good many of the apparent miracles turned merely on the utilisation of magnetic force, a force about the marvels of which science is finding out more year after year. Mdme. Blavatsky is able to utilise this force, which everyone admits is around us, in us, and in non-living things, without the apparatus used at the present time by science for its manipulation. Other of the phænomena were what she called "psychological tricks", illusions, conjuring on the mental plane as does the ordinary conjurer on the material, making people see what you wish them to see instead of what really is. Others, again, were cases of thought-transference. Another group, that including the disintegration and reintegration of material objects, is more difficult to understand. All I can say myself as to this is that when I find a person, who leads a good and most laborious life, and who exercises powers that I do not possess, telling me that this can be done and has been done within her own knowledge in a perfectly natural way, I am not going to say "deception", "charlatanry", merely because I do not understand; any more than I should say so if Tyndall told me of one of his wonderful experiments, as to which I did not understand the *modus operandi*.

There remains a great stumbling-block in the minds of many Freethinkers, which is certain to prejudice them against Theosophy, and which offers to opponents a cheap subject for sarcasm—the assertion that there exist other living beings than the men and animals found on our own globe. It may be well for people who at once turn away when such an assertion is made to stop and ask themselves whether they really and seriously believe that throughout this mighty universe, in which our little planet is but as a tiny speck of sand in the Sahara, this one planet only is inhabited by living things? Is all the Universe dumb save for *our* voices? eyeless, save for *our* vision? dead, save for *our* life? Such a preposterous belief was well enough in the days when Christianity regarded our world as the centre of the universe, the human race as the one for which the creator had deigned to die. But now that we are placed in our proper position, one among countless myriads of worlds, what ground is there for the preposterous conceit which arrogates as ours all sentient existence? Earth, air, water, all are teeming with living things suited to their environment; our globe is overflowing with life. But the moment we pass in thought beyond our atmosphere everything is to be changed. Neither reason nor analogy support such a supposition. It was one of Bruno's crimes that he dared to teach that other worlds than ours were inhabited, but he was wiser than the monks who burned him. All the Theosophist avers is that each phase of matter has living things suited to it, and that all the Universe is pulsing with life. "Superstition" shriek the bigoted. It is no more superstition than the belief in Bacteria, or in any other living thing invisible to the ordinary human eye. "Spirit" is a misleading word, for, historically, it connotes immateriality and a supernatural kind of existence, and the Theosophist believes neither in the one nor the other. With him all living things act in and through a material basis, and "matter" and "spirit" are not found dissociated. But he alleges that matter exists in states other than those at present known to science. To deny this is to be about as sensible as was the Hindu prince who denied the existence of ice, because water in his experience never became solid. Refusal to believe until proof is given is a rational position; denial of all outside our own limited experience is absurd.

Minutiæ.

Before closing this explanatory pamphlet I must allude to the kind of weapons being used against me by one or two writers in the *Freethinker*. I speak of it here, because I have no other way of answering the paragraphs which appear in that journal week after week, and I will take two or three as specimens of a kind of controversy which is not, I venture to think, worthy of the Freethought cause.

"Mrs. Besant goes in for the transmigration of souls", and then follows an absurd statement about the souls of ill-behaving Hindu wives passing into various animals. This assertion is worse than a caricature, it is a misrepresentation; and as I am told that Mr. Wheeler "knows more about Buddhism and Oriental thought generally than Mrs. Besant is ever likely to learn", I cannot suppose that the misrepresentation springs from ignorance. No Theosophist believes in the transmigration of souls, or that the human Ego can enter a lower animal; and a blunder that might pass from an ignoramus is not excusable where such great professions of learning are made. I take the above statement as a type of the caricatures of Theosophy to be found in the *Freethinker*.

There are other paragraphs which give a false idea by suppression of part of the truth. Thus: Mr. Foote states that "we do not intend to open our columns for the discussion of Theosophy" (although he had attacked it), and saying that he was going to publish a letter from a Theosophist, he adds: "The Theosophists must not expect to use our columns any further. Mr. Wheeler reviewed Mdme. Blavatsky's book on its being sent to him for that purpose, and it is not customary to discuss reviews." Putting aside the fact that Mr. Wheeler's article was an attack on Theosophy and on Mdme. Blavatsky personally, rather than a review of the "Secret Doctrine", the above sentence implies that the criticism of the *Freethinker* was challenged by the Theosophists sending the book. This was not so: Mr. Wheeler wrote saying that my adhesion to Theosophy would cause interest in the subject to be felt by Freethinkers, and asking for a copy of the book for review. This was an unusual course to take as preface to a bitter personal attack, but, waiving the question of literary courtesy, the point is that the initiative came from the *Freethinker*, not from the Theosophists. It is not consistent with Freethought traditions to gratuitously attack a person and then decline discussion. Again, Mr. Foote writes: "We do not agree with the *Medium and Daybreak* that Mr. Foote should have treated Mrs. Besant's 'apostacy with silent contempt.' A very different treatment was called for by her character and past services to the cause." The words in inverted commas do occur in the *Medium and Daybreak*, but the context considerably alters the meaning suggested by them as quoted by Mr. Foote. The passage runs:

"'MRS. BESANT'S THEOSOPHY' is the title of a 16-page two-penny worth by G. W. Foote, in which 'the Freethought party' is an ominous phrase. Like the 'Church' it stands high above truth, and Mrs. Besant is censured for treating it so 'cavalierly'. In view of the lady's new style of propaganda, Mr. Foote is anxious for the 'interests of the free-thought party'. If the 'philosophy' of that body be so 'sound and bracing', why the weakness of Mrs. Besant, and the dangerous tendencies of her new views? Mr. Foote would have shown laudable consistency, and more no-faith, if he had treated her apostacy with silent contempt."

Comment is needless.

Then we have a number of personal attacks on Madame Blavatsky; has not Mr. Foote suffered enough from the slanderous statements of opponents to hesitate before he gives currency to malignant libels on another? What would he think of me if I soiled these pages with a repetition of the stories told against him by the lecturers of the Christian Evidence Society? Yet he adopts this foul weapon against Madame Blavatsky. "No case; abuse the plaintiff's attorney." How utterly careless Mr. Foote is in picking up any stone that he thinks may inflict some slight injury is shown by the following paragraph:

"We learn on the authority of a Theosophist that Madame Blavatsky is going abroad for a few months, and has confided the presidentship of the Theosophical Society into the hands of her new convert, Mrs. Besant."

The matter is trivial enough—save for the ungenerous attempt to make out that the Theosophical Society must be hard up for adherents if it had to fall back on a new member as acting President—but it happens that Madame

Blavatsky is not the president of the Theosophical Society, and has never held that position. No "Theosophist" could have made such a blunder, but a sneer was wanted, so accuracy was thrown to the winds.

My chief reason for drawing attention to these blunders is to shew that I have some cause to ask Freethinkers not to adopt, without examination, Mr. Foote's statements about the beliefs or the lives of Theosophists, but to justify their name by making personal investigation before they decide.

To Members of the National Secular Society.

One last word to my Secularist friends. If you say to me, "Leave our ranks", I will leave them; I force myself on no party, and the moment I feel myself unwelcome I will go. It has cost me pain enough and to spare to admit that the Materialism from which I hoped all has failed me, and by such admission to bring upon myself the disapproval of some of my nearest friends. But here, as at other times in my life, I dare not purchase peace with a lie. An imperious necessity forces me to speak the truth as I see it, whether the speech please or displease, whether it bring praise or blame. That one loyalty to Truth I must keep stainless, whatever friendships fail me or human ties be broken. She may lead me into the wilderness, but I must follow her; she may strip me of all love, but I must pursue her; though she slay me, yet will I trust in her; and I ask no other epitaph on my tomb, but

She tried to follow Truth.